The European Commission, 1958–72
History and memories

THE EUROPEAN COMMISSION, 1958–72

HISTORY AND MEMORIES

Editor: Michel Dumoulin
in collaboration with Marie-Thérèse Bitsch, Gérard Bossuat, Éric Bussière, Julie Cailleau,
Yves Conrad, Anaïs Legendre, Matthieu Lethé, Wilfried Loth,
Jan van der Harst, Arthe Van Laer and Antonio Varsori

*Work undertaken on the initiative of the European Commission
with contributions from former European officials*

European Commission

The successful completion of this project would not have been possible without the great help given by three people in particular, Ms Jacqueline Lastenouse, Ms Natacha Wittorski and Mr Olivier Bailly, to whom most sincere thanks are due.

Michel Dumoulin

Translated from the French edition.

The content of this book and the views expressed in it are those of the authors alone and do not necessarily reflect the opinion of the European Commission.

A great deal of additional information on the European Union is available on the Internet. It can be accessed through the Europa server (http://europa.eu).

Cataloguing data can be found at the end of this publication.

Luxembourg: Office for Official Publications of the European Communities, 2007

ISBN 978-92-79-05494-5

Printed in Italy

<small>Printed on white chlorine-free paper</small>

Preface

José Manuel Durão Barroso
President of the European Commission

Fifty years ago, the six Member States of the European Coal and Steel Community (ECSC) decided to extend their integration into new areas. Buoyed by the new momentum imparted at Messina, they signed on 25 March 1957 in Rome the Treaties establishing the European Economic Community (EEC) and the European Atomic Energy Community (Euratom/EAEC). Building on the still recent foundations of the ECSC, they raised higher the fragile edifice of European integration and thus gave fresh impetus to a more closely knit, more open and more democratic Europe. Bolstered by their political conviction and their faith in a peaceful future, the six founding States decided there and then to conclude the new Treaties for an unlimited period.

In so doing, France, the Federal Republic of Germany, Italy, Belgium, the Netherlands and Luxembourg gave birth to the institution over which I have the honour to preside today. For it was in 1957 that the Member States decided to set up the Commission of the European Economic Community, which in 1967 became, by absorbing the ECSC High Authority and the Euratom Commission, the Commission of the European Communities, nowadays commonly known as the European Commission.

The work you are now holding traces, 50 years on, the first steps taken by that new institution, the only one of its kind at a time marked by the Cold War, the nationalism of the Great Powers, the authoritarian regimes in southern Europe, including in my own country, and the wars of independence in Asia and Africa. At a time when a new world order was taking hold for the duration, a group of men and women, defying history, embarked resolutely on an unheard-of human adventure the outcome of which looked uncertain to most of their contemporaries. This work and my message today show that they were, in actual fact, the founding fathers of a historic movement of continental scope which — half a century later — has made possible the building of a peaceful union of democratic States. I hope that this work will do them the justice they deserve and that it will bring this extraordinary human adventure to the notice of a wider audience.

Many books and studies have already been written about the history of the European Commission. Without a doubt, this one will become a work of reference. It shows the institution in a new light, thanks to the testimony of people who were there at the time and who, in the late 1950s, chose against all the odds to work — day in, day out — for European integration.

The idea behind this work, which was conceived in 2002 as the brainchild of David O'Sullivan, the Commission's Secretary-General at the time, is to piece together the collective memory of the institution. The Commission's first officials, who joined between 1957 and 1970, are now retired and many of them are no longer with us. With their passing, it is a part of the Commission's history that is being lost little by little, depriving us of precious recollections. And so, the enlightened decision to record the reminiscences of these former officials was made in 2002 with a view to writing a history of the institution's beginnings. The task was entrusted to a group of leading European historians, whom I wish to thank here for their valuable collaboration and rigorous endeavours. For almost three years, these Belgian, German, Italian, Dutch and French historians, under the coordination of Professor Michel Dumoulin of the Université catholique de Louvain (Louvain-la-Neuve, Belgium), interviewed more than 120 witnesses who had contributed, slowly but surely, to the construction of the European Commission between 1958 and 1972, the eve of the first enlargement. These interviews are now accessible to researchers at the Historical Archives of the European University Institute at Florence, for it is our duty to safeguard and pass on these memories.

At a time when the 50th anniversary of the Rome Treaties is being celebrated, it is highly enlightening to go back in one's thoughts, through this work, to the early days of the adventure that is the Commission. At the risk of repeating myself, this book gives a clearer picture of just how uncertain the new institution's future was. Everything had to be done from scratch. The scale of its twofold mission — to bring about a 'common market' with a political perspective in mind and to act henceforth solely in the 'Community interest' — led people at the time to invent a new, hitherto unknown, profile. The conquest of an identity and of a legitimacy would have been impossible without the fertile imagination of the first members of the College of Commissioners and without the fierce determination of a great many among the pioneering officials, fired as they were with a new ideal, namely that — as alive today as it was then — of the general Community interest.

Readers will find in these pages a new angle on my predecessors at the helm of the Commission, on those early officials and on a meeting of personalities shaped by their era but, at the same time, resolutely forward-looking. They will also find an analysis of and a series of anecdotes about the formulation of Community policies, some of which were barely outlined in the treaties.

For my part, I have learned with interest — and genuine curiosity — about the ups and downs of the first Colleges of Commissioners and the institutional battles they waged to assert the authority of the new institution. From the long nights of negotiations in the Council of Ministers through to the 'crisis of the empty chair', there emerges the true face of a body in search of itself, willing to make concessions but uncompromising when it came to defining the very essence of its powers and the interests of Europe. This historical retrospect is for me a wonderful pilgrimage and a particularly enriching source of reflection.

It is fascinating to discover, thanks to the reminiscences and the historians' work, that the functioning of the European Commission is still informed by the same mechanisms and the same difficulties. My predecessors thus thought from the very outset about setting up groups of Commissioners so as to improve the working of the collegiality principle. They also came up against the need for transparency following a leak to the press after the very first Commission meeting. They also perceived that the work of the Commission and of its departments would need to be coordinated through an executive Secretary at the head of a high-quality administration.

I should like to conclude by sharing with you, the modern reader, a thought drawn from my personal experience. My first contact with the European Commission dates from 1978, when — as a student in Lisbon — I came with several teachers to seek support for an association engaged in European studies. For me, the European Commission, installed in the modern Berlaymont building, in itself symbolised European integration. And even more for us who had known Portugal before the advent of democracy, the institution represented hope, a gateway to the future, to freedom.

I am pleased to say that the Commission is still today the living symbol — the very personification — of the European Union, not just in every Member State, including those which have recently joined, but also across the world, in Russia, China, Africa and beyond.

The lasting nature of this identification of the Commission with the European project after 50 years is due in large part to the fact that the Commission is seen as the archetypal Community institution, combining as it does the political answerability of an executive, administrative expertise and unwavering defence of the European project. Through its position at the interface with every Member State (whether original or new, affluent or less developed, small or large), the Commission is suited to finding compromises between all of them, being naturally disposed to combine technical expertise with political skills and being organised in such a way as to defend the general interest in strengthening the European project.

The almost carnal link between the Commission and European integration is also due to the men and women who work there. My — short but intense — experience at the head of the Commission has taught me to appreciate these officials' devotion and ability. Their contribution on a day-to-day basis is essential to maintaining and further developing the Commission's indispensable role within an enlarged Union.

The diversity in the cultural and ideological backgrounds of Commissioners and their growing number have not affected the Commission's coherence and decision-making ability — a fact increasingly recognised in the latest academic studies of the Commission's functioning. I welcome this and salute the Community spirit shown by the College's members — supported by the administration — in their effort to speak with one voice. It fills me with enthusiasm and emotion to see that the values defended by the Commission and the devotion of its members and officials have remained as intact as they are indispensable within the enlarged Union.

While acknowledging the imperfect nature of our institutions and while striving to modernise certain aspects of the Commission's functioning, I therefore wish to defend the Commission's unique role and structure against populist and simplistic attacks since, make no mistake about it, it is European integration itself, in the shape of the Commission, that is under fire.

Hence it is with great pleasure and genuine pride that I wish the Rome Treaties a Happy Anniversary. I am convinced of the increased importance of the European Commission within the enlarged Europe and of its capacity to take whatever steps are necessary to equip Europeans for the challenges posed by globalisation.

Contents

Memories for tomorrow ...

Foreword by
SOME OLD HANDS OF AN INSTITUTION WHO WERE THERE
AT THE BIRTH AND WATCHED IT GROW

The European Commission's initiative to collect and preserve its 'historical memory' was received with great interest by those who were part of the scene in the early days and who remain convinced that the institution's memory is a valuable asset for the future.

In passing on their own memories and contemporary accounts, the institution's 'old guard' provided an insider's view of the often little-known life of an institution at the heart of the Community, for they still have a vast knowledge of its history and experience and of the spirit which inspired the staff and the DGs.

As a prelude to the work of the historians, their role was to set the scene in a way that reflected their perspective on the formative years of the bold European adventure which, 50 years on, is now an established reality.

European integration was a new adventure, and the Community institutions were without precedent, but the most unusual body in the firmament, described by Jacques Delors as an 'unidentified political object', was the European Commission. It is rare in history to encounter institutions which are not rooted in any tradition or prior experience but have to invent their role as they go along. Although republics were in a similar situation when they were formed, they were normally following on from kingdoms whose powers and administrative structures they were able to inherit; virtually the only new features they had to invent were their relations with parliament and the people.

In the beginning, the Commission was unable to identify with, or define itself in terms of, a clear political model. When establishing the European Economic Community, the authors of the Treaty of Rome had opted for a functional approach, that is they had established a number of functions which they then entrusted to a given institution and they wisely endeavoured to leave no loose ends and nothing to chance, but to confer these tasks on the body which was best able to fulfil them. The tasks of the Parliamentary Assembly, the Court of Justice and the Economic and Social Committee were fairly self-evident, although the Parliamentary Assembly was treated less than generously. The problem was the Council. If the Council did not work together with a body which embodied the general Community interest, such as the Commission, the result would inevitably be an intergovernmental system, and everyone was aware of the limitations and the sticking points of such a system, which were the direct result of the unanimity rule, well known in the Organisation for European Economic Co-operation (OEEC).

The ECSC High Authority was, of course, the answer, and it served as a prototype for the Commission. Bound by very specific rules — which were only possible in a Treaty relating to a single sector, in this case coal and steel — it already carried out the three major tasks of the European Commission, namely the exclusive right of initiative as the originator of all decisions, the implementation of Community policies, the monitoring of compliance with decisions and the implementation of the Treaty.

The authors of the Treaty of Rome accordingly conferred on the Commission all the duties relating to these three tasks, all of which may be exercised only in the general interest and independently of individual and national interests.

The general nature of the Treaty of Rome, which covers all economic and social sectors, meant that, unlike the ECSC and Euratom Treaties, it could not be used to lay down a detailed economic and social policy.

The principles it established, the Commission's 'roadmap' in short, were extremely broad: promoting economic and social progress within the Community by creating a large single market through the opening of economic borders, freedom of movement for persons, services and capital, and the adoption of common policies. These common policies, which were not described in detail, were to cover the Community's foreign trade, agriculture, transport and development. Last but not least, the Treaty called for the coordination of Member States' economic, monetary and social policies.

The procedures were intended to allow the Commission to defend the general interest in both the Council and the Parliamentary Assembly, without depriving the Member States of the right to defend their legitimate interests.

Thus, the Commission held its earliest meetings, from January 1958 onwards, either at Val-Duchesse in Brussels or at the High Authority's premises in Luxembourg, not knowing where it would have its headquarters or what its budget would be, not sure as yet what sort of relationship it would have with the Council and the Parliamentary Assembly, but aware that its immediate task was to organise its internal work and set up an administration.

Although over a third of the Commission's members had been involved in drafting the Treaty of Rome, and others had attended OEEC committee and council meetings, some were discovering the Community and Europe in January 1958 for the first time.

From the start, the embryonic Commission faced three major problems: the nature of its relationship with the Council, deciding which measures should be given priority from among the vast task-sheet established by the Treaty of Rome and, last but not least, external relations. Each of these problems raised entirely new questions. Although the experience of the ECSC and the negotiations for the Treaty of Rome were some help in providing points of reference for decision-making, they offered only a very partial response to the overall problems.

First and foremost, what kind of Community were they setting out to build? A federation, a confederation, yet another intergovernmental organisation?

The interplay between the institutions was decisive in this regard, and the relations between the Council and the Commission in particular were most important of all. There was no shortage of ideas on the matter in the beginning, ranging from an intergovernmental system along the lines of the OEEC to a semi-federal system in which the Council would become an American-style Senate in the new institutional structure, while the Commission would be the executive — a weak executive but one whose strength lay in the fact that it was unopposed.

The Commission struggled to make up its mind where it was going. Faced with an all-powerful and overbearing Council, it had to fight every step of the way for the prerogatives which were, after all, its by right under the Treaty, engaging in difficult battles on every subject, but at every turn it was in danger of sparking a major political crisis, another 'empty chair', which would have jeopardised everything it had achieved.

The Council had equipped itself with a remarkable instrument, not written into the Treaty, the Permanent Representatives Committee, these being ambassadors to the Community appointed by each Member State to prepare Council decisions and, they imagined, perhaps even those of the Commission; in short to guide the Community's progress in a direct manner. There was a serious risk that this Permanent Representatives' Committee (or Coreper) might take over the Commission's executive role and transform the Commission into the Community's Secretariat-General, its administration at the service of Coreper and the Council. This at least was the policy, officially or otherwise, of some Member States, such was the difficulty at that time of conceiving and accepting the idea of an authority that would be independent of the Member States.

Borrowing a metaphor from bridge, one could say that the Commission under Hallstein, supported by all the Commissioners, played a good hand, relying on the Treaty and seeking the support of the European Parliamentary Assembly, the Economic and Social Committee, the Court of Justice and the Member States most concerned by the discussions in hand. One after the other, its proposals, defending Europe's common interest, were approved, in some cases with difficulty and only after marathon sessions and crises, sometimes with concessions, but never compromising on the Commission's role and the legitimacy of the common interest it represented.

Its proposals, whether on procedure or on substance, were difficult to draft because they were totally new and dealt with such important matters as trade policy, agricultural policy and competition. Six countries with different political traditions and conflicting interests had to be persuaded to accept them.

The responsibilities of the Commission and its embryonic services were therefore onerous indeed; at stake were the institutional future of the Community, the solidarity of its members and the long-term social, economic and legal validity of the decisions the Commission proposed.

There are few examples in history of so many fundamental reforms being initiated and adopted together, in so little time, by countries with a high level of development; the removal of all barriers to trade in the internal market, a new agricultural development policy, a common commercial policy, a competition policy which was completely new for countries other than Germany, a policy of aid to the developing countries, which was also new for most Member States. All of this, which marked a profound change in earlier practices, was achieved in under 10 years, not to mention the first steps, modest enough in themselves but very important for the future, towards the coordination of economic, monetary and regional policies, social policies, energy policy and transport policy.

In all these areas, the Commission and the Community institutions had to devise solutions and procedures for which there were no precedents and of which not one came ready made or was welcomed initially by the Member States.

This was the extraordinary challenge facing the Commission, which had sole responsibility for devising common policies and drawing up proposals. Because it was operating in an entirely new framework, it was not bound by the routines and traditions which normally shape government action. It was free but with each initiative it ran the risk of losing everything. It could not allow itself the luxury of making a mistake because those who did not believe in the Community system would have seized the opportunity to 'scrap' it and restore the intergovernmental system, as they had attempted to do during the 'empty chair' crisis.

The scope of the Treaty of Rome is so vast that it was difficult to decide to which of the priority sectors the Commission should devote most effort. Two priorities quickly emerged, however: achieving the internal market, prime objective of the Treaty of Rome, and external economic relations, pushed by non-member countries.

Abolishing all kinds of barriers to trade in goods between the six Member States was no mean feat. There was so much to do that the removal of tariff and non-tariff barriers within the Community took 10 years, which was still 18 months earlier than the cautious timescale set by the Treaty. In the case of the free movement of agricultural produce, the large internal market called for a common policy which at that time directly affected a quarter of the working population. Six national sets of rules had to be replaced by a single set of Community rules, and the different subsectors of agriculture operated in such different ways that it was necessary to create as many market organisations as there were categories of farm produce; this was achieved, with a display of financial solidarity, over a number of years, after many marathon sessions and repeated crises.

An internal market also required a Common Customs Tariff and a common commercial policy. From the very beginning, the emergence of the Community gave rise to anxiety and envy in non-member countries, and the Community institutions, first among them the Commission, had to respond to an avalanche of requests for cuts in the Common Customs Tariff, for the creation of a free-trade area, for associations of all kinds and, finally, for accessions.

The Commission was still without a real administration when it had to start work on setting up the internal market, preparing the organisations of the agricultural markets, negotiating with non-member countries in all corners of the world and laying down the principles for combating cartels, price-fixing agreements and, of course, State aid. The *cabinets* and the first Commission departments prepared copious agendas for the Commission's weekly Wednesday meeting at a frantic pace. The rigorous approach of the President, Walter Hallstein, and the Executive Secretary, Émile Noël, required that every agenda item should be accompanied by a solidly constructed dossier. Oral statements by Commissioners were concerned only with highly confidential matters or were intended to allow a preliminary exchange of views on topics which had not yet been debated. The weekly meetings of *chefs de cabinet* sorted the matters on which there was a consensus which could be decided upon without debate from those which would require a discussion and would be examined at first reading. The Executive Secretary saw to it that there was coordination at all times between departments and called meetings of the directors-general concerned whenever there was a difference of opinion.

Hallstein very quickly established a strong and highly competent administration that was able to hold discussions on an equal footing with the national administrations, and by the end of 1958 it was already a thousand strong. The multinational nature of this new administration, required to think 'European' and composed of officials whose careers and the staff regulations made them independent of their countries' civil services, guaranteed its independence. Historical differences and grievances were put aside and the sense of a shared identity would not be long in spreading through the hierarchy from top to bottom, mobilising its creativity and energy in the service of the European ideal. The enthusiasm of those days is recaptured in the chapters that follow by the many colleagues who shared with us their memories of those pioneer days.

Once the Commission had adopted a proposal or a decision, it had to be 'sold' to Member States' governments, the European Parliamentary Assembly, the press and public opinion. This meant that Commissioners, *cabinets* and directors-general alike were constantly travelling to all parts of the Community. Sicco Mansholt 'sold' the common agricultural policy not only to government ministers but also to the farmers themselves at public meetings held throughout the Community. Robert Marjolin did the same for regional, energy and monetary policy, as did Hans von der Groeben for the competition rules.

The history described in the chapters of this book is one of an incredible race against time in which the Community endeavoured to exist and to grow in a world which was itself undergoing rapid political and economic change and which had a substantial head start on the Community countries, still weakened by the war, isolated and demoralised.

The European Community has had the good fortune to be served by a host of exceptional people, whether at the Commission, the Council, the European Parliamentary Assembly or in their administrative departments, who, facing difficult circumstances but meeting tight deadlines, took the courageous decisions that made the adventure work.

It was an enormous privilege to be part of it.

'Inventing things as they went along'

Introduction by
MICHEL DUMOULIN
editor and coordinator of the project

For Paul-Henri Spaak, the signing of the Treaties establishing the European Economic Community and the European Atomic Energy Community in Rome on 25 March 1957, coming as it did after the Treaty of Paris of 18 April 1951 establishing the European Coal and Steel Community, represented the solemn affirmation of a profound solidarity between six nations that had so often in the past found themselves in opposite camps, confronting one another on the battlefield, and that were now joining forces and uniting in all their rich diversity in defence of a common human ideal [1]. In the same speech at the Capitol, the Belgian Foreign Minister, who had played a leading role in the preparation and negotiation of the Treaties, asserted that economics and technical progress would be the means of saving a civilisation, the moral order, a vision of life that was both just and in keeping with man as a fraternal being [2].

The Commission 1958–72

The signing of the Treaties signalled a new beginning, putting an end to the crisis which had followed the crushing failure of the plan to set up a European Defence Community, which in turn effectively led to the collapse of the Statute of the European Community drawn up in 1953. But, for the institutions entrusted with the task of translating the provisions of the new Treaties into reality, their implementation was to be a matter of 'inventing things as they

---

[1] *La pensée européenne et atlantique de Paul-Henri Spaak (1942–1972)*, Collection of texts edited by Paul-F. Smets, Preface by André de Staercke, Vol. 1, J. Goemaere, Brussels, 1982, p. 613.
[2] Ibid.

went along (¹). An essential role among these institutions was played by the executive, which at first meant the executives of the three Communities — the High Authority of the European Coal and Steel Community, the Commission of the European Economic Community and the Commission of the European Atomic Energy Community — and, after their merger, the Single Commission. The Commission did not confine itself to the role of guardian of the Treaties. Its working methods were not immutable, and over the years it introduced innovations which reflected not only the new demands but also the character of the individuals who shaped it (²).

This book examines the role of the Commission in implementing the Treaties and the ensuing successes and setbacks during the period from the beginning of 1958 to the enlargement from six to nine Member States on 6 January 1973.

A period of 15 years is covered. In historical terms, this is just a blink of the eye. But, in terms of the history of European integration, it is a long time. This period was also one that saw important changes at international level and within each individual country.

However, a deliberate decision was taken not to cover the wider background or the history of European construction or integration, on the assumption that readers are familiar with the general context and the main events of the construction of the European Communities. There is ample excellent literature on the subject which the reader can consult. We have chosen instead to concentrate on the history of the institution and the role of those who embodied it.

Nevertheless, certain important factors have to be mentioned because they help to explain why Europe was perceived as 'a new dawn'.

'Europe, a new dawn' (³)

By the time the Treaties entered into force, on 1 January 1958, the ECSC already had five solid years of experience behind it. It had been created for a term of 50 years and acted as the big sister and model. Based on a French proposal to pool German and French coal and steel production under the control of a common High Authority, with membership open to other partners, the ECSC was created in the context of economic reconstruction and the Cold War.

With the death of Stalin in March 1953, the Cold War evolved into a period of peaceful coexistence from 1955 to 1962, followed by détente up to 1973.

(¹) Interview with Georges Berthoin, 31 January 2004.
(²) Noël, É., *Les rouages de l'Europe — Comment fonctionnent les institutions de la Communauté Européenne*, Preface by François-Xavier Ortoli, 2nd ed., Paris — Brussels, Nathan — Labor, 1979, p. 99.
(³) Interview with Pierre Defraigne, 16 December 2004.

The world of the 1950s was dominated by the United States of America and the Union of Soviet Socialist Republics. It was a period in which the old European colonial powers, profoundly weakened by the Second World War, experienced a wave of decolonisation, while other parties sought either to differentiate themselves from the two superpowers or to seek their assistance by entering into partnerships.

In Bandung in 1955 the countries which would come to be known as the non-aligned nations stated their intention of distancing themselves from both the free-market US model and the true socialist model, while at the same time breaking once and for all with the colonial powers. The Suez crisis, which began on 28 July 1956 following the decision by the Egyptian leader, Gamal Abdel Nasser, to nationalise the canal linking the Mediterranean with the Red Sea, is a good example of this ideology. It also brought into relief two other factors: the ability of Washington and Moscow to impose order on the international scene, and the weakness of two former world powers, France and the United Kingdom.

The fiasco of the Anglo-French operation in Egypt was clearly a rebuff. It was also a sign that times were changing, not only in terms of countries' ranking in the international hierarchy but also in terms of the way people viewed the future. In this respect, the XXth Congress of the Communist Party of the Soviet Union, held in Moscow from 14 to 25 February 1956, had an important ideological and political impact, not least in western Europe.

Stalin's 'errors' and the impact of Khrushchev's report in western Europe

At the XXth Congress the Party's First Secretary, Nikita Khrushchev, presented a report denouncing Stalin's 'errors' (Stalin having died in March 1953). De-Stalinisation, which brought the dissolution of the Kominform (17 April 1956) and the brief promise of better things in Poland and Hungary, also had an impact in western Europe.

Pietro Ingrao, a leading intellectual in the Italian Communist Party, called one of his many works 'L'indimenticabile 1956' [1] (Unforgettable 1956) to convey the dramatic effect — salutary, in his view — which the publication of the Soviet report had on the development of the Left in Italy. It came, according to Giorgio Amendola, at the very height of the political and organisational crisis on the Italian Left, which was incapable of promoting the sort of structural reforms which would have satisfied the new demands being posed

[1] Ingrao, P., 'L'indimenticabile 1956', *Masse e Potere*, Editore riuniti, Rome, 1977, pp. 105–147.

by reconstruction and nascent economic growth, while preventing a situation in which this expansion, in the hands of monopolist interests, exacerbated and heightened all the contradictions in Italian society (¹).

These comments about Italy were echoed elsewhere in Europe, suggesting that the phenomenon was Europe-wide. The year 1956 was, with the benefit of hindsight, a key moment in the history of the French Left. According to the French historian, Serge Berstein, the three components of the French Left — the Parti Radical, the SFIO (French Section of the Workers' International) and the PCF (French Communist Party) — underwent a profound crisis reflecting their failure to adapt to the new realities of the situation in France in the 1950s. He goes on to say that during the crisis itself it was possible to discern the solution which was taking shape, the appearance of a new Left which was still only emerging in latent form, prevented from actual implementation by the weight of the party apparatus, but nevertheless demonstrating the existence of new potential forms that responded to new realities (²).

The Left in other European countries also experienced a similar crisis, accompanied by the first signs of renewal. At the beginning of 1955 the Belgian trade union leader, André Renard, addressed the Bureau of the Belgian Labour Federation (FGTB), pointing out that State intervention was now more extensive than it used to be, yet the holding companies were not subject to any control and the role they played was such that in a modern State they were the ones directing policy. The following year the FGTB conference on the subject of 'holding companies and economic democracy' (³), which set out its aspirations rather than any practical means, demonstrated that the problems facing the economy were clearly on a European scale.

The European dimension

One of these problems — leaving aside industrial restructuring — was Europe's ageing industrial fabric, which led to unacceptable pressure being put on workers to compensate for this disadvantage by working harder and, at the same time, to health and safety rules being flouted (⁴).

Productivity remained an important issue throughout the 1950s, largely because it raised the question of the modernisation of the productive apparatus and also the management methods and worker participation.

(¹) Amendola, G., 'Lotta di classe e sviluppo economico dopo la liberazione', *Tendenze del capitalismo italiano. Atti del convegno di Roma, 23–25 Marzo 1962*, Vol. I: *Le relazioni e il dibattito*, Istituto Gramsci, Rome, 1962, p. 194.
(²) Berstein, S., 'La Gauche française en 1956', *Ripensare il 1956*, Edizioni Lerici, Rome, 1987, p. 297.
(³) Tilly, P., *André Renard — Biographie*, Le Cri, Brussels, 2005, pp. 382–388.
(⁴) Contini, G., 'Gli operai comunisti e la svolta del 1956', *Ripensare* [...], op. cit., pp. 440 and 441.

Productivity, like growth, can be quantified. In terms of the average annual rate of growth of national product in the 1950s, Germany (7.8 %), closely followed by Italy and Austria (both 5.8 %) easily led the field in western Europe, with Belgium (2.9 %) and the United Kingdom (2.7 %) bringing up the rear ([1]). At the same time, the average rate of unemployment was 4 % of the labour force in Belgium but 7.9 % in Italy, which had the highest rate in Europe. The average was 2.9 % ([2]). There was a similar spread in average per capita income. In 1955 the figure was USD 394 in Italy, compared with USD 1 870 in the United States, USD 1 010 in Switzerland, USD 950 in Sweden and USD 800 in Belgium ([3]).

The basis on which the Communities were expected to operate was therefore far from homogeneous in terms of economic and social development. A similar diversity characterised the political situation and national ambitions, given the far-reaching changes that occurred between 1958 and 1973.

The period of the 1960s — the 'Golden Sixties' — was one in which radical upheavals in values went hand in hand with an increasingly technocratic society and ever greater material abundance.

Values turned upside down

Opening the Brussels World Fair in 1958, the King of the Belgians put his finger on the challenges of scientism. 'Mankind has entered a new era of its history', declared Baudouin I. 'More than ever before, civilisation appears to be conditioned by science [...]. Two paths stretch ahead of us: one is the path of rivalry, leading to an arms race [...] which threatens to unleash against humanity the discoveries produced by the genius of its greatest minds; the other should enable us [...] to embark on the road to understanding [...]. Technology is not sufficient for creating a civilisation. If it is to be a force for progress, there must be a parallel development of our moral thinking, our will to engage in a constructive venture together.' ([4])

The 1960s was a decade of scientific progress that was marked first and foremost by the highly symbolic conquest of space, starting with Yuri Gagarin's first flight in 1961 and culminating in Neil Armstrong's first steps on the moon in 1969. The Vatican Council II, meeting from October 1962 to December 1965, strove to adapt and revamp the moral and social order of the Catholic Church and, in so doing, caused considerable upheaval. In the second half of

---

([1]) Van Der Wee, H., *Histoire économique mondiale, 1945–1990*, Academia, Louvain-la-Neuve, 1990, p. 36.

([2]) Ibid., p. 57.

([3]) Bresciani Turroni, C., 'L'economia italiana del dopoguerra', in Banco di Roma, *Review of the economic conditions in Italy — L'economia italiana nel decennio 1947–1957*, Rome, 1956, p. 5.

([4]) *Le Soir*, 18 April 1958, p. 1.

that decade, western society and culture came in for mounting criticism. With its origins in the United States, this challenge to the establishment affected the whole of Europe even if the causes differed. It heralded the end of one world and the beginning of another. The moral crisis was said to be the result of emotional under-employment because 'there was no longer an uplifting cause to promote which could mobilise people's energy and altruism' ([1]). This was all the more true given that Communism had been in crisis since 1956 and Catholicism since Vatican II. Some people consequently saw Europe as a cause that could potentially inspire commitment in the longer term. In the words of Jean Rey at the presentation of the Charlemagne Prize in 1969: 'The Community is an essential element in the unification of Europe, but it represents only one part of Europe. We therefore think that the time has come to try to enlarge the present Community, which is in the process of being merged, and to find ways of successively admitting other European countries, step by step.' ([2])

Jean Rey had stated his conviction, but what of the 180 million inhabitants of the six countries of the Community? In 1971, according to the Commission, opinion polls showed that, on average, three quarters of the population were in favour of European unification. But even if 'it is obviously not the public that is holding back the governments, [...] the popular attitude is more one of tolerance than of actively pressing for change [and] is not sufficient to accelerate the pace of progress towards integration.' ([3]) Moreover, there were pockets of discontent here and there. Consumers blamed the Community for rapid price rises in the agricultural sector, to the point where it appeared to be first and foremost an agricultural community which did not do enough to protect the interests of consumers ([4]). Among workers, the Commission noted disappointment at the failure of social integration to keep pace with economic integration, adding that the public could not yet fully appreciate the practical objectives of, and underlying reasons for, integration at the socio-structural level ([5]).

But dissatisfaction among consumers and workers was not the only problem identified by the Commission at the start of the 1970s. Some young people questioned the very need for efforts at European unification, while others criticised the Community for failing to do enough to eliminate social tensions ([6]). Demographic and cultural changes in the Member States meant that a generation of people born after 1945 was coming of age. These people had not even started school when the Member States took their first steps towards

---

([1]) Rezsohazy, R., *Études sur les systèmes de valeurs des Belges francophones*, Cahier No 1: *La définition des valeurs — 'La méthodologie de leur étude — Leur évolution depuis 1945*, Université catholique de Louvain, Institut des Sciences politiques et sociales, service de diagnostic social, Louvain, 1976, p. 25.

([2]) Quoted by Braekman, E., 'Il y a cent ans: naissance de Jean Rey', programme 'La Voix Protestante', 15 July 2002, broadcast on RTBF-Radio (see www.protestant.be).

([3]) *Programme d'activité d'information pour 1971*, SEC(71) 590 final, Brussels, 2 April 1971, p. 6.

([4]) *Programme de politique d'information 1972*, SEC(71) 4483, Brussels, 9 December 1971, p. 2.

([5]) Ibid.

([6]) Ibid., pp. 1–2.

integration and had experienced neither the deprivations of the war nor the great debates of the post-war period. These comments on a generation which had new centres of interest which were perhaps more cosmopolitan than community-based and a highly developed critical sense which had to be taken into account ([1]), reflect the general and more specific changes between 1958 and 1973. At the same time they show that the responses at Community level had long-term implications but also represented a challenge at the level of everyday life. The poet Louis Aragon might mock the new jargon ('Ô Pool Charbon-Acier, Benelux, Euratom/Nous peuplons le vacarme avec des mots fantômes') ([2]), but these same terms had represented the high hopes of many of the generation that experienced the hardships of war and the debates of the post-war years, and these people would strongly disagree with him.

'The day-to-day reality' ([3])

Although the history of European integration, and indeed the European ideal, has given rise to an impressive number of learned publications, not to mention un-published academic research, as well as primary sources, memoirs and eyewitness accounts, the Commission history has been much less well documented. With-out going too deeply into the causes, it is safe to say that attention has focused primarily on the attitudes of the nation States to the European initiative. The first historians who worked on the subject were essentially specialists in the history of international relations. Consequently there have been many, more often than not excellent histories of European integration. But naturally enough they have devoted very little space to the history of the institutional partners themselves. If the truth be told, quite apart from the problems of access to the archives, the subject was hardly the most attractive in itself. For the unwary researcher it might seem like a matter of poring over what Boris Vian, when describing the common market, referred to as 'Nothons: strange creatures consisting of graphs, statistics, definitions and diagrams' ([4]). Nevertheless, the first attempts at writing the history of the European institutions were gradually made. The definitive work here was the history of the High Authority of the ECSC by Raymond Poidevin, a historian, and Dirk Spierenburg, who was personally involved in the institution ([5]).

The works by Peter Weilemann on Euratom ([6]) and Hanns Jürgen Küsters on the EEC ([7]) were written in a different vein, in that both consider the process

([1]) BAC 3/1978 572, *Programme d'activité d'information pour 1971*, op. cit., p. 5.
([2]) Quoted by Riccardi, F., 'Ortoli, le Français qui mène le Marché Commun', *Réalités — Revue de Paris*, No 330, July 1973, p. 44.
([3]) Interview with Giuseppe Ciavarini Azzi, 6 February 2004.
([4]) Quoted by Riccardi, F., loc. cit.
([5]) Spierenburg, D. and Poidevin, R., *Histoire de la Haute autorité de la Communauté européenne du charbon et de l'acier: une expérience supranationale*, Bruylant, Brussels, 1993.
([6]) Weilemann, P., *Die Anfänge der Europäischen Atomgemeinschaft — Zur Gründungsgeschichte von Euratom 1955–1957*, Nomos Verlag, Baden-Baden, 1983.
([7]) Küsters, H. J., *Fondements de la Communauté Économique Européenne*, Office for Official Publications of the European Communities/Labor, Luxembourg/Brussels, coll. 'Europe', 1990.

leading up to the creation of the two Communities but not the early days of their operation and still less the institutions responsible.

In addition to the general works, there have been numerous specialised studies dealing with particular policies or individuals. The bibliography at the end of this book, without pretending to be exhaustive, contains a list of these works, which were often a great help in the preparation of this study.

Terms of reference

The present study was undertaken at the instigation of Romano Prodi, when he was President of the European Commission. The idea was to trace the history of the Commission during the period when there were just six Member States. In other words, the aim was to explore the nature, the ambitions, the successes, and the disappointments and failures of the Community executive. It was, and still is, an ambitious objective. From the outset it raised a series of issues concerning sources and method. The path that was mapped out in the light of these issues determines the process, which has proved to be extremely enriching in many ways for all those who have followed it.

Sources

The history of an institution, like any other history, is never a straightforward matter, particularly when it involves the present. Some of the many witnesses and actors who were involved, are still alive. They constitute a collection of individual memories, but also a collective memory of the institution's past. These memories are a potentially vital source in that they can help to breathe life into the material furnished by the archives.

'The mouth of truth'?

The use of oral testimony, which has now joined the historian's armoury of sources and methods, is not a panacea [1]. Oral testimony, like written sources, has to be handled according to the basic principles of critical history. Just because a person has witnessed an event or a decision-making process or has held a particular office does not make their testimony a pronouncement from 'the mouth of truth', to borrow Danièle Voldman's expression [2]. But it

---

[1] Descamps, Fl., *L'historien, l'archiviste et le magnétophone: de la constitution de la source orale à son exploitation*, Ministère de l'économie, des finances et de l'industrie, CHEFF, Paris, 2001. Contains a useful bibliography on pp. 772–828.

[2] Voldman, D. (ed.) *La bouche de la Vérité? La recherche historique et les sources orales*, Cahiers de l'IHTP, 21, Institut d'histoire du temps présent, Paris, 1992.

is not just this. Since the past we are revisiting remains alive in the physical presence and voices of those who lived through it, the historian has the possibility of eliciting source material for himself (¹). The corollary to this is that the historian then feels he is under observation in that the actors can contest his assertions, dispute his interpretation and, on the basis of having actually been there when the events took place, declare at best that the author is well meaning but mistaken and at worst that he is falsifying the truth (²).

Confronting individual witnesses on the subject of a period or a field of activity often reveals contradictions, conflicting interpretations or even material errors as regards what exactly happened. Consulting archived documents, if these are accessible, can remove some of these doubts. But written sources are considered by some as being of secondary importance for contemporary history, leaving the historian without any means of deciding between two conflicting memories. Objective factors will have to play a role. These include the distinction between direct and indirect witnesses and the degree of credibility of witnesses, which is assessed on the basis of the verifiable elements in their story.

But the degree of credibility may prove to be the product of a more subtle process, in that the way the historian views certain witnesses whom he trusts for what are sometimes irrational reasons can decisively influence his choice of witnesses to consult, and the way he treats their comments.

These are the conditions in which the historian meets the different men and women he is interviewing and whose words he records and transcribes. They are his sources and they represent a remarkable cast of characters of whom La Bruyère would have been proud. The range of personalities is enormous: from the individual with a hugely inflated ego to the seemingly self-effacing person whose evidence reveals a perfect command of a sensitive dossier. The differences may be crucial, particularly as the witness in turn perceives the historian in his own particular way. The quality of the testimony thus depends also on the degree of empathy between the interviewer and the interviewee.

The testimony that is recorded and transcribed may not necessarily correspond in every case to the version which the interviewee ultimately authorises for publication. Corrections may be made to the substance as well as to the form. Sometimes the interview will have triggered further recollections which bring back memories that may have been buried, at other times the spontaneous response of the interviewee may have led him to voice opinions about individuals or the institution which, on reflection, have to be altered or deleted.

There are several reasons for the interviewees' customary discretion, including respect for the individuals concerned and the duty of reserve with regard to

---

(¹) Ibid., p. 7.
(²) Ibid.

the institution. While legitimate, these considerations can be frustrating for the historian who has to use the authorised version of the interview.

The complexity of collecting and using individual oral testimony is compounded in the case of the history of an institution by the inherent complexity of collusion between witnesses. This happens after, rather than before, the event when the witnesses discover what the historian has done with the different accounts of a particular issue. Forty years after the event, feelings of solidarity generated in the daily work which they performed with such enthusiasm will mean that today they have similar views about the meaning of the past they shared. This shared memory, which is indicative of a very strong collective identity, can cause real problems for the historian, the onus being on him to prove that a differing interpretation of the past is possible.

So there are, on the one hand, the individuals with their personal recollections who may also act as the guardians of the collective memory and, on the other, the historians with their interpretations that may or may not correspond to those recollections. The task is then to write a book commissioned by an institution that forms the third side of the triangle. This book is the result of comparing the different points of view or, in some cases, entrenched positions and will consist of a 'negotiated interpretation' because maintaining a unilateral position would provoke a crisis.

Negotiated interpretation

The concept of negotiated interpretation, in particular as discussed and conceptualised by *Public History* in America, emphasises four factors: (i) witnesses and historians engage in a joint investigation of the past; (ii) in response to a commission by an institution; (iii) to serve an educational purpose, for example for the institution's staff [1], and (iv) with due regard to the ethical rules on personal privacy.

The joint investigation leads to the negotiated interpretation, which implies that authority is shared between the witness and the historian. In other words, there is a dialogue based on a deliberate decision to relinquish some control over the product of the historical investigation. As the specialists put it, this negotiated interpretation lies somewhere 'between advocacy and mediation' [2]. This can bother the historian because 'it is a constant negotiation, based on trust and work that seems far from the historical practices we have been trained to follow.' [3]

---

[1] See Page, D. M., 'The public historian in human resource development and management', *The Public Historian*, Vol. 8, No 4, 1986, pp. 7–26.
[2] Corbett, K. T. and Miller, H. S., 'A shared inquiry into shared inquiry', *The Public Historian*, Vol. 28, No 1, 2006, p. 15.
[3] Ibid., p. 20.

This book is thus the result of a unique experiment in many ways. The presentation of this project would not be complete without a brief description of the main aspects of the way the work has been organised.

Organisation of the project

Following an invitation to tender, a consortium known as CONSHIST.COM was commissioned to gather testimony from officials who had worked in the EEC Commission between 1958 and the beginning of 1973 and, if necessary, from their colleagues in the EAEC Commission and the High Authority of the ECSC who joined their ranks as a result of the merger, and then to write this history of the Commission.

The consortium was composed of universities in Germany (Essen), Belgium (Louvain-la-Neuve), France (Cergy-Pontoise, Paris IV, Strasbourg III — Robert Schuman), Italy (Padua) and the Netherlands (Groningen), together with an institution in Luxembourg (Centre de recherche et d'études européennes Robert Schuman) and the historical archives of the European Union in Florence. It coordinated the efforts of seven academics working on the ground, all of them holders of Jean Monnet chairs in history (Professors Marie-Thérèse Bitsch, Gérard Bossuat, Éric Bussière, Michel Dumoulin, Wilfried Loth, Jan van der Harst and Antonio Varsori) and a number of other researchers. These included a number of senior figures (such as Jean-Marie Palayret) and some more junior ones, most of whom participated enthusiastically in the project [1].

The task of coordinating the organisation and work of the consortium fell to the Université catholique de Louvain (Louvain-la-Neuve) [2], with a steering committee [3] providing further assistance and advice. This was particularly valuable for drawing up lists of former officials who might be able to contribute their recollections.

The European Commission also set up a steering committee [4] which was obviously intended to monitor the progress of the project but which also proved to be a very valuable source of information on many questions of substance. In the final stage of the process, these substantive questions prompted another read-through by an ad hoc committee whose objections, comments and other suggestions prompted sometimes heated discussions with the historians — a perfect example, in fact, of the negotiated interpretation we discussed above. The entire project was overseen by the Secretary-General of the European Commission.

---

[1] Julie Cailleau, Anaïs Legendre, Veronica Scognamiglio, Corinne Schroeder, Myriam Rancon, Ghjiseppu Lavezzi, Veronika Heyde, Nienke Betlem and Mariella Smids.
[2] Michel Dumoulin, Yves Conrad, Natacha Wittorski, Julie Cailleau and Corinne Schroeder.
[3] Fernand Braun, Giuseppe Ciavarini Azzi, Jean-Claude Eeckhout, Jacqueline Lastenouse, Robert Pendville and Paul Romus.
[4] Jean-Claude Eeckhout, Antonio Marchini Càmia, Hartmut Offele and representatives of the Secretariat-General of the European Commission.

This wealth of detail about the organisation of the work is intended to show that the project was not simply a matter of commissioning a couple of historians to write the sort of study they are used to producing. In fact, the work produced on the basis of the existing literature and exhaustive archive research, for example in the historical archives of the European Commission in Brussels (where the assistance of Ms Jocelyne Collonval proved to be invaluable), took on an original character thanks in part to the content of the 120 interviews with former officials, which have now been placed in the historical archives of the European Union in Florence, and in part to the oral and, above all, written responses of members of the editorial committee.

It is, of course, up to the readers to form their own opinion of the book. But this introduction should be rounded off by highlighting a few of the specific features of the institution, the different stages of whose development and whose ultimate identity clearly emerge from the pages of the book but are not systematically spelt out at any point.

Specific features of an institution

In 1958, despite — or because of — the precedent of the ECSC, the EEC Commission and the EAEC Commission faced the essential problem of establishing their identity. Implementing the Treaties was not just a technical matter. It entailed creating and nurturing a culture which was different from traditional diplomacy. The Commission is not the executive branch of a State. Nor is it merely a technical body serving the Member States. The latter, confident in their own political and administrative cultures and jealously guarding their prerogatives and sovereignty, tended (particularly in the case of France) to downplay the role of the Commission. The Commission responded with consistent efforts specifically aimed at asserting its identity by working towards integration, which could be seen not as an end in itself but as a means of progressing from nation-based societies to a new form of society [1].

The inventiveness of the early days

As the instrument of integration, the Commission devoted much of its energy from the outset to framing common policies, a role which the Single Commission continued to pursue according to Émile Noël who, as Secretary-General, was one of the leading protagonists. As Noël put it, independently of the economic necessities, the EEC Treaty was effectively a 'framework treaty', unlike the Euratom Treaty or the Coal and Steel Treaty, which could be described as 'legislative treaties' [2].

---

[1] Kohlhase, N., 'Gesellschaftspolitische Aspekte der Europäischen Gemeinschaft', in Mestmäcker, E.-J., Möller, H., and Schwarz, H.-P., (Hersg.), *Eine Ordnungspolitik für Europa — Festschrift für Hans von der Groeben zu seinem 80. Geburtstag*, Nomos Verlag, Baden-Baden, 1987, p. 211.

[2] Noël, É., *Les rouages* [...], op. cit., p. 33.

The result was that, apart from the 'automatic' clauses on the abolition of customs duties and quotas, the whole area of economic union was left blank in the Treaty ([1]). Does this mean the Treaty was 'neutral' in terms of fundamental economic policy orientations? It is a legitimate question. There is also the matter of the relationship between the economic order and the legal order. Clearly, the founding Treaty had certain original features, not least the whole aspect of 'supranationality'.

Supranationality

This specific feature was not a natural consequence of the Treaty framework. The Treaties of Rome were conceived as a new initiative launched after the crushing failure of the European Defence Community project, which had, in turn, brought down the proposed European Political Community. In the climate that this had created, the EEC Treaty, covering the whole economy and not just a single sector like the European Coal and Steel Community, could hardly seek to create a Commission endowed with powers as great as those of the High Authority of the ECSC. The skill of the founding fathers (Monnet) and certain negotiators (Spaak) lay in creating an institution whose powers were such that they could bring the Community much greater supranationality than was initially apparent.

As one former official explained ([2]), the exclusive right to initiate legislation conferred on the Commission had the effect of giving it a greater say in the choice of Community priorities than the Council. Similarly, the fact that the Council had the right to decide by qualified majority rather than unanimity only if it stuck to the Commission's proposal tended to enhance considerably the priorities and solutions chosen by the Commission. Finally, its role as guardian of the Treaties gave it a definite advantage when it came to exploring the potential of the Treaty provisions before the Court of Justice. As von Staden put it, 'einmal ist das Recht auch eine politische Waffe' ('for once the Law is also a political weapon') ([3]).

The legal approach

The Commission still had to give practical effect to the prerogatives conferred on it by the Treaty and hence to assert its authority. To do so, the leaders of the Commission had to resort to exercising the right of initiative wisely but effectively and to exploiting the institution's role as guardian of the Treaty in order to explore the scope of its various provisions.

([1]) Ibid., p. 34.
([2]) Memo from Antonio Marchini Càmia dated 7 March 2005.
([3]) Von Staden, B., op. cit., p. 189.

The Commission followed this legal approach by adopting an interpretation of the Treaty which gave priority to the objective being pursued rather than the letter of the law. It also selected the particular cases to pursue on the basis of the light they could shed on future action, much more so than because of their intrinsic importance. It also made its position known to the Court of Justice not only in cases to which it was a party but also in all cases referred to the Court for interpretation by national courts.

In taking this approach, the Commission was supported by a Court whose interpretation amounted to nothing less than a 'peaceful judicial revolution' [1]. The frequent agreement — or complicity — between the Commission and the Court, mirroring that between Émile Noël and Joseph Mertens de Wilmars, a judge at the Court of Justice in Luxembourg, on the interpretation of the Treaty and the measures taken pursuant to it yielded rich rewards. Often the Commission would refer a matter to the Court or adopt a position which allowed, or made it easier for, the Court to deliver important judgments in individual cases, but equally the 'bridgeheads' created by these judgments often enabled the Commission to launch successfully legislative initiatives which had wider implications.

Fundamental judicial breakthroughs which today might appear self-evident were by no means guaranteed practice at the time. Two important examples amply illustrate this point: the primacy of Community law over national law and the direct effect of both Community regulations and certain provisions of directives and the Treaty itself. (The direct effect of Community law, by directly conferring on the individual the right to claim from the Court the protection afforded to him by the law, led to a proliferation of cases where the national court requested an interpretation of Community legislation from the Court of Justice, thereby making it possible to explore the limits of the Treaty.)

One only has to look at the positions defended by the Member States before the Court in the cases that produced these breakthroughs to realise to what extent the arguments advanced by the Commission and endorsed by the Court were far from unanimously accepted. The primacy of Community law over national law, for example, was challenged by the Netherlands, Belgium, Germany and Italy, and the courts in France, Italy and Germany were slow to accept it even after the Court of Justice had clearly ruled on the matter [2]. As for direct effect, it was recognised by the Court despite opposition from several Member States and even a contrary opinion from its own Advocate-General [3].

[1] Lecourt, R., *L'Europe des Juges*, Bruylant, Brussels, 1976, p. 8.
[2] Ibid., pp. 250–251 and 255 *et seq.*
[3] Ibid., p. 250.

Important though it was, the legal approach alone would not have been enough. Whatever the powers conferred on a 'supranational institution' by a treaty and whatever the nature of its decisions, the success and effectiveness of the action it takes will ultimately depend above all on the authority it can command among the Member States. This is particularly true in those areas where the Treaty assigned to the Commission a role less powerful than, or subordinate to, that of the Member States. Noël was well aware of this. 'All that counts in the final analysis, apart from the legal rules, is the technical quality and political wisdom of the proposals put forward, the calibre of the officials representing the Commission, and the personal authority and character of the Members of the Commission' ([1]).

Thus, for example, it was not by virtue of any power derived from the Treaty that the Commission was able to secure an important role for itself in the negotiations on enlargement. Having had to overcome initial opposition from France and the Netherlands in particular in order simply to obtain an advisory seat with the right to speak, the Commission gradually gained the Member States' trust and became a protagonist thanks to its command of the dossiers, the quality of the documents it produced and the objectivity and balance of the solutions it suggested ([2]). The same was true — to mention just one other example in the development policy field — of the drafting of the Yaoundé Convention in 1963. The experience and technical superiority of its officials enabled the Commission to play the major role, even though it had not been officially charged with leading the negotiations ([3]).

These comments and considerations reflect a dynamic and, in many cases, an inventiveness which could not have existed without men and women who, for all the myths surrounding the origins of the Commission, were in practice often inspired by the spirit of adventure.

Manual labourers, conspirators and other missionaries

The 120 former officials who agreed to be interviewed do not constitute a statistically representative sample. We must be careful not to generalise because, in terms of their career and involvement, they represent a body of experience which surpasses the norm, but it is nevertheless interesting to pick out a few important points.

Some of these officials, regardless of their rank in the hierarchy at the time, regard themselves as Europe's 'manual labourers' ([4]), others as 'missionaries' ([5]). Or, to use a recent expression coined by Joachim Bitterlich, 'a band of conspirators' ([6]).

([1]) See the chapters on administration and Émile Noël.
([2]) See the chapter on enlargement, pp. 539–562.
([3]) See the chapter on development, p. 377.
([4]) Interview with Georges Berthoin, 31 January 2004.
([5]) Interview with Jacques-René Rabier, 8 January 2004.
([6]) *La Croix*, 4 February 2005, p. 42.

Several factors, some of them complementary, explain this attitude, which led to a sense of solidarity in their work and to the emergence of a strong institutional identity.

In the case of some officials, as Georges Rencki repeatedly pointed out during our interviews, active involvement in the European Movement or the experience gained in the European Youth Campaign, for example, helped to preserve a particular outlook and to create alliances across the institution.

Other factors common to any enterprise culture are the charisma, competence or strength of conviction of a particular hierarchical superior. This creates a sort of vertical solidarity and helps to dispel the impression of the EEC Commission as a soulless monolith. The expressions used by the interviewees refer to the existence of groups of officials united by their common past experience — the 'veterans of Val-Duchesse' ([1]) — which reinforces solidarity across the institution, or the groups that formed around a particular individual ('the von der Groeben circle', 'the Rabier gang') illustrating vertical solidarity.

Similarly, national networks that produced EEC officials could also create loyalties based on a shared administrative culture, and these need to be borne in mind. Examples of this are the German Foreign Office and the 'high-tech Colbertism' ([2]) of the French civil service.

The oral testimony is again particularly valuable here. There is a wealth of information that does not appear and will never appear in the archives. The lunchtime conversations between officials, the meetings between Monnet, Noël and Fontaine on a Saturday morning in Paris, the Friday evening train from Brussels to Paris and any number of other details convey the mysterious alchemy at work, without which officials from six countries that had recently been at war could never have shaped the institution. So while it is true that certain major figures stand out among the ranks of the Commissioners and that interviewees frequently recalled the commanding role of the Secretary-General, Émile Noël, and the 'signorilità' of the head of the Legal Service, Michel Gaudet, it is clear that the results achieved by the time of the first enlargement were due to a much larger number of officials.

'Nobody's perfect'

This history was not designed or written as an apologia for the institution, and it would be wrong to gloss over certain controversies and even crises during the Commission's early days which still today divide historians and provoke

---

[1] Interview with Henri Étienne, 12 January 2004.
[2] According to Elie Cohen, quoted by Hougounenq, R. and Ventelou, B., 'Les services publics français à l'heure de l'intégration européenne', *Revue de l'OFCE*, No 80, January 2002, p. 8, the expression applies to the period between the nationalisations of the immediate post-war period and the 1980s.

differences of opinion between witnesses as regards the responsibility of the institutional actors involved.

As we will see in the chapter on the 'empty chair' crisis, for example, the causes of this episode continue to cause controversy. One thing, however, is clear. The crisis significantly restricted what was supposed to be an important extension of the scope for majority decision-making on 1 January 1966 [1]. As Émile Noël made clear: 'After the crisis [...], recourse to majority voting was for a long time restricted to purely administrative or budgetary measures' [2]. So, even though this was progressively relaxed in a number of ways later on [3], the Commission's activity suffered as a result during the years under consideration here because its role, which had resembled that of a referee, was in danger of being reduced to no more than a simple mediator [4].

A second example of differences of opinion, then and now, was agricultural policy. Some argue that this policy had the effect of guaranteeing excessively high intervention prices, which resulted in the development — so often lambasted in the media — of very costly cereal and butter 'mountains'.

But as the chapter on agricultural policy shows, these allegations, which place the blame entirely on the Commission, have to be challenged. Agricultural prices are fixed by the Council, not the Commission, although the Commission does draft the proposal. But 'in the majority of cases the Commission's proposals in this area were for levels much lower than that set by Parliament and, in particular, the Council. Moreover, the Council flatly rejected the proposals in the Mansholt Plan aimed at reducing supply by means of 'set-aside', for example, in order to prevent 'surpluses' [5].

The chapters devoted to these two areas may debunk the received opinions on these matters, but this does not alter the fact that reservations may legitimately be voiced about the Commission's efforts in the field of transport — one policy where the Treaty did confer significant powers on the executive — and, to a certain extent, social policy. These reservations are set out in the chapters dealing with these questions.

An educational purpose

This history and these memoirs of the Commission during the years under consideration provide examples and lessons which resemble a dialectical

---

[1] Noël, É., *Les rouages* [...], op. cit., p. 41.
[2] Ibid., p. 43.
[3] Ibid. The author added that this tendency received a marked fillip at the meeting of Heads of State or Government in December 1974, where it was felt that the practice of requiring unanimous support of the Member States for a decision should be abandoned.
[4] Memo from Antonio Marchini Càmia dated 7 March 2005.
[5] Memo from Georges Rencki dated 5 August 2006.

exchange between the past and the present on the subject of European integration. The book is neither an apology nor a manual for the perfect European, but it can serve an educational purpose by acting as a reminder, through a better understanding of the past that, while pursuing what the Member States desire and what they can agree on, we should never lose sight of what the public is prepared to accept.

The plan for the work was criticised by some actors and interviewees on the grounds that too much attention was paid to certain policies which were, at the time, no more than a vain hope. While it is perfectly true that some of these policies were still in their infancy at the time of the first enlargement, it is equally true that they subsequently experienced significant growth and have now become vital sectors. In the knowledge that we often examine the past through the eyes of the present, the authors felt that it was legitimate to adopt a perspective which, without falling into the trap of anachronism, aimed at doing full justice to the recognised achievements, but without ignoring what was still taking shape. This was effectively a way of demonstrating that the Treaty of Rome establishing the EEC was a framework treaty.

Concluding remarks

Many people have helped to make this book possible. Working on this project has forged a sense of solidarity in that none of us could have achieved this result without the help of the others. We would like therefore to express our sincere thanks to all those who contributed to what proved to be a major undertaking. It is with sadness, too, that we remember those interviewees who died between the start of the project and its completion.

The passing of these individuals brings me to my final point. The experience gained with this project shows that the memory of the Commission, like that of any other institution, needs to be carefully recorded and preserved. It constitutes an irreplaceable part of our heritage. Not least because a knowledge of what has gone before ought to form part of our baggage for the present. With this in mind, we should be urgently thinking of introducing a system of systematically gathering the testimony of officials who are about to retire. Far from being a nostalgic exercise, this living memory bank could be a tool contributing to the continuous efforts to improve governance in an institution that is constantly changing and adapting.

Part One

THE COMMISSION
AND ITS PEOPLE

CARDIFF
CAERDYDD

On 25 March 1957 the representatives of the Six sign the Rome Treaties in the Sala degli Orazi e Curiazi at the Capitol in Rome. An Interim Committee was set up to prepare the entry into force of the Treaties.
From left to right: Paul-Henri Spaak and Jean-Charles Snoy et d'Oppuers (Belgium); Christian Pineau and Maurice Faure (France); Konrad Adenauer and Walter Hallstein (Germany); Antonio Segni and Gaetano Martino (Italy); Joseph Bech (Luxembourg); Joseph Luns and Johannes Linthorst Homan (Netherlands). Another of the signatories, Lambert Schaus, is missing from the photo.

Chapter 1

The Interim Committee
(April 1957 to January 1958)

While it stands to reason that the first date in the history of the EEC Commission was its inauguration on 16 January 1958, there obviously had to be a prehistory. The prehistory consisted of a period of meetings, discussions and negotiations that filled the brief interlude between the signing of the Treaties of Rome and the new institution's inauguration. But it would be a mistake to forget that the preparations for setting up the EEC Commission coincided with those for the EAEC Commission. Especially as there was one particularly anxious and attentive observer that had been up and running since 1952 — the ECSC.

The few months separating the ceremony on Capitol Hill and the time when the new Commissions got down to work are highly significant, not so much in terms of the practical organisation of the new institutions as of designating a President and, above all, the future pattern of relations between the Council and the Commissions.

Establishing the Committee

On 7 March 1957 the Intergovernmental Committee for the Common Market and Euratom met in Brussels to consider the tasks to be performed by the Heads of Delegation as the Interim Committee once the Treaties were signed. It met again on 23 and 24 March. On 25 March the Committee of Ministers took note of the report by the Heads of Delegation and established the Interim Committee.

The option that was selected was not the obvious one, given the existence of the model of the ECSC and the experience of the Intergovernmental Committee.

The precedent of the ECSC

The first meeting of the special Council of Ministers, held in Luxembourg from 8 to 10 September 1952, instructed an ad hoc group to come up with proposals on how its work should be organised. One of these proposals was that there should be a Council of Ministers Coordination Committee (COCOR) consisting of three members per country. In addition to preparing the ground for meetings, it would coordinate the work of the various committees set up by the Council (¹), although it would also be the place

---

(¹) Spierenburg, D. and Poidevin, R., *The history of the High Authority of the European Coal and Steel Community — Supranationality in operation*, Weidenfeld and Nicolson, London, 1994, p. 60.

where complaints about the Council's loss of status to the High Authority [1] would be aired.

At the same time the COCOR, which met for the first time on 5 March 1953, developed what Ernst Haas, as early as 1958, described as 'the principle of a novel community-type organ' [2].

This new institutional culture undoubtedly influenced the organisation, composition and *modus operandi* of what is commonly known as the Spaak Committee [3], which, after the Venice Council, became the Intergovernmental Committee for the Common Market and Euratom.

The Spaak Committee (and its successor) were described as a 'rather extraordinary club' by Émile Noël, who added that it 'was both a meeting place of authorised and faithful spokesmen of the six governments and a group of militants dedicated to a vast and noble political undertaking' [4].

While Émile Noël's enthusiasm about the deeply felt convictions of certain of those involved needs tempering, the fact remains that the 'club' in question had adopted the form of a permanent negotiating body. This was why Jeffrey Lewis felt able to write that the practice established between the autumn of 1955 and the spring of 1957 was behind 'one of the less well-known political coups in the history of the EU' [5], namely the article in the Treaties establishing the EEC and Euratom that provided for 'a Committee consisting of the Permanent Representatives of the Member States [...] responsible for preparing the work of the Council and for carrying out the tasks assigned to it by the Council' [6].

This clarifies the background to the fact that the Interim Committee, which was set up on 25 March 1957 and met for the first time under its new name on 16 and 17 April, consisted of the former Heads of Delegation to the Intergovernmental Committee, faithfully preserving the atmosphere and the spirit that had prevailed since 1955, and probably earlier too, in the COCOR. What is more, the representatives of the three Benelux countries on the Interim Committee — Snoy et d'Oppuers, Schaus and Linthorst Homan — were among the signatories to the Treaties, whereas the Frenchman Marjolin, the Italian Badini Confalonieri and the German Ophüls did not have that status.

That said, before considering what the Committee actually did, it is worth mentioning the context in which they did it.

The context

The Interim Committee was operating under what were by no means the most favourable conditions.

For one thing, the national parliaments were still in the process of ratifying the Treaties of Rome [7]. The Bundestag was the first to do so, on 5 July 1957. The Dutch First Chamber rounded the process off on 4 December. But criticisms voiced in both The Hague and Brussels, without calling the Treaties into question as such, revealed the existence of serious tensions [8] which, particularly on the Belgian side, were liable to have an impact on the Committee. Without going into detail, Spaak, who took office as NATO Secretary-General in March 1957, was replaced by Victor Larock, who had great difficulty handling the

[1] Spierenburg, D. and Poidevin, R., op. cit., p. 78.

[2] Haas, E., *The uniting of Europe — Political, social, and economic forces, 1950–1957*, Stanford University Press, Stanford, 1958, p. 491.

[3] Dumoulin, M., 'Les travaux du Comité Spaak (juillet 1955–avril 1956)', in Serra, E. (ed.), *Il rilancio dell'Europa e i trattati di Roma; La relance européenne et les traités de Rome; The relaunching of Europe and the Treaties of Rome*, — Actes du colloque de Rome, 25–28 mars 1987, Bruylant/L.G.D.J./Nomos Verlag, Brussels/Paris/Baden-Baden, 1989, pp. 195–210.

[4] Noël, E., 'The Committee of Permanent Representatives', *Journal of Common Market Studies*, Vol. 5, 1967, No 3, p. 219.

[5] Lewis, J., 'National interests: Coreper', in Peterson, J. and Shackleton, M. (eds), *The institutions of the European Union*, The New European Union Series, Oxford University Press, Oxford, 2002, p. 280.

[6] Article 151 of the EEC Treaty and Article 121 of the Euratom Treaty.

[7] On the ratification of the Treaties: Küsters, H.-J., *Fondements de la Communauté économique européenne*, Office for Official Publications of the European Communities/Labor, Luxembourg/Brussels, 1990, pp. 336–347.

[8] See the concise but eloquent remarks by Bitsch, M.-Th., *Histoire de la construction européenne*, 2ᵉ éd., Complexe, Brussels, 1999, p. 123, and Gerbet, P., *La construction de l'Europe*, 3ᵉ éd., Imprimerie nationale, Paris, 1999, pp. 188–189.

'Europe united for progress and peace' proclaims this Italian poster celebrating the signing of the Treaties of Rome on 25 March 1957. It also quotes a passage from a speech given in Milan on 26 April 1953 by Alcide De Gasperi (1881–1954) to leaders of the Christian Democrats in Upper Italy: 'Europe's frontiers will finally be torn down and we will have a single Community and free movement of people and goods, and above all of labour' ('Per la legge maggioritaria', in De Gasperi, A., *Nel Partito popolare italiano e nella Democrazia cristiana*, Cinque Lune, Vol. II, 1990, Rome, pp. 473–492). The signing of the Treaties also attracted the attention of that other transnational institution, the Catholic Church. Pope Pius XII had listened closely to Spaak's speech at the Banco di Roma on 26 March on the subject of tomorrow's Europe, which had been broadcast on Italian radio. On 13 June the Pope addressed a gathering of a thousand delegates to the European Movement's Congress in Rome and gave a particularly interesting speech emphasising the idea of a spiritual and moral 'Community' and its responsibilities, particularly in Africa. He called for the ratification of the Treaties by the national parliaments and expressed a desire for a strengthening of the executives of the new Communities and hence the creation of a unifying political entity ('Die Stimme des Papstes — Stand und Aufgaben der Europäischen Einigung', *Herder Korrespondenz — Orbis catholicus*, 11th year, August 1957, p. 522).

open hostility of the Prime Minister, Achille Van Acker, to the Treaties (¹). It must also be borne in mind that some national administrations were not concealing their hostility to the prospects opened up both by the common market (²) and also by Euratom (³).

A further contributory source of uncertainty in the climate reigning in the second half of 1957 was the situation at the ECSC. In July, René Mayer, President of the High Authority for only a little more than a year, decided to step down. He made the announcement on 18 September. His successor was designated only on 7 January 1958. For more than four months the ECSC was headed by an outgoing President.

In addition, the German Vice-President of the High Authority, Franz Etzel, had been elected to the Bundestag and was waiting for an assurance of a ministerial appointment in Bonn before stepping down from his post in Luxembourg. He finally left shortly after Mayer. As Raymond Poidevin put it, the High Authority was left 'feeling rudderless for several weeks' (⁴). Above all, there was a feeling in some quarters that the first Community, a supranational experience that had aroused great hopes, would now be consigned to a mere supporting role.

The third and final factor that needs mentioning here relates to a perception noted at the time.

A bibliography of material published in the main economic weeklies and monthlies in the six Member States and the United Kingdom in 1957 reveals that the questions arousing the keenest attention among observers and commentators were the planned free-trade area and the overseas territories. Little or no interest was shown in the problem of financing for the new institutions, for example. The same can be said for the Interim Committee. This is paradoxical as the link between the work of that Committee and the planned free-trade area was far from insignificant.

The mandate of the Interim Committee and how it was exercised

The Interim Committee began work on 16 and 17 April 1957. It was chaired by Jean-Charles Snoy and met at Val-Duchesse, with a 10-point mandate.

The first point was highly technical and quickly dealt with. It concerned the drafting of the Protocol on the Statute of the Court of Justice and the Protocol on the privileges and immunities of the Communities, which had not been finalised when the Treaties were signed. There was a flurry of drafting activity in which, curiously enough, the Luxembourger Pierre Pescatore had two votes: one for his own country and one as representative of Belgium (⁵).

At any rate, the Committee, which was empowered to examine all other questions which might need a solution, but excluding any amendment of the Treaties (⁶), was instructed to look both into questions common to the two new Communities and into problems specific to each of them.

The latitude enjoyed by the Committee to look into questions other than those explicitly mentioned in the March 1957 mandate flowed directly from the EEC Treaty, and in particular Article 235, which read:

(¹) Washington, NA 755.13/3-2058, letter from Sprouse in Brussels to State Department, 20 March 1958, regarding incidents dating from October 1957 on the ratification of the Treaties.

(²) See e.g. Prate, A., *Quelle Europe?*, Julliard, Paris, 1991, p. 56 *et seq.*; Quennouëlle-Corre, L., *La direction du Trésor 1947–1967 — L'État-banquier et la croissance*, CHEFF, Paris, 2000, pp. 436–437: 'L'entrée en vigueur du marché commun est prise en compte, bon gré mal gré, dans les cadres de pensée. [...] La CEE est intégrée, même négativement, dans les raisonnements et les argumentations'.

(³) Curli, B., *Il progetto nucleare italiano (1952–1964) — Conversazioni con Felice Ippolito*, Rubbettino, Soveria Mannelli, 2000, p. 203.

(⁴) Spierenburg, D. and Poidevin, R., op. cit., p. 365.

(⁵) Pescatore, P., 'Les travaux du "groupe juridique" dans la négociation des traités de Rome', *Le rôle des Belges et de la Belgique dans l'édification européenne*, Studia diplomatica, Vol. XXXIV, No 1–4, Brussels, 1981, p. 176. See also the interview with Pierre Pescatore by Corinne Schroeder and Jérôme Wilson, 8 July 2005.

(⁶) GEHEC, PB, 23 B, Note by the secretariat of the Interim Committee for the Common Market and Euratom, Brussels, 4 December 1957, p. 5 (MAE 1293 f/57 mts).

The tasks of the Interim Committee concerning Euratom

Four of the tasks assigned to the Interim Committee by the initial mandate concerned Euratom:

— certain preparatory work for the Euratom research programme, notably as regards prototype reactors;

— preparation of a regulation on controls on the dissemination of knowledge regarded as secret;

— monitoring of the activity of the study groups on isotope separation and chemical separation;

— examination of the problems arising in the preparation of the statute of the Supply Agency.

'If action by the Community should prove necessary to attain, in the course of the operation of the common market, one of the objectives of the Community, and this Treaty has not provided the necessary powers, the Council shall, acting unanimously on a proposal from the Commission and after consulting the Assembly, take the appropriate measures.'

In April 1957 there was no Commission and no Assembly. The Interim Committee had, as it were, carte blanche. It set up two ad hoc groups, one for Euratom and one for the common market. Each was to be divided into subgroups. Four of these were directly related to atomic energy. They did not tend to produce much in the way of concrete results. Jean Rey said as much, commenting on 16 January 1958 in his inimitable dry manner, that the Interim Committee had so far had less work to do on Euratom than on the common market [1].

The common market group

The Interim Committee had to deal with two main questions relating to the common market.

The first concerned the Statute of the Monetary Committee provided for by Article 105 of the Treaty, which stated that the Committee, on which there would be two representatives of each Member State and the Commission, would be an advisory body. It would therefore issue only opinions.

The ad hoc group responsible for producing a preliminary draft decision organising the Committee made rapid progress, but in the common market group there was a major difference of opinion between the French and the Germans, more particularly between the Bundesbank's view in favour of independence and the view of the French Finance Ministry [2]. The deadlock in November 1957 meant that the Interim Committee had to leave the problem to be resolved at a later date [3].

The second question was both highly technical and particularly important. The customs subgroup

[1] CEAB, CEE/C/9f/58 ef, Draft minutes of the meeting of the EEC Commission of 16 January 1958, p. 5.

[2] Feiertag, O., 'La France, la CEE et le système monétaire international: les accords généraux d'emprunt ou l'émergence de l'Europe monétaire (1958–1962)', *Le rôle des ministères des finances et de l'économie dans la construction européenne (1957–1978)* — *Actes du colloque tenu à Bercy les 26, 27, 28 mai 1999*, t. I, CHEFF, Paris, 2002, p. 294, and Bottex, A., 'La mise en place des institutions monétaires européennes (1957–1964)', *Histoire, Économie et Société*, 18ᵉ année, 1999, No 4, pp. 754–757. On the attitude of the Bundesbank, see Dickhaus, M., 'Facing the common market — The German Central Bank and the establishment of the EEC, 1955–1958', *Journal of European Integration History*, Vol. 2, No 2, 1996, pp. 93–108.

[3] GEHEC, PB, 23 B, record of the meeting of the Interim Committee of 7 November 1957.

had to produce a draft common nomenclature and calculate the Common Customs Tariff duties for products on the general common market and for products on the nuclear common market ([1]).

After devising a specimen common tariff to serve both as a benchmark and as a common platform for future discussions within the GATT, the ad hoc group made progress towards a common nomenclature. The only remaining difficulties were with quota duties, and they were resolved only later.

A classification of products on the nuclear common market was devised and transmitted to the relevant administrative bodies in the Member States.

Thus, while emphasising that the results of its work on customs questions did not bind either the Member States or the future institutions, the Interim Committee made undeniable progress on various fronts, both in relation to the general common market and in relation to the nuclear common market. It endeavoured to take the same attitude when addressing issues common to the two institutions.

Common questions

Setting up the new institutions obviously raised practical problems. The Interim Committee does not seem to have gone into the language rules or the location of the institutions. True, in November 1957 Snoy received applications from Strasbourg and then Brussels. But the Chairman of the Interim Committee quite properly confined himself simply to taking note ([2]).

There was major preparatory work on the Staff Regulations of Officials, by contrast. The ad hoc group designated on 10 October was chaired by André Molitor. It tabled its report on 25 November. This was a substantial document in two parts.

The first was devoted to problems to be settled in the Staff Regulations. The second looked at solutions in the Staff Regulations or similar instruments at such international institutions as the ECSC, the Council of Europe, the OEEC, the WEU, NATO and Unesco, and even the draft rules for EDC civilian personnel ([3]).

Even so, when asking an ad hoc group to consider the question of Staff Regulations, the Interim Committee expressly reserved for itself — as it diplomatically put it — the examination of certain problems that would arise for the institutions once they began work ([4]).

This formulation actually expressed the ambition of the Interim Committee, and of Snoy in particular, to analyse the tasks to be accomplished by the EEC Commission in its first year of operation. A memorandum was indeed drawn up. It recommended as an example to follow the OEEC secretariat's organisational methods, thereby avoiding the risk of bureaucracy. Hallstein, to whom Snoy handed the document shortly before the Commission took office, disregarded it, as we might have expected ([5]).

What might seem at first sight to be no more than a mere anecdote was, in fact, highly indicative of the importance acquired by the Interim Committee as months went by and of its ambition of playing a leading role after it was transformed into Coreper on the basis of a Council decision of 25 January 1958.

The report presented by Snoy to the constitutive meeting of the members of the EEC Commission at Val-Duchesse on 16 January 1958 is edifying in this respect.

([1]) GEHEC, PB, 23 B, record of the meeting of the Interim Committee of 7 November 1957. Note by the secretariat of 4 December 1957, op. cit., p. 2.

([2]) Hemblenne, B., 'Les problèmes du siège et du régime linguistique des Communautés européennes (1950–1967)', Les débuts de l'administration de la Communauté européenne. Thematic issue of Jahrbuch für Europäische Verwaltungsgeschichte, 4, Nomos Verlag, Baden-Baden, 1992, pp. 130–132.

([3]) GEHEC, PB, 23 B, MAE 1281 f/57mp. Document of 69 pages. See also Sassi, S., 'Gli statuti del personale delle istituzioni comunitarie (1952–1968)', Storia, Amministrazione, Costituzione — Annale dell'Istituto per la Scienza dell'Amministrazione Pubblica, Vol. 8, 2000, Il Mulino, Bologna, 2000, pp. 205–206 (note 45).

([4]) GEHEC, PB, 23 B, MAE 1293 f/57 mts, p. 5.

([5]) Snoy et d'Oppuers, J.-Ch., Rebâtir l'Europe — Mémoires, entretiens avec Jean-Claude Ricquier, Duculot, Paris-Louvain-la-Neuve, 1989, p. 125. In the report presented to the Commission on 16 January, Snoy wrote: 'Le Comité a également estimé utile de transmettre aux institutions certaines réflexions relatives aux problèmes du démarrage'. See BA, WH, 428, CEE/C/10/d/58 mar, Report by the Chairman of the Interim Committee.

The Interim Committee meets at Val-Duchesse, an estate covering more than 28 hectares on the outskirts of Brussels. Its history dates back to 1262, when the first Dominican convent in the Netherlands was founded there. Abandoned during the French Revolution, the abbey was converted into a manor house by new owners. In 1930 the last of them bequeathed the chateau to the Belgian State by royal donation on condition that it was used as a residence for a prince of the royal family or as a reception place for distinguished guests. It was at Val-Duchesse that the intergovernmental negotiations started on 26 June 1956 to prepare the drafting of the Treaties. The first meeting of the EEC Commission would also take place here.

The Committee appears to have dealt with a singularly wide range of issues above and beyond its official mandate. To give just a few examples: the approximation of the laws of the Member States relating to foodstuffs and beverages, collective participation in the extended technical assistance programme of the United Nations, exchanges of views with the delegations of numerous governments and also preparation of common replies to the equally numerous diplomatic notes on political, economic and social aspects of the Treaties.

This effort to coordinate the attitude of the Six is also perceptible in international organisations and conferences such as the Economic Commission for Latin America, the Economic Commission for Europe and the United Nations. Coordination within the GATT was also on the agenda. As the general report by Snoy put it in January 1958:

'The Six asserted that the Rome Treaties were fully in conformity with the provisions of the GATT [...] allowing a selected number of contracting parties to establish a customs union or free-trade area without first seeking a derogation from the General Agreement. The Six stated that this conformity applied not only to the provisions of the Treaty of Rome relating to trade between the Member States themselves but also to the provisions relating to the association of the overseas countries and territories, which establish a free-trade area between those countries and territories and all the Member States. Many other contracting parties voiced fears and criticisms of the Treaty of Rome, particularly as regards the rules applicable to agriculture and the association of the overseas countries and territories. The intention of submitting the Community to periodic examinations or reports has been expressed. The Six stated that they could not agree to being submitted to a form of treatment differing from that applied to other contracting parties. The Six stood firmly by their position. This position was defended by the negotiators for the Six acting in perfect unison in a spirit of close cooperation' (¹).

While this closing observation is visibly appropriate in the case in hand, since the Six were capable of displaying solidarity when they felt themselves under attack, the coordination ambition could not be taken for granted, as became clear in the matter of the European free-trade area.

Free-trade area

On 13 February 1957 the OEEC Council of Ministers decided to open negotiations to determine on what basis it might be possible to establish a free-trade area in Europe. The Interim Committee was quickly instructed to coordinate the attitude of the six Member States towards the problems raised by the plan.

But there is now a major body of literature to show that substantial preparatory work was carried out before the negotiations on a free-trade area began.

(¹) CEAB, CEE/C/10/f/58 mb, Report by the Chairman of the Interim Committee, point II.

Jacques Donnedieu de Vabres describes the European atmosphere in Brussels between 1956 and 1958

'The negotiations involved a large number of actors from different backgrounds — politics, finance, economics, engineering, diplomacy — with a large supporting cast of confidants, extras and interpreters; a world of monologues, dialogues, complex or confused scenes: to sum up, all the elements of an epic spectacle, with passion and patience, science and circus all mixed in [...]

Brussels hosted more and more troops and sent them off into the suburbs, beyond Auderghem, to Val-Duchesse, with its lake reverting to marshland, its woods reverting to primeval jungle, and its old church, closed and virtually deserted [...] The King, the Belgian government, the Gaulois and Bois Seigneur Isaac took it in turns to host the leading actors. The rest of the cast were scattered over a prosperous and hospitable capital, around the Grand-Place and the Avenue Louise, the Rue du Pépin and the Place du Marché-aux-Poissons: they tucked into Zeeland oysters, cabbage, frites, chicory and gueuse, watched the women of Flanders knitting in their front windows, discovered the nouvelle équipe, engaged in intrigue and engaged to be married, or lost themselves in the immense Universal Exhibition Centre.'

Jacques Donnedieu de Vabres, 'Souvenirs de négociations', *Revue du Marché Commun*, No 100, March 1967, p. 118. (Translated from the French)

When on 26 June 1956 the delegations of the Six inaugurated the Val-Duchesse conference to prepare the Treaties of Rome, it was already agreed that there would be clauses providing for the accession or association of third countries.

This was the background to the decision taken by the OEEC Council on 19 July 1956 to set up a working party to study the possibility of an association between the future EEC and the other 11 OEEC members on the basis of a free-trade area.

The Commission and the practical work of the Interim Committee

'The Interim Committee took on the preparation of the work of the future Commissions. But, when the time came, the EEC Commission took virtually no notice of what had been done [...] P. Bourguignon presented the preparatory reports to the Commission when it took office, but these were eventually judged to be of no use.' (Translation)

UCL, GEHEC, Frans De Koster interviewed by Christine Machiels, 12 December 2001.

The working party was chaired by Snoy and reported on 10 January 1957. The report was then the subject of the OEEC Council decision of 13 February.

Between then and October 1957, when the OEEC negotiations began at political level in the Maudling Committee, the British Prime Minister, Harold Macmillan, committed what is now regarded as a strategic error while France, from July 1957 onwards, seriously distanced itself from the planned free-trade area [1].

Macmillan's error was that he wanted the free-trade area to be negotiated by all the 17 members of the OEEC without preparing the ground properly, as Whitehall advised. The preparation would have consisted in setting up a 'balanced group' of British, Danish, Swiss, French and German representatives, not forgetting the Chairman of the Interim Committee. In other words, Snoy would have become the ideal interface between the Six and the Seventeen.

Although the 'balanced group' never got off the ground, Snoy was nonetheless to play a role that was seen in some circles that were keen first and foremost to promote the Europe of Six as being far from clear and even ambiguous.

Snoy 'is a leading apostle of the OEEC–EFTA approach and is somewhat lukewarm on development of the Six', wrote an American diplomat [2], whereas Jean Rey, in conversation with Spaak, expressed the view that: 'Snoy had always been in favour of the OEEC Europe and his involvement in drafting the Treaty of Rome was merely a virtuous interval, after which he was now reverting to his bad old ways' [3].

The Chairman of the Interim Committee, who was also Chairman of the OEEC Trade Committee, was thus seen as a sort of Trojan Horse, an impression that was reinforced in the eyes of some by the fact that, as soon as the Intergovernmental Committee (the 'Maudling Committee') was set up in October 1957, Snoy was a member pending the establishment of the EEC. As a supporter of Greater Europe, however, Snoy regretfully had to acknowledge that establishing a common position created difficulties for the Six which would be overcome only after a prolonged effort [4]. Thirty years later he confessed that the Interim Committee had been incapable of adopting a position on the matter [5]!

The Interim Committee produced a mixed bag of results. On the one hand, there was its capacity to act as a bridge between the negotiation and signing of the Treaties and the inauguration of the new institutions. On the other hand, it failed in certain of the tasks that had been assigned to it in March 1957. But was its role really to tackle certain particularly sensitive dossiers? The question is worth asking.

Without repeating what has already been said about the continuity between the Spaak Commit-

---

[1] Maurhofer, R., 'Revisiting the creation of EFTA: the British and the Swiss case', *Journal of European Integration History*, Vol. 7, No 2, 2001, pp. 68–69.

[2] Washington, NA 755.13/10-2959, McBride memorandum for White, 29 October 1959.

[3] AULB, JR, Note for the file on the Macmillan incident, 4 April 1960, p. 2. (Translation)

[4] CEAB, CEE/C/10/f/58 mb, point I c.

[5] Snoy et d'Oppuers, J.-Ch., op. cit., p. 124.

tee and the Interim Committee, there are still a few important points to be made here.

From the autumn of 1955 onwards, the 'club' or 'clan of elders' ([1]) at Val-Duchesse had become remarkably qualified in European matters. Some of them had a political vision, so much so that, in the case of Snoy, there are all sorts of questions about which way he wished European integration to go.

In addition, the Interim Committee of representatives of the States concerned tended to see the operation of the future Community institutions in terms of pre-established formulas, as can be seen from the memorandum given to Hallstein. Yet there is even more to it than that.

As soon as the EEC Commission was set up, Snoy raised the question of Commission representation at meetings of the representatives of the Member States. It received a measured but clear response. Looking at the ECSC experience, the Commission pointed out that members of the High Authority had never attended meetings of 'alternates' unless they were being held at the invitation of one of its members. Only Marjolin, who immediately opposed this, proposed an alternative to outright refusal. A member of the Commission could attend the meeting chaired by Snoy 'specifying that he was attending without prejudice, given that the decision-making power belonged to the Council, which could not delegate it' ([2]).

This question was raised again in the run-up to the joint meeting of the Commissions and the High Authority with the Council of Ministers scheduled for 25 January. The EEC Commission again stated that any delegation of powers to what was to become Coreper would be contrary to the Treaty ([3]). And it agreed to send an official who would report to the Commission. The Euratom Commission took the same line ([4]).

The attempt by the former Interim Committee to have members of the EEC Commission attend its meetings, which rapidly came to nought, was followed by Coreper's tendency, once it was set up, to issue recommendations to the Euratom Commission ([5])! Needless to say, this provoked a sharp response.

The explanation for Coreper's attempts to assume a role to which it was not entitled is likely to be found in factors that have already been mentioned. But they do not tell the whole story.

The establishment of Coreper revealed that there was extensive manoeuvring in certain Member States regarding ways of conceiving the policy to be followed on Europe.

The first example is Belgium. Snoy, who, as we know, had played the key role, could easily have let his name go forward for a seat on the Commission — he was thinking about this in the spring of 1957 and was encouraged by Spaak ([6]). But he did not do so. Far from it: once Coreper was set up on 25 January 1958, Snoy was designated as the Belgian representative and alphabetical order meant that he became the Committee's first chairman. But his designation applied only for the common market. It was Joseph Van Tichelen, Director-General at the Ministry of Economic Affairs, where Snoy was the Secretary-General, who became the Permanent Representative to Euratom ([7]).

If we are to believe Jean-Charles Snoy, this separation of functions, which profoundly shocked him ([8]), was motivated by political considerations, Van Tichelen being seen as a socialist. But this does not explain everything.

Snoy, on the back of the competence and experience he had built up in international economic

([1]) Interview with Henri Étienne, 12 January 2004.
([2]) BA WH, 428, CEE/C 9d/58 mar, Draft minutes of the meeting of the EEC Commission of 16 January 1958, pp. 9–10. The revised minutes BA, WH, 428, CEE/C 9d/58 (rév.) mar, state that: 'La Commission estime que le Conseil a un pouvoir de décision qu'il ne peut pas déléguer.'
([3]) BA, WH, 429, CEE/C 12d/58 mk, Draft minutes of the second meeting on 24, 25 and 27 January 1958, p. 2.
([4]) CEAB, EUR/C/66/58 f., Minutes of the second meeting of the Euratom Commission, p. 6.

([5]) Ibid.
([6]) Snoy et d'Oppuers, J.-Ch., op. cit., p. 126.
([7]) Van Tichelen's appointment became effective only in March 1958. The Economic Affairs Minister taking over from Jean Rey, Roger Motz, 'n'était pas d'accord sur la nomination [...] mais il finit par s'incliner devant la volonté du Premier ministre'. Ibid, p. 127.
([8]) See footote 5, above.

negotiations since 1945, was exercising functions that brought him closer to the world of foreign affairs than economic affairs proper. And some saw the designation of Jean Rey, Minister of Economic Affairs, as Belgian member of the new EEC Commission in January 1958 as liable to strengthen even further the hold that Snoy now had over European matters. It has already been seen that the Prime Minister, Achille Van Acker, was hostile to European integration (^{1}), so there is nothing surprising about his desire to rein in a senior civil servant who had many a time demonstrated his ability to stand up to ministers whose economic policy options he did not share (^{2}).

That said, Snoy and Van Tichelen remained as Permanent Representatives until 15 January 1959, when Snoy persuaded the Gaston Eyskens government that Ambassador Joseph Van der Meulen should be Belgium's single Permanent Representative.

This decision, with its implication that the permanent representative should come from Foreign Affairs, brings us to another decision, concerning France this time.

Robert Marjolin having been appointed to the EEC Commission, the time came in 1958 for France to designate its permanent representative. The designation was the outcome of an interdepartmental battle for control of European affairs. Until April 1958 Jacques Donnedieu de Vabres, General Secretary of the SGCI, had represented his country on Coreper. But the Quai d'Orsay was keen to assert its view that the permanent representative should be under its authority. At the beginning of April 1958, Ambassador Éric de Carbonnel was appointed Permanent Representative (^{3}).

While many people saw the common market as a matter of purely technical concern, there were others who saw it as a political concern of the utmost importance. In this context, would Coreper speak for the governments, or would it be a forum for sharing opinions, and even cooperating, with the Commission? This was clearly the key issue. The answer to this would substantially determine the balance of power between the Member States and the Commission (^{4}). But it also explains the importance of the selection of the eminent persons to be appointed to the first EEC Commission, a question which was not dealt with by the Interim Committee as such but in parallel with its deliberations, thus revealing the importance of networking and of dialogue between the six capitals.

Extensive manoeuvring

One of the points that came up in the Val-Duchesse negotiations was what the members of the future Commissions were to be called. The word 'Commissioner' (*commissaire*) was not felt to be at all a good choice. Roberto Ducci felt that members would sound like senior police officers. And von der Groeben saw an even worse confusion with the People's Commissar (*Volkskommissar/commissaire du peuple*) (^{5}). In the end, Article 157 of the Treaty referred simply to 'members of the Commission'.

Once this point was settled, the question of who should be President of the EEC Commission was asked, even before the Capitol Hill ceremony. Jean Monnet was already manoeuvring. His candidate was the Dutchman Sicco Mansholt, a political heavyweight who was Minister of Agriculture in the fourth Drees government that had been put together with such difficulty in The Hague in the autumn of 1956. Over the years this seemingly immovable feature of Dutch governments since 1945 had built up a political

---

(^{1}) Prime Minister Van Acker had no compunction about stating publicly that 'the authors of the Schuman Plan should have been shot'. Cf. Dujardin, V., *Jean Duvieusart (1900–1977). Europe, Wallonie-Bruxelles, Léopold III*, new edition, Le Cri, Brussels, 2001, p. 148.

(^{2}) Van Offelen, J., *La ronde du pouvoir — Mémoires politiques*, Didier Hatier, Brussels, 1987, p. 149.

(^{3}) de Castelnau, A., 'Le rôle du SGCI dans les relations de la France avec le Marché commun (1956–1961)', *Le rôle des ministères des finances et de l'économie* [...], op. cit., I, p. 219.

(^{4}) See the study by Émile Noël, cited on page 38, footnote 4, and Zwaan, J., *The Permanent Representatives Committee — Its role in European decision-making*, Nijhoff, Amsterdam, 1995.

(^{5}) FJME, Interview with Hans von der Groeben, 22 May 1984, p. 3.

The first meeting of the EEC Commission takes place at Val-Duchesse on 16 January 1958.
The Commission invites the press to attend.
The Commissioners are seated (from left to right: Hans von der Groeben, Robert Marjolin, Piero Malvestiti, Walter Hallstein, Sicco Mansholt, Robert Lemaignen, Jean Rey and Giuseppe Petrilli), with their *chefs de cabinet* standing behind (at the back: Ernst Albrecht, Jean Flory, Jean-Claude Richard, Swidbert Schnippenkötter, Jacob Jan van der Lee, Georges Rencki, [possibly Guido Mondaini], Alex Hoven and Pierre Lucion). Michel Rasquin is not present.

entourage of relatively young members of the Labour Party (PvdA), actively militating for ever-deeper European integration ([1]). One of them was Jacob Jan van der Lee, agricultural attaché at the Dutch embassy in Rome.

In the first half of March 1957, Monnet showed keen interest in the idea of the job going to Mansholt. When the current government was being formed, Mansholt had hoped for the foreign affairs portfolio rather than being landed with agriculture for ever. But he was to be disappointed. What is more, Drees would have happily done without him altogether. In 1957, therefore, the prospect that Mansholt might leave the Dutch

---

([1]) Van Merriënboer, J. and Pekelder, J., 'Brede basis in een noodwoning — Verkiezingen, formatie en samenstelling van het Kabinet-Dress IV', *Parlementaire Geschiedenis van Nederland na 1945*, Vol. 6, Sdu Uitgevers, The Hague, 1984, p. 43.

political scene was attractive both to those who hoped to shut him up at last and to those who wished to see a Dutchman of real substance heading the future Commission.

Van der Lee was the pilotfish of operation Mansholt, while Monnet was ultimately in charge.

Between March and November 1957 the Avenue Foch was a hive of activity in support of Mansholt's candidacy. The socialist component of the Monnet network was put to work. Émile Noël played his usual vital role as intermediary and interpreter of the situation with Guy Mollet, President of the Council (Prime Minister) in France. But there was no hope without support from the Christian Democrats and the opinion of Chancellor Adenauer, the man on whom it all depended.

At the beginning of November, when Mansholt still seemed to be leading the field, the question of his candidacy became entangled with the presidency of the other two executive bodies, and even with that of the European Investment Bank. Nationality and political affiliation entered into the equation as various scenarios were mapped out in the corridors of the ECSC Assembly. For instance, if Kiesinger (CDU) were appointed to head the High Authority, the socialist at the head of Euratom would be Louis Armand and the Belgian liberal Jean Rey would have a good chance of landing the presidency of the EEC Commission [1]. But this latter hypothesis involved raising the question of where the new institutions were to be located.

Against this backdrop, Adenauer was particularly attached to the symbolic impact of the choice to be made. He saw it as an opportunity to demonstrate the equal treatment (*Gleichberechtigung*) that should be accorded to the Federal Republic of Germany in western Europe [2] without forgetting, as Monnet insisted, to see the question of the presidential appointments in aggregate terms since the individuals concerned would actually be running a joint operation [3].

In Bonn as in the other capitals, preparations were in full swing for the decisions that had to be taken in the national context so as to provide a basis for discussions in the Council of Ministers of the Six. According to the Germans, since Armand was the obvious candidate for Euratom, the pack of options should include one of the other two posts being offered to the Federal Republic of Germany. There was strong opposition to Mansholt, the Italian Carli did not seem convincing, and Jean Rey could be President of the EEC Commission only if Brussels was not the headquarters. Otherwise, Bonn was aware that it had to be prepared to assume the presidency [4]. The name to be put forward should embody the German concept of the economy, i.e. not be a socialist, and be well versed in European issues [5]. On 18 December, Adenauer discussed with President Heuss the question of putting Hallstein forward [6] as the principle of a German presidency seemed acceptable to the other European partners, including the Belgians, who were setting their sights on their capital providing the headquarters [7]. The case was heard and settled, and the name of the first President of the first Commission of the EEC was decided on at a meeting of the Member States in Paris on 6 and 7 January 1958.

MICHEL DUMOULIN

[1] FJME, AMK C 33/6/123, Jacob Jan van der Lee, memorandum for Jean Monnet, Rome, 6 November 1957.

[2] Neuss, B., *Europa mit der linken Hand? Die deutschen Personalentscheidungen für die Kommission der Europäischen Gemeinschaften*, Oldenburg, Munich, 1988, p. 244.

[3] BA, WH 1276, Jean Monnet to Konrad Adenauer, Paris, 7 December 1957.

[4] BA, WH 1092, Note by Karl Carstens for the meeting of the Federal government on 11 December 1957, p. 4.

[5] Enders, U. and Henke, J., *Die Kabinettsprotokolle der Bundesregierung*, Bd. 10: *1957*, Oldenburg, Munich, 2000, 13 December 1957.

[6] See Chapter 3, page 84.

[7] BA, WH, 1432, Walter Hallstein to Konrad Adenauer, Alpach in Tirol, 30 December 1957.

Chapter 2

The Hallstein Commission 1958–67

On 5 and 6 January 1958 the representatives of the governments of the six Member States met in Paris and designated the members of the first Commission of the European Economic Community, to be presided by Walter Hallstein, a close associate of Chancellor Konrad Adenauer. The Frenchman Robert Marjolin, the Italian Piero Malvestiti and the Dutchman Sicco Mansholt were appointed Vice-Presidents. The other Commission members were the Belgian Jean Rey, the Luxembourger Michel Rasquin, the German Hans von der Groeben, the Frenchman Robert Lemaignen and the Italian Giuseppe Petrilli. The Commission thus had one representative from each of the Benelux countries and two from each of the three larger countries.

The powers of the Commission

This institution of nine members, which operated on the basis of the principle of collective responsibility ('collegiality') and was appointed by agreement between the governments, could be seen in some ways as the successor to the High Authority of the European Coal and Steel Community (ECSC). The negotiators had taken the experience of the young ECSC and its High Authority as the starting point when determining its powers and functions. Some of its features were taken over in the new Commission while more specific powers and features were added to make this an original institutional set-up.

For one thing, the Commission, like the High Authority, was the perfect — albeit not the only — incarnation of the Community as a whole, looking beyond the specific interests of the individual Member States. It also symbolised the Community's supranational status. This was the principle that the Commission wished to use as a basis for its institutional and political legitimacy, its inspiration, from the very first years of its life.

But the negotiators of the EEC Treaty also wished to attenuate the supranational character of the new Commission in the decision-making process — though without doing away with it. This question was widely debated when the ECSC was set up. The 1951 Treaty put the High Authority at the centre of the structure, with decision-making powers. At the Paris conference on the 'Schuman Plan', the Benelux countries, who were inclined initially to distrust the supranational approach, secured provisions in the Treaty specifying, and therefore limiting, its scope of action. Once in place, the High Authority, felt by some to be too *dirigiste*, came in for criticism, especially from the large countries, which had no qualms about withholding their assent to some of the most important High Authority decisions, sometimes at the risk of weakening its position. The negotiators of the EEC Treaty did not wish to give the new Commission the same powers or quite the same role. And they were careful to rank the Commission in third place, after the Assembly and the Council and just ahead of the Court of Justice, as if to highlight the fact that it was to play a less preponderant role than the High Authority, which appears first in the description of the ECSC's institutions.

The Treaty of Rome thus took over the institutional architecture of the ECSC, but the equilibrium was subtly shifted, the decision-making capacity now going to the Council, which intrinsically weakened the supranational dimension. Even so, the Commission would maintain these powers for certain policies, such as competition policy, so as to ensure that the internal market operated smoothly and that the application of Community law was monitored on an impartial basis. Also noteworthy is that the structure of the Treaty gave the Commission a far broader power of initiative in the new Community. The Treaty of Rome concerned economic integration in general terms and not only in terms of selected industries. Unlike the Treaty of Paris, it was a framework treaty, providing the Commission with a far wider basis for developing the European Economic Community. The affirmation of the Commission's supranational status lay more in its power of initiative and in the defence of the general interest than in its decision-making power. It was, as the saying goes, an 'engine of integration'.

At the more detailed level, the Treaty spelled out the major areas of power, which it still has today, in Chapter 1 of Part Five, devoted to the institutions (Articles 155 to 163).

Article 155 outlined its functions. It began by providing that the Commission 'shall [...] ensure that the provisions of this Treaty and the measures taken by the institutions pursuant thereto are applied'. Hence it came to be known as the 'guardian of the Treaty'. According to Article 169, 'If the Commission considers that a Member State has failed to fulfil an obligation under this Treaty', it could launch infringement proceedings, the different stages of which being clearly specified by the Treaty. It could ask the Member State to give an explanation; if it considered that the Member State had not properly justified its (in)action, it could issue a reasoned opinion and ultimately, if the State did not come into line within the time allowed, it could refer the matter to the Court of Justice, which 'shall ensure that in the interpretation and application of this Treaty the law is observed' (Article 164). The Commission thus had a variety of means of exerting pressure, with different degrees of force, to secure compliance with the letter and the spirit of the Treaty, subject to review by the Court of Justice and, in some cases, with its support.

The second major power conferred on the Commission was its right of legislative initiative. The Commission thus played a pivotal role in the decision-making triangle, participating, as Article 155 put it, 'in the shaping of measures taken by the Council and by the Assembly in the manner provided for in this Treaty'. Basically, the Council took most of the decisions. In certain cases it could take decisions without reference to the Commission, which could do no more than give an opinion or make a recommendation. But most often — in a wide range of fields particularly related to economic policies — the Council could not take a decision without a Commission proposal, and it needed a unanimous vote to amend the proposal (Article 149). But as long as the Council had not reached its decision, the Commission could amend its initial proposal, in particular if the Assembly had issued an opinion on it, and the Council then had to come to its decision on the basis of the amended proposal. This opened up the possibility of a subtle interplay between the Commission, which proposed, and the Council, which disposed. Having a virtual

The EEC Commission according to the 1957 Treaty

'Article 149

Where, in pursuance of this Treaty, the Council acts on a proposal from the Commission, unanimity shall be required for an act constituting an amendment to that proposal.

As long as the Council has not acted, the Commission may alter its original proposal, in particular where the Assembly has been consulted on that proposal.'

'Article 155

In order to ensure the proper functioning and development of the common market, the Commission shall:

— ensure that the provisions of this Treaty and the measures taken by the institutions pursuant thereto are applied;

— formulate recommendations or deliver opinions on matters dealt with in this Treaty, if it expressly so provides or if the Commission considers it necessary;

— have its own power of decision and participate in the shaping of measures taken by the Council and by the Assembly in the manner provided for in this Treaty;

— exercise the powers conferred by the Council for the implementation of the rules laid down by the latter.'

'Article 157

The Commission shall consist of nine Members, who shall be chosen on grounds of their general competence and whose independence is beyond doubt.

The number of Members of the Commission may be altered by the Council, acting unanimously [...]

In the performance of these duties, they shall neither seek nor take instructions from any Government or from any other body [...]'

'Article 158

The Members of the Commission shall be appointed by common accord of the Governments of the Member States.

Their term of office shall be four years. It shall be renewable.'

'Article 162

The Council and the Commission shall consult each other and settle by common accord their methods of cooperation.

The Commission shall adopt its Rules of Procedure so as to ensure that both it and its departments operate in accordance with the provisions of this Treaty. It shall ensure that these rules are published.'

monopoly of initiative in the Community process — and all the more room for manoeuvre as the EEC Treaty was a framework treaty — the Commission could determine its priorities and the direction that Community legislation would take, particularly regulations and directives that were to apply directly in the Member States.

The third major power: the implementation of common policies. The Treaty entrusted the Commission with the implementation of the policies that it determined, including the management of certain funds, such as the European Social Fund

(ESF) and the European Development Fund (EDF), under the Convention for the Association of the Overseas Countries and Territories. Above all, the Treaty conferred exclusive powers on it in matters such as competition and the common commercial policy. The Commission actually acquired its own decision-making power through these exclusive powers and its power to monitor the sound application of Community law, using it to develop its policies and attain the objectives of the Treaty, in particular the establishment of a common market. As soon as the Treaty came into force, it had a particularly important role in

Émile Noël on the role of the Commission

'The Treaty provides the foundations, but the house itself has still to be built. Once the structure is there, the institutions will also have to frame Community policy and apply it from day to day. To guide the whole of this process, the Treaty makes the Commission today the architect of the new building and tomorrow the initiator of the common policy.

All provisions of a general scope or of a certain degree of importance must in fact be passed by the Council of Ministers, but, with one or two specific exceptions, the Council can only come to a decision on a proposal of the Commission, so it is always incumbent upon the Commission to take the initiative. If the Commission does not submit any proposals, the Council is paralysed and the Community's progress halted. And this is equally true in agriculture, transport, commercial policy or approximation of legislation.

The submission of a proposal initiates the dialogue between the national governments represented on the Council (which express their national points of view) and the Commission — a "European" body that is called upon to give expression to the interests of the Community as a whole and to seek "European" solutions to common problems. [...]

What are the consequences of this system? On the practical level, it puts the Commission in a central position within the Council, where it can permanently play the role of an "honest broker", of a mediator between governments, and also give an impulse and exert pressure to reach the agreed formulae.

The political consequences are still more important. The Commission's proposals are the expression of a policy it has framed with no other consideration in mind than the common interest of the Community as a whole. The permanent status of the Commission during its four years in office ensures the continuity of this policy, and the Council can only decide on texts submitted by the Commission, which are the means of putting the policy into effect. It is therefore not possible for the Council to adopt contradictory proposals on different subjects — by means of changing majorities or at the whim of pressure groups or struggles for influence between governments.

It is also impossible for a majority of the Council without the consent of the Commission to impose on a State in the minority any measure that would do grave harm to its vital interests. If the Commission really fulfils its obligations, it cannot be party to such an action. Its intervention is therefore an important guarantee to individual States.'

FJME, AMK 54/4/46, Speech at the Conservative Political Centre, Oxford, 7 July 1962.

monitoring the application of the competition rules (against restrictive agreements, dumping and State aid measures incompatible with the principles of competition). And it must also be remembered that the Council — in which the power of implementation was vested — could delegate its powers of implementation to the Commission in a number of fields, including negotiations with non-member countries.

Lastly, the Commission played a major role in budgetary matters. Initially at least, it had no own resources, unlike the High Authority, which enjoyed extensive financial independence thanks to the levy on the turnover of businesses in the relevant industries. The EEC operated exclusively with national contributions for the first few years (until the 1970s). Even so, it was for the Commission to establish the preliminary draft budget for adoption by the Council and to execute the budget on its own responsibility. Here again, its proposal would guide policy options and priorities for action in the emerging Community.

The Commission usually took all these decisions by a majority vote (five out of nine), unlike the Council, which decided either unanimously (by consensus) or by qualified majority (the Member States' votes being weighted). Unanimity, which was the standard requirement in the Council in the EEC's early days, was gradually superseded by qualified majority voting in more and more areas, especially after the beginning of the third stage of the transitional period in January 1966 (the transitional period was to consist of three stages of four years each, and the first of these could have been — but was not — extended by a year or two).

Although it was not the chief decision-making body in the Community, the Commission was answerable before the European Parliamentary Assembly, a representative body even though it was not elected by direct suffrage and enjoyed relatively little power under the 1957 Treaty. The Assembly — which decided on its own authority to rename itself the European Parliament in 1962 — could pass a motion of censure by a majority of two thirds of the votes cast and a majority of its members, whereupon the members of the Commission were required to resign as a body (Article 144). The Commission was also required to present an annual general report on the activities of the Community, at least one month before the opening of the annual session of the Assembly (Article 156). On the other hand, it was independent of the governments that designated its members (Article 157) but was obliged to compromise with them in order to facilitate decision-making in the Community. This situation may seem paradoxical, but it enabled the Commission to work for equilibrium in the institutional set-up by seeking support from the governments — or some of them — or from the Assembly in standing up to the governments or in bringing pressure to bear on them.

The Commission thus occupied a strategic position in the Community institutional system. Often perceived as a bastion of technocracy following in the footsteps of the High Authority, it could, if the occasion or the circumstances so required, gain democratic legitimacy through alliances with the Assembly, political legitimacy through alliances with the Member States via the Council, and legal legitimacy by referring matters to the Court of Justice. Its virtually exclusive monopoly of the right of initiative gave it powerful leverage over Council decisions. This atypical institution, which was supposed to maintain a low profile — with an insignificant name — so as to avoid upsetting the more cautious Europeans, eventually acquired far more powers than it appeared to have at first sight and, perhaps, enough trump cards to develop into a genuine political authority. As long as the headwind was not too strong, of course.

When the Commission was being set up, there were seemingly two threats to its immediate future. Since the end of 1956 the British government, supported by several small non-member countries, had proposed that a vast free-trade area be set up under the European Organisation for Economic Cooperation (OEEC), which was born out of the Marshall Plan. The idea was to extend to all the countries of western Europe the benefits of free movement of industrial products without accepting the constraints of a common external tariff or a common agricultural policy. The project, which went down well even with leading political personalities in the Community itself, such as the German Minister for Economic Affairs, Ludwig Erhard, who was widely followed in German industry, threatened to dilute the common market into a free-trade area without supranational institutions and without political cohesion. In 1958, when General de Gaulle returned to power in France, first as Prime Minister and then as President, doubts also came to the fore as the Gaullist members of parliament had vehemently criticised European integration under the Fourth Republic and voted against the Treaties of Rome in 1957. What would de Gaulle do? Respect Treaties already signed, ratified and in force, or consider repudiating them?

As soon as it was in place, the Commission thus had to face a dual challenge: how to respond to

The weekly Commission meetings are held round a table. The cabinet members form a second ring.
An interpreter is present to facilitate communication.
Clockwise from left to right: Robert Lemaignen (from behind), Hans von der Groeben, Jean Rey,
Sicco Mansholt, Robert Marjolin, Walter Hallstein, Pierre Bourguignon, Piero Malvestiti,
probably Lambert Schaus, Giuseppe Petrilli and Renée Van Hoof (interpreter).
In the background, seated, from left to right: Georges Rencki,
Jean-Claude Richard, Jean Flory and Swidbert Schnippenkötter.

these threats, and how to develop the Community potential of the Treaties.

Establishing the Commission

Hallstein was determined to place the broadest possible interpretation on the Commission's powers and to develop the emerging Community as fast as possible. The Commission, in his view, was more than just the guardian of the Treaties and the embodiment of the Community interest [1]. Its job was also to initiate the political Community and to provide input for the process of European unification. It was therefore destined to work relentlessly at extending its sphere of influence and consolidating its powers, to the detriment of the national governments and the Council of the EEC.

The members of the first Commission subscribed to this concept of a 'federalising Europe' [2] with varying degrees of clarity. Sicco Mansholt, who had been Minister of Agriculture in the Netherlands, had fought throughout the Treaty negotiations for the strongest possible Commission, one that would be as independent as possible from the Council of Ministers. Jean Rey, a former

[1] Hallstein, W., *Der unvollendete Bundesstaat. Europäische Erfahrungen und Erkenntnisse*, Econ, Düsseldorf/Vienna, 1969, p. 56.

[2] Jean-François Deniau speaking to Michel Dumoulin, 2 September 2005.

The Commission's tasks as seen by Walter Hallstein

'What do we want at the end of the day? We want to transform humanity. We want human beings, when they think of themselves as members of a polity, to identify not only as members of traditional nation States but as relatives within a broader European family. [...] The Community is a long-term construction and its fields of activity are broader and richer than anything done hitherto on the way to European integration. Our tasks, the Commission's tasks, must not, therefore, be defined in the Treaty in such a way that our attitude is determined precisely and definitively on every issue and for every specific situation. No: what our mission demands is pragmatic adaptation to ever-changing reality.'

Speech at the constituent session of the Parliamentary Assembly, 19 March 1958, in Hallstein, W., *Europäische Reden*, Hrsg. Th. Oppermann, Deutsche Verlags-Anstalt, Stuttgart, 1979, pp. 50–51
© 1979 Deutsche Verlags-Anstalt, München in der Verlagsgruppe Random House GmbH (Translated from the German)

Belgian Minister of Economic Affairs, was among the ardent apologists for federalism in Europe. Robert Marjolin, who had worked with Jean Monnet at the French Commissariat au Plan before serving as Secretary-General of the OEEC from 1947 to 1953 and then holding the Chair of Political Economics at Nancy University, was not a 'lyrical European' [1]. He saw the Commission's possibilities in a more realistic light, if only by reference to the ideas of General de Gaulle. As to the principle, however, the path that Hallstein wished to take also matched his concept, since as he was almost instinctively in favour of the idea of a European federation but feeling no less instinctively that the time was not right [2]. Hans

von der Groeben, the second German member of the Commission, who had previously headed the Europe Department of the German Ministry of Economic Affairs and had contributed much to the Spaak Report, took much the same view [3]. But, as a body, the Commission unanimously agreed with Hallstein that the main thing was to make a reality of the Treaty of Rome [4].

This consensus was opposed not only by the supporters of a minimalist interpretation of the Treaty but also by those who wished to champion national interests. When the Commission began work, the issue of its headquarters had not yet been settled. Until May 1958, it met alternately in Luxembourg, where it could count on administrative support from the ECSC High Authority, in Strasbourg, at the Maison de l'Europe, and in Brussels, where the Secretariat of the Interim Committee was located. The Commission's administration was provisionally set up in Brussels. The office premises made available by the Belgian government in the rue Belliard and at the Prieuré de Val-Duchesse quickly proved inadequate, however, and in May the Commission rented a new office complex in the rue du Marais in the centre of town. Commission members and their personal staff (*cabinets*) moved to a block in the avenue de la Joyeuse Entrée in July 1958. In December this main building was enlarged along the avenue de Cortenberg, and the Directorates-General for Competition and for Agriculture were transferred to a new block in the avenue de Broqueville in April 1959. This geographical dispersion was not exactly conducive to integration in a fast-growing administration.

In July 1958, although the Commission was de facto settled in Brussels, the French and Luxembourg governments rejected the Belgian proposal to declare that Brussels would be the single location of the Communities. It was only in February 1959 that the foreign ministers of the six Member States decided that the headquarters

---

[1] FJME, Interview with Robert Marjolin, 24 September 1984, p. 34.
[2] Marjolin, R., *Architect of European unity — Memoirs 1911–1986*, Weidenfeld and Nicolson, London, 1989.
[3] Interview with Hans von der Groeben, 16 December 2003.
[4] Marjolin, R., op. cit.

of the Economic Community would be in Brussels provisionally, for no longer than the ensuing three years, and that a definitive solution would be found within that period. But no definitive decision was reached in February 1962 and Brussels retained its status as the provisional place of work. This meant that the Commission could not acquire its own premises, and even the Belgian authorities were cautious about any investment in the future headquarters of the Community.

The national financial authorities were also quite lax in meeting their payment obligations to the Community. The Commission had to obtain an advance from the ECSC High Authority before it could start operations. It also had to address repeated urgent appeals to the various ministers of finance for last-minute assurance that at least the current month's remunerations would be paid ([1]). To cap it all, the Commission regularly encountered stiff opposition from national bureaucracies in performing the tasks assigned to it by the Treaty. Nor did national authorities make it easy for the new administration to recruit staff — far from it. There were bitter disputes about certain appointments.

The Commission endeavoured to surmount these obstacles. It took advantage both of the general lack of interest in European affairs in the last few months of the Fourth Republic in France and of the difficulties in the administrative organisation of the Council of Ministers to assert its own authority as the first truly operational institution of the new Community. The question of the allocation of portfolios to individual members, which arose at the very first Commission meetings, was settled within 10 weeks. Three weeks later, the first organisation chart was adopted. As instructed by its President, the Commission immediately appointed the directors-general, followed in the spring of 1958 by the directors and heads of division. All its senior management staff and most of

its executive staff were recruited by the autumn. When the Budgetary Committee of the Council of Ministers first met, most appointments had been made and the staff complement was virtually complete. At the end of 1958 the Commission had a staff of about 1 000. The national governments thus faced a 'fait accompli'.

Given the multitude of tasks likely to be awaiting the Commission under the Treaty, Hallstein sought to set up a *grande administration*, with a form and scale going far beyond the ECSC High Authority. An administrative infrastructure was also set up in readiness for those areas where the governments had not yet adopted a practical programme of work. A total of nine administrative departments, called 'directorates-general', were established with a director-general at the top — External Relations, Economic and Financial Affairs, Internal Market (customs, quotas and services), Competition, Social Affairs, Agriculture, Transport, Overseas Development, and Administration.

To respect the principle of collective responsibility, the Commission took inspiration from the group-based organisation of the High Authority: for each of the nine policy areas, three to five members of the Commission would form a group to prepare the decisions to be adopted by the full Commission. The chair of each group also took responsibility for the relevant directorate-general. Each Commission member had a few private staff — a *cabinet* — along the lines of the practice in Latin countries. In addition to his *cabinet*, the President was also supported by an executive secretariat, but Hallstein's experience of administration when the West German Rectors' Conference and the Foreign Office were set up in the Federal Republic of Germany led him to prevent the emergence of a high-power administrative 'supremo' who could act independently of the political direction set by the Commission ([2]).

The decision on the allocation of portfolios was also covered by collective responsibility. There

([1]) Lemaignen, R., *L'Europe au berceau — Souvenirs d'un technocrate*, Plon, Paris, 1964, p. 36 *et seq.*; Interview with Karl-Heinz Narjes, 24 May 2004.

([2]) Interview with Fernand Braun, 8 December 2003.

was never any doubt that Mansholt would hold the agriculture portfolio, and he got down to work with extraordinary determination. Marjolin, the second political heavyweight after Mansholt, originally wanted external relations. But the President opposed this, probably because he wanted to take personal charge of representing the Community on the international scene. Marjolin was compensated in the shape of the substantial economic and financial affairs portfolio [1]. Von der Groeben played his cards close to his chest and obtained the portfolio he really wanted as the spiritual father of the competition policy: restrictive practices and monopolies, State aid, the approximation of legislation and tax harmonisation [2]. External relations went to Jean Rey, a skilful negotiator who was to become one of the heavyweights of the Commission following the GATT negotiations [3]. Piero Malvestiti was given the internal market. Robert Lemaignen, the second French member of the Commission, took charge of the overseas territories, France being particularly keen on their integration. Giuseppe Petrilli, the second Italian member, was asked to look after social policy, rather less important. And Michel Rasquin, the member from the smallest Member State, handled transport, also a rather secondary portfolio at the beginning at least.

At the end of March 1958, Émile Noël, who had long worked for the former French Prime Minister Guy Mollet, was appointed Executive Secretary. When directors-general were up for appointment, attention was paid to ensuring that they did not have the same nationality as the member of the Commission, but party-political affiliations were never taken into account. What Hallstein wanted above all was to avoid national governments influencing the composition of his administration. Candidates' qualifications were what mattered to him, and he often gave preferential treatment to young candidates who combined excellent specialist knowledge with great ability

[1] Interview with Karl-Heinz Narjes, 24 May 2004.
[2] Interview with Hans von der Groeben, 16 December 2003.
[3] Interview with Fernand Braun, 8 December 2003.

Karl-Heinz Narjes on the Commission's early days

'We were able to realise that we had to act quickly and carefully and take the long-term view. Many people, both in Germany and elsewhere, opposed a consolidated and functional Commission. All those who had lined up behind Erhard or behind Euro-scepticism were identified among the opponents to rapid consolidation and a way had to be found around them. The period from the beginning of 1958 to the end of 1959 can thus be seen as an attempt to create *faits accomplis* [4] as quickly as possible before they were discovered and distorted by our opponents. The first *fait accompli*, of course, was when we established the Commission's organisation chart, its architecture, before any of the capitals realised what was going on. This was vitally important. Secondly, the Community had to be financed in such a way that nobody could use a refusal to provide finance as a lever to jeopardise or destroy the Community or impose his personal interests. These were the two main challenges.

Consolidating *faits accomplis* and establishing and fine-tuning the organisation chart were mainly down to Groeben. It was Groeben who sketched out a form of organisation chart to be taken as the basis for the distribution of tasks within the Commission. And the allocation of portfolios within the Commission was decided over a dinner in Luxembourg. At the time, we still had to go to Luxembourg occasionally and to show how neutral we were on the headquarters issue. We stayed in a really comfortable old hotel, and Commission members' portfolios were handed out in that comfortable setting, where we could enjoy a drop of cognac. The result was roughly as Groeben had envisaged. It was round about the end of January or the beginning of February.'

Interview with Karl-Heinz Narjes, 24 May 2004.
(Translated from the German)

to learn. Paradoxically enough, at the same time he was trying to recruit civil servants with sound experience in the national administrations who had acquired real authority. A rough national balance was maintained in important posts: a

[4] In French in the original.

quarter of the staff came from each of the three large countries, and the Benelux countries together provided the remaining quarter. They in general and the Belgians in particular were somewhat over-represented, but at least there was no risk of hegemony by any one Member State.

Hallstein orchestrated the formation and operation of the Commission with an authority that flowed from his masterly command of the topics for debate, coupled with a truly exceptional analytical mind. He left Commission members with considerable freedom to organise their professional lives. He respected their abilities but was highly demanding of his staff. He took personal charge at certain strategically important moments, such as the selection of senior officials, vital talks with the national governments and the presentation of the Commission's programme to the general public. When preparing his speeches, he relied exclusively on a select band of competent staff, leaving it up to Émile Noël to organise communication between departments. By combining absolute loyalty with precise specialist abilities, the executive secretary came to be the one who ensured that information flowed quickly between the two of them.

To convince the governments and the public that the Commission was needed, Hallstein not only drew attention to the quality of the work done. He also attached great importance to the formal and symbolic manifestation of its autonomy. When the Committee of Permanent Representatives of the Member States (Coreper) — an institution not provided for by the Treaty — was set up in 1958, he refused to allow Commission members to attend its meetings. As a rule, preparatory exchanges with the permanent representatives were handled by directors-general, whose status was comparable to that of the ambassadors who made up Coreper. Members of the Commission, on the other hand, would generally be in touch with ministers, both in their working relationships in Brussels and when visiting the capitals of the Member States. By the same token, when mem-

bers of the Commission visited non-member countries, it was arranged for them to be received by the relevant ministers. The President of the Commission would expect to meet the Heads of State or Government.

The rule in relations with non-member countries was that the European Community's claim to sovereignty should always be manifested. Hallstein got into the habit of receiving third-country ambassadors' letters of credence at a formal ceremony. There were other opportunities to highlight the Community's sovereignty and the authority of its executive body, e.g. when receiving State visits and organising the Commission's New Year reception. These events followed a strict diplomatic protocol. There was television coverage as Hallstein stood on a red carpet, taking care to ensure that the Commission's claims for itself were perceived in the Member States and in a large number of non-member countries. In the United States, where Hallstein deliberately paid regular visits as President of the Commission, he soon represented the Community as 'Mr Europe'.

Initiatives and successes in economic matters

Even before it had finished setting up its administration, the Commission had to devote considerable time and energy to warding off the threat that the Economic Community might be dissolved in the large free-trade area proposed by the United Kingdom. The members of the Commission spared no effort in their regular personal contacts with the national governments to persuade them to undertake to ensure that the agreements relating to the Economic Community would not be circumvented. They succeeded in having their own delegation admitted to the negotiations on setting up the free-trade area. This delegation, led by Jean Rey, kept the pressure on the Member States to stand by a common position against the British proposals. At the same time, the French Foreign Minister

On 1 February 1962 members of the EEC and Euratom Commissions, in formal dress, receive the heads of the permanent delegations of the Member States of the Communities and the heads of missions accredited to the Communities on the occasion of the annual New Year message. Hallstein's successors would carry on the tradition but without the formal dress code. To Walter Hallstein's right: Jean Rey, Robert Marjolin and Berndt von Staden; to his left: Lambert Schaus.

Maurice Couve de Murville, who met Marjolin virtually every Saturday (¹), endeavoured to convince de Gaulle that France's interest lay in becoming integrated with the Economic Community.

The turbulent times which marked the early days of the Community calmed down only when de Gaulle won Adenauer over to the idea of setting up the common market as planned, without the free-trade area. This happened at the second meeting between the two statesmen at Bad Kreuznach on 26 November 1958. The other four

governments had no objections to that decision, and the negotiations for the free-trade area were irredeemably scuppered. The Commission's role in this first manifestation of Community solidarity was quite considerable, at least according to what Marjolin tells us (²). The first step towards the customs union was taken on schedule on 1 January 1959. It was facilitated by a sharp devaluation of the French franc announced five days earlier.

In the meantime, Mansholt and his staff had been laying the foundation stones for the common

(¹) Interview with Karl-Heinz Narjes, 24 May 2004.

(²) Marjolin, R., op. cit., p. 316.

agricultural market. In July 1958, at Stresa, the Commission organised the Conference of Ministers of Agriculture of the Member States of the Community that was provided for by the Treaty. This generated the first rapprochements in preparation for a common organisation of the markets for agricultural produce. In November 1959, following extensive consultations with the ministers of agriculture, farmers' organisations and other lobbies, the Commission presented its first proposal. This was revised in response to reactions in the Council, and a new text appeared on 30 June 1960. It provided for the introduction of guide prices as a market-regulation instrument, levies on imports and guaranteed prices for producers.

The governmental negotiations on the organisation of the various agricultural product markets turned out to be distinctly arduous. It took 18 months to reach an agreement on the general principle. But the French government was firmly attached to launching the common agricultural policy. At a final Council meeting that began on 15 December 1961, the clocks had to be stopped at 31 December to respect the text of the Treaty, which provided for an agreement to be reached by the end of the first stage of the common market. Under energetic pressure from Mansholt, the compromise that finally emerged on 14 January 1962, following a legendary agricultural 'marathon', paved the way for a transitional scheme running for three years until the end of 1964. It also provided that a regulation valid until the end of the transitional period, i.e. until 1 January 1970, would be adopted no later than 1 July 1965.

A fresh crisis blew up in the autumn of 1964, when the first common prices for cereal crops were to be set. The German government refused to accept the price cuts proposed by the Commission back in March 1963. Consequently the Council could agree only on relatively high prices. The Erhard government did not accept the Commission's line until 21 October. General de Gaulle had threatened to withdraw France from the EEC if the organisation of the agricultural market was

not in place by mid-December. Hallstein kept up the pressure on the German government. He visited Bonn twice, at the end of October and in mid-November. He had talks with the Chancellor and sent von der Groeben, Commission member with responsibility for competition, to see the Minister for Economic Affairs, Kurt Schmücker. He exhorted both of them to take the French President's threat seriously. Earlier crises in the EEC had come close to blocking progress towards integration, but 'today's decision has serious consequences for the viability of the Community' ([1]). Mansholt publicly accused the German government of compromising the Kennedy Round since it opposed the setting of common prices for cereals, without which trade agreements could not be negotiated ([2]).

Hallstein's commitment to common cereal prices eventually changed Bonn's mind. It was the decisive factor. After his discussions with the Commission President, Erhard worked personally to obtain concessions from the German farming lobby. As 15 December dawned, the Council at last managed to set cereal prices at the levels proposed by the Commission. But the common price was to come into operation only on 1 July 1967, three years after the original Commission proposal, and German farmers had to receive compensatory payments from the Community for the two and a half years up to the end of the transitional period on 1 January 1970.

Once the question of cereal prices had been settled, market rules could now also be determined for a series of other agricultural products. The Council asked the Commission to put forward by 1 April 1965 proposals for the financing of the agricultural market for the rest of the transitional period (1 July 1965 to 1 January 1970). The Commission was also to produce a proposal regarding management of own resources which, under

---

[1] BA, WH 1114/1, State Secretary Fritz Neef to Minister Kurt Schmücker, 2 November 1964. Cf. Reports by Hallstein to the Commission, PV 293 EEC Commission, 9 and 13 November 1964; and PV 294, 18 November 1964.
[2] Interview with Georges Rencki, 13 January 2004.

the January 1962 decision, were to become payable to the Community once the Community tariffs for agricultural produce became effective. The Commission therefore had to consider in the light of Article 201 of the EEC Treaty how own resources might take over from financial contributions from the Member States.

While public attention was focused on the difficulties of setting up the agricultural common market, von der Groeben was able to impose the competition rules without even the hint of a public debate. That is not to say that there was no opposition. This came once again from the free-marketeers in Ludwig Erhard's entourage. They imagined that much of the inspiration for the Brussels line on competition lay in the *dirigiste* concepts of their French partner. Several governments also fiercely opposed the application of Article 90 of the EEC Treaty, which empowered the Commission to monitor compliance with the competition rules by public enterprises, and in particular State-run enterprises. But those concerned by the Commission's measures did not take their reluctance to accept them so far as to block them outright, not at any rate before Erhard became Chancellor. A major step in the implementation of the competition policy was taken with the adoption of Regulation No 17, which imposed a general obligation to report circumstances that impeded competition. Logically enough this was followed by a body of procedural law 'empowering the Commission to build up a corpus of European case-law established by the European Court of Justice, on the basis of which a transparent and thoroughly foreseeable competition law can develop' [1].

The Commission was even more successful in the implementation of the customs union. After de Gaulle had come out in favour of the rapid establishment of the common market, the timetable worked out at the negotiations in 1956 to reflect

French reservations turned out to be somewhat timorous. In March 1960 the governments reached an agreement on most of the products in 'List G' in the Treaty, on which there had been no agreement at the Val-Duchesse negotiations. In May 1960 the Council approved a Commission proposal to bring forward by one year the next 10 % cut in national customs tariffs. The first stage of the adoption of a common external tariff was also brought forward by one year. Two years later, in May 1962, the Council again agreed to bring forward by one year the subsequent stages of the duty-reduction process. Half the cuts were thus made by 1 July 1962 instead of 1 January 1965. The common external tariff was also in place three years ahead of schedule, on 1 July 1967. The last remaining duties in internal trade were abolished on 1 July 1968, 18 months before the expiry of the 12-year transitional period.

The early attainment of the customs union was closely bound up with the commercial policy. Customs union inevitably often entails taking a common stance on trade-related issues. But it was put into effect so much more quickly because of pressure from the United States and groups interested in free trade. The Commission responded initially by seeking to demonstrate that the Community wished to obtain a general lowering of barriers to trade and a climate of trust. It used the GATT negotiations at the Compensation Round (September 1960 to July 1961) and then at the Dillon Round (May 1961 to May 1962) for that purpose. Jean Rey and his staff did not confine themselves to making technical preparations for the negotiations but endeavoured to unite the national governments around a common position and defended it skilfully in the Geneva talks. At the end of the first round, it was guaranteed that the common customs tariffs would not exceed the arithmetic mean of the earlier national tariffs. The second round closed with an average cut of 7 % in common customs tariffs. Major cuts were negotiated during the third round, the Kennedy Round, which ran from May 1964 to 30 June 1967, when a general agreement was signed. Thanks to the negotiating capacity of

[1] Narjes, K.-H, 'Walter Hallstein in der Frühphase der EWG', in Loth, W., Wallace, W. and Wessels, W. (eds), *Walter Hallstein — Der vergessene Europäer?* Europa-Union Verlag, Bonn, 1995, pp. 139–163, at p. 154.

a Community speaking with a single voice, customs duties had been reduced by over 50 % for more than two thirds of the products covered by the negotiations. The reduction averaged 32 % for the full range of products and was to be applied gradually over a five-year period ending on 1 January 1972.

In some cases the Treaty itself set a timetable (¹), but in others it was the Commission which urged the governments to speed things up. In October 1962 it presented a 'programme of action for the second stage of the common market', which not only proposed a further acceleration in the customs union process but also called for monetary union to be achieved by the end of 1970. It justified the proposal by highlighting potential disruptions to the common market in the event of unilateral exchange-rate adjustments and stressed its importance for the establishment of economic union. The Commission repeated the proposal in September 1964, calling it 'Initiative 1964'. At the same time, it argued for consolidation of social policy through conversion measures in the Member States and advances in the harmonisation living and working conditions. And it called for measures going beyond the confines of the Treaty that would increase the role of the European Parliament in the Community decision-making machinery. In the Commission's view, 'The way democratic answerability is structured by the Treaty […] is all the less satisfactory each time Community activity advances a stage further into the legislative domains hitherto reserved for the Member States and the volume of budgetary resources managed by the Community expands, in particular with the establishment of European Funds' (²).

Hallstein felt that this reinforcement of Parliament's powers was within reach, especially as the customs union and the common agricultural market were in place and the customs tariff and agricultural levies were available to finance the Community. He put forward argument upon argument for not entrusting their management to the Member States, who were to collect them. As Klaus Meyer, Hallstein's deputy *chef de cabinet*, pointed out in a note to the President in August 1964, Community management of these revenue sources provided an opportunity to shift the financing of the Community towards own resources. The Commission thus had the possibility of alleviating its dependence on national contributions, which, in its view, fell short of what was needed for its ambitious programmes. The governments would then no longer be able to resist the proposal to bring the Community budget under real parliamentary control (³).

In terms of the ambitious prospects that Hallstein was conceiving for the EEC, the United Kingdom's application for accession in July 1961 was manifestly premature. Marjolin and Mansholt were worried. Implementing the common agricultural policy was, by definition, incompatible with maintaining the Commonwealth preference desired by the United Kingdom. The President was also worried that accession of the United Kingdom before completion of the customs union would weaken the Community institutions and, consequently, the prospects for the development of a political Community in the broad sense. Although the Commission was not initially involved in the enlargement negotiations, it was able to influence them. It played a major role in determining a common negotiating position for the governments of the Member States, which agreed chiefly on the defence of the *acquis communautaire*. The Commission representatives repeatedly conveyed the Community view to the British government. In 1962 Mansholt became chairman of a committee responsible for producing a compromise on the question of the United Kingdom's adaptation to the Community agricultural system. He considered that the negotiations were on the verge of succeeding (⁴).

(¹) HAEU, KM 4, EEC Commission, Commission recommendations for the acceleration of the Treaty timetable, 26 February 1960.
(²) HAEU, KM 7, EEC Commission, 'Initiative 1964', 30 September 1964.

(³) HAEU, KM 6, Notes for talks with State Secretary Alfred Müller-Armack, signed 'M 13/8'.
(⁴) Georges Rencki personal archives, Speech by Sicco Mansholt to the Dutch European Movement, Rotterdam, 13 November 1965.

The 'Initiative 1964' action programme

The introduction to 'Initiative 1964', the action programme presented to the governments by the Commission on 30 September 1964, emphasises the Commission's demand for a core position in the European integration process.

'Thanks to European policies conducted resolutely by the six Member States of our Community, but thanks also to the work done by the European institutions, the Communities today stand as a great success with a worldwide impact and have become the focus of endeavours to bring about the political unity of Europe [...] There can be no doubting that the road towards a federation in Europe passes through the existing Communities. The failure of the Communities would mean that our generation would not see a completed political Community; but, as long as the Communities live and conserve all their dynamism, there is a real prospect that a genuine federation can be achieved [...]

Halting the movement towards completion of the Economic Community would not simply mean

causing it to fail, for the Community cannot exist unless it is a dynamic one, but would also mean dismissing all prospects of achieving "political union". And we cannot take it for granted that we will achieve that. But progress towards economic integration generates and accelerates a natural progression towards full political union and offers ever more convincing reasons for achieving it.

In the current situation therefore, even though the primary concern is to avoid narrowing our horizons and losing sight of our ultimate objective, the first task awaiting the European Economic Community is to secure its dynamism. It must set an example of tenacity, calm and common sense from which the doubters can derive a sense of resolve and confidence.'

HAEU, KM 7, EEC Commission, 'Initiative 1964',
30 September 1964, pp. 1 and 4.
(Translated from the French)

When de Gaulle, at a press conference on 14 July 1963, unilaterally stated that he refused to pursue the negotiations with the British government, the Commission was rather relieved. Hallstein stated in the European Parliament that British accession was 'merely postponed' for the longer term. But he was more concerned at the way in which the negotiations had been interrupted. By going it alone, the French President had failed to observe solidarity between the Member States of the Community. Hallstein felt that this was a sign of a crisis of trust between the national governments that could complicate cooperation in the further development of the Community. To overcome the crisis, he once again asked that more powers be devolved to the Community institutions. In particular, the Commission should automatically be involved in future accession negotiations. As he once

again stated publicly, his ideal was still of a Europe democratically constituted and constructed on the federal model [1].

WILFRIED LOTH

The Commission and the Fouchet Plan [2]

Having just successfully launched the customs union in January 1959 and having brought forward

---

[1] Speech to the European Parliament, 5 February 1963; Hallstein, W., *Europäische Reden*, Hrsg. Th. Oppermann, Deutsche Verlags-Anstalt, Stuttgart, 1979, pp. 402–415.

[2] See Bitsch, M.-Th., 'Les institutions communautaires face au projet d'union politique, 1960–1962', *Revue d'Allemagne*, special issue, April–June 1997, *Du «Plan Fouchet» au traité franco-allemand de janvier 1963*, and Bloes, R., *Le plan Fouchet et le problème de l'Europe politique*, Collège d'Europe, Bruges, 1970.

the tariff cuts in 1960 and embarked on active preparations for determining the common agricultural policy, which would be adopted in January 1962, the Commission was faced with an attempt to bring about political union outside the Community context which could effectively sideline it.

General de Gaulle put forward proposals for political cooperation between the Six. After a first initiative which yielded nothing more than quarterly meetings between foreign ministers, he presented in 1960 a vast project for a confederation. Sketched out in the summer on the occasion of contacts with the other governments, the project was described in greater detail at a press conference on 5 September. President de Gaulle called for regular cooperation in four areas (foreign policy, defence, the economy and culture) to be prepared by specialist bodies consisting of national civil servants, the decisions being taken by a regular organised concert of Heads of State or Government. An assembly of members of national parliaments would be asked for its opinion, but the whole project would first be submitted to a 'solemn European referendum' [1].

The project was liable to prompt concern and misgivings among France's five partners and within the Community institutions. By bringing economic affairs within its remit, it would seem to duplicate the Communities' field of activities and bring it under an intergovernmental umbrella. By establishing defence cooperation, it could cause the Six to take a separate stance in the Atlantic Alliance and to distance themselves from the United States, which was indeed the objective being pursued in Paris. But the French proposal was not very remote from a suggestion by Jean Monnet's Action Committee for a United States of Europe, and Monnet could hardly be suspected of wanting to weaken the Communities, so this convergence could be seen as a source of reassurance [2].

Initially, the two Commissions (EEC and Euratom) and the ECSC High Authority were inclined to stay calm and adopt a wait-and-see attitude, partly perhaps because of the international context and in particular the serious crisis over Algeria, which would limit the chances of setting up a political Europe, for the moment at least [3]. The EEC Commission devoted part of its meeting on 14 September 1960 to an exchange of views on this political revitalisation of Europe and, according to Agence Europe had seen no threat to the application of the Treaty of Rome, taking the view that for the moment it would not express an official position but would simply seek to influence the proposals along the most European line possible [4]. Jean Rey, however, had been concerned back in the spring by the political weakness of the Community and now drew attention to the dangers inherent in reducing the powers of the Community institutions, which had proved their effectiveness [5].

On 12 October the Presidents of the three executive institutions set forth their views in the European Parliamentary Assembly in answer to a written question on the impact of the French plan. The President of the High Authority, Piero Malvestiti, and the President of the Euratom Commission, Étienne Hirsch, felt that the time was not ripe for political commentaries on a grand scale and contented themselves with restating their attachment to supranational bodies [6], but Walter Hallstein, who had rejected the idea of a relatively brief joint statement, took a more combative stance. While describing the current consultations as a political revitalisation of Europe, he sang the praises of the Community system, thus covertly criticising the French plan, and he warned against the temptation to abandon or sideline the existing institutions. The Commission, he said, was independent, it

[1] Press conference, 5 September 1960, de Gaulle, Ch., *Discours et messages*, t. III, Plon, Paris, 1970, pp. 244–246.

[2] FJME, AMK 55/1/32, Draft memorandum, 7 September 1960; FJME, AMK 55/3/1, Draft declaration, 6 October 1960; and FJME, AMK 55/3/9, Note, 14 October 1960.

[3] FJME, AMK 55/2/3, Conversation with Robert Marjolin, 18 October 1960.

[4] *Europe*, 15 September 1960.

[5] AULB, JR, 126 PP, VI-24, Note for the President and members of the Commission, 3 October 1960.

[6] *Les documents de la Communauté européenne*, No 6, November 1960, pp. 11–12.

Aide-memoire on the establishment of a European confederation (¹)

'I.

It is urgent for Europe to take an initiative to combat the prevailing disorder and lack of leadership in the West. So far our countries have demonstrated their dynamism, primarily in economic matters.

Today we need political action. The establishment of a European confederation will enable our countries to pursue the unification process already under way and to take a common political stance in relations with the United States, which is particularly important in our current period of uncertainty.

II.

There are certain conditions that a European confederation must meet if it is to make a substantial contribution.

There must be a popular vote. It must be democratic in nature.

It must be open to other countries, in particular England [sic].

It must have real content.

III.

A real confederation demands meetings at the highest level. The European confederation should be governed by a Supreme Council consisting of the Heads of State or Government.

The economic union that is currently being established now makes it possible to achieve a political confederation. It is essential that the current Communities — common market, Euratom and Coal and Steel Community — be preserved and integrated in the confederation. The confederation will operate all the more effectively if the various Commissions and other bodies are merged into a single executive system.

The confederation will be a reality in the eyes of the world only if it can relate to other countries as a single entity. There must therefore be a common foreign policy. This means that it must be able to come to decisions, which unanimous voting will not allow. Obviously, each country must retain its freedom of action in matters where it is the main party concerned.

If it is to be real, the confederation must have the possibility of promoting the progress of the union among its member countries. The Supreme Council must accordingly be given the power to set up the requisite bodies.

If it is to be democratic, the confederation must have an Assembly.'

FJME, AMK 55/1/26,
Action Committee for a United States of Europe,
Document, 28 July 1960.

was the guardian of the Treaty, and it supplied both the inspiration and the initiative for all Community action (²).

This determination to respect the Community system received widespread support in the European Parliamentary Assembly from its President, the German Christian Democrat Hans Fürler, from the Chairman of the Political Affairs Committee, the Italian Emilio Battista, and from the Presidents of the three political groups (the Christian Democrats, the Socialists and the Liberals) with the

(¹) In September and October 1960 several documents of the Action Committee for the United States of Europe amplify the ideas set out in the July aide-memoire, which predate General de Gaulle's press conference of 5 September 1960.
(²) BAC 118/1986 1722, Letter from Walter Hallstein to Étienne Hirsch and speech by Walter Hallstein, 12 October 1960.

exception of a few French Gaullists who were allied to the latter group. But another leading member of the Assembly, the Belgian Socialist Fernand Dehousse, realised that in foreign policy matters the governments were not ready to go any further than intergovernmental cooperation and wondered whether the French proposals, subject to a degree of amendment, might not serve as the starting point for a political Europe. The following year he was instructed to prepare a report on political union in Europe [1].

At the beginning of 1961, there was a degree of uncertainty in the air. The first conference of Heads of State or Government that met in Paris in February was the scene for a strong clash between France and the Netherlands, which defended the supranational approach to integration. Having failed to reach an agreement, the Member States instructed a committee of diplomats chaired by the Frenchman Christian Fouchet to prepare new proposals. In Walter Hallstein's view, this summit opened the way to all manner of options and made it possible to look forward with hope to a new phase in the development of Europe. The Assembly drafted a resolution on the basis of the Dehousse Report which was adopted in plenary on 29 June. This approved the principle of regular meetings provided that the Communities' supranational nature was preserved, that the two Commissions and the High Authority were associated with the discussions between Heads of State or Government as regards all questions within their remit and that the Assembly was able to organise a debate on an annual report on political cooperation [2].

At the second summit, held at Bad Godesberg near Bonn on 18 July 1961, France accepted the idea that political union should boost NATO and the EEC and signed a somewhat elaborate compromise text. The Brussels Commissions expressed satisfaction at the Bonn declaration. President

Hirsch was particularly delighted at the plans for cultural cooperation and for a European University at Florence, while the EEC Commission stressed the importance of the reference by the Heads of State or Government to the Assembly resolution of 29 June, seen as recognition of the role of the Community institutions in political cooperation [3].

The optimism faded in October, when France presented a draft treaty, known as the 'first Fouchet Plan', which did not truly match the hopes raised by the Bad Godesberg conference. The High Authority regarded it as what we would now call a WEU with small changes that could threaten the common market [4]. President Hirsch criticised the proposed name ('Union of States') and the limited involvement of the Community institutions in political cooperation [5]. And Walter Hallstein had strong reservations about the unanimity rule in decision-making, the lack of clearly defined objectives and the risk that economic integration would suffer and that the Community institutions would be weakened. The three executive bodies therefore wished to secure a few amendments to the draft to make it more palatable [6]. Their possibilities for action being limited, they were counting on France's partners to obtain alterations and encouraged the Assembly in its work on a recommendation that was eventually adopted in plenary on 20 December 1961.

This recommendation, which was approved by the EEC Commission, accepted the French draft as a starting point. It supported a Union of the Peoples of Europe and acknowledged that regular summits could make a contribution. But it called for the Atlantic Alliance to be strengthened and for the Treaties of Paris (ECSC) and Rome (EEC and Euratom) not to be called into question. It accepted the idea of appointing a secretary

[1] BAC 118/1986 1722, Debates of the Assembly, 12 October 1960 and 9 March 1961.
[2] Bitsch, M.-Th., op. cit.
[3] Europe, 19 July 1961.
[4] CEAB 2 248, Note by Edmund Wellenstein, 27 November 1961.
[5] CEAB 2 248, Address by Étienne Hirsch to the Political Affairs Committee of the Assembly, 22 November 1961.
[6] BAC 118/1986 1722, Memorandum for President Hirsch, 24 October 1961, and address by Lambert Schaus to the Assembly on behalf of the EEC Commission, 20 December 1961.

general for political cooperation, provided that he remained independent of the governments, that his functions were clearly defined and that this 'fourth executive' could ultimately be merged with the others. It also looked forward to the voting rules being changed from unanimity to majority voting and hoped that the executives would attend the Councils of Heads of State or Government when Community-related issues were up for discussion. And it called for the Assembly to be converted into a genuine parliament elected by direct universal suffrage. Finally, it considered that all the Member States should be in the political union so as to avoid a variable-geometry Europe [1].

This text stood no chance of being taken seriously. By an unfortunate coincidence, it was to be considered by the Fouchet Committee on 18 January 1962, the very day on which France presented a 'second Fouchet Plan', which reflected the positions initially taken in Paris and rejected the Bonn compromise outright. Some of France's partners were quick to respond and toughened their stance. The Netherlands and Belgium, which had regarded the British question as the top priority since London announced its membership application in the summer of 1961, were intransigent. There were only two alternatives in their view: have the United Kingdom accede rapidly to the Communities and the political Europe or abide by the supranational institutional system. Despite mediation efforts by Germany and Italy (and Jean Monnet's Action Committee), no compromise solution was found. The project appeared to be doomed when the meeting of foreign ministers on 17 April 1962 broke up in disagreement, even though from time to time — and right into 1964 — kites were flown, by the likes of the German Chancellor Ludwig Erhard and the Belgian Foreign Minister Paul-Henri Spaak, to explore the possibilities of resurrecting the idea of a political Europe.

As matters were getting bogged down at this stage, the Commission did not state an official position but its members inevitably recalled their reservations regarding intergovernmental cooperation. Addressing the Congress of the European Movement in Rotterdam in May 1962, Vice-President Sicco Mansholt denounced the French proposal, which, while claiming to advance the cause of integration, was actually minimalising and even eliminating it while giving it an exalted political name [2]. In October 1962, Jean Rey argued in a discussion that 'the best way of achieving political union would be to keep it within the Community context, [...] to proceed on the basis of the current Communities, to reinforce them by merging them and to enhance their authority by having the European Parliament elected by universal suffrage and increasing its powers and responsibilities' [3]. And in a number of speeches given that same year, President Hallstein untiringly pleaded the cause of the development of the Communities with an ultimately political objective. For him, the Economic Community was already a political reality which promoted reconciliation between Europeans, established solidarities between Member States on a broad scale and was founded on institutions that were organised in such a way as to herald a government system in which political decisions could be taken. Political cooperation, therefore, should neither weaken the existing Community nor take its place. It would be unacceptable for the Community structure to be headed, undermined or supplanted by a political structure based on ideas different from those which had governed our shared existence for 12 years (since the Schuman Declaration in 1950) [4].

There was an epilogue to the history of the Fouchet Plan. The six Member States having failed to come to an agreement, France and

---

[1] APE, *Documents de séance, 1961–1962*, Document 110, 18 December 1961.

[2] HAEC, Sicco Mansholt Speeches series, speech to the Annual Congress of the Dutch European Movement, 26 May 1962.
[3] AULB, JR, 126 PP, VI-34, Draft chapter on political union, 13 October 1962.
[4] HAEC, Walter Hallstein Speeches series, speech given on 17 September 1962 (see box p. 70). See also speeches given on 28 February, 1 March, 18 April 1962, etc.

Political union according to Walter Hallstein

'When we wonder how we can go about improving the Community's capacity and strength of action, the question ultimately boils down to a question about what is commonly referred to as political union. There is abundant scope for confusion here. What is new in these plans is not the fact that they concern a political organisation. The European Coal and Steel Community, the European Atomic Energy Community and the European Economic Community are political too. The main motivation for what is known as economic integration has always been political. This was stated in Paris and in Messina, and the preambles to the Treaties establishing the Communities say as much. The very purpose of the Community and of the action it takes is political. Customs policy, commercial policy, transport policy, agricultural policy — all these components of economic union are surely also political matters. That is why the Community too is organised on a political basis following the traditional federal model of modern history, with its own Parliament, which has, in particular, the sole power to control the Community executive through the no-confidence vote, with a Council of Ministers representing the governments of the Member States, with the executive, which I have just mentioned and which cannot receive instructions from the governments of its Member States, and with its own Supreme Court. And who nowadays would deny that the effects of this integration are political as well, for they are phenomena of economic policy and social policy (¹).

The Political Union, therefore, is not basically something new, a transition from the economic to the political. Rather the point is to complete the integration of substantial portions of the Member States' domestic policies — economic and social — and unify other areas of their policies — in particular the non-economic aspects of foreign policy (foreign economic policy already being covered by the European Economic Community as commercial policy), defence policy and cultural policy. The Community reaction to these plans is dictated by that consideration. The reaction is entirely positive.

These plans, of course, must not be allowed to weaken or destroy the successes already notched up in terms of European political union; they must not be allowed, therefore, to jeopardise the existing Communities in any way. The decisive criterion both generally and in matters of detail — including the arsenal of possible ways and means — is the progress made in the European cause as a whole.'

Speech by the President of the EEC Commission to the joint meeting of the European Parliament and the Council of Europe Consultative Assembly Strasbourg, 17 September 1962 (extract). (Translated from the French)

Germany signed a bilateral treaty on 22 January 1963, a week after General de Gaulle had vetoed British membership of the common market. This Élysée treaty — providing for cooperation in foreign policy, defence and culture and establishing the Franco-German Youth Office — irritated the members of the Commission. Mansholt regarded it as an instrument for shutting the Community out and as an expression of a Europe that claimed to place itself between East and West (²). Hallstein feared that advance consultation between the two governments could upset the balance of the Community decision-making mechanism. Addressing the European Parliament the day before the treaty was to be ratified, he urged the two

---

(¹) Original emphasis.

(²) HAEC, Speech given at The Hague, 22 February 1963.

countries to avoid interpreting and applying the treaty in such a way as to jeopardise the Community's existence, operation and dynamism [1].

The Fouchet Plan, then, like its Franco-German substitute, aroused mistrust and concern in the Community executive institutions. For the first time since its establishment, the EEC Commission felt threatened with being weakened or even sidelined. Since they could not directly oppose the French plan, the members of the Commission — and the President in particular — mobilised their energy to demonstrate the superiority of the Community method over intergovernmental cooperation as an instrument for integration and to plead in favour of consolidating the existing Communities. Dropping the Fouchet Plan marked the failure of the intergovernmental political Europe, which would leave traces like the Europe Defence Community in 1954, but at the same time came as a relief for the supporters of a supranational Europe, who could look forward to stronger Community institutions in general and a stronger Commission in particular.

Drafting the Merger Treaty [2]

Unlike the Fouchet Plan, the merger of the executives gave the Commission an opportunity to strengthen its position in the institutional set-up. Establishing a Single Commission that combined the functions of the EEC and Euratom Commissions and the ECSC High Authority would simplify the operation of the Communities, and the new institution would enjoy greater prestige and authority. The other difference from the Fouchet Plan was that the Merger Treaty was drafted mostly in the Community institutions, even though in the early days the Action Committee

for a United States of Europe was active in the debate. The three executives played an active role, without actually being in charge of the operation, which was directed by the governments. A notable feature was that the draft also concerned the merger of the Councils, but this posed hardly any problems here as the three Councils had already been operating to all intents and purposes as a single institution since 1958.

In the early period following the entry into force of the Rome Treaties, attention focused on coordination — rather than a merger — between the three executives. Regular contacts were soon established, notably in the form of meetings of the Presidents. Joint services and working parties were set up [3]. But this cooperation between three geographically dispersed institutions was sometimes difficult and occasionally provoked tensions [4]. In the autumn of 1959 the Wigny Report, which was presented to the Council by the Belgian Foreign Minister, recommended the establishment of an inter-executive committee to settle matters of common interest and facilitate the preparation of common policies [5], whereas Jean Monnet's Action Committee adopted an initial resolution supporting the merger of the executives.

The merger plan was launched by Étienne Hirsch, President of the Euratom Commission, in May 1960, when, addressing the European Parliamentary Assembly, he called for the establishment of a single executive [6]. He was immediately supported by the Assembly and by the Action Committee, though later, in the autumn, the Action Committee proposed postponing the merger and giving priority to political union. At the end of June this initiative was approved by the other two executives, albeit apparently with

---

[1] HAEC, Speech given to the European Parliament, 27 March 1963.
[2] On this question generally, see Bitsch, M.-Th., 'La création de la Commission unique: réforme technique ou affirmation d'une identité européenne?', in Bitsch, M.-Th., Loth, W. and Poidevin, R. (eds), *Institutions européennes et identités européennes*, Bruylant, Brussels, 1998, pp. 327–347.

[3] COM(58) 138, note sur les formes de coopération entre les trois exécutifs, 9 June 1958.
[4] FJME, AMK 54/4/2, Max Kohnstamm to Jean Monnet, 31 May 1959.
[5] CEAB 2 148, Wigny Report, 'Considérations sur le développement de la coopération entre les six pays de la Communauté européenne et sur leurs relations extérieures'.
[6] Speech by Étienne Hirsch to the Assembly, 16 May 1960.

some reservations. The EEC Commission at the time was interested above all in having its own powers strengthened (this was the attitude of Jean Rey ([1])), and the High Authority was concerned that it should not lose its supranational prerogatives (financial autonomy, co-optation system, etc.).

In addition, at the end of June, at the request of the Assembly and with the agreement of all the bodies concerned, the question of the merger was inserted in the programme for an interinstitutional conference to be held in November. The Assembly, the Commissions and the Council met to discuss a report on the merger of the executives prepared by Maurice Faure for the Assembly's Political Affairs Committee. Walter Hallstein presented a number of demands ([2]). For one thing, the merger should under no circumstances jeopardise the powers conferred on each of the executives. For another, establishing a single executive did not automatically have to entail broader powers for the Assembly. He saw no need for the appointment of the single executive to be confirmed by a vote in the Assembly, and Étienne Hirsch seemed to agree with him.

At the beginning of 1961, the merger proposal was taken over by the Dutch government, which intervened twice, the first time on 23 January ([3]) — a few days before the Paris summit on political union — with a note to the Council Secretariat and the second time on 27 June — three weeks before the Bonn Summit — when it presented its partners with a draft convention establishing single executives ([4]). This Dutch initiative gave the project an even more pronounced political dimension.

The merger proposal aroused little enthusiasm among the other five governments. Apart from the fact that it could be perceived as a competing project or a delaying tactic in relation to the

French political union project, several ministers felt it would be difficult to implement. Some doubted whether it was interesting in terms of efficiency and its timeliness when the United Kingdom was about to lodge its Community membership application, and they wondered whether it was expedient to amend the Treaties, even on a specific matter, in a way that could lead London to believe that the Treaty, far from being cast in stone, could be easily revised. The French government was the most hostile, considering the reform to be a window-dressing exercise unlikely to have much effect on the institutional reality. And the Luxembourg government, while less radical than Paris in its discourse, doubted the utility of the merger and was concerned at the potential damage to its country if it lost the ECSC High Authority.

Anyway, the governments had other priorities in 1961. At the end of the year, there was to be the changeover from the first to the second stage of the transitional period, which involved preparing rules for the common agricultural policy. And the six governments were in delicate negotiations both on the political union (Fouchet Plan) and on the accession of the United Kingdom, which opened in Brussels in the autumn. The Council's progress towards the merger was therefore decidedly slow and cautious.

The Council was obliged to consider the Dutch proposal and asked the Assembly and the two Commissions to give their opinions on it. This they did in the autumn of 1961; as expected, the opinions were very much in favour. The Assembly, which adopted a second Faure Report on the question, stressed the urgency of the merger, which was even more pressing than a year earlier. President Hirsch, the untiring advocate of the project, emphasised its 'technical' value in facilitating the life of the Communities and its 'political' importance in accelerating progress towards European integration ([5]). The EEC Commission

([1]) 'FJME, AMK C 33/5/134, Jean Rey to Jean Monnet, 24 November 1959.
([2]) BA, WH 178815, Note of 17 November 1960.
([3]) CEAB 2 1911, Note by Dutch government, 23 January 1961.
([4]) Europe/Documents, 26 July 1961.

([5]) CEAB 2 1912, Étienne Hirsch to Ludwig Erhard, 28 September 1961.

Walter Hallstein (President of the EEC Commission), Paul Finet (President of the ECSC High Authority) and Louis Armand (President of the EAEC Commission) at the first meeting of the presidents of the three executives on 14 January 1958.

welcomed the Dutch initiative, which opened the way to progress on a necessary reform, and the support given by the Assembly (^{1}). The High Authority, which had not been asked for its opinion, also expressed its agreement although it again asked that its supranational prerogatives be preserved. Despite this general convergence of views, it was only on 3 May 1962 that the Council placed the matter back on its agenda. It asked the permanent representatives to study the project but not to set a timetable or a deadline for a report, and so the project looked as though it had started.

At the beginning of 1963, when the political union had clearly failed and the negotiations with Lon-

don were halted, the merger project was revived. Chancellor Adenauer and President de Gaulle considered the matter at talks on 22 January, the very day on which the Élysée Treaty was signed. A month later, in an address he delivered in Paris, Michel Gaudet, Director-General of the (joint) Legal Service of the European Communities, spoke of the utility of rationalising the institutions. More significant still: the new President of the Euratom Commission, Pierre Chatenet, appointed at France's behest to replace Étienne Hirsch, who was thought to be too federalist, came out publicly in support of merging the executives. And above all, on 2 April, Gerhard Schröder, Germany's Minister for Foreign Affairs, called for the merger of the executives as a first step towards unification of the Treaties, and in July the French Foreign Minister, Maurice Couve de Murville, stated that his government had decided to go along with its partners'

(^{1}) FJME, AMK 113/2/6, Walter Hallstein to Ludwig Erhard, 10 November 1961.

views. As a result, on 24 September 1963 the Council instructed the permanent representatives to make proposals for the merger of the executives. On the same day the six ministers, despite initial reluctance from France, decided that the representatives of the two Commissions and the High Authority would be associated with the permanent representatives' discussions.

It was therefore this body — the Permanent Representatives Committee, augmented by the representatives of the three executives — that produced the report of 18 December 1963 which served as a basis for the future Merger Treaty. In less than three months, partly thanks to sound cooperation between France and Germany, all the main details of the merger were worked out. Agreement was quickly reached on the principle of a four-year term for members of the merged executive — abandoning the system of partial replacement operating at the High Authority — and on the possibility for the Assembly of censuring the executive at any time, in accordance with the EEC rules. There were three main items for discussion: the name of the single executive, the way in which its members should be designated and the number of members ([1]).

Regarding the name, the Dutch draft mentioned a 'High European Commission' and the High Authority — with support from the Luxembourg government — recommended 'European Authority', whereas France was not happy with either 'High' or 'Authority', and the German suggestion of 'Commission of the European Communities' was finally adopted. Members could be chosen by agreement between the governments, as provided in the Treaties of Rome and the Dutch draft, although some members at least could be co-opted, as at the High Authority, which was keen to maintain this procedure as a guarantee of independence of the executive; eventually, however, it was abandoned.

The number of Commission members, the trickiest question of all, was settled by the foreign ministers only in 1964. There were two theses. Paris, with varying degrees of support from Bonn and Rome as well as from the EEC Commission, and in particular Walter Hallstein, Robert Marjolin, Sicco Mansholt and the Executive Secretary, Émile Noël, defended the idea of a nine-member Commission on grounds of the efficiency, cohesion and authority associated with a smaller body ([2]). The Euratom Commission, the Netherlands and Belgium, on the other hand, preferred 14 members so that different political or regional sensitivities could be represented and also doubtless because it would then be easier to deal with certain personal problems on the day when the three executives (totalling 23 members) disappeared. The High Authority would have preferred a 15-member Commission with a co-opted member representing the trade union movement, as at the ECSC. The compromise solution devised by Germany was for a 14-member Commission for a transitional period of three years and nine members thereafter until enlargement of the Community.

Two problems of a more political nature stretched the negotiations out. The question of a stronger role for the European Parliament was less concerned with extending its powers as such, something which the governments of the day did not really want, than with election by direct universal suffrage, as called for by the EEC Commission and all the governments except the French government and as demanded quite forcefully by Italy. But the real stumbling block was the question of compensation for Luxembourg if it lost the ECSC High Authority. The Government of the Grand Duchy raised the stakes, invoking its country's 'Europeanness', its vested moral rights and its economic and political interests. If it could not obtain the headquarters of the single executive, it wanted new bodies to be set up there and at least an equivalent number of civil servants to be

---

[1] AMAEF, *Europe* Series, 1961–1965, Dossier 1964 (the entire dossier is very useful on the negotiations in the Council, Coreper, the views expressed by those involved, etc.).

[2] BAC 118/1986, Report by the permanent representatives, 25 March 1964.

Treaty establishing a Single Council and a Single Commission (extracts)

'Chapter II. The Commission of the European Communities

[...]

Article 9

A Commission of the European Communities (hereinafter called the "Commission") is hereby established. This Commission shall take the place of the High Authority of the European Coal and Steel Community, the Commission of the European Economic Community and the Commission of the European Atomic Energy Community.

It shall exercise the powers and jurisdiction conferred on those institutions in accordance with the provisions of the Treaties establishing the European Coal and Steel Community, the European Economic Community and the European Atomic Energy Community, and of this Treaty.

Article 10

1. The Commission shall consist of nine members, who shall be chosen on grounds of their general competence and whose independence is beyond doubt.

The number of members of the Commission may be altered by the Council, acting unanimously [...]

2. The members of the Commission shall, in the general interest of the Communities, be completely independent in the performance of their duties.

In the performance of these duties, they shall neither seek nor take instructions from any Government or from any other body [...]

When entering upon their duties they shall give a solemn undertaking that, both during and after their term of office, they will respect the obligations arising therefrom and in particular their duty to behave with integrity and discretion as regards the acceptance, after they have ceased to hold office, of certain appointments or benefits [...]

Article 11

The members of the Commission shall be appointed by common accord of the Governments of the Member States.

Their term of office shall be four years. It shall be renewable.

Article 13

If any member of the Commission no longer fulfils the conditions required for the performance of his duties or if he has been guilty of serious misconduct, the Court of Justice may, on application by the Council or the Commission, compulsorily retire him.

[...]

Article 15

The Council and the Commission shall consult each other and settle by common accord their methods of cooperation.

[...]

Article 17

The Commission shall act by a majority of the number of members provided for in Article 10.

A meeting of the Commission shall be valid only if the number of members laid down in its Rules of Procedure is present.

Article 18

The Commission shall publish annually, not later than one month before the opening of the session of the Assembly, a general report on the activities of the Communities.

[...]

Chapter V. General and final provisions

Article 27

[...]

2. The second paragraph of Article 24 of the Treaty establishing the European Coal and Steel Community is repealed and the following substituted therefore:

"If a motion of censure on the activities of the High Authority is tabled before it, the Assembly may not vote thereon until at least three days after the motion has been tabled and only by open vote."'

based there. At the beginning of 1965, President Hallstein, now much keener to carry the merger through, seems to have entered the arena to help bring the negotiations to a successful conclusion (¹). Several governments also wished to come to a satisfactory compromise, and agreement was reached when the Council met on 2 March 1965. The Single Commission was to be based in Brussels, but Luxembourg would retain the Court of Justice of the Communities and the secretariat of the Assembly. The Council would meet there three months every year, and a number of bodies would be based there, including the European Investment Bank, the Office for Official Publications and the Statistical Office.

The Treaty establishing a Single Council and a Single Commission was signed on 8 April 1965. In addition to merging the executives, it institutionalised the Permanent Representatives Committee, which did not exist at the ECSC, and established a single administration and a single administrative budget. The Treaty was hailed on all sides as an historic event. Following the Council meeting on 2 March, Walter Hallstein had presented the agreement between the Six as a great step forward in the history of European unification. He regarded the merger as a decisive, vital element of so-called political union (²). Comments expressed at the time reveal the extent of the hopes raised by the new Treaty: acceleration of European integration, better management of the Communities, better institutional balance between the Commission and the Council, stronger political dialogue between the Commission and the Assembly, Community identity better asserted in relation to the outside world, improved public image.

This optimism seemed to augur well for the ratification of the Treaty, basically scheduled to come into force in July 1966. Thought was already being given to the merger of the Communities, which was theoretically due to take place

three years after the merged institutions were set up. In 1960 President Hirsch, as with the Faure report, had already put the merger of the executives forward as the first stage of harmonisation of the Treaties. Several governments shared this approach from 1963 onwards, and Paris even stated that the relatively rapid merger of the Treaties was one of the conditions on which it accepted the merger of the institutions. Walter Hallstein had already been speaking along these lines since 1962, and at the beginning of 1965 he stated that the merger of the executives should make it easier to merge the Treaties. The President of the EEC Commission made his views clear at a conference organised in Liège a few days after the 1965 Treaty was signed. As he saw it, if a single Community was to be established, economic and social rules and regulations had to be unified and institutional rules, which he preferred to the term 'constitutional', had to be laid down. This merger could proceed in two stages, a report prepared by the Single Commission to identify the problems and suggest solutions then being taken as a basis for intergovernmental negotiations (³). President Hallstein, and others too (for example, the Luxembourg jurist Pierre Pescatore, at the same Liège conference), did not gloss over the difficulties inherent in this operation, which would become all the more acute following the 'empty chair crisis'. This crisis put the entry into force of the Merger Treaty back to July 1967, and there was a risk that the merger of the Communities would be jeopardised, as emphasised at a second conference in Liège and in a talk given by Émile Noël at the European University Centre at Nancy in 1966 (⁴).

Marie-Thérèse Bitsch

(¹) *Le Monde*, 3 February 1965.
(²) FJME, AMK 113/2/40, Note by Bino Olivi, No 17451, 3 March 1965.
(³) *Actes du colloque organisé par l'Institut d'études juridiques européennes de l'université de Liège, les 28-30 avril 1965*, University of Liege Faculty of Law, Liège, 1965 (speech by Walter Hallstein, pp. 215–226).
(⁴) Noël, É., *La fusion des institutions et la fusion des Communautés européennes*, European Conferences Collection, No 1, European University Centre at Nancy, 1966.

A committed generation

In the mid-1950s, as a young Secretary at the High Authority of the first of the European Communities, the Coal and Steel Community, I could see the fate of the European adventure hanging in the balance. Following the failure of the European Defence Community and its corollary, political union, the ECSC alone could not keep alive the flame of our ideal, which was to put an end to the divisions and impotence of a free Europe.

A new start was needed. What is more, international events, such as the closure of the Suez Canal in 1956 and the Hungarian uprising against Communist dictatorship in the same year, were pushing the six ECSC Member States towards taking action, while the continuing deadlock in the efforts by the Organisation for European Economic Cooperation to endow western Europe with a large dynamic market free of artificial barriers highlighted just how urgent it was for those countries that were ready to do so to organise themselves.

In 1955, Italy, in the person of Gaetano Martino, had organised the Conference of Messina, which would mark the first stage in the revival of the Community. In successive negotiations this Community would come to be constructed around two main concepts: to provide the Europe of Six with a new source of energy based on nuclear power, and to organise the economies of the Six into a customs union. The drafting of these proposals was to be the task of a conference to be held at Val-Duchesse under the chairmanship of Paul-Henri Spaak. From January 1956 onwards, the new French government, led by Guy Mollet, gave its full support to the project and managed to overcome the concerns of traditional circles in France with regard to the 'great leap forward' which a 'common market' without internal barriers would represent. The French would consult the German government under Konrad Adenauer whenever the negotiations were in danger of breaking down. The Benelux ministers (Spaak, Beyen and Bech) made sure that their notion of a customs union between the Six was implemented.

Meanwhile, Jean Monnet, the first President of the ECSC High Authority, who had resigned following

the failure of the EDC, founded his Action Committee for the United States of Europe, bringing together political and trade union leaders to promote and support a new beginning for Europe. His successor at the High Authority, René Mayer, placed ECSC experts at Spaak's disposal to help him draw up the new Treaties. Two Treaties, for the European Economic Community and Euratom, were signed in Rome on 25 March 1957 and ratified within the year.

Looking back, it is clear that only an exceptional combination of circumstances had enabled determined politicians to achieve their aim before the end of 1957. One year later these agreements would no longer have been possible, as General de Gaulle, who was opposed to supranational structures in principle, took over from the governments of the Fourth Republic in the course of 1958.

Several of the leading figures involved in the negotiations and in the early stages of European integration would find themselves working for the two new Communities, the EEC and Euratom, which came into being in January 1958. They included Walter Hallstein, the President, who had negotiated the ECSC Treaty, and Hans von der Groeben, who had defended the idea of the EEC in discussions with Ludwig Erhard, the sceptical German Economics Minister. The task of producing the final draft of the Treaties at the end of the Val-Duchesse negotiations was entrusted by Paul-Henri Spaak to Pierre Uri, from the ECSC High Authority, and Hans von der Groeben. Also at the European Commission were Robert Marjolin, who had been involved since his time at the OEEC in the moves to establish European cooperation and from 1956 in the Treaty negotiations, his colleague Sicco Mansholt, who had tried in vain during his time as Dutch Agriculture Minister to create the 'green pool' under the aegis of the OEEC, Jean Rey, another old hand from the ECSC when he was Belgian Economics Minister, and the brilliant Jean-François Deniau, one of the negotiators at Val-Duchesse, who would play a remarkable role in the successive enlargement negotiations.

Many other people who had been present at the OEEC, the Messina Conference, Val-Duchesse or the ECSC would join the ranks of the new Commission. Thus, Michel Gaudet from the ECSC would become head of the

Legal Service at the EEC Commission while Jacques René Rabier became head of the joint Press and Information Service of the three Communities. Louis Rabot and his right-hand man Helmut von Verschuer had already worked together on the 'green pool' at the OEEC. And, last but not least, Émile Noël, formerly at the Council of Europe, who had been involved in the 'political union' project since 1952 and had played a central role in the cabinet of Guy Mollet in bringing the two Treaties of Rome to a successful conclusion. The appointment of Noël to the post of Executive Secretary of the Hallstein Commission was welcomed in European circles as the ideal choice both for political reasons and because of his many personal and professional qualities. Together with his deputy, Winrich Behr, from the High Authority, Noël quickly gained the confidence of the President and the entire Commission. Consolidating his remarkable coordinating and driving role, he became and remained a pivotal figure in the continuity of the institution's operations.

I mentioned just now the 'European circles' of the time. I can bear witness to the enormous spirit of cooperation that existed in those days between all these people, members of the executives, senior Commission officials, members of the European Parliament or representatives of the Member States and even of non-member countries, who saw European integration as the only way forward for the old continent. Whether they were committed federalists or simply pragmatists, they were determined that 'their' European Community, based not on political wrangling but on the rule of law, should succeed at all costs.

This explains the extraordinary dynamism of so many 'committed' men during these pioneering times.

Written recollections by Edmund Wellenstein, July 2006.

Chapter 3

Walter Hallstein, a committed European

Walter Hallstein was one of the pioneers of European unification. He was a close colleague and adviser of Konrad Adenauer from 1950 to 1957 and one of the architects of integration of the Federal Republic of Germany with the West. Although initially regarded with great scepticism, the Federal Republic soon became a pillar of the new Europe. Between 1955 and 1957 Hallstein played a major part in drawing up the Rome Treaties, which cast the Community in its present mould. As first President of the Commission of the European Economic Community from 1958 to 1967, he contributed greatly to shaping the Community institutions and promoting integration within the Community of Six despite the many forces ranged against it. He had a forward-looking vision of how the Community's organisation should evolve and was aware of the practical and theoretical implications for the European political order.

A lawyer whose mind was open to the world

Hallstein was born on 17 November 1901 in Mainz, the son of a Protestant State architect (¹). After at-

tending grammar school, he read law and politics at the universities of Bonn and Munich and at the Friedrich-Wilhelm University in Berlin, where he quickly became assistant to the professor of civil law, Martin Wolff. In 1925 he obtained a doctorate of law with a thesis on the Versailles peace treaty and, scarcely three years later, defended a habilitation thesis on 'present-day company law'. In 1930 he was appointed titular professor at the University of Rostock, at the age of just 29. In 1941 he was appointed Director of the Institute for Comparative Law and the Institute for Commercial Law at the Johann-Wolfgang-Goethe University in Frankfurt/Main.

The meteoric rise of this brilliant and versatile jurist was then interrupted by the war. He served as a Wehrmacht officer in an artillery regiment in occupied northern France. He was taken prisoner by the American forces after the Allied landing in June 1944 and was held in Camp Como, in the American State of Mississippi,

---

(¹) For the biography of Walter Hallstein, see Loch, Th. M., 'Walter Hallstein — Eine biographische Skizze', *Wege nach Europa — Walter Hallstein und die junge Generation*, Pontes-Verlag, Andernach, 1967, pp. 5–47, and Ramonat, W., 'Rationalist und Wegbereiter: Walter

Hallstein', in Jansen, Th. and Mahnke, D. (eds), *Persönlichkeiten der europäischen Integration*, Europa-Union-Verlag, Bonn, 1981, pp. 337–378, as well as the articles in Loth, W., Wallace, W. and Wessels, W. (eds), *Walter Hallstein — The forgotten European?*, Macmillan, London/New York, 1998.

Walter Hallstein, Commission President 1958–67,
'a man of formidable energy, intellect and ambition
in the service of his institution'.
(Interview with Jacques-René Rabier, 8 January 2004)

where he organised a camp university, thus demonstrating for the first time his capacity for large-scale organisation (¹). At the age of 44, after his release in 1946, he became the first post-war Vice-Chancellor of the University of Frankfurt. In the three years during which he held this post, he not only pursued the reconstruction and democratic restructuring of his institution but also played a part in the complete reorganisation of the higher education system in the western-occupied zones as chairman of the Southern German Vice-Chancellors' Conference, Chairman of the Standing Committee of the Southern German Higher Education Congress for the American occupation zone and, finally, as Chairman of the Founding Committee of the Institute for Political Science in Frankfurt.

With no Nazi antecedents and a dynamic approach open to European ideas, Hallstein was one of the leading figures in the renascent society

of West Germany. In the spring of 1948 the Joint International Committee for European Unity asked him to attend the congress of the European Movement in The Hague from 7 to 10 May. With the German delegation, which took advantage of the congress to establish links with major west-European politicians, Hallstein first met Konrad Adenauer, then chairman of the CDU in the British zone, and others including Karl Arnold, the Minister-President of North Rhine-Westphalia, Max Brauer and Wilhelm Kaisen, the mayors of Hamburg and Bremen, and Martin Niemöller, then head of the Protestant Church in Hessen-Nassau. The congress closed with a call for a 'European assembly' (²).

Hallstein was one of the leaders whom the Western Allies sought to win over in order to make a success of their democratisation programme. This is demonstrated by the offer of a visiting professorship at Georgetown University in Washington DC, where he spent the academic year 1948–49 after completing his term as Vice-Chancellor. On returning to Frankfurt, he supported the founding of a German Unesco Commission with a view to future West German membership of the United Nations' cultural organisation. Since he already had a reputation for integrity and effectiveness, he became the first President of that Commission in May 1950, becoming actively engaged in integrating the young Federal Republic into the international community.

Europe: a common cause with Adenauer

It was thus only to be expected that Wilhelm Röpke, an economist teaching in Zürich, should mention Hallstein in early June 1950, when Konrad Adenauer, by then Federal Chancellor, was looking for a chief negotiator for the impending intergovernmental talks on the

(¹) See Schönwald, M., 'Hinter Stacheldraht — vor Studenten, Die "amerikanischen Jahre" Walter Hallsteins 1944–1949', in Dietl, R. and Knipping, Fr. (eds), *Begegnungen zweier Kontinente — Die Vereinigten Staaten und Europa seit dem Ersten Weltkrieg*, Wissenschaftlicher Verlag Trier, 1999, pp. 31–54.

(²) See Stillemunkes, Chr., 'The discussion on European Union in the German occupation zones', in Lipgens, W. and Loth, W. (eds), *Documents on the history of European integration*, Vol. 3, de Gruyter, Berlin/New York, 1988, pp. 441–465, here p. 454.

Schuman Plan. The new German State, which was still under occupation, did not yet have any well-established diplomatic machinery. Various persons whom Adenauer had at first considered proved unsuitable for various reasons: Hermann Josef Abs because he was distrusted by the French, Hans Schäffer because he was of Swedish nationality and Herbert Blankenhorn, Adenauer's most important colleague in foreign policy as head of the Federal Chancellery office for liaison with the High Commission, because, like most of the diplomats in the former Foreign Office, he had been a member of the Nazi Party. Adenauer therefore met Hallstein on 15 June 1950. Finding this former university administrator to be as persuasive, helpful and well-informed as he had been led to expect, he put him in charge of the delegation [1]. Five days later, Hallstein attended the opening of negotiations in Paris.

When leading Germany's Schuman Plan delegation, Hallstein made the acquaintance of Jean Monnet and thought highly of him, although their views could sometimes diverge, for example on the need for a European Court of Justice. He was also impressed by the atmosphere of partnership and trust in each other's European principles, which was quickly established among all the delegates to the negotiations [2]. As an organisational model, he proposed that the High Authority be responsible to an 'ECSC Congress' derived from a directly elected Parliament and a Council of Ministers, an idea developed mainly by Carl Friedrich Ophüls. In accordance with Adenauer's instructions, however, he adopted a cautious approach and supported the final compromise on the institutional architecture of the Community, which emerged early in August [3].

Hallstein's effective handling of the negotiations and his focus on results led Adenauer to entrust this skilful law professor with the operational conduct of his foreign policy. From his holiday resort at Bürgenstock on Lake Lucerne, in Switzerland, he wrote offering him the post of State Secretary at the Federal Chancellery in charge of the 'office for foreign affairs'. Out of a sense of duty and a desire to shape events, Hallstein accepted immediately. The detailed review conducted by the two men at Bürgenstock on 10 August after the first round of negotiations in Paris showed that they were in agreement on several points: the need for a Franco-German equilibrium, firm support for European unification, long-term protection of western Europe by America and a categorical refusal to contemplate a neutral Germany. Both also considered that Hallstein should retain his chair in Frankfurt so that they could work together without any personal constraints [4].

When the office for foreign affairs was separated from the Federal Chancellery in March 1951, Hallstein, now State Secretary for Foreign Affairs, was virtually in charge of a ministry. It was an odd arrangement. Adenauer remained Minister for Foreign Affairs until the Paris Treaties came into effect in the summer of 1955, but inevitably most of the routine tasks of running the department fell to Hallstein. He made a point of taking on as few as possible of the staff of the former foreign ministry and of performing these duties with the utmost rigour. With his excellent knowledge of economics, law and history, his sound classical education and his great psychological insight, he acquired unchallenged authority over the ministry and within the Federal government. He became indispensable to Adenauer in devising and implementing his country's strategy and in drawing up the Treaties binding it to western Europe.

There was no basic change in Hallstein's position when, after prolonged pressure from the coali-

---

[1] See Schwarz, H.-P., *Adenauer — Der Aufstieg: 1876–1952*, Deutsche Verlags-Anstalt, Stuttgart, 1986, pp. 723–726.

[2] Recollections of Max Kohnstamm, a member of the Dutch delegation to the negotiations, in Loth, Wallace and Wessels, op. cit., p. 5.

[3] See Küsters, H.J., 'Die Verhandlungen über das institutionelle System zur Gründung der Europäischen Gemeinschaft für Kohle und Stahl', in Schwabe, Kl. (ed.), *Die Anfänge des Schuman-Plans 1950/51*, Nomos, Baden-Baden, 1988, pp. 73–102; also Schönwald, M., 'Walter Hallstein et les institutions des Communautés européennes', in Bitsch, M.-Th., (ed.), *Le couple France–Allemagne et les institutions européennes*, Bruylant, Brussels, 2001, pp. 151–168, here pp. 152–155.

[4] See Hallstein, W., 'Mein Chef Adenauer', in Blumenwitz, D. *et al.* (eds), *Konrad Adenauer und seine Zeit, Beiträge von Weg- und Zeitgenossen*, Deutsche Verlags-Anstalt, Stuttgart, 1976, pp. 132–136.

Walter Hallstein on the goal of building a united Europe

'There is no aspect of European politics more important to us than political unity. It is the final objective, the reason behind all European endeavours. The ultimate motives for this project have always been political: peace within this united Europe, its external security and regaining its role in international politics, a role lost in two world wars. The economic benefit of this final goal, as sensational as it is, was a means to this end, an intermediate goal.'

Speech in the Bundestag on 18 June 1970,
Stenographische Berichte des Deutschen Bundestages,
6. Wahlperiode, 60. Sitzung, pp. 3336 *et seq.*
(Translated from the German)

tion parties, Adenauer passed the foreign affairs portfolio to Heinrich von Brentano in the summer of 1955. The State Secretary for Foreign Affairs retained a seat in cabinet and, above all, he still had direct access to Adenauer, who continued to have full confidence in him. Joachim Jaenicke, who left the German embassy in Washington to become the foreign affairs press officer in 1956, regarded him as an outstanding person to work for: with great powers of concentration, sparing with his words and always ready to take decisions. His standing within the Ministry of Foreign Affairs was pre-eminent, although he did make a point of loyalty to the minister, who was now his superior [1].

At that time, he left intra-German policy to Wilhelm Grewe, who since 1951 had conducted the negotiations on ending the occupation of Germany and who now took charge of the policy department of the ministry, representing the State Secretary in policy matters. According to Grewe, both shared Adenauer's view that the reunifica-

tion of Germany was not an issue with which the foreign policy of the Federal Republic could achieve any results or even success in the foreseeable future [2]. Hallstein doggedly defended the Federal Republic's claim to be the sole representative of Germany as a whole and kept open the question of Germany's eastern border. The 'Hallstein doctrine' that the federal government would suspend diplomatic relations with any country that recognised the GDR was originally formulated by Grewe. However, Hallstein adopted it unreservedly and defended it vis-à-vis both the German diplomatic service and the general public. When pursuit of this policy became a problem with the establishment of diplomatic relations between Yugoslavia and the GDR in the autumn of 1957, he ensured that the principle was put into practice.

After the occupation regime had been ended and the Federal Republic had joined NATO, Hallstein's main concern was to consolidate western integration and find a way out of the crisis into which the process of European integration had been plunged by the abandonment of the European Defence Community in August 1954. At that time, he was opposed tooth and nail by Ludwig Erhard, who resisted the creation of a European Economic Community. Theodor Sonnemann, State Secretary at the Ministry of Agriculture, and Franz Josef Strauß, who had recently been appointed Nuclear Energy Minister, also opposed him. It was only thanks to Adenauer's support that the Ministry of Foreign Affairs obtained a mandate in May 1956 to take part in the intergovernmental negotiations on the creation of a common market and a European Atomic Energy Community.

In these negotiations, Hallstein was remarkable for his single-mindedness in holding to the linkage between the Atomic Energy Community (which the French government wanted) and the Economic Community (which France sought to

[1] See Jaenicke, J., 'Remembering Walter Hallstein', in Loth, Wallace and Wessels (eds), op. cit., pp. 33–38.

[2] Grewe, W. G., 'Hallstein's conception of German–German policy', ibid., pp. 39–59, here p. 42.

delay as long as possible). He acquired a thorough mastery of his brief and so contributed to the swift conclusion of the negotiations in January–February 1957. As a matter of course, Adenauer then entrusted his State Secretary with explaining the broad lines of the draft treaty to the Bundestag on 21 March 1957 ([1]).

As regards the institutional framework, Hallstein pressed for the creation of an autonomous executive that was independent of the national authority of the nation States and under the control of a federal body operating according to the majority principle, a European Parliament and a European Court of Justice ([2]). The negotiations did not proceed entirely as he would have wished. He indeed expressed public, if restrained, reservations about the restrictions on the majority principle in the Council of Ministers and the weak position of Parliament. However, as an experienced negotiator, he knew that compromises had to be made and placed his hopes in the scope for development afforded by the Treaties. In his eyes, the Rome Treaties were not the high point of European integration, but rather a fresh start which warded off the risk of failure after the abortive attempt to create a Defence Community.

President of the EEC Commission

When Hallstein was engaged in drawing up the Rome Treaties, he was not yet aware that he himself, as the first President of the EEC Commission, would have considerable influence on how they were implemented. His appointment was again

---

[1] See Küsters, H-J. 'Walter Hallstein and the negotiations on the Treaties of Rome 1955–1957', ibid., pp. 60–81; and Schönwald, M., 'Politische oder wirtschaftliche Integration? Die Europakonzepte von Walter Hallstein und Ludwig Erhard 1950–1963', in Brunn, G. (ed.), *Neoliberalismus, die Entstehung des Maastrichter Vertrags und die Auswirkungen auf Nordrhein-Westfalen*, Nomos, Baden-Baden, 1999, pp. 11–31.

[2] Hallstein, W., *Gross und Klein-Europa: Vortrag vor dem Europäischen Forum in Alpach am 23. August 1957*, Essen, 1957, p. 10. See Bärenbrinker, Fr., 'Hallstein's conception of Europe before assuming office in the Commission', in Loth, Wallace and Wessels, (eds) op. cit., pp. 82–91, here p. 87.

Hans von der Groeben on Walter Hallstein

'Hallstein made an outstanding contribution to the process of European integration as President of the Commission of the European Economic Community. As *primus inter pares*, he knew how to merge the Commission into a working unit and how to represent our decisions to the Council of Ministers and to the public with precision and great vigour. His political speeches, in which he promoted the continuance and completion of economic and political integration, were of quality. Here his great art of expression, his comprehensive knowledge of law and his mastery of most of the languages of the Community came in useful. His colleagues gave him a great amount of freedom in representing their general political statements, even if some thought that the political landscape did not yet allow such bold objectives. From the beginning, Hallstein completely adopted the programme of the Treaty while President of the Commission. He felt it was necessary to give life to the regulations of the Treaty. Apart from this conception, he developed the idea of the Community founded upon law and, here, his knowledge and experience as a legal scholar was of great benefit to him. In my opinion, however, it would be incorrect to assume that this was his primary interest. As I know from many conversations we had, he was much more concerned with laying the foundations of European policy and he regarded autonomous European institutions as indispensable to this end. He certainly did not overestimate "material logic" but he did make use of it. It would also be wrong to assume that, from the beginning, he had utopian ideas regarding the possibility of setting up a European federal state in one stroke, as it were, by means of a constituent assembly or an intergovernmental treaty. He thought a step-by-step process much more reasonable, though he was of the opinion that the goal of a workable all-Europe would not be achieved if de Gaulle's ideas of cooperation among sovereign nation States were pursued.'

Von der Groeben, H., 'Walter Hallstein as President of the Commission', in Loth, Wallace and Wessels, (eds) op. cit., pp. 95–108, here pp. 96 and 97. (Translated from the German)

the result of a combination of circumstances. In order to ensure that the Frenchman Louis Armand was appointed President of the Euratom Commission, Jean Monnet, who had first played the Mansholt card (¹), proposed that a Belgian be appointed as President of the EEC Commission. However, the Belgian government was more interested in having the new Communities located in Brussels and therefore refrained from fielding a candidate, leaving the way clear for a German. Hallstein was available. With his specialised knowledge, his commitment and his high standing with the signatories to the Treaties, he was an excellent candidate. Adenauer discussed the question with the German President, Theodor Heuss, on 18 December 1957 and sounded out the other governments. On 6 and 7 January 1958 the foreign affairs ministers of the Six, meeting in Paris, agreed Hallstein's appointment as President of the first EEC Commission (²).

Hallstein seems to have taken only a few days to decide to accept this new task. With remarkable energy, he immediately set about welding the Commission into a working team. To a large extent, he also set his stamp on the administrative structure of the new authority. The assertive style of his relations with the Council of Ministers and the other Community bodies and the Commission's direct dialogue with the general public quickly earned him the nickname 'Mr Europe' (³), at least in the United States (⁴).

As President, he tried to make sure that the EEC Treaty was observed, in the face of ingrained nationalist attitudes and free-trade inclinations, in order to speed up the process of establishing the common market and make progress towards greater integration on the many issues which had remained unresolved in the negotiations on the Rome Treaties. He supported the establishment of a common agricultural market since he saw no

other way to ensure long-term French commitment to the Community project. He pursued the establishment of a European competition policy as a precondition for the internal market and sought to reconcile the opposing interests in the difficult areas of external trade policy, association treaties and development aid policy.

Hallstein's presidency was very successful until a crisis arose in the spring of 1965. Hallstein was trying to make use of France's interest in the establishment of the agricultural market in order to strengthen the position of the European Parliament and the Commission and, at the same time, speed up completion of the customs union for industrial goods. He was convinced that, in a number of Member States, it was not possible to gain acceptance for own-resource funding of the agricultural market without strengthening Parliament's prerogatives. He also believed that the greater integration he hoped to achieve by his initiative was a logical consequence of the practical links between the agricultural market, the general economic system and democratic accountability. He made the tactical assumption that the French President would not dare to risk delay, let alone failure, of the common agricultural policy because of the imminent presidential elections in France (⁵).

The proposal which Hallstein submitted first to the European Parliament on 24 March 1965 (⁶) was to amend Article 203 of the EEC Treaty so that Parliament's amendments to the draft Community budget could no longer be rejected by a qualified majority of the Council unless the latter endorsed the Commission's initial proposal. The Council of Ministers would no longer be able to impose its own view irrespective of the Commission's proposal and the parliamentary vote unless at least five of the six Member States agreed.

(¹) See p. 47.
(²) On this topic, see Küsters H. J., 'Verhandlungen', op. cit., pp. 103 et seq.
(³) See Chapter 2.
(⁴) Interview with Norbert Kohlhase, 26 May 2004.

(⁵) On this topic, see Chapter 4 and Loth, W., 'Hallstein and de Gaulle: the disastrous confrontation', in Loth, Wallace and Wessels, (eds), op. cit., pp. 135–150; Idem, 'Français et Allemands dans la crise institutionnelle de 1965', in Bitsch, M-Th., op. cit., pp. 229–243; Schönwald, M., 'Walter Hallstein and the "empty chair" crisis 1965/66', in Loth, W. (ed.), Crises and compromises: the European project 1963–1969, Nomos, Baden-Baden, 2001, pp. 157–171.
(⁶) Text in Europa-Archiv 20, 1965, pp. D404–D417.

Walter Hallstein attends the inauguration of the crèche set up by the EEC's Social Service. A crèche for the children of staff is an asset for officials at a time when company crèches are still a rarity.

Hallstein's gambit failed. Rather than strengthening Community bodies, it led to the 'empty chair' crisis, after which the partner governments were informed at the beginning of 1966 that the French government demanded unanimity in the Council of Ministers on issues of national importance.

Hallstein's efforts to introduce greater parliamentary control and effectiveness into the workings of the Community thus ended with a personal setback. De Gaulle vilified him as a power-hungry technocrat, the proponent of a European 'super-State' and the grand master of 'an areopagus of stateless technocrats' ([1]), who was constantly seeking greater powers for himself: 'Walter Hallstein

was the Chairman of the Commission. He was ardently wedded to the thesis of the super-State, and bent all his skilful efforts towards giving the Community the character and appearance of one. He had made Brussels, where he resided, into a sort of capital. There he sat, surrounded with all the trappings of sovereignty, directing his colleagues, allocating jobs among them, controlling several thousand officials who were appointed, promoted and remunerated at his discretion, receiving the credentials of foreign ambassadors, laying claim to high honours on the occasion of his official visits, concerned above all to further the amalgamation of the Six, believing that the pressure of events would bring about what he envisaged.' ([2])

([1]) Press conference on 9 September 1965, *Europa-Archiv*, No 20, 1965, pp. D.486–492.

([2]) De Gaulle, Ch., *Memoirs of hope*, Part 1, *Renewal 1958–1962*, Weidenfeld and Nicolson, London, 1971, p. 184.

Under fire from de Gaulle, who was further antagonised by the hostile response he received from France's five partners, Hallstein found himself caught up in a general affray. It became clear that his days as head of the Commission were numbered. In the spring of 1967, Kurt-Georg Kiesinger, the Grand Coalition Chancellor, agreed to the French President's demand for the principle of rotating the Commission's presidency to be introduced, to the extent that he wanted to allow Hallstein only a six-month term in the second half of 1967. Citing the Treaty, which provided for a two-year term, Hallstein informed Kiesinger on 5 May 1967 that he did not wish to be reappointed [1]. This meant that the Commission would no longer be able to play a decisive part in pushing forward integration and that integration would henceforth proceed at a leisurely pace.

A programme based on experience

Shortly after leaving the EEC Commission in 1967, Hallstein, at 67, was elected President of the European Movement, a position to which he was re-elected in 1970 and 1972. He also joined the Action Committee for a United States of Europe, founded by Jean Monnet. Wearing these two hats, he worked for greater European unification in his struggle with de Gaulle. In 1969, in order to support the integration movement, he collaborated with Karl-Heinz Narjes and Hans Herbert Götz on producing a work under the title *Der unvollendete Bundesstaat*, translated into English as *Europe in the making* [2], which sought to explain the principles of the building of a united Europe as an aid to completing the process.

In his book, Hallstein seeks to demonstrate that the three European Communities in fact have the makings of a federal State with all the necessary attributes. At the same time, he wished to explain how and by what means this keystone could be brought into being or, in other words, how the 'incomplete' Europe could be completed. In Hallstein's eyes, the European Communities have a 'dynamic potential' [3]: they are 'work in progress', which demands constant endeavour, as with great cathedrals. He identified the prime mover of this development as an inner logic (*Sachlogik*): a set of stages, each following on from the one before, which arise logically and are recognised and accepted by the world of politics. He regarded the Commission of the European Communities as the 'guardian' of this 'material logic', with the duty to 'represent the interests of the Community as a whole' [4].

The book met with great success. Four further editions were produced, each with extensive alterations and additions. A French version appeared in 1970, just one year after the German original. It was followed by translations into Spanish, Swedish and Italian in 1971. The British version followed in 1972, and an American edition with a detailed foreword by George W. Ball appeared in 1974. Updating the work and creating a theoretical groundwork for European unification then became a full-time occupation for the first President of the EEC Commission.

In the autumn of 1969 Hallstein allowed himself to be persuaded by Helmut Kohl, at that time Minister-President of the Rhineland-Palatinate, to head the CDU list in the Bundestag elections. He stood in the constituency of Neuwied-Altenkirchen in the Westerwald. Kohl tried to use the candidacy of this renowned advocate of European unification to cast himself in the role of Adenauer's successor. Hallstein thus hoped that, as a leading member of a party in power and perhaps indeed as a member of the government, he would again be able to help shape the Federal Republic's foreign and European policy. However, the CDU

[1] See Gassert, Ph., 'Personalities and politics of European integration: Kurt-Georg Kiesinger and the departure of Walter Hallstein 1966/67', in Loth, *Crises* [...] op. cit., pp. 265–284.
[2] Hallstein, W., *Europe in the making*, George Allen & Unwin Ltd, London, 1972.

[3] Ibid., p. 11 (Foreword).
[4] Ibid., p. 57.

Émile Noël on Walter Hallstein

'[…] this proud independence created the necessity for the Commission to assert itself on the strength of its ideas and on the quality of its proposals. The Commission (members as well as officials) therefore got to work very quickly with full force. Hallstein set a good example. He combined analytical clarity and the ability to synthesise with extraordinary efficiency. He was completely devoted to his task, whether sitting at his desk or back in his (modest) flat. He had a complete picture of all the files which lay before the Commission and he was in a position to contribute to the preparation and discussion of these files, whereby he was always mindful of ensuring the coherence and strength of positions. He knew that the new Commission was still weak and delicate — and therefore must appear all the more competent and uncompromising. [...] He also knew that the institutions — especially those which were "European" in the same sense as the Commission — had a certain responsibility which went far beyond the circumstances of the day. These institutions had to forge their own idea for the future of the Community and as far as Hallstein was concerned this could only be a quasi-federalist goal which had already been confirmed in the declaration made by Schuman and Monnet on 9 May 1950.

For nine years Hallstein led the work of the Commission (in French, which he commanded perfectly) with calm determination and great clarity. His somewhat ceremonious politeness never failed him, yet his colleagues could always express themselves openly with him. He took his decisions right away, often in discussions with the relevant Commission member. With his remarkable talent for explaining and debating, he built up to the conclusion of his lectures. In this way, the Commission never actually voted, apart from a few exceptions during the last year of his presidency. The President and the relevant Commission member reached consensus through creative and supportive proposals.

Along with the "Founders" who took the first political decisions in the 1950s, Hallstein takes extraordinary credit for having given form and substance to that which was merely ideal and hopeful expectation, and at the same time for having preserved the European message in all its power and clarity.'

Noël, É, 'Walter Hallstein: a personal testimony', in Loth, W., Wallace, W. and Wessels, W. (eds), *Walter Hallstein — The forgotten European?*, Macmillan, London/New York, 1998, pp. 131–134 (extracts).

---

lost the elections. Willy Brandt and Walter Scheel formed a socialist/liberal coalition government.

Hallstein thus found himself on the opposition benches. Within the CDU–CSU, he played the part of an elder statesman, a wise man, primarily concerned with foreign and European policy issues. He became a member of the Foreign Affairs Committee and was the European policy spokesman of the CDU–CSU group. As such, he made sure that his party's European ideology remained coherent, urged the government to take new initiatives and untiringly reasserted the aim of political union and the principles of federal organisation of the European Community. He welcomed enlargement of the Community and endorsed the Werner plan for an economic and monetary union.

Hallstein played an important part in April 1972 when the Bundestag was preparing to ratify the Treaty of Moscow, which was to form the basis for the 'new *Ostpolitik*' of the Brandt–Scheel government. Rainer Barzel, the chairman of the party and group, wanted the CDU–CSU opposition to abstain in order to avoid the collapse of the *Ostpolitik*, whereas the majority of the group was in favour of voting against. Thanks to his high standing, Hallstein was able to appeal to the sense of responsibility of the members of parliament and to marshal a large majority for abstention. This allowed the Treaties of Moscow and Warsaw to enter into force, with the consequent settlement of the Berlin question.

Though an old hand in government, Hallstein did not achieve any grassroots influence within the

The Action Committee for the United States of Europe bids Walter Hallstein farewell, 15 June 1967.
Jean Monnet on the left and Walter Hallstein on the right.

group, nor did he play a very active part in his constituency. He did not feel called upon to defend local and regional interests and remained aloof from the basic party machinery. When early elections were called in the autumn of 1972, the party leadership did not again nominate him as a candidate. Since Helmut Kohl was unable to find him a place in another region, Hallstein's parliamentary career came to an end after a single term.

On leaving the Bundestag, Hallstein remained President of the European Movement for a further two years. He gave up this position too in the spring of 1974. Though aged over 73, he did not lapse into inactivity. He was a frequent speaker at official events and, at the same time, threw himself into the task of rewriting and improving his book on Europe, the fifth edition of which was issued in 1979 under the deliberately neutral title *Die Europäische Gemeinschaft* (The European Community). He spent the last years of his life with friends in Stuttgart, and they were at his side during his distressing illness. He died on 29 March 1982, and was buried on 2 April 1982 in Stuttgart. The occasion was marked by a State ceremony.

Walter Hallstein on 'material logic' (*Sachlogik*)

'No feature of the Community is as spectacular, as thrilling as its progressiveness. This is the dynamic character of integration. It is the binding maxim of the Community. Integration is not what is, but what will be, a *création continue*. It is not a state, but rather a series, a process. Every new solution produces new requirements, which in turn demand a European solution. This is not an automatism. Nothing in politics is automatic; the human will is everywhere at play. It is, however, a gradient: new situations are always arising, new questions are always being asked which are to be answered in a European way, if reason prevails. The European challenge is constant. At the same time, the motor element, the driving force, is the most durable.'

Speech on 25 June 1970, quoted by Jansen, Th., 'Walter Hallstein after the presidency', in Loth, Wallace and Wessels, op. cit., pp. 165–180, here p. 168.

The contributions Hallstein made after he left the helm of the Commission to the debate on what was needed for the European project to succeed have, to some extent, suffered from the way in which he was caricatured by de Gaulle. The latter was regarded as an unabashed nationalist and the former as an idealistic theoretician or a power-grabber. Large swathes of public opinion were all too ready to reproach the President of the first Commission with mistakes along the way to a new Europe without giving deeper thought to what he had to say. Hallstein's legacy is thus tinged with a note of sadness.

An intellectual heavyweight on the political scene

'The main conflict inherent in his personality was his Kantian devotedness to ideas and thus the remoteness to the man in the street. He was deeply convinced that good reason and plausibility will, as a matter of fact, produce intellectual consent and thus inevitable personal respect. He suffered from the experience that this does perhaps work in a Platonian Academy, but not in politics at large. So one may not fully understand the personality nor his activities if one lacks the *sensus* for the complexity and genius of an outstanding character.

As to his devotion: who, among all the great men in contemporary history (Churchill, de Gaulle, Kennedy, Mrs Thatcher, Adenauer, Brandt, Kohl, et al.) or, for that matter, among the prominent European actors (Spinelli, Brugmans, Monnet, von der Groeben, Deniau, Albrecht and many others) have had the stamina to resist the temptation of writing their own biography to make sure history will not forget them? Hallstein did! The "Hallstein-doctrine" was not his brain-child, and the "Hallstein Commission" was invented by journalists, not by him. The idea of European integration was all that mattered to him, and this attitude and integrity, this unique mind-set, was the reason why he succeeded in making the beginning of the Community a success story, not the subtle handling of the institutional instruments. The man was what he stood for. And it is the absence of this attitude today which has brought the Community where it is now.'

Note from Norbert Kohlhase to Michel Dumoulin, 6 September 2005.

Today, there are increasing signs of interest in Hallstein's experience and insights in the arena of European politics. He is seen as more than just a major player in the history of European integration who, despite the spectacular defeat of his attempt to oppose de Gaulle, brought about remarkable successes in the consolidation of the European Communities. In view of the current debate on the European Constitution, his ideas are proving valuable and refreshing. His ability to bring interests together in a positive manner is more admirable than ever, as is his clear perception of the institutional arrangements which need to be made if the European Union is to overcome its shortfall of democratic legitimacy and political effectiveness.

WILFRIED LOTH

Chapter 4

The 'empty chair' crisis

The Council's decision of 15 December 1964 calling on the Commission to draw up proposals on financing the common agricultural policy and managing Community revenue was seen by Commission President Hallstein and his colleagues as the long-awaited chance to strengthen the Community institutions. Once German opposition to setting a common price for cereals had been overcome, which was a significant step forward for the establishment of a common agricultural market and a common commercial policy, a way had to be found of getting round the French President's legendary aversion to extending the powers of the Community. The democratic instincts of many Europeans, for whom financing from common revenues without Community parliamentary controls was inconceivable, looked like a way out. Several ministers, stealing a march on the Dutch Agriculture Minister, had already indicated at the December 1964 Council meeting that their parliaments would approve the transfer of resources to the Community's coffers only if the European Parliament's supervisory powers were increased at the same time.

Hallstein thought that, if this was the only way to make the common agricultural policy a reality, de Gaulle would be prepared to pay the price. As he saw it, the French economy's integration in the common market was so far advanced, and the common agricultural market offered France such attractive prospects, that the French President could not afford to hinder or totally block the trend towards irreversible integration permeating every sector of the economy. Furthermore, with the French elections of December 1965 in the offing, Hallstein argued, de Gaulle needed to be wary of laying himself open to criticism for an anti-European policy. As his *chef de cabinet*, Karl-Heinz Narjes, noted at the time, the French public was still so firmly convinced that such policy conflicted with French interests that de Gaulle could not afford to take that kind of decision in an election year [1]. Be that as it might, de Gaulle could only be induced to compromise on the powers of the European institutions, or indeed on any other area of policy, while the financing of the agricultural market had still not been definitively settled. Once French interests in the agricultural market had been satisfied, the Commission would no longer have any means of speeding up the integration process.

---

[1] BA, WH 1119/1, Narjes to Hallstein, 19 May 1965.

The own resources issue

Article 201 of the EEC Treaty provided that:

'The Commission shall examine the conditions under which the financial contributions of Member States provided for in Article 200 could be replaced by the Community's own resources, in particular by revenue accruing from the common customs tariff when it has been finally introduced.

To this end, the Commission shall submit proposals to the Council.

After consulting the Assembly on these proposals the Council may, acting unanimously, lay down the appropriate provisions, which it shall recommend to the Member States for adoption in accordance with their respective constitutional requirements.'

Article 2 of Regulation No 25 of 14 January 1962 on the financing of the common agricultural policy, adopted by the Council of Ministers on 4 April 1962, provided that:

'Revenue from levies on imports from third countries shall accrue to the Community and shall be used for Community expenditure so that the budget resources of the Community comprise those revenues togeth-

er with all other revenues decided in accordance with the rules of the Treaty and the contributions of Member States under Article 200 of the Treaty. The Council shall, at the appropriate time, initiate the procedure laid down in Article 201 of the Treaty in order to implement the abovementioned provisions.'

On 15 December 1964 the Council allocated the following tasks to the Commission, among others:

'The Council [...]

(g) invites the Commission to submit to the Council before 1 April 1965 [...] proposals for the financing of the common agricultural policy for the period 1965–70.'

(c) '[...] invites the Commission to submit, within the framework of its proposals on Regulation No 25 referred to in paragraph (g) of this resolution, proposals on the conditions of application of Article 2 of Regulation No 25 from the date of entry into force of the common prices for the different agricultural products.' (Translated from the German)

Hallstein's conviction that this was the case was endorsed by representatives of the Dutch government and by German political figures closely involved in European issues. Members of the European Parliament even urged him to exploit the opportunities for reinforcing the European institutions opened up by the task set by the Council of Ministers. In a parliamentary question of 15 January 1965, the Socialist Group deplored the fact that the Commission had failed to seize the opportunity offered by the proposals for establishing a precedent for a satisfactory solution to the problem of the European Parliament's powers [1]. Prompted by similar advice from Narjes, Hallstein resolved to give the most exhaustive interpretation possible to the mandate conferred by the Council on the Commission in December 1964. Initial soundings of

the French Foreign Ministry indicated that Paris might indeed accept some compromises. When, in March 1965, Narjes suggested that the financial legislation could not succeed unless France made some concessions about a stronger European Parliament, Couve de Murville showed a crystal-clear understanding of the issue, stipulating that such compromises could be tolerated in Paris only if they were framed in the most technical terms possible, avoiding any glaring publicity [2].

Hallstein's proposals

The proposals for Council decisions, drafted by Hallstein in close cooperation with Mansholt, contained five points.

---

[1] OJ EC No 79, 8 May 1965, pp. 1162–1163.

[2] BA, WH 1119/1, Narjes to Hallstein, 2 March 1965.

- To achieve a balance between the Member States and avoid undue production incentives, the price guarantee and subsidy system should first of all be applied, from 1 July 1967, to the major agricultural products for which no common market scheme had yet been adopted: milk, rice, beef and veal, and sugar. The Community should also take on all agricultural expenditure from that policy date, and in practice this would mean that the final phase of the common agricultural policy would also have to come into effect two and a half years earlier than the date set in January 1962.

- The entry into force of the customs union, which covered industrial as well as agricultural products, would also have to be brought forward to the date (1 July 1967) on which the Community prices would apply to agricultural products. Given the accelerated rate at which intra-Community customs duties were already being abolished, the completion of customs union would not be far off anyway. This strategy would also mean that all the distortions likely to arise from maintaining customs duties on agricultural and industrial products could be avoided, and export subsidies could be organised under the common commercial policy.

- Hallstein proposed allocating to the Community not only the agricultural levies but also the revenue from Community external customs duties. A complete stop would have to be put to Member States' financial contributions, and Community expenditure would be financed exclusively from own resources. While the Commission had constantly defended what it considered to be the logical and consistent system of financing, the Council, which had never reached unanimity on the subject, had left the issue of its introduction unresolved. The new system would have to be phased in gradually. In the first phase, in the second half of 1967, a proportion of the customs revenues corresponding to the balance of the amount needed to finance Community expenditure would have to be paid to the Community to supplement the levies. The proportion of the customs revenue retained by the Member States would then be reduced by one fifth each year. This meant that the transition from financial contributions to own resources should be completed by 1972.

- Given the substantial revenue that would thus accrue to the Community without being subject to national parliamentary controls, the European Parliament would have to be given greater rights of scrutiny over the drafting of the budget. Hallstein proposed amending Article 203 of the EEC Treaty in line with the proposals from Parliament and the Dutch government. This would mean that the Council would not be able to reject Parliament's amendments to the Community draft budget unless it was backed by a simple, unweighted majority vote of the Commission. The Council would no longer be able to impose its own view irrespective of Parliament's amendments and the Commission's vote unless at least five of the six Member States agreed.

- During the remainder of the transitional period from 1 July 1965 to 30 June 1967, the Commission would have to take over gradually the financing of the agricultural fund, in line with a plan of Mansholt, taking on two thirds for the 1965/66 financial year and five sixths for the 1966/67 financial year. In the case of products for which free movement of goods within the Community had been achieved before 1 July 1967, the Council of Ministers could decide by qualified majority to bring forward a full transfer of the costs by a qualified-majority vote [1].

The proposals agreed on by Hallstein and Mansholt were consistent and logical. They offered plausible solutions to the problems arising

---

[1] *Financement de la politique agricole commune — Ressources propres de la Communauté — Renforcement des pouvoirs du Parlement européen (Propositions de la Commission au Conseil)*, COM(65) 150, 31 March 1965.

The Hallstein strategy

On 19 May 1965 Karl-Heinz Narjes, Hallstein's *chef de cabinet*, prepared the following arguments for a discussion between Hallstein and the German government.

'European integration in all its forms is one of the factors most likely to affect French politics. There is no need to go into whether it would still be possible at this stage for de Gaulle, at the cost of an extraordinary deployment of political force, to slow down or completely halt the trend towards irreversible integration that permeates all sectors of the economy. Whether he could or not, the French public would now regard such measures as contrary to French interests, so much so that de Gaulle cannot afford to take decisions of this kind in an election year. [...] From year to year, interdependence is growing and the possibility of reversing this trend is diminishing.

Apart from France's own interests in continuing integration, the most powerful weapon lies in the five other governments resolutely defending the Treaty of Rome. This means both that the five governments must be willing to confront France unremittingly with the alternatives of complying with the Treaty or openly breaking with it on the international stage and that German diplomacy must effectively guide the five others from behind the scenes. [...]

Since he took office, the German Chancellor has identified himself so firmly with the objective of so-called political union that he can hardly neglect the subject in an election year. I therefore propose that he accepts the institutional part of the Commission's financing proposals and that he appropriates it as an essential step towards the democratic control of the European institutions.

In support of the Commission's financing proposals, not only must he refer to the approval in principle of the other five Member States, but also and above all he must assert that there can be absolutely no question of obtaining the German Bundestag's consent to any financial solution that does not constitute a substantial step towards increasing the European Parliament's powers of control.'

BA, WH 1119/1, Karl-Heinz Narjes to Walter Hallstein,
19 May 1965.
(Translated from the German)

---

from the decisions to phase in the customs union and the common agricultural policy gradually and were also designed to put right the democratic deficit born of the contradictory construction of the EEC Treaty. But at the same time they would require the Member States to give up a substantial part of their sovereignty and lose external customs revenue two and a half years earlier than stipulated in the Treaty. Above all, the Member States' influence over the Community budget would be reduced. Under Hallstein's proposal, the Commission would be able to impose any draft budget for which there was a simple, unweighted majority in the Council or a majority in Parliament and the support of two of the six Member States, whatever their size. Since Parliament could impose any draft for which it could secure the support of two Member States, it would acquire considerable leverage, while the Commission would take on the executive role in the Community as far as budget matters were concerned.

These challenges to the Member States led Marjolin to oppose Hallstein's and Mansholt's proposals. The French Vice-President of the Commission not only feared that General de Gaulle would oppose such major changes, he also doubted that the governments of the other Member States were ready yet to support their implementation. As he saw it, the Commission risked being defeated, which would inflict lasting damage on its authority and pointlessly paralyse the integration decisions that had already been approved. As an alternative, he recommended postponing the transfer of customs revenue to the Community until the end of the transition period and, in the meantime, leaving the fundamental questions about own resources on the back burner. However, the overwhelming majority of the Commission members felt that such postponement made no sense either theoretically or tactically [1]. The Commission adopted the proposals presented by Hallstein and Mansholt on 22 March 1965. Only Marjolin and his French colleague Henri Rochereau voted against them, and the Luxembourg Commission member Lambert Schaus abstained on the grounds that the rules and procedures for the proposed arrangements did not seem to be clear enough [2].

As the proposals' content had been prematurely revealed to the Strasbourg Parliament through the indiscretion of a few of its members, Hallstein felt obliged to give Parliament an account of the general thrust of the proposals before they were laid before the Council. It was 24 March. Hallstein gave Couve de Murville prior notice of the content of his speech in writing and offered to talk to him to explain it further. But this did not suffice to appease the French government's indignation at the Commission's arrogance in informing the Parliament of a proposal to be made to the Council. Couve gave Marjolin a thorough roasting on the occasion of Parliament's session of 26 March. He was clearly upset that the Commission had paid so little attention to his call for discretion [3].

After the drama of the public presentation, the *chefs de cabinet* put some finishing touches to the wording of the proposals, which were then adopted by the Commission on 31 March and submitted at once to the Council. The French government made an official announcement deploring the Commission's failure to discuss the matter with Member State governments before making such a radical presentation, and its disregard of the normal procedure of first submitting the matter to the Council. It 'refused to negotiate on the Community's own resources and on a strengthening of the Parliament's powers at that time: it felt that the appropriate course was simply to continue, pursuant to the arrangements worked out in the Council, to deal with the matter of financing the agricultural policy up to the end of the transitional period, i.e. for the next five years; this had to be settled, as agreed, by 30 June 1965' [4].

However, at the Council meeting on 13 May 1965, the representatives of the Netherlands and Germany opposed this view, contending that financing during the transitional period could not be dissociated from the principle of the transition to own resources during the last stage of the agricultural market and a decision was therefore also needed to increase European parliamentary control. The Dutch government even complained that the Commission proposals did not go far enough. It demanded that Parliament be given full legislative powers, be directly elected and be empowered to set up executive bodies. The Italian government welcomed the logic of the Commission's proposals and their respect for the spirit of the Community, while the Belgian government declared its agreement with almost all aspects of the proposals. Even the Luxembourg government, which had indicated that it would be satisfied with rules for the transitional period, did not object to the whole package of proposals in principle [5].

In view of all these demonstrations of support, the Commission refused to break up its

---

[1] Marjolin, R., *Architect of European unity — Memoirs, 1911–1986*, Weidenfeld and Nicolson, London 1989; FJME, ARM 21/1/22, Jean Flory to Robert Marjolin, 9 March 1965.

[2] PV spéc. 311, EEC Commission, 22 March 1965, pp. 8–10.

[3] BA, WH 1119/1, Klaus Meyer to Walter Hallstein, 26 March 1965.

[4] Von der Groeben, H., *The European Community: the formative years — The struggle to establish the common market and the political union (1958–1966)*, Office for Official Publications of the European Communities, 1987, p. 181.

[5] SEC(65) 1541, 13 May 1965.

package of proposals. Hallstein told Couve bluntly at the beginning of May that the French would have to make some concession on increased parliamentary control. Almost every week he called on the French Ambassador, who chaired the Permanent Representatives Committee in the first half of 1965, to think again about the parliamentary issue ([1]). At the same time, he asked the German Chancellor Erhard to guide the smaller EEC partners and to confront France with the choice between backing the Treaty or openly blocking it. In particular, Erhard was to make clear at the Franco-German summit of 11 and 12 June 1965 that getting Bundestag support for any financial solution which did not involve substantial progress towards greater control by the European Parliament was out of the question ([2]).

In fact, when he met de Gaulle on 11 and 12 June 1965 in Bonn, Erhard explained that the German government could not support France on the financing of the common agricultural policy unless concessions were made on industry and political union. On 15 June Couve then proposed to the Council of Ministers that the transfer of levies to the Community from 1 July 1967 should be abandoned and agricultural export subsidies should be financed from Member State financial contributions until the end of the transitional period. This would make control of own resources by the European Parliament redundant. At a meeting in Paris on 22 June, the German State Secretary for Foreign Affairs, Rolf Lahr, and the French Director of Economic Affairs, Olivier Wormser, came up with a compromise: the German government was prepared to accept financing agricultural subsidies from the financial contributions alone and, in return, the French government was ready to support the German demand that the customs union should be completed for industrial products. Germany dropped its second demand for enhancing the political side of the Community. It

seemed that hostilities between the Commission and de Gaulle could thus be suspended until the end of the transitional period in 1970.

However, when the Council of Ministers met again on 28 June, the Italian Foreign Minister Amintore Fanfani and his Dutch counterpart Joseph Luns joined in declaring that the Commission's proposals must absolutely be treated as a whole. Luns did not agree that de Gaulle should get away with not paying the political price for the common agricultural market, and Fanfani was trying to avoid the disproportionate levies which he feared would be imposed on Italy to fund the transitional arrangements. On 30 June an attempt at conciliation failed when Lahr joined those demanding that the Commission's proposals be treated as a package. The German Foreign Minister Gerhard Schröder reinforced the impression of a German U-turn by presenting to the Council a Bundestag resolution of the same day which held that the Commission's proposals for strengthening the European Parliament still did not go far enough. With an eye on the formation of a new government in Germany after the general elections in September 1965, he was keen to be seen as a 'good European'.

In view of this multiple rejection of the French compromise formula, Hallstein felt in a strong position to resist de Gaulle's hard line. When the Permanent Representatives Committee submitted a report which again tended to favour a suspension of hostilities, proposing to make both levies and customs duties available for Community objectives but without centralising them, Hallstein refused to play the role of mediator. On the contrary, he referred to the practice of previous rounds of negotiations, whereby, if an agreement could not be reached by the deadline, the clocks were stopped. In his statements he optimistically claimed that a solution would be found in a few days ([3]). When, late in the evening of 30 June,

([1]) BA, WH 1029, Walter Hallstein, Speech in Baden-Baden, 21 October 1965.

([2]) BA, WH 1119/1, Karl-Heinz Narjes to Walter Hallstein, 19 May 1965.

([3]) Newhouse, J., 'Die Krise der EWG', in Carstens, K., et al. (eds) Die internationale Politik 1964–1965, Jahrbücher des Forschungsinstitut der Deutschen Gesellschaft für Auswärtige Politik Oldenbourg, Munich/Vienna 1972, pp. 249–276, here p. 267.

Couve de Murville, who was chairing the Council under the rotation system, called a meeting of a restricted circle of ministers, State secretaries and members of the Commission, Hallstein finally declared that he was willing, at the request of Fanfani and Luns, to draft a compromise proposal, although he did not commit himself as to its content.

France suspends its participation in the Community

Nevertheless, at this point de Gaulle felt that the common agricultural market was in danger. Taken together, the concessions required by the other Member States were considerable, and there was no guaranteeing that the agreements they had concluded in January 1962 and December 1964 would hold, since, under the Treaty, Council decisions would be taken by majority vote from 1 January 1966. This meant a danger that still more burdensome concessions would then be demanded. Faced with the risk of the common agricultural market collapsing, the French President spoke on 30 June to Couve by telephone during the lunch break and gave him the go-ahead for a manoeuvre which had already been suggested as a tactical option at the end of May: a 'kind of general boycott' applied by France until things 'were sorted out' ([1]). Couve therefore rejected Hallstein's belated offer to draw up a new proposal on the basis of recent discussions, as well as his proposal to defer the meeting to the next day. Instead, at around two in the morning, he found that no agreement had been reached or could be reached, and broke off negotiations ([2]). The French government accused its partners of failing to honour their promises concerning the financing of the common agricultural policy during the transitional period and warned that there would be grave consequences. France's

---

[1] Oral statement by Maurice Couve de Murville, 16 December 1988, Institut Charles de Gaulle, Paris.
[2] Record given by Émile Noël, Doc. G(65) 329, 1 July 1965.

Hallstein and de Gaulle

On 21 October 1965 Walter Hallstein reported at the 29th meeting of Baden-Baden business leaders on his talks with Couve de Murville and de Gaulle.

'The European Parliament, as well as some of the national parliaments, has for nearly two years been focusing on the issue of parliamentary control. [...] I spoke to Mr Couve and I met him on many occasions at that time, at my place, at his and as the guest of others, and always pointed out that France could not avoid making a concession on this matter. My last conversation with General de Gaulle was devoted almost exclusively to this objective. In his own way, which makes any categorical statement impossible, the General was nevertheless perfectly aware that something had happened here. [...] I had the impression that this was the first time that [the Parliament] had been presented to the General in this light, as a thoroughly useful forum which could shape and crystallise public opinion on European affairs. And I believe that, when the French Ambassador [...] sat on my sofa every week, I never once omitted to remind him to think about this matter of the Parliament because I knew certain obstacles were being set up in Paris.'

BA, WH 1029. (Translated from the German)

Permanent Representative to the Commission was recalled, and France announced that it would not take part in the meetings of the Council, Coreper or the working parties. It believed that, by blocking the Community's activities, it would after all force its partners to approve the financing of the transitional period, without having to make substantial concessions in return.

Despite the French boycott of Community activities in defiance of the Treaty, Hallstein held on to his belief that France needed the EEC and that de Gaulle was only trying to mould it into a form that would not curtail France's freedom of action. He therefore needed the five partner governments to agree on a unanimous position about the concessions France must make in return for completion of the common agricultural market and to insist on parliamentary control of the Community budget ([1]). However, the crisis would have to be defused by postponing the thorny issue of Community own resources. The Five would have to demonstrate their capacity for action by compromising on financing and Community policy during the transitional period, thus eliminating France's pretext for blocking Community activities. Hallstein's decision to take the initiative on this was endorsed by a letter from Jean Monnet dated 13 July ([2]).

Despite Marjolin's misgivings, the Commission drew up a 'memorandum' to the Council which was adopted on 22 July. It proposed extending the transitional rules on agricultural financing until 1 January 1970 and making the transition to Community own resources only on that date. Customs union would, however, have to be completed by 1 July 1967, as the Commission had proposed in March, and the market regimes for agricultural products not yet covered by Community rules would have to enter into force between 1 November 1965 and 1 July 1967. A decreasing proportion of the agricultural fund would be financed according to the general share-out formula, and an increasing proportion according to the amount of imports from non-Community countries. The only reference to increasing the Parliament's powers stated that, as the discussion had not yet been concluded in the Council, the Commission could not adopt a new position ([3]). When the memorandum was presented to the Council on 26 July, Hallstein explained that in the current state of talks between the governments the Commission could not submit a proposal for

a compromise on Parliament's powers that would have any real chance of meeting with general approval. He nevertheless hoped that a consensus could be found when an agreement had been reached on the other issues ([4]).

In the meantime, de Gaulle had apparently taken it into his head that winning this one battle in the war over agricultural financing was not enough. As he would confide after the Council meeting of 28 July, he saw in the Commission's stubborn adherence to the conditions for the transition to own resources a better pretext than he could have hoped ([5]) for blocking the imminent changeover to majority voting in the Council. It seemed to him an opportunity to halt the trend towards a supranational Community and to replace the Hallstein Commission, which had exploited its legal rights to the full, with a more conciliatory team. At a press conference on 9 September he criticised not only the continuing hesitations of most of the Member States about the entry of agriculture into the common market but also what he saw as 'certain errors and ambiguities of principle' in the Treaties concerning the economic union of the Six. He particularly deplored the risk that majority decisions could mean that anything and everything could be jeopardised at any time, as seemed to be happening already with agricultural policy. He made France's return to the Brussels institutions conditional not only on agriculture being effectively included in the common market but also upon an end being put to 'wild and fanciful' aspirations that flew in the face of 'common sense and reality' ([6]).

Faced with this escalating crisis, the Belgian Foreign Minister Paul-Henri Spaak suggested inviting France to a Council meeting at which the Commission would not be present. Although there could obviously be no question of amending the Treaty, as de Gaulle clearly wanted, the five partners would have to demonstrate their willingness

---

([1]) BA, WH 1447/2, Memorandum of July 1965.

([2]) FJME, ARM 21/3/19, Jean Monnet to Walter Hallstein, 13 July 1968.

([3]) 'Financing of the common agricultural policy — Community own resources — Increasing the powers of the European Parliament (Memorandum from the Commission to the Council)', COM(65) 320 final, 22 July 1965.

([4]) R 802(65), 26 July 1965.

([5]) Peyrefitte, A., C'était de Gaulle, Vol. II, Fayard, Paris 1997, p. 288.

([6]) De Gaulle, Ch., Discours et messages, Vol. IV, Plon, Paris 1970, pp. 377–381.

LES INSTRUCTIONS POUR BRUXELLES

— Je suis Maurice Couve de Murville, je ne suis pas jean-foutre, je suis Maurice
Couve de Murville, je ne suis pas jean-foutre, je suis Maurice...

'My name is Maurice Couve de Murville, not Jack Ass, I am Maurice Couve de Murville, not Jack Ass, I am Maurice ...'
On 10 June 1965, at a garden party at the Élysée Palace, General de Gaulle allegedly referred to those who dreamt of a
supranational Europe as *jean-foutres*, a pejorative term for an incompetent, useless person (Le Gendre B. 'L'Europe en cinq
dates — 1er juillet 1965, de Gaulle ouvre «la crise de la chaise vide»', *Le Monde*, 11 May 2005).
Three weeks later, the crisis between France and its partners began.

to discuss possible interpretations of its wording. If the French government did not accept the invitation, the Five would be free to continue developing the Community without France (¹). Hallstein immediately blocked this proposal on the grounds that a meeting of the Council of Ministers without Commission participation would demoralise the Five (²). He did not wish to authorise an agreement between the Six which was disadvantageous to the Commission, as there was a risk that this would call into question the entire construction of the Community. His resolve to

oppose a meeting of the Council without the Commission was reinforced by confidential communications from the French deputy representative to the Commission, Maurice Ulrich, who had stayed in Brussels to provide a channel of communication with the French government. At lunch on 21 September, Ulrich told Eberhard Bömke from the German Ministry for Economic Affairs that a very large proportion of the French administration disliked the General's policy on the European Communities and indeed roundly condemned it. He also told him that no preparatory work on amending the EEC Treaty was being undertaken in Paris. Bömke immediately reported the conversation to Hallstein (³). De Gaulle

---

(¹) Herbert Siegfried, Ambassador of the Federal Republic of Germany to Brussels, to the Foreign Affairs Office, 22 September 1965, *Akten zur Auswärtigen Politik der Bundesrepublik Deutschland 1965*, pp. 1473–1476.
(²) FJME, ARM 21/4/20, Robert Marjolin's notes on the Commission meeting, 22 September 1965.

(³) BA, WH 1187/2, Eberhard Bömke to Walter Hallstein, 21 September 1965.

De Gaulle on Hallstein and his crisis strategy

12 June 1965 to Alain Peyrefitte

'Hallstein has come up with a ceremony for the presentation of letters of credence for Member States' representatives in Brussels. He takes himself for the President of a supranational government. He doesn't even hide the fact that he is planning to transpose the federal German structure to European level. The Commission would become the federal government. The European Assembly would be the equivalent of today's Bundestag. The Council would become the Bundesrat: the Senate, I mean to say [...]! It's ridiculous! But make no mistake: this institutional trend will end up winning out if we don't put a stop to it. And we are the only ones who can do it.'

7 July 1965 in cabinet

'We must use this crisis to do away with hidden political agendas. It is inconceivable that on 1 January 1966 our economy should be subject to majority rule, which will impose on us the will of our partners, who, we have already seen, are capable of joining forces against us. We must use this opportunity to review the mistaken ideas which put us in danger of being subject to the dictates of other nations. Let's review this nonsense! As to the Commission, it has

manifested a partiality which is in keeping neither with its mission nor with ordinary decency. The whole Commission must be replaced with a new one.'

21 July 1965 to Alain Peyrefitte

'What we must get rid of above all is that majority voting. France cannot allow it to call everything into question.'

28 July 1965 to Alain Peyrefitte

'A.P. — And the new Commission we are to have in January. You won't agree to have dealings with the old one?

C.d.G. — Of course not! I can't talk to Hallstein, or to Mansholt either. It's just not possible. Particularly after what they've said. [...] They have disqualified themselves as neutral senior officials, which is what they claim to be. The Treaty of Rome must be revised and that Commission must be sent packing.'

Peyrefitte, A., *C'était de Gaulle*, Vol. II, Fayard, Paris, 1997, pp. 286, 292, 294 and 297.
(Translated from the French)

therefore seemed in absolutely no position to demand amendment of the Treaty, and the French administration was indeed banking on the partners to stand firm against him.

However, Hallstein could not help it if Schröder fancied the idea of a Council meeting without the Commission, nor prevent a proposal for such a meeting from being addressed to the French government at the Council meeting of 25 and 26 October. The five foreign ministers did nevertheless secretly agree that in the negotiations with France they would not accept either a recasting of the

Treaty or an interpretation of the Treaty that limited the Commission's powers or the principle of qualified majority voting [1]. They made a statement stressing that the solution to the problems the Community was encountering had to be found within the Treaties and existing institutions. They were strongly in favour of using the Commission memorandum of 22 July as the handbook for settling outstanding disputes. But there was a hitch. It concerned the second part of the transitional period from 1 July 1967 to

[1] PAAA, B150, Bd. 62, Gerhard Schröder to Ludwig Erhard, 27 October 1965, p. 8383 *et seq.*

5ᵉ Année ★ Nᵒ 2442   **HEBDOMADAIRE : 12 FRANCS**   Jeudi 16 Septembre 1965

Pourquoi Pas?

J. Remy

Charles de Gaulle
L'Europe c'est moi !

The cartoonist Jean Remy takes Louis XIV's face and his well-known saying '*l'État, c'est moi!*' and turns them into a caricature of the French President as an absolute monarch who conceives of Europe as a Europe of nation States led by France.

1 January 1970: the Five did not want to agree in advance on continuing financing from the Member States' contributions alone. They preferred to refer back to the Commission's initial proposals for financing based on both levies and customs revenue and said that this matter should be discussed with the participation of 'all' Council members (¹).

De Gaulle did not immediately accept the invitation to a Council meeting without the Commission. With the patent intention of breaking up the Five's united front, he instructed Couve to conduct bilateral discussions with individual ministers and ambassadors. For its part, the Commission worked to convince the other governments that it was in their best interests to preserve their unanimity. In the third week of November, Hallstein went to Bonn to encourage Schröder to 'direct' discreetly and effectively the actions of the Five from behind the scenes on the basis of the Treaty. He urged him to ensure that the German government did not sanction either a veto in the Council of Ministers or any legal or practical alteration of the Commission's position. Nor was he to concede to France any direct or indirect watering down of the requirements of the Treaty concerning economic union. He also asked him to stand firm on 'personal issues' (²).

This last request referred to the attacks the French government had been making on Mansholt and Hallstein. It was clear from contacts with Couve that the open diatribes of de Gaulle about a stateless and irresponsible technocracy (³) were directed principally against the two authors of the package of proposals of 31 March. The French authorities wanted to ensure that these two figures at least would no longer be considered when the new Commission was formed according to programme on 9 January 1966 or when the two executive powers were merged. Hallstein told his German interlocutors that this was not a matter of mere personal interests, as accusations against

specific individuals would undermine the way of applying the Treaty of Rome for which they stood. To capitulate would be to make a substantial material concession and would mean a considerable loss of prestige for the Member States which had designated those individuals. He recommended coordinating with the Dutch government on the matter. The French proposal to reduce the Commission President's term of office from four years to two should be rejected come what may (⁴).

It was only after the French electorate had forced de Gaulle into a run-off after the first round of the presidential elections on 5 December that Couve agreed to a meeting with his five colleagues in January. However, to avoid any Commission influence over the decisions to be taken, he stipulated that the meeting should not be held in Brussels. Schröder opposed this demand, contending that the meeting must be a proper Council meeting prepared by the Council Secretariat and attended by the Secretary-General. On 23 December, four days after de Gaulle's election victory at the ballot, the French government accepted the invitation to an extraordinary meeting of the Council, to be held on 17 and 18 January 1966 in Luxembourg and chaired by the President of the Luxembourg government, Pierre Werner, as President of the Council.

Diverging from the position it had still defended in Couve's bilateral talks in November, France no longer called for an official revision of the Treaties of Rome at this point. However, the French government presented a catalogue of complaints and demands which amounted to a circumvention of the touchiest provisions of the Treaty known as the 'decalogue'. These '10 commandments' included the stipulation that the Commission should submit its proposals to the Member States' governments first and, only after that, to the Council. It was also to be forbidden to make any public statement without first consulting the Council, to which it should leave the task

(¹) SEC(65) 3145, 26 October 1965.
(²) BA, WH 1114/3, Karl-Heinz Narjes to Walter Hallstein, 22 November 1965.
(³) Press conference of 9 September 1965.

(⁴) BA, WH 1114/3, Karl-Heinz Narjes to Walter Hallstein, 22 November 1965.

Resolution of the European Movement

'RESOLUTION I

approved unanimously, with three abstentions

The facts have shown how effective the European institutions are. They have allowed us to move forward faster than anticipated, they have shown that the unification of the market now under way is bringing with it unprecedented economic expansion. They have shown too that without political unity the countries of Europe are not in a position to exercise decisive influence on the destiny of the world or the consolidation of peace.

All that has been built up is now threatened with destruction, and our hopes of building a political Europe, with the Communities as its cornerstone, are in danger of being severely compromised.

One member government, in defiance of the Treaty, is refusing to participate in Council meetings and threatens to paralyse the operation of the Community institutions. In response to this danger, the governments which declare themselves faithful to their European commitment — although their behaviour is not always above reproach — must not only combat the revival of nationalist trends but must set up a common front to protect the Community, without seeking on essential matters a compromise as dangerous as it is illusory.

The EUROPEAN MOVEMENT, meeting in Extraordinary Congress,

PROCLAIMS that Europe cannot be safe, or its future guaranteed without compliance with the spirit and the letter of the Treaties and that

suspending dialogue between the Council and the Commission, guarantor of the general interests of the Community and of the Member States, or extending the right of veto beyond the time limits set in the EEC Treaty would be a fatal abdication of responsibility that would block the indispensable establishment of a common economic and social policy.

URGES the governments

(a) to resume immediately, even in the absence of one Member State, regular meetings of the Council, which must adopt all the decisions, in particular concerning budgets, which the Treaty requires and allows;

(b) to act immediately in Council to examine the most recent proposals of the European Economic Commission with a view to reaching a decision as soon as possible on the financial regulation and on pending questions relating to agricultural policy;

(c) to guard the guarantees of independence provided for in the Treaty regarding the nomination of members of the Executive.

DECLARES ITS CONVICTION

that this crisis will be overcome by the irresistible pressure of the forces which constitute it and by its determination to accelerate the process of integration and democratisation of the institutions until the United States of Europe is created.'

Resolution I of the resolutions adopted by the Extraordinary Congress of the European Movement in Cannes on 3 October 1965.
(Translated from the French)

of representing the Community on the world stage. The French government further demanded that the principle of rotation be applied to the Commission presidency. Were this to happen, no-one could imagine that Hallstein's mandate would be renewed a second time. Council majority voting was to be blocked de facto by the use of a prior veto: if a Member State declared that the subject up for discussion affected its vital interests, the Council would not be allowed to vote on that subject without that Member State's consent [1].

However, at the Council meeting of 17 and 18 January 1966, these claims met with little favour. Schröder was made even more reluctant to compromise in any way by the fact that, following its memoranda on institutional issues, the French delegation also presented a timetable for dealing with the other issues which, while it did call for a compromise on agricultural financing by the end of March, made no mention at all of the need to work out common positions for the Kennedy Round. When asked about this, Couve explained that a mandate for the trade talks could be defined only once the matter of agricultural financing had been settled [2]. Schröder therefore joined Luns in categorically ruling out the veto and also refused to resolve the crisis at the Commission's expense. Attempts at conciliation by Spaak and Colombo, Fanfani's successor at the Italian Foreign Ministry, were baulked by the stubborn resistance of both sides. When the Council ended, no solution to the crisis had been found.

A difficult compromise

When the six Foreign Ministers met again on 28 and 29 January in Luxembourg, Couve and Schröder edged their way towards compromise. With discreet input from the Commission [3], the '10 commandments' were pruned down to seven that were not legally binding. They recommended that the Commission cooperate more closely with the Council, desiring that the former should consult the latter before adopting any 'important' proposals. These were to be submitted to the Council before being made public. The President of the Commission and the President of the Council were jointly to receive the letters of accreditation of ambassadors to the Communities. The Commission and the Council were to keep each other informed of their contacts with non-Community countries, consult on the form of their representation in international organisations, 'collaborate' on information policy and jointly control Community expenditure. Schröder responded to de Gaulle's fears about the principle of majority voting with a declaration of intent which provided that consensual solutions should be sought where 'very important interests' were concerned. No agreement could be reached on what was to happen if such a solution could not be found within a 'reasonable period'. However, at the last moment, at 45 minutes past midnight on 30 January, Couve agreed to resume activities in the Community institutions despite the lack of agreement on the subject of the veto. A joint statement was made announcing that some difficulties still persisted but the 'empty chair' episode was over.

Thus Couve quit blocking Community activities without any certainty as to the transition to majority voting. He also had no guarantee whatsoever concerning the dissolution of the Hallstein Commission, which he had called for again at the meeting of 17 and 18 January. Furthermore, in order to obtain consent to rapid settlement of the agricultural financing issue, he had had to promise also to give priority to customs tariff issues and the GATT talks. These were meagre pickings for the French delegation compared with de Gaulle's original aspirations. Still, the experience of the crisis had encouraged all the national governments to avoid brandishing the fundamental interests of individual Member States to an excessive degree in Council negotiations. The strengthening of the Community's institutions for which Hallstein had hoped was deferred. Hope faded of France conceding increased powers for the European Parliament in return for completion of the agricultural market.

In the short term, Hallstein's crisis management strategy had proved itself. By ensuring that the Five maintained a unified position, he had managed to fight off de Gaulle's attacks on the Treaty

---

[1] Note of 8 January 1966, cited from Bossuat, G., 'Émile Noël dans la tourmente de la crise communautaire de 1965', in Loth, W. (ed.), *La gouvernance supranationale dans la construction européenne*, Bruylant, Brussels 2005, pp. 89–113, here p. 105.
[2] FJME, ARM 21/4/50, Henri Étienne to Walter Hallstein, 18 January 1966.
[3] FJME, ARM 21/4/66, Émile Noël to Walter Hallstein, 25 January 1966.

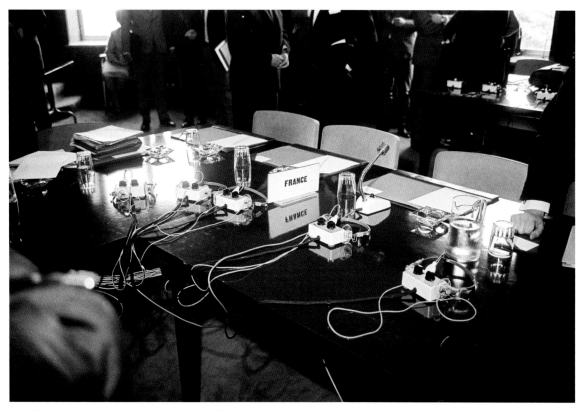

Maurice Couve de Murville at the Council on 30 June 1965: 'Mr President, there's no point in continuing. It is clear that France can no longer participate in this debate; we are leaving the table.' (Interview with Norbert Kohlhase.) With these words the French Foreign Minister was pre-empting the advice he would later give to France's Permanent Representative, Jean-Marc Boegner, on 5 July: '1. Please tell the Secretary-General of the Councils that we will no longer be participating in the meetings of the EEC Council, which will not therefore take place. [...]
2. The Permanent Representatives' meetings have no purpose; you will not therefore attend.
3. We will not be sending an observer to the negotiations that the Commission has opened or proposes to open, on the Council's instructions, with third countries. [...]
4. We will not be represented in the committees conducting general studies or preparing projects with a view to implementing common policies, e.g. the expert groups on medium-term policy or the study groups on the harmonisation of tax and social legislation'.
(Ministère des affaires étrangères, Commission de publication des DDF, dir., *Documents diplomatiques français*, t. II, *1965 (1er juillet au 31 décembre)*, PIE-Peter Lang, Brussels, 2004, pp. 42–43.)

and the Commission. The rather esoteric 'seven points' did no real harm to the Commission's way of working. In practice, the Council of Ministers made the Commission adapt its procedures in only two respects (the accreditation of ambassadors and information policy), while the other five points were soon forgotten. The Commission even had the chance to show once more, within a very short period, that it was irreplaceable: the governments proved to be absolutely dependent on its mediation in the negotiations on agricul-

tural financing, the implementation of the customs union and the negotiating mandate for the Kennedy Round.

The partners managed to reach agreement on these three issues in the course of two further negotiating marathons, from 9 to 11 May and from 23 to 26 July 1966, with the Commission making an active contribution. On agricultural financing for the transitional period, the Council essentially followed the Commission proposal of 22 July 1965.

The French government's memorandum or '10 commandments' (Luxembourg, 17 and 18 January 1966)

'1. Cooperation between the Council and the Commission is the driving force of the Community and should be manifest at every stage. Consequently, before finally adopting a proposal of particular importance for all the States, the Commission should consult the governments at an appropriate level. Such consultation would not impair the power of initiative and preparation with which the Commission is invested by the Treaty; it would simply oblige this institution to make judicious use of it.

2. It should be a rule that in no case may the Commission reveal the tenor of its proposals to the Parliament or to public opinion before they have been officially referred to the Council. A fortiori, the Commission may not take the initiative of publishing its proposals in the Official Gazette of the Communities.

3.(a) The Commission often proposes to the Council decisions which, instead of dealing with the substance of the problems posed, merely give the Commission powers to act later but without specifying the measures which it will take if such powers are conferred upon it (1963 proposal of trade; certain commercial policy proposals).

(b) In certain cases the Commission can obtain authority from the Council to put into effect the rules which the latter lays down. This delegation of powers must not imply that the tasks entrusted to the Commission will then be outside the purview of the Council. True, in certain sectors such as agriculture, the Council can intervene at executive level through its representatives on the management committees. However, it must be noted that far from being content with this system the Commission is endeavouring to replace the management committees by simple advisory committees which have no hold over it (the case of Regulation 19/65 on cartels; Commission proposal of 1965 on transport).

(c) It is important that the executive powers thus vested in the Commission should be precisely circumscribed and leave no room for discretion or autonomous responsibility, failing which the balance of powers, which is a feature of the institutional structure of the Community and a basic guarantee provided by the Treaty, would not be respected.

4. The Treaty lays down that 'directives shall bind any Member State to which they are addressed as to the result to be achieved while leaving to domestic agencies competence as to the form and means'. But we cannot escape the fact that in practice the Commission very often proposes directives which set out in detail the rules to be applied. The only freedom then left to the States is to choose the form in which the contents will be clothed and to take the necessary implementing measures.

It is evident that such practices constitute an attempt on the part of the Commission to cause the matters dealt with by such directives to slip out of national hands into the Community sphere of competence.

Such transgressions should be avoided in future.

5. In 1959 the Council laid down the rules which, provisionally, were to govern the recognition of diplomatic missions accredited to the Community. [...] These rules amount to a sharing of prerogatives between the Council and the Commission. In particular, letters of credence are presented to the President of the Commission, who has instituted for these occasions a ceremony modelled on that used between States, whereas the Treaty of Rome lays down that the Council alone may commit the Community vis-à-vis non-member countries.

A stop must therefore be put to the present practices and all prerogatives of the Council restored.

6. Consequently, any approaches by foreign representatives to the Commission must be reported with all despatch to the Council or to the representative of the State in the chair.

7. The Treaty lays down in terms appropriate to each particular case the procedure by which the Community maintains relations with other international organisations.

This situation seems to have been lost sight of by the Commission, which appears to think that it has truly discretionary powers in this field.

The Council should judge, case by case, and purely in the light of Community interests, the form and nature of the links to be established.

8. Members of the Commission must in their public statements be required to maintain a fitting neutrality with regard to the policy

followed by the governments of the Member States.

9. Information policy should not be planned and implemented by the Commission alone but jointly by the Council and the Commission. The Council should exercise effective, and not only budgetary, control over the joint Information Service of the Communities.

10. Procedures for control of the commitment and expenditure of Community funds should be revised in order to give this control the effectiveness which, as is well known, it lacks at present.'

Bulletin of the EEC,
March 1966, No 3, pp. 6–7
(published on www.ena.lu/mce.cfm).

Common prices, applicable from 1 July 1968, were set for milk, sugar, rice, cereals, oilseeds and olive oil, meaning that 90 % of agricultural production was now covered by the common agricultural policy. The date for the completion of the customs union (1 July 1968) was postponed to a year later than had been planned by the Commission. An exhaustive list of negotiating offers on industrial and agricultural products was adopted for the Kennedy Round. The greater part of the Community's external trade was thus now included in the customs tariff reductions, to which Germany in particular aspired, and the Commission's negotiating mandate was therefore strengthened. France secured just some concessions on the amounts of customs tariffs for a range of products.

The question of who would preside over the Community's destiny still remained to be decided on the basis of the Luxembourg compromise. De Gaulle did not want the Hallstein Commission to hold this role any longer. 'As for Hallstein, we've had enough,' he said to Couve

at the start of the second part of the Luxembourg Council meeting ([1]). German Chancellor Erhard took the opposite view and, at the Franco-German summit of 7 and 8 May 1966 in Paris, he strongly advocated that Hallstein should head the merged executive authorities. Luns told Hallstein that the Dutch government would not endorse a Commission of which he was not a member. As the President of the Commission could be appointed only unanimously, Hallstein would be able to hold on to his role as acting President indefinitely ([2]).

For a year it seemed that de Gaulle was yet again condemned to defeat. The decision on the entry into force of the planned merger was deferred and the Commission again tabled the issues of the agreement on agricultural financing, the completion of customs union and the GATT mandate.

([1]) Note of 26 January 1966, quoted from Vaïsse, M., *La grandeur — Politique étrangère du général de Gaulle 1958–1969*, Fayard, Paris, 1998, p. 548.
([2]) Interview with Karl-Heinz Narjes, 24 May 2004.

On 5 April 1966 the Council acceded to the French call for a two-year rotation period for the Single Commission. However, this did not rule out renewal of the Commission's term of office. The Netherlands, Belgium and Italy continued to support the German proposal that Hallstein should be President of the Single Commission for the first two years [1]. Neither Erhard nor Schröder accepted de Gaulle's compromise offer, made at a meeting with Erhard on 21 July 1966, whereby Hallstein could remain in office 'a few more months' after the merger [2]. Instead, Schröder proposed that the existing Commission should stay in office until the entry into force of the customs union on 1 July 1968.

However, when the CDU–SPD 'Grand Coalition' was formed on 1 December 1966, Germany's European policy priorities shifted. Firstly, the circles which considered it essential for the executive bodies to be rapidly merged so that a common energy policy supporting German coalmining could be launched gained importance. Secondly and most significantly, the new Chancellor Kurt-Georg Kiesinger believed that it was a matter of great urgency to re-establish good neighbourly relations between Germany and France. At a meeting of the foreign ministers of the Six on 22 December 1966, State Secretary Lahr put forward an amended version of Schröder's transition proposal, under which the merged Commission would take up its duties at the beginning of 1967 and Hallstein would retain the presidency until 1 July 1968. German demands on the duration of an extended mandate for Hallstein were thus revised downwards [3]. Kiesinger further reduced them when he referred to a term of 'slightly less than a year' at a summit with de Gaulle on 13 January 1967. However, the practical significance of this suggestion was not clear. Only on 27 April, following a long struggle, did Couve and his new German counterpart Willy Brandt manage to agree that the merger should take place on 1 July 1967

but that Hallstein would keep his post until 31 December 1967. His mandate was thus ultimately reduced by six months.

Under these conditions, Hallstein decided that there was no sense in continuing as President unless all the governments wished him to do so. When he learnt that the Belgian government was unaware of and did not support the talks between Couve and Brandt, he decided to put an end to what he felt was undignified manoeuvring over his role. On 3 May he sent a letter to Kiesinger asking him to refrain from nominating him as President of the merged Commission, pointing out that an agreement between the governments and the candidates to limit the term of office would undermine the Commission's independence and set a dangerous precedent. Furthermore, there was little chance that the merger of the former three executive bodies could be fruitfully completed within a bare six months. He declined the French proposal to make him Vice-President in the merged Commission after 31 December 1967 [4], and Kiesinger's attempts to change his mind were in vain.

Once it was certain that Hallstein was going to withdraw, the representatives of the Six lost no time in agreeing, at an Intergovernmental Conference on 5 June 1967, to appoint Jean Rey as President of the Commission. Sicco Mansholt was appointed with no difficulty at all as Vice-President. Von der Groeben, Levi Sandri, Colonna di Paliano and Rochereau also had their terms renewed. The new Commission was thus no less 'political' and desirous of consolidating the Community than the previous one. But, in terms of what the image of the Commission as the incarnation of the European project might achieve, the end of Hallstein's Commission was tantamount to a defeat. In practice, for many years the Luxembourg compromise stood in the way of majority decision-making in the Council and so significantly diminished the Commission's institutional role.

WILFRIED LOTH

[1] AAPD 1966, Rolf Lahr's comments, 6 April 1966, pp. 446–448.
[2] AAPD 1966, pp. 966–973, here p. 971.
[3] AAPD 1966, Rolf Lahr's comments, 23 December 1966, p. 1659 *et seq.*
[4] BA, WH 1126, Walter Hallstein to Kurt-Georg Kiesinger, 3 May 1966.

Chapter 5

Jean Rey, moderate optimist and instinctive European

Although his name is not widely known and he is rarely regarded as one of Europe's founding fathers, Jean Rey, who was born in Liège on 15 July 1902, was one of the staunchest promoters of European integration. He played this role with great faith and conviction throughout his long and varied career, which is regarded as something of a model in Community circles. First a member and then President of the Council, Rey then went on to serve as member and President of the Commission and, in his twilight years, as a member of the European Parliament, a record few have matched. Born in Liège to a Protestant family, a Liberal politician and proponent, even in his youth, of a federal Belgium, by 1947 he had come to the attention of the socialist Paul-Henri Spaak, who marked him down as a likely key member of a future government ([1]).

A 'serious' youth culminates in political activism

Jean Rey spent his youth in an exceptionally cultivated environment in which the culture of ideas

flourished. His father, Arnold Rey, was a clergyman of some prominence in Liège's Protestant community. His mother, Hélène, came from a Liberal family which was very active in local and national politics; her father had been Mayor of Liège during the golden years of the *Belle Époque*, and her brother, Max-Léo Gérard, was private secretary to King Albert I, editor of the newspaper *l'Indépendance Belge* and Minister for Finance. By combining his law studies at Liège University, funded by a scholarship from the University Foundation, with a stint as Secretary of the University Group for the League of Nations between 1921 and 1926, Rey built on the work accomplished by his mother, who had been active in pacifist circles before the First World War. Less than 10 years after the end of that conflict, he had no hesitation in inviting German pacifists to Liège ([2]).

True to his ideals and the family tradition, the young Rey joined the Liberal Party in 1924. At the time this was tantamount to political suicide for an intellectual, as left-leaning Walloons were

---

([1]) FPHS 677/9932, p. 10.

([2]) Balace, F., 'Jean Rey, Liégeois et protestant', in Balace, F., Declerq, W. and Planchar, R., *Jean Rey — Liégeois, européen, homme politique*, Les éditions de l'Université de Liège, Liège, 2002, p. 28.

increasingly voting socialist, partly as a result of the introduction of universal suffrage ([1]).

As such, it was not without a great deal of patience and a fortuitous combination of circumstances that he became first a town councillor in 1935 and then a member of Parliament in April 1939.

Once in Parliament, Rey spoke out on several occasions against the policy of neutrality, which was supported at the time by the bulk of the Belgian political establishment. During a debate in June 1939 he criticised government policy because it was asserted that there were no vital interests at stake for Belgium, when in fact the country had a vital interest in peace but also another, equally important interest, namely that an international system should apply in western Europe in which treaties, and the independence of small states, were respected. The Schuman Plan was still far in the future, and Europe was to suffer a vast conflagration, one that would not leave the Rey family unscathed. Jean was to be held prisoner in Germany throughout the war, and his father and mother were to die in the bombings of May 1940, but even in those terrible times he was aware that he had a part to play and understood that an international system in which treaties were respected was the only possible path to peace in Europe. Sharply critical of the so-called independence policy ([2]), he displayed a clear interest in federalism, a model he hoped Belgium would adopt ([3]).

From prisoner of war to government minister

Rey returned from captivity in 1945, but the joy of liberation was short-lived. His wife, Françoise Gevers, whom he had married in 1928 and who had borne him four children, Madeleine, Cécile, Jean-Jacques and Denise, passed away in 1946.

In the political arena, he resumed his duties as an MP and started campaigning for a federal Belgium. In October of that year he attended the Walloon National Congress, some of whose members were in favour of Wallonia becoming part of France. Inspired by the discussions he had had during captivity, he tried to persuade the audience that federalism was the right way forward. In the international camps to which the Germans had sent him while he was a prisoner of war, he came into contact with Czech, Polish and Yugoslav officers with whom he talked at length about the Slovak, Lithuanian and Croatian problems and came to the conclusion that, whenever a unitary State came up against a nationalist movement, it would inevitably break apart in the end. As he pointed out, the trick was to notice before it was too late ([4])!

Whether in government or in opposition, Jean Rey remained consistent in his approach to the highly charged issue of the monarchy. While Minister for Reconstruction in the Eyskens government, he called for a referendum on the King's return but, in the same speech, made it clear that he would accept the outcome only if both regions of the country produced a 'yes' vote. A few months later, from the opposition benches, the Liberals having rejected a proposal to allow Léopold III to resume his reign, he stated his total opposition to the sovereign's unconditional return as advocated by the Duvieusart government, since a majority of Walloons had voted against. To ensure that the nation's institutions were preserved and to restore calm to the country, he joined a call for the heir to return. As Jacques Van Offelen notes in his memoirs, Rey displayed the same qualities during the royal crisis, in which he found himself in the 'no' camp, that he would deploy throughout his career. Eschewing sloganeering, he set out the issue logically with his characteristically rapid delivery. He was imaginative, contributing new ideas; he strove to get to the heart of the matter ([5]).

([1]) Ibid., p. 21.

([2]) Rey, J., *La politique étrangère de la Belgique*, Thone, Liège, 1937.

([3]) Rey, J., 'L'État de demain', *Le Flambeau*, February 1937, pp. 160–168.

([4]) 'Discours de Jean Rey au Congrès National Wallon', in Poorterman, J., *Jean Rey nous parle*, Chez l'auteur, 1984, p. 144.

([5]) Van Offelen, J., *La ronde du pouvoir — Mémoires politiques*, Hatier, Brussels, 1987, p. 80.

Jean Rey, Belgian minister	
Minister for Reconstruction	August 1949 to April 1950
Minister for Economic Affairs	April 1954 to January 1958

By 1955 Paul-Henri Spaak perceived that Rey, together with Victor Larock, was one of the few politicians to take an interest in European affairs. Now Economic Affairs Minister, Rey provided the Belgian Foreign Minister with invaluable assistance by placing at his disposal the most gifted members of his staff, Baron Snoy et d'Oppuers and Ambassador Van der Meulen, and by making a strong case for signing the Rome Treaties at a time when the Prime Minister, who, incidentally, had for too long been left in the dark about the negotiations, was reluctant to give his approval.

From external affairs to the Kennedy Round (1958–67): a career in the ascendant

In 1957, just before the common market came into being, the Belgian government had to present its partners with a list of candidates for the posts created in the institutions established by the Treaty. Baron Snoy et d'Oppuers, who had signed the Rome Treaties and was Chairman of the Interim Committee, was interested, and told Spaak so. However, as a French-speaking Catholic, he quickly realised that his chances of being put forward by a government dominated by socialists and liberals were slim, especially since a Flemish Catholic, Albert Coppé, was already a member of the High Authority. So, during a lunch at the University Foundation, he asked Jean Rey — his minister, but also a friend — to present his application. As a Walloon liberal and convinced European who already had significant European experience under his belt as a result of his stint on the ECSC's Council of

Ministers, Rey was ideally placed to do so. He had been mooted in 1954 as a possible replacement for Monnet as head of the High Authority, but at the time the Belgian government was in favour of renewing the Frenchman's term of office. René Mayer had also put him forward as a possible President of the Commission, but at the time the Belgians were more interested in promoting Brussels as the future headquarters of the institutions than in securing the presidency of an executive body.

Rey was made Chairman of the External Relations group, apparently at his own request, but he quickly became aware that, in practice, President Hallstein regarded the EEC's foreign policy as his own domain. A power struggle ensued, aggravated by Robert Marjolin, who also brought his influence to bear on the President, while other members of the Commission, Mansholt in particular, did not resist the temptation to speak on the matter in public even without prior consultations. It was something Jean Rey, who deplored what he regarded as the President's focus on foreign policy to the exclusion of everything else, would not easily forget [1].

An episode dating from 1961 illustrates the situation well.

The Commission took the decision to entrust President Hallstein with the accession negotiations, effectively sidelining the Chairman of the External Relations group. As a former minister used to having his own portfolio and clearly delineated responsibilities, Rey found this decision hard to swallow but accepted it nonetheless because it came from the Commission as a whole. But when he discovered that the Director-General for External Relations, Günther Seeliger [2], had also been overlooked against his advice, and that Jean-François Deniau had been promoted over the heads of other, more senior

---

[1] AULB, 126 PP, VI-34, Handwritten memo by Jean Rey, 18 June 1962.
[2] Günther Seeliger, Director-General of External Relations at the EEC Commission from 1958 to 1964.

directors-general who were equally deserving so that he could take part in the negotiations, he lost patience and resigned. Accusing Hallstein of deliberately pushing him out, Rey pulled no punches:

'For five years I served in the Belgian government under two different prime ministers, neither of whom was a political ally of mine. In Belgium, overall responsibility for the administration lies with the Prime Minister, but neither of them would ever have dreamt of treating their colleague and his portfolio in such a cavalier fashion and with such a total lack of consideration.' [1]

During the early years Rey argued on several occasions with his colleagues that the Commission should devote more time to general political reflection on subjects like how the common market should develop or the Commission's internal organisation [2].

Within the Commission, he was critical of the institution's failure to intervene in European political debate. In his view, the Commission's role was to guide public opinion and the European conscience [3] and that it should therefore give vocal support to the Community dimension of the integration process. As he stated on several occasions, the Commission had to assume its take on the full political dimension, and its members should not be mere clergy, but prophets [4]. However, he also understood that it was not the Commission's role to take initiatives in the arena of political integration but that it should work to ensure rapid implementation of the Treaty of Rome in all areas and strengthen the Community by adapting, with patience and goodwill, to internal political development

ments in the Member States [5]. True to himself, he remained intransigent when it came to principles — the Commission should, he felt, prefer struggle to compromise — but be flexible about practical arrangements and formalities, perhaps in contrast to President Hallstein, for whom protocol, and what it represented for his office, was of paramount importance.

Rey took an even tougher line when addressing his fellow Commissioners in 1959, deliberately putting the cat among the pigeons by arguing that the Commission should be the leading authority of the Community; it should say what had to be done and should make the national administrations fall into line, rather like the Council of State did in France. Nor should it shrink from condemning infringements of the Treaties in public [6]. In a memo on the political situation at the time, he set out in detail his view of the Community's political development, deploring what he saw as a deliberate policy of aggression against its very political substance [7]. It was high time, he felt, for the Commission to bring its concerns to the public's attention and to make it plain that it would not stand idly by, still less collaborate [8]. Condemning the management's silence and what appeared to be resignation [9], he concluded with a sentence that went straight for the jugular: 'I am convinced that the Community will emerge from this victorious — if, that is, its bosses are prepared to come out fighting.'

But a majority of his fellow Commissioners, or at least of the most influential ones, disagreed. In January 1962, nothing having changed, he went back onto the offensive with a devastating critique to the effect that: the Commission's virtually exclusive focus on technical issues had gone hand in hand with timidity on the political front; it had sidestepped controversial issues, it had

[1] AULB, 126 PP, VI-35, Letter from Jean Rey to President Hallstein, 25 October 1961. (Translation)
[2] AULB, 126 PP, VI-34, Various handwritten memos from Jean Rey and a memo from Jean Rey to the President and members of the Commission, 15 May 1959, 6 pages.
[3] AULB, 126 PP, VI-34, Memo from Jean Rey to the President and members of the Commission, 15 May 1959, p. 2.
[4] AULB, 126PP, VI-34, Handwritten memo, 7 September 1959.

[5] AULB, 126PP, VI-34, Memo from Jean Rey to the President and members of the Commission, 15 May 1959, p. 2
[6] AULB, 126 PP, VI-34, Handwritten memo, 7 September 1959.
[7] AULB, 126 PP., VI-34, Memo from Jean Rey to the President and members of the Commission, 20 June 1960, p. 4.
[8] Ibid.
[9] Ibid. (Translation)

Returning from Geneva and the successful conclusion of the Kennedy Round talks, Jean Rey is met by the press on his arrival at Brussels airport.
(16 May 1967)

tered that real progress had been made and that it was pointless wasting energy taking a stand on the different phases of this process, i.e. the plans for political cooperation.

In October 1962, following the failure of the Fouchet Plans, the governments were still unable to make progress. Rey drafted a chapter of the Commission's programme for political union (²) in which he called on the Commission to stand firm and ensure that the integration process retained its Community dimension. More than 20 years before Maastricht, he put forward a compromise consisting of setting up a purely political pillar in the foreign policy and defence field and a second pillar strengthening the Community in its existing form, while also increasing the powers of the European Parliament, to be elected by universal suffrage, as well as the executive's economic and financial powers. In his vision, far from obstructing each other, these two structures would be complementary. They would develop in parallel, rather like the pillars of a cathedral which the builders erected sure in the knowledge that one day they would be joined by a common vault (³). He also argued against starting talks on political union with the countries engaged at the time in accession negotiations. It was, he felt, a matter for the Six alone.

On 14 January 1963 General de Gaulle vetoed the United Kingdom's accession and the talks ground to a halt. This was the Community's first, and by no means last, major setback. Behind closed doors, a row broke out between the Commissioners. Jean Rey was outraged to see the Commission's leadership role being opportunistically surrendered in exchange for the promise of a negotiating brief. He declared to his fellow Commissioners, who had rallied, under the President's leadership, to the 'wait-and-see' approach proposed by Marjolin, whom Rey regarded as having a decisive influence over Hallstein, that the Commission's silence made him ashamed. Noting the

been lacking in leadership as regards the Assembly, it had been craven in its dealings with governments and it had completely failed to lead European public opinion (¹). He deplored the lack of common positions and public memoranda. The fact that the debate on his memo was deferred for more than five months — which he regarded as unacceptable in itself — demonstrated his lack of support within the Commission. His fellow Commissioners felt that, while he was generally right on the facts, his conclusions went too far and that he painted far too pessimistic a picture of the Community. Robert Marjolin coun-

(¹) Memo from Jean Rey to the President and members of the Commission. Commission discussions on the eve of his second term, 13 January 1962.

(²) 'Action programme'. Draft chapter on political union prepared by Jean Rey, 15 October 1962, 3 pages.
(³) Ibid., p. 3.

deep divide between the French government and the Five and the immense damage done to the common market's external relations, Rey argued that the Commission should protest and defend the Community, its system and its spirit by taking more initiatives and raising its profile ([1]). But, as on other occasions, his endeavours to make the Commission pull together and work as a team came to nothing. From then on, the Commission made its views known through the personalised speeches given by the President or, in a diametrically opposed style, by Mansholt.

Two years later, with the 'empty chair' crisis showing no signs of abating, Rey was confined to bed at home in Tilff on the banks of the Ourthe. Unusually for him, he felt that the Commission was quite right to say nothing in public on the subject and become embroiled in a disagreement with the French President. It was for the governments of the Six to take the initiative; there could be no question of holding talks with the French on the basis of a unilateral infringement of the Treaty of Rome. The most urgent thing was to get the system up and running and separate the agricultural issue from the political one ([2]). Was it diplomacy or pragmatism that dictated his attitude? Whatever the reason, it did not stop him taking the view, in contrast to Spaak, that the Commission's conduct on 30 June had been beyond reproach, for only then had it become clear that no solution could be found and that the period requested by the Commission in which to put forward compromise proposals had been rejected.

From the beginning of 1958 Rey represented the Commission on the Maudling Committee. Talks were to prove difficult. Initially, even though the Commission devoted a great deal of time to the proposed free trade area — something Jean Rey subsequently regretted and apologised to his fellow Commissioners for — he had to badger the

---

([1]) AULB, 126 PP, VI-34, Handwritten memos from Jean Rey, 23 and 30 January 1963; AULB, JR, 126 PP, VI-34, Memo from Jean Rey for the UK crisis file, 23 January 1963.
([2]) AULB, 126 PP, Letter from Jean Rey to an unknown addressee (probably Joseph Van der Meulen, the Belgian Permanent Representative to the EC), 13 September 1965.

The art of persuasion

'President Rey had an apartment at the end of Brussels' rue de la Loi, on the edge of the Parc du Cinquantenaire, just a stone's throw from his office in the Joyeuse Entrée building.

One of his colleagues told me that, when he was trying to persuade the Commission to take a difficult decision but one which he felt was right and he sensed they had reservations, he would sometimes declare an hour's break, for example from 7.00 to 8.00 p.m., so he could go home and freshen up.

When he returned to the meeting, obviously he was fresher than his colleagues who were not fortunate enough to live next door to the office. Apparently that helped him on more than one occasion to persuade the Commissioners that he was right.'

Recollections of Jean-Claude Eeckhout, 31 October 2005.
(Translated from the French)

Commissioners and the President to decide on a course of action and to empower them to give instructions to his officials. There were significant differences of opinion between the Six, but the Commission, sidestepping ideological debate and focusing on practical solutions, issued a number of memoranda, probably at Rey's instigation. While open to debate, the Belgian soon became convinced that the Commission must play its role as guardian of the Treaties and press forward on that basis; that it should ensure that other institutions did not obstruct its work, and that some of the British conditions were clearly unacceptable from an economic viewpoint ([3]).

The former Economic Affairs Minister soon took an interest in the trade-related aspect of his portfolio and it was not long before he set up a 'shock division' ([4]) to conduct three sets of negotiations within the GATT framework. First, negotiations with the other directorates-general. These were

---

([3]) Speech by Jean Rey to the European Parliament, 25 June 1958.
([4]) Interview with Paul Luyten, 21 October 2004.

the easiest even though, occasionally, differences arose between Rey and the Directorate-General for Agriculture. Second, negotiations with the Member States, which were the most complex. And finally, with third countries, which proved to be the hardest of all for although some of the partners were gentlemen, others, not to put too fine a point on it, were gangsters. Jean Rey kept a close watch on developments and did not hesitate to roll up his sleeves when his colleagues, who enjoyed his full confidence, needed his support. A talented negotiator, he had the knack of tilting the scales in the Commission's favour at the crucial moment. Paradoxically, it was in the depths of the French crisis that Rey secured his place as future President of the Single Commission by speaking on behalf of the whole Commission, the successful conclusion of the Kennedy Round ([1]) being much remarked on at the time. Public opinion, and the Council members, had been impressed by his work and that of his colleagues.

A presidency cut short …

Once Walter Hallstein had rejected the compromise solution outlined by the French and German governments to extend his term of office until 1 January 1968, Rey's name was quickly put forward. As indicated above, his very positive public image worked in his favour. Jean Monnet wrote personally to Brandt, who was already almost convinced, to support Rey's nomination: 'I think that the best possible candidate is the one you mentioned to me some time ago and that is Mr Rey' ([2]). Their choice made for a certain measure of continuity in a period of crisis. Sicco Mansholt, as Vice-President, was also in the running, but the French government may have been concerned about the Dutchman's occasionally extreme political views. Above all, it probably regarded it as crucial to keep Mansholt at agriculture, where he could pursue a policy which reflected

French interests ([3]). Jean Rey, in contrast, was regarded by Couve de Murville, at least with hindsight, as very close to France and easy and pleasant to work with, even though he retained a degree of nostalgia for supranational ideals and was saddened by the French position on some issues, such as the UK's accession ([4]).

The Hallstein Commission's legacy included two poisoned chalices: the question of enlargement and the merger of the institutions' executive bodies and their respective administrations.

The 1965 Treaty had been put on the back burner and, once Jean Rey was appointed, it fell to him to implement it: this entailed not just allocating portfolios within the new Single Commission but also overseeing the merger of the respective administrations. This was a tricky matter because individuals' interests were very much at stake. Fortunately, he had the invaluable assistance of the Executive Secretary of the EEC Commission, Émile Noël, who almost two years earlier had set up a small group, with the help of the Secretaries-General of the other two executives, to prepare the reorganisation of the administration and also, to an extent, the Commission itself. Noël and Rey had gradually got to know, appreciate and trust each other over the years. Together they quickly took over the reins of what was to be the Single Commission. Émile Noël was appointed Secretary-General of the new Commission and so continued to sit at the same table as the Commissioners themselves.

The new Commission was larger and more diverse. The members had to get to know each other or catch up with old acquaintances. Having experienced the difficulties of working under a somewhat authoritarian presidency, Jean Rey tried to operate on a more collegial basis, sometimes to the detriment of his own control over Commission business. He was soon obliged to leap to the defence of Raymond Barre, who had been excoriated by the British press for taking

([1]) See Chapter 17, pp. 314–317.
([2]) FJME, AMK 112/112, Letter from Jean Monnet to Willy Brandt, 12 May 1967.
([3]) Joint interview on 15 October 2004.
([4]) Couve de Murville, M., *Une politique étrangère 1958–1969*, Plon, Paris, 1971, pp. 306–307.

orders from General de Gaulle and, shortly afterwards, Sicco Mansholt, whose comments had provoked a furious reaction from Michel Debré, the new French Foreign Minister.

Drawing on the experience he had acquired during the Kennedy Round, the new President made it clear from the outset to the Commission and MEPs that he intended to pursue dialogue with the Member States. While the Commission was determined not to give up any of its responsibilities, powers or authority, it was deeply convinced of the need for closer, ongoing cooperation with the governments of the Member States. And not just with the Council, which the Commission conferred with on a regular basis as a matter of course, but also, he stressed, with the governments ([1]). He launched this policy with a tour of European capitals in the autumn of 1967.

At the very start of his presidency, during his first press conference, Jean Rey emphasised the Commission's political role. In his view, the organisation's remit was twofold, being not purely economic but also political; its role would not be confined to economic management. Indeed, given the Commissioners' backgrounds, it had an eminently political character ([2]).

In the policy statement he made to Parliament introducing the new Commission, he called for more social progress in the Community and, above all, briefed his audience on the new opportunities that had been created by the merger of the Communities, opportunities which had to be seized immediately. This involved developing industrial policy, establishing the much coveted common energy policy, which hitherto had been obstructed by the existence of separate executive bodies, setting up a European research policy — it was time, Rey argued forcefully, to stop bemoaning Europe's backwardness in that area and

to start seeking practical solutions — and boosting regional policy ([3]). Accordingly, he made some of his colleagues responsible for overseeing change in these new or reinforced areas and set up new administrative units, or directorates-general to be more precise, to carry out these new duties in a more specialist capacity.

As regards the allocation of portfolios, as President, Rey wanted to focus exclusively on overall policy, but he retained responsibility for the Legal Service, a horizontal body essential to the smooth running of the Commission and of which he had been in charge since 1958.

To some extent, the Commission was paralysed by the issue of enlargement because it was required to submit detailed opinions on the subject, sometimes at short notice, whereas the position of the Member States, and the French government in particular, remained unchanged. Rey, who invariably sought consensus within a Community framework, was powerless to change this situation, which adversely affected the working environment and undermined trust between partners. It was his view that the Commission should direct the activities of the Community. When the situation gave cause for concern, it was his job to table proposals which reflected the — often divergent — positions of the Member States. And so he adopted a prudent approach. On occasions he took exception to comments by his fellow Commissioner, Sicco Mansholt, on French domestic policy or the possibility of a Europe without France. But the reality of the situation was that, faced with the second French veto, the Commission was powerless.

Unlike his predecessor, Rey wanted the Commission to play a role in leading European public opinion, as he had already made clear, and during his stint as President he worked to raise awareness of European issues by supporting the initiatives of the directorate-general responsible

([1]) AULB, 126 PP, VI-36, Commission of the European Communities, Speech by Jean Rey to the European Parliament, Strasbourg, on 20 September 1967, p. 14.

([2]) Commission of the European Communities, Press conference by Jean Rey, Brussels, 13 July 1967, p. 11.

([3]) AULB, 126 PP, VI-36, Commission of the European Communities, Speech by Jean Rey to the European Parliament, Strasbourg, 20 September 1967, p. 11.

for communication, but also by taking more general initiatives within the Commission itself. In 1969 the Commission published its first multi-annual action programme, in which von der Groeben first mooted the idea of examining the problems of a European constitution in the making. It also produced a number of public memoranda and considered organising conferences open to what is now referred to as civil society. Jean Rey felt that, in normal circumstances, an enlightened public was bound to opt for integration. But the fact was that the public still had to be enlightened and, in his view, that was one of the most vital tasks of future conferences (¹). Initially, the Commissioners, in line with Rey's thinking, were directly involved in organising conferences via their *chefs de cabinet*. Typically, in 1968, Rey appointed his faithful *chef de cabinet*, Raymond Rifflet, chairman of the working group responsible for preparing the Youth Conference (²), which was to take place in 1970 just before the end of his term as President. Initially, two further conferences were planned, one for the two sides of industry and the other for the farming industry.

Like other observers, Rey accepted that the Community was in crisis in 1968 but his optimism was undented, and he did not lose heart when things failed to work out as planned. Like the Commission as a whole, he worked tirelessly to improve the situation and to talk up any hopeful signs. The Community was not paralysed, he insisted; the customs union had been completed, the main agricultural market organisations had been established and customs and trade policy regulations had been adopted. The Commission was also drafting major reform programmes for agricultural structures, and work on monetary, technology, regional and energy policies was proceeding apace. However, he was not overoptimistic, as was shown by his Aachen speech in May 1969, when he explained that every step of the way had been fraught

'Building a reconciled and united continent'

Jean Rey drafted his speeches himself, sometimes drawing inspiration from memos produced by his colleagues. As a rule, he opted for a structure setting out all the points to be covered and added key words to remind him of his train of thought.

'How beautiful Europe would be if it were united, if our old continent, ravaged by centuries of conflict and whose conflicting nationalisms triggered the last two world wars, were able to rise above its past divisions and yesterday's nationalisms and build a society based on human freedom, international reconciliation and social progress! "Make that God of yours bigger if you want us to worship him," Voltaire once said to a Christian of his day. Well, *our* task is to build a reconciled and united continent, one which today's young people can see is worth working and striving for.

That was the ideal which — almost 20 years ago — inspired the founders of the European Communities, and it remains our ideal today. Have our Member States forgotten that? Can't they see that unifying our ravaged continent is the greatest political task they have undertaken since World War II, a task which has earned them the respect of the whole world and one to which they should devote their intelligence and efforts as a matter of priority!' (³)

Extract from Jean Rey's speech to the European Parliament in Strasbourg on 15 May 1968. (Translated from the French)

with difficulty; there had been the problems of merging three different administrations, which had had to be brought together to form a homogeneous single body, as well as the need to maintain the creative dynamism of an organisation which

---

(¹) AULB, 126 PP, VI–37, Memo from Raymond Rifflet to Jean Rey, 9 September 1968, p. 5.
(²) AULB, 126 PP, VII-39, Letter from Jean Rey to Marcel Hichter, Directeur général de la Jeunesse et des Loisirs (Brussels), 18 July 1968.

(³) AULB, 126 PP, VII-38, Commission of the European Communities, Speech by Jean Rey to the European Parliament, Strasbourg, 15 May 1968, p. 13.

Jean Rey at a press conference, flanked by the Spokesman, Bino Olivi, and Deputy Spokesman, Paul Collowald, together with his *chef de cabinet*, Raymond Rifflet, and Deputy *chef de cabinet*, Alex Hoven. From left to right: Raymond Rifflet, Bino Olivi, Jean Rey, Paul Collowald and Alex Hoven. (26 June 1970)

had become larger and more bureaucratic and had to deal with increasingly complex problems, an ever-increasing number of meetings and a constantly growing burden of paperwork. Last but not least, he mentioned the serious political disputes that had arisen between the governments of the Member States, disputes which had still not been resolved and which had made the task much harder, had slowed down the Community's development and had soured the atmosphere in Europe [1].

A few months before, in February 1969, he had confided to President Nixon — not that it came as a surprise to anybody — that the root of the problem was the personality of the French President, a great man but also an autocrat who was unaccustomed to pooling foreign policy, with the result that his five partners had a great deal of difficulty in getting their point of view across to him. [2]

General de Gaulle's resignation on 28 April 1969 ushered in a new era of European construction. France dropped its policy of systematic obstruction and accepted the principle that the United

[1] AULB, 126 PP, VII-40, Speech given by Jean Rey, President of the Commission of the European Communities, at the Charlemagne Award ceremony (the prize was received by the Commission as a whole) on 15 May 1969, 15 May 1969, p. 3.

[2] AULB, 126 PP, Summary of talks with President Nixon, 24 February 1969, p. 1.

Kingdom could join the Community. The Commission was now able to get back to work. It issued a new opinion to the Council on the accession applications from the United Kingdom, Ireland, Denmark and Norway. Rey argued, unsuccessfully, for the inclusion of a chapter drafted by Rifflet, which significantly boosted the institutions' powers and advocated deepening and an institutional reform, which would enable the Community to acquire the means necessary for its enlargement, since its strength and development were one of the factors of enlargement [1]. But this opinion was not shared in full by all the Commissioners and it was not long before it came under heavy attack, with Deniau taking a diplomatic line and Barre being much more outspoken [2]. At a meeting of the *chefs de cabinet*, Rifflet was practically the only one to argue with the French nay-sayers. The President was isolated, sometimes launching a frontal assault on his colleagues without first making sure behind the scenes that he carried the majority with him. Was he naive? The fact is that Rey believed that people were reasonable and intelligent. That this was one of his weaknesses, one of very few, there can be no doubt, but it also reflects his nobility of spirit.

In view of the danger of bilateral talks producing divergent outcomes, Rey regarded it as crucial that the negotiations should be conducted along the same lines as the Kennedy Round. In other words, the Commission was authorised to negotiate on the Community's behalf, keeping the Council constantly informed of developments and following its instructions. As it turned out, two years later, by which time Rey's term of office had ended, the Commission was far more closely involved in the work than in 1963, but it was not to have a mandate in the strict sense of the term.

Despite harbouring various misgivings about the role of the European institutions, President Pompidou decided to organise a summit conference, which took place in The Hague on 1 and 2 December 1969. In significant contrast to previous years, this time the Commission was present. Represented by the President, the Vice-Presidents and a number of senior officials, it was involved in some aspects of the preparations as well as the conference itself. The French government, which had initially envisaged the Commission's involvement as symbolic or at best marginal, made a concession. This was certainly at the insistence of Rey, who personally drafted the Commission's memorandum for the summit.

But, in the wake of the conference, the President's legendary optimism began to fade. His first reaction was one of disappointment. No progress had been made on political Europe, nor had there been any discussion of the need to strengthen the institutions. That was what he had really wanted to see on the table, for he was a true European federalist, even though he rarely said as much. However, in spite of his disappointment, he joined the majority of commentators in welcoming the new impetus imparted by the Hague conference.

Rey's mandate was renewed by general consent in 1970, but for just one year. As one of his friends wrote to him at the time, the French government was in favour of renewing his mandate, but the same letter stressed that Paris wanted the number of Commissioners to be reduced the following year and a new President to be appointed at that stage.

One year later Rey learnt with surprise and a certain amount of bitterness that the Belgian government had nominated Albert Coppé as the sole Belgian member of the new Commission. He had realised that the Belgian government's manoeuvres to retain a 14-member Commission were doomed to failure since Jean Monnet, via his Committee, had pressed for it to be reduced, and he regarded it as likely that the Italian government would eventually come up with a suitable presidential candidate. But he was convinced deep down that he would stay on as the Belgian

---

[1] AULB, 126 PP, VII-41, *La relance européenne: une volonté politique*, Interview with Jean Rey, President of the Commission of the European Communities, by Claude Delmas, pp. 7–8.

[2] AULB, 126 PP, VI-40, Memo from Raymond Rifflet to Jean Rey, 19 September 1969, p. 1.

member because, in May of that year, Pierre Harmel had told him he was the government's number one candidate and had opined that domestic and regional policy considerations should not come into play when the European Commissioner was appointed; all that mattered was who was the best man for the job [1]. But that was to underestimate the determination of Albert Coppé, the second Belgian member, who had joined the Commission via the ECSC, to stay on as Commissioner, his tenacity and his influence over the Flemish wing of the Belgian Christian Social Party. Rey wrote at the time that the reasons for his departure were tied up with Belgian domestic policy considerations [2]. Whatever his qualities, as a liberal at a time when the governing coalition in Belgium was of a Christian and socialist persuasion, he simply did not carry the right party card. 'I can imagine how the ship's captain must feel after guiding his vessel safely through the storm only to be denied his triumphant entry into port', wrote Étienne Davignon at the time. 'I'm deeply saddened that our diplomacy has failed to achieve its twin objectives of extending your presidency and placing the accession negotiations in your hands.' [3]

Other roads to the same European ideal

When his term ended, Rey, like other Presidents, was tempted by offers from the private sector. He accepted the posts of board member at Philips Electrical and Chairman of the Board of Directors of Société financière de transports et d'entreprises industrielles (Sofina) and Papeteries de Belgique in addition to a number of other functions, such as Chairman of the Board of the Liège-based Société d'études et d'expansion. He continued his work as President of the Administrative Board of the College of Europe, a position he had held since 1964.

---

[1] AULB, 126 PP, Memo from Jean Rey on the Commission presidency. Discussion with Pierre Harmel, Strasbourg, 14 May 1970, p. 3.

[2] AULB, 126 PP, Letter from Jean Rey to Baron Jean van den Bosch, Belgian Ambassador to London, 20 January 1971.

[3] AULB, 126 PP, VII-48, Letter from Étienne Davignon to Jean Rey, 30 June 1970. (Translation)

Étienne Davignon expresses his admiration for Jean Rey

'We always feel a certain sense of pride when someone we admire and respect discharges their duties brilliantly. So I was thrilled to see you in action: unwavering in your determination that the rights, power and prestige of the Commission, whose fundamental characteristics Mr Harmel reminded us of yesterday evening, should never be diminished; indignant whenever the Community's future was called into doubt — and there were reasons enough to fear the worst during the darkest days of Mr Couve de Murville's last presidency or when Mr Debré got carried away yet again; confident that, eventually, even the governments would be forced to acknowledge that the Community approach was the only way forward; skilful, patient and persuasive when certain delegations had to be cajoled into breaking the deadlock and a compromise had to be forced through; keeping a sense of proportion which allowed you to smile in the face of adversity and eschew triumphalism when your efforts were crowned with success. And, through it all, retaining an unshakeable sense of humour, which you shared with us yet again yesterday evening.

All these qualities, placed in the service of a great cause, have helped to get the Community back on track. Thanks largely to your faith, the Community has taken another step towards its radiant future, while losing nothing of its originality or departing from its basic objectives.' [4]

Extract from a letter from Étienne Davignon to Jean Rey, 30 June 1970. (Translation)

But, as a man of action, he voiced his concern whenever the European project appeared to lose momentum. 'Let's be frank here: the Community gives the impression of lacking leadership. It must be led, and led right now. Isn't it the role of a former President of the Commission to sound the alarm?' [5] In 1971 he invited the former Com-

---

[4] AULB, 126 PP, VII-48, Letter from Étienne Davignon to Jean Rey, 30 June 1970.

[5] AULB, 126 PP, VII-50, Rey, J., 'La communauté n'est pas gouvernée', Vision, December 1971, p. 18. (Translation)

Jean Rey leaves the Commission

'You have helped us all never to lose hope and to follow your example of clarity, courage and strength.'

(Letter from Fausta Deshormes to Jean Rey, 30 July 1970) (Translated from the French)

'Right to the last you kept hope alive, defended the institutions and valued your colleagues.'

(Letter from Michel Gaudet to Jean Rey, 2 July 1970) (Translated from the French)

'For someone like me who has devoted a considerable part of his life to the European ideal, it is extremely precious to me to see the Commission headed by a man as deeply committed to that ideal as you.'

(Letter from Michel Albert to Jean Rey, 28 July 1970) (Translated from the French)

missioners and Presidents of the Communities to meet to discuss problems of immediate relevance and to write a manifesto criticising the Communities' lack of momentum while sparing the Commission itself in so far as possible. A minority of the persons he contacted agreed to take part.

Appointed President of the European Movement in 1974, he breathed some new life back into the organisation. He focused his energies on organising the Congress of Europe, which took place early in 1976 and was attended by all the European leaders of the day. The Congress culminated in the ratification, by a comfortable majority, of a resolution which bore his stamp.

A long-standing advocate of a European Parliament elected by universal suffrage, and on the back of his European experience and commitment, Rey was elected to the prestigious assembly in 1979 with more than 40 000 preference votes. Aware of his own limitations, he withdrew from the scene a year later at the age of 78, but not without first having made his mark on Parliament's Political Affairs Committee.

The man, his faith and his loyalties

Being part of a minority on the Belgian political scene, and, for a long time, within his own party and by virtue of his faith, Jean Rey learnt at a young age to be patient or, more precisely, to persevere. His parents showed him how to live a life of action and struggle, but also one illuminated by tolerance and clear thinking.

A short text written in captivity to the memory of his parents bears eloquent witness to their decisive influence on his attitudes and character and to the depth of his faith.

Jean Rey believed in the 'primacy of the spirit' and in logic when it came to developing institutions. For him, in economics, human attitudes counted as much more important than material factors [1]. He had a spiritualist vision of the law.

Perhaps because of his rather drab sartorial style or his modest persona, he often came across to people who did not know him well as austere and serious-minded. In reality, in a small group, Jean Rey had a lively and caustic sense of humour. However, intellectually and socially, he preferred substance over style, to which he perhaps did not attach enough importance.

This explains the particularly human side which Jean Rey had as President. He was a good listener and always open to the views of Commission staff. He was not remote, as his predecessor, Hallstein, had been; on the contrary, shortly after

[1] 'Le Marché commun sera-t-il source de dynamisme économique?', Speech by Jean Rey to Société royale d'économie politique de Belgique, 20 March 1959.

taking up his duties, he met staff representatives and remained relatively available throughout his term of office.

All the evidence shows that President Rey was very well regarded by all staff at all levels. Obviously, this was particularly true of his close colleagues, even though he could sometimes adopt a somewhat managerial, even scathing tone, but he was never unkind. As one colleague reminisced, 'I've never had a boss who treated me with such consideration, took such an interest in me and showed such tolerance of my failings, while at the same time constantly reproaching me for them ([1])!'

Highly rated by his colleagues, Jean Rey repaid them with unstinting loyalty. He took part of his economic affairs team, which had followed him from the Ministry for Reconstruction, to the Commission: Pierre Lucion, the doyen of the *chefs de cabinet* and, naturally, a native of Liège, Alex Hoven, his deputy *chef de cabinet* and Miss Leveugle, his loyal secretary. Every day the group joined the President for a tea break and a chat, a habit of Rey's which dated back to his ministerial days ([2]).

His *cabinet* was more of a place where ideas were mooted and exchanged than a focal point of management or individual and/or institutional strategies. This was the case with Pierre Lucion and would be even more so with Raymond Rifflet. Hence, too, the growing influence of Émile Noël, with whom Rey got on well, on the institution and behind the scenes.

Rifflet took over from Lucion in 1967. Rey's decision to choose a socialist *chef de cabinet* — reflecting the make-up of the Belgian government of the day — was probably dictated as much by political considerations as by his natural preference for a person who shared his ideals and beliefs.

([1]) Planchar, R., 'Quelques souvenirs autour de Jean Rey', in Balace, F., Declercq, W. and Planchar, R., op. cit., p. 51. (Translation)
([2]) Interviews with Régine Leveugle, 1 October 2004, and Jean-Claude Eeckhout, 3 December 2003.

'Tea with the President'

At the Belgian Ministry of Economic Affairs in 1954

'At five o'clock the whole *cabinet*, plus Jean Rey, took tea in my office and the deputy *chef de cabinet's* office. [...] The conversation always flowed freely at these meetings thanks to the Liège faction: the Minister, invariably chatty to a fault, dispensing anecdotes to the assembled company, and his adviser, the cultivated bachelor Pierre Lucion, who had been his *chef de cabinet* at the Ministry of Reconstruction in 1949–50.'

Van Offelen, J., *La ronde du pouvoir — Mémoires politiques*, Hatier, Brussels, 1987, p. 149.

At the Commission

'Jean Rey used to interrupt his *cabinet's* work for 15 minutes during the afternoon. It was an opportunity to catch up with his colleagues and, sometimes, with some official or other who wasn't a member of his *cabinet*.

When the honour fell to me, I must admit to being somewhat taken aback. Ten minutes or so before teatime, the President's secretary phoned me and said he wished to see me. I wondered anxiously what serious mistake I must have made. But, when I entered the President's office, he said to me: at the lunch yesterday where you represented Mr Coppé it was mentioned that you're fond of sorbet. And since the kitchen has sent up to us what was left over to have with our tea, I thought you might like to join us. When I left, he said I could come and have tea with him whenever I liked. I'll never forget that little kindness, so typical of President Rey.' (Translated from the French)

Recollections of Jean-Claude Eeckhout, 31 October 2005.

In the course of his long career at the Commission, Rey also benefited from his close relationship with the Belgian Permanent Representative to the Communities, Joseph Van der Meulen. A bond of trust was established between the two men which extended beyond exchanges of ideas; they also swapped a large number of confidential documents. But it seems that most of Jean Rey's close friends were from his home town of Liège.

Indeed, he would go 'back home' every week to Liège or, more precisely, the nearby village of Tilff, where his second wife, Suzanne, whose first husband, a close friend of Rey's, had been shot by the Germans in Liège in May 1943, lived with their children. Even while he was President, Rey attended the parish meetings of his Liège church whenever possible and stood in for the organist when required. For Jean Rey was a talented musician who first learnt to play the violin but eventually came to prefer the piano. He was also a practising Protestant. Faithful to the 19th century, liberal Protestantism, which left its mark on some sections of the Belgian elite, he was tolerant and favoured an exchange of ideas which reconciled religious belief with freedom of thought, a view regarded as a pre-condition for the development of intelligence (¹).

Some contemporaries of Jean Rey maintain that his Protestant faith was a factor which influenced his solidarity with other decision-makers. It can also be safely assumed that his membership of the Freemasons played a role. Less secular in outlook (²) than his *chef de cabinet* Raymond Rifflet, as a young lawyer he had worked under the leadership of Charles

Memo from Raymond Rifflet

'Whether there are 6 or 10 of us, we can no longer wait for events to take matters out of our hands and decide for us; such events exist only in the imagination of the lazy and of history professors.' (³)

Memo to the President from Raymond Rifflet, Jean Rey's *chef de cabinet*, dated 25 September 1969. (Translated from the French)

Magnette, a pillar of the Grand Orient of Belgium. While a prisoner-of-war at Fishbeck Oflag, he founded a lodge entitled 'L'obstinée'. As in other areas, he remained true to his beliefs and commitment, for this somewhat atypical but big-hearted and decent man (⁴) believed that abiding by one's decisions was the price of future success. As he stated in an interview with a French journalist in 1969, 'I'm probably less likely to become downhearted or discouraged precisely because I've never thought the ideas I believed in were endangered just because they encountered obstacles. On the contrary, my experience as a member of a minority has taught me to struggle in the firm conviction that my ideas would have their day in the future.' (⁵)

YVES CONRAD

(¹) Fenaux, R., *Jean Rey, enfant et artisan de l'Europe*, Labor, Brussels, 1972, p. 18.
(²) Interview with Henri Étienne, 12 January 2004.
(³) AULB, 126 PP, VII, Memo from Raymond Rifflet to Jean Rey, 25 September 1969, p. 1.
(⁴) *Courrier du personnel*, No 123, 17 July 1970, p. 25.
(⁵) Jean Rey to Emmanuel de la Taille, 2 June 1969, quoted by Fenaux, R., op. cit., p. 226. (Translation)

Chapter 6

The development
of the Single Commission
(1967–72)

The establishment of a Single Commission was to be a political event of all the greater importance for European integration as it was conceived as a precursor to the merger of the Communities. But, as we have seen, the 'empty chair' crisis bore the seeds of a weaker Commission [1], a development which successive Commissions would attempt to stymie. It also delayed the entry into force of the Merger Treaty, initially scheduled for January 1966. It was only at the summit on 29 and 30 May 1967, where the 10th anniversary of the Treaties of Rome was celebrated, albeit somewhat belatedly, that the Heads of State or Government, meeting in the Italian capital, declared their intention of bringing the Treaty of 8 April 1965 on the merger of the institutions of the three Communities into force on 1 July 1967 [2].

The Single Commission took office just a few weeks after Harold Wilson's Labour government presented in May the second British application to join the Community. For five and a half years, until the enlargement of the Community from six to nine Member States actually took place, the question of the accession of the United Kingdom and the other applicant countries was a key issue for the Commission. The new executive also had to prepare the changeover from the transitional period to the definitive phase of the EEC in January 1970. Now that the common agricultural policy was operational and the customs union about to be attained ahead of schedule on 1 July 1968, it was also keen to develop new common policies and to bring in new budgetary rules following the merger of the budgets and the establishment of own resources [3]. And the Commission was under growing pressure to adjust the institutional system so as to help the Community function more efficiently.

The development of the Single Commission must be seen in the international context. Whereas the ECSC saw the light of day when the Cold War of the Stalinist era was at its height and while the two Commissions set up by the Treaties of Rome took office just before East–West tensions flared up with the crises in Berlin (1958–61) and Cuba (1961–62), the Single Commission came onto the

---

[1] See above, Chapter 4.
[2] FJME, AMK 112/4/8, Communiqué of the Conference of Heads of State or Government, 30 May 1967.

[3] On these questions, see chapters on enlargement and the various policies.

scene at a time when détente was consolidating, particularly with the strategic arms limitation talks between the superpowers (especially SALT I), the new diplomatic line being taken by certain Member States, led by the Federal Republic of Germany, where Willy Brandt, who was Foreign Minister (1966–69) and then Chancellor (1969–74), launched a bold new policy of openness to the East, and the beginnings of a dialogue between the countries in the Atlantic Alliance, the Warsaw Pact countries and the neutral and non-aligned States in Europe at the Conference on Security and Cooperation in Europe (CSCE), culminating in the Helsinki Summit in 1975.

The Rey Commission: establishment and major policy guidelines

Thought was already being given to the membership of the future Single Commission in 1966, but nothing much happened until Walter Hallstein decided not to seek reappointment. The Belgian, Jean Rey [1], who had been favourite since the Rome summit, was the obvious choice for President. He was appointed for two years and his appointment renewed for a further year in July 1969. The Commission he was to head did not look so much like a merger as a 'confluence' of two bodies into a third [2]. Of the 14 members of the new Commission, nine came from the former executives — just one from the Euratom Commission, two from the ECSC High Authority and six from the EEC Commission.

The Single Commission held its first meeting on 6 July 1967 and took the basic measures needed to be able to operate (provisional Rules of Procedure, practical organisational measures, etc.). The first delicate task of allocating portfolios was completed on 20 July. In the meantime, the Commission took the oath of office before the Court of Justice in Luxembourg, in the afternoon of 13 July. The oath was the standard practice at the High Authority and the Euratom Commission and was provided for by the Merger Treaty. But the new Commission took a vote — which passed by a majority of one, its President — to decide whether to continue with this tradition [3].

On the morning of 13 July, the Commission President presented his programme of action to the press, before fleshing it out before the European Parliament on 20 September and discussing it with the governments of the Member States during a tour of the capitals in the autumn. Jean Rey felt that the Single Commission should organise the merger of the administrations, already under preparation by the secretaries-general of the three executives for more than a year, and should consider the problems arising from the merger of the Treaties so as to put proposals to the governments. He wished to go beyond the achievements of the Hallstein Commission and to tackle industrial problems, draw up an energy policy, develop research, bring a regional policy into operation and make progress on social matters. And, at the political level, he believed that the Commission had two main dossiers to address: preparing for enlargement and strengthening the Community institutions through regular and close cooperation between the Commission, the Council and the governments of the Member States [4].

A year later, on the historic date of 1 July 1968, when the customs union was completed, the Commission spelt out its objectives and laid down a wide-ranging programme for the five years ahead, which thus seemed to bind its successor also. It wanted to advance towards economic union by harmonising monetary, tax and social policies, to make further progress towards federal institutions, to restore majority voting in the Council, to end the veto, to give the Commission executive powers, to speed up democratisation by giving the European Parliament budgetary powers, to help the people of Europe participate

---

[1] See also p. 114.
[2] *Europe*, 10 July 1967.

[3] Ibid.
[4] FJME, AMK C 33/5/153, Press conference by Jean Rey, 13 July 1967. See also *Europe*, 20 and 21 September 1967.

in Community life through direct elections and to involve economic, social and intellectual circles by organising conferences and other meetings with the social partners and with agricultural and youth organisations ([1]).

The emphasis placed by the Commission on the institutional aspects of European integration are clear evidence of its President's interest in these matters but also of the difficulties facing a Community threatened with a period of immobility after General de Gaulle's second veto on United Kingdom accession in November 1967. The political crisis linked to the disagreements between the French government and its five partners had the effect, among others, of aggravating the tendency of the decision-making process to seize up that had become apparent from 1965 onwards. In the summer of 1968 the procedure for merging the Communities provided for by Article 32 of the 1965 Treaty and presented as the logical and desirable sequel to the merger of the executives by the Rome Summit, by ministers in the Member States (such as Willy Brandt), by the European Parliament, which wanted to be involved in drafting the new Treaty, and by members of the Commission from the President down, reached an impasse ([2]). The merger was supposed to happen within three years and to improve Community integration and satisfy France, which had been calling for this since 1963. Jean Rey was aware from the outset that the merger would not be easy to bring about and would take time. But the first time he spoke to the press, in July 1967, he argued that the Commission could begin preparatory work on proposals to the governments on its own initiative without awaiting instructions from the Council.

For a year the reflections on the merger of the Communities continued in parallel in the European Parliament and the Commission. One of the points was to decide between straight harmonisation, which would probably amount to aligning the ECSC Treaty on the EEC Treaty, and drafting a new Treaty, which would require a political commitment from the Member States. The procedure and timetable for drafting the Treaty also had to be decided on. On 12 December 1967 the European Parliament's Political Affairs Committee asked the Belgian, Fernand Dehousse, to produce a report on the difficulties raised by the merger of the Treaties. He did not conceal his preference for a text that would be more than a list of amendments or additions. He raised the question of majority voting, to be entered in the new Treaty along with provisions to avert the risk of another 'empty chair' crisis or at least to attenuate its effects ([3]). The Commission also asked its Legal Service for an opinion, and this seemed to recommend a limited merger without changing anything in terms of the substance of the Treaties ([4]). This was followed by a 'stock-taking' of problems arising from the merger that was concerned chiefly with economic matters but also with the question of majority voting and that was to serve as the basis for a document to be laid before the Council ([5]). But at the end of July, as the *Bulletin* of Agence Europe tells us, Jean Rey's obstinate optimism no longer had support ([6]). The project seemed to have been abandoned de facto partly because of internal misgivings about accepting it among the former Euratom and ECSC departments ([7]) and partly because it was feared that all the governments would agree to would be no more than a second-rate Treaty that made purely technical changes on the basis of the lowest common denominator ([8]). That being so, would it perhaps be better to go for new developments in Community integration without necessarily merging the Treaties?

([1]) BAC 3/1978 44, Statement by the Commission of the European Communities, 1 July 1968.

([2]) CEAB 2 2658, Draft general report of the Single Commission, 30 November 1967.

([3]) CEAB 2 2658, Note by F. Dehousse, 19 December 1967; Minutes of EP Political Affairs Committee, 8 and 15 February 1968; EP Resolution, 15 May 1968.

([4]) *Europe*, 2 February 1968.

([5]) *Europe*, 22, 23, 24, 25 and 29 April 1968.

([6]) *Europe*, 29 July 1968.

([7]) Jean-Claude Eeckhout, group interview, 19 October 2004.

([8]) *Europe*, 29 April and 30 July 1968.

Within the Commission, the assessment of the Community's position was even more pessimistic at the beginning of 1969. For Jean-François Deniau, the question of the institutions was now the most important issue. He took the view that the Council and the Commission had become increasingly less effective for the past five years as power seemingly shifted to the Permanent Representatives even though they took no actual decisions (¹). For the Secretary-General, Émile Noël, the institutional set-up needed improving. Majority voting should be introduced in the Council. And he felt that the Commission was not working well because there were too many members and because every decision or proposal had to go before the full Commission (²).

There was no lack of internal tensions in the Commission. They were sometimes aired publicly, as when two Commissioners took up diametrically opposed positions on the supranational nature of the Community. On 10 December 1968, Raymond Barre, the French Vice-President of the Commission stated — though he specified he was speaking personally — that supranationality was a false debate, an outmoded ideological conflict dating from the 1950s. As he saw it, the problem of majority decision-making did not have the 'almost theological' importance that some attached to it; it was clear from the way the Treaties of Rome were applied that the signatory States had retained their freedom of action and that not one of them was ready for a supranational Community. On 10 January 1969 Colonna di Paliano, the Italian Commissioner, took quite the opposite personal view. For him, 'supranationality is not a fetish, it is a method', the method of a Community that could not operate on an intergovernmental basis. These disagreements prompted a Member of the European Parliament to put a written question asking the Commission to state its views, notably on its own role in relation to the Council. The Commission replied that each of

its members enjoyed extensive freedom of expression, but it also referred to its statement of 1 July 1968 and recalled that the Community was not a mere intergovernmental organisation of the traditional kind (³).

The institutional question was raised by President Rey again on 12 March 1969, when he presented the general report for 1968 to the European Parliament. Stronger institutions (stronger executive powers for the Commission, stronger powers for the European Parliament) were presented as an essential component of the Community. For Jean Rey, it was not an alternative to enlargement but it also did not complicate it. To the contrary it was a necessary condition for ensuring that the Community would not be weakened by the arrival of new Member States. Jean Rey thus launched a debate on the enlargement versus deepening issue, which would be at the heart of the deliberations of the Hague Summit in December 1969.

The Hague Summit: a challenge for the Commission (⁴)

The idea of convening a summit meeting of Heads of State or Government to find a way out of the deadlock in the Community was launched by Georges Pompidou a few days before he was elected to succeed General de Gaulle as President of the French Republic in June 1969. The newly elected President then confirmed his proposal at his first press conference and it was officially presented to the Council of the Communities on 22 July by the Foreign Minister, Maurice Schumann. The French authorities' objective was to take a less isolated position and to give fresh impetus to cooperation between the Member States on the basis of the three-pronged approach

---

(¹) FJME, AMK C 33/1/276, Note by Jacques Van Helmont of a conversation with Deniau, 28 January 1969.

(²) FJME, AMK C 33/4/186 and 33/4/200, Notes by Jacques Van Helmont after a conversation with Émile Noël, 8 February and 2 June 1969.

(³) BAC 3/1978 44, Information notes, 7 February and 28 March 1969.

(⁴) On the Hague Summit, see Bitsch, M.-Th., 'Le sommet de la Haye — La mise en route de la relance de 1969', Loth, W. (ed.), *Crises and compromises: the European project, 1963–1969*, Baden-Baden, Nomos, 1969, pp. 539–565; and *Journal of European Integration History*, 2003, Vol. 9, No 2, 2003, *The Hague Summit of 1969*, J. van der Harst.

At the summit in The Hague, Commission officials assert 'that it is possible to be a European official and to believe in Europe sincerely and unreservedly'. Konrad Adenauer is on the poster in the centre of the picture.
(*Courrier du personnel*, No 96, 7 January 1970, p. 15)
(2 December 1969)

of 'completion/deepening/enlargement'. The direction indicated by this approach coincided with France's interests but also went some way towards meeting its partners' expectations. The idea was to adopt a financial regulation before moving on to the final stage of the common market on 1 January 1970, to launch new policies aimed at deepening integration and, now that Paris had agreed to the principle, to prepare for negotiations for the accession of the United Kingdom and the other applicant countries.

Initially, the French initiative prompted a sceptical, mistrustful response from the other governments, especially in Belgium, the Netherlands and Italy, as well as from the Commission and the European Parliament. As to the substance, France was suspected of wanting to slow enlargement down by adding to the preconditions to be met.

In fact, the French government regarded completion (the financial regulation) and an agreement between the six Member States on the terms for admission as unavoidable preliminaries, but it accepted the idea of working simultaneously on enlargement and deepening. As to the details, there were even greater reservations. There were many in Europe who saw the concept of the summit, which was reminiscent of the Fouchet Plan, as having something of a Gaullist connotation and as raising the spectre of an attempted subordination of the Community institutions to an intergovernmental type of body. And they had not forgotten the Rome meeting of Heads of State or Government in 1967, which had yielded no positive benefits for Community integration.

For all these reasons, the Commission President was not keen on the idea of a summit, initially at

The Hague Summit, 1 and 2 December 1969 — European Manifesto

(Manifesto drafted at general meetings of staff to debate the issue on 28 October and distributed for signing by staff on 10 November 1969)

'On the eve of the summit conference to be held in The Hague on 17 and 18 November 1969 ([1]), the staff of the European Community institutions, bringing to bear the convictions that they have developed through years of commitment and service to Europe, publish the following manifesto:

1. Europe's objectives

The peoples of Europe need unity if they are to perform the tasks that await them on the world stage.

This holds true if Europe — which has set the example and created the hope of a new type of relationship between nations by establishing the Community of Six — is to have the political means of promoting peace between continents around the world.

This holds true if Europe — which is the world's largest trading power — is to have the political means of introducing a genuine policy for development with the less developed countries that themselves make an effort.

This holds true if Europe — the birthplace of the great ideologies and technical wonders of our time — is to have the political means to grant its peoples an ambition to give meaning to their labours, a scope which matches their ardour for progress and a hope to match the yearning of its youth for international fraternity.

By uniting to accomplish these tasks, Europe will avoid the political decadence that could transform a continent so richly endowed by nature, by its people, by its culture, its science and its history, into an aimless backwater in a world of titans.

2. Europe's difficulties

The far-from-perfect unity achieved so far, however precious, has been the expression of a shared need to remove the obstacles to the development of each of us rather than the manifestation of a shared will to build a world that is developing for us all.

This absence of a common will, following the successful removal of customs barriers, is apparent in the fact that the common agricultural policy is being hampered by the exclusively national nature of economic and monetary policies, that common energy, industrial and scientific research policies are not taking shape to replace Europe's current dependence on decision-making centres situated, by and large, elsewhere and that social policy does not look beyond the admittedly difficult task of upward harmonisation of living conditions to the transformations needed to meet the growing demand for greater responsibility in the world of employment.

This absence of a common will is also apparent in the fact that, going beyond the removal of obstacles to competition, the time has come to proceed as the ECSC did for mining and the steel industry and to convert to new activities the professions or regions which are no longer competitive, or to set up together the advanced infrastructures or facilities that cannot fit the national dimension.

This absence of a common will is also apparent in a growing institutional disequilibrium in the Community where, as the influence of the

---

([1]) The summit was originally scheduled for mid-November but was postponed to the beginning of December at the request of the Italian government as its Foreign Minister was ill.

European Parliament and the role of the Commission are played down, the Council is overburdened; and, at the same time, there is a modus operandi in which weighing up the immediate interests defended by each of our governments distracts them from devising long-term common policies.

If European integration is not to be thwarted by ever more cumbersome procedures, by ever tighter technical constraints and by ever weaker political motivation, the Hague Summit must both redefine the objectives and review the method.

3. Europe on the march

Europe's unity, which cannot be a technocratic achievement or the result of a plethora of regulations, will be brought about by the freely expressed will of its peoples.

The expression of this will presupposes that Europe's people are respected and can assert themselves not just as so many million consumers mired in moral and political apathy but as so many citizens wanting to pool their ideological and national values in a forward-looking society which makes its contribution to the world.

The expression of this will also presupposes that political, economic and technical integration is guided by the leading lights of our schools and universities, the media, the arts and intellectual circles in the historic task of creating a European personality that is both one and multifaceted and that meets the needs of our times.

And the expression of this will presupposes that the planned Single European Treaty strikes a proper balance of powers through the democratic answerability of both the Council and the Commission, through the participation of the citizens, in particular via their trade and regional organisations, in all that concerns them at European level, through the autonomy of the Commission, including in the budgetary sphere,

in managing the matters for which it is responsible, through majority voting in the Council in all areas where Community solidarity is sufficiently advanced, and through the establishment of a durable European public service responsible for devising, elaborating and proposing common solutions to the problems facing the Member States.

Thus Europe will be able to resume its march forward when the governments, guided by the freely expressed will of their people and relieving the Council of routine management questions, can address the vital issues of launching new stages in the contribution of Europe and pressing ahead with a genuine European policy in the world.

———————

It is in order to contribute to the expression of this will of the peoples of Europe that the staff of the Community institutions, in solidarity with all the citizens of Europe in their respective areas of responsibility who are striving for unity, issue this Manifesto.'

ACEU, Series Negotiations with the United Kingdom, No 21, Brussels Staff Committee, *Informations*, No 40, 6 November 1969. (Translated from the French)

least. But, since the Council appeared in practice to adopt the principle on 22 July — even though no decision was actually taken, Jean Rey immediately announced that the Commission wished to attend the conference and be involved in the preparations (¹). At the end of July, he went to Paris to meet the Foreign Minister and to plead the Commission's cause so as to ensure that, as in 1961 and 1967, it was not excluded from the summit. Maurice Schumann did not take a particularly clear position, but the French government was very reluctant and let it be known that it saw no reason for proceeding in a different manner from the Rome summit (²). However, Georges Pompidou fairly quickly suggested inviting the Commission to a technical working meeting to report on Community problems, thus giving the impression that it was being treated with respect while keeping it in the background (³). In the battle surrounding the Commission's attendance, Jean Rey obtained the support of the governments of the other Member States. Only the Belgian government seemed ready to agree that, if the summit were to deal solely with general policy options, it would be quite reasonable for the Commission not to be present (⁴).

The moment of truth came with the Council meeting of 15 September, which was to give the official decision on the organisation of the summit. The decision was taken by the Foreign Ministers over the 'white cloth' and not the 'green cloth' (as Jean Rey, who protested, put it (⁵)), that is to say at lunch, in the absence of the Commission. Maurice Schumann persuaded his colleagues to agree to a summit that all of them stated they wished to prepare as thoroughly as possible with a view to bringing their views more closely into line and achieving positive results. The Luxembourg and Dutch ministers argued for Commis-

sion participation, and this was accepted by France. Maurice Schumann reminded the meeting that the Commission was neither a super-government nor a seventh government and proposed that it attend the morning session on the second day of the summit to present a report on matters within its remit and answer questions from the governments. This was the solution adopted after the German minister, Willy Brandt, had suggested in vain that the Commission should be present at the beginning of the summit (⁶).

The Commission came up with two important papers during the preparatory stage. On 1 October it adopted the (favourable) opinion on enlargement requested by the Council on 22 July and amplifying its opinion of 1967. When reporting to the Council on 17 October, Jean Rey stated that, in the Commission's view, there was a political link between enlargement and the measures to be taken before the end of the transitional period or the decisions on deepening the Community. Strengthening the Community should not be seen as a prior condition for the accession of the applicant countries; the two processes had to run in parallel: 'according to Jean Rey, it was only by dealing with the problems facing the Community in parallel that solutions could be reached' (⁷). He also felt that de facto priority would nonetheless be given to deepening as this would be taking place in 1970–71, whereas enlargement could actually happen only after the Accession Treaties had been negotiated and ratified, which would probably mean the end of 1971 at the earliest.

The Commission also prepared an aide-memoire for the Conference of Heads of State or Government, which it discussed at its meeting on 22 October. Several speakers (Mansholt, Sassen, Coppé, Levi Sandri, Haferkamp and Colonna di Paliano — the latter in writing (⁸)) came out in favour of developing monetary cooperation or

---

(¹) ACEU, Council minutes, 22 July 1969.
(²) AMAEF, 2724, Note by the western Europe sub-directorate, 28 August 1969.
(³) CHAN, GP, 5 AG 2, 1036, Note by Gaucher, 18 July 1969, and note by President Pompidou, undated, probably early September.
(⁴) AULB, 126 PP, VII 42–43, Interview with Pierre Harmel and Willy Brandt, 3 September 1969.
(⁵) ACEU, Council minutes, 17 October 1969.

(⁶) AULB, 126 PP, VII 42–43, Note of 16 September 1969 (record of lunch, 15 September 1969).
(⁷) ACEU, Council minutes, 17 October 1969.
(⁸) AULB, 126 PP, VII 42–43, Letter from Guido Colonna di Paliano to Jean Rey, 21 October 1969.

even of establishing economic and monetary union by 1975 or thereabouts, an idea already put forward at length in a paper by Hans von der Groeben on 16 October, while Raymond Barre spelled out the detailed implications in terms of economic institutions and common policies and the necessary preparatory measures. There was a consensus in the Commission in favour of calling for stronger Community institutions, and several members were worried that the summit conference might encroach on their territory. But opinions diverged on the question of cooperation on defence and foreign policy, which von der Groeben and Levi Sandri both wanted to see. Others felt that the time was not ripe (Raymond Barre) or that it was not for the Commission to call for developments here (Sassen, Colonna di Paliano). A number of other issues were considered too, particularly the need for a solution to the difficulties of Euratom and the value of implementing industrial, social and regional policies (¹).

The aide-memoire was refined over the following weeks and finally dated 18 November before being sent to the Heads of State or Government and published in the *Cahiers de la documentation européenne*. The Commission no longer expressed reservations about the idea of the summit but hoped that it would allow recent difficulties to be overcome and a new political stimulus to be given to European integration. It set out its own vision of the 'completion/deepening/enlargement' trilogy. It proposed completing the process set in motion with the customs union by establishing economic and monetary union and determining the measures that would need to be taken in the five years ahead in the industrial, technological, social and regional fields. It called for stronger and more democratic institutions and for progress towards political union in Europe. For the immediate future, it saw a need for measures to lay down the multiannual Euratom research programme, to adopt a financial regulation based on the establishment of own resources, to increase

the budgetary powers of the European Parliament and to prepare for the reopening of negotiations on the enlargement of the Communities (²).

The Commission's staff were also involved in the debate on revitalising Europe. A manifesto (see box on pp. 130–131) was drafted at staff conferences on 28 October and distributed for staff to sign. This was not a demand for measures to benefit the staff but a profession of faith in Europe, calling for unification under pressure from the people (³). On the first day of the summit, Euratom staff demonstrated at The Hague, alongside the European Youth Movement, to express their dissatisfaction and their impatience, with slogans such as 'Assez de bla-bla, des actes', 'Euratom se meurt, l'Europe aussi', 'Contre l'Europe des trusts et des technocrates' and 'Droit de vote aux Européens' (⁴).

At the first session of the summit in the afternoon on Monday 1 December, the Heads of State or Government reviewed European problems, including Community questions naturally, but they scarcely touched on institutional questions, given France's opposition. As planned, the Commission attended only the Tuesday morning session. It was represented by Jean Rey, who was accompanied by Edoardo Martino and four officials but not by the full group of Vice-Presidents, as had been suggested. President Rey made a statement that the final communiqué drafted in the afternoon passed over in silence, although the 16 points covered (see box on pp. 134–135) extensively matched the Commission's hopes (⁵). The final communiqué confirmed the irreversible nature of the construction of the Community and its ultimate political objectives. Regarding completion, the Heads of State or Government decided to

---

(¹) AULB, 126 PP, VII 42–43, Note by Émile Noël for President Rey, 31 October 1969.

(²) BAC 79/1982 221, Aide-memoire from the Commission of the European Communities for the Conference of Heads of State or Government (transmitted for information purposes to the European Parliament).

(³) ACEU, Negotiations with the United Kingdom series, No 21, Brussels Staff Committee, *Informations*, No 40, 6 November 1969, European Manifesto.

(⁴) *Europe*, 1 and 4 December 1969.

(⁵) Ludlow, P., 'An opportunity or a threat? The European Commission and the Hague Council of December 1969', *Journal of European Integration History*, Vol. 9, 2003, No 2, pp. 11–25.

Final communiqué of the Hague Summit

'1. On the initiative of the Government of the French Republic and at the invitation of the Netherlands Government, the Heads of State or Government and the Ministers for Foreign Affairs of the Member States of the European Communities met at The Hague on 1 and 2 December 1969. The Commission of the European Communities was invited to participate in the work of the conference on the second day.

2. Now that the common market is about to enter upon its final stage, they considered that it was the duty of those who bear the highest political responsibility in each of the Member States to draw up a balance sheet of the work already accomplished, to show their determination to continue it and to define the broad lines for the future.

3. Looking back on the road that has been traversed, and finding that never before have independent States pushed their cooperation further, they were unanimous in their opinion that by reason of the progress made the Community had now arrived at a turning point in its history. Over and above the technical and legal sides of the problems involved, the expiry of the transitional period at the end of the year has, therefore, acquired major political significance [...]

4. The Heads of State or Government therefore wish to reaffirm their belief in the political objectives which give the Community its full meaning and scope [...]

5. As regards the completion of the Communities, the Heads of State or Government have reaffirmed the will of their governments to pass from the transitional period to the final stage of the European Community and, accordingly, to lay down a definitive financial arrangement for the common agricultural policy by the end of 1969.

They agree to replace gradually, within the framework of this financial arrangement, the contributions of member countries by the Community's own resources, taking into account all the interests concerned, with the object of achieving in due course the integral financing of the Community's budgets in accordance with the procedure provided for in Article 201 of the Treaty establishing the EEC and of strengthening the budgetary powers of the European Parliament.

The problem of direct elections will continue to be studied by the Council of Ministers.

6. They have asked the governments to continue without delay, within the Council, the efforts already made to ensure a better control of the market by a policy of agricultural production making it possible to limit the burden on budgets.

7. The acceptance of a financial arrangement for the final stage does not exclude its adaptation by unanimous vote in an enlarged Community, on condition that the principles of this arrangement are not watered down.

8. They have reaffirmed their readiness to expedite the further action needed to strengthen the Community and promote its development into an economic union. They are of the opinion that the integration process should result in a Community of stability and growth. To this end they agreed that, within the Council, on the basis of the memorandum presented by the Commission on 12 February 1969, and in close collaboration with the latter, a plan in stages will be worked out during 1970 with a view to the creation of an economic and monetary union.

The development of monetary cooperation should be based on the harmonisation of economic policies.

They agreed to arrange for the investigation of the possibility of setting up a European reserve fund which should be the outcome of a joint economic and monetary policy.

9. As regards the technological activity of the Community, they reaffirmed their readiness to continue more intensively the activities of the Community with a view to coordinating and promoting industrial research and development in the principal pacemaking sectors, in particular by means of common programmes, and to supply the financial means for the purpose.

10. They are further agreed on the necessity of making fresh efforts to work out in the near future a research programme for the European Atomic Energy Community designed in accordance with the exigencies of modern industrial management, and making it possible to ensure the most effective use of the Joint Research Centre.

11. They reaffirmed their interest in the establishment of a European university.

12. The Heads of State or Government acknowledge the desirability of reforming the Social Fund, within the framework of a closely concerted social policy.

13. They reaffirmed their agreement on the principle of the enlargement of the Community, in accordance with Article 237 of the Treaty of Rome.

In so far as the applicant States accept the Treaties and their political aims, the decisions taken since the entry into force of the Treaties and the options adopted in the sphere of development, the Heads of State or Government have indicated their agreement to the opening of negotiations between the Community on the one hand and the applicant States on the other.

They agreed that the essential preparatory work for establishing a basis of negotiation could be undertaken as soon as practically possible. By common consent, the preparations are to take place in the most positive spirit.

14. As soon as negotiations with the applicant countries have been opened, discussions on their position in relation to the EEC will be started with such other EFTA members as may request them.

15. They instructed the Ministers for Foreign Affairs to study the best way of achieving progress in the matter of political unification, within the context of enlargement. The ministers are to make proposals to this effect by the end of July 1970.

16. All the creative activities and the actions conducive to European growth decided upon here will be assured of a greater future if the younger generation is closely associated with them. The governments have endorsed this need and the Communities will make provision for it.'

Europe, Wednesday 3 December 1969.

adopt a financial regulation by the end of the year, to replace national contributions by own resources and to reinforce the budgetary powers of the European Parliament. To strengthen the Community, they agreed to set in train moves towards economic and monetary union, an industrial research and development policy and a European university. They agreed to open negotiations with the applicant countries without specifying a date, contrary to what five of the Member States and the Commission wanted, although France agreed that the President would announce that there was agreement that negotiations would begin as soon as the Member States had agreed on the conditions for accession, probably in mid-1970. And the summit instructed the ministers to study the best way of achieving progress in the matter of political unification and decided that the younger generation should be more closely involved in the construction of Europe.

The Commission was bound to approve of the decisions taken as they went well beyond the letter, if not the spirit, of the objectives set by the Treaties of Rome [1]. At the interinstitutional conference on 11 December, the three institutions in the decision-making triangle took stock of the summit, coming to a broadly positive conclusion. When speaking of the Commission's view, already made public on 5 December, President Rey expressed satisfaction with the agreements on completion, on the opening of negotiations and on cooperation in monetary and social matters, but he regretted the failure to come to a decision on political union and the election of Parliament by direct universal suffrage [2]. Expressing a personal opinion in a letter to Jean Monnet, Jean Rey was even more reserved. Following the Hague Summit, although he felt that he detected an atmosphere that was more conducive to cooper-

ation within the Council, he continued to reject firmly the idea of periodic meetings of Heads of State or Government that might take the place of the Community institutions and prevent any prospect whatsoever of majority voting. He also felt that the summit had been unimaginative as regards political union [3].

This balanced judgment well matched the significance of the summit, which was not the catastrophe initially feared by the Commission but did leave a threat hanging over the equilibrium of the Community system. Although the meeting of Heads of State or Government was not institutionalised, it did provide an impetus that helped Europe out of its impasse, even if Parliament was reinforced little, if at all, and the Commission's right of initiative was jeopardised. Admittedly, with support from five Member States, the Commission avoided being completely sidelined but, by fairly quickly coming round to the idea of the summit, by agreeing to participate in it and by preparing documents that were so solid that the French authorities had to respect them (particularly the opinion on enlargement [4]), the Commission was able to contribute to making a success of the summit. And the decisions taken at The Hague had a number of beneficial effects on it: greater financial autonomy and, above all, the possibility of influencing the various new projects launched. While it fell to the Rey Commission to prepare the final stages, the budgetary reforms of the spring of 1970 and the start of the accession negotiations, from July 1970 onwards it was for the Malfatti Commission to manage the problems of enlargement and deepening.

Early days of the Malfatti–Mansholt Commission

Three years after it took up office, the Single Commission was to be reduced from 14 to nine

[1] AULB, 126 PP, VII 41, Letter from Jean Rey to Jean Monnet, 29 January 1970.

[2] ACEU, Negotiations with the United Kingdom series, No 21, Information note on the Interinstitutional Conference (the annual conference between the Council, the Commission and Parliament in 1969 was devoted to the current situation and the future of the European Community following the Hague Conference and was held in Strasbourg on 11 December).

[3] FJME, AMK C 33/5/201, Jean Rey to Jean Monnet, 8 December 1969.

[4] CHAN, GP, 5 AG 2, 52, Note on the Commission opinion on enlargement.

members under Article 10 of the 1965 Merger Treaty. Under the rotation principle adopted in Luxembourg after the 'empty chair' crisis, it would be Italy's turn to designate a President. Despite these rules, there was a debate in the first half of 1970 on the membership of the Commission that was to succeed the Rey Commission at the beginning of July. The idea of maintaining a 14-strong membership until enlargement was defended by the Netherlands and above all by Belgium, with both countries wishing to retain two seats on the Commission so as to represent two different political affiliations. This would enable Jean Rey to stay on at the Commission and, in all probability, to play a major role in the negotiations that were about to start with the United Kingdom. Italy also supported this scenario, which would give it three Commissioners, and the government in Rome seemed ready even to give up the presidency [1]. Others wanted Jean Rey to stay on in a slimline nine-member Commission. Jean Monnet and those in charge at the Agence Europe were among them [2]. The Commission itself and its President seem to have avoided becoming directly involved in the discussion [3].

On 11 May the Foreign Ministers finally decided to apply the Treaty without attempting to interpret it and without making amendments that would have to be ratified in all six Member States. Italy selected Franco Maria Malfatti from among the names put forward for the presidency. He was appointed for two years but left a few months before the end of his term of office to stand in the early elections that had been called in his country. He was replaced at the head of the Commission for the remainder of 1972, until the Commission of the enlarged Community took office, by the Dutchman, Sicco Mansholt, who had held the agriculture portfolio since 1958.

On 1 July 1970 the Rey Commission held its final meeting (the 128th of the Single Commission). Five of its 14 members would stay on in the Malfatti Commission and help bring about the continuity that was symbolised by the ceremony for the transfer of powers from one President to the next on 2 July, when the nine-member Commission took office. This was a simple and sober event that took place in the President's office in the Berlaymont building. After introducing the directors-general to his successor, Jean Rey said a few words in Italian and then in French to wish the new President every success and to thank all the Commission's staff. In his reply, Franco Maria Malfatti spoke of the new frontier towards which Europe was heading: an enlarged Community which could boost and not dissipate the strength achieved by its institutions [4]. He then accompanied Jean Rey to the door, to applause from the entire staff gathered in the entrance hall [5].

That afternoon the new Commission held its first meeting (the 129th of the Single Commission), seated at a round table installed in place of the previous Commission's oval table. Once the brief opening ceremony for the press and photographers was over, it embarked on the marathon task of allocating portfolios among the members, which ended at 1.30 a.m. This rapid success was welcomed as a test case, but the Benelux leaders had some suspicion that a prior deal might have been done between the French and the Germans. In spite of those doubts, the Malfatti Commission was immediately operational, just after the enlargement negotiations had formally opened on 30 June and at a time when many projects, including those launched at The Hague, were ready to be launched and the question of the institutional balance was calling for its attention.

A few days before President Malfatti took over, Émile Noël had drawn attention to the fact that the Commission's position was being weakened and had issued a warning which was at the same

---

[1] FJME, AMK 115/3/8, Note by Jacques Van Helmont, 27 January 1970, and AMK C 33/4/222, Note by Jacques Van Helmont, 19 March 1970. See also *Europe*, 14, 20 and 23 April 1970.
[2] *Europe*, 14 April 1970.
[3] FJME, AMK C 33/5/211, Letter from Jean Rey to Jean Monnet, 11 May 1970.

[4] *Europe*, 2 July 1970.
[5] Group interview (Robert Pendville), 19 October 2004.

time a programme of mobilisation. The Secretary-General felt that the Commission's role had been under attack since 1965 but that a new stage had been reached when General de Gaulle had left office since the Commission now had less firm support from the other five governments. The Commission should try to resume its leadership in areas where its status was declining; it should participate in the enlargement negotiations, adopt a memorandum on social questions, review the transport policy and seek out a new strategy on agriculture. It should also redefine its relationship with the Council and Coreper and put an end to the guerrilla warfare waged by the two bodies to prevent the Commission from playing a role in external relations (see box on p. 142). Lastly, the Commission should assert its influence in genuinely political matters, develop its relations with the social partners, reopen the debate on institutional structures and ensure that it was not side-lined in the discussions about political union [1].

President Malfatti apparently shared his concerns. On 8 July, when the Commission made its solemn commitment before the Court of Justice and appeared for the first time before the European Parliament, he stressed the importance of a political Europe. On 15 September, in his programme address to Parliament, he stated that the Commission would not be content simply to manage routine (and technical) matters, would not agree to be downgraded to a kind of general secretariat but would embark on action to improve the institutional set-up and would not be sidelined from the process of working for a political union. He saw economic union and political union as two sides of the same coin, and the constitution of Europe could not be divorced from international reality but should rather influence it, and this warranted Commission involvement in political dossiers from which the Member States — or some of them at least — wished to exclude it [2].

The question of Commission participation in EPC and the CSCE

The question of Commission participation in the European Political Cooperation (EPC) machinery and that of the preparations for the Conference on Security and Cooperation in Europe (CSCE) arose virtually at the same time, in the autumn of 1970. Admittedly, ever since the beginning of the year, Jean Rey had been trying to get the Commission to think seriously about the action to be taken on paragraph 15 of the Hague communiqué. He thought he could provide the ministers with 'food for their imagination' [3]. He wanted political union to be defined in broad terms and not just in terms of foreign policy, and he was determined to ensure that political union should not be divorced from the Community integration of Europe, bearing in mind that economic policy had a considerable impact on external relations and that the harmonisation of foreign policies could have major repercussions for the Community [4]. But he did not receive unanimous support in the Commission, which preferred to wait and see what the Davignon Report on political cooperation might contain.

In the spring the Foreign Ministers had agreed on the general principles of political cooperation, and the Committee, comprising the six political directors, was able to draw up a report that was finally adopted by the ministers on 27 October 1970 and came to be known by the name of the Belgian director-general of policy in the Belgian Ministry of Foreign Affairs, Étienne Davignon, who had chaired the Committee. The report stated that the Communities were the original nucleus from which European unity had developed and reaffirmed the need for them to step up their political cooperation and, in the initial stage, to provide themselves with ways and means of harmonising their views in the field of international politics. According to Étienne Davignon, the project was different from the Fouchet Plan since

[1] HAEU, EN 1046, Note from Émile Noël for President Malfatti, 22 June 1970.
[2] *Europe*, 15 September 1970.

[3] FJME, AMK C 33/5/201, Letter from Jean Rey to Jean Monnet, 8 December 1969.
[4] AULB, 126 PP, VII 44, Draft by Jean Rey, 19 January 1970.

Transfer of power between Jean Rey (right centre) and Franco Maria Malfatti (left centre),
with the outgoing President presenting all the directors-general to his successor under the attentive gaze
of Secretary-General Émile Noël (centre).
(2 July 1970)

it did not simply call for consultations and did not establish new institutions separate from the Economic Community (¹). The idea was that regular information exchanges would ensure greater mutual understanding and increase solidarity by fostering a harmonisation of views, jointly agreed positions and, when it appeared feasible and de-

sirable, joint action. The project did not provide for permanent bodies but for periodic meetings of Foreign Ministers at least once every six months and of the Committee of heads of political departments at least four times a year to consult on all major matters of foreign policy. To put the political union in a truly democratic context, there were to be six-monthly informal meetings between the ministers and the European Parliament's Political Affairs Committee. The secretariat

---

(¹) HAEU, EG 104, Briefing Davignon, undated.

for political cooperation would be provided by the country exercising the presidency of the Council, and the Commission would be consulted if the activities of the European Communities were affected by the work of the ministers (¹).

The Commission was, in fact, invited to attend the first meeting of the Foreign Ministers in Munich on 19 November 1970, likewise with a delegation of five members. But President Malfatti (accompanied by Émile Noël, Renato Ruggiero and Dieter Hammer) was introduced only for the third item on the agenda, namely the economic aspects of East–West relations (²) (the other two items concerned the Middle East and the CSCE). When giving his address, Malfatti stated that it was important that the Commission should attend the ministers' first EPC meeting and he called for closer economic cooperation with the countries of eastern Europe, despite the Soviet Union's ambivalent attitude to the EEC (³).

When Malfatti returned from Munich, there was a debate within the Commission regarding participation in EPC. Reporting on the meeting, he stated that the ministers had referred the question of relations with Comecon to the Political Committee and he asked whether the heads of political departments could study economic problems placed on their agenda by the Conference of Ministers at the Commission's suggestion. He went on to ask whether the Commission should or should not attend meetings of the Political Committee (⁴). Following a rather animated discussion, especially with Sicco Mansholt, who had always taken a negative stance on the Davignon plan and regretted that the President had addressed the European Parliament on the subject without first obtaining the opinion of the Commission, Malfatti asked the members to let him have a note setting out their political views with

a view to an internal debate before he next addressed Parliament (⁵).

The Commission members thus had to set out their positions in order to clarify the debate on how EPC should operate. The idea of the interdependence between economic unification and political unification, so dear to Walter Hallstein and Jean Rey, was taken up vigorously by Altiero Spinelli, who considered that it was up to the Commission to establish links between the two processes and to align more closely decision-making procedures in a context that should become increasingly democratic. Sicco Mansholt wanted political union to be developed within Community structures and several members feared that EPC would encroach on the Communities' remit. All of them wanted the Commission to attend meetings not only of the ministers but also of the political directors, although Raymond Barre and Albert Borschette felt that the Commission should not be excessive in its demands but stood to gain more by showing how useful it was (⁶).

In 1971 there was a proliferation of attempts to secure fuller Commission participation in the activities highlighted in the Davignon Report. Before making further public statements in the European Parliament, the Commission was keen to mark out its territory. At a working dinner on the subject of cooperation on political union at Val-Duchesse on 17 February, the Commission, represented by its President, emphasised the need for convergence between political union and economic union, which should become even more marked with the establishment of monetary union and enlargement of the Communities. Malfatti restated that the Commission's role as guardian of the Treaties was to ensure that there

---

(¹) HAEU, EG 104, Davignon Report.
(²) HAEU, FMM 36, Record of meeting of 19 November.
(³) HAEU, EN 73, Address by President Malfatti, 19 November 1970.
(⁴) FJME, AMK 114/8/35, Note by Pierre Duchâteau for Jean-François Deniau, 25 November 1970.

(⁵) Ibid. President Malfatti had addressed the EP on EPC on 15 September and had appeared before the EP Political Affairs Committee on 7 September, stating that the Commission should be associated with political union (see HAEU, EG 104, Record of meeting of 7 September 1970).
(⁶) HAEU, FMM 37, Note from Raymond Barre to Franco Maria Malfatti, 17 December 1970; Note from Sjouke Jonker to Franco Maria Malfatti, 23 December 1970; Note from Albert Coppé to Émile Noël, 14 January 1971; Note from Albert Borschette to Franco Maria Malfatti, 14 January 1970; summarised, 26 January 1971.

was no encroachment on Community powers and he asked for it to be associated with all EPC machinery and with meetings of the Political Committee and the Foreign Ministers [1]. In March, not having been invited to a working lunch of the ministers at which the political and institutional development of the EEC was discussed, Malfatti protested both orally and in writing to the Council President, Maurice Schumann. However, on the occasion of the ministers' second EPC meeting in Paris, he was invited to the dinner at the Quai d'Orsay on 13 May and to the meetings on 14 May. He took the opportunity to ask that the Commission attend all Foreign Ministers' meetings [2]. The battle for Commission participation in the Political Committee raged throughout 1971, as France did not want this [3]. In 1972 Mansholt also tried to have the Commission associated with the meeting between the President of the Foreign Ministers and the European Parliament's Political Affairs Committee [4].

In Paris on 14 May 1971, President Malfatti argued for inclusion of economic cooperation on the agenda for the Conference on Security, which was later to become the Conference on Security and Cooperation in Europe. He stated that economic cooperation was a factor making for détente and security and wanted the European Community to be able to participate in the preparatory work for the conference and in the conference itself as an entity speaking with one voice. He regarded this as an opportunity for the Soviet Union to recognise the EEC, which it had hitherto always denigrated as a cold-war organisation. Maurice Schumann then asked the Commission to comment in writing on the Belgian paper that was to serve as a basic document for the Political Committee's preparatory work on the CSCE [5].

With President Malfatti attending the Munich and Paris meetings, the Commission was de facto involved in the discussion on the CSCE from the outset. But the question again arose as to the extent of its involvement. The governments had agreed to come up with a joint position in EPC and to consult together both at Foreign Minister level and at political director level. They also did not want the conference to be confined solely to security problems but to embrace economic cooperation and therefore matters within the Communities' remit. The Commission should therefore be involved in the preparatory work for the CSCE. But the fact that it had been asked to present written comments suggested that France remained opposed to its presence in the Political Committee. Moreover, the Member States decided that in the Political Committee there would be a subcommittee (without the Commission) and a 'group' which would be specifically responsible for considering the economic issues to be put to the conference and on which the Commission was represented by its Deputy Secretary-General, Klaus Meyer. Originally described as a sub-group, it was renamed an 'ad hoc group' after Émile Noël had pointed out to the Quai d'Orsay that confining the Commission's presence to a sub-group would cause problems [6]. All the delegations eventually agreed to a Commission presence in the Political Committee whenever Community matters were on the agenda. Émile Noël and Klaus Meyer were accordingly invited to Rome for the second day of the Political Committee meeting on 20 October, and from February 1972 onwards this participation seemed to be taken for granted (though still only for matters within the Communities' remit).

There is clear evidence that the Commission strongly influenced this preparatory work. In October the ad hoc group adopted a report that would then be approved by the Political Committee and that was based on a Belgian paper but extensively inspired by a Commission contribution

[1] HAEU, EN 109, Memorandum from President Malfatti, 17 February 1971.

[2] HAEU, FMM 36, Minutes of meeting, 14 May 1971.

[3] HAEU, FMM 37, Record of meeting of EP Political Affairs Committee, 16 June 1971.

[4] PV 228 EC Commission, 22 November 1972.

[5] HAEU, EN 73, Address by President Malfatti to meeting of Foreign Ministers, 14 May 1971.

[6] HAEU, EN 86, Letter from Émile Noël to Jacques de Beaumarchais (political director, Quai d'Orsay), 26 May 1971; and letter from Jacques de Beaumarchais to Émile Noël, 30 June 1971.

Relations between the Commission and the Council

In a long note addressed to President Malfatti on 22 June 1970, shortly before he took office, Émile Noël highlights the threats that the Commission will be weakened in relation to the Council. Further down the document, in a part not reproduced here, he calls for a series of measures to restore the dynamism of Commission action.

'1. The role and action of the Commission have been under attack since 1965. While the 1965 crisis, which began with very serious attacks by the French government […], prompted the other governments to form a common front in favour of the Treaties, the settlement in 1966 was very much to the detriment of the Commission's prestige, if not of its actual prerogatives.

The establishment of the Single Commission and the designation of a new President in 1967, followed by changes in the policies and style of the French government, have removed the apparent threats of institutional upheaval. Consequently, it has become easier to criticise the Commission's action and challenge its role, and there has been a growing tendency to do so since 1967, in the Council and Parliament as well as in the European and international press.

2. **Regarding the Council** ([1]), everything the Commission and its staff do is scrutinised carefully and eagerly, and less and less kindly, by the Member States' permanent delegations. Working relationships, national relationships, no less than personal relationships, are such that nothing in the Commission's intentions, hesitations and divisions is immune.

Faced with these demanding observers, rapidly transformed into censors, the Commission could a few years ago still look forward to a sort of 'unconditional support' from certain delegations by way of reaction to the French attitude. Things have not been the same since 1969. In the Permanent Representatives Committee […] and the Council, all that matters at the end of the day, beyond the purely legal situation, is the technical quality and political expediency of proposals presented, the quality of the officials representing the Commission, and the personal authority and character of the members of the Commission. […]

3. In the field of **external relations** ([1]), the Council and the delegations remain extremely reluctant to consider any increase in the Commission's responsibilities and are reluctant to see it even exercising the prerogatives that it enjoys under the Treaty.

It is possible, sometimes even easy, to uphold the Commission position when it is legally and technically watertight. […] But, where the legal basis is shaky (renewal of the Yaoundé Convention), where there has been the slightest imperfection in the technical preparation or where the political assessment of the situation is not borne out by events (e.g. the accession negotiations), the Commission is 'pushed aside'.

Here we are faced with the combined impact of the special interest that embassies and Permanent Representatives show in external relations, of the determination of the national administrations to put the brakes on out of a concern to preserve their own prerogatives and of the links between all matters such as these and questions of general policy, which, in the absence of political union, remain within the remit of each Member State.'

HAEU, EN 1046, Note for President Malfatti, 22 June 1970 (signed Émile Noël). (Translated from the French)

([1]) Original emphasis.

dating from July (¹). It was also clear that the Commission's background papers facilitated the preparatory work on economic aspects in NATO (²). The scale of the Commission's involvement can also be seen from the Commission communication to the Council on the CSCE in September 1972, which looked ahead to the multilateral preparatory work due to begin in the relatively near future. The Commission put forward proposals for trade relations, financial and monetary cooperation, energy, transport and development aid. It stressed that its proposals broadly reflected the ideas emerging from the preliminary discussions. It also outlined the spirit in which the Community would participate in the CSCE: It would play a constructive role to gain acceptance for its existence by the countries of eastern Europe but without negotiating or offering concessions in return and it would be sure to avoid encouraging greater integration within Comecon, which would strengthen the USSR's control over the people's democracies (³).

This example of Commission involvement in EPC and, in particular, in the preparations for the CSCE is a good illustration of the unremitting efforts it had to make during the Malfatti era to avoid being sidelined by the Council. It also illustrates its ability to seize small opportunities to mark out its territory and maintain its influence. At the same time as it was working on EPC, which was still seeking to work out its own procedures and guidelines, it entered into another part of the political union arena — the institutional set-up.

The proposals for institutional reform

Immediately after the Hague Summit, the prospect of enlargement and of more extensive Community powers implicitly raised the issue of institutional reform. Jean Rey, who feared that the Community would find it more difficult to function after enlargement, wanted immediate improvements to the institutional system (⁴), and in 1970 the Commission undertook to prepare a number of reforms. After new budgetary rules were adopted on 22 April, it stated that it was planning to present a proposal for a further increase in the budgetary powers of the European Parliament before the end of 1972. It also undertook to present a proposal concerning its legislative powers by the end of 1974. In 1971 the Council Resolution of 22 March on economic and monetary union and the statement by President Pompidou on the European Confederation and the appointment of Ministers for European Affairs, followed by the German proposal for a permanent EPC secretariat, all contributed material for the Commission's general review of the question (⁵).

The Commission was facing a dual challenge in the short term since, as Sicco Mansholt put it, the moment of institutional truth would come in 1973 with enlargement (⁶). Firstly, it was necessary to avert the risk that the discussions would go ahead without the Commission and to ensure that they took place within the Community framework. Émile Noël regularly asked the French, still reluctant to accept the Commission, to allow it to participate in the Foreign Ministers' discussions (⁷). Secondly, since the aim was to make the decision-making process more efficient and more democratic, it was necessary to identify the best possible options among the various suggestions for improvements made by the governments and the European Parliament's political groups and which the Commission arranged to be reviewed at the beginning of 1972 (⁸).

Having already expressed views on a number of individual ideas, notably in statements by

(¹) HAEU, EN 73, Document presented by the Commission, 19 July 1971; and note from Émile Noël to Franco Maria Malfatti, 25 October 1971. See also, HAEU, FMM 36, Political Committee Report on CSCE, 4 November 1971.
(²) HAEU, EN 1996, Note from Gian Carlo Chevallard for Klaus Meyer, 14 July 1972.
(³) HAEU, EN 1996, Proposal for a position of the European Communities, 26 September 1972.

(⁴) FJME, AMK 115/1/32, Note by Klaus Meyer, 30 June 1970.
(⁵) HAEU, FMM 37, Aide-memoire of 26 April 1971.
(⁶) HAEU, FMM 37, Note from Sjouke Jonker to Franco Maria Malfatti, 23 December 1970.
(⁷) HAEU, EN 205, Record of conversation by Émile Noël with Cuvillier and Jean-René Bernard, 7 May 1971.
(⁸) HAEU, EN 386, Document of 25 February 1972 prepared for the Commission by the working party chaired by Émile Noël.

President Malfatti in the European Parliament, the Commission asked a group of 14 eminent persons chaired by the French jurist Georges Vedel to consider the question of the powers of the European Parliament and the links with election by direct universal suffrage provided for by Article 138 of the EEC Treaty. The Vedel Report (25 May 1972) emphasised the need to increase the European Parliament's powers by improving the consultation procedure, gradually introducing a co-decision procedure with the Council, strengthening its budgetary and financial powers, and involving it in the designation of the Commission President. It did not believe that there was any automatic link between increased powers for the European Parliament and direct elections, but it stressed the importance of such elections, which could proceed in accordance with each country's own electoral system. It also suggested establishing close links between national parliaments and the European Parliament, in particular by maintaining the dual mandate. It called for the Community system to be consolidated by a return to majority voting, for no institutionalisation of summits and for respect for the Commission's proper role as a centre for policy-making, initiative, mediation and administration in Community matters [1].

There were reactions to the Vedel Report in the Commission, particularly from Spinelli, who offered to rectify its omissions and imperfections [2]. Spinelli actually redesigned the institutional architecture to avoid any separation between Community cooperation in the EEC and interstate cooperation in EPC. He rejected the idea of a confederation set up alongside the EEC, which he felt should be renamed 'European Community' rather than 'European Economic Community'. He wanted the Council of the Communities to be the body dealing with intergovernmental cooperation instead of organising parallel meetings of the Foreign Ministers, and he proposed attaching a secretariat to Coreper to handle EPC follow-up.

He also called for further progress towards Community integration, a draft Treaty revision to be produced by the European Parliament and draft legislation for direct elections [3].

In 1972 the institutional question was a source of tension between the Commission and the European Parliament, which felt that the former was not meeting its commitments and had not presented in good time significant proposals for increasing its powers, in particular in budgetary matters [4]. But in May the Commission instructed an 'administrative group' chaired by Émile Noël to draft a paper clarifying its positions on institutional matters. The paper distinguished between measures to be taken immediately to increase Parliament's powers and the efficiency of the institutions (Commission to present periodically a general programme to the Council and Parliament; EP to be involved in the legislative process through a cooperation procedure; EP to approve the Commission President, who should be given a longer term of office; more flexible unanimity rules, with the possibility for a Member State to abstain) and the measures needed to reinforce the institutional system which required amendments to the Treaty (increased powers for the EP; election by direct universal suffrage; single place of work for all the institutions; EPC to be organised within the Community context, with a political secretariat within the Council Secretariat) [5]. But this was not a genuine Commission proposal. It was its contribution to the Paris summit in October 1972 on the subject of institutional strengthening and progress towards political union and stood little chance of being accepted as it was.

The Commission and the Paris Summit

The idea of a summit at which the six existing Member States and the future new Member States

---

[1] HAEU, EN 76, Note of 10 April 1972.
[2] HAEU, EN 76, Note by Altiero Spinelli on the powers of the EP, 26 April 1972.

[3] HAEU, EN 76, Note by Altiero Spinelli, Political Union and the Communities, 26 April 1972.
[4] HAEU, EN 77, Note of 19 June 1972.
[5] HAEU, EN 76, contribution de la Commission en ce qui concerne le thème «Renforcement institutionnel et progrès de l'Union politique», SEC(72) 1597, 25 May 1972.

would come together was floated once again, by President Pompidou in August 1971, a few weeks after the end of the negotiations with the United Kingdom and a few days after President Nixon's decision to suspend the gold convertibility of the dollar. Unlike the 1969 summit, this was immediately approved by the Commission, which saw a need for a clear definition of the role and tasks of the enlarged Community so as to reinforce cohesion and solidarity between Europeans (¹). The Commission was determined to play a key role in preparing the summit. In October it decided to set up an ad hoc working party that would address the issue of the Commission's contribution (²). Four *chefs de cabinet* (Ruggiero, Cardon de Lichtbuer, Lahnstein, Duchâteau) met several times in November and December 1971 under Émile Noël's chairmanship. They produced an initial aide-memoire proposing that the Commission contribution focus on three topics: speeding up implementation of economic and monetary union and the common flanking policies, the Community's role in the world and the institutional development of the enlarged Community (³).

Once again the question of admitting the Commission to all preparatory meetings arose. On 5 November 1971 the Foreign Ministers, meeting within the political cooperation framework in Rome, decided that it would be associated with the preparations for the summit and with the summit itself on the same basis as at The Hague, which struck the Commission as too restrictive and unacceptable. At the Council meeting on 28 February 1972, President Malfatti forcefully demanded that the Commission be associated as a fully fledged participant. That morning, a first informal meeting of Foreign Ministers from the Member States and the acceding countries had just agreed on the topics for the summit, which were not very different from what the Commission had suggested: economic and monetary union and social progress in the Community, the Community's external relations and its responsibilities in the world, reinforcement of the institutions and political progress. But while the Commission was invited to play a full part in the work on the first two items, which were unquestionably matters of Community concern, the ministers reserved their decision on how and to what extent it could be brought in on the third question (⁴).

The debate came to life again when the ministers met on 20 March. Maurice Schumann now proposed that a distinction be made between strengthening the institutions, which concerned the Commission, and progress in political matters, where it could not be involved. In particular, he denied the Commission's right to speak on the possible establishment of a secretariat for political cooperation or on the question of Ministers for European Affairs (⁵). The Commission naturally rejected the French minister's contention. It challenged the possibility of clearly separating institutional strengthening from progress in political matters or foreign policy and Community powers in relation to non-member countries. It pointed out that the Treaties could be amended as regards institutional structures at the initiative of either the Commission or the Council (⁶). On 4 May President Mansholt, who had just taken over from Malfatti, wrote to the President of the Council, Gaston Thorn, to set forth the Commission's views and its vision of European integration, including the political aspects, within a single institutional set-up. But his letter went unanswered (⁷), and the Commission was not invited to the informal ministerial meeting of 26 and 27 May on political questions although it had attended the two previous meetings as a

(¹) HAEU, EN 479, Note on preparations for summit, 21 June 1972. It quotes President Malfatti's letter to the Heads of State or Government dated 10 September 1971.

(²) PV EC Commission, 13 October 1971.

(³) HAEU, EN 148, Note of 17 January 1972.

(⁴) HAEU, EN 148, Note from Klaus Meyer for members of the Commission, 29 February 1972.

(⁵) HAEU, EN 387, Note on the informal meeting of Foreign Ministers of the six Member States and the four acceding countries, 20 March 1972.

(⁶) HAEU, EN 387, Note of 26 May 1972.

(⁷) HAEU, EN 478, Letter from Sicco Mansholt to Gaston Thorn, 4 May 1972; and letter from Sicco Mansholt to the Italian Permanent Representative, 25 May 1972.

Altiero Spinelli's institutional design

Commissioner for Industrial Affairs and Research from 1970 to 1972, Altiero Spinelli also took a keen interest in the Community's institutional structure. He made a number of speeches, published articles and gave regular interviews to defend the idea of a supranational Europe and particularly to call for stronger powers for the European Parliament. His constitutionalist vision dated a long way back. In 1941, when he was held under house arrest on Ventotene Island because of his opposition to fascism, he wrote Towards a free and united Europe — a draft manifesto. *Here he described the European Federation, which he wanted to be democratic and social, as a pillar of world peace. Later, as a member of the first directly elected Parliament in 1979, he sought to turn his convictions into practice by taking the initiative of proposing a draft Treaty establishing a European Union that was approved by the European Parliament in 1984.*

In the following article, published by Le Monde *on 30 March 1971, Spinelli, reacting to a statement by President Pompidou in January 1971, defends his ideas.*

M.R.

'The Pompidou plan for Europe: an opportunity to be grasped', by Altiero Spinelli

'The discreet but widely reported attempts to consign President Pompidou's statements on the political unification of Europe to oblivion have apparently come to nought. Reactions from Mr Heath and Mr Brandt and the exchanges of views between the ministers in the Council of the EEC make it very clear that there will be a follow-up to the French President's observations.

The topic of political union and its institutions has, for some time been on the agenda of all the Community institutions and also of the Davignon Committee. It will be difficult to break the deadlock in the negotiations with Great Britain without raising the level of debate to cover the major questions of political integration in their generality. Meeting within the framework of the Monnet Committee, the leaders of virtually all parties in Europe have recently decided at last to begin a study on a draft form of political union. The great merit of the Pompidou plan is that it goes to the core of the problem by bringing in the idea of a European government whose decisions must be accepted by all Member States and by offering a roadmap for arriving there.

Working from the idea that the European government 'can proceed only from the meeting of national governments combining to take decisions that are valid for everybody', Mr Pompidou envisages three stages: (i) the Council of Ministers in its present form; (ii) a Council in which national Ministers for European Affairs would meet; and (iii) a Council whose members would no longer be members of national governments. Mr Pompidou is strictly logical and points out that this government would have to have its own executive branch separate from the national administrations and that once there is a genuine European government, there will have to be a genuine European Parliament'.

The French President seems a little too categorical when he considers that the idea that a body such as the Commission could become that government. This does not stand up to analysis on the facts. Although the Commission currently has only very limited executive powers and virtually no decision-making powers, its autonomous right of initiative gives it a political role that makes it much more than a mere technical agency. If Mr Pompidou's plan failed to succeed, we would inevitably have to resurrect the hypothesis that apparently does not hold: after all, most of our governments originally emerged from technical agencies and committees that advised absolute monarchs. But in the present-day situation there is no political or constitutional rationale for excluding a plan to confer a supranational structure gradually on a decision-making body such as the Council instead of conferring decision-making powers gradually on a supranational body such as the Commission.

[...]

What this project still lacks to make it truly operational is though a permanent, powerful political motive force.

The birth of the European government is bound to be both logical and complex for, by bringing powerful political interests into play, it will not only engender support but also arouse hostility. The meeting of ministers in the Council, however full of goodwill, will not be able on its own to overcome these obstacles. The long march towards a genuine European government will get under way only if it proceeds from the consent of the people and genuine European democratic legitimacy, that is to say a European Parliament that authentically represents the peoples of the Community. It is not reasonable to plan for this Parliament only at the third stage, as Mr Pompidou seems to propose: it must be there from the very beginning. True, it will not initially

have all the powers that it will ultimately possess, but from the outset it must be able to deliberate with authority and legitimacy on the institutional problems raised in the Council and to approve them before referring them to the national parliaments for final ratification. This constitutional role alone fully justifies having it elected without delay.

If the new political edifice is not underpinned by a European democratic body such as this, we will have to ask where this new government is going to come from, as Mr Pompidou has asked himself. If the answer is "from the secret conference of political directors in the foreign ministries envisaged by the Davignon Committee", then we are clearly not yet taking things seriously.'

(Translated from the French)

delegation of six members, equivalent to those of the Member States and although Malfatti had spoken on the Community's external relations on 20 March [1] and Mansholt on economic and monetary union on 24 April [2].

But at their meeting in June the Ministers set up an ad hoc working party which was to become the instrument for preparing the summit during the summer, and the Commission was represented by its Secretary-General, Émile Noël, who was accompanied by Klaus Meyer and Renato Ruggiero and who sat alongside the permanent representatives of the Member States, with the

Dutchman Sassen in the chair [3]. The ad hoc working party centralised proposals before drawing them together into formulations acceptable to the summit. On 7 July the Commission sent it a memorandum setting out what it saw as the objectives to be pursued in the years ahead: gradual attainment of economic and monetary union, social progress (full employment, guaranteed income for workers, and greater resources and scope for action of the Social Fund), progress towards European civic rights, narrowing of regional disparities, protection and improvement of the environment, reinforcement and integration of industrial structures, negotiations on the reform of the international monetary system, international

[1] HAEU, EN 476, Address by Franco Maria Malfatti, 20 March 1972.
[2] HAEU, EN 477, Address by Sicco Mansholt, 24 April 1972.

[3] HAEU, EN 121, Note by Klaus Meyer, 29 June 1972.

Enlargement and its impact on the atmosphere at two summits (The Hague and Paris)

'The Hague, December 1969. In a European Community virtually paralysed by tensions caused in turn by the failure of the Fouchet Plan (1962) and the "empty chair" crisis (1965), the media came in their droves to attend this historical turning point, with two new figures on the scene: Georges Pompidou (President of the French Republic following the resignation of General de Gaulle) and Chancellor Willy Brandt.

The agenda was based on the completion/deepening/enlargement trilogy and was politically highly ambitious, but there were also many technical implications where Commission staff led by Émile Noël made very valuable contributions, quite apart from Raymond Barre's efforts to make something of the hesitant first steps towards a future economic and monetary union. Bino Olivi, spokesman, and myself as his deputy went to The Hague with President Jean Rey knowing that the situation for us would be difficult and tricky.

After the official opening ceremony in the Knights' Hall, which the photographers and film crews were allowed to attend, the discussions themselves proceeded without the Commission President, who had been given a slot of one hour, no more, the next morning to speak about "the Community aspects" to the Heads of State or Government. The journalists were expecting a late night after all the delegations had given their press briefings, including the initial "confidential" statements by Georges Pompidou and Willy Brandt, backed up by their press attachés.

We devised the following scenario: as the evening went by, we would gather as much information as possible by covering all the delegations' briefings, meet for breakfast with the President to sum up the situation; then book the press room for a press conference to present the summary of the President's speech and mobilise as many journalists as possible. I will spare you the details, which would take far too long, but let me just say that the operation was a great success thanks to a number of basic factors:

— synergy between Brussels and external offices;

— efficiency of our man on the spot (R. Simons-Cohen at the time), thanks to his good relations with government departments and the national press;

— close working relations with the accredited journalists: the crowded press conference called by Bino Olivi was the perfect illustration of this.

In Paris, in the autumn of 1972, the circumstances were quite different, but once again we encountered the same attempts to sideline the Commission.

The dates had been set for the Summit Conference of the now nine Member States (Paris, 19–21 October) and preparatory work was under way, when a rumour reached us via François Fontaine, Head of the Information Office in Paris: the Commission would be allowed to attend sessions at the Summit "related to the common market", but not those dealing with political cooperation.

Without going into the details on our counter-attack, I remember meeting with Sicco Mansholt and his *chef de cabinet* to talk about, among other things, the list of acceptances to be given to 10 or so invitations. I suggested that preference be given to one in particular: the lunchtime debate with the diplomatic press in Paris. Sicco Mansholt gave me a free hand to decide on the table plan. I had learnt that *Le Monde* had put a new man in charge of its diplomatic news, Michel Tatu, who had been in their Moscow office, so I decided to seat him next to me. We had a thoroughly interesting conversation (I learnt a lot about the USSR) but, as was to be expected, Tatu did not know much about Europe — it fell to me to bring him up to date! In particular about the role of the Commission, which had been described as an "observer" at the briefing in the Quai d'Orsay.

As the summit drew nearer, the picture became more and more blurred, and I had to make an appointment to meet several journalists at the conference centre on the Avenue Kléber so as to show them the space reserved for the delegations and the Commission.

I confirmed that Sicco Mansholt, accompanied by his three Vice-Presidents Raymond Barre, W. Haferkamp, and Carlo Scarascia Mugnozza, would speak there and that Bino Olivi and I would be booking a room for a press summing-up at which the Commission President would elaborate on his contribution to the summit. Like Saint Thomas, the press wanted to see, to hear, to touch; this was the only way of making it clear where the Commission stood.

These arrangements were all the more timely as the incident with Léon Zitrone, early in the evening, revealed much about the atmosphere! The facts are briefly these. I had been present when the Heads of State or Government arrived, and I had obviously paid special attention to the arrival of the Commission President being filmed by television like the others. But there was no Mansholt on the TV news. At a reception organised at the Pré Catelan ([1]), that evening by Denis Baudouin, President Pompidou's press officer, for a large number of journalists, I went up to Léon Zitrone to tell him how surprised I was.

I asked whether it was right and proper for Sicco Mansholt, President of the European Commission, to be invisible at the summit, even though he was filmed when the delegations arrived. "What do you mean, Mansholt?", he replied haughtily, "my staff did not give me a curriculum for him! I keep my files up to date, everything is in order […] I can't accept any criticism of my professionalism!" Perhaps he was right in formal terms, but his reply brought a smile to some faces and others were clearly shocked; the representative of a German broadcaster made that clear with a particularly vulgar expletive which, fortunately, went unnoticed in the general hubbub. In the circle of journalists that had formed around us, the more polite observers simply agreed that French television was what it was, and the atmosphere generated around the Commission and its role were such that there was no need for actual directives to keep it off the screen. And off we all went to the buffet table — end of story — with the great satisfaction of having had the privilege of participating in the first summit of the nine Member States to take place after the first enlargement.'

Account of Paul Collowald in *Anecdotes européennes. Témoignages réunis par Jean-Claude Eeckhout et Jacques Keller-Noëllet*, Vol. I, Jean Monnet Chair of Contemporary European History, Louvain-la-Neuve (forthcoming).

(Translated from the French)

trade negotiations and CSCE negotiations, better cooperation with the developing countries, and reinforcement of the Community institutions ([2]).

The ad hoc working party's first report in July stated that there was a large degree of convergence between the views expressed by the different partners ([3]). The final report, dated 9 September, seemed satisfactory to the Commission though still perfectible, according to a handwritten note by Émile Noël stating that the formulas adopted were a great improvement on the July document but that in the weeks ahead the Com-

mission would deploy all its powers of persuasion to help bring views on matters of substance even closer into line and thereby enable the summit to genuinely fulfil the hopes placed in it ([4]).

The summit was held as planned in Paris on 19 and 20 October, following the ratification of the accession Treaties, and the Commission was invited to attend all but the opening session, devoted to political cooperation, on the morning of 20 October. President Mansholt spoke both at the opening session and in the discussion on external relations at the end of the second morning and again on institutional questions on the second afternoon. In his general statement on the

---

[1] A famous restaurant in Paris bearing the name of its place of location, in the Bois de Boulogne.

[2] HAEU, EN 121, Commission Communication, 7 July 1972.

[3] HAEU, EN 123, Report of 17 July 1972.

[4] HAEU, EN 124, Handwritten note by Émile Noël, 7 September 1972.

The Commission at the Paris Summit, in which it was involved from the preparatory work to the conclusions. From left to right, in the foreground: Wilhelm Haferkamp, Sicco Mansholt, Émile Noël and Raymond Barre.

first day, after the Heads of State or Government had made their statements, he sketched out the three main lines of action that the summit should lay down for the years to come. He began by explaining that everything that Europeans had achieved so far was targeted first and foremost on developing the Community into a political union. He accordingly wanted to see progress towards the formation of a truly European government answerable to a Parliament elected by direct universal suffrage, and he felt that the summit should set a deadline for the elections. He then spoke of reinforcing internal solidarity, adding to the usual economic topics (social, regional, industrial, energy and environment policies) the need for a major step forwards towards a citizen's Europe with the removal of border checks, the granting of European civic rights and cooperation in education. Lastly, opening the Community up to the outside world would help it to assert its identity [1].

The Commission in general and Émile Noël in particular seem to have made a substantial contribution to the drafting of the long final communiqué [2]. There were no great surprises, but Mansholt was disappointed by the failure to reach a decision on direct universal suffrage. A seven-point introduction restated the desire of the governments of the Member States to build a democratic Europe, to reinforce the Community by establishing economic and monetary union, to narrow disparities in living conditions, to boost the development aid effort, to promote international trade, to pursue the policy of détente and to convert, before the end of the decade, all the relationships between Member States into a European Union. The sixteen-point declaration then listed a series of projects that had been under discussion for a year [3].

---

[1] HAEU, EN 382, Statement by Sicco Mansholt, 19 October 1972.

[2] HAEU, EN 931, This contains a number of drafts for the final declaration, including some rough handwritten drafts by Émile Noël. See also collective interview (Fernand Braun, Jean-Claude Eeckhout), 19 October 2004.

[3] HAEU, EN 931, Text of final declaration.

By and large, the Commission could be pleased with how the summit had gone. One eyewitness tells us that Émile Noël was very happy. His satisfaction was justified on two counts. For one thing, the Commission had been involved in the summit proceedings much more closely than in 1969, from the preparatory stage right up to the adoption of the final communiqué. For another, the declaration set out a number of projects to be undertaken within the Community context rather than outside it ([1]).

This ambitious programme prompted the Commission — even though it was due to hand over to its successors two months later, following enlargement on 1 January 1973 — to set about straightaway preparing practical proposals on the most urgent topics, some of which were to be ready by late January or early February. On 25 October it decided to set up a working party of all its directors-general, with Émile Noël in the chair ([2]). This working party on the follow-up to the summit met first on 6 November and several more times after that, and by the end of the year it had drawn up a coordinated inventory of measures to be undertaken to give effect to the summit decisions ([3]). The essential spadework had thus been done by the time the Commission of the six-member Communities handed over to the Commission of the nine-member Communities.

———

Between 1967 and 1972, then, the single Commission was constantly grappling with the need to bolster its place in the Community institutional system. With the French authorities keen to reduce its influence, it did not always enjoy adequate backing from the other five governments, and the European Parliament was not strong enough to provide serious support. So the Commission had to rely on its own resources, the quality of the work it did, its members' positive image and moral authority, and the effectiveness of its Secretary-General. It was extremely vigilant and determined to act, in particular in institutional matters and even more so in political matters, where the Treaties did not secure its status as thoroughly as in economic matters. It was energetic in guaranteeing a place at the summits of Heads of State or Government so as to avert any risk of being sidelined and in the hope of preserving the strong points of the Community system.

MARIE-THÉRÈSE BITSCH

———

([1]) Group interview (Giuseppe Ciavarini Azzi), 19 October 2004.
([2]) HAEU, EN 481, Note by Émile Noël, 27 October 1972.
([3]) HAEU, EN 481, Coordinated inventory, 24 December 1972.

Chapter 7

Franco Maria Malfatti: a presidency cut short

Both Franco Maria Malfatti's personal reputation and his role as President of the European Commission were very deeply affected by his decision to resign in March 1972, after being in office for only a year and a half, in order to participate in the parliamentary elections in Italy that spring, following the early dissolution of the Italian parliament. This decision — often interpreted as an indication of a lack of commitment to his post in Brussels — has led the majority of historians to disregard Malfatti's work at the head of the Commission or even to assess it negatively [1]. If one leaves aside the decision which brought his European tenure to an end and focuses instead on the activities of this Christian Democrat leader during the brief period in which he presided over the Commission, a less one-sided verdict emerges.

Malfatti's nomination took place at a particularly difficult time in the life of the Community, just a few months after the Hague Summit of December 1969 and the adoption of the three celebrated objectives of 'enlarging, completing and deepening' the European Community [2]. Accordingly, it was the first few months of 1970 that saw the launching of the process that would lead inter alia to the opening of negotiations for accession to the EEC, to the ECSC and to the EAEC on the part of the United Kingdom, Ireland, Denmark and Norway, to creating instruments for the funding of the Community budget and to the first proposals for monetary union and forms of closer political cooperation. Alongside these important objectives, there was the need to deal with a complex international situation characterised by increasing economic instability and by serious disagreements between western Europe and the United States, then led by Richard Nixon, with regard to the monetary and commercial relationships between the two sides of the Atlantic. Early

---

[1] See, for example, the verdict in a recent volume: Dinan, D., *Europe recast — A history of European union*, Palgrave/Macmillan, London, 2004, p. 144: 'By common consent it was Italy's turn to nominate a candidate for President in 1970 when Jean Rey stepped down. No prominent Italian wanted to go to Brussels. Eventually the government nominated Franco Malfatti, the minister for post and telegraphs. A good speaker, Malfatti liked to orate about the lamentable state of European integration. Beyond that he had little impact on the Community. He resigned as Commission President in 1972 to return to Italian politics.'

[2] On this subject, for example, see special issue 2/2003 of the *Journal of European Integration History* and Guasconi, M. E., *L'Europa tra continuità e cambiamento — Il vertice dell'Aja del 1969 e il rilancio della costruzione europea*, Storia delle relazioni internazionali, 8, Polistampa, Florence, 2004.

Franco Maria Malfatti [1]

Franco Maria Malfatti was born in Rome on 13 June 1927. As a journalist, he became involved in politics at an early age: a national delegate of the *movimento giovanile* of the DC (Christian Democrat youth movement) in 1951, he was elected to Parliament for the first time in 1958.

In addition to his parliamentary activities, he was given governmental responsibilities in 1963, when asked to join the first Moro government as Under-Secretary for Industry and Commerce, a role he also carried out in the third Moro government. He was Under-Secretary for Foreign Affairs in the second Leone government and the first Rumor government until 14 February 1969, when he was appointed Under-Secretary for the Budget.

He achieved ministerial rank for the first time in 1969 with the *partecipazioni statali* portfolio (State shareholdings in enterprises) in the second Rumor government. He was subsequently Minister for Post and Telecommunications in the third Rumor government until June 1970, at which point he was appointed President of the Commission of the European Communities, a post he held until March 1972.

In 1973 he returned to the government as Education Minister in the fourth and fifth Rumor cabinets and in the fourth and fifth governments led by Moro. Reappointed as Education Minister in the third Andreotti government, he became Finance Minister in the two following Andreotti cabinets. In the first Cossiga government (1979), he was entrusted with the Ministry of Foreign Affairs, a post he resigned for health reasons in January 1980.

In 1987 he was asked to lead the Italian delegation to the Western European Union before being appointed, in 1989, to head the political secretariat of the Christian Democrat movement.

As a member of the governing council of the Christian Democratic party, he headed its campaigning service, its cultural activities service and the Catholic publishers *Cinque Lune*. As editor of the *Il Popolo* and *La Discussione* newspapers, he published articles on the history of the Christian Democrat movement in a number of the party's journals.

He died on 10 December 1991 in Rome.

1970 saw the end of the term of office of the Commission presided over by the Belgian Jean Rey and it had been decided that the new Commission should have only nine members rather than 14. It was suggested that the presidency should go to an Italian and the names of leading politicians such as Emilio Colombo and Giuseppe Petrilli were put forward, together with that of Lionello Levi Sandri, who had served as a European Commissioner for 10 years [2]. However, the government parties vetoed each other's nominations, while some candi-

dates seemed less than keen to go to Brussels and thus be exiled for a period from Italian political life. It was only with difficulty that the candidacy of Franco Maria Malfatti won support. Born in Rome on 13 June 1927, he was 43 years of age and one of the youngest and most brilliant representatives of the Christian Democrat movement. Having entered politics very young, he was elected to Parliament for the first time in 1958. During the 1960s he was Under-Secretary of State in a number of governments. In 1969 he was appointed to head the very important *Partecipazioni Statali* ministry (State shareholdings in enterprises) in the second Rumor cabinet, subsequently serving from March 1970 in the third Rumor cabinet as Post and Telecommunications Minister, a portfolio that belies its apparently secondary rank.

---

[1] See HAEU, biographie de l'inventaire du Fonds Malfatti; www.democraticicristiani.it; www.esteri.it

[2] Both Petrilli and Levi Sandri were members of the European Commission, Levi Sandri also being its Vice-President. Emilio Colombo had played an important role not only in the negotiations for the first UK application to join the EEC but also in bringing about what would be known as the Luxembourg compromise.

Early in his political life, Malfatti was active on the left wing of the party before becoming a faithful supporter of Aldo Moro. During this period the latter was Minister for Foreign Affairs and it was he who managed to convince a hesitating Malfatti, reluctant to forsake the national political stage, to accept the Brussels post. The appointment was confirmed at the meeting in Bagnaia in late May 1970 of the foreign ministers of the Six. The new Commission came into being on the first of July. Apart from the President, the institution saw the confirmation of quite a number of other posts: Sicco Mansholt from the Netherlands, undoubtedly one of the outstanding personalities, Raymond Barre and Jean-François Deniau from France, the Belgian Albert Coppé, Germany's Wilhelm Haferkamp, but also a number of important new figures such as Albert Borschette from Luxembourg, the famous German intellectual Ralf Dahrendorf and the Italian federalist leader Altiero Spinelli. In many cases, the people Malfatti was dealing with were eminent figures highly experienced in European issues; in others, they were individuals with strong opinions, and here one cannot fail to mention the Secretary-General, Émile Noël. In tackling his new task, Malfatti was assisted by a highly experienced Italian diplomat, Renato Ruggiero, who had previously been working in the Coreper and who would work closely with the President as the head of his private office [1].

In managing the activities of the Commission, Malfatti felt that he could employ the approach that suited him best and one which was based on his experience of the Italian political world. It had indeed been a valuable apprenticeship because the Christian Democrat movement was driven by factions whose existence and behaviour required a constant striving for balance and compromise. The Christian Democrat leader was consequently often required to mediate and to show a willingness to find a compromise solution wherever possible. Early on, especially, this approach seemed to conflict with the methods adopted by his predecessors, who tended to appear before the Commission with tightly-defined proposals, rather than allowing decisions to emerge from discussions within the institution. This approach, characterised by mediation and compromise, was interpreted by some officials, and by a couple of Commissioners, as a weakness [2]. In fact, although Malfatti was reluctant to clash with other people or to confront opponents head-on, he arrived in Brussels with certain specific objectives which he sought to maintain throughout his period in office. Aware that the Community was going through a critical phase, he strove on the one hand to implement as far as possible the decisions taken at the Hague Summit in 1969 and, on the other, to defend and to strengthen where possible the role and prerogatives of the Commission, particularly in the light of the attempts by certain Member States to treat the institution as some kind of auxiliary structure with a purely technical and administrative role [3].

That Malfatti was committed to these objectives is evident, for example, from his comments on the way the press treated the work of the Council and that of the Commission [4]. His concern for the prerogatives of the Commission even led to a clash between him and one of the Commissioners, Germany's Haferkamp, whereby he took the latter to task for criticising within the Commission the nomination of an Italian official as the Commission's representative to the US government. In a personal letter sent to Haferkamp, Malfatti not only defended his choice and the selection procedure adopted but also stated 'through the nomination of our envoy to Washington, we have won a battle that began as early as the Hallstein presidency; this appointment constitutes a gesture with regard to the United States that President Nixon himself has welcomed both in public and private. I therefore expected that every

---

[1] See the interview with Renato Ruggiero, 15 July 2004.

[2] Ibid. These assessments clash with a number of unfavourable opinions expressed in 1972 by some journalists who referred to disagreements between Malfatti and European officials arising from the President's presumed desire to be accorded the privileges and formal recognition due to his 'rank'. See HAEU, FMM 6, 'Démission du Président Malfatti'.

[3] See, for example, the first declarations by Franco Maria Malfatti in HAEU, FMM 2, 'Mise en place de la Commission'.

[4] HAEU, FMM 4, 'Notes confidentielles', Letter from Bino Olivi to Renato Ruggiero, 20 September 1971.

member of the Commission would fully understand and support this approach. It is inconceivable that the Commission itself should now want to cast doubts on its own decision.' ([1]) This episode also demonstrates that Malfatti was not always inclined to follow the path of compromise if he felt that the fundamental interests of the institution over which he presided were at stake.

Given that it is impossible to analyse in detail the various aspects of Malfatti's work, one has to focus on some of the many problems with which he was confronted ([2]), of which the most important were the relations between the Community and the United States, the plans for economic and monetary union and the enlargement process.

Transatlantic relations

As far as the partnership between America and Europe was concerned, the relationship was clouded at the time Malfatti took office not only by Washington's doubts about the attitude of certain European partners and by European suspicion of the Nixon administration but also by the existence of specific economic and commercial difficulties relating to the role of the dollar and the protectionist approach of the US government. Against this background, and despite his desire to develop positive relations and full cooperation with the United States, Malfatti did not shrink from encouraging the Commission, in turn influencing the standpoint of the Council, to take a firm line on certain protectionist measures, particularly the possible adoption of the Mills Bill. Although such legislation was not adopted, protectionist tendencies on the American side be-

came more evident between late 1970 and early 1971, to the point that Malfatti decided to travel to the United States. Ruggiero undertook a prior exploratory visit, while the President called a meeting of the Foreign Ministers of the Six in order to agree a Community standpoint ([3]). Having obtained the agreement of the Six to this proposal and to his initiative of appointing a high-level Commission representative to the United States ([4]), Malfatti left in April 1971 for Washington ([5]). Discussions with the representatives of the US government proved far from easy. Although both sides had a positive view of political developments within the Community, economic issues gave rise to a series of obstacles and misunderstandings. While the Americans appeared preoccupied with their problems and annoyed by an alleged lack of flexibility on Europe's part, Malfatti emphasised that it was essential for the United States to refrain from applying protectionist provisions, which moreover were not compatible with the GATT negotiations then under way ([6]). Eventually, a 'general agreement to avoid subsequent worsening of differences' was reached. The Americans were, however, not the President's only concern. Indeed, with regard to both commercial issues and the designation of an official Commission envoy to Washington, it was important to show consideration for the Six by taking care not to exceed his powers. Especially at the level of diplomatic representation, considerable symbolism was at stake. The Commission's position had to be safeguarded without injuring the susceptibilities of each of the countries maintaining bilateral diplomatic relations with Wash-

---

([1]) HAEU, FMM 4, 'Notes confidentielles', Letter from Franco Maria Malfatti to Wilhelm Haferkamp, 24 July 1971.

([2]) It is revealing that the day after the resignation, perhaps to counter an impression of an unremarkable presidency, Commission officials wrote an assessment of Malfatti's work, highlighting in particular three fundamental aspects of his involvement. See HAEU, FMM 3, 'Réforme de la Commission', 'Note de couverture pour le dossier "Primi elementi per la cronistoria della Commissione Malfatti"', addressed to Renato Ruggiero.

([3]) HAEU, FMM 4, 'Notes confidentielles', 'Éléments pour la conversation du Président Malfatti avec les ministres des affaires étrangères sur le voyage aux États-Unis', March 1971.

([4]) The nomination of a Commission representative to the United States was the subject of difficult negotiations because of French opposition. In resolving this issue, probably at Malfatti's request, a key role was played by the Italian government, Ralf Dahrendorf and Émile Noël; see HAEU, FMM 4, 'Notes confidentielles', Note from Émile Noël, 1 March 1971, 'personal'; Note from Klaus Terfloth addressed to Renato Ruggiero, 1 April 1971.

([5]) HAEU, FMM 4, 'Notes confidentielles', 'Éléments pour la conversation du Président Malfatti avec les ministres des affaires étrangères sur le voyage aux États-Unis', March 1971.

([6]) HAEU, FMM 3, 'Réforme de la Commission', document referenced above in note 2, p. 156.

Franco Maria Malfatti (standing) taking the oath before the Court of Justice in Luxembourg on 8 July 1970. When a new Commission takes office, its members take the oath before the Court of Justice and the European Parliament. Article 157 of the EEC Treaty provides that 'When entering upon their duties, they shall give a solemn undertaking that, both during and after their term of office, they will respect the obligations arising therefrom and in particular their duty to behave with integrity and discretion as regards the acceptance, after they have ceased to hold office, of certain appointments or benefits.'
Behind Malfatti, from left to right, in the front row: Jean-François Deniau, Wilhelm Haferkamp, Sicco Mansholt, Raymond Barre, Albert Coppé; in the second row: Walter Much, Émile Noël, Albert Borschette, Altiero Spinelli and Ralf Dahrendorf.

ington. This aspect was quickly and satisfactorily settled. The Commission was able to state that 'the reception by the ambassadors of the Six was excellent and, despite certain reservations, the principle of close cooperation with the future Commission delegate had been accepted.' (¹)

Particularly on the initiative of Malfatti, the Commission subsequently sought to maintain good relations with Washington by encouraging the

Community to show a measure of 'goodwill' in respect of certain agricultural products, as had been requested by the Nixon administration (²). In adopting this approach, Malfatti had to confront the opposition of a number of Community partners including France and his own Italy. Moreover, during the summer of 1971, the

(¹) HAEU, FMM 3, document referenced above in note 2, p. 156.

(²) The positive reaction of the Nixon administration to the visit by Malfatti is confirmed by the memoirs of the Italian ambassador to Washington, Egidio Ortona; in this context, see Ortona, E., *Anni d'America*, vol. III, *La cooperazione 1967/1975*, Il Mulino, Bologna, 1989, pp. 296–297.

US government took a number of important decisions that included protectionist measures and the abandonment of the gold standard for the dollar. Within the Commission, it became Malfatti's task to draw up the initial measures to respond to the American U-turn and show a united and unanimous European front. The President took the issue extremely seriously and acted on a number of occasions to make his standpoint publicly known. Meanwhile, the Commission also acted as mediator to avoid any further deterioration of relations with Washington, a role in which Malfatti made a major contribution. He contacted the American authorities — for example, the American ambassador William Eberle [1] — or exploited his links with the Italian Foreign Minister [2]. Over the next few months, however, there was increasing dissent within the Six as to the position the Community should adopt when dealing with the United States and it was again thanks to the Malfatti Commission that it proved possible to agree a common position and thus negotiate the Smithsonian Institute agreements in December 1971 [3].

The origins of monetary union

A further problem facing Malfatti was the launching of the plan for economic and monetary union. The Commission seemed to be fully aware of what was at stake and of the need to achieve progress, while at the same time being equally aware that different and often opposing viewpoints had quickly arisen, particularly between those who feared excessive supranational powers and those who, on the contrary, regarded EMU as an ideal instrument for achieving decisive progress towards a federal Europe, not to mention the differing standpoints of the 'monetarists' and the 'economists' as to the shape of the plan. Once again, Malfatti chose to take a middle line that was subsequently adopted once disagreements within the Commission itself had been settled.

As is shown by an internal document, Malfatti's approach involved the following objectives: giving a political dimension to the discussion and defusing the tension between economists and monetarists by ensuring that economic and monetary union develop completely in parallel, seeking gradual progress and demonstrating flexibility with regard to institutional issues by postponing their definitive solution, taking specific measures initially and recognising the need for structural action [4]. Once this approach had been adopted by the Six, the Commission would then seek to overcome the differences that had emerged between Member States, most especially French hostility to radical institutional reform. Largely based on the Commission position, an agreement in principle was adopted at the Council of Ministers in February 1971, again reflecting the many discussions Malfatti conducted with leading figures of the Six and with other personalities at Community level. However, the EMU project was threatened in the spring of the same year by the monetary difficulties experienced in certain countries and by the sharp disagreement about the position of the German mark that arose between Germany, on the one hand, and France and Italy, on the other. Malfatti renewed his efforts on behalf of the Commission to avoid a permanent rupture between Community partners, seeking to find common ground that would allow the renewal of negotiations; among the points he stressed was that the obstacles facing the European Community should be seen in the context of more widespread difficulties that thus required joint effort by the Six. In fact, the Commission's analysis proved accurate because within just a few months the American decision to abandon the gold standard for the dollar merely emphasised the urgent need for a far-reaching Community initiative. As new divisions between the

[1] HAEU, FMM 4, 'Notes confidentielles', Memo for the record, 29 September 1971.

[2] HAEU, FMM 4, 'Notes confidentielles', Letter from Franco Maria Malfatti to Aldo Moro, 25 January 1972 and a letter from Franco Maria Malfatti to Giorgio Bombassei, 25 January 1972.

[3] An analysis of the problem in general may be found in James, H., *Rambouillet, 15 novembre 1975 — La globalizzazione dell'economia*, Il Mulino, Bologna, 1999, pp. 135–164.

[4] HAEU, FMM 3, document referenced above in note 2, p. 156.

Franco Maria Malfatti and his colleagues celebrate the first anniversary of the presidency.
From right to left: Franco Maria Malfatti, Renato Ruggiero, Mario Santi, Malfatti's secretary and Giampaolo Fontana Rava.
(2 July 1971)

Member States emerged, the Commission took the initiative of putting forward five principles around which to structure currency exchange rates: fixed parities for Community currencies with scope for adjustments when desired, flexible exchange rates between the Community and the outside world, measures to counter excessive outflow of capital, concerted action by central banks to support Community currencies, and im-plementation of a financial solidarity mechan-ism ([1]). Despite the failure of an initial meeting of the Council of Ministers held in mid-August, the Commission's viewpoint was eventually accepted at a subsequent meeting, held in September, of those responsible for the economy in each of the Six.

___

([1]) Ibid.

This approach facilitated the launching of negotiations with the American authorities and the signature of the Washington agreements. This result was a useful basis for the decisions to be taken by the Six during the first few months of 1972, especially after the apparent solution of the disagreements between France and Germany. On the eve of his resignation, Malfatti seemed to be relying on firming up the future currency 'snake' and he stressed in particular the need for the Six to adopt a 'monetary identity'. The position adopted here by Malfatti clearly indicates that he had a political goal in mind but his departure from the Commission meant that developments in this field could not reach maturity.

Enlargement

One final area in which Malfatti's achievements are particularly notable is that of the enlargement of the Community. In fact, the Italian statesman took office when the negotiations had barely commenced. Despite Jean Rey's urging, the Commission had been assigned only limited responsibility, reflecting the fear among a number of people that the Commission might become the conscience of the enlargement operation [1]. Under Malfatti, it therefore sought not only to provide vital technical assistance but also to emphasise to the British authorities the goodwill of the Six by supplying the Community governments with the necessary input to overcome the obstacles that rapidly arose. In this context, Malfatti's visit to London in March 1971, designed to show the Commission's goodwill with regard to the United Kingdom, was essential. Moreover, the Commission President strove to intensify his contacts with both the Commission negotiators and with the British delegation, 'links which proved significant in overcoming the many difficulties during the negotiations'. This visit also contributed greatly to resolving various technical problems such as Caribbean sugar production,

the position of New Zealand and the British contribution to the Community budget [2].

No sooner had the most crucial problems concerning the negotiations with the candidate countries been resolved than there arose the issue of the signing of the Accession Treaties, scheduled for January 1972. The Commission's objective was to participate in the official ceremony but this was vetoed by France. During the subsequent row, Malfatti tried to pressure the other five Member States and so marshal clear support for the Commission's views but his efforts met with a 'lukewarm response' from Germany, Italy and the three Benelux countries. Accordingly, the Commission had to accept 'the procedure whereby the President of the Council (would sign) on behalf of the Community'. Nevertheless, during Malfatti's speech at the ceremony, he emphasised the need to continue to examine the role of the enlarged Community and the risks it faced if it did not equip itself with more robust institutions and a coherent political plan [3]. Within a few days, Malfatti was again confronted with proof of the Commission's weakness and of the national governments' intention to retain full control over the political aspects of the European project. It was only through a confidential tip-off by Gaston Thorn that the President of the Commission learned of a meeting that had been held between the Ministers of Foreign Affairs and the Coreper representatives at which, in particular, discussions had begun on the calling of a European summit. Malfatti's annoyance and bitterness were obvious [4]. Having already been snubbed in connection with the ceremony celebrating the enlargement of the Community, this new episode demonstrated the point to which the Commission, despite the significant progress made on building the Community, risked being sidelined by governments.

---

[1] HAEU, FMM 3, document referenced above in note 2, p. 156.

[2] Guasconi, M. E., op. cit., pp. 207–208 and pp. 217–218.
[3] Document referenced above in note 2, p. 156.
[4] HAEU, FMM 4, 'Notes confidentielles', note of 3 February 1972.

Extracts from the interview with Renato Ruggiero on the subject of Franco Maria Malfatti

The meeting between Malfatti and Nixon on enlargement issues: 'At the time, we were experiencing great difficulties with the United States, the preferential-system component of a regional agreement proving a significant problem.' Malfatti recognised this immediately and we decided we had to go to Washington and talk to Nixon about it. Malfatti commented at one stage, 'Well, I think one way of getting round the problem is to launch multilateral discussions as soon as possible — and I would like to suggest that these negotiations be called the Nixon Round.' Nixon replied, 'In fact, I think it would be more accurate to call them the Malfatti Round because you were the one to suggest them.' At that point, with his usual modesty and simplicity, Malfatti said 'No, no. I think that even the most flattering outcome for me would be for them to be known as the Nixon–Malfatti Round, but certainly not the Malfatti Round.' They were actually then called the 'Tokyo Round'.

The difficulties initially experienced by Malfatti in Brussels: 'I would say, quite sincerely, that Malfatti arrived with a background in Italian politics and that at that time in particular there was a considerable difference between the way politics functioned in Italy and in other European countries. Early on, he encountered this problem of seeking a compromise, even before knowing the issues, whereas others would first want to start a discussion of the issues and then perhaps try to find a compromise [...]'

As far as Malfatti's resignation is concerned: 'I can assure you that he said "I believe it is my duty to return to Italy because, now that I have gained this experience, I believe I can help to raise awareness of the nature of the European ideals and by so doing improve politics in Italy". When the day scheduled for his press statement arrived, there were rumours that the press would attack him. The man was seized, as it were, by an attack of nerves and refused to attend. I have to say that Bino Olivi was also unwilling to go, one of his comments being "I am an Italian and therefore a target." It was therefore decided to send the deputy spokesman, a rather uncommunicative individual... This gave rise to an even worse reaction on the part of the journalists. He [Malfatti] had prepared a very good speech clearly setting out the grounds for his action. Basically, the step he took was fully justified. The President of the Commission has a political role and, as with all political roles, there are political agendas that must be borne in mind. Anyway, at that time a President of the Commission had only a 50th of the prestige he now has. And he [Malfatti] felt that his main mission, the goals I referred to earlier, had in effect already been achieved and therefore there was no longer an agenda that required him to stay on...'

Interview with Renato Ruggiero, 15 July 2004.

Grounds for his resignation

It is difficult to assess what influence the above incidents had on Malfatti's decision some weeks later to resign the post of President of the Commission in order to participate in the Italian elections. In a letter to Moro, he stated his 'profound conviction that in this way I can continue to contribute actively to the development of Europe over the years to come.' [1] The way in which Spinelli justified the choice of Malfatti in a letter he sent to the President of the socialist group of the European Parliament, Francis Vals, is revealing: he noted that 'this is indeed the weak point of our system, it is not a matter of a choice between a European political career and one in national politics. It involved a choice between completing a European term of office, amounting to the pure and simple abandonment of any subsequent political activity, or returning earlier than planned to national life'. [2].

[1] HAEU, FMM 6, 'Démission du Président Malfatti', Letter from Franco Maria Malfatti to Aldo Moro, 2 March 1972.

[2] HAEU, FMM 6, 'Démission du Président Malfatti', Letter from Altiero Spinelli to Francis Vals, 9 March 1972. Spinelli asked Vals to ensure that the socialists did not criticise Malfatti at the Strasbourg Assembly.

Extracts from press articles on the occasion of Malfatti's resignation

'He [Malfatti] is a sensitive, cultivated man, respected for his intelligence and integrity. But his apparent lack of self-confidence has undoubtedly helped to prevent him from being an effective President. His chief fault in this post has been his complete failure to provide the sort of leadership required to weld the Commission into the homogeneous, tightly knit team which it needs to be.'

The Times, 6 March 1972, p. 21.

'The Commission in Brussels has no direct contact with the European population [...]. The consequence of this, however, is that the politicians entrusted with European tasks at the top in Brussels lose contact with politics in their home countries and eventually no longer have influence anywhere. This fate, suffered for example in all its severity by the former presidents Rey and Hallstein, is one that Malfatti now intends to avoid. [...] Malfatti has made his choice: rather than sacrifice himself in Brussels and therefore sign his political death warrant, he is rushing back to Italy. In taking this step in such a pivotal year for the EEC year as 1972, he is seeking to portray it as a demonstration aimed at Europe's governments and peoples from which they should draw the lesson that the EEC cannot be allowed to remain a mere administrative superstructure but that it must instead be filled with democratic life.'

Luxemburger Wort, 6 March 1972, p. 1.
(Translated from the German)

'By leaving, Malfatti not only weakens the position of the Commission at a critical time but he also gives the most conservative wing of the French government new ammunition in its campaign to limit the powers of the Commission, just one week after the Commission's presence at the first meeting of the Foreign Ministers of the Ten [...] was considered undesirable. Malfatti will feature in the contemporary history of Europe as the individual who put the interests of his party before his responsibilities to Europe.'

De Nieuwe Gids, 8 March 1972, p. 2.
(Translated from the Dutch)

'Malfatti's behaviour is, in fact, no different from that of others who have preceded him at the head of European Community institutions; men who, when the opportunity presented itself, switched their attention back to the domestic politics of their home countries, clearly recognising that European posts, to which one is appointed rather than elected, can only be a staging post on the road to the exercise of political power. Thus far (i.e. for as long as there are no direct European elections and a democratic, parliamentary basis is accordingly lacking), Brussels continues to be known as the politicians' grave for those who remain there too long and therefore lose direct contact with their political parties and with the political ebb and flow in their home country.'

Süddeutsche Zeitung,
6 March 1972, p. 7.
(Translated from the German)

Although there were realistic grounds for the action taken, certain parts of the press criticised Malfatti, sometimes very harshly. A number of members of the European Parliament also expressed their disappointment. The resigning President therefore chose a variety of settings to defend his decision. Addressing the Assembly in Strasbourg, he did not assess the work conducted during his term in office as unsatisfactory and continued to defend, for example, the tasks and prerogatives of the Commission. He concluded by stating: 'Accordingly, I am profoundly convinced that I am not leaving behind a weakened Commission, but rather a Commission which has taken up its role as political initiator in a full and concrete manner and will, I am confident, continue to do so.' [1]

---

[1] HAEU, FMM 6, 'Démission du Président Malfatti', text of a speech given at the European Parliament.

The Malfatti presidency as seen by Emanuele Gazzo

'Under the leadership of President Malfatti, and despite very difficult circumstances, the Commission **succeeded** ([1]) in obtaining recognition of its role as an autonomous and responsible initiating force. This is clear from an objective examination of the documentation (for the first time, the Commission took a direct part in preparing the summit meeting; it was involved at all levels of political union; it provided decisive political support for enlargement; it foresaw the necessary decisions in relation to economic and monetary union; and it was the first to urge that Europe should launch its own dialogue with the United States, rather than merely drawing attention to its existence, etc.). All of the above is confirmed by the fact that the Commission, more than ever in the past, is now being attacked by those who regard it as the most serious obstacle to cosy intergovernmental cooperation dominated by the deals arranged by the so-called great powers.'

Europe, 3 March 1972.
(Translated from the French)

While Malfatti was definitely not the most notable President, it is undeniable that during a difficult stage in the development of European unity, and taking account of the brief period he was in office, he did his best to confront the many problems facing the European Community at the beginning of the 1970s and that he sought, to the extent his powers permitted and in a spirit of mediation, to defend the interests of the Commission and the goal of greater integration. An analysis of his involvement does, to some extent, give due credit to a period too often described as having had little influence on the fate of the Community.

ANTONIO VARSORI

([1]) Original emphasis.

Chapter 8

Sicco Mansholt: courage and conviction

Sicco Leendert Mansholt was one of the leading lights in the early history of the European Commission ([1]). His name will forever be linked to the common agricultural policy (CAP), which took shape in the 1960s under his vigorous stewardship. In the eyes of many, including those within the Commission's apparatus, Mansholt **was** the CAP. Besides being Agriculture Commissioner, he was Vice-President of the Commission of the then six-member Community and was even President for a while.

Besides highlighting certain episodes in his Brussels career, we should underscore his position, his contribution to building the Commission's apparatus, its working methods, the ties he kept with French and Dutch politics and, more generally, with European public opinion, his concern at the developing global situation, and the nine-month period during which he was Commission President ([2]).

From The Hague to Brussels

Before being appointed to the Commission, Mansholt spent twelve and a half years in the Dutch government as Minister for Agriculture, Fisheries and Food Distribution. During this period, from 1945 to 1957, he was a key member of successive cabinets. He was largely responsible for the growing prosperity of the rural population in the post-war period. The socialist Mansholt knew agriculture inside out. He was the son of a farmer and, before becoming minister, managed a farm for several years. While he was minister, agriculture moved from production shortfalls to export-led abundance. Mansholt became known at the same time as an advocate of the European ideal. In 1950 he proposed creating a 'green pool' to rationalise west European agriculture on a supranational basis.

He was well known as a dynamic and creative organiser and for his strength of conviction. Although he managed to modernise Dutch agriculture in an exemplary way, his policy was contested. His Cabinet colleagues reproached him for overregulating the agricultural market, making farmers dependent on price guarantees and

---

([1]) A major biography on Mansholt has been published since editing this chapter: Merriënboer, J., *Mansholt: een biografie*, Boom, Amsterdam, 2006.

([2]) Mansholt's key role in the CAP is considered at pp. 317–337.

subsidies, even though this was the case in virtually all the industrialised countries. His Social-Democrat friend, Prime Minister Willem Drees, regularly got angry with him as he noticed with regret that domestic agricultural policy had created enormous export surpluses and become 'terribly costly'. When the European Commission came into being in January 1958, he had no objection to Mansholt leaving The Hague for Brussels. One day he said to his Economic Affairs Minister Jelle Zijlstra: 'What a relief! We've got rid of him.' Zijlstra replied: 'What do you mean, rid of him, you've got another think coming, he'll come through the back door'. (¹) Zijlstra meant that in Brussels Mansholt would do all he could to carry out his agricultural plans at European level. Which is what happened.

Despite Drees's and Zijlstra's scepticism, Mansholt was the ideal Dutch candidate for the post of European Commissioner. A number of eminent members of his party, the Dutch Labour Party (Partij van de Arbeid — 'PvdA'), even tried to get him appointed first Commission President. Alfred Mozer, who was later to be his chief of staff and who cultivated broad international contacts, approached Chancellor Adenauer about him, but Adenauer said no.

As the Chancellor said, 'A farmer and a socialist, that is too much for one man (²).' The highly influential Jean Monnet, after playing the Mansholt card (³), plumped for a German candidate (⁴). Even his own government refused to back him. This was due to the position of the negotiations in the Benelux context. As it seemed that the Commission would be based in Brussels, it was not clear that Benelux could also ask for the Commission presidency.

When the foreign affairs ministers met in Paris in January 1958, the German Walter Hallstein was appointed President. According to State Secretary Ernst van der Beugel, standing in for the unwell Minister Luns, he was the man for the job. The die was cast but, according to van der Beugel, Mansholt had caused problems as he had his eyes on the presidency whatever the Cabinet in The Hague thought (⁵). His close collaborator, Jaap van der Lee, who had known Mansholt for some while, testified much later that Mansholt was not the right candidate for the President's job, at the beginning at least (⁶). He was flamboyant, impatient and sometimes not very diplomatic, which led to conflicts.

Creating the apparatus

On 16 January 1958 the EEC Commission held its first meeting at the château of Val-Duchesse in Brussels. Everything had to be created from scratch. A working party was set up to allocate the tasks among the Commissioners. It consisted of Commissioners Malvestiti, Mansholt, Marjolin, Rey and von der Groeben. In sharing out the portfolios, it had to decide whether to follow the High Authority's loose structure or to give each Commissioner a very precise task. A compromise formula was chosen, with each Commissioner dealing with several fields while being in charge of one specific sector (⁷). Another working party of three Commissioners — Mansholt, Marjolin and von der Groeben — was also set up to prepare a work programme. This working party was also asked to consider the status and importance of the *cabinets* (⁸).

For his own *cabinet*, Mansholt chose Jaap van der Lee and Georges Rencki. Van der Lee had been his principal adviser while he was minister

(¹) Interview with Jelle Zijlstra, in Harryvan, A. G., van der Harst, J. and van Voorst, S. (eds), *Voor Nederland en Europa — Politici en ambtenaren over het Nederlandse Europabeleid en de Europese integratie, 1945–1975*, Instituut voor Nederlandse Geschiedenis, The Hague/Boom, Amsterdam, 2001, p. 347 (Horizonreeks, 2).

(²) Ein Bauer und ein Sozialist, das ist des Guten zuviel.

(³) See Chapter 1, p. 47.

(⁴) Interview with Jacob Jan van der Lee, in Harryvan, A. G. et al., op. cit., p. 73.

(⁵) Interview with Ernst Hans van der Beugel, in Harryvan, A. G. et al., op. cit., p. 53.

(⁶) Interview with Jacob Jan van der Lee, in Harryvan, A. G. et al., op. cit., p. 73.

(⁷) Interview with Jean Flory, 3 December 2003.

(⁸) IISG, AM 104, Resumé Jacob Jan van der Lee, 18 January 1958.

in the Netherlands and showed enormous interest in the construction of Europe. He became Mansholt's first *chef de cabinet*, but only for a short period. Rencki was number two in the *cabinet*. He had been recommended by Robert Schuman, who was President of the European Movement at the time and therefore indirectly responsible for its international secretariat for youth, the European Youth Campaign, to which Rencki belonged. The choice of Rencki, a Frenchman of Polish origin, was particularly interesting. In making this choice, Mansholt was the only one of the first batch of commissioners to appoint a non-compatriot to his *cabinet* ([1]). Mansholt considered that, given the crucial position of the French farming sector, Rencki was key to setting up a European policy ([2]).

In addition to his cabinet, which fulfilled a political function, Mansholt tried to appoint the best people in his DG, the Agriculture DG (DG VI). He had green fingers, so to speak. Louis Rabot, whom Mansholt knew from the 'green pool' negotiations and who had enjoyed a good reputation in the field of agriculture, was named Director-General. Other noteworthy figures included Berend Heringa, from the Dutch Ministry of Agriculture, and the German von Verschuer. Mansholt thus surrounded himself with devoted and competent fellow workers. DG VI occupied from the outset a leading position in the Commission's apparatus.

As early as April 1958, van der Lee let it be known that he was seeking another post within the Commission. He had come to Brussels as Mansholt's trusty right-hand man but he now wanted to cut loose from his boss and make his own way. Commissioner Robert Lemaignen, who held the portfolio for the associated countries, offered van der Lee a directorship in DG VIII, which he readily accepted. Very quickly, Mansholt had to find another *chef de cabinet*. The PvdA proposed Alfred

Sicco Mansholt was a cartoonist's dream. No doubt the responsibilities he held within the Commission contributed to fuelling their eloquence, but Mansholt's physical appearance and his legendary pipe were also a source of inspiration.

Mozer, who had put in a good word in his favour with Adenauer. Mozer had had a hectic life and a chequered career. Of German Jewish origin, he had fled the Nazis in the 1930s to become a Dutch citizen. He had played a key role in the European Movement and was at the time international secretary of the PvdA. Van der Lee, who left DG VI, was not at all in agreement with the choice of Mozer and tried to dissuade Mansholt in April and May 1958. According to van der Lee, Mozer was too tarnished politically. He wrote to Mansholt: ' Mozer is himself a politician and used to considerable independence. He is not methodical and is not used to working with a big administration. He would be happy in this post only if he could continue to use and develop his contacts. This would rapidly lead to misunderstandings. He does not know the Community's economic issues and would not be firm enough in

([1]) Interview with Jacob Jan van der Lee, 15 December 2003.
([2]) Interview with Jean Flory, 3 December 2003.

Mansholt on the subject of the three institutions

'I should like to express myself on the subject of the construction of all the bodies [...]. The final decisions are taken by the Council. It can therefore be said to express the will of the Community. Secondly, there is the Commission, the executive body. It has to take the initiative [...]. I would call that the intelligence. Thirdly, there is Parliament, which has a supervisory function: it should be the conscience.'

Speech given by Sicco Mansholt at the general meeting of the Netherlands district chamber of the Netherlands–German Chamber of Commerce, Scheveningen on 12 September 1958, p. 6, IISG, AM, 147. Speeches, 1958–1971. (Translated from the Dutch)

managing the study of economic problems, the main job of your Cabinet.' Van der Lee feared that Mozer's appointment could weaken Mansholt's position in the Commission, given the background of the other *chefs de cabinet*, 'all young people with great experience in the economic and administrative fields'. 'Your cabinet, he continued, can only give you modest political support. You need someone to chat with in confidence and who knows you well enough to speak frankly and without hesitation on the basis of this relationship of confidence about things which are not right. You need someone who will not take you too seriously and can from time to time take the risk of making fun of you.' According to van der Lee, Mozer was not the man for the job (¹). To boot, he had a linguistic handicap: he did not have good enough French or English (²).

Instead of the socialist Mozer, van der Lee thought it wiser to appoint a *chef de cabinet* from a Catholic background. It would be better for Mansholt's future career. For what would happen to Mansholt after his first term of office at the Commission would depend on the support he would receive from the Catholic People's Party KVP, the largest Dutch political party after the PvdA. 'If you want to be Prime Minister, you must be acceptable to the KVP (Katholieke Volkspartij) (³).' Van der Lee proposed among the competent young Catholics the names of Charles Rutten from the Foreign Ministry and Wim van Slobbe from the Economic Affairs Ministry. Rencki, who had just been appointed, would become the third, instead of the second, most important man in the *cabinet*. Van der Lee was not in agreement but saw no other solution. He wrote of Rencki: 'I have a lot of respect for his work but I don't think it is possible to keep him as number two in the *cabinet* given the political traditions in the Netherlands (⁴).'

Van der Lee sized up Mansholt psychologically: 'Fortunately, the outside world does not see how difficult it is to work with you. Working with you means being on the ball the whole time because you are extremely intelligent and physically tougher than anyone I know. When you have the wrong ideas in your head and they have been there for a long time, it takes a very careful man to change your mind (⁵).' Van der Lee pointed out that methodical governances were alien to Mansholt. 'As befits a politician, you work on impulse and political conviction, and it is to your credit that you are more competent than anyone in the field for which you are responsible. However, your logic is essentially "home-made". It is to your disadvantage that you do not have any academic qualifications or the discipline of systematic thought. So I honestly believe anyone wishing to be independent and not wishing to

(¹) IISG, AM 205, Letter from Jacob Jan van der Lee to Sicco Mansholt, 23 April 1958.
(²) Interview with Willem-Jan van Slobbe, 6 January 2004.

(³) IISG, AM 205, Letter from Jacob Jan van der Lee to Sicco Mansholt, 9 May 1958.
(⁴) Ibid.
(⁵) IISG, AM 205, Letter from Jacob Jan van der Lee to Sicco Mansholt, 23 April 1958.

belittle himself (Mozer) cannot be your *chef de cabinet*. You need a kind of intelligent slave and, above all, someone systematic' (¹). Van der Lee was no doubt thinking of the kind of co-worker he was when he arrived in 1950 to join Mansholt.

Despite these warnings from within his inner circle, Mansholt finally opted for Mozer. This appointment was well received within the PvdA, with which Mansholt maintained close links. Mozer was also known for his networking (he knew everybody, even the Pope), his speeches, his humour and his easy contacts with the press. He would remain *chef de cabinet* until 1970, when Sjouke Jonker succeeded him. The Catholic economist Wim van Slobbe became second-in-charge, and Rencki was appointed head of division for relations with the agricultural sector in DG VI, but he would work directly with Mansholt until 1968 (²).

The Commission moved into a six-storey building in rue Belliard in Brussels. To begin with, the Commissioners and civil servants were somewhat disoriented: the nine-member Commission met in a room on the first floor that was too small. There was a table and a few chairs. There were no secretaries yet, and no paper and pencils. Mansholt tells how he called a lift boy, gave him 20 francs and sent him to the nearest shop to buy the first office supplies. Mansholt looked around his colleagues: 'Robert Marjolin, I know; Hallstein [...] I am not sure who he is; Jean Rey already almost an accomplice; Petrilli the Italian, a total stranger, Émile Noël, the first Secretary-General, [...] an astonishing man: never gives way. [...] nine men around a table with a huge job to accomplish (³).'

(¹) IISG, AM 205, Letter from Jacob Jan van der Lee to Sicco Mansholt, 23 April 1958.
(²) Interview with Georges Rencki, 13 January 2004.
(³) Mansholt, S., *La crise — Conversations avec Janine Delaunay*, Stock, Paris, 1974, pp. 86–87.

Working together in the Commission in 1958

'In the large six-storey building we chose two rooms on the first floor, very small ones. Hallstein's habit was to meet in rooms that were too small, which made Jean Rey moan. […]

We had to work out procedures, prepare and install an administration, find technical staff. We thus had the time to get to know each other. Our families were not yet with us. There were no secretaries, so no temptation to show off in front of staff, nine men face to face, with a major task to perform. Despite our past experience, we were very confident, very optimistic.

We lived together, lunched, dined and spent entire evenings discussing all the problems. A small political team is extraordinary, quite ideal for working well. Ten years later the Commission had become a vast administration where Parkinson's law held sway. But I always sought to maintain small nuclei or teams and I got them together in an office at a round table every week. I had real leaders — five, eight, ten, no more — to discuss issues that really were very complex. Politics is now a matter of teamwork, we have to live close together, share our thoughts, develop ideas, however absurd they may be. And discuss them, influence each other.'

Mansholt, S., *La crise — Conversations avec Janine Delaunay*, Stock, Paris, 1974, pp. 86–87. (Translated from the French)

Stresa: the Commission consolidates

Although the Treaty of Rome left it up to the Commission to shape the future agricultural policy, it had, before setting about its task, to consult Member States at an agricultural meeting of the Six. Mansholt and DG VI went about this task energetically. The intention was first to hold the meeting in Rome but, on a proposal from Germany, it was moved to Stresa on Lake Maggiore in northern Italy. This was a much more pleasant place as the meeting was held in midsummer, from 3 to 11 July 1958. Everybody who was anybody in the world of agriculture was present. The six Member States but also the Commission had trouble keeping down the numbers in their delegations. The Commission feared that the budget would be overrun and made it known in good time to the Italian government that it was not ready to assume the extra expenditure ([1]). Between the various discussions and meetings of working parties there was also time to relax. Mansholt managed to put on a show of his own. To impress the female guests, the German civil servant von Stülpnagel tried frequently but without any success to do waterskiing. Mansholt had never ever put on skis but he too tried. At the second attempt, he got up, remained upright and skied in wide circles around the lake. He was loudly applauded on his return. This earned him respect and contributed subtly to strengthening his position ([2]).

What the conference actually achieved was highly significant in terms of content. The Commission, the Member States and the agricultural organisations which were invited as observers at Mansholt's insistence ([3]) reached an agreement on the outline of a European agricultural policy and the procedures to be followed. Their aim was to set up a common market for agricultural produce and a production modernisation policy.

Mansholt's power was further bolstered by the ease with which he was learning French, the Commission's lingua franca. When he arrived in Brussels, he could hardly put two words together in French but did not consider that to be a problem. 'When French had to be spoken, he spoke French and that didn't bother him,' said van Slobbe ([4]). After three months at the Commission, he was managing to express himself adequately. His colleagues were impressed. As one of them said, 'He really murders spoken French, but it is fluent ([5]). But he continues to make mistakes, sometimes very funny ones. One day he told a colleague: "I'm getting by with my

Mansholt as Commissioner

'He was surrounded by a small circle of close colleagues with whom he developed and tested his policy through constant discussion. He delegated really well and left them substantially free to put the policy into practice. It was really fine teamwork.'

Van der Lee, J. J., *Mijn herinneringen aan Sicco Mansholt*, S and D 10, 1995, p. 491, IISG, AM. (Translated from the Dutch)

French, it is just the sex that's causing me problems." Of course, it was the gender of French words he meant.' ([6]) He sometimes used French deliberately — e.g. at the Council — to be able to say, if the negotiations were not going his way: 'Sorry, that's not quite what I meant to say' or 'Sorry, I didn't quite understand' ([7]). On the other hand, according to Rencki, some misunderstandings arose with the farmers because Mansholt often replied 'd'accord', meaning 'I agree' when he really meant 'I understand' ([8]).

Mansholt was known for his heavy work rate and for his tireless desire to explain the CAP to his colleagues, to ministers, to farmers and to consumers. He had a mission to accomplish ([9]). He travelled from Schleswig-Holstein to Sicily, discussing the issues in depth and never fearing to clash with those who did not share his views. He had a small group of confidants at the Commission with whom he outlined the policy around a table specially designed for the purpose: in DG VI these were above all Rabot, Heringa ([10]), von Verschuer ([11]) and Rencki ([12]). There were 100 or

---

([1]) PV 21 EEC, Commission, 19 June 1958.

([2]) Molegraaf, J. H., *Boeren in Brussel — Nederland en het Gemeenschappelijk Europees Landbouwbeleid, 1958–1971*, Proefschrift Universiteit Utrecht, 1998, p. 46.

([3]) Interview with Georges Rencki, 13 January 2004.

([4]) Interview with Willem-Jan van Slobbe, 6 January 2004.

([5]) Interview with Jean Flory, 3 December 2003.

([6]) Interview with Jean-Claude Séché, 8 June 2004.

([7]) Recollection by a member of the Marjolin cabinet interviewed in January 2004.

([8]) Interview with Georges Rencki, 13 January 2004.

([9]) Interview with Willem-Jan van Slobbe, 6 January 2004.

([10]) Interview with Johannes Westhoff, 7 January 2004.

([11]) As assistant to Rabot, von Verschuer was a permanent member of the 'round table', which was joined by the relevant director and head of division depending on the topic under discussion (Note from Helmut von Verschuer to Michel Dumoulin, 3 September 2005).

([12]) He was there firstly as member of the *cabinet* and then because of his relations with the farming world (Note from Georges Rencki to Michel Dumoulin, 31 August 2005).

so meetings between 1958 and 1961, 36 of them in 1959 alone ([1]). Mansholt delegated easily: Mozer and van Slobbe often took part in the Commission's meetings when he was abroad. He maintained good contacts with the press and sometimes 'flew a kite' to test proposals ([2]). His iron constitution enabled him to stand the heat longer than his negotiating colleagues at marathon meetings, for example on cereal prices, and thus obtain key results in the small hours. Mansholt could also get very angry and impatient. Ferrandi described him as 'this bull-necked Dutch giant who went red in the face very quickly, very impulsive and very authoritarian' ([3]). He sometimes feigned anger to force the pace and move forward in discussions that had stalled. He regularly used the system of linked transactions to gain the acceptance of certain countries for agricultural proposals. All this was very time consuming and energy consuming and cost a lot of money. Agriculture swallowed up the bulk of meeting time and of the Community budget, especially at that time. Mansholt was the spider in the web.

Mansholt and France

In shaping the CAP, Mansholt could count on the support of France and the Netherlands while resistance came from Germany. Solid links were created between Mansholt and the French Agriculture Minister, Edgar Pisani ([4]). Despite their convergence of interest, there were regular clashes between the French government and Mansholt. The de Gaulle government's opposition to a supranational Europe exasperated him, whereas Paris criticised the Commission Vice-President for meddling in the domestic policy of the Member States, in this case France. At times this gave rise to serious controversy, for example during a speech Mansholt made in Rotterdam in May 1962,

openly criticising President de Gaulle, and the French government and political system. He emphasised the limited powers of the French parliament 'which is more like the *ancien régime* than a democratic structure'. As for the political union project, this was the period of the negotiations on the Fouchet Plan. Mansholt said that de Gaulle's ideas on the subject 'were designed in reality to minimise, if not destroy, the integration process with a political coronation'. He also expressed an opinion on the accession negotiations with the United Kingdom. He himself supported UK accession and wondered whether French policy in this regard was defined by economic considerations or rather by France's desire to become a nuclear power, this latter assumption being the preferred one.

Paris was 'not amused' by Mansholt's intervention. The French Foreign Minister, Maurice Couve de Murville, let it be known by letter that he was very disturbed by the remarks addressed to France. He felt that the statements, coming from a member of the Commission, 'were quite serious' but he wanted to avoid a diplomatic incident.

In his response to Couve, Mansholt defended himself by saying that 'as a member of the Commission, I'm not bound by a national government, that of the Netherlands. I'm not a civil servant of any government [...] but, as a citizen of my country, I feel I have the right to speak my mind when a political development which affects my country and my fellow citizens is up for discussion. I am not criticising France's Head of State or its government but a concept with which my country and my fellow citizens will have to live in the future. In my accepting this post within the European Commission, I and my compatriots are convinced that we haven't lost the right to say what we think about a project which will be crucial for the future of more than one country in Europe'. ([5])

([1]) Note from Georges Rencki to Michel Dumoulin, 31 August 2005.

([2]) van Merriënboer, J. C. F. J., 'Het avontuur van Sicco Mansholt', http://www.ru.nl/contents/pages/22864/mansholt_.pdf, p. 13 (article published in *Politieke Opstellen*, Nos 15–16, pp. 136–168).

([3]) Interview with Jacques Ferrandi, 28 and 29 May 2004.

([4]) Interview with Paul Collowald, 2 December 2003.

([5]) IISG, AM 113, Letter from Maurice Couve de Murville to Sicco Mansholt, 8 June 1962, and Sicco Mansholt's reaction.

Mansholt on the organisation of the Commission in agricultural matters

'On 14 January last year a decision was taken concerning a common mechanism for the most important products, and on 1 August it became operational. [...] I believe that our successes can be put down to two main reasons: firstly, from the outset we have kept the industry, farmers' organisations and manufacturers informed. And we have had regular discussions with consultative bodies that include professional organisations. We have involved national administrations in our activities [...] We can draw conclusions for the future from our experiences on these two fronts: national administrations and industry must be integrated into the process of devising the Community policies.

We have set up management committees. This is a nice name but they don't manage anything, they can only give an opinion. Opinions that we don't need to heed. If we do not follow an opinion, they can appeal to the Council against our decisions, but all that is secondary. What is important is that we never take decisions without consulting these committees. We discuss matters with experts — eggs, pork or poultry — and that gives the impression that they cannot be manipulated but that the common policy has been devised jointly by national administrations and the Commission.

One thing worries me. We have a good relationship with those who produce and administer but it is difficult to establish the same links with those who consume. [...] The big question of the day is how consumers can make their voices heard. In my opinion, that is possible only through better parliamentary representation.'

Rede uitgesproken door de heer dr. S. L. Mansholt te Leuven op 22 January 1963, pp. 10–11, IISG, AM, 149. Stukken betreffende gehouden toespraken 1958–1971. (Translated from the Dutch)

Mutual irritation escalated during the summer of 1965, after de Gaulle showed his repugnance at the growing power of the Commission — and of Mansholt and Hallstein in particular — in the field of farm funding. As a reprisal, he recalled the French Representative to the Council for six months. This was the period of the 'empty chair' crisis. Mansholt felt that de Gaulle's intervention was a bad thing for the Community and showed his displeasure at the French attitude at several times and places. Delivering a speech in July 1965, he warned that nobody should be allowed to block European unification as that would be 'the greatest act of destruction in Europe since Hitler' [1]. The French were furious. Putting de Gaulle on a par with Hitler was unacceptable.

But Mansholt did not give up. In September 1965 he went to The Hague and made direct contact with the Dutch government to ask it to adhere strictly to a hard and consistent policy and not yield to French demands. He was worried about Belgium, where minister Spaak seemed to be quite receptive to the wishes of the French. On the other hand, the Netherlands had to demonstrate a consistent attitude designed to produce total unanimity among the five Member States. According to Mansholt, such an attitude would end in an independent decision being taken by the Five 'not only when a majority vote was provided for but also when unanimity was required'. He stressed that the Commission's lawyers were convinced that such decisions by the Five would be legal 'as France was violating the Treaty by her absence'. The Dutch government shared Mansholt's opinion, of course, but considered that

---

[1] IISG, AM 452 (1966), Klein, W., *De Super-Boer Sicco Leendert Mansholt*, Elsevier, 29 January 1966, p. 21.

the European Commission was being too unsubtle in the circumstances. Prime Minister Joseph Cals said that the 'empty chair' policy was above all a political problem, and legal issues which Mansholt was highlighting played a secondary role. Joseph Luns had doubts that a united front of the Five was possible, given Spaak's position [1]. But it was decided that 'tactically one should avoid giving the impression that the Netherlands was ready to sign any kind of compromise' [2]. This was not the first and certainly not the last time that Mansholt would visit government representatives in The Hague. After the talks they often dined together in the Royal restaurant in the city centre.

Mansholt's trips to The Hague did not go unnoticed. In November 1965 State Secretary Leo De Block wrote a letter in which he said that 'leading officials in France have stated maliciously that Mansholt has regularly exchanged ideas with the Dutch government on the problem relating to the EEC crisis. This is seen as a sign that the Dutch member of the Commission is not rising above party relationships as he ought to be and as the Netherlands considers that a Commission member ought to do as one of his main duties'. Although De Block added that the French should be feeling guilty given the close ties between Brussels and Paris (for example, the relations between Hirsch and Chatenet), he considered that Mansholt should remain very careful in future. De Block wished that the next exchange of views should take place in a discreet place, certainly not in the Royal restaurant, and that those taking part would be asked not to mention this meeting [3].

Occasionally Mansholt tried to influence The Hague. The contrary was rarely the case. According to Mansholt, Dutch governments had always been very correct from 1958 onwards: 'They never put pressure on me. Sometimes they

approached me to draw my attention to a particular issue but I considered that normal. When a matter didn't concern me directly, I always addressed them to my colleague who was responsible' [4]. Mansholt had the feeling that his independent attitude increased his power within the Commission but also within the Council. He was annoyed by certain colleagues who would seek instructions in their country's capital. He thought this was bad for the Commission's image [5].

In 1967 Jean Rey succeeded Hallstein as the new Commission President. Mansholt who was the main candidate of the Benelux countries and even acceptable to the Germans encountered opposition from de Gaulle. France even wanted Mansholt to go at the same time as Hallstein, but the Dutch government was against this. Mansholt would remain Vice-President thanks to a sleight of hand: unlike in the case of the Merger Treaty, four Vice-Presidents would be appointed instead of three [6].

In July and August 1968 a conflict erupted between Mansholt and Debré, who had just been appointed Foreign Minister by de Gaulle. The new President Rey was to play a thankless role in this conflict. The starting point was an interview by Mansholt on the meaning of the elections organised in France in June. De Gaulle had won them but only at the second round (the bulk of the farming vote had gone to Lecanuet, his Christian Democrat opponent) [7]. On that occasion, Mansholt said that for years there had been the divergences of opinion between France and the other Member States on the structure of Europe's future (a Europe of nation States or a federal Europe) and on majority voting in the Council as regards the United Kingdom's accession and on the level of democracy in the future Community. Mansholt felt that, as long as key political disputes

[1] IISG, AM 120 (1965–66), Kort verslag van informele bijeenkomst in het Kabinet van de Minister-President, 14 September 1965.
[2] IISG, AM 120, Letter from Leo De Block to Sicco Mansholt, 9 November 1965.
[3] Ibid.

[4] Mansholt, S., *De Crisis*, Contact, Amsterdam, 1975, pp. 41–42. (Translated from the Dutch)
[5] Ibid.
[6] Van Merriënboer, J. C. F. J., op. cit., p. 19.
[7] Interview with Georges Rencki, 13 January 2004.

were not ironed out, there was little real hope of establishing quickly a united political Europe. De Gaulle's election victory would result in the same form of government as before, which Mansholt deplored.

Debré reacted as if he had been bitten by a snake. In a letter to Rey he wrote: 'Vice-President Mansholt has said unacceptable things as a Commission Vice-President and has no right to pass judgment on the domestic policy of a Member State.' Mansholt, in Debré's eyes, had acted in a partisan manner. 'His words were seriously offensive to national sentiment as Gaullism is an expression of our gratitude to a man who represents not only our honour, our freedom but also the honour and freedom of Europe. He also symbolises the patriotic sentiment of the French people which benefits the whole of Europe. By what authority does the Vice-President condemn millions of voters who have expressed confidence in General de Gaulle?' ([1])

Rey was in a difficult situation. He wanted to reassure Debré without disowning his colleague Mansholt. He finally wrote a letter which satisfied neither of them. He replied to Debré: 'I can of course understand that the French government did not appreciate the statements of my colleague Vice-President Mansholt on the subject of French politics. For years, Mr Mansholt has been making such statements from time to time. They have created worries for me and for my predecessor.' He pointed out that Mansholt did not speak for the Commission but in his own name, that he alone was responsible for his statement and that 'our Commission refrains from making statements on the domestic policy of Member States'. He added that 'Mr Mansholt is an energetic and combative political figure and we have benefited from his dynamism in integrating Europe while we have had to put up patiently with certain disadvantages'. Rey added that he did not understand the furious reaction, as the Commission had recently satisfied certain French demands ([2]).

Mansholt was very disappointed with Rey's answer to Debré. He wrote to the Commission President that he was not speaking personally: 'I have enough sense of irony to put up with an attack by an exchange of judgments on a member of the Commission between the Commission President and a minister in one of the Member States. That final judgment remains on the whole "satisfactory": difficult but not exactly blameworthy.' He thought it unfair that Rey had accepted Debré's interpretation both as to his interference in domestic policy and to his impartiality and neutrality. 'In accepting Debré's views on the subject of the rights of Members of the Commission, you brought this organisation down to the level desired by the French government.' Finally, Mansholt was astonished that Rey had alluded to certain identical situations which had arisen under his predecessor Hallstein: 'I had disagreed with Hallstein on the advisability of this or that statement but never on the right to express a political opinion.' ([3])

In a long reply to Debré, Mansholt also denied having meddled in domestic politics: he wanted to draw conclusions on the foreign policy of one of the Member States concerning Europe. Mansholt felt that, as a Member of the Commission, he also had to be impartial, of course, but that did not mean remaining neutral: 'to serve the interests of Europe, it is essential to express political opinions. In its absolute independence, the Commission itself will judge what that meant' ([4]).

This was clearly not the reply that Debré was expecting. In a final polemical outburst, he wrote to Mansholt: 'I read your letter with surprise. I was expecting, if not an apology then at least an expression of regret. I have taken cognisance of your lengthy explanations: [...] which explain nothing. If I were to reply to you at similar length, I would have to state certain truths which might be hurtful. I prefer not to do so but simply to say that I fully stand by the very moderate terms of my letter to President Rey.' ([5])

([1]) IISG, AM 99, Letter from Michel Debré to Jean Rey, 8 July 1968.
([2]) IISG, AM 99, Reply from Jean Rey to Michel Debré, 15 July 1968.

([3]) IISG, AM 99, Letter from Sicco Mansholt to Jean Rey, 30 July 1968.
([4]) IISG, AM 99, Letter from Sicco Mansholt to Michel Debré, 30 July 1968.
([5]) IISG, AM 99, Letter from Michel Debré to Sicco Mansholt, 20 August 1968.

The conflict became more bitter and questions were put in the European Parliament. Things never improved between Mansholt and Debré. With General de Gaulle the position was less clear. He would have agreed to meet Mansholt, this 'Batavian' for whom he had a degree of respect ([1]).

The limits to growth

A very difficult period began for Mansholt. The success he had achieved during the first 10 years in setting up the CAP turned against him now. These difficulties were the result of agricultural surpluses caused by high prices, with the substantial expenditure which that entailed, and also of monetary instability (revaluation and devaluation) — whereas prices were expressed in units of account.

Mansholt understood that changes were needed. To reform the policy on a structural basis, he drew up in December 1968 a detailed plan to lower prices, modernise farms and provide aid for the worst-hit farmers. However, this plan came up against resistance from part of the farming population in the Member States and, since he lacked support from the governments, he was obliged to adapt certain of his proposals. In May 1971 the plan was accepted but it did not manage to put an end to the surpluses owing to the opposition of governments to lower prices and reductions in the areas under cultivation ([2]). For Mansholt this was not about to be a very happy period. He had health problems. Moreover, he was more and more 'worried by the future of the global economy and the European economy' and was wondering what type of growth should be promoted in future. On top of his older concerns about the demographic explosion, food shortages, pollution and future energy shortage, there was now the global analysis by the MIT (Massachusetts Institute of Technology), 'The limits to growth' drafted under the editorship of

D. L. Meadows for the Club of Rome, of which he was a member. He fully shared its conclusions and those of Professor Tinbergen, winner of the Nobel Prize for Economics, and other Dutch socialist leaders.

Growth had to be made more compatible with energy and food supply limits and with natural environmental resources. Mansholt felt that this was a challenge for the Commission. In 1972 he wrote a long and detailed letter to President Malfatti in which he asked that these issues be the theme of the Commission's political testament when it left office on 1 January 1973. The testament should emphasise the key problems of the day in the context of North–South relations and demographic growth. He stressed that the per capita consumption of raw materials and energy in the industrialised countries was around 25 times more than the average. He wrote that society could no longer be based on growth, at any rate material growth. In his eyes, it was vital to reduce consumption of material goods ([3]). The authorities also needed to intervene on a grand scale to provide tax incentives to firms to provide longer-life goods and avoid waste ([4]). 'If we want to meet the fundamental demand of justice, our economy should develop in such a way as to give everybody the same opportunities. In so doing, sharing out raw materials and capital goods between the public and private sectors, can no longer be avoided. Moreover, planning should be geared to ensuring that goods and services are produced using a minimum of raw materials and energy. To compensate for the decline in prosperity, more care should be devoted to intellectual and cultural growth ([5]).' Instead of gross national product (GNP), Mansholt proposed henceforth using GNH (gross national happiness). The Commission should make a proposal for a European development plan and a new system of production (CR: clean and recycling) exempt from VAT and based on a recycling economy.

---

[1] Note from Georges Rencki to Michel Dumoulin, 31 August 2005.
[2] See above, Chapter on agricultural policy, pp. 333–337.

[3] IISG, AM 100, Letter from Sicco Mansholt to Franco Malfatti, 14 February 1972.
[4] Ibid.
[5] Ibid.

Mansholt closed his letter to Malfatti by wishing that they devote that last year to these issues in order to come up with fully thought-out proposals [1].

Mansholt's letter did not have the desired effect. Reactions within the College of Commissioners were lukewarm, even hostile. The most detailed commentary was by Vice-President Raymond Barre, Commissioner for Economic and Financial Affairs, who severely criticised Mansholt's ideas [2]. He downplayed the seriousness of the problems identified and warned against exaggeration and dramatisation. Barre noticed furthermore that his colleague had not taken account of 'the interaction between social progress and technological development', which could remove the perceived threats. Barre also wondered to what extent the extrapolations made by Mansholt on the basis of current conditions and of his vision of the future situation could be extended. He had strong doubts, for example, about the pollution issue. Regarding energy stocks, there were grounds for being reasonably optimistic, according to Barre. He drew attention to the coal and oil reserves that were available and to the solutions offered by fast-breeder reactors and solar energy. There were certainly dangers — water, air quality, food, raw materials and even vital living space — but nowhere in the world was there a threat of inevitable disaster [3]. By dint of this criticism, which had support from various quarters, Barre dealt a severe blow to the Mansholt Plan [4].

Another reaction came from Altiero Spinelli, Commissioner for Industry, Technology and Scientific Affairs. Spinelli was more moderate than Barre and felt that Mansholt's ideas matched recent Commission communications concerning environmental issues [5]. Mansholt diverged from them on two points: first, he chose a more integral approach on account of the attention devoted to demographic problems and, second, he took a more *dirigiste* approach than his Italian colleague [6].

Several people noticed that Mansholt had changed. Many, including his former *chef de cabinet*, Mozer, were astonished at the neo-Marxist tone [7] of his speeches and papers. Initially a social democrat, Mansholt's political views had become more radical [8]. He was reproached for surrounding himself with poor staff. Even his faithful member of staff, von Verschuer, no longer recognised Mansholt after this brusque ideological shift [9], which seemed to correspond to his intention of creating a European party that would represent his ideas [10].

It was a real surprise that the presidency, which he had long coveted, was given to him at this time. On 17 March 1972 Malfatti resigned. Three days later Mansholt learnt that the Council, on the initiative of the French government [11], had decided to appoint him President. Mansholt's mandate would cover only a short period: on 31 December of the same year, the Commission's term of office came to an end because of the accession of three new Member States. Mansholt remarked ironically that he had become acceptable because he was being offered a short term of office and was not seeking an extension [12]. He was probably right. According to Barre, it was quite right that a man like Mansholt, above all as he was leaving, should end his career as Commission President [13].

[1] Ibid.

[2] See the chapter on industrial policy, pp. 374–376.

[3] IISG, AM 100, Reaction from Commissioner Barre to Sicco Mansholt's letter, 9 June 1972.

[4] Interview with Philippe Bourdeau, 5 March 2004.

[5] Spinelli refers to documents SEC(71) 2616 final and SEC(72) 666 final.

[6] IISG, AM 100, Reaction from Commissioner Spinelli to Sicco Mansholt's letter, 26 June 1972.

[7] IISG, AM 1, Letter from Alfred Mozer to Sicco Mansholt, 24 January 1972.

[8] Van Merriënboer, J.C.F.J., op. cit., p. 21.

[9] Interview with Helmut von Verschuer, 3 March 2004.

[10] Interview with Karel Van Miert, 19 August 2005.

[11] Mansholt, S., *La crise* [...], op. cit., p. 125 (Mansholt, S., *De Crisis*, p. 91).

[12] Ibid.

[13] Interview with Raymond Barre, 20 February 2004.

Le Club 30 JOURS D'EUROPE

ouvrira, dans la deuxième quinzaine de mai, un débat sur :

LA RECHERCHE DU "BONHEUR NATIONAL BRUT" EN EUROPE
proposée par Sicco Mansholt

Pour recevoir une invitation
écrire au Club 30 Jours d'Europe
61, rue des Belles-Feuilles - Paris-16ᵉ

Les comptes rendus des précédents débats
sont disponibles à l'adresse ci-dessus

Spring 1972. Against a backdrop of protest against the values on which European societies are built, in particular liberal capitalism, Sicco Mansholt proposes a different approach: to replace gross national product by gross national happiness.

'Focus on what really matters and always say what you think'

'Then Mansholt came. He was 62 years old when he became President and the only reason the ministers chose him was his seniority: "They chose the oldest guy they could find," he himself remarked. But he quickly revealed his concept of the Presidency: do not leave the Community to mere customs problems but focus on what really matters and he always said what he thought. There was no doubting his visionary side. When he envisaged reforming agriculture, he saw it as a transformation of lifestyle in the countryside which allowed farmers to take the weekend off and go on holidays in the Balearic Islands, while at the same time remodelling the landscape by recreating woods and forests. When, at the Unctad conference in Santiago, the Community was unable to agree on a generous plan for the Third World, he got on a plane, rushed to the venue and promised what he felt he had to promise without waiting for authorisation from the governments. This Dutch giant with fair hair and blue eyes, who found cocktail parties boring and hid away in Sardinia to make furniture as soon as he found the time had made it impossible for Europe to go back to manufacturing useless things. He took the debate on the future of the industrial society away from the experts and gave it its proper political dimensions. We may smile at Mansholt's expression "gross national happiness", but the politicians, employers and trade unions are obliged to base their programmes, promises and projects on concepts which seem to have been forgotten: individual development, quality of relations between people and between peoples, renaissance and respect for all cultures, priority for lifestyle over the purely material standard of living.'

Riccardi, F., 'Ortoli, le Français qui mène le Marché commun', in *Réalités — Revue de Paris*, No 330, July 1973, p. 45.
(Translated from the French)

During his short presidency, Mansholt had time to achieve only a few things. He had the misfortune that European integration was going through a long period of crisis. He was certainly more than a caretaker President and behaved like a true President [1]. He made a remarkable speech at the first major global conference on the environment in Stockholm, where he reiterated his idea that, for the poorest countries to be able to grow, there was a need to slow down the growth of pollution in the rich countries [2]. He was acclaimed by young demonstrators and exceeded his allotted time to the great discontent of the chair [3]. But his time as a European was over. At the European Summit in Paris in October 1972, he made concrete proposals to put integration back on track — abolishing passport controls, mutual recognition of diplomas and conferment of civic rights on foreign workers — but failed to get the governments to support him [4].

At the end of his term of office Mansholt was already distancing himself from the Community machinery, which he felt was too centralised, and adopting more radical political stances.

A great 'old boy'

The happiest and most successful years Mansholt spent at the Commission were undoubtedly the early years, when Hallstein was President. Although they had completely different personalities, Mansholt and Hallstein had an excellent working relationship based on mutual respect. Their ideal was a Europe unified not only economically but also politically. Mansholt got on very well with another leading light of the early Commission, the Frenchman Robert Marjolin [5]. His knowledge of agricultural problems and his attitude to work enabled Mansholt to obtain impressive results throughout that period.

---

[1] Interview with Paul Collowald, 2 December 2003.
[2] Interview with Georges Rencki, 13 January 2004.
[3] Interview with Michel Carpentier, 5 January 2004.
[4] Mansholt, S., *De Crisis*, op. cit., pp. 60–62.
[5] Interview with Robert Toulemon, 17 December 2003.

Mansholt was a man of the land but also a man of the sea. He had a passion for sailing and owned a *hoogaars*, a traditional Dutch flat-bottomed ship built in the 1930s. He was very much a handyman and used to maintain the *Atalanta* himself. Despite his very modern political ideas, on a boat he was a traditionalist: he would favour rigging made of hemp as opposed to nylon, sails made of cotton as opposed to terylene. He also sculpted decorative elements for his wooden boat. Mansholt had a perfect understanding of currents and tides, which enabled him to negotiate the sandbanks of Zealand. One of his close colleagues recalls the suggestion Mansholt made to him on several occasions, and in particular at the end of a marathon agriculture meeting at five in the morning: 'Let's go sailing!', he said. And the two men set off for Breskens, at the mouth of the river Schelde, where Mansholt's boat was moored. After the hectic world of Brussels, navigation was 'a perfect way to wind down: it was a different world, another language, a complete change of universe'. (Reminiscences of Georges Rencki, September 2006.)

After Hallstein and Marjolin left, Mansholt felt less and less at ease in the merged Commission. He found it cumbersome, unwieldy, bureaucratic and non-democratic. In his eyes, the powers of the European Parliament should be extended considerably. He was irritated also by the fact that several of his colleagues listened to what was being decided in their home countries and did not always act very independently. At the same time he discovered that the agricultural policy, which had been set up with so much dynamism and success under his stewardship, was starting to display serious weaknesses. Mansholt immediately saw the need for a thoroughgoing reform and in 1968 proposed an overall comprehensive solution to the farming problems ('Agriculture 1980' memorandum). This Mansholt plan was designed to modernise the structure of agricultural produc-

tion and to reduce surpluses. At another level, Mansholt came to the conclusion that the limits to economic and demographic growth had been reached and that the Commission should consider an economic policy compatible with environmental equilibrium. 'Europe has a mission to accomplish', he wrote in a letter to Malfatti.

Mansholt criss-crossed Europe to get his plan accepted by the farmers. Applauded in Italy, rejected in Germany, welcomed with some interest and scepticism (according to the farmers' organisations) in France. But it was European agriculture overall (20 % to 30 % of the population at the time) which took part in the debate. Despite these difficulties, in 1972 Mansholt succeeded in getting the Council to adopt the key elements of his structural reform. But the idea of reducing the surface area given over to agriculture, shocking at the time, had to wait 20 years to be accepted. This delay had crucial repercussions for the CAP.

Mansholt was probably the first politician (holding high level office) to ask the question publicly (there were many press articles on the subject) of the type of European growth and world growth to be envisaged for the future. He prompted a debate which rapidly became a public debate on energy constraints, food constraints, and atmospheric and land pollution constraints affecting growth. For several weeks the Commission was the focus point of a major debate on societal issues.

Within the Commission he tried to put over his new ideas, without much success. The respect

and prestige which he enjoyed in the early years was in decline. The presidency, which was given to him in 1972, had less impact than it would have had in the previous phase of his Brussels career. To many, it was a consolation prize for this 'grand old man' of the European Community.

Mansholt left a considerable achievement behind him. In difficult moments he was also able to make his voice heard, the voice of the great politician, the voice of the Liberal Socialist convinced that the future lay in socialism and in European integration ([1]).

JAN VAN DER HARST

([1]) Doutrelant, P.-M., 'M. Sicco Mansholt, un socialiste libéral', *Le Monde*, 23 March 1972.

Chapter 9

The College of Commissioners: a new type of public authority

The organisation of the Commission and its method of operation were laid down by the 1957 Rome Treaties (in particular Articles 155 to 163 of the EEC Treaty, derived in part from the 1951 ECSC Treaty), the 1965 Merger Treaty (Articles 9 to 19) and the successive rules of procedure that the Commissions themselves adopted. But it was the personalities of the members of the Commission and the international climate, particularly the policy of the Member States, that clearly shaped its history.

Composition of the Colleges: diversity and continuity

The EEC Commission which took office in January 1958 had nine members, the same as the ECSC High Authority established in 1952, although the Euratom Commission numbered only five. Unlike the members of the High Authority, however, the Commissioners were all appointed 'by common accord' of the governments of the six Member States. None were co-opted. They were appointed for a renewable four-year term of office, while the President's term was renewed every two years. In practice, each government would choose those of its own nationals that it wanted to have a seat in the College and its proposals would be ratified by the five others, which therefore were not really exercising their power of scrutiny or veto implicit in the text of the Treaties [1]. This approach would eventually be condemned and criticised by the Commissioners, including Étienne Hirsch, President of the Euratom Commission, when his term of office was not renewed by the French government at the end of 1961 as his commitments were considered too federalist [2].

In the EEC Commission, each of the three largest Member States was entitled to two Commissioners, while the three Benelux countries were allowed only one each. In the Euratom Commission, each Member State other than Luxembourg appointed one member. Following the merger of the three executives [3], the Single Commission

---

[1] Braun, N.-C., *La fonction supranationale*, Thesis, IEP Paris, 1967, pp. 27–28. See also the box on the 'Appointment of Commissioners and the principle of collective responsibility', p. 188.

[2] AHUE, CEAB 2 248, Speech by Étienne Hirsch to the European Parliamentary Assembly, 20 December 1961.

[3] For the creation of the Single Commission, see Chapters 2 and 6 above.

The composition of the Commissions ([1])

The first Hallstein Commission (10 January 1958 to 9 January 1962)

The Commission led by Walter Hallstein took office on 10 January 1958. Its term of office was renewed as stipulated four years later, on 10 January 1962, at the end of the first phase of the transitional period. Specialised working groups operated within the Commission at this time. Each Commissioner chaired one of these groups (see below) and was a member of other groups.

Commissioner	Portfolio	Chef(s) de cabinet
Giuseppe Caron (I) (Vice-President) took office on 9 December 1959, replacing Piero Malvestiti	Internal market	Maurizio Bucci (I), 1961–62
Walter Hallstein (D) (President)	Presidency Administration Secretariat-General	Swidbert Schnippenkötter (D), 1959–60 Berndt von Staden (D), 1961–62
Robert Lemaignen (F)	Overseas development	Jacques Ferrandi (F), 1959–61
Lionello Levi Sandri (I) took office on 22 February 1961, replacing Giuseppe Petrilli	Social affairs, then Administration	Lamberto Lambert (I), 1961, 1962 a.i.
Piero Malvestiti (I) (Vice-President) held office until 15 September 1959, replaced by Giuseppe Caron	Internal market	Guido Mondaini (I), 1959
Sicco Mansholt (N) (Vice-President)	Agriculture	Jacob Jan van der Lee (N), 1958 Alfred Mozer (N), 1959–62
Robert Marjolin (F) (Vice-President)	Economic and financial affairs	Jean-Claude Richard (F), 1959–62
Giuseppe Petrilli (I) held office until 8 February 1961	Social affairs	Antonino Arena (I), 1959 and 1960
Michel Rasquin (L) held office until 27 April 1958, replaced by Lambert Schaus	Transport	Fernand Braun (L), 1958
Jean Rey (B)	External relations Legal Service	Pierre Lucion (B), 1959–62
Lambert Schaus (L) took office on 19 June 1958, replacing Michel Rasquin	Transport	Camille Dumont (L), 1959–60 Lucien Kraus (L), 1961–62
Hans von der Groeben (D)	Competition	Ernst Albrecht (D), 1959–62

[1] The information on the *chefs de cabinet* was compiled from the available Commission organisation charts. These charts are more concerned with the organisation of the directorates-general than of the *cabinets*. They remain one of the only sources of information on the *chefs de cabinet*, as consultation of personnel files is not allowed. In 1958, in the early days, the Commission was still engaged in organising its structure, so there was not yet any organisation chart. An organisation chart for the Rey Commission, under which the executives were merged, is available for April and August 1968 only. Some uncertainty remains, therefore, concerning the actual periods of office of the *chefs de cabinet* concerned. Organisation charts only provide a snapshot of the situation at a given time and do not actually reflect any changes that might have occurred between the two dates for which information is available.

The second Hallstein Commission (10 January 1962 to 5 July 1967)

Commissioner	Portfolio	Chef(s) de cabinet
Giuseppe Caron (I) (Vice-President) held office until 16 May 1963, replaced by Guido Colonna di Paliano	Internal market	Maurizio Bucci (I), 1962
Guido Colonna di Paliano (I) (Vice-President) took office on 9 September 1964, replacing Giuseppe Caron	Internal market Industrial affairs	Rinieri Paulucci di Calboli (I), 1965–67
Walter Hallstein (D) (President)	Presidency Administration Secretariat-General	Berndt von Staden (D), 1962 Karl-Heinz Narjes (D), 1963–67
Lionello Levi Sandri (I)	Social affairs, then Administration Internal market, a.i. (replacing Giuseppe Caron, before the appointment of Guido Colonna di Paliano)	Lamberto Lambert (I), 1962–64, 1966 a.i. Giovanni Falchi (I), 1967
Sicco Mansholt (N) (Vice-President)	Agriculture	Alfred Mozer (N), 1962–67
Robert Marjolin (F) (Vice-President)	Economic and financial affairs	Jean-Claude Richard (F), 1962 Robert Toulemon (F), 1963 Jean Flory (F), 1964–67
Jean Rey (B)	External relations Legal Service	Pierre Lucion (B), 1962–66 Raymond Rifflet (B), 1967
Henri Rochereau (F)	Overseas development Social affairs	(Jacques Ferrandi (F), 1962) Jean Chapperon (F), 1963–65, 1966 a.i., 1967
Lambert Schaus (L)	Transport	Lucien Kraus (L), 1962–67
Hans von der Groeben (D)	Competition	Ernst Albrecht (D), 1962–67

The Rey Commission (6 July 1967 to 1 July 1970)

As a result of the merger of the executives, the Single Commission had 14 members for the first three years before it was again reduced to nine. The first Single Commission held office from 6 July 1967 to 1 July 1970 under the presidency of Jean Rey. It more or less abandoned the organisation by specialised working groups in favour of a system of portfolios.

Commissioner	Portfolio	Chef(s) de cabinet
Raymond Barre (F)	Economic and financial affairs Statistical Office	Jean-Claude Paye (F), 1968–70
Victor Bodson (L)	Transport	Henri Entringer (L), August 1968
Guido Colonna di Paliano (I)	Industrial affairs, until 7 May 1970	Rinieri Paulucci di Calboli (I), April 1968

The Rey Commission *(continued)*

Commissioner	Portfolio	Chef(s) de cabinet
Albert Coppé (B)	Press and information Credit and investment Budget Administration, from July 1968	Daniel Cardon de Lichtbuer (B), 1968–70
Jean-François Deniau (F)	Foreign trade Financial control	Claude Trabuc (F), 1968
Hans von der Groeben (D)	Internal market and approximation of legislation Regional policy	Manfred Caspari (D), 1968–70
Wilhelm Haferkamp (D)	Energy Supply Agency Euratom safeguards	Willy Schlieder (D), 1968
Fritz Hellwig (D)	General research and technology Dissemination of knowledge Joint Research Centre (JRC)	Wilhelm Krafft (D), April 1968
Lionello Levi Sandri (I)	Social affairs Administration, until July 1968 Personnel Industrial affairs, from 8 May 1970	Giovanni Falchi (I), 1968
Sicco Mansholt (N)	Agriculture	Alfred Mozer (N), 1968
Edoardo Martino (I)	External relations	Paolo Antici (I), 1968
Jean Rey (B)	President of the Commission Secretariat-General Legal Service Spokesman's Group Security Office	Raymond Rifflet (B), 1968
Henri Rochereau (F)	Development aid	Jean Chapperon (F), 1968–70
Emmanuel Sassen (N)	Competition	Josephus Loeff (N), 1968

The Malfatti/Mansholt Commission (2 July 1970 to 5 January 1973)

On 2 July 1970 the new Commission had nine members, as stipulated. It held office until 5 January 1973, when it was succeeded by the Commission of a Community enlarged to include the United Kingdom, Denmark and Ireland. Its President was Franco Maria Malfatti until 21 March 1972, then Sicco Mansholt.

Commissioner	Portfolio	Chef(s) de cabinet
Raymond Barre (F)	Economic and financial affairs Statistical Office	Jean-Claude Paye (F), 1970–72

The Malfatti–Mansholt Commission *(continued)*

Commissioner	Portfolio	Chef(s) de cabinet
Albert Borschette (L)	Competition Press and information Dissemination of knowledge Regional policy	Guy Mines (L), 1970 Robert Sünnen (L), 1971 and 1972
Albert Coppé (B)	Social affairs Transport Personnel and administration Credit and investment Budget Financial control	Daniel Cardon de Lichtbuer (B), 1970–72
Ralf Dahrendorf (D)	External relations External trade	Klaus Terfloth (D), 1970–72
Jean-François Deniau (F)	Coordination of enlargement negotiations Development aid	Claude Trabuc (F), 1970 Jean Chapperon (F), 1970–72
Wilhelm Haferkamp (D)	Internal market and approximation of legislation Energy Euratom Supply Agency Euratom safeguards	Willy Schlieder (D), 1970 Manfred Lahnstein (D), 1971 and 1972
Franco Maria Malfatti (I) held office until 21 March 1972	President of the Commission Secretariat-General Legal Service Spokesman's Group Security Office	Renato Ruggiero (I), 1970–March 1972
Sicco Mansholt (N)	Agriculture, until 11 April 1972 From 12 April 1972: President of the Commission Secretariat-General Legal Service Spokesman's Group Security Office	Sjouke Jonker (N), 1970–72
Carlo Scarascia-Mugnozza (I)	Agriculture, from 12 April 1972	Giuseppe Jacoangeli (I), 1972
Altiero Spinelli (I)	Industrial affairs General research and technology Joint Research Centre (JRC) From 24 February 1971: Industry, technology and science Joint Research Centre (JRC) Administration of the customs union Group on teaching and education, from 22 July 1971	Gianfranco Speranza (I), 1970 Christopher Layton (UK), 1972

The capital letters in parentheses next to the names of Commissioners and *chefs de cabinet* indicate their nationality:
B = Belgian, D = German, F = French, I = Italian, L = Luxembourgish, N = Dutch.

provisionally consisted of 14 members (3 German, 3 French, 3 Italian, 2 Belgian, 2 Dutch and 1 Luxembourger), before its numbers were cut to nine in 1970 until the enlargement of the Community on 1 January 1973. Once appointed, the members of the Colleges were completely independent in the performance of their duties. In the words of the Treaties, 'they shall neither seek nor take instructions from any government or from any other body' nor, during their term of office, could they engage in any occupation, whether gainful or not. But this did not mean that they could have no contacts with the authorities, administrations, political parties or various pressure groups in their countries of origin. On the contrary, many Commissioners had close relations with national leaders. This was certainly true in the case of Hallstein, at least until the last days of the Adenauer era, Belgium's Jean Rey and many others too. Robert Marjolin and Raymond Barre regularly saw the French Foreign Minister, Maurice Couve de Murville, while Barre sometimes also met with General de Gaulle and later Georges Pompidou at the Élysée ([1]).

Practically all of the members of the first EEC Commission belonged to the generation born between 1899 and 1913. Only Robert Lemaignen was in his sixties while France's other Commissioner, Robert Marjolin, and one of Italy's, Giuseppe Petrilli, were the youngest (47 and 45 respectively). President Walter Hallstein, at 57, was just a few months off the average age, which was virtually the same in the 14-man Single Commission that came into office in 1967 (see Chapter 6). Although two of its members, President Jean Rey and Luxembourg's Victor Bodson, were already 65, a number of 'youngsters' also joined the Commission: France's Jean-François Deniau (39), Raymond Barre (43) and Germany's Wilhelm Haferkamp (44). The maximum age spread was therefore quite large (26 years). It fell slightly in the next Commission — back to nine members again — in which the average age was signifi-

cantly lower (51) when the Commission was formed. The ranks of the twenties' generation, first seen in the Rey Commission, were strengthened by the arrival of Germany's Ralf Dahrendorf, Luxembourg's Albert Borschette and Italy's Franco Maria Malfatti (53), the President of this College.

The Commissions at this time were all-male preserves composed largely of senior officials and politicians who had proven their mettle in their countries of origin. Almost all political leanings were represented, apart from the far left and the far right, but there was less variety in terms of career backgrounds. There were many Commissioners who had studied law or law and economics. Many had been lawyers or university professors before embarking on their careers in government or politics. The Commission headed by Professor Walter Hallstein, a Christian Democrat, for example, included one other Christian Democrat, Italy's Piero Malvestiti, a political disciple of Alcide De Gasperi, as well as the Belgian liberal, Jean Rey, and several socialists (the Netherlands' Sicco Mansholt, Luxembourg's Michel Rasquin and France's Robert Marjolin). Almost all the members of this College were firm Europeans; a number were committed federalists (Hallstein, Mansholt, Rey, etc.); some had close links with Jean Monnet and his Action Committee for a United States of Europe; others with the European movement. Only Giuseppe Petrilli appeared less committed in this respect, though he was no eurosceptic, unlike Ralf Dahrendorf, who was probably an exception.

The men established a pattern of continuity from one Commission to the next. In 1967, nine of the 14 members of the first Single Commission came from the former executives, including five from the EEC Commission, amongst them Jean Rey, the new President. In 1970, out of the nine members of the new smaller Commission, five belonged to the previous Commission. But the big names in the single Commission — other then Mansholt — were the newcomers, Raymond Barre, Jean-François Deniau, not to mention Altiero

([1]) Interviews with Raymond Barre, 20 February 2004; Paul Collowald, 2 December 2003; and Jean Flory, 3 December 2003.

Spinelli (¹). None could beat the long-service record of Albert Coppé, a member of the High Authority from 1952 to 1967, then of the Single Commission from 1967 to 1972, or Sicco Mansholt, in office from 1958 to 1972 throughout the period of the EEC of Six, but several served more than 12 years, from January 1958 to July 1970, in one or the other of the executives: Jean Rey, Hans von der Groeben and Emmanuel Sassen (who started in the Euratom Commission), while Hallstein and Marjolin stayed in Brussels for almost 10 years, from 1958 to 1967.

Meetings: the College at work

The EEC Commission met for the first time on 16 January 1958 at Val-Duchesse. A number of the Commissioners were already familiar with the place, having taken part there in the negotiations on the Rome Treaties, in particular Marjolin, Hallstein and the other German member, Hans von der Groeben. At this first meeting, the Commission laid down practical arrangements for the organisation of its work and decision-making procedures but did not see fit to adopt any rules of procedure immediately, believing it premature as the rules could not be established until some experience had been gained of the workings of the Commission (²). It referred to the precedent set by the ECSC High Authority, which had not drawn up its rules of procedure until 5 November 1954, more than two years after taking up office. The Commission's first meeting was also marked by a small incident. Jean Rey had been instructed by the President to prepare a discussion on the Commissioners' salaries but had printed only four copies of the proposal, for himself, Hallstein, Mansholt and Marjolin. But at the end of the morning, when the item came up for discussion, 'someone brought in a copy of *Agra-Europe,* which had published the memo [...] Hallstein was furious' (³). This first leak in the history of the

EEC Commission probably did little to soften Walter Hallstein's stance, who was very wary of the press and somewhat inclined to secrecy (⁴). But the culture of secrecy was not the prerogative of the EEC Commission. It existed at Euratom (⁵) too, but the leaks — which intensified during the Rey Commission and some of which were probably organised (⁶) — were never discussed by the full Commission (⁷).

During its few first months, the Hallstein Commission was a genuine itinerant college. The Foreign Ministers of the Six had decided in January 1958 that the EEC and Euratom Commissions would hold meetings in Luxembourg and Val-Duchesse alternately until June (⁸). In reality, the meetings took place all over Europe. In Val-Duchesse, especially in January. In the Maison de l'Europe in Strasbourg during sessions of the European Parliamentary Assembly. At rue Aldringen in Luxembourg, where each of the Commissioners also had an office (⁹). More and more frequently in Brussels, Walter Hallstein's preferred venue, at 51 or 53 rue Belliard or at 69 rue du Lombard. But also in Rome, on the first anniversary of the signing of the Treaties or in Paris and Stresa in July. It was in the summer, the first time on 15–16 July, then regularly from the start of September, that the EEC Commission moved into 24 avenue de la Joyeuse Entrée (although the Euratom Commission stayed in rue Belliard). This complex of offices, recently constructed by the Royale Belge insurance company, was able to accommodate the Commission, which occupied the 7th floor, and its administrative departments. Witnesses fondly recall the warm atmosphere in Joyeuse Entrée in those days where everybody knew everyone else (¹⁰). Others remember the somewhat formal etiquette. Walter Hallstein's usher wore a morning coat and it was not the

---

(¹) Interview with Pierre Defraigne, 16 December 2004.
(²) PV 1 EEC Commission, 16 January 1958, I.
(³) Interview with Georges Rencki, 13 January 2004.

(⁴) Interviews with Bino Olivi and Georges Rencki, 13 January 2004.
(⁵) Interview with Jacques-René Rabier, 8 January 2004.
(⁶) Interview with Pierre Defraigne, 16 December 2004.
(⁷) Interview with Frans De Koster, 14 November 2004.
(⁸) Lethé, M., *L'Europe à Bruxelles dans les années 1960*, History degree dissertation, UCL, Louvain-la-Neuve, 2003, p. 54.
(⁹) Interview with Robert Pendville, 16 December 2003.
(¹⁰) Interview with Jacqueline Lastenouse, 21 January 2004.

The appointment of Commissioners and the principle of collective responsibility

'The way the Commission works is hampered by the need to submit all decisions and proposals for discussion by all the members.

In the early 1950s this totally collective system was the antidote to any national tendencies on the part of the members of the Commission. Nowadays, nobody thinks or believes that the members of the Commission reflect their government's views. The system of collective responsibility has become the antidote to the circumstances under which the Commission is appointed.

The Treaties stipulate that the members of the Commission are to be appointed by common accord of the governments. In fact, the governments rarely appoint the Commission together. Each nominates one or more members of the Commission and the others endorse the choice that each government makes.

The Commission is therefore formed in a very different way to a government. Forming a government in each Member State involves putting a team together to carry out a programme. The practice for appointing the Commission adopted until now has therefore little to do with political choice and amounts to appointing civil servants.

The composition and the operation of the Commission could be improved if its members were to receive individual assignments when appointed. Rather than just a list of names, the act of appointment could indicate each commissioner's assignments after their name.

This would force each government to pay attention to the choice of every member instead of being solely concerned by the choice of its own nationals. In the functioning of the Commission, collective responsibility would be confined to general guidelines and establishing the overall programme.

If this change were made, it would no longer matter how many members of the Commission there are, the same as in a government. As far as the functioning of the Commission is concerned, such a reform would make it possible for more countries to be accepted into the Community. It would not prevent the risk of the Council being paralysed as a result of the increase in the number of member countries.'

FJME, AMK C 33/4/200,
Note by Jacques Van Helmont, 2 June 1969, about a conversation with Émile Noël on 31 May 1969.
(Translated from the French)

done thing to take the lift with the President ([1]). But the sense of hierarchy was further heightened when, in 1969, the Commission moved — again to the top floor — into the Berlaymont, a flagship building constructed in the vicinity of the then rue de la Loi roundabout (now the Schuman roundabout), the area soon to become Brussels' European district ([2]).

Not counting extraordinary sessions, the Commission normally held its meetings on Wednesday mornings, traditionally also the day on which the Council of Ministers met in Paris. These meetings were held in closed session and could last 'hours and hours, all day long, late into the evening [...] part of the night' ([3]). Other participants, besides the Commissioners, included a number of senior officials, starting with the Executive Secretary (with his deputy). Belgium's Pierre Bourguignon — who had the President's confidence, was to stay on in his *cabinet* and 'kept

---

([1]) Interview with Jean-Claude Eeckhout, 3 December 2003.
([2]) Interview with Jacques Vandamme, 21 January 2004.

([3]) Interview with Frans De Koster, 14 November 2004.

Hallstein very well informed' (¹) — was replaced in this post after three months by France's Émile Noël (²), who would remain in it until well after the Europe of Six and was given the title of Secretary-General after the merger of the executives. Other participants included: the Registrar, Frans De Koster (³), whose job was to draft the minutes of the meetings on Wednesday night for them to be revised by Noël and distributed on Thursday, the Head of the Legal Service, the very influential Frenchman, Michel Gaudet (⁴), the Commission's spokesman, Italy's Giorgio Smoquina and then, from 1961 onwards Bino Olivi (⁵), not to mention the interpreters or the officials invited according to the agenda under discussion.

The seating arrangements around the table were soon quite fixed, it would appear (⁶). Alongside President Hallstein, on a slightly raised chair because of his relatively small height (⁷), sat his compatriot Hans von der Groeben, so close that, if he defended the position of the 'country he knew best' (the hallowed expression used by a Commissioner so as not to name his own country) too enthusiastically, Hallstein could put his hand on his to tell him to stop. The two Frenchmen would also sit side-by-side, separated by the interpreter, who interpreted from German. The table had to be adapted to the number of members. The 14-man Rey Commission opted for an oval table, which was replaced again in 1970 by a round table.

The working language was mainly French and to a lesser extent, German. The two other official languages — Italian and Dutch — were used much less often. Walter Hallstein, who spoke all four languages, chaired the meeting in French (⁸) but liked to be able to use his mother tongue with his immediate colleagues. A good knowledge of German could be an asset for anyone wishing to hold a position of responsibility with the President (⁹). Sicco Mansholt, who spoke little French when he arrived in Brussels, learnt the language fast and did not hesitate to speak it in defending his ideas (¹⁰). Von der Groeben always spoke German, while the Italian members of the first College spoke French, though quite badly. Language was not a problem for the members from Belgium and Luxembourg.

Witness accounts illustrate the atmosphere in the Commission and the relationships developing between colleagues. Many of them highlight the desire for consensus, the climate of trust, even the friendships being struck up. According to one witness, there was a very pleasant atmosphere within the Commission. One striking point was how much they admired each other. But the Commission was not without personality clashes, differences of opinion, sometimes even tension and disputes. In the Hallstein Commission, the President sought to prevent an organised opposition emerging. His leadership was supported by the strongest personalities in the Commission, in particular Mansholt, a fellow federalist, and Marjolin. Although Hallstein had less immediately in common with Marjolin, who was a pro-European socialist but no federalist, the two men understood each other well enough (at least until the 1965 crisis) to carry issues forward, so much so that one senior French official referred to this Commission as the 'Grand Duchy of Marjolin-Hallstein' (¹¹). The usual atmosphere of complicity did not prevent Robert Marjolin from making 'a scene in a meeting held in camera' to stop Hallstein appointing General von Stülpnagel's nephew as spokesman (¹²). Relations between

(¹) Interview with Georges Berthoin, 31 January 2004.
(²) See Émile Noël's biography below (Chapter 10).
(³) Frans De Koster joined in 1959.
(⁴) Interviews with Giuseppe Ciavarini Azzi, 6 February 2004, and Frans De Koster, 14 November 2004.
(⁵) Interviews with Bino Olivi, 26 January and 9 February 2004.
(⁶) Ibid.
(⁷) Ibid.
(⁸) Interview with Jean Flory, 3 December 2003.

(⁹) Interviews with Bino Olivi, 26 January and 9 February 2004.
(¹⁰) Interview with Jean Flory, 3 December 2003.
(¹¹) Interviews with Jean-François Deniau, 3 and 10 November 2004 (the quotation is from Olivier Wormser).
(¹²) Interviews with Bino Olivi, 26 January and 9 February 2004 (General von Stülpnagel brought back bad memories for the French: he was the commander of Paris during the Second World War and was executed because of his presumed involvement in the plot against Hitler).

Hallstein and Jean Rey, another heavyweight who had no hesitation in criticising the President, were somewhat tense ([1]). Sometimes there was mistrust between members. On Raymond Barre's arrival in 1967, two years after the empty-chair crisis, many of the Commissioners were wary of the Frenchman whom they suspected would 'report back to de Gaulle' ([2]). Although he soon won the trust of the President, Jean Rey, and managed, through his intelligence and intellectual honesty, to win his colleagues over within a year ([3]), there was no lack of disagreement with some of them, e.g. with Mansholt on zero growth ([4]) or with Colonna di Paliano on the issue of supranationality ([5]).

Collective responsibility and decision-making

The principle of collective responsibility, inherited from the ECSC High Authority, was the basic rule governing how the Commission worked. It meant that all measures taken by the Commission in the exercise of its powers must be adopted by the full Commission, by a majority of its members ([6]), who thus shared joint responsibility for the decision taken. The concept did not preclude delegating the work of preparing and implementing decisions. However, on a maximalist interpretation, decisions were also prepared by the full Commission and supported by all its members in the other Community institutions and in contacts with the public. With this in mind, the ECSC High Authority had introduced the system of working groups comprising several members of the executive to prepare proposals.

At its first meeting, the EEC Commission decided to postpone the adoption of its rules of procedure and to follow the example of the High Authority as a starting point for drawing up its working arrangements ([7]). Several Commissioners, in particular Mansholt, Rey and Marjolin ([8]), set great store by the system of collective responsibility and, in March 1958, the Commission decided to set up working groups on the model used by the ECSC, where they worked well, for the task of preparing decisions on a collective basis ([9]). Each working group had its own sphere of competence and comprised a maximum of five members, one of whom was the chairman (see box on working groups, pp. 194–195). A directorate-general was set up for each sphere of competence, although its head could not have the same nationality as the chairman of the working group ([10]).

In practice, according to several accounts, the working groups did not work in the best possible fashion. The Commissioners were not interested in them and often delegated the task to their colleagues. One witness commented wryly that these working groups had one main advantage: they allowed each Commissioner to take a turn in the chair ([11]). A system for dividing up the work by portfolio very soon emerged. However, in July 1962, at Jean Rey's request, the Commission held a meeting to rethink its working methods. At the meeting, President Hallstein talked of the importance of the system of collective responsibility and the Commission decided to keep the working groups, which would now meet more frequently ([12]). At the same time, however, it also agreed to organise meetings between members of the Commissioners' *cabinets* to prepare for the meetings of the full Commission ([13]). In the early days, therefore, the organisation of work seemed to be a matter of trial and error and some hesitation between a system based on groups and a system of portfolios.

_____

([1]) Group interview, 19 October 2004.
([2]) Interview with Jean Degimbe, 15 December 2003.
([3]) Interview with Michel Albert, 18 December 2003.
([4]) Ibid.
([5]) See Chapter 6.
([6]) EEC Treaty, Article 163.
([7]) See document referred to in note 2, page 195.
([8]) Interviews with Georges Rencki, 13 January 2004.
([9]) Conrad, Y., 'L'organizzazione amministrativa della Commissione europea (1958–1961)', *Storia Amministrazione Constituzione*, 8/2000, Il Mulino, Bologna.
([10]) Ibid. (see Chapter 11 on the directorates-general).
([11]) Interviews with Jean-François Deniau, 3 and 10 November 2004.
([12]) PV spéc. 172, EEC Commission, 5 July 1962, XX, pp. 7–12.
([13]) For the role of the cabinets, see end of chapter (pp. 195–204).

The Hallstein Commission (1958–62)

1) Renée Van Hoof (interpreter)
2) Giuseppe Petrilli
3) Jean Rey
4) Piero Malvestiti
5) Hans von der Groeben
6) Walter Hallstein

7) Émile Noël
8) Robert Lemaignen
9) Robert Marjolin
10) Lambert Schaus

(Mansholt is absent)

The Hallstein Commission at the Joyeuse Entrée: the Commissioners meet round three assembled tables. An interpreter is present. Hallstein presides with a bell.

In January 1963 the Commission adopted its rules of procedure ([1]). Modelled on the last rules of procedure of the High Authority ([2]), they confirmed existing practices. They were renewed by the next two Commissions, subject to minor amendments relating in particular to the change in the number of Commissioners, which affected the quorum and the majority. Article 1 enshrined the principle of collective responsibility: 'The Commission shall act collectively in accordance with these rules.' But the rules did not specify either of the two working methods. Article 13 stated that 'The Commission may assign to its members responsibility for the preparation and implementation of acts of the Commission in particular fields.' Article 14, on the other hand, provided for the possibility of setting up working groups.

In 1967, when the executives were merged, Émile Noël realised that, unlike in the High Authority, decisions in the EEC were not prepared by the full Commission, but each Commissioner had a specific sphere of competence and was responsible solely for drawing up the proposals to be submitted in that sphere. While he believed that the requirements of collective responsibility probably corresponded to the current state of European integration, he acknowledged the virtual impossibility of preparation by the full Commission in a Community with such wide-ranging jurisdiction on account of the growing number of decisions to be taken and the need to act fast ([3]).

This admission of failure did not, however, prevent the Rey Commission from setting up working groups, although not until September 1967, once the portfolios had been allocated. The tasks of these groups, which could now contain a maximum of seven Commissioners, had moreover been redefined. Their main responsibility consisted in preparing issues relating to several sec-

tors by coordinating proposals and summarising positions ([4]). One member of this Commission explained: 'We worked together in groups of two or three Commissioners who believed that the issues at stake were issues that concerned us. And it went well. I have no recollection of any tension or any wish on the part of the groups to take the place of the Commissioners. The groups were there to help the members of the Commission, and then the members of the Commission would assume responsibility' ([5]). The role of the groups was clearly quite secondary. The main concern was the allocation of portfolios, which was thrashed out after lengthy consultations in 1967 and which would take less than 24 hours to resolve in July 1970, no doubt following a certain amount of prior wheeling and dealing ([6]).

In successive Commissions, the allocation of portfolios was decided on the basis of recognised spheres of competence, although this did not prevent some being regarded as private preserves. President Hallstein kept administration for himself, wishing to develop it in the German mould, with a precise organisation chart, in stark contrast to Monnet's idea for the High Authority, where he had recruited on a needs-must basis ([7]). Economic and financial affairs was always the domain of a top French Commissioner. The two areas were considered inseparable, as Raymond Barre recalled: 'All my colleagues knew I was an economist, that I had held posts in the economic sphere in France. They understood my asking for the economic and financial affairs post. They understood all the more because I was following on from Marjolin. [...] The question arose because a German Commissioner, Hellwig I think, wanted them to split the economic and financial affairs portfolio into two, one part dealing with monetary affairs, the other with economics and planning. I argued my corner. I explained to my col-

([1]) They were adopted by the College on 9 January and published in the *Official Journal of the European Communities* on 31 January 1963.
([2]) *Official Journal of the European Communities*, 3 May 1960.
([3]) Noël, É., *La fusion des institutions et la fusion des Communautés européennes*, Publications du Centre universitaire de Nancy, No 1, 1966, pp. 8–9.
([4]) PV spéc. 7, EC Commission, 1967, XVIII, pp. 10–13.
([5]) Interview with Raymond Barre, 20 February 2004.
([6]) See Chapter 6.
([7]) Interviews with Jean-François Deniau, 3 and 10 November 2004, Jacques-René Rabier, 8 January 2004 and Henri Étienne, 12 January 2004.

The Hallstein Commission (1962–67)

1) Walter Hallstein
2) Emile Noël *secrétaire exécutif de la Commission de la CEE*
3) Jean Rey
4) Sicco Mansholt
5) Henri Rochereau

6) Robert Marjolin
7) Lambert Schaus
8) Lionello Levi Sandri
9) Guido Colonna di Paliano
10) Hans von der Groeben

Meeting of the second Hallstein Commission; the Commission has moved to a round-table format.

leagues why I considered that it was unreasonable to do this. I was ready to discuss the matter with my colleagues. There was no need to divide it up because that would be tantamount to losing cohesion, which was of fundamental importance.' ([1]) Successive Frenchmen took overseas development too (Lemaignen, Rochereau), while Italians took social affairs (Petrilli, Levi Sandri) and Luxembourgers (Rasquin, Schaus, Bodson) transport, the portfolio it seemed nobody wanted ([2]). No-

body dreamt of taking agriculture off Mansholt, who kept it under his charge from the outset until his appointment as President in 1972.

While responsibility for preparing proposals lay more with members of the Commission working in an individual capacity (with their *cabinet* and directorate-general) than with the full Commission or the working groups, decision-making was the true prerogative of the Commission. It was the President's job to convene meetings and draw up the agenda (Rules of Procedure, Articles 3 and 4). However, any Commissioner unable to attend

---

([1]) Interview with Raymond Barre, 20 February 2004.
([2]) Interview with Henri Étienne, 12 January 2004.

Working groups in the Hallstein Commission

To assert its collective nature, the Hallstein Commission adopted a system of working groups. Each Commissioner chaired one of these groups and was a member of other groups. Each group had a specific remit (external relations, agricultural policy, competition policy, etc.).
It would examine the dossiers prepared by the directorate-general that dealt with the same subject area and then prepare the decisions that would subsequently be adopted at the meetings of the College.

External relations	— Jean Rey (Chairman of the working group)
	— Robert Marjolin
	— Giuseppe Petrilli, until 8 February 1961 Giuseppe Caron, 1 March 1961 to 15 May 1963 Guido Colonna di Paliano, from 9 September 1964
Economic and financial affairs	— Robert Marjolin (Chairman)
	— Sicco Mansholt
	— Piero Malvestiti, until 15 September 1959 Giuseppe Caron, from 9 February 1959 until 1 March 1961 Lionello Levi Sandri, from 1 March 1961
	— Hans von der Groeben, from 10 January 1962
Internal market	— Piero Malvestiti (President), until 15 September 1959 Giuseppe Caron (President), from 9 December 1959 Guido Colonna di Paliano (President), from 9 September 1964
	— Jean Rey
	— Lambert Schaus, from 19 June 1958
Competition	— Hans von der Groeben (President)
	— Robert Marjolin
	— Jean Rey
Social affairs	— Giuseppe Petrilli (Chairman), until 8 February 1961 Lionello Levi Sandri (Chairman), from 22 February 1961
	— Robert Lemaignen, until 9 January 1962 Henri Rochereau, from 10 January 1962
	— Sicco Mansholt
Agriculture	— Sicco Mansholt (President)
	— Hans von der Groeben
	— Robert Lemaignen, until 9 January 1962 Henri Rochereau, from 10 January 1962
	— Lambert Schaus, from 19 June 1958
Transport	— Michel Rasquin (Chairman), until 27 April 1958 Lambert Schaus (Chairman), from 19 June 1958
	— Robert Lemaignen, until 9 January 1962 Henri Rochereau, from 10 January 1962
	— Piero Malvestiti, until 15 September 1959 Giuseppe Caron, from 9 December 1959 until 15 May 1963 Guido Colonna di Paliano, from 9 September 1964

Overseas development	— Robert Lemaignen (Chairman), until 9 January 1962 Henri Rochereau, from 10 January 1962
	— Hans von der Groeben — Giuseppe Petrilli, until 8 February 1961 Giuseppe Caron, from 8 February 1961 until 1 March 1961 Lionello Levi Sandri, from 1 March 1961
Administration	— Walter Hallstein (Chairman)
	— Sicco Mansholt — Robert Marjolin — Piero Malvestiti, until 15 September 1959 Giuseppe Caron, from 9 December 1959 Giuseppe Petrilli, until 8 February 1961 Lionello Levi Sandri, from 5 July 1961

could ask for an item to be placed on the agenda of a later meeting because, although they could be represented by members of their *cabinet*, the *cabinet* member was only allowed to speak, not vote (Article 9). Only Commissioners could vote. Decisions were taken by absolute majority (five votes in the nine-member Commission), while the quorum required to make the meeting valid was also set at five (Articles 6 and 7).

Discussions could be lengthy and animated. Although Hallstein was regarded as very authoritarian, he would allow members to have their say but would then sum up and draw the conclusions of the debate before taking a vote [1]. Hallstein frequently sought to reach a consensus too [2], as a rule through debate. In 1972, however, a report found that the Commission did not debate long enough or well enough — at any rate, not early enough in the process of preparing proposals — so that discussions dwelt too much on the precise decisions to be taken, rather than on the general policy direction [3]. Some decisions did not even come up for discussion at a Commission meeting. The use of the written procedure to 'reduce the workload' [4] curtailed discussions. Devised in

1959 and widely used from the summer of 1960, this procedure was subsequently incorporated in the rules of procedure (Article 11). It involved sending a proposal to all the members and, provided that none of them expressed any reservations by a given deadline, the proposal would be considered adopted by the Commission. The President could also decide to take a vote without debate on a decision unanimously approved by a meeting of the *chefs de cabinet*, a forum that was introduced gradually but assumed growing importance.

The role of the cabinets

The abandonment of working groups favoured the rise of the Commissioners' *cabinets*. The *cabinet* had many roles: not only did it deputise for the Commissioner, liaise between 'le patron' and his administration, i.e. the directorate-general covering the same sphere of competence, and cooperate with the other *cabinets* and the Secretary-General of the Commission, but it also made contacts with the outside world, with civil society organisations and with the administration in the Commissioner's country of origin. But while the mandate of the *cabinets* was clear, the way they operated was not immediately evident, the more so because of differences in practice between the six Member States. With the post of

---

[1] Braun, N.-C., op. cit., p. 167.
[2] Interview with Fernand Braun, 8 December 2003, and group interview, 19 October 2004.
[3] AHCE, BAC 158/1990, dossier 19 (Poullet Report).
[4] Ibid.

chef de cabinet not existing in the traditional German set-up, Walter Hallstein preferred a French-style organisation, but not an exact copy of the Parisian model.

At Hallstein's request small *cabinets* limited to four to five persons were the rule initially [1]. In April 1958 the Commission confirmed that those recruited to work directly for its members would have the title of *chef de cabinet* and deputy head, rather than director as in France. The rest of the *cabinet* staff consisted of a secretary and one other employee, while the President had an additional administrative assistant. Some members, notably Robert Lemaignen, insisted time and time again that they needed more staff to cope with the workload, which was necessarily heavier if the Commissioner's work entailed frequent trips abroad. The *cabinets* continued to expand, particularly when the executives merged in 1967 and again in 1970, when the number of Commissioners was reduced from 14 to nine, prompting a broadening of their areas of responsibility and the need to recruit some of the staff of the former *cabinets*.

In the early days, the teams tended to be 'of a uniform colour' [2], i.e. with each Commissioner preferring to recruit his immediate staff from his own country and even from his own political party. There was one notable exception: Sicco Mansholt selected a *chef de cabinet* of German extraction, Alfred Mozer, who had emigrated to the Netherlands under the Nazis, while the deputy head was a Frenchman, Georges Rencki, both men being long-standing supporters of the European movement [3]. Other noteworthy exceptions included the following: in 1972, shortly before the first enlargement, Altiero Spinelli recruited a British *chef de cabinet*, the economist Christopher Layton, another fervent pro-European, while, throughout his whole period of office from 1967 to 1972, Raymond Barre's *cabinet* included

a Belgian, Jean Degimbe, who had previous experience in Europe in the ECSC and good union contacts [4].

Time spent in a *cabinet* could kick-start a career. It was not long before the Commission decided that members of *cabinets* were Commission officials, later to be covered by the staff regulations, a cause of some disquiet to the administration, which found this system of 'parachuting' unfair, especially as people were often 'parachuted in' at high career grades and steps, to the detriment of candidates from the directorates-general. Many directors and directors-general started out as members of *cabinets*. Some quickly made director-general, e.g. Jacques Ferrandi, François-Xavier Ortoli, Ernst Albrecht, Karl-Heinz Narjes, Raymond Rifflet and Fernand Spaak; others were not promoted until the end of their careers, e.g. Robert Toulemon, Fernand Braun and Lamberto Lambert. Conversely, an official joining a *cabinet* could earn extra consideration from his colleagues [5].

Some left the Commission after several years, occasionally leaving the *cabinet* weaker. President Hallstein's first two *chefs de cabinet*, for example, like him ex-members of Germany's Foreign Office, returned to the diplomatic service. Renato Ruggiero, Malfatti's *chef de cabinet*, unanimously regarded as a man of exceptional personal qualities, went on to pursue a career both in the public sphere (Trade Minister, Director-General of the World Trade Organisation, Foreign Minister) and in the private sector (board member at Fiat, Chairman of ENI, Chairman of the board for Citigroup in Zurich). Ernst Albrecht, von der Groeben's *chef de cabinet*, was to become Prime Minister of Lower Saxony. Manfred Lahnstein would be appointed Chancellor Helmut Schmidt's Finance Minister. Jean-Claude Paye, Raymond Barre's *chef de cabinet*, became Secretary-General

---

[1] Braun, N.-C., op. cit., p. 213 et seq.
[2] Interviews with Jean Flory, 3 December 2003, and Pierre Defraigne, 16 December 2004.
[3] Interview with Georges Rencki, 13 January 2004.

[4] Interview with Jean Degimbe, 15 December 2003.
[5] Interview with Fausta Deshormes, 2 February 2004.

The Rey Commission (1967–70)

1) Jean Rey
2) Emile Noël secrétaire général de la CCE
3) Emmanuel Sassen
4) Victor Bodson
5) Edoardo Martino
6) Henri Rochereau
7) Fritz Hellwig
8) Sicco Mansholt

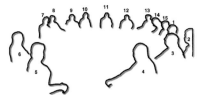

9) Raymond Barre
10) Hans von der Groeben
11) Wilhelm Haferkamp
12) Jean-François Deniau
13) Guido Colonna di Paliano
14) Albert Coppé
15) Lionello Levi Sandri

The number of Commissioners having increased to 14, the Rey Commission meets round an oval table. The round table was now no longer big enough.

of the OECD, while Daniel Cardon de Lichtbuer, Albert Coppé's *chef de cabinet*, would become the chairman of Banque Bruxelles Lambert.

The accounts of many of those involved agree that life in the *cabinets* was hard, exhausting, yet exciting: 'Twelve hours a day dealing with new and complex problems in six cultures and four languages — nothing was really easy'; but there were some major compensations: 'We managed to get things moving in an extraordinary manner because it was a period of intense creativity, amazing innovation, [...] it was like a honeymoon

period for Europe at the time' ([1]). Another of those present at the time remembers: 'I attended all the night sessions of the common market over 15 years. The *chef de cabinet* was expected to be there. It was amazing. I was tired out when it finished. It was unimaginably exciting, extraordinary' ([2]).

The *cabinet's* main task, as a rule, was to ensure that its Commissioner could go into the weekly

---

([1]) Interview with Jean Flory, 3 December 2003.
([2]) Interview with Daniel Cardon de Lichtbuer, 12 November 2003.

Jean Monnet, the Action Committee for the United States of Europe and the Commission

In 1955, after standing down as President of the ECSC High Authority, Jean Monnet, the inspiration behind European integration, set up the Action Committee for the United States of Europe. Comprising leaders of political parties or non-communist trade unions, the ACUSE set out to promote a stronger role for the European Communities.

Throughout the period 1958–72, Monnet, together with his close collaborators Jacques Van Helmont and Max Kohnstamm, maintained a very close relationship with the Commission, where he had many friends who shared his European ideal. Through correspondence, exchanges of letters, telephone conversations and meetings — e.g. with Émile Noël whom he often met in Paris on Saturdays, or with Walter Hallstein, Albert Coppé and many others — Monnet exerted an inestimable, but undoubtedly very great influence.

1. Letter from Jean Monnet to Walter Hallstein, President of the Commission, 23 May 1960

'My dear friend,

I found Hirsch's ([1]) speech at the Assembly excellent, particularly the passage about the merger. I am delighted that the three political groups unanimously adopted his ideas and underlined the urgency of merging the executives.

[...]

I agree with you that the Commissions must play a major role in this procedure. [...] Do you intend to announce publicly that the Common Market Commission will do its utmost to facilitate the merger of the executives, as Hirsch has done?

And if you do, will you do it at the next Assembly or earlier?

It would send a very important message if the Commissions of the Common Market and of Euratom were both in favour of a single executive.

I should like to discuss this matter with you by phone as soon as possible; or, if possible, I would prefer to meet with you. [...] In the meantime, I am sending you the draft resolution on the merger of the executives that I propose to table at the next meeting of the Committee. As I have not shown this draft to the members of the Committee, I can make any changes that you think necessary to it, either in the substance or the wording.'

(FJME, AMK C 33/2/136)

2. Interview with Giuseppe Ciavarini Azzi (extract dealing with the empty chair crisis)

'We had prepared a file for Monnet in August [1965]. He tried to get in touch with his contacts in Paris to emphasise France's interest in putting an end to the empty chair problem. At Émile Noël's request, we had prepared a whole file with Henri Étienne, all sorts of things that might help Monnet. I remember taking it to Monnet's house in Paris.'

Interview with Giuseppe Ciavarini Azzi,
6 February 2004

([1]) Étienne Hirsch, then President of the Euratom Commission, had been a close colleague of Monnet in the 'Commissariat général au plan', the French Planning Commission.

3. Letter from Jean Monnet to Willy Brandt, Foreign Minister, Bonn, 12 May 1967

'My dear Minister,

Kohnstamm and I intend to be in Bonn on Thursday the 18th and Friday the 19th of May. I hope very much that we will have an opportunity to see you on your return from Tokyo. But if this is not possible, I want to write to you what I would have liked to say to you verbally.

Now that Hallstein has resigned from the European Commission, and that other members will also leave, the question of who is going to be appointed:

a) as Chairman of the Commission

b) as a German member to replace Hallstein

is absolutely of major importance.

[…]

I think that the best possible candidate is the one you mentioned to me some time ago and that is M. Rey. I suggest to you that a great effort should be made to have him appointed. I think Lunds would go along with you, and probably also the Belgium and Luxembourg governments. […]'

(FJME, AMK 112/1/2, extract of the original English, uncorrected)

4. Statement by Jean-Claude Eeckhout

'I met Monnet when I was at Albert Coppé's (¹) in 1967. I remember that there was this whole ritual whenever Monnet came to the Commission. Coppé would go down to greet him, take him up to his office, speak to him in private for a while, and then the other employees would be given the opportunity and the honour to be summoned and to be present at a discussion between Coppé and Monnet. […] I know that they exchanged papers. Then they would say, Let's both read this, then we'll speak on the telephone. But I don't have any actual memories in detail. I just remember the ritual and it didn't happen that often. I think it was five times a year. […]

Monnet and Coppé often rang each other. I often heard Coppé say to Monnet, 'I'll have a word with Brandt, then I'll call you back.'

(Group interview, 19 October 2004)

M.–Th. B.

(¹) From 1952 to 1967, Albert Coppé was a member of the ECSC High Authority, of which Monnet was President from 1952 to 1955. He was subsequently a member of the Single Commission.

Commission meeting with a clear, self-explanatory agenda, by underlining the important points and marking up passages in the documents that had to be read ([1]). The *cabinet* staff also assisted the Commissioner at the European Parliament's meetings in Strasbourg and in the various meetings of the Council of Ministers: the *cabinets* would gather all the documents together, do the calculations and swap with their neighbours, etc. They would shield the Commissioners, erecting a formidable barrier between the Commissioner and the administration, especially on sensitive issues like the budget, information, etc. But they did not simply focus on issues within their Commissioner's remit. When Robert Toulemon became Marjolin's *chef de cabinet* in 1962, Marjolin said to him: 'There is no need for an intermediary between my director-general and me in anything to do with economics, finance and monetary matters, […]. It would only confuse things. You have absolutely no need to concern yourself with matters within my remit. Your job is to keep me informed of what my colleagues are up to, what they are proposing, what they are about to propose and to give me your opinion' ([2]). Not all the members of the Mansholt *cabinet* dealt with agriculture either ([3]).

Cabinet staff also had the job of establishing ties and arranging consultations with various bodies outside the Community, primarily the Member State governments. According to Jean Flory, a member of Robert Marjolin's *cabinet*, '(In Paris,) we mostly ended up seeing the members of the SGCI, the interministerial secretariat for European affairs, which was the interface, via the permanent representation, for almost every matter arising between the French administration and the European institutions. All legal, financial, economic matters, etc. had to be discussed with them. They would send out the instructions to the permanent representation. Sometimes, we had to go higher and see this or that ministerial *cabinet* or admin-

istration' ([4]). The *cabinets* were also in contact with civil society organisations, in particular, trade associations. In Sicco Mansholt's *cabinet*, Georges Rencki was responsible for negotiating with the farmers. 'First of all, our idea was not to work in a vacuum — we wanted information — and secondly, we wanted to let our intentions be known and see the reaction. Informally, to start with, by encouraging organisations covering the Six to be set up, but then more formally by setting up advisory committees attached to the Commission. […] That kept us informed about possible compromises between them, while we would let them know the general outline of proposals quite early on, before the Council, so that when our proposals were published, they would already understand what they were all about' ([5]).

The role of the *cabinets* gradually increased in importance. By the early 1970s, their stature was impressive. They had the advantage of handling all the major issues, they had an overall, more political perspective than the directorates-general. Yet they had less authority than the French model. Jean Chapperon, who had served in a French ministerial *cabinet*, admitted that, 'almost automatically, without even having to think about it, we would pick up the phone, call a director-general and give him instructions. It was as if the minister himself had spoken and then I realised that, in Brussels, it couldn't work like that' ([6]). In fact, the Commission was careful to specify in 1962 that the *cabinets* could — in fact, should — contact the officials in charge of a file direct to obtain the technical information they required, but without discussing policy aspects or influencing their attitude. On the other hand, a *cabinet* was not authorised to organise meetings with groups of officials from a directorate-general other than the one answerable to its Commissioner. If they wanted to, they had to obtain the prior agreement of the Commissioner responsible ([7]). According to Fernand Braun, although the *cabi-*

([1]) Interview with Jean Chapperon, 23 January 2004.
([2]) Interview with Robert Toulemon, 17 December 2003.
([3]) Interview with Georges Rencki, 13 January 2004.

([4]) Interview with Jean Flory, 3 December 2003.
([5]) Interview with Georges Rencki, 13 January 2004.
([6]) Interview with Jean Chapperon, 23 January 2004.
([7]) PV spéc. 185, EEC Commission, 11 April 1962, XXV-2, p. 25.

The Malfatti Commission (1970–72)

1) Franco Maria Malfatti
2) Émile Noël secrétaire général de la CCE
3) Albert Borschette
4) Altiero Spinelli
5) Wilhelm Haferkamp

6) Sicco Mansholt
7) Albert Coppé
8) Ralf Dahrendorf
9) Jean-François Deniau
10) Raymond Barre

The Malfatti Commission, comprising nine members, returns to the round table. The Commissioners can listen through headphones to a translation provided by interpreters working in the cabins at the back of the room.

nets on the whole increased their influence over the directorates-general following the establishment of the Single Commission in 1967, there were several variants: the weaker Commissioners no doubt relied on their *chefs de cabinet* to keep the directorates-general under control, but the stronger Commissioners were in direct contact with their administrations ([1]).

The role of the *cabinets* was defined through the efforts of Émile Noël. To facilitate collective deci-

sion-making, the Secretary-General succeeded over time in putting over the idea of organised *chefs de cabinet* meetings. To start with, these were informal meetings dealing with specific issues. In 1962, the Commission decided to put meetings of *cabinet* members on a more systematic basis ([2]), in advance of its own meetings, but it was only with the advent of the Single Commission in 1967 that this was formalised on the basis of a weekly schedule with the specific aim of preparing the Commission's discussions. On

---

([1]) Group interview, 19 October 2004.

([2]) PV spéc. 185, EEC Commission, 11 April 1962, XXV-2, p. 25.

6 July, at its first meeting, the Commission decided, on a proposal from its President, Jean Rey, who most likely was asking on the advice of Émile Noël, that *chefs de cabinet* would meet every Tuesday morning — later to become Monday afternoons — to prepare for the meetings of the Commission itself. It was also agreed that the *chefs de cabinet* could be accompanied by a senior official or an expert from the directorate-general answerable to their Commissioner. The Legal Service was also to attend, while the secretariat would be provided by the Secretariat-General, which was responsible for drawing up a summary report to serve as a basis for the Commission meeting. If the *chefs de cabinets'* discussions led to unanimous agreement, it was decided that the President could propose the decision for adoption at the meeting without a debate. If the *chefs de cabinet* could not agree, the Commissioners would continue the discussion on the basis of the various positions adopted and alternatives proposed in the report. These meetings would be chaired by the Secretary-General, Émile Noël or, in his absence or if the nature of the questions so required, by the President's *chef de cabinet*. Some Commissioners, notably Albert Coppé and Emmanuel Sassen ([1]), would have preferred the second alternative but the first prevailed. So, 'Émile Noël had found a useful tool, meetings of the *chefs de cabinet*. They [...] met every week. [...] And that was how Émile Noël prepared all the meetings. Nothing happened in the Commission unless it had more or less been planned. It was masterful' ([2]). In these meetings Noël would quickly identify 'the points of convergence and the differences. He was a genius, not just with words [...] but ideas too. He would come up with ideas that pulled things together or set them apart. And he could memorise everything that was done and everything that was said [....]' ([3]).

The political future of Commissioners

'As things now stand, the national politician who becomes a European politician has no future or prospects from the moment he breaks with his own party and his electors, his term of office as a European Commissioner being, in any case, of limited duration.

We are perfectly aware that *this is a bad and unsatisfactory situation* ([4]), but the first thing to do is to recognise that it exists and to think what can be done to change it. We must recognise that the promised *European future* of politicians involved in European politics is non-existent. A politician's aim is, by definition, to *take part in the management of political power*, even when in opposition, something that would be impossible if he were excluded from national political structures, given the absence of a *European political structure* that is not obliged to work through national structures. At best, he might be able to devote himself to propaganda and spreading the European message, or running pressure groups, which naturally would not satisfy everyone.

So the direction we have to go in is this: we have *to try to create that European political structure* in which politicians could move freely, which would be influenced by political and social forces and which would be the expression of a genuine European power.'

Emanuele Gazzo in *Europe*, 4 March 1972, on the resignation of Franco Maria Malfatti ([5]).

([1]) Interview with Jean-Claude Eeckhout, 3 December 2003, and group interview, 19 October 2004.
([2]) Interview with Daniel Cardon de Lichtbuer, 12 November 2003.
([3]) Interview with Jean Chapperon, 23 January 2004.

([4]) Original emphasis, *et seq.*
([5]) See Chapter 7.

The Mansholt Commission (1972–73)

1) Sicco Mansholt
2) Émile Noël secrétaire général de la CCE
3) Albert Borschette
4) Altiero Spinelli
5) Carlo Scarascia-Mugnozza

6) Raymond Barre
7) Albert Coppé
8) Ralf Dahrendorf
9) Jean-François Deniau
10) Wilhelm Haferkamp

The Mansholt Commission retains the customs of the other Commissions; Émile Noël, the Secretary-General, sits beside the President.

Émile Noël was thus largely responsible for ensuring the Commission's cohesion. Besides the Monday meetings of *chefs de cabinets*, he also chaired the Thursday meetings of directors-general — which enabled him to keep the administration informed about the decisions taken by the Commission at its Wednesday meeting — and the meetings of the assistants of the directors-general on Fridays, not to mention the numerous ad hoc committees of which he was the chair and lynch-

pin ([1]). Émile Noël knew everything that was going on, he was the best informed person in the Commission and he was an inexhaustible source of ideas for it ([2]). The most remarkable thing was that the Secretary-General's calm but all-pervading authority appeared to be accepted without question by all the members of the Commission.

([1]) See, for example, the ad hoc groups on institutional and political matters in the early 1970s in the chapter on the Single Commission.

([2]) Interview with Giuseppe Ciavarini Azzi, 6 February 2004, and group interview, 19 October 2004.

Émile Noël was the confidant and adviser to most of the Commissioners ([1]). They trusted him and would happily come to talk with him in his office. He worked closely with successive Presidents. Although Walter Hallstein would probably have preferred Pierre Bourguignon as his executive secretary, the two men enjoyed a mutual trust and held broadly similar views on European integration ([2]). Noël had an easy relationship with Jean Rey, whom he helped through a difficult succession ([3]), while the Malfatti Commission, under the leadership of a relatively weak President, worked well, guided by the partnership which Noël managed to develop with the *chef de cabinet*, Renato Ruggiero ([4]).

Marie-Thérèse Bitsch,
with the collaboration of Yves Conrad

([1]) Interview with Fernand Braun, 8 December 2003, and group interview, 19 October 2004.

([2]) Interview with Jean Flory, 3 December 2003, and other interviews.

([3]) Interviews with Giuseppe Ciavarini Azzi, 6 February 2004, and Frans De Koster, 14 November 2004.

([4]) Interview with Giuseppe Ciavarini Azzi, 6 February 2004.

Chapter 10

Émile Noël, a loyal servant of the Community of Europe

'Writing about Émile Noël means, first and foremost, daring to write about Émile Noël.' This is how the Belgian Ambassador to the Communities, Paul Noterdaeme, describes the difficulties involved in depicting the man and his achievements [1]. Nevertheless it is an enormous intellectual and emotional challenge to try to understand this Frenchman of the Jean Monnet mould, who shaped, over 30 years, the most innovative of the European Community institutions, the European Commission. How best to learn about the life and work of the Executive Secretary to the Commission of the European Economic Community (EEC) and subsequently Secretary-General of the Commission of the European Communities after the merger of the executives than through those who knew him? Émile Noël was one of the founders of the Community of Europe between January 1958 and January 1973, a dynamic and productive period of the Europe of Six.

What was Émile Noël's background?

Émile Noël was born in what was Constantinople (now Istanbul) on 17 November 1922 to a Bel-

gian father and a French mother and died in Agliano (Tuscany) on 24 August 1996. After attending secondary school in Aix-en-Provence, he passed the entrance examination for the École Normale Supérieure in Paris in 1941, where he studied sciences. He graduated in physics and mathematics. During the war, at the age of 21, having refused to do compulsory labour service, he joined the Resistance (forming part of the Maquis in Isère and then in Vaucluse, fabricating false papers, organising escape routes and the clandestine press in Paris). He led the Resistance network at the École Normale Supérieure after Michel Voisin's arrest.

After the war, in a desire to promote education for young working-class people, he set up and led the Camarades de la liberté (Cam' Lib), a secular and humanistic youth movement which had grown out of the Resistance (Mouvement de libération nationale, Libération Nord, Organisation civile et militaire des jeunes, ceux de la résistance and Nouvelle jeunesse), which popularised the idea of youth clubs and rural centres, and organised open-air holiday camps. Noël, who was inspired by the ideals of the Resistance and democracy in a united Europe, organised a

---

[1] Noterdaeme, P., 'Farewell Mr Noël', *Courrier du personnel*, September 1987, Special edition, No 488, p. 76.

travelling youth train in 1948, which visited 100 cities in France, Belgium and Switzerland to provide information to young people about job opportunities on the French labour market.

For a few months in 1949 Noël worked for the international secretariat of the recently created European Movement and was assisted by the Deputy Secretary-General, Georges Rebattet. He then became Secretary to the General Affairs Committee of the Consultative Assembly of the fledgling Council of Europe. In 1952 he became Director of the Secretariat of the Constitutional Committee of the ad hoc Assembly charged with producing a blueprint for a European Political Community in 1953. He then served as *chef de cabinet* to the socialist Guy Mollet, President of the Consultative Assembly of the Council of Europe, from 1954 to 1956.

When Guy Mollet became Prime Minister of France on 31 January 1956, a post he held until 21 May 1957, Émile Noël went with him, serving as his *chef de cabinet* and then Deputy Director of *cabinet*. Alongside Alexandre Verret, Noël played a leading role in the negotiation of the Treaties of Rome. He was Guy Mollet's right-hand man. Robert Marjolin, a member of the French delegation led by Maurice Faure, State Secretary for Foreign Affairs, described him as 'a "European" from the start, ardent in his convictions beneath an affable and tolerant exterior, clear-sighted and keen, he helped, often decisively, to get the President of the Council to take decisions that enabled the Brussels negotiators to carry out their task effectively'. Jean Monnet, who was the driving force behind the launching of the European project, considered Émile Noël to be a 'very valuable link' for the Prime Minister (¹). In this role he wrote for Guy Mollet on various aspects of governmental policy. He also proposed ideas in confidential exchanges with Guy Mollet, with whom he became close friends, and other members of

the *cabinet*. He was also responsible for vital diplomatic missions, which only persons with discretion could carry out on issues such as the Franco-British intervention in Suez and the Algerian question.

Once the Treaties of Rome had been signed, Robert Marjolin supported Émile Noël's nomination for the post of Executive Secretary of the Commission of the European Economic Community because of his knowledge of European affairs. Noël took up his post in March 1958, a few weeks after the Hallstein Commission entered office. When the institutions of the three Communities were merged, Émile Noël became Secretary-General of the Single Commission of the Communities in early 1968. He remained in this post until 1987. For nearly 30 years he was the highest-ranking official in the Community administration and applied himself — in Monnet style — 'with a tenacity as great as his modesty, [...] to make the Community's institutions both supple and strong' (²).

As only part of his career and achievements will be discussed below on the basis of the interviews I have conducted, it will obviously give only a partial view of the man's work. This covers the period from January 1958 to January 1973, during which four Commissions served: the Hallstein Commission (January 1958), the Rey Commission (July 1967), the Malfatti Commission (July 1970) and, finally, the short Mansholt Commission (March to December 1972). During these founding years of the Europe of Six, Émile Noël put in place an effective and multinational European administration combining, according to Jacques Rabier, 'tenacity, modesty, efficiency and flexibility' (³). These qualities gave the European Commission, despite the problems it faced, undisputed credibility as its work was well prepared and solutions were worked out in confidence and with efficiency both within the institution and with the other Community institutions (the Court

(¹) Marjolin, R., *Architect of European unity — Memoirs 1911–1986*, Weidenfeld and Nicolson, London, 1989, p. 298; Monnet, J., *Memoirs*, Collins, London, 1978, p. 417.

(²) Monnet, J., *Memoirs*, Collins, London, 1978, p. 418.
(³) Rabier, J.-R., 'La mémoire et notre avenir', article prepared for the Jean Monnet Association, Paris, 14 November 1996.

of Justice of the European Communities, the European Parliamentary Assembly and the Council of Ministers) and with the other European Communities (the ECSC High Authority and the Euratom Commission until 1967). Since he was initially responsible for organising the Commission's agenda and keeping a faithful account of decisions taken at meetings, Noël attended the meetings of the Commission. He was always present at the meetings of the General Affairs Council (Foreign Affairs Ministers) and occasionally at those of the other Councils. As a key figure, Noël regularly attended the European Parliamentary Assembly and also fostered contacts with the Council of Europe. He represented the Commission abroad. Lastly, he maintained contacts with representatives from non-Community countries and had a productive relationship with Jean Monnet, Altiero Spinelli, Alexandre Marc and other proponents of European unity.

When Émile Noël left his post as Secretary-General of the European Commission in 1987, he became President of the European University Institute in Florence, where he remained until 1993.

An exceptional figure

How are Émile Noël's achievements and personal qualities assessed by the many persons who agreed to be interviewed? Firstly, he was extraordinarily methodical. We must rely here on the accounts from his immediate entourage, who were best acquainted with the Secretary-General in his working environment. Other accounts are based on more general impressions or his reputation. Nevertheless, everyone describes him as exceptional, with a sharp intellect, high moral principles and legendary discretion, which made him a man on whom Commission Presidents could rely.

Admiration

There was virtually nobody outside the Commission's Secretariat who did not express boundless admiration, sometimes in familiar but very signifi-

cant terms, in the interviews. 'A genius in the Commission' said Pierre Wathelet, a Head of Division and trade unionist, who spoke about his 'extraordinary cold seduction' [1]. 'A fascinating person' explained Heinrich von Moltke, a former official at Euratom, 'he knew everything' [2]. 'The most extraordinary man I have ever met', said Gianluigi Valsesia, who was an administrator in Ispra at the Joint Research Centre (JRC), 'he was an absolute genius' [3]. 'A patrician', added Claude Brus, of the Directorate-General for Administration and, for many years, a staff representative [4]. He was also admired by Marcello Burattini, who worked in external relations [5]. 'Émile Noël was a wonderful man', remembered a colleague of Robert Marjolin [6]. The Head of the Interpreting Service noted that 'in the institutions we need strong, not popular people, who are firm [....] Noël was extraordinary' [7]. Émile Noël's reported skilfulness and the care he took of his officials were admired. Those who knew him best shared the same opinion of Émile Noël. Jacques-René Rabier, Director of the Joint Information Service, called him 'an extraordinary man' [8]. 'An extraordinary personality' is what Robert Toulemon, at the time Director for industrial, technological and scientific affairs, said. He revealed another side to Noël's character, noting that Noël was 'a fairly secretive but very discreet man' [9]. He was also grateful to Noël for having warned him and Guido Colonna di Paliano, Commissioner for industrial policy, that their grandiose industrial policy projects would not succeed [10].

A demanding man

Their admiration was based on the view that the man was demanding of himself and others. He listened carefully to his interlocutors out of

---

[1] Interview with Pierre Wathelet, 8 June 2004.
[2] Interview with Heinrich von Moltke, 22 January 2004.
[3] Interview with Gianluigi Valsesia, 4 December 2003.
[4] Interview with Claude Brus, 5 December 2003.
[5] Interview with Marcello Burattini, 18 February 2004.
[6] Interviewed in January 2004.
[7] Interviewed in February 2004.
[8] Interview with Jacques-René Rabier, 8 January 2004.
[9] Interview with Robert Toulemon, 17 December 2003.
[10] Ibid.

politeness or principle. He never got annoyed or, if he did, all I heard him say was: 'Yes, of course'. 'He never went any further', said Clément André, who was responsible for staff training and the *Courrier du personnel* ([1]).

This quality gave him impartiality. 'He was a man who was totally, but totally, independent and dared tell Commissioners when he didn't agree', said Jean Degimbe, Special Adviser to the French Commissioner Raymond Barre in 1967, admiringly ([2]). He even demonstrated his independence by speaking forthrightly to the Presidents themselves, reported Renato Ruggiero, who at the time was *chef de cabinet* to President Malfatti: 'Mr President, of course you must know what Mansholt, Deniau, and others think. But the most important thing is what do you think?' ([3]).

This sometimes made him difficult to get on with. Jean-Claude Séché, Assistant to the Director-General of the Legal Service, reminisces that Noël 'was not always very easy' ([4]). Frans De Koster, Head of the Registry in the Commission's Secretariat-General until 1972, noted that Émile Noël had such a huge personality that he helped his colleagues in many ways but that they were in danger of losing some of their independence of thought ([5]). Gérard Olivier, Deputy Director-General in the Commission of the European Economic Community's Legal Service, noted that 'in his relations with Commission officials, Noël was the type of man who would go easy with you if you showed any resistance. You had to stand up to Noël, otherwise he would dominate you.' ([6]) Degimbe agreed with Gérard Olivier: Noël had 'a fantastic intellect, he was a human computer, extraordinary, but very demanding, very authoritarian, in fact extremely authoritarian' ([7]).

A more critical picture is painted by Hubert Ehring, who was Financial Controller at the time: 'Noël was also a solitary man. You must have been aware of that. He didn't have any friends. He was an unconditional integrationist.' ([8]) The secretive and reserved side to his character and his European ideals could make him too demanding. 'Noël lived alone, he had absolutely no personal or social life. He lived entirely for his work. He spent his weekends in Paris. Then he would return to Brussels', explained Gérard Olivier ([9]). This view of Émile Noël by someone who was not one of his friends is based on a misconception. Noël had childhood friends, friends from his time in the Resistance or the Cam' lib (Camarades de la liberté), Socialist friends and people whom he had got to know when he worked at the Council of Europe and whom he saw when he was at the Commission. During the holidays and on some long weekends he liked to return to the Charentes, where he had a home on which he liked to work himself. This was where his family lived. Edmund Wellenstein, who at the time was Secretary-General of the ECSC High Authority, wrote that he had happy memories of a man who liked his food, was witty and was extremely hospitable ([10]). When he joined the Commission, Noël became friendly with his two colleagues from Euratom and the ECSC, Giulio Guazzugli-Marini and Edmund Wellenstein. They met regularly, creating a sort of regular link between the three executives at the time through their secretariats. This helped them to draw up a joint report on the integration of the three administrations when the two Commissions and the ECSC High Authority were to be merged in 1967. The 'monk-like' existence which some people claimed he led was without foundation. Noël had a much richer personal life than these views would lead us to believe. It was discretion combined with a huge capacity for work which created a false image of someone who lived only for his work.

([1]) Interview with Clément André, 9 February 2004.
([2]) Interview with Jean Degimbe, 15 December 2003.
([3]) Interview with Renato Ruggiero, 15 July 2004.
([4]) Interview with Jean-Claude Séché, 8 June 2004.
([5]) Interview with Frans De Koster, 14 November 2004.
([6]) Interview with Gérard Olivier, 4 December 2003.
([7]) Interview with Jean Degimbe, 15 December 2003.

([8]) Interview with Hubert Ehring, 4 June 2004.
([9]) Interview with Gérard Olivier, 4 December 2003.
([10]) Letter from Edmund Wellenstein to the author, 28 July 2005.

A very loyal friend

'Émile Noël was a very loyal friend. I often had lunch with him in Brussels (but usually somewhere near his office…). He had an admirable ability to theorise but "in practical terms". It was the Community institutions which counted; I remember that from 1972 onwards he called on us to be less punctilious in our way of legislating and pointed to the risk of taking too uniform an approach to very diverse national situations.'

Interview with Georges Rencki, 13 January 2004.

The image of hardness, distance and coldness that some attribute to him is dispelled by Émile Noël's intellectual and emotional collaboration with a group of senior officials who were 'motivated by similar experiences [....] and wanted to do everything they could to make this new adventure on which the European Communities had embarked work', as Michel Gaudet, Winrich Behr (his first Deputy Executive Secretary), Louis Rabot, Helmut von Verschuer and Fernand Spaak, alongside Fernand Braun, Robert Toulemon, Jacques-René Rabier, Klaus Meyer, Walter Much and Gérard Olivier, report [1].

'He always saw the interests of the institution as also being those of the Community', added Henri Étienne, Head of Division in the Secretariat-General [2]. This was reflected in a huge capacity for work and complete mastery of European matters which made his contributions both within and outside the Commission exemplary [3].

Political commitment

Émile Noël was also a committed socialist who renewed his membership card with the SFIO (French Section of Workers International) every year even if he did not give the appearance of being a fiery Socialist [4]. Who was aware of this at the Commission? Noël seemed to be 'more a Monnet man than a militant socialist' but he was very close to Guy Mollet, reported Karl-Heinz Narjes, Head of Hallstein's *cabinet* [5]. His socialist leanings did not facilitate his initial contacts with the Christian Democrat, Walter Hallstein, who was EEC Commission President. However, this political obstacle was soon overcome as the Community of Europe was an all-embracing religion, explained Marc Sohier of the Legal Service [6]. After the Greek colonels' coup on 20 April 1967, Noël and others, including Sicco Mansholt, Alfred Mozer and Bino Olivi opposed, on the grounds of their political views, the granting of loans by the European Investment Bank (EIB) to Greece [7]. Despite his political commitment Noël did not, however, show any political preferences in the appointment of officials [8] since, as Clément André indicated: 'he never made a thing of his political or other views'. [...] The Commission always came first. He only had one thing to say: 'the Commission.' [9] Nevertheless, Noël maintained contact with the Parisian Left and Centre opposition. During the Presidential electoral campaign in 1965 he prepared briefings on Europe for Jean Lecanuet and François Mitterrand, who were standing against de Gaulle. Noël worked for the 'Europeans' in France and never hesitated to provide Gaston Defferre (a socialist) with information he could use in face-to-face talks with Michel Debré (a Gaullist) [10].

A man in the shadows

Observers unanimously agree that Noël was a man of influence, secretive and perhaps feared,

[1] Edmund Wellenstein had much evidence to show how Noël colluded with other senior Commission officials.
[2] Interview with Henri Étienne, 12 January 2004.
[3] Interview with Gianluigi Valsesia, 4 December 2003.
[4] Interview with Henri-Marie Varenne, 17 December 2003.
[5] Interview with Karl-Heinz Narjes, 24 May 2004.
[6] Interview with Marc Sohier, 3 June 2004.
[7] Interview with Bino Olivi, 26 January 2004.
[8] Interview with Fernand Braun, 8 December 2003.
[9] Interview with Clément André, 9 February 2004.
[10] FMJE, AMK C 33/4/150, Van Helmont to Émile Noël, 24 October 1966, and reply in C 33/4/151, Émile Noël, 28 October 1966 to Van Helmont.

but certainly astute. 'An *éminence grise*', said Robert Toulemon, 'a man of few words but always well aware of what was going on, a man who had succeeded in gaining Hallstein's confidence.' ([1]) Klaus Meyer, Deputy Secretary-General, said 'he was a very fair man, very intelligent, a mathematician with a slightly dark, mysterious side.' ([2]) 'He was a monk, a secular European monk', explained Jean Durieux, Director in the Directorate-General for Development ([3]). This image is reinforced by the seemingly austere life he led, according to observers. Noël lived in a small, modest, one-room apartment in the avenue Charlemagne. Every weekend he returned to Paris to join his wife and two daughters, taking with him work in a small suitcase, reported his colleague Giuseppe Ciavarini Azzi ([4]). But sometimes he dropped his guard and his colleagues at the Commission were surprised, reported Daniel Cardon de Lichtbuer, *chef de cabinet* to Albert Coppé, after the Paris Summit in December 1972: 'Then I saw something nobody had ever seen. Noël so happy, and a Noël who was so reserved we didn't even know whether he was married or not, he lived in a small apartment, he worked night and day, etc. Noël said to us all: "come to my place" and we had dinner in Noël's apartment in Paris, a slightly shabby academic's apartment on the Left Bank with Madame Noël, his wife. Yes, there was a Madame Noël. This was all very mysterious. But that's how it was. We knew nothing about his life.' ([5]) Secretive, industrious, an *éminence grise* for the cause of Community integration, 'Machiavellian' ([6]) and 'Byzantine ([7]), a new Talleyrand according to some' ([8]), but, as Jean Chapperon, *chef de cabinet* to Henri Rochereau and then Jean-François Deniau, said, 'a sort of secular saint working for the European cause' ([9]).

The key to his influence

In what way did Noël exert an influence?

Firstly, he made sure he was informed about what was going on and he kept others informed. Noël was a good listener, 'hearing others' confessions' ([10]). He had an extremely detailed knowledge of every area in which the Commission was involved. 'Without Noël, the Commission would never have been able to function as it did', was the view of Francesco Fresi, Head of Division for external relations ([11]). Noël also briefed the new Commissioners, who received their initial dossiers from the Secretariat-General, and this was an opportunity, said Henri Étienne, 'for Noël to put forward some of his ideas' ([12]). He had greater influence than his office would have suggested ([13]). He knew how to insinuate ideas. 'He would whisper in your ear, saying "I wouldn't do that, I would do this. Why did such a Commissioner take such a position? He would have been better to have done something else." ' ([14]). His authority was, however, challenged by Michel Gaudet, Director-General of the Legal Service ([15]). Relations between the two men were like 'two emperors trying to get along', said Gérard Olivier. Was this true? It is believed that they held each other in mutual respect by virtue of their respective abilities and impartiality. There was no rivalry between Noël and Edmund Wellenstein, who was Secretary-General of the ECSC High Authority at the time the executives were merged in 1965, even if Wellenstein knew full well he himself would have made an excellent Secretary-General of the Single Commission ([16]). He must certainly have come up against another strong personality, Altiero Spinelli, who became a Commissioner in 1970: 'Wellenstein and Spinelli got on like a house on fire, Spinelli got on well with Wellenstein, much better than he did with Noël — he didn't

---

([1]) Interview with Robert Toulemon, 17 December 2004.
([2]) Interview with Klaus Meyer, 16 December 2003.
([3]) Interview with Jean Durieux, 3 March 2004.
([4]) Interview with Giuseppe Ciavarini Azzi, 6 February 2004.
([5]) Interview with Daniel Cardon de Lichtbuer, 12 November 2003.
([6]) Interview with Jean Stenico, 24 February 2004.
([7]) Interview with Norbert Kohlhase, 26 May 2004.
([8]) Interview with Marcello Burattini, 18 February 2004.
([9]) Interview with Jean Chapperon, 23 January 2004.

([10]) Interview with Henri-Marie Varenne, 17 December 2003.
([11]) Interview with Francesco Fresi, 5 February 2004.
([12]) Interview with Henri Étienne, 12 January 2004.
([13]) Interview with Fernand Braun, 8 December 2003.
([14]) Interview with Frans De Koster, 14 November 2004.
([15]) Interview with Jean-Claude Séché, 8 June 2004.
([16]) Interview with Gérard Olivier, 4 December 2003.

Walter Hallstein (on the left) and Émile Noël (on the right) were both born on 17 November; Hallstein in 1901 and Noël in 1922. Here they exchange birthday greetings in the Commission's meeting room on 17 November 1961.

get on with Noël, there was a deep mutual mistrust and antipathy,' said Ricardo Perissich, who was a member of Spinelli's *cabinet* ([1]). This view seems rather odd as Spinelli wrote to Noël in 1975, 'After being a guardian of the Treaties for so long, you have not only guarded them but also looked beyond them.' ([2])

The second key to Émile Noël's influence was his knowledge of the Commission's administrative functions: 'Émile Noël was the real head, as it were, of the Commission, as regards administrative and day-to-day affairs.' ([3]) His very detailed knowledge of the Commission explains his ability to propose just the right solution. Émile Noël's influence was due to his organisation of the Ex-

ecutive Secretariat, which became the Secretariat-General, the engine room of the Commission's administration. He began by setting up a registry of documents as the official memory that could be relied on in any circumstances. He also introduced internal coordination between all Commission departments and coordination of relations with other Community institutions. These three instruments made the Secretariat-General a mandatory control and transit point. Although he sought to establish a strong Secretariat-General, Émile Noël did not develop very elaborate or rigid administrative structures within the Secretariat-General. His concern was to ensure efficiency based largely on direct contacts with colleagues ([4]). It is said that relations with Noël in the Secretariat-General were based on trust but

([1]) Interview with Riccardo Perissich, 2 February 2004.
([2]) Marianne Noël private archives, signed letter from Spinelli to Noël, 26 June 1975.
([3]) Interview with Jacques Ferrandi, 28 and 29 May 2004.

([4]) Interview with Giuseppe Ciavarini Azzi, 6 February 2004.

were always demanding (¹). Noël stayed in the office late into the night and required officials to be available (²). He relied on his assistant, Nadine Verbeeck, whom he trusted implicitly, for day-to-day work (³). He worked with two secretaries who took it in turns to work either in the morning or the afternoon and evening; the secretary who worked in the evening would stay until the morning to finish the previous day's correspondence, so it is said.

The third key to his influence was his Community convictions. He had come from the Council of Europe, had been the personal representative of the French Prime Minister, Guy Mollet, in the negotiations of the 1957 Treaties of Rome, and had decided to do all he could to ensure European integration was a success. His language never revealed his federalist convictions. Henri Étienne took a radical view: 'Monnet never used fine words. Hallstein did and we know where that led. But Jean Monnet, never. […] And as for Noël, he was the ultimate incarnation of all that.' (⁴) Noël's authority was based on his conviction that the Secretary-General was the guardian of Community doctrine.

The fourth key to his influence was his networks. Networking was part of his tactics to achieve the 'European ideal', in the view of the assistant to the Director-General of the Legal Service (⁵). His networks were not solely socialist, even if Noël continued to write many articles in Guy Mollet's name, for *Le Populaire,* the SFIO's daily newspaper, in the 1960s. Nor did he use the media, even though he exerted an influence on the information put out by Emanuele Gazzo's Agence Europe (⁶). Émile Noël was not a communicator. As Paul Collowald, Deputy Spokesman and subsequently Director-General for information, said: 'I had much admiration for Émile Noël, although

sometimes I felt he was distrustful, disinclined even to work with me.' He went on to say 'he was not necessarily an ally in relations with the press and information' (⁷). On the other hand, Noël belonged to the Monnet network. As a young Executive Secretary, he was often asked to come on Saturdays to Avenue Foch in Paris at the headquarters of the Action Committee for the United States of Europe. He kept him regularly informed about the Communities' activities (⁸). He also received strategic information from Jean Monnet. We have some idea of his telephone conversations with Monnet or Van Helmont, Secretary-General of the Action Committee for the United States of Europe (⁹). Noël was able to give him everything. In October 1960 he drafted for Monnet an outline of the Action Committee's conclusions on the latest French initiatives on European matters (Gaullist proposals for political union and criticisms of the Atlantic Pact) (¹⁰). He also suggested to Monnet that he take the initiative to link the Élysée Treaty of January 1963 with the Treaties of Rome (¹¹). This was the ardent pro-European speaking, not the Executive Secretary. During the 'empty chair' period, Noël had his colleagues, Henri Étienne and Giuseppe Ciavarini Azzi, draft memos to Monnet to bring pressure to bear on Paris (¹²). Their relationship was so strong that in 1962 Monnet asked Noël to work with him, but he refused (¹³). Émile Noël was not part of the third circle of the Monnet network, as Éric Roussel wrote (¹⁴), but one of its secret pillars.

(¹) Interview with Jean-Claude Eeckhout, 3 December 2003.
(²) Interview with Yves Desbois, 3 December 2003.
(³) Interview with Margot Delfosse-Frey, 25 October 2004.
(⁴) Interview with Henri Étienne, 12 January 2004.
(⁵) Interviewed in June 2004.
(⁶) Interview with Pierre Defraigne, 16 December 2004.

(⁷) Interview with Paul Collowald, 2 December 2003.
(⁸) FMJE, AMK, C 33/4/89, Émile Noël to Jean Monnet, 8 February 1962.
(⁹) FMJE, AMK, C 33/4/102, record of conversations between Émile Noël and Jacques Van Helmont, 15 February 1964, on the institutions after the merger; FMJE, AMK, C 33/4/101, Jacques Van Helmont, record of conversations with Émile Noël, 10 November 1963, record of 2 December 1963, Émile Noël raises questions about the CAP, relations between the United States and the Commission, and the Kennedy Round.
(¹⁰) HAEU, EN 878, Brussels, memo of 27 October 1960 to Jean Monnet, Chair of the Action Committee for the United States of Europe (CAEUE), 3-page document attached.
(¹¹) HAEU, EN 878, Émile Noël, May 1964, suggestions made in a discussion with Jean Monnet on initiatives to be taken relating to the ratification of the Franco-German agreement of 1963, Émile Noël.
(¹²) Interview with Giuseppe Ciavarini Azzi, 6 February 2004.
(¹³) FJME, Jacques Van Helmont agenda, p. 135, 22 October 1962, Houjarray, meeting with Jean Monnet, Émile Noël and Jacques Van Helmont.
(¹⁴) Roussel, É., *Jean Monnet,* Fayard, Paris, 1996, p. 703.

Chapter 10 — Émile Noël, a loyal servant of the Community of Europe

A good knowledge of the institution was Noël's final way of exerting influence. His long period as Secretary-General is certainly one reason why he knew everything about the institution, but another reason was his custom of referring to the discussion of the College of Commissioners which were carefully recorded in green notebooks and became a legendary source of reference. This enabled him to explain why a particular decision had been accepted or rejected in the past. Because he was the institution's memory, he was indispensable to the new Presidents [1].

As a result, Noël had such absolute mastery in his area of expertise that Klaus Meyer was prompted to say 'If Émile Noël worked something out or did something, it couldn't be improved, changed or rejected. It had to be accepted as it was.' [2] Noël was considered by some to be the 10th member of the Commission of Nine, as Marc Sohier indicated [3]. But he was much more, said Francesco Fresi: 'He was Number Two in the Commission, after the President.' [4] He was 'much more than a Commissioner', added Pierre Defraigne, who worked for several *cabinets* [5]. All this demonstrates the special place and influence Émile Noël had among the Commissioners.

Émile Noël, an enterprising Executive Secretary

Émile Noël was appointed Executive Secretary of the EEC Commission in February 1958, against the initial wishes of Hallstein and von der Groeben, and became Secretary-General of the Commission of the European Communities in 1967 [6]. His nomination in 1958 was supported by Robert Marjolin and by Guy Mollet. Jacques Ferrandi, first Director of the European Development Fund (EDF), considered his appointment to be commensurate with his previous position in Guy Mollet's *cabinet* and at the Council of Europe [7]. Wellenstein noted that the presence of a 'committed and capable Frenchman in this post was crucial' [8]. He took up his post on 26 March 1958 [9]. His duties as Executive Secretary were defined on 25 January 1958 by the Commission: the Executive Secretary would carry out only auxiliary administrative tasks and would not have authority over the entire administration [10]. As Edmund Wellenstein recalls, his office did not have the calibre of that of a Secretary-General: 'the Commission did not want a NATO — or OECD-type Secretary-General, who would be head of the entire administration' [11]. Hallstein even imposed the term Executive Secretariat [12]. However, once he arrived, Noël began to make his mark, as the Head of the Interpreting Service confirmed: 'That is where real power lay. Without Noël, nothing whatsoever would have got done.' [13] How did he achieve this? In 1967 he was appointed Secretary-General of the Single Commission. Despite the speculation in Commission circles, Wellenstein, as he himself said, considered Noël to be the natural candidate for this office, which he had never, therefore, considered for himself.

Establishment of the institution

His effective organisation of the institution is the reason for the power he exercised. A mere 48 hours after he arrived, Noël drafted the Com-

[1] Interview with Klaus Meyer, 16 December 2003.
[2] Ibid.: 'If Émile Noël decided or wanted to do anything, no improvement, change or rejection was possible. It had to be accepted as it was.'
[3] Interview with Marc Sohier, 3 June 2004.
[4] Interview with Francesco Fresi, 5 February 2004.
[5] Interview with Pierre Defraigne, 16 December 2004.
[6] Interview with Jacqueline Lastenouse-Bury, 21 January 2004.

[7] Interview with Jacques Ferrandi, 28 and 29 May 2004.
[8] Letter from Edmund Wellenstein to the author, 28 July 2005.
[9] 'Au revoir M. Noël', *Courrier du personnel*, September 1987, Special Edition, No 488, p. 17. As regards the date of appointment, Fernand Braun, interview on 8 December 2003. Marianne Noël-Bauer archives, letters from friends in Brussels to Émile Noël, March 1958 and 24 March 1958: 'At last! Your appointment has been confirmed before you leave for Rome.' PV 11, EEC Commission, 24–27 March 1958, arrival of Emile Noël, 26 March 1958.
[10] PV 2, EEC Commission 2, 24–25 January 1958, quoted by Conrad, Y., 'Première esquisse de l'organisation administrative de la Commission européenne "marché commun", Méthodes de travail et mise en place de services communs (1958–1961)', draft article for *Storia amministrazione Constituzione*.
[11] Letter from Edmund Wellenstein to the author, 28 July 2005.
[12] Interview with Henri Étienne, 12 January 2004.
[13] Interviewed in February 2004.

mission's internal rules of procedure under Article 162 and they were accepted virtually in their entirety ([1]). Originally, the structure of the Commission's administration had been defined according to President Hallstein's ideas. The Commission was organised like a government, the Commissioners were the ministers and the directors-general the state secretaries (according to the German system of classification, senior officials, not politicians). Noël was not involved in the allocation of portfolios to Commissioners in the first Hallstein Commission because he was not there in January 1958! But he certainly was for subsequent Commissions, as Klaus Meyer confirms. He trained the first officials in the Executive Secretariat in the summer of 1958: 'At the moment they're not yet any help, indeed they are more of a burden — we have to train them, i.e. get them to carry out tasks (not very well) and leave them to their own devices, in the hope that, in the long term, this effort will be rewarded by more independent thinking', he wrote to his wife Lise ([2]). He set up an Executive Secretariat, which was taken as a model by the Secretariat-General of the Single Commission after the merger of the executives ([3]).

To facilitate the Commissioners' decision-making, he suggested, as Marc Sohier confirms ([4]), that a system of written procedure be introduced. This involved circulating among the Commissioners, for adoption, draft decisions of Commission proposals which had been approved by the directorates-general concerned and the Legal Service. He also provided internal information to Commission officials by inventing some years later the so-called 'informaphone', a telephone number providing a brief resumé of the decisions adopted by the Commissioners at their weekly Wednesday meetings, and his very rare lectures were popular because they were prodigious, as one

person said ([5]). Noël kept a watchful eye over the Commission's administration even if there was a Director-General for administration and a Director of personnel ([6]). 'The big boss was Noël', said Jean Degimbe ([7]). Why? 'The Commission's main task', explained Noël, 'was policy-making, the drafting of legislation or regulations and overseeing of their implementation. This meant there had to be a strong headquarters in Brussels with able officials and competent departments to deal on an equal footing with national administrations or even to get the better of them.' ([8])

Recruitment of officials

The Staff Regulations of European officials were adopted by the Council in 1962 ([9]). They were based on the regulations for European officials working for the ECSC drawn up earlier under René Mayer, Monnet's successor as President of the High Authority. Noël had a hand in their drafting.

Noël recruited officials, whether they were recommended or not, according to the basic criterion of their commitment to the European project. If he considered that a particular candidate would be useful to the Commission, he got him or her accepted. He persuaded a Commissioner to accept a nomination simply by telling him 'I could work with him.' The Commissioner was then bound to express considerable interest ([10]).

The Secretary-General involved staff representatives in the annual promotion rounds for category A officials by bringing together directors-general and the staff delegation ([11]). In the 1971 strikes at the Commission, in order to persuade governments to accept an automatic salary review pro-

([1]) Interview with Karl-Heinz Narjes, 24 May 2004; interview with Klaus Meyer, 16 December 2003.
([2]) Marianne Noël-Bauer archives, letter from Émile Noël to Lise Noël, 1 September 1958.
([3]) Interview with Giuseppe Ciavarini Azzi, 6 February 2004.
([4]) Interview with Marc Sohier, 3 June 2004.
([5]) Interview with Guy Levie, 3 March 2004.
([6]) Interview with Claude Brus, 5 December 2003.
([7]) Interview with Jean Degimbe, 15 December 2003.
([8]) Interview with Émile Noël by Roger Morgan, 4 July 1991, numéro thématique du *Jahrbuch für Europäische Verwaltungsgeschichte*, *Les débuts de l'administration de la Communauté européenne*, Nomos, Baden-Baden, 1992, p. 156.
([9]) Interview with Henri Étienne, 12 January 2004.
([10]) Interview with Norbert Kohlhase, 26 May 2004.
([11]) Interview with Jean Degimbe, 15 December 2003.

cedure, Noël negotiated with the Council but also consulted the staff representatives. Jacques Ferrandi, drawing on his personal experience at the Commission in managing failing officials, reported this remark by Noël: 'Jacques, you know in 5 % to 10 % of cases there are members of staff who have problems and who need social rather than professional help. From time to time you have to show some tolerance' ([1]). Pierre Duchâteau, *chef de cabinet* to Jean-François Deniau, Jean Degimbe and Yves Desbois, Head of Division in the Personnel Directorate, noted that Noël was extremely concerned about the impact of the merger on officials from the former institutions ([2]). Noël was well acquainted with the files of officials who were about to be promoted: 'When one of his colleagues was pushing a particular official for promotion, he would let him speak and then say: 'For what reason did you say that in the staff report at the time?' ([3]). Staff representatives quickly realised that Noël was fully acquainted with the difficult cases.

Relations with Commission Presidents

Noël, a loyal servant of Europe, soon gained President Hallstein's confidence. He implemented Hallstein's ideas and offered him many suggestions. 'I believe Hallstein always appreciated working with Émile Noël,' said Giuseppe Ciavarini Azzi ([4]). Noël gained and retained Hallstein's trust.

Relations with Jean Rey, Hallstein's successor and first President of the Single Commission, were easier because, according to Ciavarini Azzi, Jean Rey 'regarded Émile Noël as a godsend' during a very difficult succession ([5]). Is it true, as Marcello Burattini suggests, that 'the President had no

powers compared with Noël. Noël did and undid everything.'? This might be an exaggeration but there is no doubt that, although every President dreamed of making his mark and doing without Noël, he would soon realise that without him the Commission would not be able to do anything ([6]). After the Hallstein period, Émile Noël became 'the confidant of all Presidents and all Commissioners. Everyone turned to him for advice to ensure that they did not get into difficulties', explained Fernand Braun ([7]). During the Commission of Franco Maria Malfatti, a weak Commission President, the Noël – Ruggiero (the President's *chef de cabinet*) team kept everything going: 'I might even say that the President was superfluous, almost' said Jean-Claude Eeckhout, who was a member of Coppé's *cabinet* at the time ([8]). This relationship with a weak President might account, according to Gérard Olivier, for the fact that, after Sicco Mansholt's brief presidency, some doubts were expressed about the continued presence of Émile Noël at the head of the Secretariat-General ([9]). Edmund Wellenstein did not agree, even if there was speculation about whether two important posts should be given to persons of the same nationality. Nevertheless, it is common knowledge that the new President, François-Xavier Ortoli, benefited from Noël's experience. Was he 'irreplaceable', as Klaus Meyer thought ([10])? Everyone I interviewed and who played a central role at the Commission stated unreservedly that Noël inspired confidence in Presidents but kept a suitable distance in order to ensure that the institution could function.

The Commission's rites

Émile Noël stamped his authority on the workings of the Commission through the rites he created. Noël gradually introduced a series of

---

([1]) Interviews with Jacques Ferrandi, 28 and 29 May 2004.
([2]) Interviews with Pierre Duchâteau, 22 December 2003; Yves Desbois, 3 December 2003; Jean Degimbe, 15 December 2003.
([3]) Interview with Yves Desbois, 3 December 2003.
([4]) Interview with Giuseppe Ciavarini Azzi, 6 February 2004.
([5]) Ibid.

([6]) Interview with Marcello Burattini, 18 February 2004.
([7]) Interview with Fernand Braun, 8 December 2003.
([8]) Jean-Claude Eeckhout, in a group interview on 19 October 2004.
([9]) Interview with Gérard Olivier, 4 December 2003.
([10]) Interview with Klaus Meyer, 16 December 2003.

'A familiar gesture of Émile Noël, showing his ability to listen and the great deal of attention he used to bestow on his interlocutors and expressing his train of thought in the search for answers and solutions. Behind this reflex of his hands, Émile Noël no doubt also hid his legendary modesty and his concern to give others time to catch up with his thinking and reasoning. It was his way of making his point of view known, acting with his usual reserve, without imposing it on anyone.'
(E-mail from Jacqueline Lastenouse, 24 October 2006.)

meetings which formed the basis for his management and influence.

Émile Noël attended the Commissioners' weekly Wednesday meetings with the Head of Registry, Frans De Koster, the Director-General of the Legal Service and the Spokesman. Noël, seated to the left of the President, remained silent but, if a serious problem arose, would interject: 'Mr President, if you would allow me…', 'Yes, Secretary-General, what's the problem?' was the reply. 'I believe that on this item the Commission would be well advised to consult the Legal Service again.' 'Yes, yes!' was the President's response.

'On which particular item?' There was no more discussion and the item was adopted the following week, according to Jean Chapperon (¹). It is also reported that 'if Mr Noël wished to intervene on a particular point at the Commission meeting without asking to take the floor, he usually indicated this before the meeting to a Commissioner. When the point was raised, the Commissioner would ask the President 'Perhaps Mr Noël has something to say on the matter?' (²)

Very rapidly, Émile Noël instituted meetings of the directors-general on Thursday mornings. When the Hallstein Commission took office, he also instituted meetings of assistants to the directors-general, following the procedure used by the High Authority, on Friday mornings, according to Jean-Jacques Beuve-Méry of the Legal Service (³). He considered this to be extremely important as the assistants acted as intermediaries and were particularly effective in getting Commission policy accepted by Commission departments. He gathered vital information about how departments were working from these meetings. 'Émile Noël reported on the Commission's meetings', explained Giuseppe Ciavarini Azzi, 'although he was known for his rather pedantic manner, he could also introduce a note of humour' (⁴). 'The idea was also to find out what was happening: a sort of progress report as it were', said Pierre Wathelet. The whole scenario would begin with Noël saying 'this is what the Commission said on Wednesday'. He could be unbelievably coy: in front of him was a huge notebook in which he recorded everything. And he would be able to relate everything without opening his notebook. We would get through 18 items, including agricultural policy. He would then turn elegantly to the assistant of Directorate-General VI (agriculture), saying 'if I am not mistaken, was there not an item on […] also?'. It was pure affectation, he knew full well (⁵).

It became standard practice for the Commissioners' *chefs de cabinet* to meet on Monday afternoon (extremely useful, according to Jean-Claude Eeckhout (⁶) after the merger (⁷). As their bosses' political right-hand men, they were not prepared to be manipulated by the Secretary-General. Nevertheless, Noël succeeded in chairing this meeting every week, despite resistance from Commissioners Albert Coppé and Emmanuel Sassen, as he had gained recognition 'at a higher level than any of the *cabinets*' (⁸). In this way, Émile Noël created an unofficial College on which he 'stamped his mark' but in which everyone derived real authority from their Commissioner (⁹). These meetings played a vital role as Noël attempted to find areas of agreement which would not have been accepted by the Commission, explained Gérard Olivier (¹⁰). Renato Ruggiero thought that this was the way Noël controlled 'the entire Commission machine' but that he did so 'with style, exceptional ability, rare courtesy and without embarrassing any of his interlocutors' (¹¹). However, Noël was insistent that Heads of Cabinet be fully briefed before the meetings. When a member of the Malfatti *cabinet* was inconsistent in a meeting, Noël asked him: 'Are you a member of the President's *cabinet*?' The official replied 'yes'. 'Prove it', retorted Noël' (¹²). Paul Collowald noted that there was a change in Émile Noël's attitude to information. When the Monday meetings of the *chefs de cabinet* were introduced, Émile Noël agreed to the Deputy Spokesman being present to ensure that the Spokesman was fully briefed on the Commission's meeting on the following Wednesday as he had to give a statement the following day in the press room. Daniel Cardon considered that the 14-man Commission worked well, precisely because of the *chefs de cabinet* meetings (¹³). Émile Noël and the

(¹) Interview with Jean Chapperon, 23 January 2004 and interview with Francesco Fresi, 5 February 2004.
(²) Account provided by Jean-Claude Eeckhout, 24 February 2006.
(³) Interview with Jean-Jacques Beuve-Méry, 3 March 2004.
(⁴) Interview with Giuseppe Ciavarini Azzi, 6 February 2004.
(⁵) Interview with Pierre Wathelet, 8 June 2004.

(⁶) Interview with Jean-Claude Eeckhout, 3 December 2003.
(⁷) 'Au revoir M. Noël', *Courrier du personnel*, September 1987, Special Edition, No 488, p. 20.
(⁸) Interview with Jean-Claude Eeckhout, 3 December 2003.
(⁹) Interview with Pierre Defraigne, 16 December 2004.
(¹⁰) Interview with Gérard Olivier, 4 December 2003.
(¹¹) Interview with Renato Ruggiero, 15 July 2004.
(¹²) Interview with Jean-Claude Eeckhout, 3 December 2003.
(¹³) Interview with Daniel Cardon de Lichtbuer, 12 November 2003.

Deputy Secretary-General assisted with all the meetings of the Council of Foreign Ministers with the directors-general concerned.

This was how he built up his networks of influence and consolidated them after the merger of the institutions in 1967.

This organisation of the Commission's internal workings, Émile Noël's strong personality, his obvious devotion to the Community of Europe, his attention to detail and his meticulous presentation had such an influence on young officials that there was a sort of Émile Noël school ([1]). Jean Durieux summed up in a few words the feelings of the persons interviewed and of Noël's close colleagues which perhaps confirm in some way the nickname of monk he was given: 'He was a towering figure. Nobody of his calibre exists any longer. What I mean is that nobody has replaced him. He was called the 10th Commissioner, member of the Commission, and indeed he was. He was the Commission's conscience and memory. [...] He lived only for that. He worked 15 hours a day. He knew everything. He was eminently respected by everybody, Commission officials and Commissioners alike, and also by the Member States' Permanent Representatives. He was a really exceptional [man] who developed an administration with rules which were not too bureaucratic but with a highly developed ethic. Certainly all those who knew Noël and who can see how the Commission works today often look back nostalgically to the time of his administration' ([2]).

This chapter has focused on Émile Noël's central role in the Commission. He played a role not only in politically sensitive affairs such as the 'empty chair' period in 1965–66, when he maintained links with the French government and regularly met Maurice Ulrich, France's Deputy Permanent Representative, but also in more sectoral issues for which he was not directly responsible, such as the restructuring of the Euratom Joint Research Centre. At the Paris summit in October 1972 he instituted the attendance of the Secretary-General of the European Commission at summits of Heads of State and used this opportunity, which continued uninterrupted until 1988, to contribute personally to the drafting of the final communiqué.

Émile Noël was a reserved man by temperament with a keen intellect and a fervent believer in the Community of Europe. Whether his convictions derived from his past as a member of the Resistance, from his socialist leanings, from his work at the Council of Europe and with Guy Mollet, which he continued with Jean Monnet, is irrelevant. Noël was literally consumed by a passion that burned in him to the end of his days: 'to build Europe'. For him, this meant firstly 'to build the Commission', reported Giuseppe Ciavarini Azzi ([3]). Émile Noël and Jean Monnet belonged to a generation of pioneers, some of whom worked in the shadows of others and others who took more centre stage — Hallstein, Marjolin, Mansholt, Rey and Spinelli. They took to heart the lesson they had learnt from the 'century of extremes' that Europe could only play a future role in history commensurate with the splendour of its past if it were united.

GÉRARD BOSSUAT

([1]) Interview with Umberto Stefani, 20 January 2004.
([2]) Interview with Jean Durieux, 3 March 2004.

([3]) Interview with Giuseppe Ciavarini Azzi, 6 February 2004.

Chapter 11

The administration

In 1958, once the College of Commissioners had been set up, the administration of the EEC Commission had to be created from scratch. Having said that, a precedent already existed in the form of the High Authority, and the interim committee had set to work on the Staff Regulations of its future officials. A number of governments, and most notably that of the Federal Republic, had also done their best to provide the new institution with officials.

At the same time, the new Commissions had been expected to perform as from the earliest days of their existence the tasks conferred on them by the Treaties. An example of this was the organisation of the Agricultural Conference of Member States, convened by the Commission at Stresa from 3 to 12 July 1958. As Hallstein wrote after the conference, everything had to be set up, even though the Commission administration was not yet in place [1].

The original estimate was that between 1 000 and 2 000 officials would need to be recruited [2].

By 31 December 1958 there were 1 051, and thereafter the numbers grew rapidly, reaching approximately 2 900 on the eve of the merger, 4 900 after the merger and almost 5 800 on the eve of enlargement.

Exactly what sort of administration did the members of the Commission want to create? Just as the organisation and working methods of the College itself were of decisive importance, so were the choice of administrative structure and the status of the staff, who could potentially breathe life into the organisation.

1958–67

For Klaus Meyer, it was basically very simple — as simple as a diagram of a government with its constituent parts. Right at the top, the Commission itself. The individual members of the Commission were like ministers; then there was the director-general, who was like a State Secretary, and below that the breakdown into directorates and departments [3]. So does that make the President the head of government? Not exactly,

---

[1] Personal archives of Georges Rencki: letter from Walter Hallstein to Georges Rencki, asked by the Commission to take charge of the practical organisation of the conference, 17 July 1958.

[2] BA, WH 2432 fiche 1, Émile Noël to Christian Calmes, Brussels, 2 April 1958.

[3] Interview with Klaus Meyer, 16 December 2003.

Staff numbers — EEC Commission and then EC Commission (1958–72)

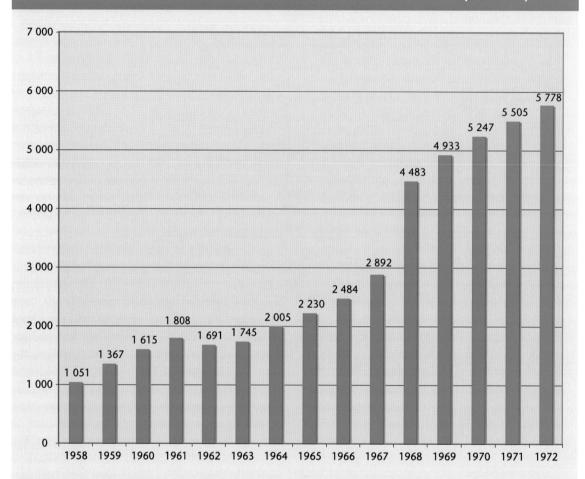

For the years up to 1967 these figures are a conservative estimate. The figures in fact vary, sometimes quite considerably, depending on the sources used. Those published in the General Report each year include in some cases the staff in the EEC branch of the joint services. The same applies to auxiliaries and local staff. The figures based on the reports of the Audit Board relating to the accounts for the financial years 1961 to 1966 do not include those from the joint services but do correspond, with only the occasional very minor difference, to the figures produced by DG IX (Administration). The comparison shows that the Audit Board counts only officials, thus excluding the 11 categories of 'other staff'. There is also the fact that the statistics were not compiled on the same date each year. While the Audit Board consistently based its figures on the situation as at 31 December, the Annual Report did its count on different dates: 28 February (1959), 31 March (1965–67) and 15 April (1961), before finally adopting the date of 31 December too. The figures used are those of the Audit Board for the years 1958–66 and then those of the Annual Report on permanent posts in categories A to D and in the language service (category L/A).

because it fails to take account of the principle of collective responsibility and the supranational aspirations of the Commission. A perfect example of this is the story of how, when von der Groeben began to defend the German position a little too strongly, Hallstein touched his hand and said 'genug' — enough.

When it came to allocating the portfolios, Hallstein himself took charge of administration, an area close to his heart. He also made sure that he kept control of the Personnel Directorate of DG IX Administration after he had delegated other areas to Levi Sandri in 1963 (¹).

Many contemporary observers confirm that the President played a decisive role in setting up the administration. He wanted a 'great administration', recalled Émile Noël (²). It must be strong, like the Commission which he envisaged as the incarnation of the European project, since, as he would have said, 'a man who lacks vision is not a realist' (³). Strong and also hierarchical, he was inspired by the German Foreign Ministry, which he had created as State Secretary and which he regarded as a model. Each level had its own responsibilities, dossiers were to move up and down the levels and there were not normally any advisory or ancillary positions (⁴). This was in marked contrast to the situation prevailing at the ECSC, according to Edmund Wellenstein (see his recollection opposite).

The question of organisational structures did not feature in the minutes of Commission meetings; it was jealously guarded by Hallstein, who intended to retain control himself. There was to be no role for the Council in a study of the departmental

Coordinating nine columns

'Hallstein's idea of a highly hierarchical administration organised into vertical columns contrasted, for example, with that of the High Authority, whose members were not individually responsible for a sector or department of their own but worked in groups of four members, with the directors of the various departments responsible for related areas. The problem for Noël, with his officially very lowly status, was to ensure coordination between these nine vertical columns. He succeeded, in parallel with similar efforts in the Legal Service, by insisting on reports and proposals being presented to the Commission's weekly meeting, by convening weekly meetings with the assistants to the directors-general (following the example of the High Authority), with the chefs de cabinet and, finally, with the directors-general themselves (again, as in the final years of the High Authority). But this final stage, which was the result of careful and systematic efforts, took shape only after the merger.'

Edmund P. Wellenstein, written recollections, 16 January 2006, p. 3.

structure; instead the task was entrusted in 1960 to a specialist consultancy answering to the President and three directors-general. All the signs point to the close involvement of the President in the creation of the administration. Although the first organisation chart was drawn up quickly enough, it then took much longer to implement the structure in practice.

The organisation chart

According to Georges Berthoin, it was Hallstein who introduced the concept of the organisation chart (⁵). With its directorates-general composed of directorates, which in turn consisted of divisions, the Commission developed a structure that seemed impersonal compared with that of the

(¹) PV 234, EEC Commission, 1963, Hallstein delegates management of the budget and finance and of internal affairs.
(²) Noël, É., 'Témoignage: l'administration de la Communauté européenne dans la rétrospective d'un ancien haut fonctionnaire', Les débuts de l'administration de la Communauté européenne, Jahrbuch für Europäische Verwaltungsgeschichte, 4, Nomos Verlag, Baden Baden, 1992, p. 150.
(³) Interview with Franz Froschmaier, 19 January 2004.
(⁴) Noël, É., 'Témoignage: l'administration de la Communauté européenne dans la rétrospective d'un ancien haut fonctionnaire', op. cit., p. 151.

(⁵) Interview with Georges Berthoin, 31 January 2004.

High Authority as conceived by Monnet. The highly hierarchical structure brought the risk of compartmentalisation of the directorates-general, which the physical dispersal of the DGs around Brussels did nothing to alleviate. It also created a class element, in that senior officials did not fraternise easily with those ranking beneath them in the hierarchy (¹).

Originally, the Commission consisted of nine directorates-general, numbered I to IX, including the DG for Administration. The Executive Secretariat, the Spokesman's Group and three EEC branches of the joint services — the Legal Service, the Statistical Office of the European Communities and the Joint Press and Information Service — completed the structure. It was not all plain sailing. There was a long power struggle with the High Authority before the EEC Commission secured the chairmanship of the board of administration of the Joint Press and Information Service (²), brought the Legal Service under its authority and left the chairmanship of the board of administration of the Statistical Office to its counterpart in Luxembourg (³).

Executive Secretariat

In January 1958 the new Commissions had to be equipped with a secretariat in which there was a careful balance between nationalities. In the first instance, before any names had been put forward, the secretariat of the Interim Committee was asked to assist the EEC Commission (⁴). Hallstein's *chef de cabinet*, Schnippenkötter, stepped into the breach. Then, when the President requested a secretary *ad interim* (⁵), the Commission nominated the Belgian, Pierre Bourguignon (⁶). This solution was temporary by

definition, and the task a difficult one, so Marjolin (if we are to believe his *Memoirs*) put forward the name of Noël (⁷), a candidate who undoubtedly enjoyed the support of Guy Mollet. But Noël had his doubts. Hallstein had already made it clear at the end of January how he viewed the job. It was not to be a secretariat like that of other international institutions such as NATO, the UN or the OEEC. The position was not that of a general secretary, the tasks would be purely administrative and auxiliary, and the incumbent would have no authority over the administration (⁸). These limitations were obviously unpalatable to Noël, who said as much. Marjolin took the matter up with the President. It was decided that the secretary would be 'executive', a term which suggested to the French Vice-President a role comparable to that of the *secrétaire du gouvernement* in his own country (⁹).

At the start of the third session of the Commission meeting at the Villa Madame in Rome on 26 March 1958, President Hallstein welcomed Mr Émile Noël, who would in future be in charge of the Commission's Secretariat (¹⁰). The decision was formally ratified on 10 April. It specified that Noël was appointed as 'Executive Secretary of the Commission' (¹¹). This was the start of an extraordinary career. He was even referred to as the 10th Commissioner. Assisted by a deputy secretary-general and a registrar, the Secretariat-General, with its highly multinational staff (¹²), was in charge of internal communications within the Commission and interinstitutional relations. It also drafted the regular reports.

(¹) Interview with Jean Degimbe, 15 December 2003.

(²) See pp. 515–516.

(³) De Michelis, A. and Chantraine, A., *Mémoires d'Eurostat — Cinquante ans au service de l'Europe*, Office for Official Publications of the European Communities, Luxembourg, 2003, p. 28.

(⁴) PV 1, EEC Commission, 16 January 1958, p. 8.

(⁵) PV 4, EEC Commission, 7–10 February 1958, p. 2.

(⁶) PV 6, EEC Commission, 24 February 1958, p. 6.

(⁷) Marjolin, R., *Architect of European unity — Memoirs 1911–1986*, Weidenfeld and Nicolson, London, 1989, p. 298.

(⁸) Conrad, Y., 'L'organizzazione amministrativa della Commissione europea "mercato comune" (1958–1961)', *Storia, Amministrazione, Costituzione — Annale dell'Istituto per la Scienza dell'Amministrazione Pubblica*, Vol. 8, Il Mulino, Bologne, 2000, p. 172.

(⁹) Belin, D., 'Organisation et fonctionnement de la Commission des Communautés', in Cassese, S. (ed.), *The European administration — L'administration européenne*, Bruylant, Brussels, 1987, p. 62.

(¹⁰) PV 11, EEC Commission, 24–27 March 1958, p. 8.

(¹¹) PV 12, EEC Commission, 9–10 April 1958, p. 7. The minutes of the first 12 Commission meetings were not adopted until 18 April 1958, by which time Émile Noël was fully established in his new position.

(¹²) Interview with Manuel Santarelli, 4 March 2004.

Organisation charts are a valuable graphic presentation of the structure of the administration: directorates-general, directorates, divisions. They also give the name of the official holding each of the managerial positions. When the administration is being restructured, they become very difficult to draw up: everybody has to be given a function corresponding to his or her status and grade, depending on what posts are vacant and what jobs need doing.

'Merging three institutions was not a simple task. Each of them had its own administration. At Euratom, there were no auxiliary staff and no agency staff. Virtually all the posts were occupied. But at the common market there were 300 auxiliary staff, and they had university graduates in B grade posts and non-graduates in A grade posts! We had six months to sort out all these problems.'
(Interview with Yves Desbois.)

Michel Gaudet

Born in Paris on 24 December 1915, Michel Gaudet studied at the Sorbonne, in the Law Faculty and in the École libre de sciences politiques in Paris. His military service began in 1937 and finished in 1939, just before the outbreak of the war. He was taken prisoner in 1940 and spent 18 months in Dresden. At the request of the Red Cross, he was sent to the free zone and became auditor at the Council of State in 1942. He spent the rest of his career within this institution, an organisation with which he felt a close bond despite the periods of secondment which he enjoyed.

In 1945 he was the legal adviser to the French protectorate in Morocco. Promoted to the position of 'master of requests' in the Council of State in 1948, the following year he became head of the private office of the State Secretary for Finance and Economic Affairs, only to return to the Council of State in 1950 to serve as government commissioner in the litigation section. After returning to the position of 'master of requests' in 1952, he was named a Councillor of State in 1964.

Michel Gaudet was one of Jean Monnet's close associates and maintained regular contact with him. Among his associates figured Max Kohnstamm, whom he met particularly frequently [1]. He found himself working for the High Authority in 1952 where he was in charge of its Legal Service. Having been involved in the drafting of the Treaties at Val-Duchesse, he became, at the request of Jean Rey, Director-General of the EEC Commission's Legal Service in 1959.

Many of his colleagues from that period are effusive in their praise for him. Michel Gaudet was 'quite remarkable', 'a great man', 'a fine mind', 'a strong character' [2]. He was highly regarded particularly for his way of working.

'He was a man who wanted to understand. He took great care to be understood. [...] He had this way of not launching straight into the crux of the problem but explaining. [...] When everyone shares the same cultural references, you can go quite fast but, when they don't, this can be a source of misunderstanding. You mustn't go too fast. He learnt all this at the ECSC.' [3] He took also 'great trouble over recruitment. It was crucial. To recruit people who worked well, who appreciated a high standard of work and who believed in Europe, who were there not for the money but who wanted to be part of this great venture [...]. These were the people you wanted on your team. [...] You can be demanding but you must respect their work. And you must make sure there is absolutely no question of favouritism, national or otherwise. [...]. And keep them informed of everything that concerns them [4].' His un-hierarchical methods set the standard for many years after his departure [5].

He was 'highly intelligent, very well-balanced. He was both deeply European and, at the same time, very aware of the need to soothe national sensibilities, to be tactful in dealing with the Member States, and particularly France and the French administration. He was really a man of the highest calibre, an outstanding lawyer and a source of inspiration.' [6]

He was sometimes referred to as the 11th Commissioner. Because of his position he was able to assess the legal validity of a decision and to exert a certain influence, particularly as he

---

[1] Interview with Jean-Jacques Beuve-Méry, 3 March 2004.

[2] Interviews with Gérard Olivier, 4 December 2003, with Jean-Claude Séché, 8 June 2004, with Marc Sohier, 3 June 2004, and with Claus-Dieter Ehlermann, 29 January 2004.
[3] Interview with Jean-Jacques Beuve-Méry, 3 March 2004.
[4] Ibid.
[5] Interview with Jean-Claude Séché, 8 June 2004.
[6] Interview with Gérard Olivier, 4 December 2003.

had the ear of Walter Hallstein first; and then Jean Rey after. Both Presidents had a legal training (¹).

The reasons for his departure in 1969 are rather obscure. He claimed to be resigning on personal grounds. According to his assistant at the time, Jean-Claude Séché, Gaudet thought he was about to be replaced and pre-empted the move. Actually, the two most important directors-general, namely the Secretary-General and the Director-General of the Legal Service, were both French. To amend this situation, it seemed obvious that a choice would have to be made

and, in view of his influence and his high profile, Émile Noël was bound to retain his post (⁵).

In 1970 Gaudet became President of the French Federation of Insurance Companies. From 1978 to 1982 he was also President of the European Insurance Committee. Finally, from 1977 to 1989 he succeeded Jean Rey as President of the Court of Arbitration at the International Chamber of Commerce (⁶).

M.R.

One department that was important not for its size but for its function was the mail service, which one commentator, alluding to its head, Max Sicar, compared to the French secret service, *la Piscine* (²). This perhaps surprising comparison nevertheless conveys the perceived importance of this department, which handled all of the institution's incoming and outgoing mail.

The Legal Service

The EEC branch of the Legal Service was headed by Michel Gaudet, who had come from the ECSC and was close to Jean Monnet. In Brussels he served under Jean Rey and remained there until his departure at the end of 1969. 'A fine lawyer' who enjoyed a very high standing among the directors-general (³), Gaudet was described by some as the 11th Commissioner (⁴). He was assisted by a Deputy Director-General, the German Hubert Ehring. The Legal Service had a flat organisational structure consisting of a series of often tiny teams of just two or three officials (⁷). In its early

days it was the keeper of the knowledge, the repository of the collective wisdom.

With its dual role of warning the Commission against making mistakes and defending it when it does, the Legal Service has no authority over the Commission's other departments. It does, however, have enormous influence over the course that is taken. In this sense, its participation in Commission meetings and its meetings with the *chefs de cabinet* enhance still further the visibility of a service that in some ways embodies the fundamental principle of the EEC as a Community based on the rule of law. As Jean-Jacques Beuve-Méry put it, 'Gaudet was determined there should be a clear and simple rule about the role of the Legal Service in the Commission. No document was to be submitted to the Commission without having been seen and checked by the Legal Service. This was very simple, but it gave the service considerable power over the working of the Commission and the administration'. Hence the system of prior consultation by the directorates-general, albeit to varying degrees. In fact, as time went by, the central role of the Legal Service

---

(¹) Interviews with Claus-Dieter Ehlermann, 29 January 2004, with Jean-Claude Séché, 8 June 2004, and with Marc Sohier, 3 June 2004.
(²) Interview with Jean Stenico, 24 February 2005.
(³) Interview with Claus-Dieter Ehlermann, 29 January 2004.
(⁴) Interviews with Marc Sohier, 3 June 2004, and Guy Levie, 3 March 2004.

(⁵) Interview with Jean-Claude Séché, 8 June 2004.
(⁶) Interview with Michel Gaudet, 20 and 26 January 1998, 'Voices on Europe' programme, HAEU.
(⁷) Interview with Claus-Dieter Ehlermann, 29 January 2004.

declined to some extent as the number of law-yers in the DGs increased (¹). In addition, the empty-chair crisis was followed by a crisis of confidence in the director-general (²), although no commentator could put their finger on the cause. Gaudet left the Commission at the end of 1969, leaving the field entirely open to Noël (³).

Recruitment

The question of the administrative structure may have been relatively straightforward, but the same could not be said of recruitment. Hallstein wanted to recruit people who held important positions in the Member States, on the grounds that they would ensure the high calibre of the institution and would have the necessary authority to stand up to the representatives of private interests. Noël, who drew a distinction between officials in positions of responsibility and initiative and other staff (⁴), shared this view.

The directors-general

Hallstein's vision was not easy to put into practice. As well as those who were obviously unwilling to chase shadows, there were others who faced a barrage of questions and insults from their national colleagues on why they were going to join the 'federasts' (⁵).

Nevertheless, the calibre of the first directors-general was, as Hallstein himself said, undeniable. The President was personally responsible for selecting them and the directors, leaving the *cabinets* to sort out the rest of the problems between them (⁶).

One important principle was that the director-general must not have the same nationality as the Commissioner. As an intermediary between the

directorate-general which he heads and 'his' Commissioner, but also the other members of the Commission, he enjoys an autonomy subject to the constraints set by the boss. Jean Degimbe explained that a good director-general 'either leaves if he does not agree or applies the Commissioner's policy [...]. The room for manoeuvre is awfully small. We are a bit like lawyers. You plead a case which is the Commissioner's' (⁷), although Paolo Clarotti qualified this by pointing out the opposite was sometimes true too (⁸).

The large countries had two posts, Belgium and the Netherlands one each, while the Director-General of Administration (DG IX) and the Executive Secretary were excluded from the quota. The top officials included a number of diplomats: the Germans, Seeliger (DG I), 'more of an artist than an official' (⁹), and Allardt (DG VIII), famous for his scar (¹⁰), and the Italian, Franco Bobba (DG II). Others had vast experience in their field: Renzetti (DG VII), who had headed the Italian State railways, Rabot (DG VI), head of the Agriculture Department at the OEEC, and the Dutchman VerLoren van Themaat (DG IV), an eminent lawyer. The same could clearly not be said of the Belgian De Muynck, who headed DG V (¹¹). Lastly, in the Administration DG two Dutchmen (Maurits van Karnebeek and Antoon Smulders) followed one another in quick succession before the Belgian Joseph van Gronsveld held the post for many years.

With distinguished careers already behind them, the directors-general were hardly in the first flush of youth. So it was impossible to predict how these highly experienced but relatively elderly people would adapt to a job that was very different from what they had done before and for which no real precedent existed (¹²). Some of

(¹) Interview with Jean-Jacques Beuve-Méry, 3 March 2004.
(²) Interview with Claus-Dieter Ehlermann, 29 January 2004.
(³) Ibid.
(⁴) Noël, É., *Les rouages de l'Europe*, 2nd edition, Paris, Nathan, 1979, p. 89.
(⁵) Interview with Pierre Duchâteau, 22 December 2003.
(⁶) Interview with Erich Wirsing, 2 March 2004.

(⁷) Interview with Jean Degimbe, 15 December 2003.
(⁸) Interview with Paolo Clarotti, 28 November 2003.
(⁹) 'Mehr Künstler als Beamter', von Staden, B., *Ende und Anfang — Erinnerungen, 1939–1963*, ipa, Vaihingen/Enz, 2001, p. 178.
(¹⁰) Interview with Pierre Cros, 8 December 2003.
(¹¹) Interview with Paul-Henri Buchet, 20 January 2004, and Noël, É., 'Témoignage: l'administration de la Communauté européenne dans la rétrospective d'un ancien haut fonctionnaire', op. cit., p. 150.
(¹²) Noël, É., 'Témoignage: l'administration de la Communauté européenne dans la rétrospective d'un ancien haut fonctionnaire', op. cit., p. 151.

them failed the test. For others, it was their finest hour. And age was not necessarily the deciding factor. For example, the French, with the exception of Rabot, stood out because of their youth. Ortoli (DG III) was 33 and the Executive Secretary 35. Both fell into the category of what the Germans referred to with tongue in cheek as the 'young French geniuses'. The phenomenon became more widespread lower down the hierarchy, the most famous example being Jean-François Deniau, a director in DG I. With his background in the Finance Inspectorate, he belonged to that formidable French elite drawn from the most prestigious institutions of State, which the Germans might laugh at but which nevertheless impressed them (¹). As they said, this was an administration of 'énarques' (²).

While the reasons for the failure of some and the success of others had little to do with age, they were certainly related to the new administrative and institutional culture. The directors-general were responsible for recruiting their own staff but were bound by the constraints of a multinational organisation and by administrative rules which seriously restricted their freedom of choice (³). Even though the actual system adopted worked relatively well (⁴), the directors-general did not immediately appreciate the difficulties entailed in recruiting officials in the Member States and getting them to work together (⁵).

Getting people to work together

There is nothing unusual about an administration having difficulties with recruitment or with officials who are less competent or less motivated than others. But in 1958, despite the precedent of the High Authority, certain other problems arose.

The first was the obvious matter of staffing levels, which was the subject of complex negotiations between the Council and the EEC Commission. This remained an issue throughout this period. One moment the Council would be generous, the next it would be imposing stringent cuts. However, having attended to the most urgent matters in 1958, the EEC Commission had a recruitment plan by February 1959.

Then there was the problem of officials' terms of employment. This covered not only their everyday working conditions but also their administrative status and salaries. On the question of pay, the point of reference was the salaries paid by international organisations and particularly the High Authority of the ECSC.

Were the Staff Regulations that entered into force on 1 July 1962 purely fortuitous or did they draw judiciously on other sources of inspiration?

With the proviso that staff matters were the private prerogative of Hallstein, which explains why Noël did not become closely involved, the Staff Regulations were largely modelled on those of the ECSC officials, which had been adopted under the presidency of René Mayer (⁶). Consequently, they drew heavily on the staff regulations of the French public service, for example in the sections on the role of the official, on recruitment by competition — a typically Franco-Belgian idea — and on the General Regulations and the Staff Regulations of the ECSC (⁷). The same commentator also noted that German inspiration, by contrast, was less apparent and that, for example, the distinction in the German system between *Beamte* and *Angestellte* was not adopted and instead everyone who worked for the institutions, from the director-general down to the doorman, chauffeur or technician, was classified as an official (*Beamte*) (⁸).

On the basis of the Staff Regulations, the staff of the administration were now classified into four catego-

---

(¹) Von Staden, B., *Ende und Anfang [...]*, op. cit., p. 178.

(²) Coming from ENA, the French École nationale d'administration. Interview with Erich Wirsing, 2 March 2004.

(³) Interview with Manuel Santarelli, 4 March 2004.

(⁴) HAEU, FMM 3, *Rapport sur l'organisation des services de la Commission de la Communauté Économique Européenne*, (1961), partie A, p. 18.

(⁵) Interview with Armand Saclé, 28 January 2004.

(⁶) Edmund P. Wellenstein to Ivo Dubois, 16 January 2006; Ivo Dubois to Catherine Day, 5 January 2006, p. 7.

(⁷) Ivo Dubois to Catherine Day, 5 January 2006, p. 7.

(⁸) Ibid.

ries (A to D) covering a total of 22 grades. Officials would receive a pension after 33 years of service.

But it was not just a question of finding and appointing candidates. This was the height of the Cold War, and candidates had to be beyond reproach. This was not such a problem in the case of candidates plucked from the Council of Europe or the High Authority as it was for officials coming from the national administrations. Security checks had to be carried out with these administrations. The EEC Commission complained that this could take months, but the delays were even longer in the case of candidates from outside the public sector. Were these checks really necessary or was this just paranoia about 'the Red menace'? It is very hard to say. It is impossible to generalise from the isolated examples cited by Pierre Duchâteau, most of which concerned German officials who had been imprisoned by the Russians during the war and on whom the Russians exerted pressure [1].

But the communist threat was not the only reason for vigilance. The war had only recently ended and, as Bino Olivi remarked, memories of the war period were still very fresh in the minds of the French [2]. Elaborating on this point, Jean Degimbe commented that the question of who did what in Germany still touched a raw nerve [3]. It was not just the psychological aspect of throwing together the occupied and the occupiers; the position of the Italians was ambiguous, as was that of ex-Vichy officials, while the Germans suffered from a guilt complex, according to Daniel Cardon [4]. The question of who did what under the Nazi regime was obviously important, not just on moral grounds but also because the European institutions could not run the risk of embarrassment by tolerating the presence among their officials of people with guilty secrets in their past. Unlike the High Authority, which provoked a scandal by accepting Speer's former associate and honorary SSer, Karl-Maria Hettlage, Adenauer's State Secre-

tary for Finance, as one of its members from 1962 up to the merger [5], the EEC Commission let through only a few isolated undesirables and got rid of them as soon as the truth came out.

In order to incorporate into the new system the staff of the Communities who were already in service on 1 July 1962, an integration procedure was applied to all staff of the 'new Communities' who had been recruited on a provisional basis pending the entry into force of the Staff Regulations. This implicitly resolved the cases of delays or difficulties related to the security checks to which the EEC Commission attached particular importance. Once they got the green light, the staff became established officials with retroactive effect. This system could produce anomalies: staff who might have been positively assessed on the basis of the work they had done might receive an unfavourable recommendation from the integration committee which could lead to a salary cut!

By the spring of 1961 most of the recruitment had been completed [6] and it was time to prepare the next stage: setting up the programme of internal competitions. However, some time was to elapse before these got under way.

All of this took place without any systematic consultation with the staff. The Commissioners were divided on the issue. As a result, a staff committee was set up and occasionally consulted, but up until 1967 it was only able to voice its opinions in informal meetings.

The administrative machinery

As we have seen, setting the machinery in motion was no easy matter, and maintaining the dynamic

---

[1] Interview with Pierre Duchâteau, 22 December 2003.
[2] Interview with Bino Olivi, 9 February 2004.
[3] Interview with Jean Degimbe, 15 December 2003.
[4] Interview with Daniel Cardon de Lichtbuer, 12 November 2003.

[5] See in particular the organ of the Belgian Socialist Party, *Le Peuple*, 26 and 27–28 October 1962, reporting the information published by *La voix internationale de la Résistance*. See also Carbonnel, M., 'Karl-Maria Hettlage (1902–1995): Un expert au service de l'Europe et de l'Allemagne', *Journal of European Integration History*, Vol. 12, No 1, 2006, pp. 67–85.
[6] HAEU, FMM 3, *Rapport sur l'organisation des services de la Commission de la Communauté Économique Européenne*, (1961), partie IX, p. 3.

proved equally difficult. In his role of liaising between the Commissioner and the administration under his command (¹), the director-general, who was often poorly prepared for leading very large teams (²), was, of course, perfectly free to take the initiative of convening his colleagues, but equally he could choose not to do so. In other words, everything depended on the man himself — and at this stage there were still very few women.

In an administration of the sort that was created in 1958, the Executive Secretary planned to play a leading role, particularly in relation to the directors-general. Of course, the directors-general were in contact with their Commissioner or his *cabinet*, which consisted of a very small number of people. But formally they had no contact with their fellow directors-general, largely because of the structure imposed by Hallstein. Noël took the initiative of bringing them together. His aim was to pass on information but also to gather information for himself. He would explain what the College of Commissioners had decided, had given its interpretation of developments and had answered the questions put. He thus ensured that a sense of collective responsibility prevailed at the level of the directors-general. But it was an uphill struggle. He sensed a certain reticence on the part of these senior officials (³). A polite way of saying that, by casting himself in the role of coordinator, as we would now describe it, he was in danger of treading on people's toes. But, despite their heavy workload, the directors-general assiduously attended these meetings over the years.

The assistants: a different atmosphere

During the meetings with the assistants, which he started in 1959 and which were held in his office, the Executive Secretary did the same thing as

with the 'bosses'. What was different, however, was the ambiance. The atmosphere was described as friendly, unrestrained and confidential, which is not to say that Noël could not be firm and assertive at times (⁴). With his pedagogical bent and occasional flashes of humour (⁵), Noël would address the assistants and listen to them. He was trying to ensure proper coordination (⁶), which was felt to be essential between such officials, who came from every background, had different cultures and different working methods (⁷). The concern for cohesion and information was palpable, all the more so as Noël and his small staff also used these meetings to learn more about what was happening in the departments. As the assistant to the Director-General of the Legal Service put it: 'We would tell Noël and his colleagues what we had done that week in the Legal Service and the others reported on their directorates-general. For us assistants, it was useful because we didn't have any information other than what reached us through our director-general.' (⁸)

(¹) Interview with Jean Chapperon, 23 January 2004.
(²) Daniel Cardon de Lichtbuer to Jacqueline Lastenouse, 4 January 2006, p. 1.
(³) Interview with Jean Chapperon, 23 January 2004.
(⁴) Interview with Giuseppe Ciavarani Azzi, 6 February 2004.
(⁵) Ibid.
(⁶) Interview with Henri Étienne, 12 January 2004.
(⁷) Interview with Jean-Jacques Beuve-Méry, 3 March 2004.
(⁸) Interviewed in June 2004.

These meetings of the assistants, which were not minuted, 'were sacrosanct because they set the tone Noël wanted, which then spread through all the directorates-general' (¹). A policy some referred to as 'rule by the mayors of the palace' (²), which also explains why 'everyone would talk to him, from the President and the Commissioners down to the lowliest official' (³).

Noël therefore coordinated from below what went on up on high.

Meetings of the *chefs de cabinet*

Faced with a huge increase in the number of dossiers and hence of items (some of them very minor) on the Commission's weekly agenda, the Commission decided in July 1960 to have greater recourse to the written procedure, which could be combined with preparatory work by the *chefs de cabinet* (⁴), when it came to matters which did not require the attention of all of the Commissioners.

Seizing this opportunity, Noël took the initiative, with the support of the Commissioners, of convening the *chefs de cabinet* (⁵). The Deputy Director-General of the Legal Service was also invited. Members of the Press and Information Service would occasionally attend too and report on the latest developments on a particular issue, as would the Spokesman or one of his deputies (⁶). These meetings were informal before the merger but were institutionalised thereafter. Whatever their status, these meetings were highly important, bringing together as they did a group of young men who were particularly brilliant, as their subsequent careers would demonstrate, and above all dedicated to the general interest of the Commission and to European integration, some-

The important role of financial control, as recalled by its first Director-General

'[…] There was an accounting system in the Directorate-General for Personnel and Administration, but there was no financial control. There was just an audit. There were no checks on sound financial management or regularity in the sense of compliance with the terms of the budget. Let me explain.

(When I became Director-General,) I found 300 staff at Ispra who had been in regular employment for years but without being included in the organisation chart. They were paid from the appropriations designated for spare parts, claiming that they manufactured spare parts in Ispra's workshops. This was the sort of fraud I came up against. […] The Directorate-General for Press and Information employed […] a number of staff far in excess of its organisation chart who were paid from appropriations for consultants. I don't know what their exact title was. This was perhaps one of the first clashes.

In my first year I refused to sign hundreds of authorisations. I would not authorise the list for paying these *appaltati*, as they were called in Ispra. The administration also did more or less what it pleased. One day Mr Schwenck, who was in charge of the administration, came to me with an authorisation for paying the removal expenses of a secretary who was leaving Luxembourg for Brussels; these included the costs of exhuming her late husband's body from the cemetery in Luxembourg, transporting his coffin and burying him again in Brussels. That's what I call marital fidelity! It was hard to object. But it was the sort of administration that did whatever it pleased. I wouldn't call it corruption, but it was typical.'

Interview with Hubert Ehring, 4 June 2004.

thing which could not always be said of certain directors-general or indeed certain members of the Commission (⁷). It was hardly surprising, according to Daniel Cardon de Lichtbuer, that the

(¹) Interview with Henri Étienne, 12 January 2004.
(²) Ibid.
(³) Interview with Giuseppe Ciavarani Azzi, 6 February 2004.
(⁴) PV 112, EEC Commission, 18 July 1960, VI, p. 6.
(⁵) PV 192, EEC Commission, 4 July 1962.
(⁶) Interviews with Pierre Cros, 8 December 2003, and Paul Collowald, 2 December 2003.

(⁷) Daniel Cardon de Lichtbuer to Jacqueline Lastenouse, 4 January 2006, p. 2.

chefs de cabinet had a decisive influence on the management of the Commission and were to play a crucial role in bringing about the merger (¹).

These meetings were a way of exchanging information and, above all, of settling disputes and hence working out a consensus, which was all the more necessary given von der Groeben's tendency in the early years to rant about the delays in providing the German versions of the preparatory documents for decisions.

The system devised by Noël for communicating with both the Commissioners and the directorates-general was a remarkable interface but, of course, the administration consisted of more than just directors-general and their assistants, on the one hand, and Commissioners and their *cabinets*, on the other. Two matters, at least, needed attention: the nationality of officials and other staff, and the vexed question of languages.

Nationality of staff

Just over a year before the merger an analysis of the nationality of officials outside the joint services revealed that the Belgians led the field. They were very closely followed by the Germans. Then came the French and Italians, almost on a par with each other. The Dutch were under-represented and the Luxembourgers brought up the rear.

However, the overall picture requires some qualification. When the figures are broken down by category, including linguists, it becomes clear that the Belgians occupied the C grade positions and, together with the Italians, the D grades, while the French led the field in the A grades and the Germans in the B grades and also, significantly, among the linguists.

In the joint services the Germans were heavily represented and the Belgians still outnumbered the French and the Italians.

Concern about the balance (or rather imbalance) between the nationalities was apparent from the fact that DG IX (Administration) quickly compiled statistics (first manually and then using the new technologies that were emerging) on the staff serving in the Commission and the EEC branch of the joint services. They were produced monthly and provided a scoreboard showing the absolute number of officials and other agents by nationality and, in an accompanying column, the percentage this represented. If a nationality appeared to be under-represented in categories A or B a Commissioner faced with confirming an appointment or endorsing a promotion might take offence. While the Luxembourger occasionally expressed his disappointment, the Italians in particular were capable of leaping to the defence of their national interest. Commission meetings may not exactly have deteriorated into a slanging match, but there were times when the exchanges were far from civil. In 1966, for example, Carlo Facini was appointed Director of the Budget and Financial Control, a directorate which was to enjoy autonomy from DG IX. The Luxembourger, Lambert Schaus, unkindly nicknamed by some 'le petit Schaus', strongly objected, asking whether the candidate owed his appointment to the fact that his father-in-law was an Italian government minister or to the good offices of Confindustria, the Italian employers' association. The mood was tense (²).

Of course, the complicated balancing act was inspired by a desire for fairness. But it would be naïve to ignore the role of power and influence. DG VIII, for example, was said to be a French stronghold. It had a French Commissioner and its director-general was German, but the French were very prominent in the other departments too and the European Development Fund was almost entirely under French influence (³). The situation also bothered the Belgian government,

(¹) Ibid.

(²) BA, WH 1265, fiche 1, Note to Walter Hallstein, 4 May 1966.
(³) BA, WH 1261, fiche 2, Note from Antoon Smulders to Walter Hallstein, 27 March 1963.

which made its concerns known (¹). Power and influence? When Britain first applied to join, the prospect of one day having a British director-general at the head of DG VIII was a significant consideration (²).

Given that the question of nationality was not taken lightly, particularly because of languages, it comes as no surprise to learn that senior German officials were given regular briefings, while one commentator recalls that in September 1958 Marjolin invited all the French officials to the cafeteria to hear him deliver a speech opposing the return of General de Gaulle. The initiative was very badly received by the French officials (³).

Languages

From the moment the High Authority was set up, the proposed language regime differed from that of the other major international organisations. A protocol was adopted on the basis of a draft produced by a committee of lawyers. It provided for four official languages (German, French, Italian and Dutch) but left the practical arrangements to the rules of procedure and to custom and practice (⁴).

In theory, the four official languages were also the working languages. In January 1958 the first regulation adopted by the Councils of Ministers of the new Communities was devoted to the language regime. It drew heavily on the High Authority's protocol. There was no doubt that French would be easily the most widely used working language. After all, the Treaties had been drafted in French, the cities that hosted the EEC Commission's departments were predominantly French-speaking, and 'the Germans, in any case, did not

psychologically have a right to use their language. It was not appropriate to speak German' (⁵).

Several commentators confirmed that Hallstein spoke excellent French, chaired the Commission meetings in French and switched to German only rarely in order to explain highly technical questions. Others, like von der Groeben, deliberately used their mother tongue for less legitimate reasons; obviously, regardless of their nationality, not all officials and other staff necessarily spoke a second language. A prime example being the French, 'the only monoglots in the Commission' (⁶). This is probably going too far. Among the Germans the situation varied widely, from those with no knowledge or a passing knowledge of French to those with a good command of the language. This led to problems. Quite apart from von der Groeben's criticisms, the use of French caused serious problems of translation and interpreting, although the same could be said of the reverse situation, when staff were working out of German. As everyone knows, words do not necessarily have the same meaning in all languages. Some people felt they were witnessing the birth of a European language, a progressive mix of idioms and national cultural traditions which in time would lead to the formation of a corps of officials with its own jargon (⁷), but the general feeling was that, if the institution were to work properly, it would have to build up a team of highly qualified linguists.

Translation and interpretation

Translating and interpreting are two very different jobs.

The translation service consisted of four language sections, one for each language, each containing three or four translators, one reviser and a secretary. In the early days the translations were dic-

(¹) BA, WH 1261, fiche 3, Note on the visit of the Belgian Permanent Representative, 7 May 1963.
(²) BA, WH 1261, fiche 1, Berndt von Staden to Walter Hallstein, 5 June 1962.
(³) Interview with Manuel Santarelli, 4 March 2004.
(⁴) CEAB 2 144, Protocole sur le régime linguistique de la CECA, 24 July 1952.

(⁵) Interview with Norbert Kohlhase, 26 May 2004.
(⁶) Interview with Paul-Henri Buchet, 20 January 2004.
(⁷) Interview with Marcell von Donat, 18 February 2004.

One of the stages involved in a recruitment competition is the oral test. Candidates have to face a selection board and show what they are capable of. Here, candidate interpreters (facing us) are being evaluated by Commission officials (seen from behind).

tated to a typist, sent to the reviser, returned to the translator with any corrections and then sent back to the requesting department. The Dictaphone was then introduced and gradually replaced the old method.

There was something monastic about the work. Translators had their little rooms furnished with a chair and a desk. Their equipment consisted of a few dictionaries, a telephone and, presently, a Dictaphone. There were a number of colourful characters in the service. The head of the French section, Daniel Berbille, was outstanding. Origin-

ally from the Basque region, he came from the ECSC and was highly gifted. His speciality was the President's speeches, which he translated impeccably, with a very faithful rendering of the text. Others were less competent. The selection procedure became ever more rigorous and standards rose. At the same time, the specific nature of the subject areas covered by the Commission called for a great deal of work on the terminology and linguistic sensitivity of the four languages. At the end of the 1960s, when part of the service had been installed in Luxembourg, the basis was laid for a common terminology bank. The High

'Women in the kitchen'

Renée Haferkamp Van Hoof recounts the following telling anecdote about her first meeting with Albert Coppé:

'When I was presented to him, he said, "What are you doing here?" I replied that I had been recruited as a conference interpreter. "But, my dear, your place is in the kitchen," he retorted. An unbelievable response.

I met him again at the European Movement when he was President of Honour. I said to him, Monsieur Coppé, I'm pleased to see you again even if my recollection of you is not the warmest. You told me when I was 24 that my place was in the kitchen.

He responded immediately, "Madame, don't you think everyone should get a second chance?"

"But of course," I replied.

And we've worked well together ever since.'

Recollection by Renée Haferkamp, in Tindemans, L. and Cardon de Lichtbuer, D. (eds.), *Albert Coppé*, Garant, Antwerp Apeldoorn, 2006, pp. 34–35.

Authority had promoted the creation of a system called Dicautom, the brainchild of Albert Bachrach, whereby the translator could consult an electronic dictionary. This was the prototype of what was to become the Eurodicautom terminology database, which has been adapted with every enlargement.

In terms of staff numbers, the number of posts actually filled was for years lower than the number provided for in the organisation chart. For example, in October 1963 the staff establishment plan provided for 137 posts, but only 101 of these were filled. In 1966 there were 110 vacant posts out of a total of 284.

Overall, the figures increased very significantly after the merger. Taking the translation and inter-

pretation services together, the number of posts rose from 467 in 1968 to 561 in 1972 and 707 in 1973, after enlargement. Provision for this had been made in advance, and considerable effort was devoted to translating the text of the Treaties and secondary legislation into English, Danish and Norwegian. Finally, a new role emerged for 'lawyer-linguists', who were responsible for ensuring the consistency of Community acts in all the different language versions.

The role of the interpretation service was to facilitate verbal exchanges in meetings, regardless of the language skills of the participants. Here, too, there was plenty of work to be done. It was not a matter of just providing interpretation for Commission meetings, a responsibility which fell to Renée Van Hoof, an emblematic figure in the history of the EEC Commission and later the Single Commission. It was just as much about ensuring the smooth running of the increasingly numerous meetings of national experts from the Member States and other countries. The figures speak volumes. In October 1963 there were only 22 serving interpreters out of the 67 provided for in the organisation chart. Of these 22 people, four were Swiss and one Austrian. The interpretation service, like its translation equivalent (which contained eight Britons and one stateless person) had to turn to nationals of non-member countries.

The growth of the interpretation service was quantitatively and qualitatively important. Demand grew. And Renée Van Hoof came to dominate the service over the years. Despite her evident qualities, she came up against the glass ceiling. Clearly, it was no easy matter being a woman in the 1960s, and the fact that the organisation employed many female interpreters made no difference. In fact, quite the contrary.

Making improvements

Clearly, many people involved in the birth and development of the EEC Commission wanted this

Reasons for the 'drift' in certain Commission departments in 1960

'There are objective reasons for the drift which will make it very difficult to eliminate the problem altogether. We know what they are: a degree of inertia typical of multilingual organisations, where differences in training lead to difficulties of amalgamation; the nature of the Commission's powers, which are powers of initiative rather than decision or management; the nature of the institution in that the type of responsibility that exists, collective down to the smallest detail, unduly extends the direct competence of the Commission, and the Commission, for all its high calibre, has only a limited capacity to give direction and provide leadership and it reserves this capacity for the major issues; finally, what we might call the rotation of problems, the piecemeal mobilisation of the administration from one period to the next, and a failure in many cases to follow up policymaking and negotiating tasks with management tasks.'

HAEU, FMM 3, [F.-X. Ortoli],
Rapport sur l'organisation des services de la Commission de la Communauté Économique Européenne, (1961),
1ère partie, p. 3.
(Translated from the French)

to be an efficient, rational and skilled process. The willpower of Hallstein and Noël alone was not enough. Others had to pull their weight too, helping to create a strong institutional identity. An illustration of this was the Commission's decision at the end of 1960 to launch a job description survey with the help of a private firm.

This seemed to be a good moment. Most of the recruitment had been completed. The results would carry all the more weight as a result. They were examined by a committee on rationalisation consisting of Bobba, VerLoren van Themaat and Ortoli, assisted by officials of DG IX's organisation department. The outcome, the *Rapport sur l'organisation des services de la Commission de la Communauté Économique Européenne* (known as the Ortoli Report), contained various general and specific conclusions. We shall consider only the general ones here.

The Commission's successes had all been achieved in 'the small number of collective operations which gave an impetus to the common market [...] and in managing the tasks circumscribed by a timetable and resting on binding clauses in the Treaty'. These successes all relate to the same types of problem 'they were important, urgent, the aims were clear, and they were sure to result in a decision, there were clear guidelines and the Commission was in control'. In this area the Commission justifiably gave the impression of speed and coherence in its work (¹).

By contrast, where there were no clear orders, there was a feeling of 'drift' that was, if not general, at least widespread. These departments had slipped into 'the international routine, organising themselves around studies, operating like the secretariat of a meeting of six States'. This had regrettable consequences: low morale, pointless work, slowness and indifference. This demoralised officials who had entered the Community administration with the aim of building Europe and the illusion of building it fast (²). Three recommendations were made to remedy this state of affairs: remove staff who were underperforming, redistribute certain tasks and refocus activity.

The report served its purpose. Reforms were successfully introduced. But just when the EEC Commission seemed to have put its house in order, the Council decided on 24 September 1963 to start the preparations for the merger, now that British membership was no longer on the cards.

(¹) HAEU, FMM 3, *Rapport sur l'organisation des services de la Commission de la Communauté Économique Européenne*, (1961), partie A, p. 2.
(²) Ibid. p. 4.

From merger to enlargement

Noël began working on the merger in October 1963. In July 1964 he was instructed to carry out in a strictly personal capacity a preparatory study with a view to reorganising the services, in conjunction with Wellenstein, the Secretary-General of the High Authority, and Guazzugli-Marini, the Executive Secretary of the EAEC Commission. Although the final report was dated 1 July 1967, it was the culmination of a long period of reflection about what was a major decision.

It would be impossible to analyse this 150-page report in detail here. But a number of points should be mentioned because they concern important pointers for future developments.

The number of directorates-general doubled, while the joint services ceased to exist in their previous form and were incorporated into the new institution. The Press and Information Service became DG X, with the Statistical Office and the Legal Service remaining as special cases. The Spokesman and his deputy acquired a larger staff.

Four Euratom departments and one ECSC department were not directly affected by the merger. The Supply Agency, which was legally and financially autonomous, remained in existence. The Safeguards Directorate, which monitored the use of nuclear material, and the Security Office, which was responsible for preventing the disclosure of data that might be detrimental to the defence interests of one or more Member States, were directly answerable to the Commission and the President respectively. This provoked some hilarity at a time when Europeans were fascinated with the exploits of James Bond.

Euratom's Dissemination of Knowledge DG became DG XIII, and the ECSC's Credit and Investment DG became DG XVIII. Both remained in Luxembourg.

For the rest, certain existing DGs, such as DG VI (Agriculture) and DG VIII (Overseas Development), were hardly affected by the merger and others experienced limited changes. The main exceptions were the financial and economic DGs, namely DGs II, III and IV [1].

New DGs were set up largely because responsibilities were reassigned or in order to stimulate developments that were already well under way, as in the case of the Directorate-General for Regional Policy (DG XVI).

One area of Euratom which employed a particularly large number of officials and local staff was its Research and Education DG. When the staff of the four research establishments are included, this sector accounted for a total of 2 500 officials and 600 local staff. The creation of the new DG XV did not resolve the matter of the sheer number of officials. This continued to cause problems in the ensuing years, which were marked by recurrent industrial unrest, particularly in Ispra, in Italy. This also shows that the merger seems to have been a more traumatic experience for many officials from the EAEC Commission than for the ECSC.

Apart from the changes in the organisation chart, the merger also encouraged a new approach and the adoption of new measures to improve the procedures for preparing proposals for submission to the Commission. This was all the more necessary given that the Commission would now have 14 members and its deliberations would necessarily be more drawn out [2]. The written procedure was therefore used to settle everyday or minor problems, while the meeting of *chefs de cabinet*, which had become a regular feature of Tuesday mornings and was chaired by the Secretary-General, was used to deal with matters of medium importance. At the same time, the members' private offices (*cabinets*) expanded their membership, supposedly to be drawn from the DGs but certain exceptions were made.

---

[1] *Rapport du Secrétaire général de la Haute Autorité et des Secrétaires exécutifs des Commissions de la CEE et d'Euratom sur l'organisation des services de la Commission des Communautés européennes*, SEC(67) 3001, 1 July 1967, p. 11.
[2] Ibid.

Aladdin represents the 'typical' civil servant in the Commission *Courrier du personnel*, pictures sometimes speaking louder than words. The cartoonist satirises the post-merger staff rationalisation. In 1958 staff had to be found, but in 1967 cuts have to be made: one in four will probably have to go. The measures thought up to help resolve the crisis include Articles 41 and 50 of the Staff Regulations, whereby, provided certain conditions are met, an official can leave the Commission and be paid an allowance when a restructuring operation is launched.

Noël wanted to increase the role of the Secretariat-General in order to help settle differences between departments. This called for organisational measures: setting up permanent interdepartmental committees, chaired by the lead DG and served by the Secretariat-General. Proper management committees were also set up within the Commission to run activities affecting several departments (¹). Other examples, such as the proposal to attach the Press and Information Service and/or the Spokesman's Service to the Secretariat-General, show that Noël regarded the merger as a good opportunity for carrying out reforms. The prevailing impression was that Noël, while

encouraging the work of horizontal services, was keen to secure the future of the Secretariat-General. Commissions would come and go, but it would endure. However, as Edmund Wellenstein points out, 'I never saw any permanent interdepartmental committee in operation' or a 'genuine management committee to run activities affecting several departments' (²).

Quite apart from these considerations, the merger posed certain purely administrative challenges and raised certain psychological issues. It was no mean feat. On 13 July 1967 Jean Rey addressed

---

(¹) Ibid., p. 12.

(²) Written recollections of Edmund P. Wellenstein to Ivo Dubois, 16 January 2006.

his officials: 'We must not stitch together or simply maintain three separate administrations [...]. On the contrary, we must merge them, fusing those departments that have to work together, leaving separate those that have to remain separate [...] but, clearly, we have to rethink our administration so that it becomes a single administration.' (¹)

This declaration of intent was not enough to reassure the staff. The business of transferring officials from Luxembourg to Brussels and vice versa and the individual problems that arose as a result of differences between the grades of officials from the different executives would take up the second half of 1967 and all of the following year (²). There was a real risk that the Commission would be able to work on little else apart from the merger — or takeover, as the other two executives saw it (³).

The work was completed more or less according to the timetable set by the three Secretaries-General or Executive Secretaries. The real problem was the rationalisation associated with the revision of the Staff Regulations. The negotiations with the Staff Committee internally and Coreper externally, and the 'wait and see' attitude of the European Parliament's Committee on Administration and Budgets dragged the proceedings out over many months. The Staff Regulations were adopted in February 1968, pending a review planned for the end of that year. However, the organisation charts and rationalisation of the administration were the subject of several stormy Commission meetings. The Council stood its ground: cuts had to be made in staff numbers. Of course, this was partly inspired by the desire for rationalisation, but, as illustrated in the chapters on policy, a determination on the part of France in particular to bring the Commission to heel also played a part.

The adoption of the establishment plan by the Commission on 23 January 1968 was far from painless. The sharp cuts in the number of posts had to be achieved by natural wastage; in other words, staff who left would not be replaced. But this was not enough, and redundancies could not be avoided. Von der Groeben, supported possibly by Hellwig or Sassen, rounded on his fellow Commissioners and the President: the problems were being placed before the Commission much too late, leaving time for nothing more than an emergency debate, but above all the procedure adopted was all wrong. The Commission found itself negotiating with the Council from a position of weakness, armed with only feeble arguments, whereas it ought to have defined the tasks to be performed, and their respective importance, and calculated the corresponding staff requirements beforehand. It would then have had a solid basis on which to enter into the discussions with the Council.

Events proved von der Groeben right. Despite the very firm position taken by Levi Sandri in Coreper and the urgent efforts by the Commissioners to impress upon their national governments the impossibility of further staff reductions, nothing could be done. Some Commissioners probably compared Coreper to Moloch, imagining that a few more sacrifices would be made and then the score would be settled. The Commission ultimately confirmed that there would be no redundancies for officials below grade A3, but it left the door open to all who wanted to resign, provided that this did not jeopardise the working of the administration. There were a total of 254 voluntary departures, and 488 people changed their place of work.

To complete the arrangements, the Commission officially appointed the directors-general in March 1968, and Noël assumed his position as Secretary-General. Other appointments followed in the period up to June. Two strict rules were applied: officials were to remain in their original department for as long as possible, and the transfers were made without promotion. Lastly, although this question was not directly linked to rationali-

(¹) AULB, 126 PP, dossier VI.36.
(²) Report of the Secretary-General of the High Authority and the Executive Secretaries, op. cit., p. 14.
(³) Interview with Henri Étienne, 12 January 2004.

The administration consisted of four categories (A to D) covering a total of 22 grades.
After the merger this category-based structure became more pronounced, especially where ex-Euratom staff were concerned, for they were less used to this kind of hierarchy. The cartoonist, a Commission official, suggests that the motto for D staff should be 'modesty in dignity' and for C staff it should be 'the Community interest comes before our own interest'. Categories A and B are at the top of the hierarchy. Grades A1 to A5, the managerial posts, are open 'by invitation only', whereas the 'intermediate' Grades A6 to B1 are 'by order of merit'.

sation, Coreper proved very parsimonious as regards any salary increase. The rise that was finally agreed was modest and was not retroactive. The Commission was diplomatic about the outcome: 'this decision will bring only limited satisfaction to staff […]' (¹).

This period of unrest was also marked by tensions between the Commission and the Staff Committees of the three executives, which resigned on 15 February 1968. This minor crisis was resolved in April with the adoption of the rules of procedure of the new Staff Committee and the election of its members.

Lastly, Levi Sandri asked to be relieved of the responsibility for personnel and administration in July 1968, citing pressure of work in his social affairs portfolio. Nobody was deceived by this excuse; the Commissioner had had enough. In the end, a compromise was reached: the Italian kept personnel and Albert Coppé took over administration.

As Raymond Barre put it, 1968 had indeed been a dreadful year (²). And not just because of the events of May. Or perhaps it would be better to borrow Marcell von Donat's description and refer to it as 'chaotisch' (³).

No sooner had conditions in the Commission improved in 1969, than a new dossier — enlargement — appeared on the horizon, and the Summit in The Hague chose this moment to tackle a series of sensitive issues which included own resources.

At the same time, the Commission underwent further reforms of its administrative structure by incorporating certain departments into existing DGs or regrouping DGs.

MICHEL DUMOULIN

(¹) PV 18, EC Commission, 20 May 1968, 1, XIV, p. 17.

(²) Amouroux, H., *Monsieur Barre*, Robert Laffont, Paris, 1986, p. 98.
(³) Interview with Marcell von Donat, 18 February 2004.

Chapter 12

Like strangers in the city? European officials in Brussels

The structure and organisation of the work of a civil service, and the way in which they evolve, make up one aspect of a reality which includes another, equally important aspect, namely the way in which men and women personify what the public has long known by the blanket expression 'the common market'.

At the beginning of 1958, as we saw in the previous chapter, everything was still to do. The two Commissions, provisionally established in Brussels in offices which were scattered across the city, had each to implement a different Treaty. At the risk of oversimplification, Euratom seemed more fragile but younger than the EEC Commission. More fragile because the creation of a 'community' in the nuclear sector was at the time a response to considerations that were, above all, political and contradictory. Wanted by Monnet and promoted by France, the EAEC seems, with the benefit of hindsight, to have been condemned from the start to miss out on the extraordinary potential of the Treaty that set it up [1]. At the time, these visions of the future were inspiring and attracted public support. The future belonged to the atom. After all, the coal mines were destined to close and the 1956 Suez crisis had exposed the weakness of the West with regard to oil.

Euratom's intention was to recruit high-calibre staff: nuclear researchers and experts in the supply of fissile materials, nuclear safeguards and health protection. Some of those who joined the EAEC came from the embryonic nuclear industry or specialist national institutions such as the Commissariat à l'énergie atomique (French Atomic Energy Agency) or the Centre d'études nucléaires/Studiecentrum voor Kernenergie (Belgian Nuclear Research Centre). Others were engineers, fresh from university. Their training, if not actually in nuclear physics, was scientific. They were ideally suited to the task and eager to embark on this new adventure [2]. Is that why the profile of Euratom staff was younger and more dynamic? There are those who think so [3]. The disappointment that quickly set in, as described in the chapter on research [4], was all the greater because, initially, the climate in Europe at the end of the

[1] Interview with Ivo Dubois, 22 December 2003.

[2] Interview with Manfredo Macioti, 6 July 2005.
[3] Interview with Ivo Dubois, 22 December 2003.
[4] See the chapter on research, pp. 497–511.

1950s was profoundly influenced by the hope that scientific and technological progress would take mankind forward to greater things. Ten years later the situation had changed radically. By the time of the merger, Euratom was in the grip of profound disillusionment, which, on top of the problems inherent in any large-scale administrative restructuring, explains a great deal.

The EAEC Commission was therefore developing a separate culture at the same time as the EEC Commission was searching for a culture of its own, and in January 1958 almost the only source of inspiration — whether or not one chose to follow it — was the experience of the ECSC High Authority, now a little peeved that it was no longer the sole embodiment of the European project.

The situation we must try to describe was therefore more complex than it might appear at first sight. In a relatively short time, Brussels had attracted a substantial number of young and not-so-young men (there were strikingly few women) from six countries that the last war had brought to the brink of ruin. These 'Europeans' were joining institutions with different tasks. As with any new project, achieving these tasks was a challenge. Although the degree of success depended on the qualifications, motivation and courage of all levels of the hierarchy, it was also affected by the general working environment and organisation, not to mention everyday life. It was not easy for an official who was not Belgian to find his feet in a living environment, Brussels, and in a working environment, an institution where everything had to be built up from scratch, which required him to leave his personal and professional roots behind.

Not for the first time and certainly not for the last, Brussels in 1958 was a vast building site. Imposing building works were being completed ready for the World Fair, which opened in the Heysel park in April. The ECSC also had a pavilion there. Most of the new European officials joined the 42 million visitors to the World Fair during its brief

six-month existence. The impression created by the Belgian capital was deceptive. In normal times, its pace was less hurried, more sedate. Some would say more boring. The fact was that post-war reconstruction was at its height in Belgium and in Brussels at that time. The 'golden sixties' were just around the corner. Unemployment was negligible, public services were expanding rapidly, the generous social security system provided a high standard of protection. Values were bourgeois, the pillars on which society was built were catholic, liberal and socialist. This division into pillars began at school. The Church, the Congo, the King, the Société Générale de Belgique and one or two other institutions still constituted an 'obstinately traditional structure in the style of "old Europe"' [1]. A sort of 'old chateau and its accoutrements from a bygone age' [2], rather like Val-Duchesse, where young officials starting out on their career at the Economic and Social Committee before moving on to the Commission of the Communities (after 1967) cut their teeth in working conditions which no doubt make them smile today but, at the time, felt as if they were stepping through a looking-glass into another age [3].

The men and women who arrived in Brussels in steadily increasing numbers from the beginning of 1958, including a number of translators from Switzerland, have a story to tell. In other words, they inspired a long list of questions and the answers to these questions often differed depending on whom we asked.

Who were these officials? Where did they come from? Why had they come? How many were there? How were they recruited? What became of their initial enthusiasm? How did their careers develop? What was their experience of relationships between the different nationalities in the workplace and outside? How did they organise them-

---

[1] Fox, R. C., *Le Château des Belges — Un peuple se retrouve*, Duculot, Brussels, 1997, p. 27.
[2] Ibid.
[3] Interview with Guy Vanhaeverbeke and Lydia Vanhaeverbeke, 25 February 2004.

Expo 58 was inaugurated on 17 April 1958 and had received 42 million visitors by the time it
closed on 19 October. Surveying the nations for a more human world, the exhibition, as King
Baudouin said in his inaugural address, was to 'prompt a spirit of cooperation and peace' since
'civilisation cannot be built up on technical achievements alone. If it is to be a factor for progress,
it needs us to work at the same time on our ethical conceptions, our desire to make a
constructive effort together'. A message which the ECSC pavilion also sets out to illustrate.
(Poster by Bernard Villemot for the Brussels Universal Exhibition, 1958)

selves to defend their interests? What was their reaction to the various crises of the 1960s? These are some of the questions; the answers given provide only a rough sketch of the overall picture.

Going to Brussels — a difficult decision!

Most of the original senior officials or members of the Commissioners' staff came from national civil services or were on permanent loan from existing European institutions such as the ECSC High Authority or the ECSC Court of Justice. 'Nearly all the rest had been civil servants before they arrived as *chefs de cabinet*. I was probably the only one, or almost, who hadn't,' says Fernand Braun [1]. 'Where is *Le Monde*'s former Strasbourg correspondent?' asked Marjolin, who was looking for a spokesman. 'He's with Grabbier at the High Authority,' came the reply, and it would be many long weeks before he could be poached away from Luxembourg [2]. Other ECSC officials felt the wind of change and rushed to join the new Community executives.

Each Member of the Commission, in consultation with his home country's foreign ministry or economics ministry or both, drew up a list of potential national candidates for the top jobs in the embryonic administration and invited applications for the less important positions. The information was circulated first of all within the Member States' civil services, and this had a major influence on initial recruitment to the new Commissions. Far fewer senior officials were recruited from industry or the trade union movement than had been the case with the ECSC High Authority in 1952.

This should be seen in context. International organisations were few and far between. With the exception of diplomats and miners, very few people went abroad to work, especially as there

was no employment shortage, except in southern Italy. Seeking one's fortune in Brussels was therefore not an economic necessity. Moreover, the prospect of leaving their roots held little appeal for those who came from the most far-flung regions. Why leave your home to go to a distant, cold, dark, damp, rainy country where they can't cook spaghetti, where tomatoes are sold individually like Fabergé eggs and where there's no garlic and no artichokes [3] is what many Italians asked themselves. You had to really believe in what you were doing [...], you had to want to get to know other people, to enter a Tower of Babel where they might not speak your language, where you would come up against different nationalities, ways of life, attitudes, etc. [4]

Whether they worked in a ministry or in a bank, their colleagues, and indeed their families, found their decision difficult to understand. Europe was an adventure, it was not dependable like the bank, the Bar, the Council of State or the Finance Inspectorate. Europe was a 'Trip to the Moon', to quote the title of a book presented to a future Commission employee by his former colleagues [5]. Europe was a place of banishment, far from the political and administrative contacts which were essential for a national career. Granted, there was a structure in Brussels but it was still embryonic. According to a senior official from Germany, it did not guarantee stable employment like a job in the German civil service [6]. Besides, who of those recruited could claim to want a career in Europe? The ship had left port. Some would stay aboard, others would leave. It was, after all, a time of new beginnings. As a general rule, those who came to Brussels did so with the intention of doing a good job, whether or not they were firm supporters of the European cause, since even those who were not particularly committed generally proved to be open to other cultures and had as a common point of reference the memory of the Second World War.

---

[1] Interview with Fernand Braun, 8 December 2003.
[2] Interview with Paul Collowald, 2 December 2003.

[3] Interview with Marcello Burattini, 18 February 2004.
[4] Ibid.
[5] Interview with Yves Desbois, 3 December 2003.
[6] Interview with Axel Herbst, 25 May 2004.

'Never again!'

The scars of the Second World War were still fresh. It had left its mark on that generation which had 'gone to the 1914–18 War as a twinkle in their father's eye and had a front-row seat for the Second World War' (¹). Soldiers, POWs and members of the Resistance had left part of themselves behind in the war. Their deepest conviction was that it must never happen again. Very quickly, usually but not always before they took up their duties in Brussels, they realised that they were working on a project that could outlaw war. One of those who was there at the time commented that the European motivation of German colleagues who had been in the forces between 1939 and 1945 was also to be found in their own past, and he went on to say that people did not become militant Europeans without a reference to, or a reaction against, that earlier era (²). The same was true of the younger staff, as confirmed by a former official from Germany, who said: 'We had emerged from this experience deeply marked by the war but not having to apologise wherever we went. At 17, we were "morally intact" despite the experience' (³). In fact, these converts were all the more committed because they had opted for Europe. It was a sort of knock-on effect. With their plan for a Coal and Steel Community, Monnet and Schuman had set in train a process whereby the former combatants, 'winners' and 'losers', were placed on an equal footing. It was a bold gesture and it is difficult today to gauge just how ambitious and profoundly significant it was, particularly as it was not merely a formal gesture but a fundamental principle on which the structure of the Community and, ultimately, the daily lives of the officials in Brussels were based.

Nevertheless, the war was ever-present, if only in the background. It was seldom, if ever, discussed. However, Georges Berthoin recalls discussing the matter and feels that it is important to remember

Brussels or bust

'One day I was stopped at the French border by a customs official who opened the boot of my car and saw an old boat pump. He asked me to accompany him into the customs post, where a very pleasant duty officer was waiting. "Forgive me, sir," he said, "you see, I would very much like a job with the common market. You told my colleague that you work there and, as I am looking for a job, I've asked all my officers to stop people like you in the hope that they will be able to help me!"'

Anecdote recounted by Georges Rencki in a note of 15 January 2006. (Translated from the French)

it today. 'Do we forgive? Do we forget? I was one of those, and it is easy to agree, who said that we couldn't forget. We couldn't forgive […]. Most of the French or Dutch who were there were people who had suffered personally from the German occupation […]. We said, "We can't forgive, we can't forget, but we have the great good fortune — and we were all young — that we can build the future together"' (⁴). Others felt the same (⁵). That was the most important thing for them.

Among the rumours, slander and concealment, there were nevertheless a small number of cases of European officials with a 'murky' past which occasionally surfaced. Mansholt apparently dismissed on the spot, as an example to others, an official who had played a role in the rationing that the people of Brussels faced during the war. A very small number of those interviewed also expressed surprise at the backgrounds of some of the Italian senior officials who had been diplomats in Berlin before the war.

Many reasons for working for Europe

Michel Albert told us that, for a young man like himself, the hope that the European ideal embodied

(¹) Interview with Claude Brus, 5 December 2003.
(²) Interview with Frans De Koster, 14 November 2004.
(³) Interview with Norbert Kohlhase, 26 May 2004.
(⁴) Interview with Georges Berthoin, 31 January 2004.
(⁵) Interview with Paul-Henri Buchet, 20 January 2004.

was something very special compared with the misfortunes of his childhood, the defeat, the memory of the war, and so on ([1]).

The opportunity to 'do something' for the newly emerging Europe while in a rich cultural and professional environment, coupled with excellent material conditions (comfortable salary, wide choice of housing, etc.), played a role in the choice of what was not yet a career but simply a job, varying in importance depending on the individual's grade.

Prior to taking up their duties, a small but very active minority of officials had been involved in movements promoting European unity, such as the European Movement, Europa-Union or the Campagnes européennes de la jeunesse.

They threw themselves with passion into a career in Europe and some of them continued their campaigning activities at the same time. A European section of the Union of European Federalists was thus set up in Brussels. Rudolf Dumont du Voitel said that in his day there were about 30 officials who agreed to incorporate into the work of the Community and vice versa ideas which had originated with Europa-Union as proposals and suggestions ([2]).

For others, 'enthusiasm for Europe did not come at once but developed over the years. By the end of the 1960s, let's say, I was completely European, enthusiastic and convinced of the need for and the usefulness of even the purely procedural instruments provided by the Treaty [...] This enthusiasm for Europe was created on the spot, on the job. And I still feel it! I am still convinced even now that the system that was set up is a good system, despite the problems in the sector for which I was particularly responsible' ([3]).

'I did it,' says Jean Durieux, 'because I made a much better living than in Belgium. I had three children, I had to build a house, my job was great, I met some amazing people, people such as I'd never met in the Belgian civil service. My colleagues were really of a calibre you seldom find in the Belgian civil service. [...] It was tremendously enriching. People from different cultures lived and worked alongside each other. It was one of the first things I noticed' ([4]).

However, limiting ourselves to these reasons gives rather an incomplete picture and the wide range of individual situations provides plenty of other examples.

At 39, Berndt von Staden knew nothing about European integration. He worked for the German Foreign Office in the East–West relations department, and in particular on the Soviet desk. The two areas were highly compartmentalised. For health reasons, he asked to return to Brussels, where he had started his career at the Federal Republic's Embassy. When his request was refused, he claims to have left his job ([5]).

Von Staden's boss, his head of division in Brussels, was Jean-François Deniau. He was 30. Having followed the Val-Duchesse negotiations as a member of the staff of several ministers, including Maurice Bourgès-Maunoury, French Prime Minister from June to November 1957, he chose the following year to respond to an appeal from Marjolin rather than join the cabinet of Antoine Pinay, General de Gaulle's Finance Minister. 'In Paris I was finished!' he wrote ([6]).

It was quite usual for individuals not to understand the decisions of friends and colleagues. Henri Étienne, a Luxembourger, was 'practically recruited off the street'. 'A friend of mine who was a director in Brussels said "Wouldn't you like

([1]) Interview with Michel Albert, 18 December 2003.
([2]) Interview with Rudolf Dumont du Voitel, 1 December 2003.
([3]) Interview with Nicola Bellieni, 19 December 2003.

([4]) Interview with Jean Durieux, 3 March 2004.
([5]) von Staden, B., *Ende und Anfang — Erinnerungen 1939–1963*, IPa, Vaihingen/Enz, 2001, p. 176.
([6]) Deniau, J.-Fr., *Mémoires de 7 vies — 2. Croire et Oser*, Plon, Paris, 1997, p. 183.

to join us?" "Yes, I don't mind," I said. I was free, I was single. Everyone said "You're completely mad to go to the EEC." Because at that time the only thing that was taken seriously was Euratom. The common market was just a pile of papers that no one had ever read. I'd never read the Treaty.' (¹)

Another young Belgian was under 30 when he was recruited in December 1958 by Émile Noël. A doctor of law with a degree in political sciences, he had been Political Secretary, Private Secretary in other words, to the Belgian Foreign Trade Minister Hendrik Fayat until May 1958. Following the change of government he found himself with no prospects other than the Bar. However, through the contacts he had made while working for the minister, he was able to let Jean Rey's entourage know that he was looking for a job with the EEC Commission (²).

Then there was the young Italian chemical engineer who worked at the Patent Office in Rome. His sister had married a senior Italian official with the High Authority. While visiting them, he heard about the opportunities on offer in Brussels and decided to try his luck (³).

Another young man, a German lawyer, had obtained a doctorate in a topic relating to industrial property. He worked as a lawyer and part-time assistant to Professor Ullmer in Munich, who encouraged him to reply to an offer from Brussels for a lawyer dealing with the approximation of laws. The chain of contacts worked well. Hallstein rang the State Secretary for Justice in Bonn, who rang Ullmer, who said that his protégé would do very nicely. The young man, who had little taste for a career as a lawyer and wanted to leave the Bavarian capital, told himself it was now or never (⁴).

This case is typical of the role played from the outset by the university network, both in the very early days and later. The College of Europe, the Strasbourg Institut des hautes études européennes, the Centre européen universitaire in Nancy and other institutions were specialising in training high-calibre young people in European affairs. In other universities too, teaching staff who were aware of the importance of what was at stake were giving encouragement to young graduates.

Universities were not only a rich breeding-ground for the talent recruited by the Community institutions, they were also a natural pool of potential young trainees, or *stagiaires*. Some did not stay in the institution beyond the end of their training period, which really was a total immersion in Europe, but others were offered temporary contracts, which could be renewed until such a time as their hitherto precarious situation could be regularised. Some senior officials, including directors-general, used to scout for talented youngsters and use their influence to have them recruited.

However, it was not only academics and men who joined the embryonic European civil service. Women were recruited to what might be called subordinate posts. Let us not forget that in several countries women were still far from equal to men, particularly from the legal point of view. Although less important than in the past, the golden rule for women was still the three Cs: children, church and cooking. Nevertheless, some of the women who joined the EEC Commission, whether as secretaries or graduates, became an essential part of the machinery, not least because of their ability to find pragmatic solutions where some men clung to the rules.

The circumstances which led people to choose to come to Brussels were therefore many and varied, although we can attempt to identify certain national strategies and profiles.

(¹) Interview with Henri Étienne, 12 January 2004.
(²) UCL, GEHEC, Interview with Frans De Koster by Christine Machiels, 12 December 2001.
(³) Interview with Manfredo Macioti, 6 July 2005.
(⁴) Interview with Franz Froschmaier, 19 January 2004.

Stagiaires were part of the family

Karel Van Miert, a member of the Commission from 1989 to 1999, took his first steps in the institution as a *stagiaire* in 1967. As a student at the Centre européen universitaire in Nancy, he had met Émile Noël, who was lecturing there and who offered him a six-month period of in-service training (known as a *stage*) with the Secretariat-General. Karel Van Miert remembers this time as a valuable experience which taught him a great deal about the European institutions. He was able to attend a wide range of important meetings, including the weekly meetings with the directors-general. Occasionally he would accompany Émile Noël to the Council or to Coreper. The training was very general. Van Miert was not the only one to attend all these meetings, a number of other *stagiaires* were also allowed to do so. At the time, *stagiaires* really did feel like part of the family.

There were about 80 *stagiaires*, and it was quite a close-knit group. Everyone knew everyone else. The *stagiaires* also put a great deal of effort into organising leisure activities on top of their apprenticeship within the Commission's departments — kayaking on the Lesse, a trip to Holland, etc. Karel Van Miert recalls that the stage was not confined to work, there was more to it than that.

Interview with Karel Van Miert, 19 August 2005.

J.C.

In search of national strategies and profiles

In the case of officials from Germany, it is essential to make a distinction between two generations. The first is made up of the senior officials, recruited initially for their experience and because they had a past officially 'unblemished' by any active collaboration with the National Social-ist Party. They did not all come on their own initiative. They came out of a sense of duty or because they were pushed into it. At that time, anyone with an important position in the German federal administration did not want to be banished to Brussels. It did not help their career and they sometimes felt, usually wrongly, that they would encounter hostility. They feared that the open or unspoken question about what they had done between 1938 and 1945 would be constantly hanging over them. It also seemed tactless to speak their own language. As a result, many officials jumped the Community ship at the earliest opportunity.

The profile of the next generation and the role they played are quite different from those of their elders. With their training, and in some cases their first working experience, in international or European affairs, they had come to Luxembourg or Brussels by choice. Younger than their predecessors, but marked nonetheless by the horrors of the Second World War, they had realised the importance of the European dynamic. By helping to build a new Europe and being treated as equals by their colleagues, they were setting themselves free from a generation which still bore the stigma of the war.

It seems too that the German government played a not inconsiderable role in the selection, and even promotion, of officials within the European Commissions. As early as 1958, the German Foreign Office asked President Hallstein's Private Office for a list of all German staff recruited by the Commission. Some witnesses insist that Bonn made a preliminary selection of applications with the aim of deliberately allowing the best candidates to leave for Brussels and then controlling their careers in collusion with the President's office. This was made all the easier by the fact that among the few powers Hallstein had was ultimate control of personnel management.

The Italians in Brussels were also divided into two groups. The first was made up of A-grade officials recruited in Italy. Eye-witness accounts

```
        ... à tous ceux qui savent que l'horaire actuel est impossible, mais
        qui peut-être n'ont pas imaginé ce qu'était réellement la vie d'une
        femme-fonctionnaire-mère-de-famille devant concilier vie profession-
        nelle et vie privée


    ┌─────────────────────────────────────────────────────────────────┐
    │ Journée type d'une femme-fonctionnaire-mère-de-famille            │
    │                                                                   │
    │ 6h30 : (lever, soins matinaux, préparation du déjeuner enfants : toi-│
    │         lette des bébés, surveillance des + grands ; préparation du │
    │         lunch à emporter à l'école ou de certains éléments du dîner │
    │         du soir)                                                    │
    │                                                                   │
    │ 7h30 : déjeuner                                                    │
    │                                                                   │
    │ 8h   : départ, conduite des enfants à l'école                     │
    │                                                                   │
    │ 8h30 : arrivée au bureau, travail intensif                        │
    │                                                                   │
    │ 13h30 : (                                                          │
    │          pose du midi : temps libre : trop ou pas assez...        │
    │ 14h30 : (                                                          │
    │          retravail intensif                                       │
    │ 18h30 : (                                                          │
    │ ou                                                                 │
    │ 18h45 : ici débute la 2ème journée de travail de la femme-fonction-│
    │          naire.                                                    │
    │                                                                   │
    │ 19h15 : petits achats indispensables                              │
    │                                                                   │
    │          (ensuite rentrée au domicile pour se partager entre : la  │
    │          préparation du dîner, les devoirs et les leçons des en-   │
    │          fants à revoir, le bain des plus jeunes à donner ou celui │
    │          des plus grands à surveiller ainsi que le repas des jeunes│
    │          enfants à servir et les coucher)                         │
    │                                                                   │
    │ 20h00 : dîner de la famille                                        │
    │                                                                   │
    │ 20h30 : coucher des plus âgés - vaisselle                         │
    │                                                                   │
    │ 21h00 : divers menus travaux indispensables au choix : repassage,  │
    │          petite lessive, petits nettoyages, raccommodages, comptes à│
    │          faire, classement des papiers.                           │
    │                                                                   │
    │ 22h30 : la nuit s'ouvre devant elle pour se cultiver, se mettre au │
    │          courant de la vie politique - se relaxer et... dormir    │
    │                                                                   │
    │                 - tout le restant : samedi et dimanche            │
    └─────────────────────────────────────────────────────────────────┘

    PITIE POUR ELLE : NE VOULEZ-VOUS VRAIMENT PAS L'AIDER ?
    Si oui... raccourcissez-lui son horaire !
            Signé : un-groupe-de-demmes-fonctionnaires-mères-de-famille.
```

… to all those of you who know that the current working hours are impossible, but perhaps have never thought about what it is really like for a woman who is both an official and a mother trying to juggle her private and professional life:

Typical day of a woman who is both an official and a mother

6:30: get up, shower and dress, prepare the children's breakfast, change, wash and dress the baby, supervise the older children, make packed lunches for school or prepare part of the evening meal; 7:30: breakfast; 8:00: leave the house and take the children to school; 8:30: arrive at the office and get straight down to work; 13:30: lunch break: free time (too much or too little …); 14:30: back into a heavy work programme; 18:30 or 18:45: this is when a female official's second day's work begins; 19:15: quick trip to the shops for a few essentials; — then go home to tackle: preparing supper, checking the children's homework, giving the younger children their baths or supervising the older ones, giving the smaller children their supper and putting them to bed; 20:00: supper for the rest of the family; 20:30: put the older children to bed — washing up; 21:00: long list of essential jobs ranging from ironing, washing, housework and mending to accounts and paperwork; 22:30: she has the whole night ahead of her to improve her mind, catch up on the latest political events or — to relax and … SLEEP; — all that's left: Saturday and Sunday

HAVE PITY ON HER — SURELY YOU MUST WANT TO HELP HER?
If so … reduce her working hours!
Signed: a group of women who are both officials and mothers

A debate gets under way in the readers' letters columns of the *Courrier du personnel* about working hours and the continuous working day.
A group of female officials bringing up children also make their voices heard.

seem to suggest that the best candidates did not really come forward in the beginning. Italians with a job in the civil service in Italy were even more reluctant than the Germans to come to work in Brussels. Senior officials of Italian nationality were as hard to find as Commissioners, let alone a President, but the recruitment of younger officials and B-grades was not so difficult.

On the other hand, the Italians, along with the Belgians, were heavily represented among the messengers and drivers. Originating in the very large Italian community in Belgium, mainly to be found in Wallonia, they spoke French in addition to their own language. Following a familiar pattern, the first to arrive created family groups in the broadest sense of the term: brothers, uncles, cousins, all came north one after the other. Then there was the Italian *mamma* with her culinary skills. Brussels had been home to a number of high-quality Italian restaurants since before the First World War, and now the arrival of the European executives had encouraged the opening of small *trattorias* where the cuisine was simple and appetising, the atmosphere welcoming. Some of these places soon became rallying points, not only for officials but for journalists too. In the early days — for the practice was soon banned — some messengers would disappear mysteriously in the middle of the day to help *mamma*, who could not do everything by herself (¹).

As repeatedly pointed out at meetings of the EEC Commission, and the Euratom Commission for that matter, the balance of nationalities in senior positions was often unfavourable to the Italians and the Luxembourgers. This was the result as much of the mediocre calibre of the candidates as of the lack of influence of the Luxembourg and Italian Commissioners in the EEC Commission. The latter spent more time organising the recruitment of lower-grade staff to satisfy the expectations of friends back home. For senior posts, they often recommended 'worthy' compatriots,

---

(¹) Interview with Margot Delfosse-Frey, 25 October 2004.

whereas the French and the Dutch put forward experienced people. It was an uneven contest.

The Luxembourgers, few in number, had to fight hard. It was not until 1973 that Luxembourg got its first director-general post. This omission could, of course, be attributed to a lack of real support within the institutions for nationals of the Grand Duchy, but this would be to overlook the fact that Luxembourg, as a member of both European and international institutions, did not have an inexhaustible supply of top-flight candidates. This was unfortunate since, as a general rule, Luxembourgers, who were obliged to study at foreign universities, were greatly appreciated within the Community administration for their excellent command of French and German and their sense of proportion.

With a few exceptions, the Belgians did not shine in managerial posts in the early years. Selection and recruitment left much to be desired. Jean Rey and his cabinet took little interest and some of the choices made occasionally proved to have been unwise. Nevertheless, Belgians with university training were much appreciated. However, they tended to be promoted more slowly than officials of other nationalities and there were a large number of Belgians in middle-ranking posts.

The early senior officials of Dutch nationality were known in particular for their competence and discretion. In contrast to their colleagues of other nationalities, they were obliged, on taking up their duties, to sever all ties with their national administration. They could not, therefore, be 'seconded' to the European institutions.

From the outset, the senior French officials chosen by Robert Marjolin were highly qualified civil servants, mostly graduates of the *grandes écoles* and the great institutions of the Republic, and utterly committed to the European cause. Most accounts, from all nationalities, agree. The French had one advantage, of course — they could work in their own language. But that was not all. Marjolin had an intuitive ability to spot good candidates. For him, there was only one criterion for recruitment or promotion: ability first and last. The decisive influence of France at that time was very largely founded on its choice of people. Like his colleague von der Groeben, Marjolin also managed to persuade Hallstein to appoint brilliant youngsters to positions of responsibility. It was an uphill struggle in the beginning. Some of the Germans, and Belgians too, accustomed to age taking priority, were shocked. When von der Groeben wanted to appoint Albrecht as his *chef de cabinet*, he was told by Hallstein that it could not be done, that he was too young. But, little by little, Hallstein was eventually won over by the quality and efficiency of the candidates — not that the role of the Executive Secretary and later the Secretary-General, as well as of certain directors-general, did not prove to be very important on quite a few occasions.

The Staff Regulations, a legal document serving a permanent civil service

The introduction of the Staff Regulations, and hence the establishment of a genuinely permanent European civil service, is provided for in the Treaties of Rome, although, as a minor point of interest, they are said to have been added after the Treaties had been formally signed. As Hubert Ehring, Head of the Council Legal Service at the time, explains: 'I attended the signing of a Treaty which still included blank pages. [...] It was only after the signing that they filled in the blanks with the Staff Regulations, Privileges and Immunities, things like that. [...] It's an interesting fact. It's not a State secret.' ([1])

However, in comparison with the Coal and Steel Community, the new Communities had lost some of their autonomy on administrative matters. It would now be the Council which, at the end of the procedure and on a proposal from the Com-

mission, would determine not only the number of staff but also their salaries and would deal with questions arising in relation to the Staff Regulations. There was no equivalent in Brussels of the so-called Commission of the four Presidents (the Presidents of the Court of Justice, the High Authority, the Joint Assembly and the Council), with its supranational overtones, which had existed in Luxembourg.

The EEC Commission and the Council which had set up a Staff Regulations Committee or Working Party, and the EAEC Commission for that matter, spent the first few months, indeed the first few years, humming and hawing about the question of salaries and the Community tax. The EEC Commission felt that net salaries should be sufficient to attract high-calibre staff, more generous than those paid by the European intergovernmental organisations and preferably equivalent to those paid by the High Authority ([2]). But the pioneers of the Communities-based Europe had set the bar very high and by the end of the 1950s some governments were extremely reluctant to adopt the same salary scale, although in fact during the early years — and in the absence of any decisions to the contrary — it was that scale that was used as a point of reference. As regards the Community tax, the Commissions were in favour of a genuine tax with a rate that varied according to salary. However, they vigorously opposed the introduction of a retroactive tax.

As regards the Staff Regulations proper, the EEC Commission, like the Euratom Commission, came down in favour of a single set of rules for all three Communities ([3]). It decided to adopt as a working basis the existing ECSC Staff Regulations ([4]) with as few changes as possible. However, it did introduce a distinction in the texts between officials, who were employed on a permanent basis and occupied a post in the establishment plan, and other servants, who consisted of temporary

---

([1]) Interview with Hubert Ehring, 4 June 2004.

([2]) PV spéc. 41, the EEC Commission, 10 December 1958, Item VIII, pp. 3–4.
([3]) PV 49, EEC Commission, 11 December 1958, Item IVa, pp. 3–4.
([4]) PV 38, EEC Commission, 19–20 November 1958, Item VIII, p. 9.

and auxiliary staff, local staff, experts, etc. ([1]). It was also in favour of filling vacant posts by giving priority to the promotion or transfer of Commission employees ([2]) and supported the principle of paying pensions out of the Community budget ([3]), whereas, under the ECSC rules, pensions were financed with the aid of a pension fund.

The French were initially opposed to a permanent civil service. They felt that European officials should remain in close contact with their national administrations. The Dutch, on the other hand, advocated setting up a genuinely independent civil service. Consequently, since the temporary arrangements could not go on for ever, Albert Borschette, the Luxembourg Permanent Representative, was given the task in October 1961 of looking into ways of bringing about an agreement between the EEC and EAEC Councils and the ECSC Commission of the four Presidents. A shrewd negotiator, he brought all his skills to bear to reconcile the different positions. He knew that a staff rotation system would damage the newly created institutions but realised too that it would be difficult to sever all ties between the national and the Community authorities. Fortunately, he had the confidence of most of the players, including Walter Hallstein, President of the Commission, who felt that the Commission should trust Mr Borschette's judgment since he was familiar with the Commissions' concerns and the needs of Community staff and should give him a free hand in the negotiations he was about to undertake ([4]). For once, the auspices were favourable; the Staff Regulations of Officials of the European Communities were adopted on 18 December 1961 and entered into force on 1 January of the following year. The Staff Regulations were a single document. However, they included certain provisions which were specific to the officials of each executive. These provisions were standardised as part

of the revision exercise which took place in 1968 following the merger of the executives.

The EEC Commission was sometimes reluctant to make changes to the Staff Regulations. It did not want to play into the hands of the Council since the Council was able, by unanimous vote, to amend any Commission proposal in this area. This was a real danger since some Member States wanted the institutions to recruit staff on the basis of lists of candidates drawn up by the Member States, for example ([5]).

Some claim that the Germans had a major influence, from the President's *cabinet* to the head of the Staff Regulations division, while others maintain that the Staff Regulations owe a great deal to Émile Noël. However, the 1962 Staff Regulations were very similar to the earlier ECSC Staff Regulations, which were originally intended to be truly unique and multinational. In Luxembourg, Monnet, as was his wont, invited the first rapporteurs, Paul Finet, a member of the High Authority, and Jacques Rueff, a judge at the Court of Justice, together with their colleagues, to meet him one evening to discuss the texts and, ultimately, to influence their political content. He was taking a long-term view: 'The Staff Regulations of officials of the [ECSC] Community should be concerned less with resolving the short-term problems of managing the staff of the ECSC institutions than with laying down the rules for the creation of a body of officials to serve all the European institutions.' ([6]) The early versions of the Staff Regulations were regarded in some quarters as too rigid, however, and it was not until the new President of the High Authority, René Mayer, submitted a much more flexible, more 'administrative', text which respected the autonomy of the individual institutions that the ECSC Staff Regulations were adopted on 28 January 1956. The final version of this text had been produced by the departments of the High Authority under the supervision of

---

([1]) PV 99, EEC Commission, 29–30 March 1960, Item IV, pp. 6–9 and PV spéc. 99, EEC Commission, 29–30 March 1960, Item IV, pp. 3–4.
([2]) Ibid.
([3]) Ibid.
([4]) PV 160, EEC Commission, 12 and 13 October 1961, Item VII.2, p. 8.

([5]) Interview with Yves Desbois, 3 December 2003.
([6]) HAEC, CEAB 3 415, Report by Paul Finet and Jacques Rueff on progress on drafting the Staff Regulations, 30 September 1954, p. 3.

André Rossi, a close colleague of René Mayer and future member of the European Parliament. The French influence was therefore undeniable and, in the view of people who had spent their entire career implementing the articles of the Staff Regulations, many of these articles had their origins in Belgian and French law.

From his appointment until his death, and sometimes even beyond (through survivors' pensions, allowances for handicapped children, etc.), the life of the European civil servant was governed by the Staff Regulations. They differed from the various national rules in the major respect that they were based on a broader legal framework which included, for example, their own pension scheme and health insurance scheme distinct from those of their place of employment; in the Member States such texts were normally separate legal documents. The aim was indeed to create an elite civil service independent of the Member States. 'We had more or less drifted into the idea of Staff Regulations "by analogy" and out of a desire to create a situation which was closer to that in the national administrations than to that in international organisations. We considered that a supranational civil service was, in fact, a sort of national civil service whose nationality was "supranational"', wrote Jacques Rueff in 1953 [1]. 'It was a gem [...]. It was a genuine model. [...] It really set the European public service apart, a body with rights but also with duties' [2]. However, this did not mean that career structures which were well designed but badly implemented, for example, could not be criticised [3].

Between 1958 and 1962 staff were recruited on fixed-term contracts. Each member of staff received a contract in the form of a letter of recruitment, known at the time as a *lettre de Bruxelles*. For the rest, they had to manage as best they could with the resources available, not least as regards the payment of salaries. Those who were there at the time remember it very well. 'Our salaries were paid at a little window manned by the famous Mr Leistikow, who gave us our money. I can't even remember in which year I opened a bank account.' [4] At Euratom, 'the same task was performed by the unfailingly pleasant Mr Guillemin', insisted Ivo Dubois [5]. And Jacques Ferrandi recounts: 'In Brussels, in the early days, nobody had a flat. We were all in hotels. I remember one amusing detail. None of us had a bank account in Brussels. We got around the problem in rather a novel way. At the entrance to the Commission's meeting room there was a Belgian official called Mr Cheval — not a name you forget — who had at his feet a huge metal trunk full of notes from the six Member States [...]. Every one of us, members of the Commission and *chefs de cabinet*, would take from the trunk whatever we needed. We merely signed a piece of paper that Cheval kept safe and the amount was then deducted from our monthly salary, of course.' [6]

The staff mobilise, organise and unionise!

Paradoxically, both at the High Authority in 1956 and the 'common market' Commission in 1962, the Staff Regulations led to the formation of trade unions even though they recognised neither the right of association for officials [7] nor the right to strike. A trade union presence was established as a result of the first elections to the Staff Committee and to the other committees set up under the Staff Regulations, although the number of actual members remained small. One of the pioneers of the FFPE (Fédération de la fonction publique européenne, or European Civil Service Federation) recalled that the elections were fought in a way which, if not exactly bitter, was nevertheless lively [8].

[1] Remarks by Jacques Rueff, Judge at the Court of Justice (HAEC, CEAB 12 73, Record of the 'Staff Regulations' meeting, 28 October 1953, p. 49).
[2] Interview with Claude Brus, 5 December 2003.
[3] Ibid.

[4] Interview with Ursula Thiele, 20 October 2004.
[5] E-mail from Ivo Dubois to Michel Dumoulin, 23 February 2006.
[6] Interview with Jacques Ferrandi, 28 May 2004.
[7] Not included in the Staff Regulations until 1972 (Article 24a).
[8] Interview with Paul-Henri Buchet, 20 January 2004.

Even before the Staff Regulations were adopted, Horst Siebel was encouraged by the Director-General for Administration and Personnel of the EAEC Commission to set up a staff organisation (¹). At the EEC Commission, as the number of staff was increasing rapidly, there were those who felt the need to join forces to help this or that colleague who was having problems with his superiors or to ensure that the staff could be consulted on decisions which concerned them. In the beginning, this was done on an informal basis via a staff association but it quickly became clear that, in order to take effective action — particularly in relation to the Council, which was responsible for salaries, staff numbers and the Staff Regulations — it was necessary to establish structured trade unions. As a general rule, it was people with experience of trade union activity at national level who became involved in the setting up of the staff associations of European officials following traditional national divisions. By the end of the first year, two trends had emerged, one more left wing which would become the Union Syndicale and would join the International Confederation of Free Trade Unions (ICFTU) and the other more catholic in outlook, the Alliance, which would become the Syndicat des fonctionnaires internationaux européens (SFIE) and would join the International Federation of Christian Trade Unions (CISC). The Fédération de la fonction publique européenne (FFPE), which was more like a professional organisation or a German civil service association, claimed to be neutral but in the beginning was made up primarily of liberals. The driving force behind it was a larger-than-life figure who is still remembered by many of the old guard, Theodor Holtz, 'big Theodor', the 'phantom translator', well connected and always hard at work running the federation and defending the staff. Another figure who is still remembered is Arlette Grynberg, who was ever willing to take to the barricades on behalf of the Union syndicale.

In fact, in the early days European officials had little inclination to join a trade union. They enjoyed a relatively high standard of living, they were committed to their work, which they found absorbing, and they were swept along by the European project. However, as European integration faltered and occasionally stalled, the morale of the staff wavered, and this, coupled with seemingly endless discussions on salary adjustments and uncertainty surrounding certain categories of research staff at Euratom, strengthened the role of the trade unions, which held all the seats on the Staff Committee.

In some cases, both the High Authority and the members of the so-called 'Brussels' Commissions tacitly supported the would-be strikers as the action was directed against the budgetary authority, namely the Council. Stoppages, supported by virtually all the staff, were held in April 1964, February 1965 and March 1966. Émile Noël, although he requisitioned essential staff to maintain a minimum service, backed the strike — to the great surprise, not to say displeasure, of certain directors-general. So, according to one account, 'Noël, who had called a meeting of directors-general — this was after 1967 — asked his colleagues to donate to the strike fund a proportion of their salary corresponding to the number of strike days as an expression of solidarity since it was impossible for a director-general to take part in a strike. I don't think many colleagues did so.' (²)

Likewise, Fritz Hellwig, Vice-President of the Commission, and a number of Members of Parliament took part in the first Extraordinary General Assembly of Community staff, held on 17 December 1968 in the Salle de la Madeleine in Brussels following the failure by the Council to adopt a decision on the Joint Research Centre (³).

The union action ranged from the good-natured — like the picnic at the foot of the Berlaymont building to protest at working conditions in the new complex — to the more resolute, when the interpreters boycotted the interpreting booths in the same building. Negotiations, too, could be

(¹) Letter from Ivo Dubois to Michel Dumoulin, 18 July 2005.

(²) Interview with Hubert Ehring, 4 June 2004.
(³) Courrier du personnel, No 48, 13 January 1969, p. 6.

Staff fairly quickly begin to complain about working conditions in Berlaymont: the lifts are unsafe or too slow, there are no opening windows, the airconditioning system is inefficient, there are rumours about excessive CO_2 concentrations, the interpreters have to work in the basement [...] they fear they will have to spend their lives underground and never see daylight. (Interview with Anne Maria ten Geuzendam, 17 December 2004)
(Demonstration by officials in Brussels)

bitter, like the wage negotiations, or more dramatic, as at Ispra, where staff held hunger strikes and occupied buildings.

Ups and downs of the embryonic European civil service

In the early 1960s, says Robert Marjolin, although the material circumstances of Community officials were satisfactory, the air of uncertainty surrounding their future status did little to create a good working atmosphere [1]. Although there was not yet any real unrest, some of the administrative provisions adopted at that time would have damaging consequences when the initial momentum of European integration began to wane.

In January 1962, for example, Jean Rey observed that the overburdening of certain sectors of the Commission administration had become a real problem, while at the same time some officials seemed to be permanently underemployed [2].

In 1969 a relatively large survey based on anonymous replies from 412 members of staff showed that 96 % of those who replied felt that there was real discontent among European officials in Brussels. It found that this discontent was widespread among all categories and ought to be taken seriously. In some cases it was severe. In all cases it was worrying, particularly since it was the younger officials who seemed to be most affected. The dissatisfaction was due in large part to the perception by officials of deficiencies in the administration, and especially in personnel policy — recruitment, promotion, organisation of departments, increased bureaucracy and hierarchical rigidity. It was also the result of awareness on the part of these officials that the political integration of Europe had stagnated, and had even taken a step backwards, in recent years. But this did not seem to be the principal cause of the

malaise [3]. Nonetheless, the vast majority of the staff still placed great importance on their work, the purpose it served and especially the international nature of interpersonal relationships [4].

A far-sighted Michel Gaudet observed at the time that political disenchantment made people more sensitive to administrative shortcomings and difficulties while administrative irritations which it was possible to live with at the height of the storm led to annoyance when the restoration of calm allowed time to think about them [5].

From the French veto to the Luxembourg compromise

General de Gaulle's press conference on 14 January 1963, which de facto put an end to enlargement negotiations with the United Kingdom, was the first real blow, and according to some the most severe blow, to the morale of the Communities' staff. 'At that time — I remember it very well — morale in the Commission's departments was at its lowest ebb [...]. I'm not saying that the crisis was caused by the rejection of British accession. It was the way in which it was done and also the more general climate at that time. On the whole, the Commission's departments felt that it was a good thing that the negotiations had failed at that time [...]. In addition, Walter Hallstein's relationship with Chancellor Adenauer had already cooled. It was difficult for him to restore the confidence of his troops.' [6]

The 'empty chair' policy created a new crisis to which reactions in the administration varied. For some, it was obvious that a solution would be found — the show would go on [7]. For others it was a time of intense anxiety, with some officials

---

[1] AULB, 126 PP, VI.34, Memorandum from Robert Marjolin concerning the restructuring of the Commission's administration, 19 February 1960, p. 1.

[2] AULB, 126 PP, VI.34, Memorandum from Jean Rey to the Presidents and Members of the Commission, 13 January 1962, p. 4.

[3] HAEU, JG 224, *Les fonctionnaires européens et leur situation, Recherches communautaires européennes*, p. 2.

[4] Ibid., p. 3.

[5] HAEU, JG 224, Report by Michel Gaudet, *Le fonctionnaire européen et les problèmes psycho-sociologiques des grandes organisations*, p. 4.

[6] Interview with Frans De Koster, 14 November 2004.

[7] Interview with Marcello Burattini, 18 February 2004.

EUROPA

Poem written by a Commission official

Rappelle-toi Europa

Il pleuvait sans cesse sur Bruxelles ce jour-là

Et tu marchais souriante

Épanouie, ravie, ruisselante

Sous la pluie

Rappelle-toi Europa

Il pleuvait sans cesse sur Bruxelles

Et je t'ai croisée rue de la Loi

Tu souriais

Et moi je souriais de même

Rappelle-toi Europa

Toi que je ne connaissais pas

Toi qui ne me connaissais pas

Rappelle-toi

Rappelle-toi quand même ce jour là

N'oublie pas

Un directeur au Berlaymont s'abritait

Et il a crié ton nom

Europa

Et tu as couru vers lui sous la pluie

Ruisselante, ravie, épanouie

Et il t'a parlé du 'Feoga'

Rappelle-toi cela Europa

Et ne m'en veux pas si je te tutoie

Je dis tu à tous ceux qui s'aiment

Même si je ne les connais pas

Rappelle-toi Europa

N'oublie pas

Cette pluie sage et heureuse

Sur ton visage heureux

Sur cette ville adipeuse

Cette pluie sur le Conseil

Sur la Commission

Sur le taxi d'en bas

Oh! Europa

Quelles conneries ces réunions

Qu'es-tu devenue maintenant

Sous cette pluie de décisions

De papiers et de règlements

Et celui qui te serrait dans ses bras

Amoureusement, le Président

Est-il mort ou disparu ou bien encore vivant

Oh! Europa

Il pleut sans cesse sur Bruxelles

Comme il pleuvait avant

Mais ce n'est plus pareil et tout est abîmé

C'est une pluie d'incohérence terrible et désolée

Ce n'est même plus l'orage

Des discours et des communiqués

Tout simplement des nuages

Qui viennent de chez les Anglais

Des anglais qui rouspètent

Et vont crier au loin

Au loin très loin de Bruxelles

Vers le grand large

Europa Europa

Pour qu'il n'en reste rien

Pierre Cros — Brussels, (*Courrier du personnel*,
No 99, 29 January 1970, pp. 13–14.)

genuinely fearing for the survival of the Communities and hence for their jobs. 'It was a very difficult time which affected us a lot, including professionally, since for years afterwards we were just marking time. And that's not much fun, especially at the age we were then — between 30 and 40. I recall that that was the time when I seriously considered the possibility of giving up on the Commission and going home' (¹), said an Italian official. 'We had the feeling at the Commission that we were all going home' (²) declared another. Some officials even considered halting the construction of their new houses (³). But, 'in spite of all that,' said a German official, 'it was interesting, and the more severe the crisis and the greater the fear that it was all going wrong, the more interesting it was.' (⁴) The officials closed ranks to counter the lack of good faith on the part of some governments, France in particular.

The Luxembourg compromise left the 'old guard' feeling betrayed. There was a genuine rift, and the Commission, in an attempt to achieve its objectives, had to tread carefully, sacrificing sound personnel management in the process. 'In some cases, in fact, even recruitment and the careers of officials, particularly in the higher grades, became bargaining counters, part of the negotiations.' (⁵) As this report makes clear, certain 'coalitions' within the Commission were able to keep 'weak' officials of certain nationalities in key posts (⁶).

Merger — an unavoidable but difficult transition

In July 1967 the Single Commission was given the onerous task of organising the merger of the administrations. Fortunately, the ground had been discreetly prepared by the Executive Secretaries and Secretaries-General of the different executives. It was a vast undertaking which had direct implications for the lives of the officials of the various institutions, in particular those of the High Authority, the Euratom Commission and the European Investment Bank. Although only 10 % of staff were actually to be reassigned, it was a time of real anxiety. Officials were left wondering where they would be working in future, what the timetable for any change would be, and whether there would be compensation or changes to the Staff Regulations, given the differences between the rules for the ECSC and those for the EEC. The lack of information meant that rumours were rife within the departments.

People were not at all happy about the merger of the executives (⁷). Among some categories of official a feeling of rivalry grew up where once they had felt they were building Europe together (⁸). 'They were fighting over chairs because there wouldn't necessarily be two chairs in one office. If they were the same grade, they had to have chairs of the same quality or there would be trouble' (⁹), observed a former official dryly. 'I was aware of quite a few little dramas going on around me — people who were being forced to leave or to do something else which didn't always interest them.' (¹⁰)

The staff of the European Atomic Energy Community were dispersed across the various departments and were not at all happy about it (¹¹). As one former official said, 'It was rather a sad state of affairs; the ECSC and EAEC people felt that they had been "swallowed up" by the EEC under the efficient leadership of Émile Noël, popular and admired as he might have been in other quarters.' (¹²)

For this official, originally from the ECSC, the merger was a time of insecurity. Many officials

---

(¹) Interview with a former Italian official, January 2004.
(²) Interview with Paolo Clarotti, 28 November 2004.
(³) Interview with Claus-Dieter Ehlermann, 29 January 2004.
(⁴) Interview with Marcell von Donat, 18 February 2004.
(⁵) HAEU, JG 224, Report by Enrico Angelini, *Le fonctionnaire euro-péen et les problèmes psycho-sociologiques des grandes organisa-tions*, pp. 2–3.
(⁶) Ibid.

(⁷) Interview with Paul-Henri Buchet, 20 January 2004.
(⁸) Ibid.
(⁹) Ibid.
(¹⁰) Ibid.
(¹¹) Ibid.
(¹²) Letter from Ivo Dubois to Michel Dumoulin, 18 July 2005.

had expected to work for the High Authority until they retired, since the lifetime of the Treaty of Paris was 50 years. The situation was chaotic (¹) and people feared for their jobs (²). Some left the High Authority as quickly as they could: 'I phoned the newly appointed Director-General in the Regional Policy DG in Brussels and asked if I could join him. He said yes, so I gathered up all my clothes in Luxembourg, took my secretary with me, and we simply went to Brussels' (³). Some ECSC officials who had been there from the start would find it hard to leave the Grand Duchy, but the merger was the result of unavoidable institutional change. 'We knew too that life was not over for us. We could see that the High Authority was moribund. That's why we all wanted to join the Commission quickly. We were still officials in Luxembourg but we were already buying plots of land in Brussels' (⁴). Nevertheless, for the rest of their careers they would continue to harbour a certain nostalgia for the Place de Metz and the working methods established by Jean Monnet and his colleagues. The administration in Luxembourg was not huge and hierarchical, it had a family atmosphere. Former officials report that every morning they would encounter the bishop, who eventually took to greeting them each day. They would walk to the office with a member of the High Authority whom they met in the street and who also used to walk to work. Accustomed to living and working together in an environment that some might consider provincial, they continued to meet in Brussels and established a circle of friends firmly rooted in Brussels community-based life there. 'Our friendships were all with people we had known in Luxembourg. They continued in Brussels. We were all getting married at the same time, we were having children at the same time. [...] And now (in retirement), we are calling each other again.' (⁵) Some people, though, had difficulty fitting into the structure of the merged administration and left the Communities

altogether. Jacques-René Rabier recalls that in the early days in Luxembourg there were 'missionaries' and 'adventurers'. It was the latter who now, one by one, moved on to pastures new, like Michel Bonnemaison.

The Hague: a new optimism

In January 1970, in his New Year message to staff, the President of the Commission, Jean Rey, was aware of the situation but could see a glimmer of hope. General de Gaulle was gone and the results of the conference in The Hague looked promising. 'An air of pessimism seems to hang like a cloud over everybody and everything. The Community's grand venture goes on, with little sign of progress and with no creative satisfaction for those who have made the task their own. But just as 1969 was drawing to a close, something changed. The mists of uncertainty and unease are lifting. 1970 is dawning to a bright future.' (⁶)

At the mercy of the vagaries of European integration, the Communities' staff became aware that their objective was more remote than they had thought and that they were in fact facing a long-term challenge. It would be an unremitting battle. They would have to be on their guard and remain faithful to their convictions and to their faith in Europe. Every day the battle had to be fought and won. This was the dominant impression of 600 colleagues who wanted to show by their presence in The Hague that it was possible to be a European official and to believe in Europe sincerely and unreservedly (⁷).

The balance of nationalities and its effects

Article 27 of the Staff Regulations provides that officials must be recruited on the broadest

---

(¹) Interview with Marcell von Donat, 18 February 2004.
(²) Ibid.
(³) Ibid.
(⁴) Ibid.
(⁵) Ibid.

(⁶) Message from the President of the Commission, *Courrier du personnel*, No 96, 7 January 1970, p. 4.
(⁷) *Courrier du personnel*, No 96, 7 January 1970, p. 15.

Staff policy or staff without a policy?

'The serious flaws in staff policy have been common knowledge since the publication of the "Round table report". Seldom has a report produced by a working party been read so avidly by the staff — especially one that is 50 pages long. We did not expect this lucid analysis. Perhaps the fact that it exists at all is a good sign. Be that as it may, it highlights a flaw which I feel is as serious, relatively speaking, as the decline in the European ideal in recent years: the disenchantment of the staff in the face of an impenetrable bureaucracy, its feeling of being left to its own devices. Paternalism almost starts to look attractive. Balancing acts and legal smoke and mirrors are no substitute for a staff policy. This is the main lesson of this report, a lesson we must on no account forget during this restructuring, which I for one prefer to call a tidying-up operation.'

Guggenbuhl, D., *Courrier du personnel*,
No 123, 17 July 1970, p. 24.
(Translated from the French)

possible geographical basis. However, since the establishment of the High Authority, it had been common practice to distribute senior posts especially according to rules which were both flexible and unwritten [1]. Thus the formulation of decisions relating to the balance of nationalities remained intentionally vague. Unlike the High Authority and the Commission of the common market, which used to examine the question only when a member — usually an Italian — complained of an imbalance, the Euratom Commission considered this balance to be essential and therefore discussed it openly.

As early as 1958, the EEC Commission had decided that Germany, France, Italy and the whole of Benelux would have 25 % of posts each [2]. The original aim was to establish an integrated multinational administration, with staff of every nationality in every department. As Michel Gaudet explained to his colleagues, a dossier had to travel up through the hierarchy, via officials of different cultures, so at the end of the day it was a good document, a balanced document which took account of the sensitivities and traditions of the different countries [3].

Unfortunately, once this balance had been achieved, it was sacrosanct. The situation became entrenched, at the expense of a fair promotion system: 'The Commission had a real nationality list for filling director-general, director and head of division posts in the establishment plan. There was practically a national flag on every job. Changing the nationality of a post was an extremely sensitive business [...]. This system slowed down the promotion of many a good official [...]. To have a successful career it was helpful to have the right nationality at the right time' [4]. The ECSC Commission was in a similar situation.

Consequently, careers were not linear. Officials had to be able to accept a change of directorate, or even directorate-general. Commission officials advanced crabwise — never in a straight line. For some, passionate about and expert in their field, there was no question of changing, for others it was the best way of advancing their career. In both cases, a sense of bitterness remained, though some felt it more than others.

What is more, the system known as 'parachuting', whereby members of the Commissioners' private offices (*cabinets*) were found permanent jobs in important posts, heightened this sense of injustice. That the pressures were enormous [5] and

---

[1] CEAB 2 713, Minutes of an informal meeting between the members of the High Authority, 5 December 1952, Item 6.

[2] PV 10, EAEC Commission, 23 April 1958, item 3.
[3] Interview with Jean-Jacques Beuve-Méry, 3 March 2004.
[4] Interview with Frans De Koster, 14 November 2004.
[5] Interview with Yves Desbois, 3 December 2003.

the influence of the *cabinets* was 'a scourge' ([1]) is confirmed by former officials. In the early years, however, the scale of the phenomenon remained fairly modest because, under Hallstein's influence, the *cabinets* were made up of no more than two or three people, even though a good many directors-general learnt the ropes, as it were, as a member of the Commission's immediate circle.

But then there was also the day-to-day work which had to be done, and which provided a source of motivation ([2]). European officials were very close to the decision-making process. They experienced it directly, for example in the Council of Ministers; they had to argue their case, defend themselves, go on the offensive, work out compromises, and so on ([3]). It was a fascinating job. In the early years, a young administrator was doing virtually the same job as a director, or even a director-general, would do in years to come. Naturally, it was very rewarding.

Work, leisure and solidarity

People worked very late. It was not unusual to spend one's evenings at the office. The example was set at the highest level. Hallstein and Noël lived in and for the Commission: 'I saw Hallstein three or four times and it was always at 10 o'clock at night' ([4]); 'he had a bed in his office' ([5]); '(in the Secretariat-General) you had to keep up; if you once fell behind, you were lost.' ([6]) And it was true, particularly in the early days, for a large number of administrators and their assistants. The working hours were often impossible for the staff in the upper echelons of the administration and for those who were involved in trade negotiations, for example. They threw themselves into their work with a passion, often at the expense of their family life — if they had one, and that is a

valid question. The Commission ran on French time. The working day began at about nine, with a long lunch break from 1 p.m. until 2.30 p.m. — in the days of the High Authority this was to allow staff to go home for lunch — and ended officially at about 6 p.m., although in reality it was often an hour or two later. The Cortenberg self-service restaurant was open in the evenings. The lights went out in some windows in Berlaymont much later. Noël often left the building, accompanied by his faithful secretary, between 10 p.m. and 11 p.m.

Under the circumstances, there was not much time for leisure activities ([7]). According to some French officials, there was not a lot to do in Brussels after 8 p.m. in those days. 'When we went out there was no one around. Everything was shut.' Consequently, the Eurocrats in exile in the Belgian capital had to make their own entertainment. In the beginning, they used to meet privately for a drink in multinational groups — old 'colonials' from Directorate-General for Development or old 'railwaymen' from the Directorate-General for Transport. Once the activities began to include families — dinners or parties, for example — they preferred to meet in groups of the same nationality or, more precisely, of the same language. Although virtually all Community officials spoke a second language, their spouses often spoke only one and social life necessarily included spouses ([8]). This was particularly true of the Germans. Berndt von Staden was led to wonder whether the Germans' tendency to keep to themselves was the result of memories of the recent past or of traditional German provincialism ([9]).

Far from their families but also from their local parish, devout officials very quickly formed religious groups. The German Protestant and Catholic communities opened their doors to their fellow-countrymen, while the Foyer catholique

([1]) Interview with Claude Brus, 5 December 2003.
([2]) Interview with Frans De Koster, 14 November 2004.
([3]) Interview with Marcell von Donat, 18 February 2004.
([4]) Interview with Paul-Henri Buchet, 20 January 2004.
([5]) Ibid.
([6]) Interview with Frans De Koster, 14 November 2004.

([7]) Ibid.
([8]) Interview with Marcello Burattini, 18 February 2004.
([9]) Von Staden, B., op. cit., p. 187.

européen (European Catholic Centre), set up in the early 1960s on the initiative of Catholic officials, brought together French, Belgian and Italian officials through its pastoral activities. Its role within the Catholic community that was working for the European institutions was very broad. It was more than just a congregation, it was a family — a highly dynamic family, offering in addition to philosophical and spiritual choices a place where people could meet or hold discussions, parties or conferences.

As the months went by, the ranks of officials working for the new Communities swelled and, often at the instigation of unmarried members, they began to set up sports clubs and other groups of their own. These proved to be a real melting pot in which the European identity of the Communities' staff was forged. 'The point of contact was no longer nationality but leisure interests, and sport is a great cohesive force, a great bond.' (¹) In their lunch break, in the evening or at the weekend, officials would meet around a table, a judo mat or a football pitch. The *Courrier du personnel* of the day provides an insight into the exploits of the Eurobasket Club, winner in 1969 of the Robert Schuman Challenge Cup, the atmosphere surrounding Community derby between FC Euratom and Marcom (the telegraphic address of the common market) or, for motor sports fans, the peregrinations of the Scuderia Europa car rally. Volleyball, basketball, skating, yoga, riding, dancing, tennis, not to mention stamp collecting, drama, music and photography — the activities offered were many and various. In Luxembourg, the Cercle sportif Richard Merten was the home of the main sports clubs organised for and by officials from 1958 onwards. In Brussels, the aim of the Club carrefour européen, for example, was to organise the leisure activities of young and not-so-young European officials, including staff from embassies and permanent representations, and it hosted dances, parties, exhibitions and a film club, among other things. Until 1967 it held its events at the Foyer européen in

---

(¹) Interview with Clément André, 9 February 2004.

'On my first evening I left the office at 11 o'clock'

'The phone call came on 4 May (1958). I arrived in Brussels on the evening of 18 May and the following morning I started work. It was all very formal. I was sent to rue Belliard, where I was told that I would be working for Walter Hallstein's press officer, Mr von Stülpnagel [...]. He wrote the President's speeches. When I first arrived, it was all very temporary. There were two Dutchmen who looked after the money. They gave me a form which said that I had been recruited as a C3, I would be earning 8 300 Belgian francs plus daily allowances, I was entitled to a trip home once a fortnight, I could buy myself a train ticket and I was urgently awaited in a particular office. When I arrived in the office, Mr von Stülpnagel [...] said: "I must dictate something to you at once." He didn't ask me any questions, he just said "This is so urgent, this speech must be finished this evening." I left the office at 11 o'clock that first evening. At about 8 pm he asked me if I couldn't type faster. I'd already done 31 pages or more and it was not possible. At 10.30 he called in another secretary from Hallstein's cabinet to dictate more letters. It was like that for the first six months. There was no fixed timetable but we didn't mind. It was fascinating.'

Interview with Ursula Thiele, 20 October 2004.

the rue du Marais (close to rue Neuve and the Development DG). Arts and crafts enthusiasts, on the other hand, patronised another club, the Atelier européen. In 1969, following the merger of the administrations and the 'voluntary' or 'compulsory' transfer of several hundred people, a number of officials took the initiative of organising a welcome and support group known as Amitiés européennes. Its first tasks were to provide a welcome for new arrivals, to find friendly meeting places for unmarried staff, to encourage the Europeans to get to know each other better and to establish a local support structure, in the various municipalities and districts of Brussels. By 1970 the group had 100 members and it opened

The cafeteria is a place where officials from different directorates-general can meet and chat in a relaxed atmosphere.
On 12 June 1972 a new cafeteria, the 'Rotonde' with space for 400 people, is inaugurated in Berlaymont at the same time
as a self-service restaurant and a meditation centre.
(Cafeteria of the European Commission)

its doors to all Europeans who did not belong to the Communities but who shared the same spirit of European solidarity (¹).

This spirit of solidarity was also turned outwards, with the creation of bodies such as the Association Europe/Tiers-Monde, launched on the initiative of staff members in DG Development. The aim of this body was to make the staff of the European institutions more aware of the problems of the Third World and to forge direct links with Third World communities, particularly through practical aid (²). By March 1968 the association had 250 members, with each of them undertaking to pay over to it 1 000th of their monthly salary; it organised tombolas and sold greetings cards at Christmas and New Year. It continued to be very active, supporting projects such as the setting up of facilities for raising laying-hens in India or the provision of study grants for students in Cameroon (³).

By the end of the 1960s a large number of officials were supporting charitable organisations. They wanted to do something worthwhile. Contrary to what some people thought, they were, for the most part, well aware that they were privileged and privilege brought certain obligations. 'We have been given so much and now it is our turn to give. Europe's wealth must not make us into a closed and privileged victors' club. We must not forget the misfortunes of the Third World or, on our own doorstep, the dispossessed of the Marolles. We must not become "glorified" migrant workers and, leaving aside our material comforts, we must not overwhelm with our knowledge those less knowledgeable than ourselves. Let us sometimes look beyond the job to see the man beneath. [...] Of course, European officials, already under pressure as a result of leaving their roots and of the contrast, not to say clash, of cultures may well be tempted to seek to avoid that tension, essential nevertheless, gener-

ated by the pricking of a conscience which never sleeps.' (⁴)

For some, this was carried over into the realities of the administration of the Communities in the form of a militancy which went beyond the mere financing of charitable projects. There was a desire to implement policy measures, even if they did not, strictly speaking, fall within the remit of the Communities. It was against this background that Albert Coppé, a member of the Single Commission, met Fr Wresinski, the founder of the ATD Fourth World Movement, at the instigation of officials who were concerned about the problems of the Fourth World and underprivileged children. This marked the beginning of a new dynamic which a few years later led to the first European Commission poverty relief programme.

A small group of officials committed both to Europe and to the furtherance of social justice found inspiration at that time in the personalist movement, which originated in France between the wars. Although Emmanuel Mounier, the founder of the movement, did not develop a specific theory on Europe, through his thought and actions he was instrumental in giving it a soul, in the words of Jacques Delors. Some, like Jacques-René Rabier, worked after the war on the magazine *Esprit*; others took part, and in some cases still do, in the activities of the Jean Moulin Club, Citoyen 60 or the popular education movement Vie nouvelle, while still others, the younger ones in many cases, were simply under the spell of a philosophy to which they could rally. At the beginning of the 21st century Michel Albert, Michel Camdessus and Jean Boissonnat declared, in accordance with their Catholic and humanist traditions, that the development of the individual occurred in a complete relationship with others, based on responsibility and giving. The consequence for society as a whole was that peace

---

(¹) *Courrier du personnel*, No 99, 15 January 1970, p. 9.
(²) *Courrier du personnel*, No 20, 15 May 1968, p. 16.
(³) *Courrier du personnel*, No 91, 21 November 1969, pp. 15–16.

(⁴) André, C., 'Le fonctionnaire européen au travail', *Courrier du personnel*, No 107, 1 April 1970, p. 22.

1er JUILLET 1971 - M. COPPE INAUGURE L'INFORMAPHONE

The Informaphone is a phone-based internal information service inaugurated on 1 July 1971 by Albert Coppé, who launched it. The three-minute tape-recorded message begins with the words: 'Ici, l'Informaphone. Service information du personnel', followed by the date and 'Voilà les informations de la journée'. As the success of the Informaphone grows, a second telephone line is added and languages other than French are offered. In 1971 the record number of daily callers — 1 350 — is reached. The Informaphone also offers interviews with Commissioners, directors-general and so on. Every Wednesday evening Émile Noël records a report on the day's Commission meeting, so that everybody is informed by Thursday morning.

—Prenez chaque jour 3 minutes pour vous informer sur l'actualité communautaire.

—Nehmen Sie sich täglich 3 Minuten Zeit und informieren Sie sich über das Zeitgeschehen in der Gemeinschaft.

—In tre minuti sarete informati ogni giorno sulle attualità della vita Comunitaria.

—Neem iedere dag 3 minuten de tijd om naar het laatste nieuws over de Gemeenschappen te luisteren.

INFORMAPHONE 4551 4651

could not be real without social justice (¹), thus confirming their positions taken in the 1960s.

The European School: a unique cultural achievement

In the early days the Commission recruited expatriate administrators, people with a certain amount of experience. As a result, it was not long before the question arose as to how to educate their children. Alongside the education provided by the Belgian school system, Brussels in 1958 already boasted a *lycée français*, a German school and an international school. However, these did not meet the specific needs of all the staff of the new Communities, particularly as they were aware of the Luxembourg experiment, often cited as exemplary.

On the initiative of parents working for the European Coal and Steel Community, the first European School (consisting of a kindergarten and a primary section) had been opened in Luxembourg in 1953. It had received the blessing of Jean Monnet and Paul-Henri Spaak, the Presidents of the High Authority and of the Joint Assembly respectively, and financial support from the ECSC institutions and the Luxembourg government. From the legal point of view, however, it was a private initiative run by a non-profit organisation set up for the purpose under Luxembourg law, the Association des intérêts éducatifs et familiaux des fonctionnaires de la Communauté. The experiment was so successful that a secondary school — set up with the support of the Member States' governments — was opened in the autumn of 1954. To complete the creation of this unique educational system and ensure the recognition of the school-leaving certificate and access to higher education, a convention defining the statute of the European School was signed in April 1957 and the European *baccalauréat* was introduced a few months later. Two men fought to keep this initiative alive, Marcel Decombis, a

member of Jean Monnet's *cabinet*, who initiated the idea and subsequently became the first headmaster of the European School in Luxembourg, and Albert Van Houtte, the Registrar at the Court of Justice and Chairman of the above association, who through their perseverance and diplomacy succeeded in convincing the Member States' delegates of the need for a specific and completely new statute. Paradoxically, the European School had its own legal personality. It was not in the strict sense an institution of the Communities, but an institution of the Member States. It was the first official intergovernmental school.

It was originally divided into four language sections — German, French, Italian and Dutch — in order to provide children with a basic education in their mother tongue while following the same curriculum and timetable. It emphasised the learning of a 'vehicular' or common language — either German or French — in which primary pupils were taught the so-called 'European hours' (including music, handicrafts and physical education), where the different sections were mixed together, and in which secondary pupils took actual classes, such as history and/or geography.

On the eve of the entry into force of the new Treaties, the structure was already in existence. All that was needed was to adapt it to the situation in Brussels. President Hallstein was aware of this fact and in May 1958 contacted the representative of the Board of Governors of the European Schools, Albert Van Houtte. 'It is also the wish of our Commission,' he said, 'that its officials should have the opportunity to place their children in a common school where the ethos strongly encourages mutual understanding and therefore the aims set by the European governments when establishing the Communities.' (²)

However, the French government was not convinced. It feared that the new school would compete with the existing *lycée français* in Brussels

---

(¹) Albert, M., Boissonnat, J. and Condessus, M., *Notre foi dans ce siècle*, Arlea, Paris, 2002, p. 198.

(²) BAC 118/1986 2166/1, Letters from Walter Hallstein to Albert Van Houtte, 23 May 1958 and undated.

The Brussels (now Brussels I) European School is inaugurated in September 1958, originally in a house in the rue du Trône/ Troonstraat before moving the following year to the former Devis family residence in Uccle. The words of Jean Monnet expressing the essential aims of the European Schools have been sealed, in parchment, into the foundation stones of all the Schools: 'Educated side by side, untroubled from infancy by divisive prejudices, acquainted with all that is great and good in different cultures, it will be borne in upon them as they mature that they belong together. Without ceasing to look to their own lands with love and pride, they will become in mind Europeans, schooled and ready to complete and consolidate the work of their fathers before them so as to bring into being a united and thriving Europe.'

and in particular it had reservations, as always, concerning any move which might reinforce the position of Brussels as the de facto seat of the new executives. In January 1960 Jacques-René Rabier and Albert Van Houtte decided that they needed the backing of Jean Monnet, as the French government had declared that there was no question of financing a European School in places where there was already a *lycée français*, for example in Brussels. In other words, 'foreigners' would just have to come and immerse themselves in French culture in French schools ([1]), and both the Germans and the Belgians seemed likely to back the French position.

However, there was no denying the success of the Luxembourg 'Schuman Plan' school, as it was known, and it was clear that this was the way ahead. The first classes opened in Brussels in September 1958. The Belgian government was in favour of the scheme and even offered to make the Val-Duchesse site available for the future school, but it was decided to opt for a provisional site on the rue du Trône, close to the Quartier Léopold station — now the Gare du Luxembourg — before the final move to a site in Uccle, flanking the Chaussée de Waterloo, in 1959.

The Statute of the European School, signed in Luxembourg on 12 April 1957, made no provision for the setting-up of schools outside the Grand Duchy, however, and a supplementary protocol was required. Signed in 1962, it entered into force only after completion of the deposit of the instruments of ratification in December 1975. The Statute, which had for a long time been 'non-contractual', stated that 'for the education and instruction together of children of the staff of the European Communities, establishments bearing the name "European Schools" may be set up on the territory of the contracting parties' and, in a new departure, 'other children, irrespective of their nationality, may also be admitted to them' ([2]). The principle of a social mix was therefore accepted, although as early as 1962 a commentator pointed out that the European School entailed the risk that the children, who would receive an excellent education, might unwittingly have instilled in them the notion that they belonged to a special and pampered group, a 'Eurocrat' elite ([3]), even though a real effort was being made to open

the school to local children and the school brought together the children of officials of all grades. Jean Monnet and Albert Coppé, for example, had sent some of their children to the European School in Luxembourg and others would do the same in Brussels.

The existence of a European School was particularly important where parents had no real alternative. The Euratom Commission accordingly insisted that sister establishments be set up at the places of employment of Community staff, leading to the creation of the European Schools at Varese, close to the Ispra Centre (1960), Mol/Geel in Belgium (1960), Karlsruhe in Germany (1962) and Bergen in the Netherlands (1963). According to Ivo Dubois, the two Commissions had every respect for these establishments, which were essential for the recruitment of staff, especially to the Joint Research Centres; they accordingly paid that part of the running costs of the schools not covered in the annual budget by the equivalent of the national salaries which the Member States, who provided teaching staff on secondment, paid as their contribution to the budget of the school, the teachers receiving a 'European salary' set out in specific rules. The representatives of the Commissions were given one seat on the Board of each school. They were responsible for ensuring sound financial discipline. Discussions with the representative of the Board of Governors, Albert Van Houtte, who defended 'his' European School tooth and nail, could be hard work ([4]).

In Brussels, staff who — at the outset, at least — planned to return home after a few years or who wanted a 'national' education for their children would sometimes put them in the *lycée français*, the German school or the Juliana School; others, preferring to integrate into their host country, enrolled their children in Belgian schools.

First-hand accounts suggest that, while the European School experience was unique, it was also as a result somewhat different from the national

([1]) FJME, AMK, V 33/5/60, Letter from Jacques-René Rabier to Jean Monnet, 8 January 1960.
([2]) Article 1 of the Protocol on the setting-up of European Schools.
([3]) *Trouw*, 27 November 1962, quoted in *Scholae Europaea Luxemburgensis 1953–1963*, Luxembourg, 1963, p. 66.

([4]) E-mail from Ivo Dubois to the author, 23 February 2006.

education systems. One parent says that he was satisfied because he expected no more from the European School than it was able to provide (¹); even though the aim of the school was to prepare pupils as effectively as possible for higher education in their countries of origin, it might not have been the best preparation for university in France. At the European School the emphasis was more on the ability to communicate, for example through language teaching.

The development of this specialised school structure proved to be a constant academic challenge, given the need to coordinate age-old traditions of schooling and find a sort of common denominator, which called for understanding and concessions on all sides (²). It was the first real attempt at integrated education at European level. It was not only the educational approach, but also the fact that the pupils were of different nationalities and the teachers, the inspectors and, of course, the parents were from different cultural and linguistic backgrounds, that made the European School into the cradle of an emerging European identity.

But beyond the common misconception of tiny tots of all nationalities singing 'Frère Jacques' in four languages, the standard also varied, as in other school systems, according to the period, the people and the establishment. While the Luxembourg experience continued to be remembered as outstanding, the Brussels school, though carrying on the same educational traditions, quickly found itself having to cope with a larger number of students and an increase in the number of language sections, which led in turn to fewer contacts between the sections. The chemistry between the various players (pupils, teachers, inspectors and parents) from the six founding Member States often worked, but we should not deceive ourselves about the many problems which could occasionally have an impact on re-

sults and teaching standards. Sometimes, as in Karlsruhe in 1968, there were problems recruiting teaching staff and, according to the parents, the pupils suffered as a result of the inconsistencies of an education provided, within a single language section, by teachers and inspectors employed by two different governments, Belgian and French (³). In fact, strictly speaking, there was not a French section at all but a Franco-Belgian section, just as there was a Belgo-Dutch section. The selection of teaching staff by the national ministries of education and the — sometimes too frequent — rotation of these staff also had a somewhat damaging effect on teaching, as a Parliamentary report pointed out at the time (⁴).

In Brussels, to overcome the fact that the school was a long way from the European quarter and poorly served by public transport, the parents gradually set up a private bus service to collect pupils from different parts of the city.

A former pupil confirms the paradoxical absence of lessons on European integration and the Communities (⁵). Indeed, for many years pupils followed syllabuses based on national curricula in which 'Europe' played only a minor role. Fortunately, the children met fellow-pupils of different nationalities in language classes, at playtime and on school trips. Although such meetings were beneficial, they could occasionally be difficult as children are not always kind. But, in the end, national prejudices became blurred; children are more open-minded. They were able to really get to know fellow-pupils of other nationalities and communicate with them in their own or a common language. It was not much but it was more than one might have hoped for.

While the children went to school, their parents too were completing their education. A consider-

(¹) Interview with Jean-Claude Séché, 8 June 2004.
(²) Bourrinet, H., 'L'École européenne [...] vue par les professeurs', in Scholae Europaea Luxemburgensis 1953–1963, Luxembourg, 1963, p. 83.

(³) Courrier du personnel, No 20, 15 May 1968, pp. 3–5.
(⁴) Merten, H., Rapport parlementaire sur les écoles européennes et leur développement, Documents de séances 1966–1967, Document No 8, 7 March 1966.
(⁵) Benoit, P., 'L'École européenne [...] vue par les anciens élèves', in Scholae Europaea Luxemburgensis 1953–1963, Luxembourg, 1963, p. 101.

Discovering the United States — Leaders' grants to promote transatlantic relations

'The Department of State hereby awards a United States Government Grant for the purpose of enabling you to participate in the Mutual Education and Cultural Exchange program ([1]).' These words, from the Office of European Programs, marked the beginning for EEC officials, including Émile Noël and Bino Olivi, of a unique experience — a two-month study visit to the United States laden with information visits and meetings — thanks to a leaders' grant. It was an opportunity offered to people with a promising future ([2]) and to young people in the administrations and professional organisations who were considered by ambassadors anywhere in the world to have the makings of a future leader ([3]).

Camille Becker explained the decision-making process for leaders' grants. The US ambassadors would choose graduates who had already made a promising start in their careers and who were expected to rise quickly through the ranks. If Washington approved of the choice, the ambassadors would be given perhaps six leaders' grants. Mr Schaetzel, head of the US Mission to the Communities, had 7, 8, 9, 10 leaders' grants and would ask his colleagues which of the Commission, Council and European Parliament officials he should choose ([4]). The Office of Cultural Exchange of the Leaders and Specialists Division of the Department of State ([5]), with organisational assistance from a non-profit

association, the Government Affairs Institute ([6]), then took charge of organising the trip.

As regards the itinerary, Guy Vanhaeverbeke explained that the successful candidate chose the theme of the visit. It then had to be accepted ([7]). Indeed, the US Mission in Brussels insisted that the grant recipients should provide it with details of the places they wished to go and the people they wished to meet ([8]). The Government Affairs Institute also gave advice to successful candidates on drawing up their itinerary ([9]). Daniel Cardon de Lichtbuer, for example, was interested in the Californian administration ([10]). Émile Noël, on the other hand, visited the Massachusets Institute of Technology and established contacts with academic circles ([11]). Fernand Braun studied Boeing and met one of the founders of GATT, Bill Clayton ([12]).

This type of exchange reflected not only the importance of the Community for the United States but also served quite specific objectives. In addition to establishing contacts or friendships between the US and European 'elites', John Tuthill, the US Representative to the Communities, told Émile Noël that 'We hope that it will enable you to become better acquainted with our institutions and the ways of life of our people. (I express the hope) that your experience will contribute to strengthening the mutual understanding between the people of the United States and the people of the European

---

([1]) HAEU, EN 1584, *Copy for grantee*, US Department of State, 20 July 1965.

([2]) Interview with Fernand Braun, 8 December 2003.

([3]) Interview with Guy Vanhaeverbeke, 25 February 2004.

([4]) Interview with Camille Becker, 4 March 2004.

([5]) HAEU, EN 1584, *United States Mission to the European Communities, memorandum for participants in the US State Department's Leader Program*, attached to a letter from John W. Tuthill, US Representative to the European Communities, to Émile Noël, dated 27 July 1965; HAEU, EN 1661, Letter from Émile Noël to Hans Tabor, dated 2 August 1965.

([6]) HAEU, EN 1660, Letter from Leonard Tennyson to Émile Noël, dated 13 July 1965.

([7]) Interview with Guy Vanhaeverbeke, 25 February 2004.

([8]) HAEU, EN 1669, Letter from Émile Noël to an unidentified correspondant, 23 July 1965.

([9]) HAEU, EN 1661, Letter from Émile Noël to Hans Tabor, dated 2 August 1965.

([10]) Interview with Daniel Cardon de Lichtbuer, 12 November 2003.

([11]) HAEU, EN 1660, Letter from Émile Noël to Thomas W. Fina, 17 August 1965.

([12]) Interview with Fernand Braun, 8 December 2003.

Communities' ([1]). On the European side, Ivo Dubois felt that the United States was trying to 'pick our minds' to win Europe over to the American cause ([2]). In the view of Émile Noël, the prime objective was to obtain an overall view of US foreign policy. With his special interest in European and US problems, he wanted to extend his knowledge and understanding of the global approach to problems of a world power like the

United States ([6]). For Heinrich von Moltke, the leaders' grant was a stroke of genius and the impression the trip made on him is with him still ([7]).

C.S.

able number of European officials apparently benefited from leaders' grants from the American institution. A two-month stay was offered to promising young graduates. It gave Community officials the opportunity to familiarise themselves with the American perspective on their area of activity within the EEC or Euratom Commissions. A specialist in combating cartels could learn about US anti-trust laws, for example, including raids on companies ([3]). Someone else might renew his interest in regional policy ([4]). The field of study was broad, the benefits unquestionable and the importance of this network of special contacts for relations between the USA and the European Communities considerable.

Making Europe work in daily life; the secret of a new solidarity

'Institutions are more important than men […]. But some men have the power to transform and enrich what institutions pass on to succeeding generations' ([5]). This extract from Jean Monnet's *Memoirs* acknowledges the importance of individual players but also their transience. And yet, without individuals to create them, develop them, to breathe life into them and give them a soul,

there would have been no institutions. 'It was a European attitude, the fruit of working together and above all of having to reach a common conclusion after long discussion and widespread consultations' ([8]), declared the father of the Schuman Plan. At work, at play and in the classrooms of the European School a common spirit developed, marked by a shared determination to succeed in the European project, and new ties were forged in defiance of national prejudices. Were these the beginnings of a real European identity? It certainly seemed so in Luxembourg in the days of the High Authority. It was probably the same in Brussels, too — the old guard remember it that way — but it was less apparent. The city was larger and the rapid increase in staff allowed a number of cliques to remain in place. In time, a certain spirit, albeit different from the pioneering spirit of the early days, spread through the Communities' corridors. Even in 1970, when a feeling of malaise had descended on the Commission, the international and multicultural character of the institution was never really in doubt. On the contrary, it was a real source of commitment.

In the words of Walter Hallstein, it was within the institutions, through the frequent, almost daily,

---

([1]) HAEU, EN 1584, Letter from John W. Tuthill to Émile Noël, dated 27 July 1965.

([2]) Interview with Ivo Dubois, 22 December 2003.

([3]) Interview with Jacques Vandamme, 21 January 2004.

([4]) Interview with Paul Romus, 20 January 2004.

([5]) Monnet, J., *Memoirs*, Collins, London, 1978, p. 471.

([6]) AUHE, EN 1584, Émile Noël, *Objectifs généraux du voyage*, 6 July 1965.

([7]) Interview with Heinrich von Moltke, 22 January 2004

([8]) Ibid., p. 377.

contacts between leading figures of all the Member States, that the European spirit essential to the success of the Community developed and the growth of the European awareness so vital for the current generation occurred. By making Europe work, the officials and business leaders of the Six were able to see the deeper reasons for the Community and the fundamental solidarity which bound the Member States together ([1]).

MICHEL DUMOULIN,
with the collaboration of YVES CONRAD

([1]) Hallstein, W., 'L'évolution des Communautés européennes', *Annuaire européen,* 1958, Title VI, p. 10.

Chapter 13

The question of location

The minutes of the first meeting of the EEC Commission, which was held at the Château of Val-Duchesse on 16 January 1958, record that, after a lengthy debate on which city should be the venue for Commission meetings, the members of the College adopted the formula put forward by Marjolin: meetings would take place in Brussels when the services of the Interim Committee were required and in Luxembourg when those of the High Authority were called upon ([1]).

From the very outset, Hallstein had drawn a very clear distinction between the designation of a place of work for the Commission, which the Commission itself should determine, and the location of the Community's seat, which was a matter for the Council of Ministers ([2]).

First, therefore, the delicate issue of the seat was raised, or rather revived. In 1952, the designation of Luxembourg as the seat for the High Authority had already been discussed at the end of a meeting of the ministers of the Six, which verged on the surreal. The Belgian Minister for Foreign Af-

fairs, Paul van Zeeland, constrained by domestic considerations, had been obliged to defend Liège as a candidate. His colleagues had favoured Brussels, which had many advantages in terms of geographical position, communications, infrastructure and services. Van Zeeland had fought tooth and nail against the Brussels bid! Luxembourg's minister, the jovial, canny Joseph Bech, had made the best of the situation and, in order to break the deadlock, had proposed Luxembourg as the seat for the High Authority, on a provisional basis ...

The intention had been that the decision of 1952 would be renegotiated soon afterwards, but it was not seriously raised again until 1958 — although plenty of people had had afterthoughts. Some contemplated the idea of multiple locations, others a single seat.

The seat of the EEC and Euratom institutions

The sensitive issue of where the new institutions should be located was broached neither at the Val-Duchesse negotiations nor in the interim period, for fear of disrupting the ratification

---

([1]) Minutes of the EEC Commission's 1st meeting, 16 January 1958, Item X, p. 6.
([2]) Ibid., p. 5.

process. Officially there was, therefore, a total blackout on the subject until the beginning of December 1957 and as a result there was barely a month left before the Treaties came into force. An informal meeting did take place unofficially after a NATO meeting on 20 December in Paris, but all they managed to decide was to meet again at the same place on 6 and 7 January 1958.

Heading for the inevitable status quo

When the Paris negotiations began on 6 January, no official candidates were presented, although candidates did exist: Brussels, Strasbourg, Turin, Milan, Monza and Stresa. Luxembourg, which wanted to keep the ECSC at any cost, was, however, unwilling to accept all the institutions: public opinion was afraid there would be a massive influx of foreigners which would overwhelm the small country. It would, therefore, become a candidate only if discussions definitely pointed towards the designation of a single seat and hence the loss of the High Authority. One final city did make an impressive bid: Paris, or rather Chantilly, which lies some 40 kilometres north of the French capital in the department of Oise. Here the French authorities were willing to build from scratch the whole infrastructure necessary for a European district.

For two days the negotiations marked time. Everyone agreed on the principle of a single seat, but as soon as they tried to apply it no one could agree. On the one hand a single seat could not be created overnight and on the other it would mean one side got everything and the rest nothing.

The Paris Conference ended in a failure barely mitigated by the appointment of the members and Presidents of the Commissions. The institutions could therefore begin work, but in which city? The ministers, as we have seen, had decided that the EEC and Euratom Commission meetings would alternate between Luxembourg and Brussels. The final press release referred more specifically to Val-Duchesse rather than Brussels.

The Common Assembly would hold its meetings in Strasbourg. As for the Council of Ministers, it would be convened on the initiative of the presiding country. For the first six months of 1958, Belgium held the presidency. This situation, which favoured Brussels somewhat, was to continue until 1 June 1958, the date on which the ministers were to meet again to discuss the question of the seat. They were to be helped by a group of town planning experts who had been given the task of deciding between the candidate cities on non-political grounds. At the same time, the Presidents of the institutions were also to give their views.

The day after the Paris Conference, the Luxembourg government realised that it was losing ground to Brussels. It therefore decided to officially present Luxembourg as a candidate for the single seat. This created yet one more stumbling block in the negotiations due to take place on 1 June. Until that time, the two cities which shared the Commissions would do everything possible to accommodate the Communities' needs and consolidate what they had just accomplished.

In the meantime, however, on 11 February 1958, the Six reached an unofficial agreement. On the assumption that once the final seat was agreed on it would take at least two years for the buildings to be built, they decided that Brussels would house — at least for the next two years — the Secretariats of the Councils of Ministers and the Commissions of the common market and Euratom. The decision was of course welcomed in Belgium, particularly as the Six no longer talked about Val-Duchesse but about Brussels.

Slightly later than scheduled, the opinions requested in Paris at the start of January began to filter through from May onwards. Although the committee of experts had obviously tried to avoid offending anyone's sensibilities, its results were not unfavourable to Brussels. Unlike the other candidates, Brussels had a large number of advantages: its central geographical position, a developed communications network, the status of

Pour la publication immédiate   Union Paneuropéenne
Lundi, le 12 Mai 1958   2 Leimenstrasse, Bâle

Quelle sera la Capitale de l'Europe?

A la veille du scrutin de l'Assemblée Parlementaire Européenne sur la question du siège de la future Capitale de l'Europe, l'Union Paneuropéenne publie les résultats définitifs de son Enquête Parlementaire sur ce sujet.

L'Union Paneuropéenne s'était adressée au 2996 parlementaires des six pays faisant parti du Marché Commun Européen.

Les 768 réponses obtenus se répartissent de la façon suivante:

Parlementaires	Paris	Bruxel-les	Stras-bourg	Luxem-bourg	Autres villes	Total
Allemands	36	44	88	14	4	186
Belges	--	123	--	--	--	123
Français	171	3	80	--	5	259
Italiens	52	15	14	4	15	100
Luxembourgeois	--	--	--	12	--	12
Néerlandais	9	58	16	4	1	88
Total	268	243	198	34	25	768

Les autres villes sont:

Milan – 9 I, Turin – 2 I, Rome – 2 I, Stresa – 2 I,
Nice – 2 F, Lyon – 1 F, Dijon – 1 F, Fontainebleau – 1 F,
Vienne (Autriche) – 3 A, Saarbruck – 1 A, Rotterdam – 1 N.

R. Coudenhove-Kalergi

Richard de Coudenhove-Kalergi
Président de l'Union Paneuropéenne

For immediate publication   Union Paneuropéenne
Monday, 12 May 1958   2 Leimenstrasse, Basle

Where will the capital of Europe be?

On the eve of the vote by the European Assembly on the location of the future capital of Europe, Union Paneuropéenne is publishing the final results of its parliamentary survey on the subject. Union Paneuropéenne questioned 2 996 Members of Parliament from the six countries of the European Common Market. The 768 replies received are broken down as follows:

Members of Parliament	Paris	Brussels	Strasbourg	Luxembourg	Other cities	Total
German	36	44	88	14	4	186
Belgian	–	123	–	–	–	123
French	171	3	80	–	5	259
Italian	52	15	14	4	15	100
Luxembourg	–	–	–	12	–	12
Dutch	9	58	16	4	1	88
Total	268	243	198	34	25	768

Milan – 9 I, Turin – 2 I, Rome – 2 I, Stresa – 2 I,
Nice – 2 F, Lyon – 1 F, Dijon – 1 F, Fontainebleau – 1 F,
Vienna (Austria) – 3 G, Saarbrücken – 1 G, Rotterdam – 1 N.

Richard de Coudenhove-Kalergi
President of Union Paneuropéenne

Results of the survey on the location of the future capital of Europe carried out by Union Paneuropéenne among members of Parliament from the six Member States.
(Richard de Coudenhove-Kalergi, *Quelle sera la capitale de l'Europe?*, 12 May 1958.)

Joyeuse Entrée and Belgique joyeuse

When the EEC Commission moved to the avenue de la Joyeuse Entrée, Jean Rey was reported to have had difficulty making his colleagues, who were unfamiliar with the constitutional charters of Brabant, understand that their new address was not 'l'Entrée joyeuse' and that it had nothing to do with la Belgique joyeuse, which at the time was the venue for another kind of activity ([1]).

La Belgique joyeuse was the name given at Expo 58 to a very small village consisting of reconstructed facades typical of 16th and 17th century Belgian architecture and a series of bars, restaurants and other places of festivity. The Joyeuse Entrée referred to the charter by which the new sovereign of Brabant confirmed the privileges granted to his subjects at the time of his inauguration — his 'joyous entry' into Brussels. It defined not only the mutual obligations of sovereign and subject but also the latter's freedoms and served as a constitutional reference work.

According to M. Lethé, *L'Europe à Bruxelles dans les années 1960: le pourquoi? et le comment?*, UCL, Louvain-la-Neuve, 2003 (History degree dissertation), p. 133.

an international metropolis for more than a century, a building stock with interesting prospects for Europe, the sociocultural infrastructure of a capital city, and a sociological environment favourable to the European idea. The Presidents of the three European Commissions also viewed Brussels quite favourably, especially Walter Hallstein:

'When studying the various bids for the seat, I have been guided by the idea that, as far as possible, the choice must not depend on any consideration of prestige and that a balance must be maintained within the Community. This is why I do not think any of the three big Community countries should be chosen. Of the cities proposed, Brussels meets particularly well the requirements that a city must satisfy to become the seat of all the European institutions, from the point of view of geographical position, ease of access, and the immediate availability of office space and living accommodation' ([1]).

As for the Assembly, after a complicated vote, it gave further support to the Brussels bid, but in a less demonstrative, more equivocal manner.

On 1 July 1958, the ministers met. However, Italy, which was in the midst of a serious government crisis, did not send a representative to the meeting. It was therefore impossible to decide on the seat, as unanimity was required. The question was, thus, deferred. In the meantime the existing situation persisted, and Brussels continued to do everything to ensure that the institutions operated smoothly there. Maintenance of the status quo was clearly in its favour.

At the end of 1958, the executives of the EEC and Euratom no longer met anywhere other than in Brussels — thereby waiving the principle of alternating with Luxembourg ([2]). The Assembly met in Strasbourg and its Secretariat was well established in Luxembourg, but for the sake of simplicity its committees worked alongside the Commissions in Brussels.

This split between three cities appeared to suit the Member States and the European executives. Only the Assembly was inconvenienced, since it was divided between three nerve centres. It was, moreover, the Assembly that regularly raised the issue. In May 1959, it passed the following resolution: 'Noting that the governments have not yet decided where the single seat for the Community institutions should be located, the Parliamentary

---

[1] 'Monsieur Rey nous parle du Marché commun' (Mr Rey tells us about the Common Market), *Le Soir*, 27 April 1958. (Translation)

[2] Archives of the Ministry of Foreign Affairs, Brussels (AMAEB), file 6641 1.G.2.

[3] However, two meetings took place in Strasbourg at the Maison de l'Europe on 22 and 23 October 1958 and 16 and 17 December 1958.

The Commission moves into the Joyeuse Entrée building in July 1958. An extension on the avenue de Cortenberg/ Kortenberglaan is added. The Commission also has 100 offices in the rue du Marais/Broekstraat. In April 1959 two directorates-general are transferred to the avenue de Brocqueville/Brocquevillelaan.

Assembly, of the opinion that this is seriously detrimental to the activity which the European Parliamentary Assembly has the obligation and right to carry out, […] requests the Committee of Chairmen (of each Parliamentary Committee) to appoint a delegation to submit the present resolution to the governments of the six Member States and to state firmly that if, after a reasonable period of time, they have not taken any decision regarding the seat of the Assembly, the Assembly will decide on the venue for its part-sessions and how they are organised, so that it always has available the premises it requires both to hold Assembly and committee meetings and to provide permanent, suitable accommodation for its Secretariat.' (¹)

However, the Assembly was ignored and it put its threat into action. Subsequent attempts to put the question back on the agenda of ministerial meetings came to nothing. The provisional situation dragged on until the merger.

The merger of the executives and the seat of the Single Commission

The merger of the executives inevitably meant changes to their geographical location. The main issue lay in the choice between Luxembourg and Brussels. The problem of the European Parliament in Strasbourg ought really to have been no more than a side issue in the final settlement, but in the end, Parliament became the very nub of the problem, used as bargaining fodder in the trade-offs between Brussels and Luxembourg.

The Luxembourg capital had a lot to lose. The most important executive body was now that of the EEC in Brussels and as a result the High Authority had become a less significant institution which no longer had the status it had enjoyed in the process of European integration prior to 1958. Brussels was therefore the centre of gravity and if a move was necessary, logically it would be in that

direction. Aware of the irreversibility of this situation, the Luxembourg authorities gradually stopped calling for the ECSC to be kept in Luxembourg. Belgian diplomacy prevailed and Luxembourg now concentrated on gaining compensation.

Luxembourg wanted compensation for two types of loss: material damage and prestige. In losing the ECSC High Authority, it would also lose 1 100 officials who, together with their families, worked, lived and consumed locally. The High Authority had also enhanced the prestige of the Grand Duchy's capital and given it a place on the international stage, increasing this small country's standing. To make up for this loss, the presence of one particular institution appeared to be appropriate: the European Parliament. Parliament held its part-sessions in Strasbourg, but its Secretariat was located in Luxembourg. Bringing them together would be the ideal solution. Obviously, however, such a solution would not be to the liking of Strasbourg and the French government.

When the negotiations on the merger of the executive bodies began on 20 September 1963, the problem the ministers of the Six had to tackle was particularly complex. By now, practically no one envisaged a single seat for the Council, the Commission and the Assembly. Moreover, only Luxembourg, Brussels and Strasbourg were still in the running, although no official decision had ever ruled out the other cities considered in 1958.

Not surprisingly, Strasbourg rejected Luxembourg's proposal outright. Another solution had therefore to be found — a task to which Coreper applied itself energetically. It made a series of proposals meeting Luxembourg's desire to maintain its moral rights — i.e. preserving its prestige — and the material benefits resulting from the presence of the High Authority. At the Council of Ministers meeting in February 1964, Coreper proposed that Luxembourg should keep the Court of Justice and the Assembly's Secretariat and that the European Investment Bank and a series of other institutions of lesser importance should also be located there. Luxembourg rejected the proposal,

---

(¹) AMAEB, file 6641 1.G.2. (Translation)

Brussels, 30 September 1964, Berlaymont under construction. It is built wing by wing. Originally scheduled for 1964, the first wing is completed only in 1967. The Directorate-General for Agriculture settles in there.

its representative making it amply clear that such an offer was beneath it ([1]). For Luxembourg, only the part-sessions of the Assembly could be seen as reasonable compensation.

A new idea then started to gain credence in some diplomatic circles: that of a two-centred seat. If a single seat was not possible, they had to aim for as little dispersal as possible and the institutions had, at the very least, to be grouped logically. One city could, therefore, house all the executive bodies and another one the supervisory, judicial and parliamentary bodies. No one contested Brussels' suitability as the executive centre. Indeed, this was already a fait accompli. As for the other centre, Luxembourg was emerging as the most likely candidate, but France was, of course, opposed to this.

It was at this point that the Parliamentary Assembly, weary of fruitless negotiations and tired of being pushed around without being consulted, decided to take things into its own hands. As we have seen, in 1959 it had issued a serious warning to the ministers. On 13 September 1964, on the basis of the principle agreed in January 1958 that there should be a single seat, it threatened to decide itself where it would meet. Given that the institutions were centred around Brussels, it was there that it would aim for if it were put under pressure.

However, at the same time another solution was emerging in Coreper: this consisted of splitting either the Assembly's part-sessions between Strasbourg and Luxembourg or the meetings of the Council of Ministers between Brussels and Luxembourg — or both. Unofficially, this solution seemed to appeal to Luxembourg's representatives. However, officially they continued to demand all of Parliament's part-sessions. For its part France still opposed a division, while Belgium reluctantly accepted the principle of conceding

some of the Council of Ministers meetings, as the Belgian Coreper representative said to his minister: 'The Belgian delegation finds itself obliged — as otherwise it would be accused of defending its own self-interest — to agree to sacrifices which go no way towards reaching a sound decision. […] The solution — now proposed in order to accommodate France's calculated intransigence concerning Strasbourg and Parliament's preferences runs counter to the Communities' interests.' ([2])

Nevertheless, Parliament's action took shape on the basis of Coreper's suggestion. The Assembly finally gave its verdict in November, following a close vote: 74 of the 142 members of the European Parliament stated their preference to remain in Strasbourg rather than travelling between Strasbourg and Luxembourg. It is worth noting that the Brussels option was not even mentioned in the resolution, otherwise it would probably have won.

However, the confused, rushed nature of the vote considerably undermined the position of Parliament, whose resolution was in no way binding. Admittedly, the ministers could not disregard its opinion and the proposal to divide part-sessions between Luxembourg and Strasbourg was therefore scrapped, to the great annoyance of the Luxembourg delegation. However, from then on the ministers were able to work without the prospect of a hostile vote from Parliament. One source of irritation had been removed.

At the same time, however, a possible solution had also disappeared. There was only one option left: to divide meetings of the Council between Brussels and Luxembourg. This was unacceptable for the Luxembourgers, who did not consider this adequate political compensation. They reached stalemate.

For over a month the situation remained at a standstill. It was not until January 1965 that

---

[1] CEAB 2 2775, AFP-AP dispatches on the meeting of the Council of Ministers of 24 February 1964; collected by the Commission of the European Communities, 25–26 February 1964.

[2] AMAEB, file 6641 1.G.2, document A.Q.QC.12/8.694, serial No 620. (Translation)

The 'Quartier Schuman'/'Schumanwijk' signpost goes up at the entrance to rue Juste Lipse. The Schuman district, where the European institutions are located, is in the heart of Brussels, between the Cinquantenaire Park and the Royal Park.

Coreper put forward a new proposal, which was quite similar to the previous ones. However, the Belgian delegation added a touch which accentuated the policy angle: 'The best solution would most probably be to seek an organic and operational presentation that would be clearly perceived as favourable to Luxembourg in terms of its European role' ([1]).

It was little more than a question of presentation. The European bodies located in Luxembourg would be grouped according to specific fields of policy. Grouped around the financial pole there would be the EIB, the European Development Fund and other financial institutions to be created in the future. Council meetings of European Finance Ministers could also be held in Luxembourg. The same principle would apply to legal matters, based around the Court of Justice.

---

[1] AMAEB, file 6641 1.G.2, document C.QC.12/9.841, serial No 40. (Translation)

This new proposal meant that an agreement could be reached at the meeting of the Council of Ministers on 1 and 2 March 1965. A month later, the Six signed the Merger Treaty, which stated that Luxembourg, Strasbourg and Brussels remained the provisional working places of the Community institutions. Brussels was to be the seat of the European Commission. Parliament was to have its seat in Strasbourg but its Secretariat would be located in Luxembourg, while the Council's seat would be in Brussels but it would automatically hold its April, June and October meetings in Luxembourg.

The main victim of the agreement was definitely the European Parliament. It ended up scattered around, with its part-sessions in Strasbourg, its Secretariat in Luxembourg and its committee meetings in Brussels. The Commission of the European Communities, on the other hand, came off best, with everything in Brussels. Until the end of the 1980s — notwithstanding a few adjustments in the interim — the Community institutions continued to be divided in this provisional manner. It was not until 1992, at the Edinburgh Summit, that the question of the seats was settled once and for all.

The Six had wasted precious time over this issue. It had taken seven years — from 1958 to 1965 — for a decision to be made, and even then it was only provisionally. Throughout that time, European integration had been unable to make any steady progress, the various Member States being constantly side-tracked by practical issues and matters of prestige. Even back in January 1958, the day after the Paris Conference, the Brussels daily newspaper, *Le Soir*, was well aware of the extent of the problem. At the time it had proposed a solution which, in the end, was very close to that adopted in March 1965:

'True, rationally speaking, it would be preferable for all the institutions to be concentrated in one place. Surely the solution would therefore be to find a fair balance between the need for rationalisation and the requirements of national prestige? Such a solution does not look impossible. Apart from the central administrations of the three Communities, which practically have to be located in the same place, there is a whole series of European institutions (the Court of Justice, the Assembly, the Bank, technical bodies, etc.) which could be spread around without doing serious damage.

The advantages of such a dispersal would considerably outweigh the minor inconveniences. First, the city housing the European Commissions would no longer be unique — an honour too great in the present climate, given the sensitivities of the parties concerned.

Furthermore, such a solution would share out the cake, a method not that morally wrong if — as is the case — very respectable acquired rights exist. [...] There would certainly be no great harm done if the Assembly of the Six continued to meet in the Alsatian capital. And it would be no more damaging if, in exchange for the ECSC High Authority, Luxembourg obtained various institutions of similar status and material significance.

This appears to be the direction in which we should be moving to break the deadlock. Otherwise it could last forever and compromise the very future of Europe's revival.' [1]

Brussels welcomes Europe

Brussels already enjoyed a central position on the international stage. Since the end of the 19th century it had been famous for its economic and industrial dynamism, the political ideas that had found currency there, the number of artists choosing to live there, the intellectual activity of its scientific institutions and, already, the number of international congresses and conferences taking place there. This activity, overflowing in all fields, diminished considerably as a result of the First World War. However, it soon picked up again

[1] *Le Soir*, 14 January 1958. (Translation)

Pensionnat de Berlaymont — Façade rue de la Loi

The Belgian State is looking out for land in Brussels where the European institutions can be housed. It opts for the property owned by the Canonesses of Saint Augustine, where there are two hectares on which to construct a building for the Commission with a minimum of compulsory purchases. The Berlaymont convent, day school and boarding school then move to Waterloo, but the name is left attached to both sites. The Ladies of Berlaymont had settled in the centre of Brussels in 1624 and moved to the Minimes and rue aux Laines district in 1808, from where they had been forced to leave in 1864, when the Palais de justice (Law Courts) was being built. That was when they moved to the rue de la Loi/Wetstraat.

afterwards, moving into the tertiary sector: bankers, businessmen and traders met in Brussels, where they had all the infrastructure they needed.

On this basis and strengthened by the surreal experience of 1952, the Belgian government immediately accepted the Brussels bid in October 1957 and undertook to present and defend it vis-à-vis the other Member States. It decided to do its utmost to ensure the bid's success. Unfortunately for it, the problem was much greater in 1958; Luxembourg and Strasbourg had already accommodated some institutions for several years. They therefore already had their noses in front.

The Belgian State possessed a number of sites where large buildings could be accommodated if there was to be a single seat. The press cited several, but those in which the authorities were really interested were the Heysel plateau, where the Universal Exhibition was taking place, and the plaine des Manœuvres, formerly a military training area. However, even if the governments of the Six decided that the institutions would be located in Brussels, it would be impossible for practical reasons to construct a European quarter in one of these places immediately. The Belgian government therefore opted to rent enormous buildings which were already or almost completed, which it did even prior to the meeting of 6 and 7 January 1958.

It was these buildings, not far from the rue de la Loi roundabout (the future rond-point Schuman), that the EEC and Euratom Commissions were to occupy from January 1958. Ten floors were available immediately, providing a total of 203 offices. A building was also in the throes of completion just a few hundred metres away. From May 1958, the eight floors of that building housed the EEC Commission departments and the first building was left for the Euratom Commission. By June 1958, two new buildings would provide over

The ECSC pavilion at Expo 58 as seat of the European Parliamentary Assembly?

The ECSC was represented at the 1958 Universal and International Exhibition in Brussels in a structure made entirely of glass and steel (see p. 535), suspended on a set of six pillars symbolising the six Member States of the Community. Although the pavilion had been designed as a temporary building, which its owners were contractually obliged to demolish at the end of the Expo, a number of projects were considered for its subsequent use. The Belgian government first envisaged incorporating the pavilion in a university complex for science and technology in the Heysel district, but this plan never materialised. The High Authority, for its part, thought of offering it to the EEC as a meeting and congress centre. The institutional section of the pavilion would be converted into a European hemicycle to solve the problem of a seat for the European Assembly. Although the Heysel site was a long way from the centre of Brussels, this was offset by the fact that access to it was easy and there were good parking facilities. The refurbishment of the ECSC pavilion would provide a solution to the shortage of office space

for the Communities in Brussels and constitute a further point in favour of the Belgian capital as the seat of the institutions.

However, all these projects required financial investment — particularly to ensure the durability of the building, something in which neither the Belgian authorities nor the European institutions appeared to be interested. The sole remaining possibility was that the High Authority should itself make the investments — an idea quickly dismissed since 'the ECSC would have no direct interest in the use of the refurbished pavilion.' (¹)

The High Authority finally decided to have the pavilion dismantled on 6 May 1959, as the deadline for demolition could be postponed no further.

N. W.

According to V. Hellemans, *La CECA à l'Exposition universelle et internationale de Bruxelles 1958*, UCL, Louvain-la-Neuve, 1995 (History degree dissertation), pp. 132–142.

400 offices, a figure that would reach 1 000 by the end of the year.

The most economical solution for the European Communities would have been to buy these buildings immediately. However, since the question of the seat had not been resolved, they could not make a commitment in favour of one city or the other city. They could not even rent a building, as a decision could be taken at any time and they could find themselves obliged to break a series of leases. The solution adopted for these buildings and for a good number of subsequent ones was that the Belgian State bought or rented the buildings and then let or sublet them to the Communities. This required a considerable outlay on the part of the Belgian State. However, to the minds of its leaders, these sacrifices would be

advantageous when the Six had to decide on the final seat of the institutions.

Very soon the departments in Brussels were short of space. From the outset it had been planned that the number of officials would grow rapidly, but the proportions surprised both the European and Belgian authorities. The Belgian State therefore had to find office space that could satisfy the Communities. From April 1958 it rented two new buildings, which were distant both from each other and from the rue de la Loi roundabout. Distance was a permanent hindrance to the smooth functioning of the institutions. It gave rise to considerable travel costs and waste of time. The Belgian State was very much aware of this. Despite

---

(¹) CEAB 3 1160, letter from Joseph Dinjaert to Albert Wehrer, 6 May 1959.

Construction of the Berlaymont building, designed by the architect Lucien De Vestel. In conjunction with Jean Gilson and Jean and André Polak. This cross-shaped building of 13 storeys consists of four wings of different dimensions, standing on pillars. While it is being built, the Belgian government makes a number of other changes to the area — the rue de la Loi is widened, two road tunnels and a tunnel for the Metro are built and an old railway station is reopened.

the apparent satisfaction of the European administrative departments, which was probably due to the fact that the buildings were very comfortable inside, in June 1958 it began to look for a large area that could suit the new institutions and informed the President of the EEC Commission that it was ready to have an administrative complex built. The reply was cautious. Once again, the Commission was faced with the precarious nature of the status of Brussels as the seat of the institutions.

Belgium went to great lengths to prove itself and stand out among the candidate cities. Obviously it would welcome the go-ahead from the Commission for the institutions to be grouped together in one specific place: this would increase the chances of Brussels becoming the final seat. That

was why, despite the ambivalent response of the European leaders, the Belgian authorities went ahead and looked for land not far from the rue de la Loi roundabout. Five of Brussels' eight 'European' buildings were already located in this district. Moreover, most European officials lived in the eastern and south-eastern communes of Brussels, in other words the city's wealthiest and most comfortable districts. It was therefore logical for the complex to be built in that area.

Less than a hundred metres from the roundabout lay a two-hectare property belonging to the Sisters of Berlaymont which housed an educational establishment. In December 1958, the State expressed its interest in buying the property and after several months of negotiations a transaction was signed in May 1960.

The Belgian authorities did not wait until they were actually owners of the property before commissioning studies on the future building. A committee was formed at the beginning of 1959 to draw up the plans for the future Berlaymont complex. Its remit was to prepare for the construction of a prestigious building that could accommodate all the European departments but which could, if necessary, be rapidly converted to house a national administrative body. The Belgian State thus committed itself to a massive investment without really knowing what was going to happen.

The enthusiasm and enormous publicity surrounding the Berlaymont building soon turned sour. It rapidly became clear that the building would not be completed according to the schedule set out in the Belgian government's three-stage plan. According to the plan, the first stage was to be completed between March and November 1961. It was not started until February 1961 and even then only the contracts for the initial excavations were awarded. Actual work did not begin until the end of April. Not surprisingly, the Belgian government had to field a series of urgent enquiries over the summer of 1961 from the Communities, which wanted precise details about the completion dates of each stage of the Berlaymont. In fact, the Belgian State was short of funds. It had to resort to external financing and the conclusion of the agreements took time. Once again, it went to extreme lengths for Europe and did not falter at the idea of getting into debt. Nevertheless, such delays clearly did not impress its European partners nor, indeed, the institutions themselves.

By April 1962, however, the State had found a private partner for constructing the complex. According to the estimates, the first wing could be available by around May 1964. However, this did not take into account the lack of coordination between the Berlaymont building site and adjacent works concerning the railways and public transport. Yet another delay was announced. In the end it was not until 1 February 1967 that the first wing of the Berlaymont was completed. The first officials moved in there in August. In the months that followed and up to the end of 1969, the offices in the four wings of the building were gradually completed and occupied by 4 000 officials. The Commission had finally moved in.

But what about the other institutions in Brussels? Originally it had been planned that the Berlaymont would accommodate all the Commission's officials and the Secretariat of the Council of Ministers. With the increase in the number of officials, however, an alternative solution had to be found quickly. The problem was that, even before it was completed, the Berlaymont had acquired international recognition and both institutions wanted to benefit from this. Lengthy, laborious negotiations began, during which the possibility was considered of sharing the building but keeping the two institutions totally separate from each other — at great expense. It was finally decided that the Commission would have exclusive use of the Berlaymont and the Belgian State would have another building built opposite the rue de la Loi for the Council of Ministers. The Commission had won. As for the Council of Ministers, it had to wait over 20 years more before it could move into the Justus Lipsius building.

MICHEL DUMOULIN and MATTHIEU LETHÉ

Part Two

THE COMMISSION
AND ITS POLICIES

Scene from the 1951 film *Le banquet des fraudeurs* (Smugglers' Ball), directed by Henri Storck (screenplay and dialogue by Charles Spaak). In real life the three frontiers in question are the point where the municipalities of Vaals (in the Dutch province of Limburg), Plombières (in the province of Liège, Belgium) and Aachen (Germany) intersect. In the film this becomes the imaginary village of Dorpveld.

The film had its first showing in Brussels on 5 April 1952 and opened in Paris on 9 July. The leading roles were played by Françoise Rosay, Jean-Pierre Kérien, Christiane Lénier, Paul Frankeur and Raymond Pellegrin.

Storck spoke at length about the film's origins and the reasons behind it and described how it evolved from a documentary to a piece of fiction: 'It was the directors of the Marshall Plan's film department who suggested in 1949–50 that I make a documentary about the birth of Benelux [...]. I was lucky enough to persuade [...] Charles Spaak to take part in the project [...]. We contacted the Benelux committees in Belgium, and their chairman, Mr Van Dorpe, agreed to produce the film, together with the European Cultural Centre in Geneva, which was run by Denis de Rougemont [who] [...] put us in touch with the President of the European Union of Federalists, Dr Eugen Kogon, in Frankfurt [...]. In order to produce the film, Dr Kogon set up [...] a production society [...] called Europafilm [...].'

Storck and Charles Spaak conducted detailed research among the Dutch and Belgian political, economic and social milieus involved in the Benelux experiment, but they were left with the problem of how to present these problems, and particularly the economic issues, in a fictional film. As Henri Storck explained: 'We were really stuck when, quite by chance, we discovered on our travels that there actually was a village which had three border posts with all the usual features: barriers across the road, passport controls, customs officers [...]. And there were three different worlds living side by side in this village: the workers, the customs officers and the smugglers [...]. What would happen if opening the border between the Netherlands and Belgium were to cause economic difficulties for the workers? And if the closed border with Germany was only a sham, because smugglers were crossing it every day in their hundreds? Would it be possible, under the guise of a classic cops and robbers adventure, to engage the audience and hold their attention while telling them about all the issues which our story raised? And finally, would we be able, in the background, to sketch the broad outlines of the Benelux problem in relation to Germany by showing that the solution proposed was only an initial stage in the process driving all of Europe towards unification?' (Henri Storck, 'Présentation du film *Le banquet des fraudeurs*', *Jeune Cinéma*, No 189, October 1988, pp. 47–48).

Chapter 14

Not quite
a common market yet

The establishment of a large internal market has been at the root of all projects undertaken since the interwar period to lay the necessary foundations for economic prosperity in Europe, following the example of the United States, which has provided the benchmark since the start of the century. The customs union projects devised since the 1920s thus came to fruition, with the creation in the 1960s of the common market involving six countries. However, the aim of economic efficiency could not be limited to the free movement of products of industrial origin. In addition to the common market in agricultural products, the free movement of services, labour and capital also had a fundamental role to play in economic integration.

The dynamics of the customs union

The Community activity report for the year 1958 [1] states that 'the implementation of the common market in the field of the movement of goods is not a spectacular affair'. It was, however, a difficult task considered to be the cornerstone

of the Community project and was to be completed ahead of the schedule set under the Treaty of Rome, 18 months before the end of the transitional period. This vast enterprise consisted essentially in dismantling quotas and customs duties within Community territory, while at the same time introducing a Common External Tariff. Europe's past had prepared it poorly for such a massive operation: the crisis of the 1930s, economic difficulties and post-war shortages had led the Member States to build up vast arsenals of protectionist measures. National traditions and cultures differed, with France and Italy taking a protectionist approach, while their partners tended more towards the free-trade philosophy. In addition to this, the fragility of the balance of payments in France and the sectoral interests defended by influential trade organisations in each country made the enterprise so difficult that some observers doubted its chances of success. On the other hand, the habits of cooperation and the experience acquired under the auspices of the OEEC, which had been responsible for economic matters in western Europe since the early 1950s, facilitated dialogue.

Taken together with customs duties, quotas represented a formidable weapon of protectionism

---

[1] EEC, Commission, *First General Report on the Activities of the Community*, 17 September 1958, p. 51.

which allowed Member States to impose quantitative restrictions on imports. During the 1950s, their dismantling had been partially achieved under the auspices of the OEEC. However, the process was not yet complete as the Treaty of Rome required their definitive discontinuation. Therefore, each country had to pool its quotas, until then allocated individually to each of their partners in the Community, following which the permitted import quantities were to be progressively increased until the complete abolition of quotas was finally achieved.

The Treaty also laid down precise objectives concerning the removal of customs barriers. From a status quo based on the duties applied by the Member States, customs duties affecting the movement of products within Community territory had to be abolished by the end of a transitional period. The Treaty scheduled a reduction of 30 % in the first stage (1958–61), 30 % in the second (1962–65) and total abolition by 31 December 1969.

Having followed the establishment of the common market from the French customs directorate, Claude Jacquemart, head of division responsible for customs matters in the Directorate-General for Industry since 1966, explained the extent to which the tradition of cooperation between national customs services since the 1950s had paved the way for the implementation of the Community programme: 'One important, shared regulatory asset therefore already existed and was already facilitating international trade and bilateral or multilateral negotiations. It very clearly extended efforts in Europe to dismantle tariffs and quotas stemming from international agreements, which had a wider scope in geographical terms [...]. The customs officers of the six Member States therefore had an advantage over their counterparts elsewhere. They knew and met each other, established friendships [...]' (¹).

Once the Treaty was signed, the shared working patterns facilitated the application of the programme laid down by the Treaty, through the establishment of close cooperation between Commission and national officials: 'The method [...] consisted in sending national officials with a certain level of experience to Brussels [...]: Secondly, [...] committees were set up and entrusted with preparing the projects which were then proposed to the Commission by its services.'

'These meetings were prepared carefully, often through bilateral contacts. As the responsible head of division, I made it my duty as of 1966 to meet each of the heads of administration [...] in order to devise compromise formulas.' The last or penultimate negotiations on the basic texts 'generally took place at the meetings of the Customs Questions Committee before the actual proposals went through the official procedure [...], not to mention that contacts [...] were established where necessary with the relevant trade circles' (²).

The successful implementation of the customs union would, therefore, be attributable to the Commission's effective use of old working relations and friendships between national customs officials, some of whom had joined the Community administration. It should be added that the directors-general of the national customs authorities were in the habit of meeting informally in the so-called Club of Directors-General, a structure which allowed them to resolve difficulties in an informal manner (³). Another factor was the flexibility of the Treaty itself, which in Article 155 provided for the delegation of power to the Commission, subject to the opinion of, and qualified majority vote in, each committee responsible for examining the problems of implementing the Treaty with regard to customs rules (⁴).

The strong impetus given by the Commission to this process, reinforced by the free-trade tradition

(¹) Jacquemart, C., 'Le rôle des douanes dans la construction européenne, 1957–1978', *Le rôle des ministères des finances et de l'économie dans la construction européenne (1957–1978)*, Vol. 1, 'Histoire économique et financière de la France', Animation de la recherche, CHEFF, Paris, 2002, pp. 462–467.

(²) Ibid.
(³) Ibid., p. 465.
(⁴) Ibid., p. 464.

'The Community shall be based upon a customs union which shall cover all trade in goods and which shall involve the prohibition between Member States of customs duties on imports and exports and of all charges having equivalent effect, and the adoption of a common customs tariff in their relations with third countries.' (Article 9(1) of the EEC Treaty.)

of some countries and a favourable economic climate, made it possible to move ahead of schedule. Most of the work was achieved in the first few years, which were marked by two successive accelerations in the process. While the initial decisions on the dismantling of trade barriers were taken according to the schedule set by the Treaty, namely 1 January 1959 and 1 January 1960 for quotas and 1 January 1959 for the first reduction in intra-Community customs duties, the process speeded up for the first time on 12 May 1960. On this date, the Council decided to abolish the quota system altogether, and to introduce an additional 10 % reduction in customs duties on 31 December 1961, the starting date for the second stage of the transitional period. Another decision to accelerate the process was taken on 15 May 1962, allowing a further 10 % reduction in customs duties on industrial products on 1 July. Intra-Community protection of industrial prod-

ucts, thus, fell to half of its original level well before the deadline of two and a half years. The subsequent stages led to the total abolition of duties within Community territory on 1 July 1968. In actual fact, almost all the Member States added to these measures with voluntary and unilateral provisions to dismantle customs restrictions, thereby strengthening the dynamic created by the joint measures: Germany did so from 1957 and then in 1964, France in 1961, and Italy in 1962. By the start of the third stage of the transitional period, intra-Community trade was consequently affected only by duties which were generally below 5 % [1].

The introduction of the Common External Tariff (CET) would allow the Community to be identified

---

[1] Nême, J. and Nême, C., *Économie européenne*, PUF, Paris, 1970, p. 54.

France and the common market: unjustified apprehension

'The first round of tariff cuts and quota dismantlements took effect on January 1, 1959. The Community served notice that it did not intend to practise a protectionist commercial policy by broadly extending these derestrictions to trade with third countries. Once under way, the movement rapidly gained pace. At France's suggestion, the timing of intra-Community tariff reductions laid down in the Treaty of Rome was accelerated twice, in 1960 and in 1962. By the end of 1961, quantitative import restrictions had been completely removed; France, whose economy had been rigorously protected by measures of this kind up until 1958, made a remarkable effort in helping to see that this target was met. The Common External Tariff was gradually coming into being. By mid-1962 intra-Community customs duties had already been reduced by 50 %.

This movement of trade liberalisation would continue as scheduled, or faster, throughout the rest of the sixties, with the result that the customs union and the common agricultural policy were in place by 1 July 1968, a year and a half ahead of the time limit set by the Treaty. Intra-European trade grew rapidly during those years. Although trade with the rest of the world grew more slowly, it too increased very considerably, showing that the common market was a factor in the world's prosperity as a whole.

Along with trade, productivity and output in the Community grew at unprecedented rates. I shall come back to this subject later on when I attempt to take stock of what the common market contributed to Europe. But here and now I wish to emphasise that France's initial misgivings proved to be unfounded. True, Germany is still the most powerful industrial country in Europe, but the gap between France and Germany, far from having widened, has to a great extent been bridged. The living standards of the French are almost equal to those of the Germans, while those of the two countries are now not very far short of American living standards. It can be said, without exaggeration, that of all the countries of the Community, it was France that derived most benefit from the trade liberalisation which the Treaty of Rome prescribed or indirectly brought about.'

Marjolin, R., *Architect of European unity — Memoirs 1911–1986*, Weidenfeld and Nicolson, London, 1989, pp. 322–323.

as a single customs entity vis-à-vis the rest of the world. So as not to infringe GATT rules, the Treaty provided that common tariff duties would be established on the basis of the arithmetical average of the duties of the four merged customs areas: Germany, France, Italy and Benelux. The CET's overall impact would therefore be no greater than that of the previous national tariffs. However, the Treaty, established on the basis of the duties applicable on 1 January 1957, was undermined by a number of exceptions. These exceptions were grouped into a series of product lists for which the CET could not exceed a rate of 3 %, 10 %, 15 % and 25 %. List F covered a series of products for which the protection level was predetermined, while List G was for products requiring negotiation between members once the Treaty entered into force. In addition to a range of raw materials and food products, List G included important industrial products for which it had not been possible to reach an agreement during the negotiations: motor vehicles, aeroplanes, machine tools, aluminium, etc. This series of exceptions was introduced on the initiative of Spaak during the negotiation of the Treaty in order to avoid a stalemate over details 'because Mr Spaak was a nervous man who wanted to push ahead. When there was a meeting at Val-Duchesse, he just wanted to keep moving forward [...] When a problem arose, Mr Spaak said: "List F! List G! We have to sign the Treaty. Let's not get stuck on trivial matters"' [1]. As a result, in order to determine the fate of these products, the Treaty provided for negotiations to take place before the end of 1959.

---

[1] Interview with Camille Becker, 4 March 2004.

The first activity report of the Commission showed the degree of difficulty involved in developing the CET, a project undertaken before the Interim Committee had implemented the Treaty. In fact, it involved creating a working tool which could be used by the customs officials and economic stakeholders concerned and was based on four tariffs with differing specification details. It was, therefore, a matter of concentrating a body of around 20 000 positions representing a mere juxtaposition of the current tariffs into one document of around 7 000 positions. The General Report of 1958 included the following observation: 'This requirement greatly complicates the apparently simple problems connected with the calculation of an arithmetical average; instead of a purely mechanical operation, it necessitates delicate decisions in the economic and customs fields' (¹).

Most of the work on the CET was completed in early 1960. The Council of 13 February validated the draft tariff for products whose protection level was fixed using the arithmetical average. On 2 March 1960 matters were likewise settled for the majority of products on List G. The outcome for the most difficult cases was to be decided between 1960 and 1964.

The effective establishment of the CET took place at an accelerated pace and on more liberal terms than those laid down in the Treaty. The first move towards an alignment of national tariffs with the CET was made on 1 July 1961. This was done on the basis of a CET reduced by 20 % in order to demonstrate the liberal spirit of the Community initiative within the GATT. Further alignments took place on 1 July 1963 and 1 July 1968. As a result of the negotiations conducted within the GATT in the Dillon Round and then the Kennedy Round, the global impact of the CET was significantly reduced in comparison to its initial bases.

The implementation of the customs union also involved the adoption of common rules with a view to the uniform application of the CET, which required work on the harmonisation of national customs legislation. This work started at the beginning of the transitional period and was completed for the most part in 1968 and 1969. In the first phase of the transitional period, care was taken to specify the rules for the free movement of goods from the six Member States and for imported goods for which duties upon entry into the Community customs territory had been paid. Likewise, an initial series of difficulties concerning processing traffic was resolved in 1960, allowing imported goods to be processed in the Community and then re-exported free of duty. A number of regulations adopted in June 1968 led to the harmonisation of national interpretations with regard to customs valuation (i.e. establishing the value of an imported product subject to customs duty) and to the definition of product origin. The directives and regulations adopted in March 1969 laid down the rules concerning warehousing, free zones and transit zones and the payment of customs duties, and completed the provisions governing processing traffic (²).

Initial difficulties and unfinished work

Completing the free movement of goods

The implementation of the customs union and the definition of common rules with regard to the application of the Common External Tariff did not in themselves ensure the effective free movement of goods within Community territory. Since the debates over the Single Act, the European public had become accustomed to dealing with numerous other obstacles to the movement of products. These were to be removed under the Treaty of Rome by the end of the transitional period, although there was no precise definition of how or in what stages such a process would

(¹) EEC, Comission, *First General Report on the Activities of the Community*, 17 September 1958, p. 57.

(²) Nême, J. and Nême, C., op.cit., pp. 67–71; 'L'élaboration d'une législation douanière communautaire', *Bulletin des CE*, April 1969, pp. 33–36.

The interpenetration of trade flows

In 10 years, the effects of the establishment of the internal market became apparent in trade flows, which were developing at a much faster rate between the Six than between the Six and the rest of the world. (*Source: Dix ans de marché commun*, Statistical Office of the European Communities, Luxembourg, 1968.)

EXTERNAL TRADE BY PRODUCT CATEGORY

(million USD)

Country	Total		Food, beverages, tobacco (Sect. 0 + 1)		Energy, lubricants (Section 3)		Raw materials, oils, fats (Sect. 2 + 4)		Capital goods (Section 7)		Other products (Sect. 5, 6, 8, 9)	
	1958	1967	1958	1967	1958	1967	1958	1967	1958	1967	1958	1967
Intra-Community imports												
Germany	1 896	6 868	504	1 442	120	337	183	484	209	1 295	880	3 310
France	1 227	5 374	92	446	281	291	79	237	305	1 667	470	2 733
Italy	687	3 390	78	482	42	71	111	440	162	981	294	1 416
Netherlands	1 518	4 546	80	302	107	207	82	205	454	1 379	795	2 453
BLEU	1 462	3 984	156	420	195	258	166	319	385	1 246	560	1 741
EEC	**6 790**	**24 161**	**909**	**3 091**	**745**	**1 164**	**622**	**1 685**	**1 515**	**6 568**	**2 999**	**11 653**
Intra-Community exports												
Germany	2 406	8 003	66	285	397	485	108	381	897	3 114	938	3 738
France	1 136	4 702	122	890	96	158	204	515	186	1 111	528	2 028
Italy	608	3 373	190	459	19	208	37	89	136	1 014	226	1 603
Netherlands	1 337	4 003	421	1 061	150	257	123	393	187	645	456	1 647
BLEU	1 377	4 433	88	421	120	97	111	276	214	893	844	2 746
EEC	**6 864**	**24 513**	**886**	**3 116**	**783**	**1 205**	**584**	**1 655**	**1 620**	**6 777**	**2 991**	**11 760**
Extra-Community imports												
Germany	5 465	10 483	1 440	2 139	630	1 398	1 712	2 261	375	1 207	1 308	3 478
France	4 382	7 004	1 321	1 424	826	1 505	1 315	1 474	374	1 070	546	1 531
Italy	2 528	6 307	468	1 297	580	1 520	853	1 624	179	636	448	1 230
Netherlands	2 107	3 791	479	840	508	661	465	718	250	620	405	952
BLEU	1 674	3 182	312	562	229	357	432	672	206	451	495	1 140
EEC	**16 156**	**30 767**	**4 020**	**6 262**	**2 773**	**5 442**	**4 777**	**6 750**	**1 383**	**3 984**	**3 203**	**8 329**
Extra-Community exports												
Germany	6 401	13 733	117	255	183	244	127	306	3 060	6 668	2 914	6 260
France	3 985	6 676	543	878	225	190	166	245	979	2 193	2 072	3 170
Italy	1 969	5 329	321	444	161	325	74	154	544	1 940	869	2 466
Netherlands	1 881	3 285	473	667	273	316	123	252	350	841	662	1 209
BLEU	1 675	2 604	65	133	71	98	74	139	212	477	1 253	1 757
EEC	**15 911**	**31 627**	**1 519**	**2 377**	**913**	**1 172**	**563**	**1 095**	**5 146**	**12 119**	**7 770**	**14 864**

take place. The obstacles in question were taxes with an effect equivalent to that of customs duties that were applied specifically to a product imported from a member country but not to the similar national product and, therefore, had the same effect as a customs duty on the free movement of products [1]. These obstacles also included a whole series of measures with the same potential effects as quotas, such as public-sector or technical regulations, State monopolies, and public procurement regulations and practices. It was common practice for Member States to use some of these measures for protectionist purposes. The abolition of customs duties and quotas was liable to give fresh impetus to this tendency even within Community territory.

As the Commission was perfectly aware of the scale of the task before it and as the process leading to customs union appeared by then to be long since under way, a 'work programme for all aspects relating to the internal market and competition sectors with a view to the complete abolition of barriers to trade before 1970' was established by the Directorates-General for the Internal Market and for Competition in early 1965. This was such a wide-ranging programme that the directorates-general concerned pointed out that the completion of the work by the planned deadlines depended on a number of factors most of which could not be influenced: the feasibility of organising meetings with national experts; translation and interpretation resources; staffing problems in the relevant departments; resources available to the national authorities for accompanying and following up on their work [2].

Such was the workload that, even when setting priorities and assuming compliance by the Commission departments and by the Member States, Hans von der Groeben, Commissioner for Competition, was of the opinion that, even then, it was obvious from this inventory that it would be impossible to resolve all these problems by 1970 [3].

The difficulties were not only administrative or institutional in nature. There was hardly any doubt that, once the tariff barriers and quotas had been abolished, the Member States would be reluctant, for all their apparent wish for non-discrimination, to let go of any remaining means of protection. As we know, the economic crisis of the 1970s would consolidate this tendency.

Article 28 of the EEC Treaty, therefore, required the elimination of measures having equivalent effect to quantitative restrictions. However, under the guise of regulations applicable to all products with no apparent distinction as to their origin, the Member States often tried to favour national production. For example, a measure adopted by the Belgian government stipulated that the nitrogen content of all fertilisers to be sold in Belgium had to be at least 24 %. Before, they had produced fertilisers with a nitrogen content of 16 %. They had, therefore, increased the nitrogen content to 24 %. The measure was to be applied indiscriminately and was pursued with a legitimate objective. It, therefore, did not appear to be protectionist. But its aim was to oblige the producers from the other Member States, in particular French producers, to adapt their production, as France was producing fertilisers with a 22 % nitrogen content and would, therefore, have had to adapt. This example led to Directive 70/50/EEC of December 1969, which defined the concept of effect equivalent to quantitative restrictions and created a link between the Member States' intended objective and the measures taken to achieve it by using the idea of proportionality between the intended objective and the regulations adopted at national level. 'For chemical fertilisers in Belgium, the Belgians were perfectly able to achieve the objective [...] by choosing a nitrogen content of 22 %' [4].

[1] Judgments in Cases 2 and 3 of the Court of Justice of the European Communities, 1962. Quoted by Nême, J. and Nême, C., op. cit., p. 56.

[2] Programme de travail pour l'ensemble des matières relevant du marché intérieur et de la concurrence, note du secrétariat exécutif, SEC(65) 297, 2 February 1965.

[3] Ibid.

[4] Interview with Alfonso Mattera Ricigliano, 25 November 2004.

Technical barriers to trade, which represented one of the main issues under the programme to complete the internal market, were linked to the concern of the authors of the Treaty to take account of the legitimacy of Member States' action to subject certain types of goods to import controls for reasons of safety or public health. However, Article 36 of the Treaty specified that related checks and national legislation must not constitute a disguised restriction on trade. The tariff dismantling required to implement the customs union gradually revealed the potential impact of technical regulations and requirements, some of which could be formidable instruments of indirect protectionism. In fact, it was only possible to eliminate these barriers through the approximation of national legislation. This required a great deal of patience and dogged determination as approximation took place on a case-by-case basis, thus making it possible to establish criteria of a more general nature. On the back of the progress made, the Commission developed a programme which the Council endorsed on 25 March 1969. It entailed the Member States' acceptance of a status quo in terms of regulations and the mutual recognition of controls if rules on the marketing of a product were equivalent or made equivalent by a Community measure. It also included a flexible procedure for updating directives, so as to allow the rapid adaptation of regulations to technological developments, and an extensive development programme for directives covering priority sectors, to be completed by 1 January 1970. However, this programme was quickly marked by such considerable delays that, at the end of December 1970, the Commission acknowledged that 'the results obtained fell considerably short of that which should have been achieved by now' (translation) [1]. This situation was caused by the volume of work outstanding, which was growing on a virtually continual basis. The following observation was made in late 1970: 'Although the programme made it possible to de-fine a certain order of priority […], it needed to be supplemented […]. Take motor vehicles, for example: 25 directives were planned by the programme, whereas now there are plans for around 70.' Furthermore, the extension of national legislative action to new fields such as the environment served only to exacerbate the problems. With the customs union in place, the legislative field covering technology seemed to have become the sticking point in the bid to balance national economic interests, thus slowing the process of completing the internal market. A progress report drafted by Spinelli's services for his colleagues expressed regret over this matter, stating that, as soon as a draft directive was referred to the Council, the positions adopted in the preparatory meeting tended to change and there was an increasing risk that an outcome based on 'package deals' rather than decisions on the merits of the directive concerned would gradually take shape. There was, moreover, a marked tendency to reserve all decisions for the highest level [2]. At the end of 1970, the Commission consequently prepared to draw the institutional consequences of these difficulties by taking a stance in favour of using qualified majority voting if the current difficulties were to persist. Article 100 of the Treaty of Rome concerning the harmonisation of legislation actually required unanimity for all Council decisions in this field despite the usually technical nature of the range of options from which to choose [3].

Practices tending to favour national suppliers in connection with public procurement were another of the Commission's concerns at the start of the 1970s. These practices were common in all Member States and were sometimes prescribed by national legislation, such as the Belgian measure of 1935, confirmed in October 1955, which entrusted a committee of civil servants with the task of examining tenders from foreign businesses for public contracts. Apart from the discrimin-

[1] *Note concernant l'état d'avancement du programme général relatif à l'élimination des entraves techniques aux échanges.* Communication from Mr Spinelli, SEC(70) 4532, 8 December 1970.

[2] Ibid, p. 15.

[3] Toulemon, R., 'Des idées nouvelles en politique industrielle', *Revue du Marché Commun*, September 1970, pp. 386–387.

The success of the single market

'All customs duties between the Member States were abolished on 1 January 1968, in other words two years ahead of the negotiators' most optimistic predictions. The quantitative restrictions that existed above all in France had likewise taken only a few years to disappear (end of 1961), whereas, in this case too, a long transitional period had been envisaged. This resulted in the rapid development of trade between the Member States, which increased twice as fast as world trade. Particularly high growth occurred from 1962 onwards, when the abolition of quantitative restrictions and a sufficient decrease in customs duties created undeniable material ease.

However, we cannot neglect the psychological aspect either: the feeling that the six countries were truly engaged in the creation of a customs union generated awareness and positive reactions which resulted in the Treaty taking effect more quickly and extensively than could logically be justified by the detailed provisions. One of the unquestionable virtues of the common market, at least as important as improved trade opportunities, was its timetable, which set precise obligations for fixed dates. Its other strength was that we believed in it. Thanks to this belief, many economic operators made the necessary efforts, particularly in France, and anticipated its results, thereby fostering its overall success.'

Deniau, J.-Fr., *L'Europe interdite*, Éditions du Seuil, Paris, 1977, pp. 86–87 (Translated from the French)

atory character of the procedure, this Belgian system gave national businesses a preference margin of 10 % in terms of price ([1]). Such practices, irrespective of whether they were laid down in national legislation, affected not only public procurement but also the main businesses in the capital goods sector. 'For them, life continued as if the common market did not exist', explained Robert Toulemon in 1970 ([2]). Remedying this state of affairs was a major challenge because it required a complete change of spirit. However,

this was not supported by the Member States, which were soon to be confronted with the economic crisis of the 1970s.

National monopolies of a commercial nature gave rise to the same type of problem. They were targeted by the Treaty less in terms of their existence than in terms of the likelihood that they would generate discrimination against nationals of the Member States. Some of these monopolies involved taxation and concerned tobacco, matches or alcohol. Others were monopolies linked to the implementation of a national policy in a sector of strategic importance such as gas or petroleum. In the latter case, the State import monopoly established in France since 1928 formed the basis of a policy to favour national groups for economic and security reasons. At the end of the 1950s, this monopoly was used as a way of selling off Saharan petroleum. One of the difficulties here lay in the differing interpretations of Article 37 of the Treaty, even within the directorates-general concerned. Should the monopolies be adapted so as to put an end to all discrimination affecting Community suppliers or should they simply be abolished ([3])? In spite of the difficulties, the Commission did achieve some results here. For instance, the Italian government agreed to abolish the import monopolies on bananas and quinine. Generally speaking, however, the partial adjustments undertaken by the governments still left significant areas of discrimination by the end of the transitional period. Difficulties in defining a European energy policy would, therefore, stand in the way of an end to discrimination in this field for a long time to come ([4]).

Overall, although the achievement of the customs union is rightfully presented as a major success for the Commission, the completion of the internal market started to falter by the end of the 1960s in the face of various points of resistance on the part of Member States, which had not

([1]) Nême, J. and Nême, C., op.cit., p. 121.
([2]) Toulemon, R., op. cit., p. 387.

([3]) COM(61) 181, *Problèmes de la mise en œuvre de l'article 37 CEE*, Communication from Mr Caron, 26 November 1961.
([4]) EEC, Commission, *Third General Report on the Activities of the Community*, May 1960, pp. 88–91.

relinquished all possible means that could help them defend their interests, including their own interpretation of the Treaty. Coupled with institutional uncertainties, this explained the emerging stalemate, which was exacerbated by the crisis of the 1970s. To these problems must be added the difficulties experienced by the Europeans in agreeing on new common policies the implementation of which could have facilitated work on the completion of the internal market.

Labour, services and capital

The free movement of workers is enshrined in Articles 48 to 51 of the EEC Treaty. In so far as its purpose is to allow mobility of labour as a production factor, it is complementary to the establishment of the market for industrial products, agriculture and services. Workers from the Member States must be able to take any employment available in the Community, with the exceptions laid down by the Treaty, such as public-service employment. This freedom was largely achieved in three stages.

Initially, Regulation No 15, adopted by the Council in August 1961, maintained the priority given to nationals. A worker from another Member State could be employed only in the absence of a suitable national candidate. Regulation No 38 of April 1964 essentially brought an end to the priority enjoyed by nationals, to a large extent assimilating the treatment of Community workers to that of nationals in terms of rights at work and facilitating family reunification. The provisions of 29 July 1968 completed the work accomplished one and a half years ahead of the schedule planned by the Treaty and placed Community workers on a completely equal footing with national workers by abolishing work permits for Community nationals, establishing freedom for Community nationals to seek employment anywhere on Community territory and even giving priority to Community workers over those from third countries.

These provisions were all the easier to implement given that, in general, the Community suffered

from a considerable shortage of labour in the 1960s, so much so that it was resorting widely to workers from third countries.

Freedom of establishment and freedom to provide services are in many respects complementary to the free movement of goods, if only through the possibility for businesses to develop commercial networks or offer services linked to the sale of their products. These two freedoms, therefore, also featured in the objectives to be achieved after the transitional period, with priority given to the activities of greatest use 'to the development of production and trade' (¹). The Commission, therefore, devised a programme for the progressive abolition of restrictions on these freedoms that was approved by the Council in December 1961. Covering the period 1963–69, only a fraction of the programme was carried out depending on the sector of activity and the profession concerned. The effective implementation of these freedoms, in fact, required the approximation of national legislation, particularly in certain professions or for certain categories of companies, whether it was a question of the medical, technical or legal professions, banking or certain distributive trade activities such as pharmacy, etc. The resistance of a number of categories, some of which had a long-established structure organised at national level, and the difficulty in harmonising diplomas or company law, thus, constituted major obstacles to the completion of the common market.

The free movement of capital had wide-ranging effects on the achievement of full economic union at Community level. It was the essential counterpart to the payments linked to everyday commercial transactions involving goods or services. It also complemented the free movement of persons and particularly workers, who had to be able to transfer their personal property and the product of their work from one country to another. But such freedom could also be envisaged with a view to creating a homogeneous econom-

(¹) Article 54 of the EEC Treaty.

ic area within which economic stakeholders could obtain financing on similar terms. Thus, the free movement of capital gradually came to be viewed as one of the conditions for the establishment of an industrial area or even of a Community industrial policy [1]. However, such freedom gave rise to some tough questions as it entailed a minimum of economic policy coordination between the Six and therefore the acceptance of less autonomy for the Member States in this field.

Unlike the free movement of goods, the aims, means and stages of establishing the free movement of capital were not specified in great detail in the Treaty. At the end of the transitional period, the restrictions on capital movements were to be abolished 'to the extent necessary to ensure the proper functioning of the common market' [2]. Although it was understood that this objective had to be achieved progressively, only the first stage in the process was defined by the Treaty: the freedom of current payments linked to the free movement of goods, services and workers had to be accomplished by the end of 1961. The Treaty also included the principle of non-discrimination within the Community. The liberalisation process was initiated by two directives adopted on 11 May 1960 and 18 December 1962. The first set out measures for the unconditional liberalisation of movements of a personal nature, direct investments, operations in listed securities, real-estate investments and credits linked to commercial transactions. The conditional liberalisation system, on the other hand, concerned unlisted securities, the issue of foreign securities and financial credits, in other words credits not linked to commercial transactions. For these categories, the Member States could impose restrictions if they considered that these movements might form an obstacle to the achievement of their economic policy objectives. The 1962 directive,

---

[1] This concern is reflected in the Memorandum on the industrial policy of the Community of March 1970: *La politique industrielle de la Communauté, Mémorandum de la Commission au Conseil*, COM(70) 100, 18 March 1970. See also Toulemon, R., op. cit.

[2] Article 67 of the EEC Treaty.

An incomplete single market

'Incentives to encourage the effective creation of the single market — which is far from being a European reality, despite the progress that has been achieved — can take either a negative form, such as the elimination of any differences in standards which still exist between countries and which distort competition, or a positive form, such as the establishment of a tax framework. These incentives must encourage competition even at consumer level. At present, competition exists at producer level, but the continuing protectionist approach to transport or trade channels creates preferential conditions for some of these producers or distributors, rather than for the individual buyers. When, for example, German manufacturers of electrical or photographic equipment sell products on the French market at prices comparable to those charged in France even though they could sell them for 30 % less — an assumption based on the prices charged on the German market — we cannot claim that the public is benefiting from competition as much as could rightfully be expected. Furthermore, governmental bodies and the Commission of the European Communities need to foster competition between channels of distribution to match that between production companies. In this respect, mail-order sales, which allow direct contact with the consumer, should for instance be encouraged.

The single market also works on the assumption that people can move freely and establish their residence anywhere for the purpose of work. The remaining barriers relating to educational qualifications are therefore taking too long to dismantle.'

Armand, L. and Drancourt, M., *Le pari européen*, Fayard, Paris, 1968, pp. 212–213. (Translated from the French)

which complemented the 1960 directive, extended liberalisation to new stakeholders and lines of activity. It should be noted that some of the Treaty requirements and the provisions subsequently adopted at Community level were largely commensurate with the obligations imposed by the IMF on its members or were included in the OECD Code of Liberalisation of Capital Movements of July 1964: the identification of the Community in relation to the rest of the world was, therefore, weak in this field.

In actual fact, France, the Netherlands and Italy announced their decision to abide by the unconditional requirements for the liberalisation of capital movements provided for in the 1960 directive. This minimal interpretation explains why the first version of a third directive on liberalisation drawn up in early 1964 was not approved by the Council in March 1965. The capital market within the Community consequently remained compartmentalised. It was far from satisfying the Commission's desire to see the development of a European capital market able to provide the necessary means of financing for businesses. The expert group chaired by Claudio Segré, Director in the Directorate-General for Economic and Financial Affairs, worked between 1964 and 1967 on identifying the very complex problems raised by such a project. As Segré explained, 'We realised that the movement of capital depended on the institutional structure of the markets. [...] The obstacles were sometimes of a regulatory nature. Sometimes, they quite simply stemmed from the market structure. If, for example, an insurance company in country X does not have the right to invest in foreign securities, it immediately faces a major hindrance. It was not just about the obstacles. It was about a different approach. Some markets lay entirely in the hands of the State. For others, this was much less the case. In some, there was an aim for liberalisation. Others, in contrast, were under increasingly strict control. And then there were all the issues of power and the national authorities' control over certain things. It was a period during which every country had the underlying impression that it was short of capital.' [1]

Immediately following the work of the Segré Committee, the Commission proposed an amended version of the third directive on the liberalisation of capital. It asked the Member States to discontinue controls both on the issue of their national market of equities from other EEC countries and on minor credit operations which were not linked to commercial transactions. All measures were subject to a ceiling. The amended version also included the elimination of a number of discriminatory measures regarding access to the financial markets for issuers of securities in the EEC. Two years later, a memorandum from the Commission drew the Member States' attention to the need for an agreement on the third directive and called for a round of harmonisation concerning the fiscal organisation of capital markets from the viewpoint of taxation and regulation [2].

The crisis of May 1968 in France, followed by the growing strains on the international monetary front in the early 1970s, placed the project to create a unified European financial area in question once again, owing to the unilateral measures taken by each of the Member States to isolate their market from destabilising speculative movements of capital. Most of these measures made no distinction between capital flows from Community countries and those from other countries: the prospect of unification for the European capital market became more distant again for a number of years [3].

Éric Bussière

[1] Interview with Claudio Segré, 3 March 2004.
[2] 'Commission memoranda on the capital market and the taxes affecting it', *Bulletin of the EC*, No 5, 1969.
[3] Bakker Age, F. P., *The liberalization of capital movements in Europe*, Kluwer Academic publishers, Dordrecht, 1996, pp. 116–118.

Display at the Innovation department store in Brussels in 1960, 'Common Market Month'. The shop was established by the Alsatian François Bernheim in the rue Neuve/Nieuwstraat in the 19th century at the historic headquarters of a chain distributing novelty fashions before the group diversified across a wide range of segments of the distribution business. In the interwar years the group was run by Émile Bernheim (1886–1985), who was already actively involved in 'Europeanising' the large-scale distribution business, and by the 1950s it was working for closer links between national distribution companies, promoting the concept, among others, of European buying associations through the Association commerciale internationale, established in 1953.

Chapter 15

Competition

In his retrospective analysis of the Commission's activities during the first stage of its history — where he played a leading role — Hans von der Groeben described the creation of a competition policy as a 'struggle', a term he used in the title itself of his work. The importance of competition rules and competition policy to the development of the common market had, he wrote, variously assessed. The proponents of a market economy regarded as essential the introduction and safeguarding of healthy and fair competition. Others were inclined to accord greater importance, when it came to creating a vast economic area, to direct economic policy intervention or to agreements between enterprises. As a member of the Commission, he had made up his mind to translate the Treaty rules in that area into practice, notwithstanding the difficult nature of the task ahead given the considerable differences of opinion and conflicts of interest [1].

Von der Groeben outlined light-heartedly the way in which portfolios were distributed among Commissioners, saying that he behaved like a rag-and-bone man, picking up anything and everything. And that was how he had managed to gather together under the roof of his directorate-general cartels and monopolies, State aid, the approximation of laws and tax harmonisation. Those were, in his view, the ingredients that subsequently ensured the Community's viability, no less. Intriguingly, Hallstein, who could not have failed to notice this fact, did not let on to von der Groeben. The others, however, were so convinced that these were matters which had to be governed from on high that they made a grab for the posts where they thought they could hold the reins from Brussels. Von der Groeben's entire philosophy — which was no secret — was, however, diametrically the opposite, being based on the idea that the conditions had to be put in place so that economies could grow gradually side by side into an economic area. Genuine integration, to his mind, started from the ground upwards, and what he and his fellow Commissioners had to do was to establish the ground rules and nothing more [2].

---

[1] Von der Groeben, H., *The European Community — The formative years — The struggle to establish the common market and the political union (1958–66)*, European Perspectives, Office for Official Publications of the European Communities, Luxembourg, 1987, pp. 59–61.

[2] Interview with Hans von der Groeben, 16 December 2003.

Thus armed with powers over restrictive practices, aid, taxation and the approximation of laws, the competition policy department's responsibilities overlapped in almost every area with those of other directorates-general, whether they were concerned with general economic policy, structural policy, industrial policy, energy policy or regional policy. Competition policy was therefore at the crossroads between many areas of responsibility. Its successful pursuit would depend on all the Commissioner's strength of conviction and on his capacity for dialogue, both with his colleagues and with the economic operators concerned.

The goal he set himself was to create conditions identical to those existing in national markets [1]. Competition policy was, therefore, in von der Groeben's view, part and parcel of the policy aimed at establishing the single market as well as of general economic policy, competition being for him a powerful factor in the development of structures and hence in their modernisation. He pursued this goal by taking two complementary courses of action. The first consisted in combating practices aimed at distorting or preventing competition between market operators and the second in harmonising the conditions of competition in relation to taxes, State aid or law-making — that is, State intervention. The policy on restrictive practices and mergers and the harmonisation of the bases of common taxation through VAT were his two most outstanding achievements.

Restrictive practices, abuses of dominant positions and State aid

Introducing rules applicable to enterprises ('undertakings') in the area of cartels or other private restrictive practices and in that of abuses of dominant positions was one of the Commission's main priorities and one that was most difficult to implement. Article 85 of the Treaty prohibited agreements or concerted practices between undertakings having as their object the restriction or

distortion of competition within the common market. Article 86 dealt with abuses of dominant positions. These two articles were directed at practices born of different situations but with potentially similar effects. In the former instance, undertakings sought to organise the market through manifold private agreements containing, say, provisions for dividing up markets or fixing selling conditions or even prices. In the latter instance, in a highly concentrated industry, an undertaking might be tempted to exploit a borderline monopoly in order to derive the same kind of benefits. Since 1945, these two situations had been the target of national laws, especially in France and Germany, where the underlying philosophies bore witness in fact to different industrial structures. In Germany, a law of 1957 prohibited cartels as a matter of principle except where they had been exempted by the Federal Cartel Office. In France, legislation introduced in 1953 governed not so much the principle of a cartel as the abusive practices that the Technical Commission for Restrictive Practices was charged with preventing. The French authorities were thus more sensitive to the concept of abuse of a dominant position, as covered by Article 86 of the Treaty, than were the German authorities. They took a sympathetic view of cartels because these often acted as substitutes for a merger and their economic impact could sometimes be considered beneficial. Owing to the more dispersed nature of their industry, the French were more sensitive to the effects of domination, from which foreign businesses, being often much more highly concentrated, could profit, as in the case of German or American firms.

The difficulty in implementing Articles 85 and 86 stemmed mainly from the fact that three EEC Member States did not as yet have any domestic laws on the subject and to the differences of approach between France, followed for a time by Luxembourg and Belgium, on the one hand, and Germany and the Netherlands, on the other. What, moreover, were the respective roles of the Commission and the Member States to be once the Community apparatus was operational? From

[1] Von der Groeben, H., loc. cit.

Pressure from firms on the Directorate-General for Competition

When asked whether firms exerted pressure on the Directorate-General for Competition, Ivo Schwartz replied that they did, very much so. Being still young at the time, he found it most disagreeable. There were already some very difficult negotiations and discussions going on. And then there were the bilateral lobbies. For example, the whole of German industry was represented by one man who was forever on the doorstep asking to see everyone and Schwartz in particular. His name was Eichner. Diplomacy was called for in dealing with him without overly compromising the Commissioner's position. The staff were there to do a job and they could not afford to argue among themselves and create internal divisions. That was unthinkable. But Schwartz's Bonn experience, during which he had observed at close hand the negotiations between Germany and the Allies, came in very handy in that respect.

Interview with Ivo Schwartz, 16 January 2004.
(Translated from the German)

1958 onwards the Commission was careful to coordinate closely its work and that of the Member States by gathering together national experts in these areas at regular intervals to discuss points of law and procedure. While agreement was quickly reached on Articles 85 and 86 of the Treaty being directly applicable legal provisions, difficulties arose as soon as the discussion turned to the manner of their implementation. The Commission, faced with the lack of any legislation in Belgium, Italy and Luxembourg, strove to speed up the drafting and enactment of the necessary instruments in those countries. But the situation was seized on by those countries which did have the necessary legal arsenal as a pretext for not taking any action. Von der Groeben said in February 1960 that, by invoking the principles of equality of treatment and reciprocity, the other Member States were holding back from applying the provisions (¹). In those circumstances, although the Treaty provided that, until such time as Community rules were adopted, it was for the Member States to ensure compliance with the provisions of Articles 85 and 86, their inaction risked seeing relations between Community undertakings crystallise in the form of cartels that neutralised the removal of obstacles to trade by the Member States through tariff dismantling (²). The risk was all the more serious at the time owing to the acceleration of the process of opening up frontiers decided on in May 1960. A second, related difficulty lay in the differences between national laws. The application of national laws, where they existed, implied a minimum of concerted action if there was not to be any inequality of treatment from one Member State to another for one and the same infringement. Von der Groeben explained that it was inadmissible, for example, that one Member State should apply to a cartel the prohibition in Article 85 when that same cartel was, by contrast, authorised in another Member State, was considered not caught by Article 85(1) in a third and was simply turned a blind eye to in a fourth (³). The Commission felt, therefore, that the solution lay in unofficial consultations between national experts in the hope that an open, in-depth discussion of the issues might result in a broad meeting of minds. It was hoped to achieve this through the examination of a few case studies. As well as making it possible to lay down a common approach, this method was also a tactical means of inducing Member States to pursue an active policy towards Articles 85 and 86.

To the extent that the Treaty also provided that it could carry out investigations on its own initiative, the Commission hoped to be able to count on Member States' cooperation to supplement its own evidence-gathering. It soon came to realise that this was a vain hope. It was hard to get Member States to cooperate in gathering information on cartels and dominant market positions because some of them did not yet have any

---

(¹) *Cartels policy, Communication from Mr von der Groeben*, COM(60) 17, 15 February 1960.

(²) Ibid.
(³) Ibid., p. 11.

The debates on competition in the European Parliament in 1961

'The debates in the European Parliament on the implementation of the Treaty articles on competition were very lively occasions. They took place between supporters of the principle of the prohibition of cartels and those who placed the emphasis on abuses of dominant positions. The part played by the Commission in regulatory and investigatory matters was also debated.

In Parliament as elsewhere, opinions diverged on this fundamental issue. The rapporteur of the internal market committee, the German MEP, Arved Deringer, tried to work out in his report a draft compromise which, on the basis of the prohibition principle, made concessions to the proponents of the abuse principle via provisions on the retroactivity of the exemption authorisation. At the plenary sitting in Strasbourg on 19 October 1961, the two sides clashed as usual. It was a great day for Parliament. There was no demagoguery, only technical exchanges, firm but polite. On the questions of principle, a small majority favoured the Commission's viewpoint, and in the final vote, which took place during the night, the Deringer Report was approved, with a few amendments, by a large majority. Parliament came out unequivocally in favour of the Commission having sole decision-making power, with the possibility of appeal to the Court of Justice. The House was full, and the press reports were comprehensive and objective. The general public and the interests concerned took part extensively in the discussions, which were fuelled by sound arguments on all sides. These debates give some idea of the important role the European Parliament — thanks among other things to direct universal suffrage, which was already in the pipeline — could have played in the integration process if the Member States had succeeded in implementing political cooperation. In this instance, as in many others, the Commission did everything in its power to help Parliament play its part as a constitutional body participating in the decision-making process through an intensive information campaign, frequent debates in committee and the personal commitment of the responsible Commissioners. In fact, the Commission stated that it was ready in this case too to take account of Parliament's positions in the discussions within the Council. Parliament's debates and its resolution therefore contributed in no small measure to the compromise finally reached by the Commission and the Member States at the Council meetings in December.'

Extract from Hans von der Groeben's work: *The European Community — the formative years — The struggle to establish the common market and the political union 1958–66*, European Perspectives, Office for Official Publications of the European Communities, Luxembourg, 1987, p. 122.

competent national authorities or sufficient procedural rules. Hence the observation that the hope of seeing Member States submit specific cartel cases to the Commission had still to be realised (¹).

Starting in the early 1960s, the Commission therefore took it upon itself to act, deeming itself empowered to open investigations and to enter into direct contact with the undertakings or other bodies concerned, no matter what action the Member States might themselves take. The objective was, according to von der Groeben, to open an investigation into a few major cartels which were particularly damaging to the establishment of the Community so as to make it clear to Member States that a passive attitude on their part would not prevent the Commission from pursuing an active cartels policy and to show the business world that the Commission would not content itself with investigating, in response to complaints, cartel cases of no importance (²).

The speeding-up of the market-opening process and Member States' passivity forced the Commission, however, to broaden the scope of its action and present a proposal for a regulation in the

(¹) *Cartels policy, communication from Mr von der Groeben*, COM(60) 17, 15 February 1960, p. 14.

(²) Ibid., p. 15.

autumn of 1960. Von der Groeben thus explained to his colleagues that the Commission was currently stymied by its enormous dependence on the effective collaboration of the Six's national authorities. The Member States' efforts so far did not entirely correspond to what was needed. It was therefore essential, on the one hand, to increase the amount of information available to the Commission on existing cartels and, on the other, to put an end to the legal uncertainty about which industry frequently complained [1].

The Commission's proposal for a regulation was discussed in the Council, the Parliamentary Assembly and the Economic and Social Committee, where advocates of the abuse theory clashed with supporters of the prohibition theory. In the end, Regulation No 17 of 21 February 1962, more commonly known as Regulation 17/62, which laid down rules for the application of Articles 85 and 86 of the Treaty, was based on the principle that all cartels were prohibited. Anticompetitive agreements between undertakings therefore had to be notified to the Commission, which decided what action to take on them. Following notification, the Commission could either decide not to act or to authorise the agreement if its overall effects were considered to be favourable, or else to prohibit it or initiate proceedings. Regulation 17/62 provided for the possibility of proceedings in response to complaints by interested third parties or Member States, own-initiative proceedings opened by the Commission itself, and the possibility of sector enquiries, which were better suited to detecting abuses of dominant positions.

The enactment of Regulation 17/62 was a victory for the Commission. It gave it a wide range of powers and centralised in its hands the lion's share of the decision-making process in the name of efficiency and of the unity of the case-law to come. It nevertheless remained determined to promote a joint effort with the Member States by hosting regular meetings of government experts

and by relying on employers' organisations to disseminate information among the business community. Von der Groeben's legitimate concern was to avoid a direct confrontation with the latter. This cautionary attitude showed itself, according to an entertaining account by Ivo Schwartz [2], in the way he would put off reaching a decision on individual cases. What, he asked Schwartz — just as he had asked others at the very beginning — was really behind the youthful European Economic Community? The answer was, if one looked more closely, the economy mainly. The Commission was therefore faced with a choice between eradicating as quickly and as energetically as possible the existing array of cartels and monopolies, thereby running the risk of undermining the economy; proceeding steadily in that direction, step by step; and maintaining support for the economy and, in particular, for industry and commerce for Europe's and the European Community's sakes.

In the event, the Commission chose to embark on an educational campaign and to enter into a dialogue with the interests concerned. A document entitled 'Initial comments on the first regulation applying Articles 85 and 86 of the Treaty of Rome' was thus drawn up by UNICE, in partnership with the Directorate-General for Competition [3]. All in all, it is DG IV that seems to have launched, in early 1962, the initiatives that helped competition policy to take off successfully. Witness a remark by Kohnstamm to Monnet — commenting on the fact that the anti-cartel legislation had been adopted unanimously — to the effect that everyone seemed to think that the legislation was good and that the final text was, if anything, an improvement on the Commission's original proposal. Many people, he added, thought that von der Groeben had prepared the ground very well with the various governments [4].

---

[1] Regulations implementing Articles 85 and 86 EEC, Communication from Mr von der Groeben, COM(60) 138, 9 September 1960.

[2] Interview with Ivo Schwartz, 16 January 2004.
[3] BAC 89/1983, Initial comments on the first regulation applying Articles 85 and 86 of the Treaty of Rome, 17 April 1962.
[4] FJME, MK 20, Max Kohnstamm to Jean Monnet, 5 January 1962.

P. VerLoren van Themaat on the ideas behind the drafting of Regulation 17/62 on competition

VerLoren van Themaat recollected that two major problems that arose when a start was being made on drafting Regulation 17/62 stemmed from the fact that there was at that time only one country, namely Germany, with the beginnings of a policy that could be compared, in terms of its principles, with the principles underlying Articles 85 and 86 of the Treaty of Rome. Three countries had no competition policy aimed at the business sector, while the remaining two had policies which differed widely. Overall, the Member States' policies contained absolutely no indication as to how to resolve any issues that might arise.

When it came to the crunch and ideas were called for, the idea that was chosen (and this proved important to what came afterwards) was that anything that might be interpreted as an attempt to approximate national laws should be avoided. The starting point was instead that firms could not be allowed to re-erect barriers that governments were forbidden to erect, such as entry barriers to national markets, price barriers, quantity barriers, etc.

Accordingly, in Regulation 17/62, the first implementing regulation, which was still in force at the time of VerLoren van Themaat's recollections, emphasis was placed on the impact that firms' practices had on trade between Member States. The interesting thing about this was that, as far as those practices were concerned, both the business world and private individuals were so enthusiastic about the opportunities provided for moving into new markets that the number of decisions started to increase rapidly. But after several decades — and this was something that had not been expected when the 1962 roadmaps were being drawn up — the Member States themselves (Luxembourg being — VerLoren van Themaat believed — the forerunner of this new, independent national development) began to adopt, at the national level, the principles laid down in Articles 85 and 86, not in the context of dealings of transnational interest, but in the national context.

The scope of European competition law according to P. VerLoren van Themaat, in Commission européenne, DG X (ed.), *40 ans des Traités de Rome ou la capacité des Traités d'assurer les avancées de la construction européenne/40 years of the Treaties of Rome or the capacity of the Treaties to advance the European integration process*, Action Jean Monnet series, Bruylant, Brussels, 1999, p. 80. (Translated from the French)

However, Regulation 17/62 proved difficult to implement in practice. Rules on the subject were new in Europe, experts in the field were few in number and the information transmitted by interested parties to the Commission was not always sufficient. The Commission wished to take every precaution inasmuch as the first decisions would set a precedent. The compulsory notification of agreements caused, moreover, a major organisational headache. More than 35 000 notifications were sent to Brussels following the regulation's enactment. Simply processing that amount of information was problematic for want of enough trained staff. Von der Groeben acknowledged these difficulties, stating on more than one occasion that investigations were as a rule very time-consuming, more so than had at first been supposed, and that interpreting the Treaty provisions raised many tricky questions and called for detailed studies and discussions. The directorate-general's staffing levels unfortunately did not reflect the workload ([1]). The Commission's departments nevertheless came up with answers to this challenge. In July 1962, Schumacher, head of DG IV's antitrust directorate, informed a meeting of national experts that it had been decided to proceed by category, or type, of agreement as this would make it possible to deal with a very large number of cases at any one time. It had also been decided to take a limited number of individual decisions so as to demonstrate the Commission's determination to act and to provide guidance to undertakings. Regulation 67/67 of 22 March 1967 thus made it possible to deal en

---

([1]) 'Competition policy, an integral part of economic policy in the common market', Speech given by Hans von der Groeben to the European Parliament, 16 June 1965.

bloc with 13 041 cases involving exclusive dealing agreements, and a decision taken in 1968 enabled the file to be closed on a further 12 000 such agreements.

The finding of infringement made in September 1964 against the Grundig-Consten agreement, an exclusive dealing agreement with absolute territorial protection between a German firm and a French distributor which led to a partitioning of the market and substantial price differentials between France and Germany for the same product, was the first in a series of proceedings, the exemplary and dissuasive effect of which enabled the Commission to act subsequently by dissuasion. Armed with Court of Justice judgments on appeal upholding its decisions, the Commission succeeded even in persuading many cartels to dissolve or to change their ways so as no longer to infringe the rules. Nevertheless, the decision to prosecute the Grundig–Consten agreement was not an easy one to take. Manfred Caspari was part of von der Groeben's inner circle and saw how it was that his colleagues' exhortations induced him to act. Caspari recalled that it was Ivo Schwartz who handled such cartel cases in the Commissioner's private office. The case was, of course, a complex one in that it involved patents, licences, etc. Von der Groeben was extremely hesitant, as was the responsible head of division, a German official. But, thankfully, there was another person in their midst, a Dutchman, who did an excellent job. The entire private office, moreover, was in favour of taking a decision. It was an uphill struggle to get von der Groeben, in the interests of the Community, to give his agreement to a decision being taken, but in the end he did just that (¹).

This willingness to forge ahead was shared by the officials working for the DG. Young lawyers for the most part, they had gained a modicum of experience either in their home countries or on the job, while some of them had been to the United States on a leader's grant to see how anti-trust proceedings were conducted there (²). DG IV thus learned how to use the carrot-and-stick approach, i.e. education, on the one hand, and fear of the policeman, on the other. Some of the officials were the very embodiment of the idea. Jacques Vandamme — Head of the EEC Controls Division (1961–67), then of the EEC Inspections Division (1968–73) — recalled, for example, how visits used to go. Some were simply information-gathering exercises. Firms would be asked whether they were prepared to receive Commission officials without the latter having to exercise their powers of enquiry. They would be told that such and such an industry was being scrutinised. In most cases, all went well by and large. If it came to an investigation — that is, where there was sufficient prima facie evidence of wrongdoing — officials would carry out raids on firms, often coming up trumps. They had smelled a rat, and their reward was an unexpected pay-off in the form of actual proof of an infringement. The officials concerned were generally mature individuals with a certain amount of seniority given that the tasks they had to perform were highly sensitive. There would come a point during the course of an investigation when they would have to ask the managing director to open certain filing cabinets to show what was in them. As a rule, people could be induced to hand over their files voluntarily without the need for coercion (³).

But, apart from the policeman's role of the Commission and the judgments of the Court of Justice, a series of favourable decisions made it possible to determine the limits and the meaning of the rules (⁴).

Once its role had been recognised by the institutional and private interests concerned and its working methods had been perfected, the Commission was able to set out more clearly its position on all aspects of agreements between undertakings. Cooperation agreements were thus

---

(¹) Interview with Manfred Caspari, 18 February 2004.

(²) Interview with Jacques Vandamme, 21 January 2004.
(³) Ibid.
(⁴) Nême, J. and Nême C., *Économie européenne*, PUF, Paris, 1970, pp. 99–105.

The Commission squares up to the French oil monopoly

In France, State intervention in the oil sector was born of the traumatic experience of the shortage of petroleum products during the First World War and of the preponderance of foreign, and in particular US, companies on the French market during the interwar period. The legal regime put in place by the Law of 30 March 1928 had the twofold aim of guaranteeing the country's security of supply and of strengthening the position of domestic companies on the market. The law established a State oil monopoly, the management of which the State delegated to oil companies in return for certain commitments. The law also brought in import and distribution licences that made it possible to monitor French and foreign operators' market shares.

When the Treaty of Rome was signed, the French authorities' primary concern was to safeguard the monopoly system. France made sure that the French oil regime came under Article 37, which provided for the progressive adjustment of State monopolies, and not under Article 30, which concerned quantitative restrictions on imports. In the former case, the Commission simply made recommendations as to the manner in which and the timetable according to which the adjustment was carried out, whereas in the latter case it had binding powers which would have obliged the French State to comply with its instructions.

On the eve of the first oil crisis, despite three recommendations (of April 1962, July 1963 and December 1969) from the Commission, France enjoyed almost total freedom to adjust its oil regime. A degree of flexibility was introduced in 1959 with the opening of an overall EEC quota and subsequently with the disappearance of discrimination such as the prohibition on using non-French equipment or the French nationality requirement for oil company managers. However, European liberals, especially in the Netherlands, felt that these measures did not go far enough and advocated dismantling the quota system. France made further movement on its part conditional on the introduction of a common energy policy.

From being very hostile to the French position, the Commission became more receptive to France's concerns when at the end of the 1960s the problem of defending European oil companies against the US majors came to a head. The Communities' activity report for 1967 stated, for example, that, as far as the import regime for French oil products was concerned, progress needed to be made towards a common energy policy before a fresh recommendation was sent to the French government.

Throughout the 1960s France lobbied very actively for a common oil policy incorporating the fundamentals of the Law of March 1928.
On 11 July 1967, for example, it secured from the Council of Ministers a definition of Community company that was limited to enterprises whose fundamental interests coincided by their very nature permanently with those of the Community, which implied that they would be controlled by Community nationals or a Member State government and that they would have their decision-making centre in a Community country. The 1973–74 oil crisis strengthened the French conviction that the maintenance of a national oil policy underpinned by the principles of the Law of 30 March 1928 was justified.

A. D.

the subject of discussions which culminated in the publication of a document by the Commission in July 1968 specifying that agreements between undertakings whose activities accounted for only a small part of the European market were not caught by Article 85. The aim here was to help SMEs adapt to the new conditions of the European market.

Besides cartels, the effects of concentration on competition were one of the Commission's major concerns. For a while it was feared that the Commission might adopt a rigorous attitude — a stance which some Member States considered potentially harmful to European industry with its often overly dispersed structures. However, the studies carried out by the Commission on concentration in Community industry led it to adopt a more subtle approach which took into account a twofold concern: (i) the need to bridge the gap between Europe and the United States in a number of areas and hence the need for a higher degree of concentration in certain sectors so as to achieve a critical mass internationally, and (ii) the need also to escape from the mindset centred on national champions and European monopolies. As von der Groeben stated in June 1965, the increase in trade and competition with the rest of the world called for a corresponding increase in the number of enterprises and, in many cases, the existing economic structures in Europe did not yet reflect that twofold rejigging of the world economy (¹).

This realistic analysis reassured economic operators and national public authorities alike and met the expectations of Parliament, which wanted merger policy to take account of the impact of competition from non-Community enterprises. Be that as it may, such an approach raised the difficult question of the application of Article 86 on abuses of dominant positions. As von der Groeben explained before Parliament in 1965,

the closer a dominant firm came to constituting a monopoly by joining forces with another firm, the more likely it was that the dominant firm would commit an abuse as a result of the merger (²). Consequently, the Commission had to take steps to prevent monopoly situations from arising in a given sector and to seek to promote the emergence of a structure of competition between oligopolistic European (and no longer national) firms — a structure suited to promoting technical and economic progress (³).

Articles 92 et seq. of the Treaty of Rome contained a series of provisions on the prohibition in principle of State aid. The aim was to ensure that governments did not prevent the further development of intra-Community competition brought about by abolishing customs duties. The Treaty accordingly stated that 'any aid granted by a Member State [...] which distorts or threatens to distort competition by favouring certain undertakings or the production of certain goods shall, insofar as it affects trade between Member States, be incompatible with the common market'. It provided, however, for a number of exceptions to this prohibition in principle, such as aid having a social character, aid linked to regional development or aid to promote the execution of projects of common European interest. It also laid down that the Commission had to keep under review, in cooperation with the Member States, all existing or planned aid schemes, that it could ask the Member States concerned to alter or abolish them and that it could, if necessary, initiate proceedings before the Court of Justice of the Communities.

Such arrangements could not but meet with resistance from certain Member States, which viewed aid as an instrument of economic and social or regional planning policy. Sometimes the difficulties stemmed from governments' inability to resist the temptation to satisfy one or other request. The Commission strove here also to work with

---

(¹) 'Competition policy, an integral part of economic policy in the common market', Speech given by Hans von der Groeben to the European Parliament, 16 June 1965.

(²) Ibid.
(³) Ibid.

national authorities in order to draw up an inventory of measures existing in the different countries. As early as 1959, it sent governments a questionnaire which, despite the tardy and incomplete nature of the initial replies, gave an insight into the veritable jungle formed by national schemes, many of which were long-standing, complex and constantly changing. There was export aid, aid for economic expansion (guarantees, loans on preferential terms, grants, etc.), regional aid, sectoral aid, and so on and so forth. Persuading national authorities to cooperate proved difficult and, on occasion, a source of conflict, as when the Commission decided not only to scrutinise a general aid scheme but also to carry out an in-depth, case-by-case investigation. In the spring of 1965, von der Groeben took stock of the work done, counting some 450 aid schemes, of which 13 had been abolished as being incompatible with the common market and 60 or so had been amended at the Commission's request. As in the field of company mergers, however, the Commission did not simply act as a policeman. Firstly, the exceptions provided for by the Treaty placed a huge range of tools in the hands of the Member States. Secondly, and more importantly, the Commission adopted a favourable attitude towards regional and structural aid. Consisting as it did in coordinating and harmonising the measures existing within Member States, avoiding distortions and encouraging selective and degressive measures, aid policy helped to gradually define the bases of both a regional policy and an industrial policy.

Towards a common tax system

Applying the same reasoning as he did to cartels, von der Groeben urged Member States to act in the field of taxation by telling them that the abolition of tariff barriers and quotas was not in itself sufficient to create a common market. Just as producer cartels could kill off competition by sharing markets, taxation, if skilfully manipulated, could be a means whereby Member States cancelled out the effects of the removal of tax frontiers. Steps therefore had to be taken to prevent

Young lawyers in DG IV

Franz Froschmaier began lecturing in 1954 at the Munich University institute for international and comparative industrial property and copyright law, where he very soon became interested in the European patent. In early 1958, he read in the German press that the Commission was looking for staff. He telephoned the Foreign Ministry in Bonn, where he was told that it was the Ministry of Economic Affairs that was dealing with the matter and that he should contact such and such a person, which he did. He was then summoned to an interview in Bonn with seven other applicants. He picked up a pile of information on the EEC and read it on the way to Bonn. When he arrived for the interview, he knew more about the subject than the team that was asking questions.

Interview with Franz Froschmaier, 19 January 2004.

Aurelio Pappalardo recalled that the early years were devoted to exploring the possibilities, without any specific objectives. He arrived at a time when serious work had begun on the contents of the basic competition instrument, Regulation No 17 of 1962. As a young lawyer interested in international issues, which he found extremely stimulating, he made the following discovery almost every day: they were a small group of people, and they realised, albeit still vaguely, that together they were laying the first bricks of an edifice. It was not known what that edifice would turn out to be, but what was known was that an important building project was under way. And that was definitely the feeling that remained with him and others for many years.

Interview with Aurelio Pappalardo, 26 January 2004.

the advantages gained by dismantling tariff barriers and quotas from being nullified by the manipulation of drawbacks and countervailing charges. Distortion of competition had to be eliminated; in merchandise trade, fair competition had to prevail ([1]).

([1]) 'Harmonisation of turnover taxes in the Community', extracts from a statement by Mr von der Groeben in the European Parliament, 17 October 1963, *Bulletin of the EEC*, December 1963.

Although it was taken into account in the Treaty of Rome, the issue of tax frontiers had not gone away, allowing an unsatisfactory and intractable situation to continue. In 1958 all the Member States had turnover tax systems with structures, levels and collection procedures that varied from country to country. The smooth functioning of the common market required that these differences did not distort intra-Community trade: the same product had to be taxed according to the same system and at the same rate, whether it was of domestic origin or sourced from another EEC Member State. Tax neutrality could therefore be achieved, in theory, by remitting the tax on exported goods and applying the importing country's taxes once the frontier had been crossed, but implementing such a system posed formidable technical problems, while at the same time offering Member States enormous scope for distorting competition. This was the case especially with those countries which applied a system of cumulative cascade taxes, that is, all the EEC countries except France. Inasmuch as such taxes were levied on a given product at each stage in its manufacture, the amount of tax included in the price of the finished product was very difficult to assess and could vary in the case of one and the same product depending on the number of stages in the manufacturing process. Consequently, the amount of tax to be remitted on exports or the amount of tax to be applied on imports could be determined only approximately using averages. That is what the Treaty provided for in Article 97. Unlike the cascade tax system, the VAT (value added tax) system applied by France since the mid-1950s, under which tax was levied on a product only once when it reached the final consumer, made it possible, on the contrary, to carry out taxation and tax remission operations with much greater accuracy.

Pierre Guieu was principal administrator and then head of division responsible for VAT matters at the Commission between 1959 and 1973. The adoption of a taxation system common to the Six was, he wrote, inescapable. The priority task of the departments was to bring some order to the flat-rate taxes applicable to, among other things, international trade. The Commission was therefore given a mandate to look for a way of calculating the effective amount of tax contained in the value of a good or a service. This gave rise to endless discussions. A system of calculation had to be developed whereby a weighting was assigned to the amount of tax that could be borne by each product manufactured in integrated economic circuits and in non-integrated economic circuits since, in order to assess that amount of tax, it had to be known how many times the tax had been collected. This was because tax was collected at each stage of manufacture, and the longer the economic circuit, the more tax there was incorporated in the price of a product. Existing taxes were so untransparent and so difficult to manage in international trade that, although a common calculation method had been drawn up, another system of taxation just had to be devised [1].

Quite apart from their technical complexity, the operations of taxation/tax remission at frontiers posed formidable competition problems insofar as Member States could play on the uncertainties surrounding the levels of adjustment at frontiers in order to improve the competitive position of their domestic products by overestimating the amount of tax remission on their exports and the amount of tax payable on imports. Attending to the most urgent matters first, the Commission persuaded finance ministers to introduce a tax standstill in June 1960, while the Member States gave a commitment to cease modifying countervailing charges at frontiers except for purely technical reasons. But this did not really put an end to suspicions of manipulation. It was not until March 1968 that the Commission succeeded in inducing Member States to accept a directive laying down rules for calculating countervailing charges on imports and drawbacks (refunds of tax) on exports in the area of turnover taxes.

[1] Guieu, P., 'La Commission européenne et l'harmonisation fiscale', *Le rôle des ministres des Finances et de l'Économie dans la construction européenne (1957–1978)*, CHEFF, Paris, 2002, p. 57.

In reality, the adoption of a uniform system of indirect taxation proved to be the only way of resolving this thorny problem once and for all. While the Commission and Member States alike called for such an initiative, opposition to its aims and methods was voiced from various quarters. Should the aim be simply one of neutrality, or should one go a step further and remove tax frontiers as well? The Directorate-General for Competition and Commissioner von der Groeben favoured the latter option. Von der Groeben felt that the disparities between indirect tax systems and rates could engender distortions of competition between the individual countries' industries, necessitating drawback and equalisation payments at frontiers and therefore frontier controls. Tax harmonisation had two objectives: first, in the shorter term, the elimination of distortions of competition, and second, the removal of tax frontiers [1].

The two working hypotheses (simply aiming at tax neutrality or removing tax frontiers) were already being debated at the time the Treaty of Rome was being negotiated. Tax neutrality could be achieved simply by harmonising tax systems, the taxation of products in the country of destination making it possible for each country to retain control over the rates charged within its borders. Removing tax frontiers entailed taxing in the country of origin and hence approximating rates sufficiently so as to avoid competition between national tax systems and the resulting tax dumping. The Commission favoured the more ambitious approach and announced its stand in 1959. Supported by the Federal Republic of Germany, it faced opposition from France, which wished to retain its tax autonomy by continuing to perform adjustment operations at its frontiers. The Commission tried to find a solution by turning to a committee of independent experts chaired by Professor Fritz Neumark, whose report, which was published in 1962, advocated removing tax frontiers. It also relied on a group of experts

drawn from national tax authorities which recommended abandoning cascade taxes and replacing them with a generalised VAT system.

In November 1962 the Commission tabled a first proposal for a directive aimed at generalising VAT throughout the Community, together with the removal of tax frontiers. Rejected by France, the draft was resubmitted in the form of two proposals in June 1964 and April 1965. These provided for the introduction of a common VAT system by 1 January 1970 and laid down implementing procedures. Both directives were finally adopted by the Council on 9 February 1967. Von der Groeben welcomed their scope. The common system would, he said, make possible exact tax equalisation at frontiers. The application of 'flat-rate' equalisation measures to imports and exports between the Member States would then no longer be allowed [2]. For von der Groeben, the objective of the complete elimination of tax frontiers still remained to be attained, and this would be done by approximating rates, which in turn would make it possible to charge tax in the country of origin [3].

The removal of tax frontiers necessitated, however, an additional step, which governments, and the French government in particular, were reluctant to take.

Philippe Rouvillois, who at that time was technical adviser in the private office of French Finance Minister Michel Debré, reminiscing about the talks leading up to the adoption of the 1967 directives, said that, during 1966 and up until the directives' adoption in February 1967, something of a guerrilla war was waged between the Commission's departments — backed discreetly, but not so much as to jeopardise Franco-German cooperation, by the Germans — and the other Member States, which broadly favoured the French position. A compromise was finally reached in the form of a proposal on the condi-

[1] Von der Groeben, H., 'Introduction of the common value added tax — a decisive step on the road to the complete elimination of tax frontiers', *Bulletin of the EEC*, May 1967.

[2] Ibid.
[3] Ibid.

'Buy European'. The 1930s remain in our memories as the time when domestic goods were being promoted in a protectionist environment, but the early 1960s witnessed the promotion of the 'product of Europe' label.

tions under which harmonisation could, rather than should, lead to the removal of tax frontiers, etc. For good measure, this was coupled with a reminder that, when the matter was dealt with, account would have to be taken of the relationship between direct and indirect taxes, which differed according to the Member State, and of the impact on tax and budgetary policy. This was a discreet way of saying that France in general, and Mr Debré in particular, supported on this point by the President of the Republic and the Prime Minister, was not ready for too large a dose of supranationalism [1].

One of the French government's fears was that harmonisation might pave the way for the introduction of a European tax collected directly by Brussels. As late as April 1970, Dominique de La Martinière, Director-General of Taxes, told his Minister that the Commission's true motives in this area were political. The removal of tax frontiers was, in his opinion, a way of engaging Member States in a process of transferring their financial and economic powers to a Community political authority, and it would lead logically to a vast European budget fed by harmonised VAT resources. De La Martinière added that it was not for him to assess those political motives, but the discussion would be all the clearer for being viewed from the outset against such a background [2].

---

[1] Rouvillois, P. and Debré, M., 'La mise en œuvre de la loi du 6 janvier 1966 et l'adoption des premières directives, 1966–1968', *Le rôle des ministères des Finances et de l'Économie*, op. cit., p. 41.

[2] Cited by Tristram, F., *La Direction générale des Impôts et la politique fiscale en France de 1948 à la fin des années 1960*, Thesis, Paris X, 2003, p. 594.

Even if the Commission had to give up the idea of dismantling tax frontiers for the time being, it still considered it to be a desirable objective. But this meant going through a difficult process of harmonisation involving not only VAT rates but also the main consumer taxes on alcohol, tobacco and petroleum products. The Commission also wished to carry out an approximation of direct taxation. The harmonisation programme launched in 1967 dealt with the question of the taxation of income from capital in order to promote the free movement of capital and the establishment of a European market. A further aim was to approximate corporation tax rules so as to promote closer relations between European enterprises [1].

Von der Groeben highlighted the overall difficulties of tax harmonisation in an address he made to the European Parliament on 2 July 1969 [2]. He told his audience that harmonising the rates of the future European VAT and of indirect consumer taxes posed problems which were difficult to resolve as they were often political in nature. Cooperation in the area of corporation tax was seriously hampered, he said, by the Member States' very different systems for determining and monitoring the basis of tax assessment. To that end, the Member States had not only to accept the economic and technical arguments, but also to endorse the policy itself. Von der Groeben also drew an explicit link between the measures to be taken in the area of the taxation of income from capital and future prospects for economic and monetary cooperation. In the Commission's view, he warned, it was impossible as well as pointless to advance further in the tax field if no progress was made with regard to economic and monetary policy. All in all, at the end of the transition period, although the steps needed to make the common market function had been taken, further progress towards the establishment of an economic union called for new breakthroughs. These depended on an awareness and a willingness on the part of the Member States. On the Commission's part, there was a need to exercise intellectual leadership and a certain amount of caution. Von der Groeben showed great lucidity when he explained that the margin for budgetary manoeuvring still freely available to the Member States would be limited to a certain extent by tax harmonisation. Care would have to be taken that tax harmonisation did not so limit the scope of budgetary administrations as to deprive them of such room for manoeuvre [1].

As in the case of the internal market, the Commission's work in the area of competition and taxation plateaued before tailing off in the face of the inertia caused by the economic crisis of the early 1970s. The compromises gradually reached with the Member States in the mid-1960s in regard to both competition and taxation rested on the lucid appraisal of the constraints of external competition, especially from the United States, and of the need for autonomy felt by Member States in the tax sphere. These compromises left the door open to new developments. But progress in the early 1970s depended on successful conclusion of the economic and monetary union project and on being able to launch new common policies in the energy, industrial and regional spheres. The difficulties experienced in opening up these fresh vistas help to explain the deadlocks that hampered completion of the internal market in competition and tax policy during the 1970s.

ÉRIC BUSSIÈRE

[1] 'Programme for the harmonisation of direct taxes', *Bulletin of the EEC*, September–October 1967.
[2] 'Tax harmonisation and the common market, an address by Hans von der Groeben to the European Parliament', *Bulletin of the EEC*, September–October 1969.

[1] Ibid.

Chapter 16

The common agricultural policy: a leading field of action

Agriculture is covered by Articles 38 to 46 of the Treaty. The key goals of this policy are to increase productivity, ensure that the farming population enjoys a reasonable standard of living and maintains prices at a level acceptable to consumers. These were the fundamental issues — drafted to be broad and deliberately vague — which Commissioner Sicco Mansholt and his directorate-general (that of agriculture or DG VI) worked on over the years [1]. It was not the first time that Mansholt had tried to introduce a common farm policy at European level. At the beginning of the 1950s he was behind the discussions among 15 European countries to create the 'Green Pool', discussions which came to nothing other than the creation of a Ministerial Committee for Agriculture and Food within the OEEC. The standpoints of the different member countries were still too far apart. Later, however, the analyses of agricultural structures, markets and policies in the various countries and the personal contacts made during the conference on the 'Green Pool' would turn out to be very useful.

The Treaty of Rome and the creation of the EEC opened up new prospects because agriculture could no longer be thought of as being managed separately but as forming part of the broader Community agenda. The technique of the package deal was now available to break down any obstacles that might arise. It was clear that an independent Commission would be able to play a leading role using this instrument.

The Stresa conference in July 1958, the Commission proposals of 1960, the 'night of the cereals' in 1964, the Community crisis of 1965 and the Mansholt Plan of structural reforms in 1968 show this approach in operation, driven by the directorate-general responsible for agriculture.

The creation and composition of DG VI (agriculture)

The most important official in DG VI under the tutelage of Mansholt was its Director-General, Louis Rabot. Before coming to Brussels he had

---

[1] On the first years of the common agricultural policy (1958–68), see Ludlow, N. P., 'The making of the CAP: towards a historical analysis of the EU's first major policy', *Contemporary European History*, Vol. 14, No 3, 2005, pp. 347–372. It should be noted this article was published after drafting this chapter.

Articles 38, 39, 40 and 43 of the EEC Treaty

TITLE II — Agriculture

Article 38

1. The common market shall extend to agriculture and trade in agricultural products. 'Agricultural products' means the products of the soil, of stock-farming and of fisheries and the products of first-stage processing directly related to these products.

[…]

Article 39

1. The objectives of the common agricultural policy shall be:

(a) to increase agricultural productivity by promoting technical progress and by ensuring the rational development of agricultural production and the optimum utilisation of the factors of production, in particular labour;

(b) thus to ensure a fair standard of living for the agricultural community, in particular by increasing the individual earnings of persons engaged in agriculture;

(c) to stabilise markets;

(d) to assure the availability of supplies;

(e) to ensure that supplies reach consumers at reasonable prices.

[…]

Article 40

1. Member States shall develop the common agricultural policy by degrees during the transitional period and shall bring it into force by the end of that period at the latest.

2. In order to attain the objectives set out in Article 39, a common organisation of agricultural markets shall be established.

This organisation shall take one of the following forms, depending on the product concerned:

(a) common rules on competition;

(b) compulsory coordination of the various national market organisations;

(c) a European market organisation.

3. The common organisation established in accordance with paragraph 2 may include all measures required to attain the objectives set out in Article 39, in particular regulation of prices, aids for the production and marketing of the various products, storage and carryover arrangements and common machinery for stabilising imports or exports.

The common organisation shall be limited to pursuit of the objectives set out in Article 39 and shall exclude any discrimination between producers or consumers within the Community.

Any common price policy shall be based on common criteria and uniform methods of calculation.

4. In order to enable the common organisation referred to in paragraph 2 to attain its objectives, one or more agricultural guidance and guarantee funds may be set up.

Article 43

1. In order to evolve the broad lines of a common agricultural policy, the Commission shall, immediately this Treaty enters into force, convene a conference of the Member States with a view to making a comparison of their agricultural policies, in particular by producing a statement of their resources and needs.

2. Having taken into account the work of the conference provided for in paragraph 1, after consulting the Economic and Social Committee and within two years of the entry into force of this Treaty, the Commission shall submit proposals for working out and implementing the common agricultural policy […].

The Council shall, on a proposal from the Commission and after consulting the Assembly, acting unanimously during the first two stages and by a qualified majority thereafter, make regulations, issue directives, or take decisions, without prejudice to any recommendations it may also make.

[…]

been a director in France's Ministry of Agriculture, Chairman of the Interim Committee for the 'Green Pool', then Director for Agriculture at the OEEC. He arrived in Brussels just before the Stresa conference. His eligibility for the job was helped by his international renown. He was also strongly supported as a candidate by the French government. The appointment of a Dutchman to the post of Commissioner in charge of agriculture was a sore point for Paris. Indeed, that appointment would never have been made if a Frenchman had not been chosen for the most important job in DG VI. For Mansholt this posed no problems. He knew and trusted Rabot. The documents of the time and our interviews show that they were generally in agreement on management matters. Rabot was a competent director-general within DG VI. He combined knowledge of the field with natural authority and a personal aura. He was good at delegating and made sure that the directorate-general's officials kept in close touch with Mansholt through round-table discussions. These were typical of the way DG VI worked. They facilitated consensus on management matters and increased its effectiveness [1].

Rabot toured the national capitals explaining the Commission's policies and collecting national points of view. Very soon his staff were receiving frequent invitations to meetings with national representatives of agriculture. From the start, Rabot developed a deliberate strategy on this. He told his assistant von Verschuer not to be too close with the representatives of Member States, non-member countries and farming organisations, to avoid playing the game of invitation and counter-invitation, even if it appeared useful in the interests of the service. This strategy not only saved time and energy but also strengthened the image of an independent Commission [2].

Although suffering from health problems, Rabot performed his duties in full and gained the grudging respect of his staff. For instance, at the beginning of the 1970s a member of staff came to see him about a promotion, pointing out that he had been in the same job for many years. After listening politely, Rabot replied: 'Well, there's not much I can do. Look at me, I have been Director-General since 1958 and I still haven't been promoted.' Having been thus put in his place, the official said nothing and never brought the subject up again [3].

At Rabot's side was another important figure of the early DG VI years, Berend Heringa. Heringa had worked with Mansholt over a long period as an adviser in the Dutch Ministry of Agriculture but made up his mind, after considerable hesitation and under pressure from Mansholt, to leave his job in The Hague in the summer of 1958 for a career in Brussels. Although Heringa was of a different political stripe than his boss — he was a Christian Democrat while Mansholt was a Social Democrat — and did not share Mansholt's boundless enthusiasm for the European idea, they understood each other perfectly. This was due without question to their common origins: they were both sons of peasant farmers from the Province of Groningen in the northern Netherlands. Their personalities were very similar. Heringa knew from experience that Mansholt could not stand yes-men and liked to debate issues with his staff as long as they had a solid grip on their brief. In other words, he expected them to pull their weight. With his detailed knowledge of price support systems, Heringa was a good example of the trust, respect and support that Mansholt was prepared to invest in those working for him. The difficult post of Director for Agricultural Markets enabled Heringa to play a leading role in developing the common agricultural policy. The first plan that the Commission developed in this area in 1959–60 is sometimes called the 'Mansholt–Heringa bible', which gives a hint of the latter's importance behind the scenes [4]. In 1963 Heringa was appointed Deputy Director-General.

[1] Interview with Helmut von Verschuer, 3 March 2004.
[2] Ibid.
[3] Interview with Michel Jacquot, 19 December 2003.
[4] Molegraaf, J., 'Boeren in Brussel — Nederland en het Gemeenschappelijk Europees Landbouwbeleid, 1958–1971', doctoral thesis, Utrecht, 1999, p. 75.

This post included responsibility for discussions with the national representatives in the Special Committee on Agriculture.

There were a few Germans too who played an important part within the DG: Martin Meyer-Burckhardt (Director for General Affairs), Hans-Broder Krohn (running agricultural markets under Heringa, later to become Deputy Director-General) and in particular Helmut von Verschuer (assistant to Rabot and later Director for International Affairs). All three were pro-Europe and for this reason were looked on suspiciously in Bonn. The Federal Republic of Germany was at this time the Member State which most feared the adoption of a common European farm policy. The relationship between Mansholt and Meyer-Burckhardt was in any case a difficult one. Mansholt did not hesitate to bypass his German Director when it suited him ([1]). Sometimes he avoided consulting him if it was a question of developing a new form of market management and preferred to speak instead to his head of department, in whom he had more confidence ([2]).

Georges Rencki, who has been mentioned before ([3]), occupied a prominent position in the DG. For a while he was Mansholt's deputy *chef de cabinet*, but, after the departure of Van der Lee at the end of 1958 and the arrival of Mozer and van Slobbe, he was appointed to head the division dealing with relations with non-governmental organisations. This division was to have an important role in the DG because of its close contacts with the lobby groups in the agricultural world, to which Mansholt attached a great deal of importance, especially when they were transnational. The 'Rencki Division' was, of all the divisions in DG VI, the one most closely associated with the Mansholt cabinet. In all other areas, the cabinet and the DG operated separately. Mozer and van Slobbe did not understand much of the details of agricultural policy. They concentrated on the political side, in the broad sense of the

---

([1]) Interview with Johannes Westhoff, 7 January 2004.
([2]) Interview with Willem-Jan van Slobbe, 6 January 2004.
([3]) See Chapter 8, p. 166.

The Mansholt method

'He is a virtuoso of political planning and preparation and tactical changes of position, a practitioner of modern-style teamwork, working with a highly qualified staff under his intellectual direction. Hence the devotion and enthusiasm with which his team hold to him through thick and thin.'

Freisberg, E., Die *Grüne Hürde Europas. Deutsche Agrarpolitik und EWG*, Westdt., Cologne, 1965, p. 21.
(Translated from the German)

term, within the Commission: contacts with the other cabinets and preparing the weekly meeting of the Commission, for example. When Mansholt was not there, they replaced him at Commission meetings even when the agenda included specifically agricultural issues. Rabot or one of the directors of DG VI would often be hovering nearby as 'prompters' ([4]).

A certain amount of time was needed before the directorate-general was complete. This was down to the procedure which Rabot and von Verschuer used to recruit new staff. Applications followed a very precise pattern. Candidates were received first by von Verschuer, who opened a file and set a date for the interviews. These were successively with Rabot, von Verschuer, the director of the division where the vacancy was and the head of that division. After the interviews, the four officials met to reach a decision. One important criterion was that the new recruit should integrate well into the team. If they were not unanimous about the best candidate, the decision was taken by majority vote; but the casting votes were those of the director and the head of division who would be working directly with the recruit. Nationality was a consideration only if two candidates were of equal quality. Preference then went to a person whose nationality was under-represented in the DG. In all other respects, quality was decisive. The procedure was rather complicated but it produced the right results. Rabot also had a drawer

---

([4]) Interview with Willem-Jan van Slobbe, 6 January 2004.

in his desk for letters of recommendation. These letters remained systematically unanswered, even if they came from the prime minister of a Member State. But, from time to time, Rabot would nonetheless open this drawer and invite a recommended person to an interview ([1]).

The Stresa conference

Under Article 43(1) of the EEC Treaty, the Commission was required to organise a conference of the Member States to determine the broad outlines of the common agricultural policy. Mansholt and his officials saw this as a unique opportunity to give more prominence at an early stage to the Commission's views on agriculture. He started by setting up a small working party drawn from his cabinet and the DG to prepare for this conference under his direction. Van der Lee and von Verschuer had a leading role in the working party. The actual organisation of the conference, given that the new Commission had no real administration as yet, was entrusted to Rencki, who also liaised with the agricultural lobby organisations. Meetings began early in the morning and ended late in the evening. They would open at 9 a.m. in the office on rue Belliard, adjourn for lunch in the 'Grand Laboureur' near the Quartier Léopold Station (nowadays the Luxembourg Station), then it was back to rue Belliard for the afternoon session. Dinner was taken in a restaurant on the avenue des Nations (later to be called avenue Franklin Roosevelt). The day's discussions would be rounded off at the home of either Mansholt or Van der Lee. At midnight the tireless Mansholt would dismiss them all because he had still to deal with his correspondence of the day. This routine went on for weeks. The working party examined all the issues, leaving nothing to chance. A final declaration was drafted, to be pulled out at a suitable moment during the meeting ([2]).

As a result of his job as Minister for Agriculture and his experience with the 'Green Pool', Mansholt knew almost everyone in the agricultural sector. It therefore fell to him to deal with the invitations. Apart from the ministers of agriculture of the six Member States, he also invited their Permanent Representatives in Brussels, national officials and representatives of interest groups. He immediately told the agricultural organisations that he would prefer to deal with European-level bodies rather than national-level ones. His aim was to stimulate the formation of associations which would give their input directly at the Commission's own level, rather than nationally and would help shape workmanlike compromises. This strategy quickly paid off. Even before the meeting convened, 14 transnational groups had applied to the Commission to take part. Most of them had been set up in haste. Shortly after Stresa, in September 1958, the organisations of agricultural producers were induced by the Commission to form the Comité des organisation professionnelles agricoles (Committee of Professional Agricultural Organisations, or COPA).

The problem, however, was that the number of participants was in danger of becoming very big. The Commission had decided that it was going to fund the conference, but its resources were not unlimited. Up to the last moment, it tried to control the number of participants and persuade the Italian government to make up any overshoot of the budget ([3]). Since the Commission's staff was still small, it called in officials from the ECSC and even students from the College of Europe to help the team in charge of organising and coordinating the meeting.

President Hallstein opened the conference with a long speech to the delegates in which he explained the general political importance of agriculture to society. Taking a wider view than just European agriculture, he spoke out against those who wanted to separate agriculture from general

---

([1]) Interview with Helmut von Verschuer, 3 March 2004.
([2]) Ibid.

([3]) PV 21, EEC Commission, 19 June 1958; ABZN, Code 996.412.0, File 1135, Mansholt letter, 4 June 1958.

economic policy. He also stressed the growing opinion that national economic policy was no longer sufficient to face up to the challenges of the modern world:

'We are surrounded by vast economic regions which benefit fully from enormous resources of production and generous prospects for expansion. Today the geographical distances which used to protect us from these competitors no longer exist; the world has actually become smaller. The various countries of Europe have reached the limits of their possibilities. They can no longer grow alone. They can only do this by collaborating.' [1]

Mansholt's turn came on the third day, 5 July, with a long and very detailed speech in which he reacted to what had been said over the first two days by the agriculture ministers. He reminded his audience that Article 43 of the EEC Treaty provided for fixing the outlines of a common policy and comparing the agricultural situations and policies of the various Member States. It would then be the role of the Commission to make proposals which reflected the outcome of the conference.

Mansholt pointed to the simultaneous increase in agricultural output and shrinkage of the farming population. He wondered why the level of incomes in the agricultural sector was declining relative to other sectors instead of rising, and he suggested that the Commission should start doing research on the subject. The guarantee of a reasonable income and standard of living for the farming community must be the cornerstone of the CAP. These objectives, he stressed, could not be achieved by a policy of high prices because:

'Price policy is obviously a major element in our market management policy. But it is also a risky instrument. We want to encourage reasonable earnings for farmers and farm labourers, but the big danger is that, if prices are fixed centrally, then producers on the one hand and consumers on the

other may lose touch with market forces. When setting a given price, we must not forget what the consequences will be for production, in particular if that remains linked to market forces.' [2]

In this Mansholt showed he had a premonition about the issue, and he opposed putting up the level of prices for fear of stimulating surplus production. However, we know that later he was not able to keep price movements within reasonable bounds because major disparities emerged between the prices in different Member States.

Mansholt also mentioned the need for a structural policy which, by modernising farms without putting up prices, would bring farm incomes closer to those of other occupations. In his speech he was careful not to alienate the farming organisations by maximalist calls for rationalisation. He defended the solidly run family farm and argued conservatively that only less than marginal holdings would be forced to disappear. Mansholt concluded:

'We need to understand that we do wrong to agriculture if we regard it purely as an economic factor, in particular as a provider of food and clothing. We need to see the farmer as, both sociologically and politically, an essential part of our increasingly technological world, not a museum relic or a piece of rural nostalgia but a healthy and strong independent figure. [...] Let us all agree here that we must allow the farmer to develop his own strengths.' [3]

The agenda of the conference was heavily laden. Work was conducted in plenary sessions and in three working parties. Mansholt chaired the conference. Louis Rabot acted as general secretary, assisted by von Verschuer. The aim in particular was to harmonise the various national points of view but not to seek single common solutions or undertake detailed market analysis [4]. The national standpoints were in any case well known

---

[1] ABZN, 996.412.0, 1135, Hallstein speech in Stresa, 3 July 1958.

[2] ABZN, 996.412.0, 1135, Mansholt speech in Stresa, 5 July 1958.
[3] Ibid.
[4] ABZN, 996.412.0, 1135, Comments by the Commission, 25 June 1958.

H. de Koster   Haimel Ma Mansholt   Mansholt   J. Rey L. Homan

↑
Albrecht.   Morer   Lübke

Heringa   Mansholt
mevr. mansholt
v. Verhage

The Stresa conference: 'All the farmers' unions in the Community, relevant industries and ministries were represented.
The conference generated a consensus, a friendship between farmers across Europe who had not met before.'
(Interview with Jean Flory, 3 December 2003)
Stresa conference (3 to 12 July 1958), photographs from Sicco Mansholt's album.

Émile Noël remembers Stresa

'Another memorable operation was the Stresa conference […]. An ongoing dialogue had been started between politicians and farming industry leaders, orchestrated by Presidents Mansholt and Hallstein. It was a heady mix of debates and decision-making, breakthroughs in thinking and detailed point-by-point discussions. From it emerged the broad outlines of what was to become the common agricultural policy. It was an amazing cultural melting pot. We never saw anything like it over the next 30 years.'

Extract from an interview given by Émile Noël to the *Courrier du personnel*, No 488, September 1987, pp. 23–24.

to everyone from the discussions over the 'Green Pool'. Thus, the host country Italy was concerned about excess labour in agriculture and was looking for structural reform of the sector. Germany wanted to safeguard the small family holding and was defending the maintenance of a high price level for agricultural products. As a net importer of agricultural products, it was also opposed to any discrimination with respect to third countries. The Netherlands was likewise afraid of a protectionist EEC. But, unlike Germany, it was against small farms and favoured the modernisation of production. The Dutch Minister, Vondeling, thought that the Commission had a vital role to play in attaining these ends. As a result, only proposals free from the pressures of national 'protectionist' interest groups were able to emerge. At the time of Stresa, France was deeply involved with internal political problems following the Algeria crisis and the transition from the Fourth to the Fifth Republic. It was not yet clear at that point if de Gaulle — about to make his return to the French political stage — would really accept the EEC Treaty [1].

The conference took a somewhat disordered course, with masses of reports and documents circulating among the delegations and being translated into the four official languages of the day. There was not enough comparative statistical data. Most of the figures circulating were based on individual national situations, making reliable comparisons impossible [2]. In consequence, the results of the conference for the situation in the various agriculture sectors were poor. This meant that the conference took on a mainly informative character, as a venue where specialists could meet and where points of view could be exchanged. It became a place where lobbying and intrigue abounded [3]. The attendance of representatives from the farming organisations was also very enriching for the Commission. The lobby groups, now organised at transnational level, contributed to legitimising the pioneering role played by the Commission in building the agricultural consensus. The agriculture ministers themselves, faced with discontent among their farmers at home, did not a priori block a central role for Brussels. For one thing, unloading certain issues on Mansholt and his team made it possible to divert attention from a number of domestic problems, especially the constantly growing gap in earnings between agriculture and other sectors of the economy. For another, it was a tempting road to take for governments trying to reduce the burden on national budgets. Mansholt did not hesitate for a moment. This was a unique opportunity to define the broad outline of a common policy, to block in its main principles. As a result, while the Stresa conference did not produce immediate results, it was crucial to setting the stage for the medium and long term and for developing a negotiating method.

One eyewitness remembers that, when the Commission made concessions to the Member States, this was only seemingly so. Because their reactions had been discounted in advance, the compromises which the Commission proposed ap-

[1] Lauring Knudsen, A.-Chr., *Defining the policies of a common agricultural policy — A historical study*, doctoral thesis, EUI, Florence, 2001, p. 155.

[2] Ibid, p. 157.
[3] Interview with Jean Flory, 3 December 2003.

Stresa conference
From left to right: Walter Hallstein (seen from behind), Émile Noël, Robert Lemaignen, Renée Van Hoof, Swidbert Schnippenkötter and Lambert Schaus.

peared to come from them. This was the supreme art of political psychology (¹).

As for setting the stage for the future, the final resolution, drafted by a committee under Rabot, set out a list of general propositions and gave the Commission two years to turn them into specific proposals.

On the whole, Stresa was a success measured against the context and its ambitions. It was to Mansholt's credit that the conference turned out to be more than a simple exchange of information. From the beginning, he set his own stamp on the discussions and secured the agreement of the six ministers on important points of doctrine for the future common policy. The final resolution bears this out:

— agriculture certainly has specific character but should be considered an integral part of the economy;

— the implementation of the Treaty should lead to a gradual growth of trade within the Community; at the same time, the need to maintain commercial relations and contractual, political and economic links with third countries must be taken into account; so must the possibility of protection against unfair competition from them;

(¹) ABZN 996.412.0, 1135, Linthorst Homan report, 12 July 1958.

Chronology

1958	**3–11 July:** Stresa conference.
1960	**30 June:** The Commission submits the final text of its proposals for a common agricultural policy to the Council ('Mansholt–Heringa bible').
	19–20 July: Inception of the Special Agriculture Committee (SAC).
1961	**18 December:** First agriculture marathon.
1962	**14 January:** The Council decides that the conditions are met for the second phase of the transition period, as provided for in the Treaty of Rome. Decisions are taken on various market organisations: cereals, pigmeat, poultrymeat, eggs, fruit and vegetables.
	14 January: The EEC accepts the basic principles on which a common agricultural policy will be based.
1963	**16–23 December:** Second agriculture marathon: overnight from 21 to 22 December, a package deal proposed by the Commission moves the negotiations along and finally enables an agreement to be reached between the French and German ministers. Decisions are taken on milk products, beef and veal, and rice.
1964	**4 May:** Beginning of the Kennedy Round (lasting until 15 May 1967).
	12–15 December: Third marathon: Council decision on common cereal prices.
1965	**31 March:** The Commission proposes a new regulation on financing the CAP with own resources and budgetary control by the European Parliament.
	30 June: Beginning of the 'empty chair' crisis.
1966	**17–18 and 20–29 January:** Negotiations in Luxembourg lead to the 'Luxembourg compromise'. On the basis of an agreement to disagree, it is decided that work within the Council will resume.
	May to July: Provisional fixing of a financial regulation. Agreement on a common agricultural policy.
1967	**1 July:** A common market starts for cereals, pigmeat, eggs and poultrymeat.
1968	**18 December:** Memorandum on the reform of agriculture called 'Agriculture 1980' (the 'Mansholt Plan') proposed to the Council.
1969	**1 and 2 December:** Conference at The Hague. Consensus on a regulation on financing the common agricultural policy, including an own-resources system for the EEC and a degree of oversight by the European Parliament over Community expenditure.
	19–22 December: Agriculture marathon: the Council decides to open the final phase of the common market.
1970	**29 April:** The Commission submits a reform proposal, the Mansholt Plan.
1972	**13–15 March:** Agriculture marathon.
	20–24 March: Council decision on social and structural measures and prices.
1973	**22–24 January:** First agriculture marathon with nine Member States.

— the efforts made to increase productivity should permit the application of a price policy which would simultaneously avoid over-production and leave room for competition;

— the improvement of agricultural structures should keep incomes comparable with those obtainable in other sectors of the economy, thus anticipating the future Mansholt Plan.

The Commission proposal of 1960

Mansholt and his staff immediately set to work to achieve some results within the time frame that had been set. During this interlude the Council of Ministers held back, in expectation of receiving concrete proposals from Brussels. Between Stresa and the unveiling of the plan, only a few informal Council meetings concerning a future CAP took place. No final decisions were taken at those meetings. This gave a free hand to the Commission. Through Rencki, it kept close contact with the non-governmental organisations such as COPA. In addition, some 30 inter-trade advisory committees were created under the Commission's aegis. The Commission also took account of the opinions of the Economic and Social Committee ([1]).

Mansholt presented the Commission proposals in June 1960, and they included variable levies to protect the European market against excessive imports from outside. The stress was on a common policy for market management and price support that was intended to contribute to stabilising agricultural markets and guaranteeing a reasonable income for farmers. For a transitional period that was to last until June 1967, it was planned to introduce single prices gradually for a number of basic products, starting with cereals. The level of EEC prices was to be higher than on the world market. These proposals were obviously favourable to farmers, who could hope for improved profitability for their products, but less

---

([1]) Interview with Helmut von Verschuer, 3 March 2004.

Mansholt on decision-making involving the CAP

'I am convinced that I would never have got the agricultural policy going and certainly not its market management components if I had not had to force the Council of Ministers, by dint of preparation, incitement and persuasion, to take certain decisions. It is important to know that the Council cannot take decisions except on the basis of Commission proposals. According to the Treaty, the Council can take a decision in line with a Commission proposal by majority vote, but it can depart from the proposal only if the vote is unanimous. Here resides part of the power of the Commission. But this power was weakened and that was what President de Gaulle was after in requiring unanimity in all cases. Not only did this make the Council practically unable to function, it also prevented the Commission from exerting a very major influence. At the same time, thanks to the rule of unanimity, the Commission is able to build a position which gives it major influence. If, for example, we had simply put forward proposals on each common organisation of the market, there would probably never have been any decision. The Treaty does not, in fact, say that the Council has to adopt a decision on a proposal. And my fear was always that a policy might not be pursued for lack of decisions being taken by the Council. This has actually happened in a number of cases. But, at the time when we were tabling the proposals on the CAP, we, by which I mean the Commission, always took care not to make them in a vacuum but to link them to other proposals, to other necessities. Not formally linked, but I always tried to construct a political link and I often pulled it off.'

Mansholt, S. L., *De Crisis*, Contact, Amsterdam, 1975, pp. 43–44.
(Translated from the Dutch)

favourable to consumers in the importing countries, who would have to pay more for their food. It was feared that this would increase the cost of living in these countries. Many attributed this complex system to the influence that the Frenchmen Marjolin and Rabot had over Mansholt. The Commissioner, Robert Marjolin, had already said out loud that the EEC 'could be free-trading in the industrial sphere but protectionist in the agricultural sector' ([1]). Rabot was very well informed about what French agriculture circles were thinking, and he knew that French farmers like their colleagues in other countries and more generally across the industrialised world were not attracted to a system open to the world market.

The plan was criticised within the Commission, in particular by Hans von der Groeben, who became a partisan of the system applied in the United Kingdom, i.e. deficiency payments as direct aid to farmers. Compared with the price policy proposed by Mansholt, this system would allow free imports of products at world market prices. But, aside from his compatriot Hallstein, von der Groeben found only scant support for his ideas. In the college of Commissioners, his amendments were systematically rejected ([2]). In fact, the 'deficiency payments' system was practical only in a country with net imports like the United Kingdom. Mansholt believed that the world price was merely the unstable result of the dumping policies practised by all the large producing countries. The world market was nothing but a 'wastepaper basket', he said ([3]).

The main attention was on market and price policy, but the Commission plan also made a little room for structural measures. The Commission would be making annual recommendations to intensify structural activities on the ground and special aid was to be granted for improving structures through a specially created section of a European fund, the EAGGF. It was clear that the Member States intended to remain the main authorities responsible for these measures. At an earlier stage, Mansholt had said that a common structural policy was at least as important as a price policy, because structural measures would help to lower farm prices. But this idea remained

> ### Commission proposal on the price mechanism
>
> 'In order to achieve, in the interests of Community producers and consumers, the necessary stabilisation of agricultural markets, the excessive influence of fluctuations in world market prices on the agricultural markets of the Community must be warded off.
>
> In addition, account should be taken of the fact that the production conditions and characteristics of the Community's farming enterprises are not the same as in some non-European countries which are major agricultural exporters. Furthermore, the prices of agricultural products on the world market are often distorted artificially. This is why, generally speaking, prices for agricultural products inside the Community cannot have the same level as those obtaining on the world market but must be stabilised at a higher level. All the efforts made must, however, aim at improving the conditions of production and the productivity of Community agriculture and at obtaining a normalisation of conditions on the world market.'
>
> Translation (from the French) of an extract from AHCE, COM(60) 105, 30 June 1960, Part II, paragraph 43.

a dead letter despite an agreement wrung from the Council to allocate one third of EAGGF spending to structural measures ([4]). The Member States just did not want to play along. Years later, Mansholt was to say that he had acted deliberately. He wanted first to make the marketplace the driving force so as to be able to harmonise and modernise production structures at a later stage. He felt the reverse would not have been possible ([5]). But, in practice, it quickly became evident that the lack of suitable structural measures would weigh very heavily on the developing CAP.

([1]) ABZN, 996 EEG 1955-64, 1138, Codebericht Linthorst Homan 289, 4 November 1959.
([2]) PV 63, EC Commission, 10 and 11 June 1959; PV 76, EEC Commission, 5–7 October 1959; PV 78, EEC Commission, 22–24 October 1959; PV 80, EEC Commission, 2–3 November 1959.
([3]) Interview with Georges Rencki, 13 January 2004.

([4]) Ibid.
([5]) Mansholt, S. L., De Crisis, Contact, Amsterdam, 1975, pp. 88–89.

The night of the cereals

The question of the price of cereals occupied a central place in the implementation of the market and price policy. It was of capital importance to introduce common prices for the main cereals (wheat, rye, barley, maize) because they would determine the price levels of almost all the other agricultural products and indirectly the level of external protection. For a long time the Commission put off tackling this issue because of the expected resistance from the Member States, especially Germany. The Germans had a high guaranteed price for cereals at national level and their farmers did not want this interfered with at European level. At the end of 1963, however, Mansholt proposed harmonising prices in one step with effect from the 1964 harvest. He thought uniform prices would help with social harmonisation since it would be a way of levelling out incomes. Mansholt's tough stance caused astonishment and opposition all round, right to the core of the Commission. Among the Commissioners, the heaviest resistance came from Hallstein and von der Groeben, who, for political and psychological reasons, insisted that farmers affected by a price drop should be given fulsome compensation [1]. The opposition of the German Commissioners to Mansholt's proposal on prices did not come out of the blue. Through their *cabinets*, they had been attentively following the situation at home. And the Commissioners' independence clearly had its limits. Heringa in DG VI wondered whether it was clever to take on the Member States in this way [2]. But Mansholt held firm. By dint of majority votes, he forced the German Commissioners to accept his proposal [3].

The Commission had an excellent trump card to make the ministers agree. The Kennedy Round was looming, when questions of trade — and of customs tariffs — would be negotiated at world level, in particular with the United States. If the European countries maintained their point of view and did not find a consensus in time, this could harm cooperation at world level and the individual positions of the Member States, more especially since the German government attached great importance to the success of the Kennedy Round in view of the likely cut in tariffs for industrial products round the world.

But the German Agriculture Minister, Werner Schwarz, fought his corner tooth and nail. Under heavy pressure from the farming unions, he adopted a very radical position in the discussions within the Council over the price of cereals. A slightly lower price level than in Germany was acceptable only if at the same time Brussels would set up a very generous system of protective measures to compensate for farmers' losses. He demanded for this purpose an annual amount of DEM 700 000 000 up to 1970. It was a stand with which he could win few friends, especially within the Commission, in France and in the Netherlands. The Dutch wanted to lower these prices considerably and did not want to enter into long and expensive commitments to compensation. Paris was particularly determined. At this point, France had the lowest prices in the Community and France's interests were therefore diametrically opposed to those of Germany. De Gaulle and his Agriculture Minister, Pisani, feared an unacceptable rise in consumer prices in France and threatened to sabotage the Kennedy Round that was just beginning and to which Germany attached such great importance. They made it a firm condition that the common market in agriculture should start at the same moment as the common market in industrial goods.

The negotiations in Brussels made painfully slow progress. The issue became still more complicated when Italy came up late in the day with new demands concerning its fruit and vegetable sector. The Italians also felt that the possible introduction of common prices for cereals could wait several more years. Germany called for a

---

[1] PV 247, EEC Commission, 30 October 1963; PV 248, EEC Commission, 4 November 1963.

[2] Molegraaf, J., op. cit., p. 162.

[3] COM(63) 430 of 11 November 1963. Von der Groeben did not give up easily. When his colleague Hallstein was absent, he proposed that he cast his vote by telephone. However, despite Hallstein's vote, von der Groeben did not manage to secure the necessary majority.

Chancellor Erhard on the pricing of cereals (March 1964)

'The current prices of cereals in Germany are not thought to be excessive in view of relative output and costs. The Federal government will therefore not approve any price reduction in cereals for the 1964 and 1965 marketing years. And I have no way of knowing at this juncture at what date and on what terms the Federal Republic of Germany might be prepared to adopt different arrangements on this issue.'

Müller-Roschach, H., *Die deutsche Europapolitik 1949–1977 — Eine politische Chronik*, Europa Union, Bonn, 1980, p. 85. (Translated from the German)

postponement until 1970. The differences of opinion were worsening the whole situation. The Commission was waiting for the most opportune moment to propose a final compromise.

As already said, Mansholt intended to profit from the Kennedy Round in a bid to secure agreement on single prices for cereals. He knew that these trade talks, to which the German government was attached not only for economic but also for political reasons, were not likely to succeed if the agreement was confined only to industrial products.

He argued that it was not possible to negotiate the level of protection for Community agriculture if common farm prices were not fixed first (at least for cereals given their essential role) because these were precisely the prices which would determine the degree of protection in agriculture. This put Germany in an embarrassing position as the country refusing to complete the CAP by blocking common prices.

Mansholt piled on even more pressure: he declared publicly that he doubted the political will of the German government to negotiate with the Americans in the GATT! This statement immedi-

ately garnered a public protest from the finance minister, who said he was 'outraged' by Mansholt's speech. The future would show that the tactics were right, as the debate in the Council began under better auspices.

By the last phase of this exhausting battle, on 15 December 1964, there were only Mansholt and the six ministers left in the room ([1]). All the officials had been sent home. Mansholt kept trying in his droning voice to win over the negotiating parties and, like a true schoolmaster, explained the intricate problems at a blackboard ([2]). In the meantime, he had made the Italian proposal for a delay his own. The new rules would not be introduced until 1967. During one of the many adjournments, late into the evening, Mansholt, his confidant Rabot and Heringa met in a Provençal restaurant on the Petit Sablon to see what room for negotiation still remained. The three diners were of one opinion. Each minister should be able to return home to his country with some result. Nobody should lose, no minister could be left by the wayside against his will ([3]). As far as possible everybody had to be satisfied, with a small compensatory levy here and a customs duty there ([4]).

Mansholt remembers: 'After an hour of work, I went back to the room at the Council where the ministers were waiting. They were ready to explode. I thought: "This is the best moment. Let's go for it!" I had not even been able to consult my colleagues and they had no idea what I was going to do. That night I achieved something I was never able to carry off again. I said: "Gentlemen, we have to arrive at a conclusion. I will make a proposal but it will be all or nothing. I no longer want to hear further discussions. It is only on these terms that I will table this compromise proposal."' ([5]).

---

[1] Actually there were five ministers left since Schwarz, the German Agriculture Minister, was replaced in the last phase of the negotiations by his State Secretary, Rudolf Hüttebräuker.
[2] Molegraaf, J., op. cit., pp. 9–10.
[3] Interview with Rudolf Dumont du Voitel, 1 December 2003.
[4] Interview with Jean Flory, 3 December 2003.
[5] Mansholt, S., *De Crisis*, op. cit., p. 86.

France's ultimatum (October 1964)

'Without prejudging the outcome of the talks, General de Gaulle, Mr Pompidou and the government once again stressed that France would cease to participate in the European Economic Community if the common market in agriculture were not to be organised as it has been agreed that it would be organised. The resolution adopted by the Council was expressed in the most unequivocal way, such as to make the common market in agriculture the touchstone of future European integration and the very precondition for it. This was an unequivocal reaffirmation of the view which has always been held by France, the firmness of which has however been doubted by some of our partners. There is no possibility of negotiating usefully with the United States until the European Economic Community, agriculture included, is fully in place. These two issues are considered key, and France will hold this line.'

Extract from ABZN, 913.100, blok II, 6383, Het Franse dreigement van 21 oktober 1964, 21 October 1964. (Translated from the French)

After 10 minutes of hesitation, this unusual ultimatum was accepted. Dawn was breaking outside. Amid a deathly hush, Mansholt read the proposal out. He then looked at the ministers one after the other. The German still seemed to have serious doubts.

'I said: "[…] It is a question of yes or no." The Commission could withdraw its proposal at any moment and then there would be no more proposals. Deathly silence […] The session broke up […] for half an hour. We then resumed and went round the table. There were six yeses […] we had won.' (¹) In practical terms, the Council had agreed on the prices for cereals and decided to implement the single market in agriculture as from 1 July 1967. This meant three years gained on the date originally foreseen of 1 January 1970 (²).

Mansholt believed that this night had been decisive for the common agricultural policy itself. If he had not won through at this point, it would have been practically impossible to complete the CAP. The dominant role played by the Commission is once again in evidence. Since then, it has become current practice for the Commission to table compromise proposals in order to foreclose interminable negotiations in the Council.

Mansholt's enormous personal contribution to this success does not, however, fully explain it. Other factors also counted. The German minister, Schwarz, met with a great deal of opposition in his own country, in industry circles and even within his own government. President de Gaulle too put a very clear ultimatum to Chancellor Erhard: if there were no resolution over the price of cereals, French collaboration in all other fields would be threatened. The alliance between Mansholt and the two Frenchmen made a major step forward in the agriculture sector possible. The Dutch Agriculture Minister was an equally enthusiastic supporter of a common policy. Contrary to their consumer organisations, the French and Dutch farmers found higher cereals prices very tempting. It was mainly German agriculture which, having become accustomed to a higher price level than the one agreed, had to make an effort. For non-member countries, the EEC decision fell short. The agreed European price was well above the world average and the EEC market was protected from imports by the variable external tariffs (levies).

(¹) Mansholt, S., *De Crisis*, op. cit., p. 86.
(²) Georges Rencki's course on the CAP, College of Europe, 2005, and interview with Georges Rencki, 13 January 2004.

The 'empty chair' crisis and the Luxembourg compromise

Meanwhile, agriculture was increasingly becoming the driving force of European integration. In the mid-1960s, the EEC was above all about agriculture. It accounted for 95 % of the budget, 90 % of legislation and 70 % of ministers' meeting time ([1]).

During the marathon on cereals prices in December 1964, the Council of Ministers asked the Commission to produce a proposal on financing agriculture for the period up to 1 January 1970. A decision on this had to be taken by 1 July 1965. Under the leadership of Hallstein and Mansholt, however, the Commission decided to propose an earlier date. Fired by the harmonisation of cereals prices, as recounted above, and by other favourable developments, it cherished the hope that the transition phase could be terminated in July 1967. To this end, it proposed advancing rapidly to a permanent financial settlement involving own resources for the Commission, to come from customs duties and agricultural levies. These would also help fund the CAP ([2]). Another important part of the Commission's proposal was the budget powers conferred on the European Parliament.

When these proposals began to leak out at the beginning of 1965, the Commission did not hesitate: it sent all its proposals to Parliament without any political preparation. This behaviour by the Commission, perceived as brazen and authoritarian, caused great irritation to President de Gaulle. At this point there had, in fact, been a kind of alliance between de Gaulle and Mansholt because of their convergent interests. But this alliance came to an end in 1965. The French President considered the package of Commission proposals to be pure blackmail. Although he supported a final settlement on financing the CAP, he could not accept that the Commission was proposing a greater supranational role for the Community. It was quickly obvious that the imminent extension of majority voting as a general rule within the Council of Ministers was the determining factor in de Gaulle's opposition to the Commission's plans. Paris found it unacceptable to give up its veto within the Council. Relations between Paris and the EEC Commission quickly cooled ([3]).

By January 1966 the Community was back at work again even though the Luxembourg compromise was anything but a compromise. Mansholt described it publicly as 'an agreement to disagree' ([4]). Some thought that de Gaulle had come out the clear winner and that he had firmly put the Commission in its place. Edmund Wellenstein did not share this view. He even called the compromise 'a total defeat for de Gaulle'. Wellenstein pointed out, that despite the uproar, the French President had accepted that the Treaty should be applied in accordance with the wishes of the other five Member States. The '10 commandments' that France had put on the table and were intended to limit the powers of the Commission contained few substantial points. Its importance was more cosmetic than substantive. The consternation caused by France's blocking of majority decision-making within the Council is put in perspective by Wellenstein. Ultimately, the national delegations agreed in Luxembourg that, if unanimity appeared unattainable, their difference of opinion would not prevent the work of the Commission from resuming according to the normal procedures. The Five did not give up majority voting ([5]).

But the position of Hallstein and Mansholt, whom France regarded as the instigators of the crisis, was undeniably weakened. After it, Hallstein decided not to seek a further term as President. Mansholt stayed on but he no longer played the role of lead policymaker. His former ally, Pisani, was obliged by de Gaulle to leave the field.

([1]) Merriënboer, J. C. F. J. (van), 'Het avontuur van Sicco Mansholt', http://www.ru.nl/contents/pages/22864/mansholt_.pdf, p. 16 (article published in *Politieke Opstellen*, No 15–16, 1995–96, pp. 136–168).

([2]) Molegraaf, J., op. cit., pp. 187–188.

([3]) See Chapter 4.

([4]) Personal files of Georges Rencki, manuscript of the speech by Mansholt to the fifth general meeting of the free trade unions.

([5]) Interview with Edmund P. Wellenstein, 17 December 2003.

The agriculture talks started up again on 30 January 1966. The Commission and Mansholt persuaded the Council to agree on the financial issues for the period up to 1970, with own resources included. Between the end of 1966 and July 1968 the single market gradually came into effect for agricultural products.

A structural policy for agriculture (the Mansholt Plan)

Once common farm prices were finally introduced in 1967 (a harmonised price was henceforth set for products other than cereals), the Commission and Mansholt turned their attention to the long-deferred question of social and structural policy. This issue had already been raised at an earlier stage, in particular in Stresa. But concrete results had not ensued. Guaranteed prices at too high a level were creating surpluses which the Commission and the Member States could not control. Very quickly there were 'butter mountains' to cope with. The EEC intervention agencies were required to buy-in some of the surpluses at intervention prices and bear the costs of storage. Most of the rest was sold on the world market (where prices were lower) with the help of export subsidies ('export refunds'), which was tantamount to dumping. In this way, the CAP became very expensive while at the same time harming the environment and discriminating against non-member countries. Moreover, the hoped-for parity of incomes was de facto an illusion. Despite the protection at EEC borders and the unlimited funding of production, the standard of living of the farming population remained below that of other commercial sectors. Smallholders especially were struggling, with intervention proving most rewarding for large producers. The CAP had the perverse effect of encouraging the big to the detriment of the small [1]. So much so that Heringa admitted that the EEC had lost its

way: 'The French call it a cul-de-sac. It gave the feeling of leading nowhere.' [2]

It was absolutely essential to curb production. Mansholt came under heavy pressure from all sides to come up with an answer. On 10 December 1968 he proposed a plan (the Agriculture 80 memorandum) which raised a major debate in European agriculture circles. He put forward an overall solution to the agriculture problem. The 'Mansholt Plan' was written in collaboration with everybody in the directorate-general, Rencki being appointed head of the division for production structures. The Commission forecast that by around 1980 almost half of the 10 million producers in the EEC would have given up farming.

The Mansholt memorandum was based on three considerations. Each one was matched by a different type of aid.

— Since a steady growth in guaranteed prices was no longer politically acceptable, it was vital to provide aid towards investment in modernising holdings (and in marketing) for farmers who intended to remain in farming. The aim was to help them attain an income comparable with incomes in other sectors of the economy.

— The CAP was to be given the means to support those who wished to leave farming, either because of their age (over 55) or because they were going into another activity.

— Energetic measures would be taken by the Community to reduce production surpluses by ensuring a better balance between demand and the volume of output, by withdrawing 5 million hectares from production out of a total of 70 million, in particular by reafforestation, and getting rid of approximately 3 million dairy cows.

[1] Remarks made to Michel Dumoulin by Hartmut Offele on 3 May 2005.

[2] Quoted from Westerman, F., De Graanrepubliek, Atlas, Amsterdam, 2003, p. 171.

These latter measures, designed to counterbalance the effect of aid towards modernising holdings, which would often lead to increased production, were considered by the Commission to be absolutely essential.

Financing these measures was to be achieved partly by cutting prices and limiting surpluses and partly by an extra financial contribution from the Member States.

Mansholt travelled throughout the Community trying to get his plan accepted by the farmers. But the initial reactions that he met with were very mixed. He found support from all the Italian agricultural organisations, with the 'agriculture godfather' Bonomi in particular convinced of the need to make adjustments. Of all the Member States, Italy was the one which, having invested least in its own structural policy, had most to gain from an EEC policy. Although the Netherlands backed structural reforms, the Dutch thought that they should be achieved through national policies, above all for financial reasons. In France, Minister Pisani, Mansholt's long-time ally, had disappeared from the scene and the government was sceptical; although accepting structural measures of this kind, it feared the high cost of the European reform plan. Mansholt also had the support of the leading French cereals producer, who had helped him in 1964 by putting up cereals prices, and the general secretary of the French farmers' union (FNSEA), Debatisse, as well as from within the young farmers' trade union (CNJA).

During a special meeting held at Val-Duchesse between Mansholt and COPA, it became obvious that some of the dissatisfaction in agriculture stemmed from the slowness of progress in coordinating economic policies: excessive currency fluctuations, the generalised inflation which adversely affected agricultural production costs, etc. COPA called for a significant price increase, referring to the general rise in wages and prices in the Member States. It wanted to make the structural measures — which it thought desirable — conditional on such an increase. The calls were especially strong in Germany and Belgium, where small-scale farmers had for a long time been facing major difficulties in the management of their holdings. They were afraid that the Brussels plan, involving a cut in prices, would prove the last straw. German farmers had bad memories of the price cut that Mansholt had imposed on them a few years earlier. Tension was rising and opinions were becoming politicised. The leaders of the German 'Bauernverband' accused Mansholt of wanting to introduce 'kolkhozes' and demanded his resignation. During a public event at the Ostseehalle in Kiel, Mansholt was prevented from speaking for four hours. Scuffles broke out and the police had to intervene to calm things down. The Belgian farmers' union also focused on him and organised huge demonstrations. The ways of expressing discontent were sometimes unconventional. When Mansholt gave a speech in Flemish Zeeland, near the Belgian border, farmers threatened to block the ferry boats and the speech had to be moved further north under heightened police surveillance. The denigration and threats against Mansholt personally from the agriculture organisations of certain countries mounted, while the European trade unions of farm labourers and European consumer organisations supported him. As did UNICE and the EEC craft industry.

And the agriculture ministers themselves? They were careful not to compromise themselves by backing a controversial plan. Even the departure of de Gaulle did not improve the climate. In autumn 1969, as a result of the devaluation of the French franc and the revaluation of the German mark, the Community market and price policy came under heavy pressure. For a time, Germany was even threatening to introduce its own prices policy. In all the member countries irritation was growing. COPA called for the convening of a conference of the Six to discuss a common monetary policy.

Despite all these difficulties, after a 45-hour Council marathon and thanks in particular to the dogged support of the Italian minister, Natali,

A surprise visitor to the Council meeting on agriculture on 15 February 1971 — a cow accompanies the group of farmers invading the meeting room and holding up proceedings. Michel Cointat, French Minister of Agriculture, looks thoughtful, to say the least.

Mansholt succeeded on 24 March 1971 in having the essence of his agricultural structural policy accepted.

The Council adopted three of the four so-called 'socio-structural' directives; these set out the measures to be implemented by the Member States, i.e. investment aid under a 'development plan' designed to make a holding viable, an early re-tirement scheme predicated on handing over the holding to new entrants to farming under the 'development plan', and the creation of a body of socioeconomic advisers.

The adoption of these texts, which formed the starting point for other measures, in particular concerning the less-favoured areas, should not disguise the fact that the 'market' part did not match the 'structures' part. The national governments refused in fact to take action on those Commission proposals, to which the Commission attached great importance and which were designed to reduce production potential (premiums for reducing the area under cultivation and the slaughter of dairy cows), because of the sharp reactions within the agriculture sector. As a result, the atmosphere of riot and mayhem which reigned in Brussels during the final phase of the adoption of the Mansholt Plan has remained graven in people's minds. The Belgian capital was transformed into a battlefield. The confrontations between the gendarmerie and 100 000 angry farmers, mostly from Belgium and France and calling for an increase in prices and more effective farm structures, resulted in one death and at least 10 people injured. The damage to property was considerable. While expressing his satisfaction with the decisions taken by the Council, Mansholt was profoundly saddened by this unhappy turn of events.

———————

Mansholt focused his attention after that on the type of economic growth that Europe could hope for in future given the resources available, the limits to which he stressed prophetically ([1]). On becoming President of the Commission in March 1972, he turned away from the problems of agriculture for the first time since 1945. The Commission noted with regret that its reform plans were unable to bear proper fruit. As far as the agriculture ministers were concerned, price support and market management had priority because — in contrast to the measures for improving agricultural structures — they were 100 % funded by the Community budget. Additionally, right around the time of enlargement, the world market saw farm prices for several important products rise to much higher levels than in the Community. This provided the pretext not only for increasing Community prices substantially in the spring of 1973 but also for introducing an intervention system for beef and veal and for reinforcing the guarantees under the common organisation of the market in sugar. At this point Pierre Lardinois was the Commissioner responsible for agriculture and Jacques Chirac was one of the agriculture ministers. Then, in July 1973, the Community introduced export levies for cereals, rice and sugar with a view to safeguarding the security of supplies, after the United States brought in a ban on soya exports in June 1973. The work achieved by the six governments and the Commission was considerable. If the CAP was not always entirely rational (as regards prices in particular), that can be explained by the forces that were operating and the state of thinking at the time. Adjustments would come later. The CAP was by now the best known of the Community's activities (the daily lives of almost a quarter of the population were affected by it). The creation of the CAP was a major contribution through which the divergent interests of the Member States became, to a great extent and almost miraculously, mutually complementary. It is worth underlining that the spillover effect from the agricultural policy helped bring about European integration. As one of the insiders said: 'It represented real experience of Community cooperation without which Europe would not have […] achieved the progress that it did and continues to achieve.' ([2])

Agriculture provided a stimulus to later integration, and Mansholt and his DG VI were largely responsible.

Jan van der Harst

———————

([1]) See the chapter on Sicco Mansholt, pp. 175–178 and the box on pp. 414–416.

([2]) Pisani, E., *Persiste et signe*, Odile Jacob, Paris, 1992, p. 214.

At a farmers' demonstration in 1971, one of the banners reads:
'Mansholt, you are depriving the farmers around Courtrai of their income. Here are the gallows you deserve.'

Chapter 17

The Commission's role in external relations

If, as Émile Noël wrote in July 1958, the common market was as important politically as it was economically [1], it is clear why the Commission should have wanted to develop its presence in the world by various means and why non-member countries were so eager to be represented in Brussels and to negotiate agreements with an organisation on the rise. Moreover, the Treaties provided for the Commission to negotiate association and trade agreements with Greece, Turkey, the Associated African Countries and Madagascar (AACM), and the Mediterranean countries [2].

The Commission takes steps to organise itself

It is therefore necessary to understand how the Commission set about devising a foreign trade policy and laying down the principles guiding its external action, in short, how it tackled four issues: the offer to create a free-trade area in western Europe, the reciprocal liberalisation of trade under the General Agreement on Tariffs and Trade (GATT), non-

member countries' requests for association and relations with international organisations.

The Commission's international role was underpinned by Article 110 of the EEC Treaty, which defined its missions as follows:

'By establishing a customs union between themselves, Member States aim to contribute, in the common interest, to the harmonious development of world trade, the progressive abolition of restrictions on international trade and the lowering of customs barriers.

The common commercial policy shall take into account the favourable effect which the abolition of customs duties between Member States may have on the increase in the competitive strength of undertakings in those States.'

In the words of Edmund P. Wellenstein, 'This article sets out a wide-ranging political agenda that will attract attention all over the world. Structures left totally fragmented by the Great Depression of the 1930s and the war are going to be turned upside down by the emergence of a major new trading power proclaiming its readiness to negotiate the

---

[1] FJME, ARM 19/2/1, memo by Émile Noël on current European issues, 26 July 1958.
[2] See the Sequence of events.

Members of the Commission responsible for external relations and trade 1958–72

1. **Jean Rey** in the first and second Hallstein Commissions (10 January 1958 to 9 January 1962, then 10 January 1962 to 5 January 1967).

2. **Jean-François Deniau** at Trade and **Edoardo Martino** at External Relations in the 14-member Rey Commission (6 July 1967 to 1 July 1970)

3. **Ralf Dahrendorf** at External Relations and Trade in the Malfatti Commission (2 July 1970 to 21 March 1972) and the nine-member Mansholt Commission (to 5 January 1973)

gradual abolition of barriers to international trade. The Commission will play a key role in the process. Article 111 would apply from the very start of the Community's internal transitional period.' [1]

If Member States abolished or reduced quantitative restrictions in relation to third countries, they were required to inform the Commission beforehand and accord the same treatment to other Member States.

After the transitional period, Article 113 would enter into force:

'1. After the transitional period has ended, the common commercial policy shall be based on uniform principles, particularly in regard to changes in tariff rates, the conclusion of tariff and trade agreements, the achievement of uniformity in measures of liberalisation, export policy and measures to protect trade such as those to be taken in case of dumping or subsidies [2].'

The Commission, Article 113 continues, 'shall submit proposals to the Council for implementing the common commercial policy', negotiate agreements with third countries with the Council's authorisation and 'conduct these negotiations in consultation with a special committee appointed by the Council'. From the start of the transitional period [3], the Commission strove, against the opinion of the leading governments, to extend the scope of its exclusive powers in international trade negotiations. It sought to tighten control over the Member States' use of derogations under Article 115. It asked to negotiate economic and industrial cooperation agreements and trade agreements. It called for the transitional period to be cut short and got its way. Cut from 12 years to ten and a half, the transitional period ended on 1 July 1968.

Preparing trade negotiations

Trade negotiations were prepared by the EEC Commission's directorates-general and by the Commissioners' *cabinets*. Jean Rey, the member of the Hallstein Commission (1958–67) responsible for external relations, conducted the common commercial policy with the help of Directorate-General I (External Relations). Under the responsibility of Günther Seeliger, who was DG I's director-general from 1958 to 1964, GATT negotiations were handled by Theodorus Hijzen, the head of Directorate A (General affairs, multilateral trade policy). De-

---

[1] Memo from Edmund P. Wellenstein to Julie Cailleau and Natacha Wittorski, late February 2006, p. 5.

[2] Article 113, *Extraits du traité instituant la Communauté économique européenne et documents annexes*, 25 March 1957, published by the Secretariat of the Interim Committee for the Common Market and Euratom, Brussels.

---

[3] Article 8 of the EEC Treaty laid down a 12-year transitional period.

Article 111 of the EEC Treaty

'The following provisions shall, without prejudice to Articles 115 and 116, apply during the transitional period:

1. Member States shall coordinate their trade relations with third countries so as to bring about, by the end of the transitional period, the conditions needed for implementing a common policy in the field of external trade.

The Commission shall submit to the Council proposals regarding the procedure for common action to be followed during the transitional period and regarding the achievement of uniformity in their commercial policies.

2. The Commission shall submit to the Council recommendations for tariff negotiations with third countries in respect of the common customs tariff.

The Council shall authorise the Commission to open such negotiations.

The Commission shall conduct these negotiations in consultation with a special committee appointed by the Council to assist the Commission in this task and within the framework of such directives as the Council may issue to it.

3. In exercising the powers conferred upon it by this Article, the Council shall act unanimously during the first two stages and by a qualified majority thereafter.

4. Member States shall, in consultation with the Commission, take all necessary measures, particularly those designed to bring about an adjustment of tariff agreements in force with third countries, in order that the entry into force of the common customs tariff shall not be delayed.

5. Member States shall aim at securing as high a level of uniformity as possible between themselves as regards their liberalisation lists in relation to third countries or groups of third countries. To this end, the Commission shall make all appropriate recommendations to Member States.'

---

partments were, Edmund Wellenstein explains, organised in such a way that responsibility for issues was always combined with geographical responsibilities. The departments responsible for the GATT, for instance, were also responsible for relations with the United States, Canada, etc., for textile arrangements with Hong Kong, etc [1]. When Jean Rey became President of the new European Commission (1967–70) resulting from the merger of the three executives, DG I was split in two. The newly created DG I, headed by Axel Herbst, was placed in the hands of Commissioner Edoardo Martino. A new DG for Trade, headed by Edmund P. Wellenstein, former Secretary-General of the High Authority of the ECSC, was assigned to new Commissioner Jean-François Deniau, who was responsible not just for trade but for relations with the United States, Canada, South Africa, Australia, New Zealand, Japan, the Far East and the state-trading countries (the Eastern Bloc), for GATT negotiations and for relations with the OECD. In 1970, in the Commission headed by Franco Maria Malfatti, Ralf Dahrendorf, the Commissioner responsible for external relations, worked with DG I and DG XI (Trade). Jean-François Deniau had, in the meantime, been asked to set up a much needed task force headed by Edmund Wellenstein to prepare accession negotiations with countries wishing to join the Communities. Hijzen therefore replaced Wellenstein as Director-General of DG XI (Trade).

The Commission conducted trade negotiations in consultation with a special committee appointed by the Council to assist the Commission in this task [2]. Made up of officials of the Member States and the Commission, the special committee (initially referred to as the '111 Committee', it became

---

[1] NB: This text owes much to Edmund P. Wellenstein, who agreed to supplement it and suggest changes in four letters to the author dated 28 July, 10 and 25 August and 7 September 2005. Letter from Edmund P. Wellenstein to the author, 25 August 2005, p. 1.

[2] This special committee was cited twice, in Articles 111 and 113. Article 111 was repealed in 1992 because it referred to the transitional period.

Organisation chart of the Directorates-General for External Relations and Trade from 1958 to 1972
Organisation chart of the Directorate-General for External Relations (DG I)

Director-General for External Relations	1958–64: Günther Seeliger (German) 1965–69: Axel Herbst (German) 1970–72: Helmut Sigrist (German)	
	DIRECTORATE	**DIRECTOR**
Directorate A ([¹])	1958–64: General affairs, relations with international organisations	1958–67: Theodorus Hijzen (NL)
	1965–67: General affairs, multilateral trade policy	
	1968: General affairs, external relations in the scientific, technical and nuclear fields	1968–72: Walter Pauly (D)
Directorate B	1958–64: Relations with third countries	1958–64: Jean-François Deniau (F)
	1965–67: Western Europe, accession and association	1965–68: Robert Toulemon (F)
	1968–70: External relations with European countries, accessions, association, preferential agreements	1969–70: Roland de Kergolay (F)
	1971: Relations with the Mediterranean countries.	1971: Josephus Loeff (NL)
Directorate C	1958–64: Bilateral relations	1958–72: Robert Faniel (B)
	1965–67: Trade policy towards developing countries	1963–72: Mattia Di Martino (I)
	1968: General policy towards developing countries, bilateral relations and economic organisations of the United Nations	
Directorate D (1958–67) ([¹])	Trade policy (negotiations)	1958–67: Wolfgang Ernst (D)
5th Directorate until 1965	Director earmarked for a posting abroad, responsible for special coordination tasks	1958–64: Riccardo Luzzatto (I) 1964–65: Adolphe De Baerdemaeker (B)

([¹]) In 1967 these two directorates and their staff merged to form the new Directorate-General for Trade.

Organisation chart of the Directorate-General for Trade (DG XI), set up in 1967

Director-General for Trade	Edmund Wellenstein (Dutch), **1967–73** (Theodorus Hijzen, ad interim, **1970–73**)	
	DIRECTORATE	**DIRECTOR**
Directorate A	Commercial policy: Multilateral questions and agricultural questions	**1967–73:** Theodorus Hijzen (Dutch)
		1971: Alexandre Stakhovitch (French of Russian origin)
Directorate B	Commercial policy: Objectives, instruments and industrial questions	**1968–72:** Wolfgang Ernst (German)

DG XI was also responsible for relations with the non-member countries and international organisations handled by these directorates, namely:

— the United States of America, Canada, Australia, New Zealand, South Africa, the Far East, Japan and the countries of eastern Europe;

— GATT and the OECD.

the '113 Committee' when the transitional period expired) met for the first time in February 1959. Senior officials from Member States and DGs could also attend informal meetings chaired by the Commission [1].

Starting in 1962, negotiations were prepared inside the Commission by a Trade Policy Committee (TPC), which was made up of officials from the directorates-general involved and which reported to the more political External Relations Group [2]. The TPC comprised Commissioners Rey, Marjolin, Petrilli (succeeded by Colonna di Paliano from 1962 to 1967) and Caron. In 1967 the Single Commission set up an internal commercial policy group to coordinate the activities of the External Relations and Trade DGs, and in 1971 a working party headed by the Director-General of DG Trade drew up the objectives of external economic policy [3].

This organisation did not prevent friction between the Commission and the Council. When the Permanent Representatives Committee (Coreper) asked the Commission to present the second memorandum on the common commercial policy to the European Parliamentary Assembly, it was told that the Commission had the absolute right to decide, if it saw fit, to transmit the memorandum to the European Parliament [4]. It reminded Coreper that it alone was entitled to make proposals to the Council [5]. The Commission also had to defend its position as sole GATT negotiator, which France contested on the grounds that such negotiations were not just a matter of international trade but of international economic relations [6].

---

[1] 'Trade policy issues', COM(60) 129, 22 July 1960.

[2] PV 257, EEC Commission, 15 January 1964, XVII, pp. 23–24.

[3] 'Organisation of Directorates-General for External Relations and Trade', SEC(71) 3603/2, 15 October 1971.

[4] PV 192, EEC Commission, 4 July 1962, III.4, p. 11.

[5] PV spéc. 292, EEC Commission, 3–4 November 1964, VII, p. 7; PV 303, EEC Commission, 1965, VIII.3, pp. 18–19, shift by the Commission towards the Harkort compromise; PV spéc. 303, EEC Commission, 1965, XVIII.2, p. 10.

[6] PV spéc. 326, EEC Commission, 19 and 22 July 1965, IX, pp. 31–32; Commission's 1962 reply, used again in 1965: PV spec. 206, EEC Commission, 14 November 1962, XIII, pp. 8–9.

The joint working parties and Commission working groups produced drafts which, if approved by the College, became Commission proposals to the Council. But the ultimate instrument available to the Commission was the extraordinary power of being the Community's sole negotiator in matters of commercial policy. As Wellenstein remarks, 'I do not believe the authors of the Treaty of Rome foresaw the scale of the Community's role in the world under Articles 110, 111 and 113' [1]. Its external negotiating powers were, Wellenstein underlines [2], strengthened by the Court of Justice of the European Communities, which ruled that logically the Communities' external powers extended to areas governed by Community regulations.

Commission missions and information offices

The Commission also took organisational steps in order to exercise diplomatic and public influence outside the Community by setting up Community missions and information offices abroad. In November 1958 the Common Market Commission invited the other two European Communities to establish joint diplomatic representations abroad (the High Authority already had a fine representation in London). Euratom opened a representation in Washington in the wake of the agreement with the United States on cooperation in the peaceful applications of atomic energy. For the European Economic Community, everything began with the Communities' information offices, which were organised by Jacques-René Rabier, head of the Joint Press and Information Service, and the Commissioners responsible for the three

Communities' external relations: Rey (EEC), Wehrer (CECA) and Krekeler (Euratom) [3].

In London there had been a diplomatic representation of the High Authority since 1955, headed by Ambassador Eelco van Kleffens, a former foreign minister of the Netherlands and a figure of international standing, who was accredited by the ECSC only [4]. There was also a Communities' information office, headed by Roy Price, later succeeded by Derek Prag. Georges Berthoin, Head of the Communities' Delegation in London from 1971, recounts his freedom of action. 'The fact that I had started out in Luxembourg meant that I had no hierarchical position,' recounts this intimate of Monnet, whom he briefed on all the most sensitive developments [5]. But, at the time of the merger of the executives, Hallstein tried to assign the task of representing the three Communities to the new head of mission in London, Johannes Linthorst Homan, and to have him exercise the representative powers conferred by the ECSC Treaty on the High Authority alone. This doctrine was immediately contested by France, which refused to boost the Single Commission's diplomatic influence. Émile Noël notes that the incident 'illustrates how alert the French government is to anything with a bearing on the Community's external representation. This is no surprise to us.' [6] Jean-François Deniau reports France's reaction on another occasion: 'When I went to Washington — I was a member of the Commission at the time — to negotiate with the United States on the GATT and all that, they put me up at Blair House. The French ambassador wrote a report, made a great fuss. Yes, since they put me up like a Head of State. The Americans were still playing that old game. France was furious.' [7]

---

[1] Letter from Edmund P. Wellenstein to the author, 10 August 2005, p. 5.

[2] AETR judgment of 31 March 1971, ECJ: There was no act authorising the Community to conclude external transport agreements, but the Community had already begun laying down rules on the welfare of lorry drivers. The ECJ therefore ruled that the Community, rather than the Member States, was competent to conclude such external agreements. This judgment was of general application (see letter from Edmund P. Wellenstein to the author, 7 September 2005, p. 2).

[3] Interview with Jacques-René Rabier, 8 January 2004.

[4] Legendre, A., *Jalons pour une histoire de la diplomatie européenne: la représentation des Communautés européennes à Londres (1954–1972)*, forthcoming; *The Times*, 19 April 1971; FMJE, AMK C 8/3/68.

[5] Interview with Georges Berthoin, 31 January 2003.

[6] HAEU, EN 1158, Émile Noël to Jean Rey, 17 September 1968, incident with Jean-Marc Boegner and deputy PR Gabriel Robin; letter of 13 September 1968 from Émile Noël to Jean-Claude Paye, Barre's *chef de cabinet*.

[7] Interview with Jean-François Deniau, 3 November 2004.

Representations and liaison offices (1958–72)

Offices abroad

Cities of residence	Heads of mission
London Heads of the ECSC High Authority's delegation in the United Kingdom, which became the European Communities' delegation in 1967	**1958–59:** Jonkheer Hendrik L.F.K. van Vredenburch **1959–67:** Eelco van Kleffens **1968:** Interim head of delegation: Georges Berthoin **1970:** Johannes Linthorst Homan (Deputy head of delegation: Georges Berthoin) **1971:** Georges Berthoin
Paris Liaison by DG External Relations with the OEEC, later the OECD in Brussels The liaison office set up in 1965 became the delegation to the OECD in 1968.	**1958–65:** Theodorus Hijzen **1965–68:** Helmuth Cammann **1968–72:** Adolphe De Baerdemaeker
Geneva From 1965 onwards: liaison office with GATT (Geneva). 1968: delegation of the EC Commission to international organisations in Geneva	**1965–72:** Pierre Nicolas
Washington Prior to 1968, ECSC–Euratom representation From 1968 onward: EC Commission liaison office in Washington 1970: delegation	**1954–67:** Leonard Tennyson **1968–70:** Curt Heidenreich **1971–72:** Aldo Maria Mazio
Santiago Prior to 1968, delegation of the ECSC High Authority. After 1968, EC Commission liaison office in Santiago.	Wolfgang Renner **1968–72:** Wolfgang Renner

The fledgling Common Market Commission also recommended that a head of mission, with the rank of ambassador, be appointed to represent the three Communities in Washington, as had been done in London (¹). When Hallstein opened the joint mission in February 1960 without the Council's backing, two Member States (France and the Netherlands) approached the State Department to oppose full diplomatic recognition. There was already an ECSC information office, headed by an American, Leonard Tennyson, recruited by Jean Monnet in 1954 on the recommendation of George Ball, an old friend of the President of the High Authority. Monnet encouraged Rabier to expand the Washington office so

(¹) PV 19, EEC Commission, 11 June 1958, VIII.b; PV 62, EEC Commission, 4 June 1959, IV, pp. 5–6.

Diplomatic relations: Asserting the Commission's international role ...

'Asserting the Commission's international role [...]

[...] with the backing of Jean Monnet [...]

"The time has come for you to take a broader view of our action in America. I must repeat that, for the first time since we began this venture together in 1950, the Americans feel that their interests are at stake. This is a new prospect to which you must adapt." (¹)

[...] but without encroaching on national prerogatives in matters of diplomacy [...]

Jean Flory analyses the difficulties encountered by Hallstein in establishing EC representations abroad: "Hallstein played up the institutional side of the Commission, with official representatives, delegations that were yet to be called embassies, although he would very much have liked them to be. The French response was 'Nothing, no way'. Hallstein said, 'That is simply not possible. We have to have a presence in Washington. We have to have a presence in London, if you want us to be able to state our case. And we have to have a presence in would-be member countries, in order to prepare for accession." (²)

[...] and without offending the sensibilities of certain Member States [...]

Hallstein was always looking for protocol arrangements worthy of a sovereign state. Georges Berthoin tells the following story: "When he went to the United States for the first time, I believe Eisenhower was still President, though you would have to check [...] The President of the United States received Hallstein like a Head of State, and de Gaulle didn't like it — and Hallstein was in office for 10 years, he was becoming President of Europe. [...] In the case of Hallstein, it was consistent with the initial thinking [...]. So the Americans, who at this time were always ahead of the game, accorded Hallstein all the courtesies normally reserved to a Head of State. So he went to Blair House, the whole palaver. It is quite funny because, when Jean Rey became President, General de Gaulle welcomed him to the Élysée with a guard of honour. We played with this fact. Indeed, on that occasion — Jean Rey told me — he wanted to arrive by car, but the problem is that you need a flag on a car. So he flew today's European flag, which was not that of the European Community, which did not have one, but of the Council of Europe. You had to have a flag. You cannot arrive at the Elysée in an official car without a flag. And there was the Republican Guard, etc. It was de Gaulle's idea because he was buttering up the Commission at the time, etc." (³)

When a residence had to be found for the Communities' representation in Washington, Guy Vanhaeverbeke recounts: "We visited one of the possible residences. It was across the road from the offices of the French trade adviser, Belmont Road, you had to climb a few steps [...] The residence, Dillon Villa, was really perfect and not oversized either. As we were going up the steps, Cardon said: 'This is what we need. This is what we need, it's slightly supranational.' (⁴) *And that is the one that was chosen."'*

---

as to stir the US public's interest in the Communities as they prepared their enlargement to include the United Kingdom, Denmark and Ireland. Another of this mission's tasks was to lobby Congress, for which it employed first the Roy Bernard public relations firm and then the law firm Clearly, Gottlieb, Steen & Ball. As Jean Flory saw it, that firm, backed up by a Community office in Washington headed by Tennyson, played a very important role in persuading American political circles and the Senate that the Community should definitely not be destroyed (⁵). In 1971, the Commission was at last represented in Washington by a real head of delegation, former Italian diplomat Aldo Mazio. In this delegation, Pierre Malvé hand-

---

(¹) See FMJE, AMK C 335/67 of 9 January 1962.
(²) Interview with Jean Flory, 3 December 2003.

(³) Interview with Georges Berthoin, 31 January 2003.
(⁴) Interview with Guy Vanhaeverbecke, 25 February 2004.
(⁵) Interview with Jean Flory, 3 December 2003.

led commercial policy, while the press and information office was handled by Leonard Tennyson (¹). This delegation incorporated the Euratom Office, later known as the 'Euratom Liaison Office', which was initially a 'foreign agent' and therefore subject, as a result of McCarthyism, to tight control by the US Department of Justice. The office was created from scratch by Curt Heidenreich. Employed by Euratom from the outset, he was posted to Washington in autumn 1958 to liaise with the US authorities on such issues as the supply of special fissile materials to the Community and the related security controls after Euratom and the United States had concluded a cooperation agreement. Under Article 86 of the Euratom Treaty, 'special fissile materials shall be the property of the Community'. More generally, however, Heidenreich kept Brussels informed, long after the single delegation was established following the merger, of developments he thought might be of interest, including political reports on, for instance, the Vietnam War and all sorts of hearings on this and other subjects. He had excellent connections in government and political circles. This did not always make for an easy relationship with Leonard Tennyson's Information Service, Tennyson claiming a precedent dating back to the time of Jean Monnet and George Ball. Curt Heidenreich was successively assisted by Gabriele Genuardi and Giorgio Longo and, following the merger, by Ivo Dubois, who specialised in political, judicial and supply matters, and Giorgio Boggio, who specialised in technical and scientific matters.

In Latin America, where the ECSC already had a liaison office in Santiago in 1960, an information office was opened in Montevideo in 1965; in 1967, the two were merged under Wolfgang Renner, the head of the ECSC mission (²). At the request of Turkey's business elite, the Commission opened a

European Documentation Centre in Ankara in 1970, with a branch in Istanbul (³). Edmund Wellenstein recalls the ECSC's legacy in the Communities' external policy and the organisation of the Communities' representations abroad; before the EEC, the ECSC had maintained very close relations with Sweden, Austria, Japan, Switzerland, the United States, the United Kingdom and other countries (⁴).

In 1971 the Communities were still represented by a mix of heads of delegation and heads of information offices, all of them referred to as heads of mission, whereas non-member countries were represented in Brussels by heads of diplomatic missions.

Foreign representations to the Commission and the Council

The EEC's worldwide role in trade made it advisable for non-member countries to be represented in Brussels. The United States, which was already represented at the ECSC, showed its interest in the EEC and Euratom by accrediting a representative, Walton Butterworth, on 3 February 1958 (⁵). Greece did likewise. From 1959 all countries of the free-trade area, and then New Zealand, Canada, the Latin American countries, Israel and Morocco, were represented in Brussels (see pp. 348–349). The influence of the US head of mission quickly made itself felt, even if, Francesco Fresi explains, 'we didn't say so or weren't aware of it at our level. We did, however, begin to feel US pressure for Great Britain to successfully catalyse all this renewal in Europe into forms that were not hostile to US policy. ' (⁶) It had no cause to regret this pressure (⁷), even if the Commission managed to assert its own objectives vis-à-vis the United

(¹) Interview with Guy Vanhaeverbeke, 25 February 2004; additional remarks by Edmund P. Wellenstein, February 2006.

(²) PV 140, EC Commission, 28–29 October 1970, V.1, p. 8; 'Memo to the Commission from Mr Borschette and Mr Dahrendorf concerning the Commission's representation in Latin America', SEC(70) 3836, 22 September 1970; a number of Commissioners took a dim view of Salvador Allende's election. PV spéc. 140, EC Commission, 28–29 October 1970, V, p. 4.

(³) HAEU, EN 1063, Émile Noël, conference in Turkey, memo to Albert Coppé of 7 January 1970; PV spéc. 224, EC Commission, 1972, XVI, p. 7.

(⁴) Letter from Edmund P. Wellenstein to the author, 10 August 2005.

(⁵) William Walton Butterworth (1951–62) was followed by John Tuthill (1962–66) and J. Robert Schaetzel (1966–72).

(⁶) Interview with Francesco Fresi, 5 February 2004.

(⁷) HAEU, EN 2561, Émile Noël to Jean Rey, 27 March 1969; P/227/69, organisation of regular contacts with the US mission, speech by Ralf Dahrendorf to the American Bar Association on the European Community in the world, Chicago, 26 March 1971.

Countries accredited to the EEC and the

(a) Establishment of non-member and associated country missions or representations to the European Economic Community
(the year is that in which the letters of credence were first presented)

1958:	Greece, United States
1959:	Denmark, Ireland, Israel, Japan, Norway, Sweden, Switzerland, United Kingdom
1960:	Austria, Australia, Brazil, Canada, Morocco, New Zealand, South Africa, Spain
1961:	Chad, Colombia, Congo (Leopoldville) [Democratic Republic of the Congo], Dahomey [Benin], Gabon, Cote d'Ivoire, Madagascar, Mauritania, Mexico, Niger, Senegal, Somalia, Togo, Upper Volta [Burkina Faso]
1962:	Argentina, Burundi, Cameroon, Central African Republic, Ceylon [Sri Lanka], Chile, Congo (Brazzaville), Costa Rica, Dominican Republic, India, Iran, Lebanon, Pakistan, Portugal, Thailand, Tunisia, Venezuela
1963:	Haiti, Iceland, Mali, Nigeria, Peru, Ruanda [Rwanda], Uruguay
1964:	Algeria, Ecuador, Finland, Korea (South), Philippines, Turkey
1965:	Guatemala, Salvador, Trinidad and Tobago
1966:	Paraguay, United Arab Republic [Egypt], Sudan
1967:	Jamaica, Panama, Saudi Arabia, Syria
1968:	Ghana, Indonesia, Kenya, Libya, Malaysia, Malta, Tanzania, Uganda, Yugoslavia
1970:	Cyprus, Ethiopia, Nicaragua, The Holy See
1971:	Fiji, Iraq, Jordan, Malawi, Mauritius, Sierra Leone
1972:	Singapore

Source: European Commission, Secretariat-General, Protocol Service, Historical table of the establishment of non-member and associated country missions to the EEC (compiled in June 1991), internal document.

(b) ⌂ : List of cities in non-member countries in which the Commission had a delegation or representation: Washington, London, Geneva (GATT), Paris (OECD), Santiago (Chile)

© Communautés européennes • Cartographie: Guillaume Balavoine

Communities' delegations and press and information offices abroad in 1972

States. The Commission, as a mouthpiece, prevented the Member States from reacting to US demands and initiatives in a piecemeal manner that would have weakened their position ([1]).

Very soon, however, the Commission and the Council found themselves in a dispute over the presentation of letters of credence by representatives of non-member countries ([2]). The Commission recommended that non-member countries present letters of credence to the Commission President, who would then inform the Council. This solution was applied until the 'empty chair' crisis ([3]). Hallstein seized the opportunity to implement a protocol on the presentation of letters of credence that was quite similar to that applied by States. A witness, Armand Saclé, who sensed the growing hostility of the French, told Hallstein's *cabinet*: 'The General is not at all happy, and he is going to say so. What is more, he feels that President Hallstein is rather overdoing the protocol, especially the audiences he grants non-member countries' representatives and his desire to appoint pseudo-ambassadors to non-member countries.' ([4]) The Luxembourg arrangement of 30 January 1966 concerning 'the Heptalogue' — the list of French grievances against the Commission — decreed that letters of credence be presented, without ceremony, to the Presidents of the Commission and the Council. The Communities' success, which was apparent by the early 1970s, convinced many non-member countries to climb on board ([5]). By 1972 there were 85 ambassadors accredited to the Communities.

––––––––––

The three highly enterprising commissioners Robert Marjolin, Jean Rey and Jean-François Deniau, backed by the Commission, made full use of the internal and mixed instruments for analysis and action conferred on the Commission by the Treaty for the management of external trade relations. The Commissioners worked hand in glove with the heads of the DGs' directorates, who were of various nationalities: Rey with Seeliger, Herbst, Hijzen, Di Martino and Ernst; Martino with Sigrist and Di Martino; Deniau with Wellenstein, Hijzen, Ernst, de Kergolay and Caspari; Dahrendorf with Hijzen, Sigrist and Ernst; Mansholt with Rabot, Heringa and von Verschuer ([6]). The Commission managed to be represented in key countries. Its overriding motive was to embody the Community's aspirations and do all in its power to win influence in European and international institutions.

The Commission adopts principles for external relations

The Commission was eager, for the post-transition stage of the common market, to establish a common commercial policy founded on 'uniform principles' ([7]) but encompassing areas additional to those expressly cited in the Treaty. The issues it handled during the transitional period gave it the opportunity to lay down Community principles for the future, which it began setting out in a series of memoranda with self-explanatory titles in 1958 ([8]).

Opening up to the world and Community integration

First principle: on the basis of the objectives laid down in Article 110 of the Treaty, the Commission proposed building a commercial policy that

––––––––––

([1]) Letter from Edmund P. Wellenstein to the author, 10 August 2005, p. 4.

([2]) PV 36, EEC Commission, 5 November 1958, V, p. 6.

([3]) 'Memo from Jean Rey on the draft agreement between the three European Communities on the establishment of joint representations', COM(58) 258, 24 November 1958; 'Memo from Jean Rey on the organisation of the Community's external relations', COM(59) 37, April 1959.

([4]) Interview with Armand Saclé, 28 January 2004.

([5]) Dahrendorf, R., Speech, 25 January 1971, Deutsche Gesellschaft für Auswärtige Politik (Bonn), published in *Europe Document*, 12 March 1971.

([6]) As recalled by Edmund P. Wellenstein, letters to the author, 25 August 2005, p. 2, and 7 September 2005, p. 5.

([7]) In Article 111.

([8]) 'Memorandum from the Commission to the Council concerning methods for unifying the Member States' trade policies in respect of non-member countries', COM(58) 229 rev., 27 October 1958; COM(61) 48 of 17 April 1961; PV spéc. 142, EEC Commission, 27 March 1961, XI, p. 9; PV 144, EEC Commission, 26 April 1961, XXI, p. 25; PV 151, EEC Commission, 27 June 1961, XIV, pp. 16–19; 'Second memorandum from the Commission to the Council concerning an action programme in the area of the common commercial policy, drawn up by virtue of Article 111 EEC', COM(62) 10, 21 March 1962.

Visiting Washington in April 1963, Walter Hallstein presents his book
United Europe: Challenge and Opportunity to Dean Rusk, US Secretary of State.

was integrated and open to the world. Marjolin, who was firmly behind this proposal, called for the United States, the EEC and the Commonwealth to agree a common commercial policy [1]. He wrote to Jean Monnet that it was in the world's interest that American exports rise and that it was therefore urgent to make the United States fully eligible for all the trade liberalisation measures that the European countries had reached among themselves over the past four years [2]. These principles informed the management of quota increases and tariff cuts [3]. The Commission proposed, for the purposes of the GATT negotia-

tions, that a contact commission be set up between the EEC and other European countries. It invited the Community to develop trade with the planned economies [4]. Jean Rey would have liked to integrate the EEC economies with those of non-member countries at the same pace, but he recognised that the Community's integration was a precondition for its being able to pursue a liberal policy towards the outside world [5]. The Commission therefore resolutely asserted the principle of opening up trade and its prerequisite, Community integration and therefore trade differentiation.

[1] FMJE, AMK C 33/3/290, Letter accompanying a memorandum to an unidentified French addressee, possibly Jean Monnet, 4 August 1959.

[2] FMJE, AMK 62/1/1, Letter from Robert Marjolin to Jean Monnet, Brussels, 9 June 1959.

[3] COM(59) 123 rev., 22 September 1959.

[4] Hallstein, W., 'Customs union and free-trade area', *Bulletin of the EEC*, No 1, 1959, p. 5.

[5] Rey, J., 'The external relations of the Community', *Bulletin of the EEC*, No 4, 1959, pp. 6 and 20.

Promoting developing countries' trade

The second principle was the Commission's backing for long-term aid to all the developing countries. For the 1964 United Nations Conference on Trade and Development (Unctad), the Commission drew up a 'doctrine' for increasing developing countries' export earnings by carefully organising international trade in commodities. The Commission was in favour of market agreements, and Hallstein, very wisely, advocated a policy of support for developing countries' exports ([1]). 'And we, as a Salvation Army for the developing countries, thought it a good thing', explains Jean Chapperon, Rochereau's *chef de cabinet* from 1962 to 1970 and Deniau's until 1974 ([2]). In 1972 the Commission welcomed the calls of the Group of 77 for generalised preferences to be extended to all developing countries ([3]). It also very logically supported the creation of an International Trade Organisation (ITO) ([4]). Jean-François Deniau claims that he thought up the Stabex mechanism that Commissioner Claude Cheysson introduced in the Lomé Conventions: 'It was Cheysson who implemented it. There was a meeting and it was approved. It wasn't easy: the Dutch weren't too keen and the Americans were totally against. They were trigger-happy, the Americans. For them, the idea that we were going to stabilise commodities was an act of aggression. Even the Dutch minister came round. So the principle was established: there would be Stabex.' ([5])

Pre-empting economic and trade problems

The third principle of external trade policy was to pre-empt problems. The Commission wanted to go further than drawing up the common external tariff (CET) and piloting it through the GATT. Hallstein called for a common external economic and commercial policy that took account of agricultural and industrial issues but also of the business cycle and international monetary relations ([6]). Marjolin explained in 1965 already that the turbulence in the international monetary system (IMS) gave the Communities responsibilities in the matter of its reform ([7]). As Deniau saw it, the new challenges concerned the standardisation of the Community's instruments for external action. Although the Treaty did not place instruments such as price and exchange-rate guarantees, industrial and scientific cooperation agreements and financial, technical and cultural assistance policy in the Community sphere, it was becoming increasingly obvious that the scope of 'commercial policy' was expanding rapidly ([8]). In 1972 Commissioner Ralf Dahrendorf also stressed the need for a broader understanding of commercial policy ([9]).

Three principles underpinned the common commercial policy: the mutual liberalisation of trade between developed countries, special trade arrangements for developing countries and the abandonment of commercial policy in favour of external economic policy.

First challenge: the free-trade area

Guided by these principles, the Commission soon had to rise to four major challenges. The first challenge to be met by the fledgling Commission concerned the project for a free-trade area between the common market and the European non-member countries belonging to the Organisation for European Economic Cooperation (OEEC).

A generous position

This project, which originated with the United Kingdom, was proposed when the European

([1]) Hallstein, W., Speech, Strasbourg, 26 November 1963, *Bulletin of the EEC*, No 1, 1964, p. 12.
([2]) Interview with Jean Chapperon, 23 January 2004.
([3]) HAEC, DGER, memo to Commissioner Ralf Dahrendorf on discussions in the Commission concerning the President's attendance at the third Unctad, 10 April 1972.
([4]) The WTO would be set up in 1994.
([5]) Interview with Jean-François Deniau, 10 November 2004.

([6]) Hallstein, W., Speech, Strasbourg, 26 November 1963, *Bulletin of the EEC*, No 1, 1964, p. 12.
([7]) Marjolin, R., 'The EEC and international monetary questions', Commission Vice-President Robert Marjolin, statement to the European Parliament, 23 March 1965, *Bulletin of the EEC*, No 5, 1965.
([8]) Deniau, J.-Fr., 'A new stage in the implementation of the common commercial policy', *Bulletin of the EC*, No 2, 1970, pp. 5–7.
([9]) PV spéc. 232, EC Commission, 1972, XXIV, pp. 21–22.

**Robert Marjolin defends the common market
free-trade area and common market (May 1958)**

'Discussions in the Organisation for European
Economic Cooperation with a view to establishing
a free-trade area have been under way for over
18 months now. [...] It is understandable, indeed
inevitable, that these discussions should seem
extremely confused to outside observers who
cannot study the texts themselves. All they see in
this confusion are a few simple features which the
mind seizes on, ignoring the real complexity of
the issue, oversimplifying and making up for the
lack of clarity with passion and indignation.

A few features and a few thoughts may shed a
little light on the subject. Let us begin with the
facts:

The common market is an open structure. More
specifically, any European country may join it and
enjoy all its advantages, provided it is ready to
accept the obligations of membership.

The difficulty lies in the fact that the OEEC
countries other than the Six that concluded the
common market Treaty do not feel able to accept
all the obligations laid down in the Treaty or
simply do not wish to do so. In particular, they
cannot or will not unify the common customs
tariff that they apply to non-member countries,
merge their extremely disparate import rules and
practices into a single commercial policy or
accept the authority of institutions to which
governments had delegated a major part of their
economic and financial responsibilities.

What we are looking for is a formula that will
associate the OEEC countries other than the Six
with the common market, without their having to
accept the provisions of the common market
Treaty, which their circumstances or public
opinion prevent them from doing.

There would therefore be nothing illogical or
unfair in introducing the Treaty of Rome's
provisions on customs duties and quotas verbatim
into the association agreement since other, no
less essential, provisions would be omitted. The
different articles of the Treaty of Rome form an
indivisible whole. Those concerning the freedom
of trade within the Community cannot remain
intact if the others are amended or deleted.

It should also be pointed out, without going into
the details, that the concept of a free-trade area
presents technical problems not encountered in a
customs union.

The main problem with a free-trade area is its lack
of political content, the prospect of full union
between Member States, in economic matters at
least, which has enabled the six countries to
overcome the objections raised by the trade
aspects in various sectors of public opinion [...].

FJME, ARM 26/4/31, 'Free-trade area and common
market', *Appel pour l'Europe*, May 1958.
(Translated from the French)

Economic Community became a certainty. The GATT stipulated that the bulk of trade had to be covered. Customs duties would be abolished between member countries, which nevertheless remained free to adopt different customs duties in respect of the outside world. The European Economic Community therefore had no objection in principle to such an area. But it did run into an obstacle of British origin: During a press conference British Prime Minister Harold

Macmillan insisted that the free-trade area had to exclude agricultural products in order to maintain the preferences enjoyed by the Commonwealth countries on the British market ([1]). This would, in the United Kingdom's view, avoid awkward negotiations on very different

([1]) Clavel, J.-Cl., and Collet, P., *L'Europe au fil des jours — Les jeunes années de la construction européenne 1948–1978*, Notes et études documentaires, No 4509–4510, La Documentation française, Paris, 1979, p. 21.

agricultural rules. The Commission's view was that the Treaty of Rome had to be defended because it was not discriminatory (¹). To prove its point, it offered the other countries of the OEEC, and indeed other parties to the GATT, the 10 % tariff cut that the Six were to grant each other on 1 January 1959. It was even prepared to introduce special arrangements for agricultural products (²). In September 1958 a Commission working party, chaired by Jean Rey, invited the Six to pool their quotas and increase them by 20 % for the future free-trade area (³). But the Commission made sure that the Community figured as an institution in the future intergovernmental cooperation machinery for the area, renamed the European Economic Association. The unity of the Six was sorely tried by the United Kingdom's diplomatic manoeuvres. In the words of Jean Flory, Marjolin's *chef de cabinet*, 'the Community at that time had great difficulty maintaining cohesion between the Six in order that what had been agreed at Community level could not only be conserved but enter into force.' (⁴)

Playing down the setback

France, backed by Germany, responded to the unrelenting hostility shown towards the common market by the UK delegation headed by Reginald Maudling by breaking off negotiations on 14 November 1958: 'It was a dialogue of the deaf', recalls Jean Flory. 'All the Six had done to grow closer, to build something together was completely ignored and disowned by the English.' (⁵)

Faced with a fait accompli, the Commission reiterated the goodwill measures in favour of the EEC's OEEC partners planned for 1 January 1959. There would be a 20 % cut in customs tariffs on imports

of manufactured goods, subject to reciprocity, from OEEC countries, on top of the 10 % reduction in national duties offered to all GATT members (3 and 4 December 1958) (⁶). The Commission also decided to prepare the gradual abolition of quotas between the Six and the 11 OEEC members. The matter of the free-trade area vindicated Hallstein, who wrote: 'We regard the reproach of splitting Europe as unjust in view of the fact that, as a result of the establishment of our Community, thousands of kilometres of customs frontiers will disappear [...]' (⁷)

Second challenge: promoting trade in the mutual interest, cutting tariffs in GATT

The Commission's task was to contribute to the harmonious development of world trade and to negotiate reciprocal cuts in customs tariffs. Before going to the GATT, the Six adopted a theoretical common external tariff at a weighted average rate of 7.4 %, a rate more advantageous than the 9.1 % arithmetical average of national tariffs. The Member States' tariffs were gradually aligned on the common external tariff over the 12-year transitional period to 1970. Since, however, certain tariff rates in the Member States had to rise gradually to reach the common level (German and Benelux rates) and others to fall (French and Italian rates), negotiations had to be opened with non-member countries on compensation to be given or received (⁸). 'You know that the GATT rules mean there is a price to pay when you set up a free-trade area, and that price had to be paid', explains Jean Flory (⁹). The negotiations to bring the Community into line with the GATT provisions on customs unions took place at the GATT in 1961 under Article XXIV-6 of the agreement. This complex matter, with consid-

---

(¹) PV 4, EEC Commission, 9 February 1958, 12, p. 7; PV 9, EEC Commission, 17 March 1958, VI, pp. 3–4.
(²) Doc. 190/58; PV 28, EEC Commission, 9 April 1958, p. 4.
(³) COM(58) 176 in Annex 1 PV to 28, EEC Commission, 9 September 1958.
(⁴) Interview with Jean Flory, 3 December 2003.
(⁵) Ibid.

(⁶) 'Memorandum from the Commission to the Council of Ministers, measures to be taken on 1 January 1959 in the Community's external relations', COM(58) 259 rev., 27 November 1958, Annex I to PV 39, EEC Commission.
(⁷) Hallstein, W., *Bulletin of the EEC*, No 1, 1959, p. 11.
(⁸) Letter from Edmund P. Wellenstein to the author, 10 August 2005, p. 5.
(⁹) Interview with Jean Flory, 3 December 2003. The common market is a customs union, which is subject to tighter rules than a free-trade area.

erable political implications, showed the central position of the recently established Community and the United States in international trade relations. There were four problem issues at the GATT: the common tariff, import levies, agricultural export refunds and the preferential association with the overseas territories.

The EEC, a new heavyweight in the GATT (May 1961)

The common external tariff and the prospect of a common agricultural policy gave rise to much apprehension in the GATT. The Commission had to reassure its partners that it would stick scrupulously to the rules but that it was fully entitled, without restrictions, to establish a customs union. Deniau, who went to Geneva with Snoy et d'Oppuers, attests that they were obliged 'not just to wage a legal battle but to make clear, especially to the underdeveloped countries, that we could benefit them and that we were derogating from the most-favoured-nation clause in their favour. We were up against frenzied opposition from the British, the Commonwealth and the Nordic countries. The Swiss took a moralising stance: "You're dividing Europe, you should be ashamed of yourselves"' [1]. Feeling the negotiations would enhance his organisation's prestige and professional standing, the GATT General Secretary, Wyndham White, would help the Commission. The Community was able to prove that the mooted common tariff did not increase the Community's level of protection, save on certain specific headings, and that it was set to fall further [2]. It unilaterally decided a 10 % cut in such national duties as were higher than those of the common customs tariff that was to enter into force only at the end of the transitional period. It agreed to negotiate future cuts in duties on the basis of the proposal by Douglas Dillon, the head of the US delegation, to reduce tariffs by 20 % over four years. It even pre-empted the result of

the Dillon Round negotiations by making its first tariff cuts before 31 December 1960 [3]. The negotiations under Article XXIV-6 were completed in May 1961. The agreement would be signed a year later, at the same time as that closing the Dillon Round with the United States. The common market was no fortress.

The Dillon Round, a partial success (May 1961 to July 1962)

The Dillon Round (May 1961 to July 1962) produced a Community–United States tariff agreement to cut by 20 % the duties on the manufactured products of which the United States was the main producer; that cut could be automatically extended to other GATT members. Identical agreements were concluded with the United Kingdom and later with other countries. The Commission, at its cost, waived the principle of strict reciprocity of concessions in order, says Marjolin, to secure US political support for European unity. The success would have been complete had the United States not gone back on its concessions a fortnight later, a move roundly condemned by Jean Rey [4]. The Commission would take retaliatory measures [5]. New talks on agricultural products were planned, after the establishment of the CAP. To reassure the Americans, the Commission agreed to conclude interim (one-off) agreements on certain agricultural products — wheat, maize, sorghum, rice and poultry. An agreement on international trade in cotton was concluded in the GATT cotton textiles committee on 9 February 1962. The final act of the Dillon Round was signed by the parties in Geneva in July 1962.

---

[1] Interviews with Jean-François Deniau, 3 and 10 November 2004.
[2] Hallstein, W., 'Trade policy issues', *Bulletin of the EEC*, No 1, 1960.

[3] Rey, J., 'The EEC and the Tariff Conference', *Bulletin of the EEC*, No 6/7, 1960, p. 5.
[4] Rey, J., 'The conclusion of a tariff agreement between the Community and the United States of America', *Bulletin of the EEC*, No 4, 1962.
[5] Draft aide-memoire from the European Economic Community to the Government of the United States of America, approved by the Commission on 29 March 1962.

The Kennedy Round, the masterpiece (4 May 1964 to 30 June 1967)

The Dillon Round raised the real issues. The Commission and the Council agreed to address them in new negotiations, which began on 4 May 1964.

The Commission had high hopes of the US Trade Expansion Act of January 1962, which authorised President Kennedy to abolish all duties on products in which the US and the Community accounted for 80 % of world trade and gradually to reduce tariffs on other products by up to 50 %. There were three items on the agenda: tariff cuts, the organisation of trade in agricultural products and trade with the developing countries. The Commission and the Council placed the emphasis on reducing disparities between the contracting parties' tariffs in respect of duties affecting a given product and on non-tariff protectionist measures. The Commission knew it would have difficulty negotiating specific agreements with the developing countries because it was bound to honour the preferences granted by the Community to the Associated African Countries and Madagascar (AACM). It wanted, at the very least, to create better conditions for the developing countries' exports (¹).

The United States, which dearly wished to come to the main negotiations in 1964 with an agricultural agreement already signed with the European Economic Community, offered product agreements in exchange for a review of the common agricultural policy. The Commission refused, and relations with Kennedy's personal representative to the GATT, Christian Herter, deteriorated. He accused the Community's CAP levies of harming US exports of poultry to Germany and flour to the Netherlands (²). The United States contested the Community's right to grant preferences to the AACM. High-level talks between Walter Hallstein, Robert Marjolin, Jean Rey, Sicco Mansholt

and their US counterparts got nowhere. The result was a 'poultry war' which lasted from 25 June 1963 to 7 January 1964. The Americans suspended the application of USD 26 million worth of tariff concessions to the Community. As Michel Jacquot recalls, US taxes on cognac lasted for 16 years. Jean-François Deniau, while acknowledging the assistance given by the United States to building Europe, recalls a member of the US Administration saying, with reference to the US protection for Berlin, 'If you don't take our chickens, we'll take our troops back' (³).

The Commission pointed out that the United States was refusing to discuss its own system of farm support while denouncing the Community's. Each producer country left the importer countries to deal with the problem of imbalances on international agricultural markets. The US negotiators claimed they would never be able to persuade their exporters to comply with minimum prices or to impose new costs on US importers. Yet, by the end of the poultry war, they had promised Denmark and the Community to respect a 'minimum export price'.

The Kennedy Round ended on 15 and 16 May 1967. 'From the Community angle, their effect will be an approximate 35 % reduction in the common customs tariff duties on industrial products and a reduction of up to 50 % on certain products such as motor vehicles; thanks to the Community's insistence, this will also apply to the United States', explained Jean Rey, who saw it as a success (⁴). The agreement was to be implemented over five years. The United States announced that it would forgo the American selling price in trade in chemical products, and the Community bound eight tariff quotas (⁵). The agreement also provided for a code stipulating the implementing arrangements for GATT anti-

(¹) Rey, J., 'Statement of the EEC Commission at the inaugural session of the Kennedy Round', 4 May 1964, *Bulletin of the EEC*, No 6, 1964, p. 5.
(²) PV spec. 228, EEC Commission, 1963, VIII., pp. 7–10.

(³) Interview with Jean-François Deniau, 3 November 2004.
(⁴) Rey, J., 'The successful conclusion of the Kennedy Round', *Bulletin of the EEC*, No 6, 1967, p. 5.
(⁵) The 'American selling price' was a reference price for domestic and imported chemical products used by the United States to calculate customs duties.

Jean Rey and Robert Marjolin visit Washington for the Kennedy Round negotiations.
From left to right: John W. Tuthill (United States Representative to the European Communities),
Jean Rey, George Ball (US Deputy Secretary of State) and Robert Marjolin.

dumping rules to be adopted in order to prevent arbitrary practices in that matter. Though a success in terms of dismantling customs barriers, the agreement was a failure in terms of the international organisation of agricultural markets. A general agreement on cereals had been prepared by the Commission in March 1965 in an attempt to balance international supply and demand ([1]). The general agreement that was signed merely set a minimum selling price. There would also be a bilateral agreement on the export to the EEC of US animal feeds (soya, manioc, etc.), which was presented to European farmers as the concomi-

tant of a Community beef production plan. The final act of the Geneva Conference was signed on 30 June 1967.

Agriculture was therefore continuing to poison relations between the Community and the United States since the US challenged the system of protection applied at the Community's frontiers for trade in agricultural products. It forced the Commission to accept the idea of quotas for managing trade in steel and textiles, and the Commission tried to organise consultations on aid measures for agricultural exports ([2]). The

([1]) PV 312 final, EEC Commission, 31 March 1965, and Annex 1: SEC(65) 1200, 9 April 1965.

([2]) PV spéc. 12, EC Commission, 1967, XXVI, pp. 12–13.

GATT negotiations

Cooperation between directorates-general

Paolo Clarotti recalls: 'DG External Relations was to take part for the first time in what was known at the time as the Dillon Round. It was the first round of global negotiations within the GATT framework. They very quickly realised in 1960–61 that DG I's structure was extremely limited. As I remember it, there was a head of division, whose name was Donne, and a deputy, Schlösser. Sadly, Donne died soon afterwards. Schlösser, who later became director-general, had three or four colleagues [...]. On the US side, there were hundreds of people at work. So they said they were technically unable to conduct multilateral negotiations. They really didn't have the resources [...]. The Commission decided that the other DGs would have to help. The directorate-general that helped most in the end was DG Internal Market. Two [...] directorates were placed at DG I's disposal — Industry and Customs. The first comprised three divisions — industry, trade and small businesses, in the original set-up, which was more or less theoretical and bore no relation to reality. Mr Ortoli said to us: "You have got to go over there, you have to help them compile and prepare files on all the products, etc." So all these files had to be prepared.' ([1])

Exceptions and disparities:
14 days of non-stop meetings

Fernand Braun recalls: 'It was the Kennedy Round that really changed things. Millet, myself and Jean Durieux worked on what are known as exceptions and disparities. We went through all manufacturing sectors. We got the Council to give us a mandate for exceptions and disparities. It was under the German Presidency. State Secretary Neef was President at the time. We did that in almost 14 days of non-stop meetings which almost every night went on until three in the morning. And then, between four and five in the morning, we would go back to the drawing board, then we would go to bed for three hours and come back later the same morning. It is something you can do when you are involved in a great project and you are only forty or forty-two years old. It is a great effort and not one you can make at any age' ([2]).

Jean Rey at GATT

Raymond Barre tells the following story: 'We were in the middle of the Kennedy Round, he was Commissioner for trade and, naturally, he was well regarded not just by his colleagues but by the governments, whose respect he had won. And especially the French government ([3]).' *Fernand Braun adds: 'If the truth be known, Rey really came to the fore during the Kennedy Round. For the Presidency, that was when he won his spurs' ([4]). This view is endorsed by Cardon de Lichtbuer: 'The Kennedy Round was his lucky break'. ([5]) But it would be an exaggeration to attribute the opening-up of the Community to international trade to Rey.*

([1]) Interview with Paolo Clarotti, 28 November 2003. Clarotti started work at the Commission in 1959. He was an administrator in DG Internal Market before becoming the first head of the Banking and Insurance Directorate.

([2]) Interview with Fernand Braun, 8 December 2003 (Translation). Mr Braun began his career in Rasquin's *cabinet* before joining the Commission's Secretariat-General, in which he held a number of posts. In 1961 he became head of a directorate at DG Internal Market before joining DG Industry as a chief adviser. He became Deputy Director in 1970.

([3]) Interview with Raymond Barre, 20 February 2004 (Translation). Raymond Barre was Vice-President of the Commission of the European Communities responsible for economic and financial affairs from 1967 to 1972.

([4]) Interview with Fernand Braun, 8 December 2003.

([5]) Interview with Daniel Cardon de Lichtbuer, 12 November 2003. Cardon joined the Commission as an economist in 1958. He was Albert Coppé's *chef de cabinet* from 1960 to 1972.

Commission went along with targeted negotiations that reduced levies on imports of US tobacco, tinned ham and poultry ([1]). But it was all to no avail. The United States introduced countervailing duties on a number of bound tariff headings (tinned tomatoes imported from Italy, dairy products) and quantitative restrictions. It even tried to oppose the introduction of value added tax in Germany, a move foiled by the Commission. The Commission accepted that US reactions were political but also prepared an appeal to the GATT ([2]). In the meantime, there was increasing disruption on international agricultural markets when the United States and Canada decided to sell their wheat below the price agreed in the international cereals agreement. It is also true that the CAP was creating imbalances that the Community was slow to correct, for instance the overproduction of dairy products. Export refunds were driving agricultural prices down. The preferential arrangements on citrus fruits between the Community, Spain and Israel were also contested by the United States.

One might wonder why the United States was complaining, since the CAP did not stop it selling USD 1.982 billion worth of agricultural products in 1970, whereas the EEC's exports totalled only USD 437 million. According to Guy Vanhaeverbeke, the US view was that 'this surplus would be even greater if you weren't so protectionist because our agriculture is much more competitive' ([3]). It was not until 1972 that a bilateral agreement between the EEC and the United States committed the two parties to settle their differences by negotiation. The GATT had therefore been a key arena for the Commission. While commitments had been made to liberalise trade, Hallstein continued calling for greater flexibility to facilitate growth in the developing countries and militating for unilateral preferences in their favour. The Kennedy Round had been a great success for the Commission in its role as negotiator and a success for the Community, which, despite serious shortcomings, had presented a united front to non-member countries. In a similar vein, the Malfatti Commission had advocated the organisation of a new set of world trade negotiations after enlargement; this project was endorsed by the summit convened by President Pompidou in late 1972, and the negotiations were launched by the GATT in 1973 as the 'Tokyo Round'.

The dismantling of tariff barriers had therefore made headway. The Commission had been able to apply the trade-defence measures warranted by the attitude of the United States. But it failed to gain acceptance from the GATT, and more specifically the United States, for international agreements to stabilise prices for the main agricultural products, either because its powers of persuasion had proved inadequate or perhaps because the Council was not convinced of the need for them.

Third challenge: establish ties with Europe and the world

The third challenge involved establishing fruitful long-term relations with all European countries (OEEC, the Eastern Bloc and Spain) and the rest of the world. The Commission had to reassure its partners by concluding different types of agreement. The European Economic Community also had to be able to get ready to admit new members. And so association agreements were signed, development was promoted, unity of action in trade matters was sought and, last but not least, a Mediterranean development policy was devised ([4]). Thus, the entire period from 1958 to 1974 is marked by a series of almost never-ending negotiations between the Commission and dozens of partners all over the world.

([1]) PV spéc. 13, EC Commission, 1967, XXXI, pp. 36–37.
([2]) PV spéc. 35, EC Commission, 1968, XIII1, pp. 8–9; PV spéc. 56, EC Commission, 1968, XXI, pp. 16–17; PV spéc. 20, EC Commission, 13 November 1968, XI, pp. 5–8.
([3]) Interview with Guy Vanhaeverbecke, 25 February 2004.

([4]) The legal framework for relations with Africa is based on the Treaty, the Yaoundé Conventions and the Arusha agreements.

The association agreements in preparation for membership of the Communities

Greece became a candidate for association in June 1959. It began by seeking access to loans from the European Investment Bank; the Commission responded unenthusiastically owing to the country's enormous debt. Greece felt itself hard done by, yet provisions allowed it to export manufactures to the Community free of customs duties, without immediate reciprocity, and to receive financial and technical aid for its development with a view to future accession [1]. Italy demanded a general safeguard clause in respect of Greek wines, which was refused by both the Commission and Greece. Greece wanted to maintain its trade with its traditional markets outside the EEC, as did the United Kingdom subsequently [2]. The Commission, without the approval of the Council or the special committee, initialled an agreement [3]. Jean Rey also fended off French demands that responsibility for monitoring the agreement be shared by the Council and the Commission. The association agreement with Greece was signed in Athens on 9 July 1961 [4]. The Commission felt it had avoided the proliferation of special arrangements that would have served as precedents for subsequent agreements. This agreement was political in that it took account of the strategic concerns of the 'Free World' engaged in the Cold War. Greece, the first associated country, managed to have the objective of its eventual accession one day expressly written into the Treaty.

The Colonels' coup in 1967 obviously disrupted relations. As Robert Toulemon [5] and, later, Umberto Stefani [6] attest, both Émile Noël, the Secretary-General, and Jean Rey lobbied for sanctions. The Commission suspended financial relations, meetings of the association council and the customs union. France would have preferred the Commission to give the Member States a free hand because diplomacy was not the Commission's responsibility; Germany felt the same way but was motivated by a desire to hang on to its contracts with Greece. The Commission renewed its protests after the arrest of figures it held in great esteem, although two Commissioners, Raymond Barre and Jean-François Deniau, abstained, Barre because it was for the Council to make such a statement and Deniau because the means were not appropriate to the ends [7]. The arrest, in May 1972, of the former head of the delegation responsible for the association agreement outraged the Commission [8].

Exploratory talks with Turkey opened on 28 September 1959 [9]. The Commission proposed that the association agreement be less binding than that with Greece [10]. Jean Rey spoke of an association agreement based on the Community's assistance and not on a customs union [11]. Turkey, however, presented it as the way to move towards membership. The preamble to the draft, identical to that in the Greek agreement, states that the agreement's purpose is to support the Turkish people's efforts to improve their standard of living and subsequently to facilitate Turkey's accession to the Community, a concession on the Community's part that continues to have repercussions in the early 21st century. A customs union would be phased in [12]. The agreement was signed in Ankara on

---

[1] BAC 26/1969 263, Vol. 2–3, State of negotiations with Greece (July 1960, report by the External Affairs DG, COM(60) 112).

[2] BAC 26/1969 264, Vol. 2–3; BAC 26/1969, 262, Vol. 1, September 1959, first meeting of the Commission on the problems posed by the association of non-member countries with the EEC, and in particular the possible association of Greece.

[3] Initialled on 30 March 1961.

[4] BAC 26/1969 268, Statement of the grounds for the agreement (S/360/61).

[5] PV spéc. 284, EEC Commission, 9 September 1964, VI, p. 3.

[6] Interview with Umberto Stefani, 20 January 2004.

[7] PV spéc. 117, EC Commission, 15 April 1970, XXXII, p. 25; SEC(70) 1403, 14 and 15 April 1967.

[8] PV spéc. 205, EC Commission, 10 May 1972, XII, p. 11.

[9] HAEC, Secretariat I/S/06648, memo to the Commission concerning Turkey's association with the Community, Brussels, 5 October 1959; DG I, summary record of exploratory talks between the delegations of Turkey and the Commission (28–30 September 1959), 3 October 1959.

[10] HAEC, SE, I/S/07997, memo to the Commission concerning association with Greece and Turkey, draft agreement, 14 December 1959.

[11] HAEC, DGER, I/S/0827/61, Association Agreement with Turkey, 10 February 1961.

[12] BAC 11/1966, Vol. 1, mandate from the Council of 27 February 1963, S/165/63.

The delegation of the European Communities in London and the attitude of the British Prime Minister at the time of the United Kingdom's first application

(a) Georges Berthoin, a key figure in the London office, tells the following story:

'One day I was in the countryside — because in England everything happens in country houses at the weekend — and I am sitting next to a charming young girl of nineteen or twenty. I didn't really know what to say to her. So I asked her: 'When you're dancing, do you prefer the man to talk or not to talk? It is important.' And she said: 'It is funny you should ask me that. You know who I danced with last night? The Prime Minister, Mr Macmillan.' I asked her: 'So, does he talk or doesn't he?' She replied: 'I was terribly intimidated.'

[You may not know this, but upper-class English girls are not always highly educated. But there is a trick they learn: they glance at the headlines on the front page of the Daily Telegraph. They skim the article that they more or less understand and, should they run into a man of importance, they ask him a question, the man of importance talks for two hours and everybody is happy. Anyway, she had seen something about joining the common market, etc.]

And she said: 'Oh! Prime Minister. Are we going to join the common market? It's awful!' And he squeezed her in his arms and replied: 'Don't worry my dear, we shall embrace them destructively!' And she said: 'Don't you find that funny?'

The next day I wrote a personal letter to Hallstein and Jean Monnet.' ([1])

(b) The letter sent by G. Berthoin to Jean Monnet on 17 June 1960

ADK C 3012/474
17 Juin 1960

Cher Monsieur,

Les suggestions PROFUMO paraissent se développer et les Six, en difficulté pour en esquiver les conséquences qui présentent beaucoup de danger. A ce sujet M; van Kleffens vient d'envoyer à la Haute Autorité et à Monsieur Hirsch un télex dont voici une copie.

Par ailleurs, on m'a rapporté hier soir, d'une source dont je suis sûr, cette phrase - (ou boutade) - du premier Ministre Mac Millan, prononcée ces jours derniers en privé, à propos des Six et des projets dintégration de la Grande-Bretagne dans la Communauté : " We must embrace them, destructively."

Ceci représente parfaitement bien l'état d'esprit des milieux officiels tel que nous le constatons ici.

Bien fidèlement votre
Georges Berthoin

P.S. Est-ce que Marianne a déjà fixé la date de son voyage en Angleterre ? Anne et moi serions très heureux de la voir.

FONDATION JEAN MONNET
POUR L'EUROPE
Ferme de Dorigny
CH-1015 LAUSANNE

Translation:

Dear Sir,

The Profumo proposals appear to be evolving and the Six are having great difficulty escaping what could turn out to be very dangerous consequences. Mr van Kleffens has just sent the High Authority and Mr Hirsch a telex of which I attach a copy.

Yesterday I learnt from a reliable source that at a private function a few days ago, when Mr Mac Millan [sic] was talking about the Six and the plans for Britain to join the Community, he came up with the witty suggestion that 'We must embrace them, destructively'.

That perfectly reflects the attitudes in official circles here as we perceive them.

Yours truly,
Georges Berthoin

PS. Has Marianne already set the date for her visit to England? Anne and I would be so glad to see her.

([1]) Interview with Georges Berthoin, 31 January 2003.

12 September 1963. Camille Becker recounts an anecdote on the subject: 'There were still two or three odds and ends to settle with the Turks. Our Member States' embassies told us: "The Turks are listening in! And not just behind the door."' So he and Borschette, when communicating with André Feipel of the Council's General Secretariat in Brussels, spoke Luxembourgish ([1]). The Commission was receptive to Turkey's accession owing to the secular regime established by Ataturk. An additional protocol was signed on 23 November 1970. Turkey also asked to be involved in the discussions on European political cooperation in order to be considered an associate on the road to accession ([2]). Nobody at the Commission, claims Robert Toulemon, considered the political consequences of the customs union with Turkey.

Negotiations with Malta and Cyprus culminated in association agreements on 5 December 1970 and 19 December 1972 respectively ([3]). The new agreements were intended to foster stability and prosperity in the Mediterranean basin through financial, technical, environmental and employment measures ([4]). They did not yet prejudge the issue of accession. However, while General Franco's dictatorial regime made it impossible to grant Spain's request for association, a trade agreement was concluded in June 1970 ([5]). The Commission believed it could secretly influence the Spanish government to prevent the execution of Basque militants ([6]). The lack of an association agreement by no means signified that Spain (and Portugal) were ineligible for association and accession, but the circumstances were not yet right.

The Commission considered that the European countries of the OEEC (now the OECD) were eligible under the Treaty to join the Community, despite the failure of the large free-trade area in November 1958. The non-Community OECD members had, however, formed a small free-trade area of their own, the European Free Trade Association (EFTA), and sought closer ties with the Community. Austria, Switzerland, Portugal, Iceland and Finland, which had been isolated since the United Kingdom, Ireland, Denmark and Norway had applied to join the Communities, applied in their turn for association or membership ([7]). 'Later', explains Jean-François Deniau, 'when I was a member of the Commission responsible for negotiating with the United Kingdom and, since EFTA was on the way out, the Nordic and neutral countries, I proposed a plan for association with the neutral countries. This was a lifeline for them because, once the United Kingdom, Denmark, etc. had joined, 80 % of their trade was with the Community.' ([8]) But some demanded strict respect for their neutrality or insisted on their freedom in external tariff matters. On 22 July 1972, after the United Kingdom, Ireland, Denmark and Norway had signed a treaty of accession to the Communities, free-trade agreements were signed with Austria, Switzerland, Sweden and Iceland ([9]). A Norwegian referendum would later reject accession, and association agreements would be signed with Finland in October 1972 and Norway in 1973.

Association with Austria raised two awkward questions: the maintenance of trade flows with the state-trading countries and the sensitivity of the USSR to what it saw as a new *Anschluss*. But, according to Camille Becker, the official responsible for negotiations, the Soviet reaction was moderate. He tells how, when lecturing in Graz, he saw white posters with big red letters reading:

([1]) Interview with Camille Becker, 4 March 2004.
([2]) HAEC, Secretariat-General, Émile Noël, Memo to Helmut Sigrist, DG External Relations, concerning Turkey's involvement in the Ten's discussions on political cooperation, 28 June 1972.
([3]) PV spéc. 172, EC Commission, 15 July 1971, XXIV, p. 18; SEC(71) 2614, 12, 14 and 15 July 1972.
([4]) PV spéc. 199, EC Commission, 8 March 1972, XIX, pp. 6–9; SEC(72) 799-945, 8 March 1972.
([5]) PV spéc. 179, EC Commission, 28 February 1962, VI, p. 6; S/961/62 – S/01109/62, 28 February 1962.
([6]) PV spéc. 144, EC Commission, 1970, XVI, p. 11; PV spéc. 144, EC Commission, 25 and 27 November 1970, XX, 15, p. 24.

([7]) *Bulletin of the EEC*, No 3, 1963, p. 27; SG of the Commission, 'Agreements with the EFTA states not applying for membership', *Bulletin of the EC*, No 9, 1972.
([8]) Interview with Jean-François Deniau, 3 November 2004.
([9]) SG of the Commission, 'Agreements with the EFTA states not applying for membership', *Bulletin of the EC*, No 9, 1972.

'The EEC without Austria', which was the title of his lecture, albeit without the question mark initially announced. One listener asked him what the Soviets would do if Austria were to apply for accession and Brussels accepted. He answered: 'Ich glaube nicht, das sich die Panzer in Bewegung setzen werden' [1]. The next day a newspaper headline read: 'The tanks won't start rolling.' [2] But Jean Flory takes a different view: 'As soon as we started talking about Austria's rapprochement with the common market, the Russians said: "Watch out, it is a *casus belli*, it's *Anschluss*, you are bringing Austria and Germany together again". And that stalled everything for 10 years' [3]. The agreements with the EFTA countries provided for the dismantling of tariffs for manufactures. The agreements made no provision for agricultural harmonisation. This did not, as Wellenstein explains [4], preclude special 'tailor-made' arrangements for specific products. Only the agreements with Portugal (tinned fish, tomatoes, wine) and Iceland (fishery products) and minor arrangements with Austria and Switzerland partly concerned agriculture [5]. Portugal, with which association was impossible for the same reasons as with Spain, secured a free-trade agreement as an EFTA member on 27 September 1972.

International trade and development

Opening up to the world demanded that the Commission address underdevelopment. The Commission therefore attached considerable importance to its status as member of the Development Assistance Committee (DAC), an OECD group responsible for coordinating financial aid to the developing countries. The Six discussed beforehand issues of special interest to the common market, discussions in which France and Belgium demanded a

degree of freedom of action [6]. It was fundamentally in favour of agreements to stabilise commodity prices. The Commission had observer status with the International Coffee Council and the International Sugar Conference, speaking on the basis of positions prepared by the internal trade policy committee. There was even an article in the agreement giving it the possibility of becoming a party to the agreement. The Commission also tried to maintain cohesion between the Member States at the 1972 United Nations conference on cocoa.

It did not succeed in becoming the Community's sole representative in Unctad or in ironing out the differences in the Member States' development policies. At the 1964 Unctad in New Delhi, the developing countries asked for 'generalised preferences' for their exports to the industrialised countries. Determined to improve the prices paid for developing countries' products, the Community granted tariff preferences for a number of processed agricultural products and all manufactures from developing countries [7]. But these draft international product agreements were not accepted. Disappointed with the outcome of the April 1972 Unctad in Santiago, the Commission stated that the Community and its Member States had failed to project the image of a group of countries capable of pushing through a coherent policy for the developing countries [8].

Trade agreements with the Eastern Bloc: the awkward shift to a Community approach

Relations with the state-trading countries depended on the political will of the partners. They

---

[1] 'I don't think the tanks will start rolling.'
[2] Interview with Camille Becker, 4 March 2004.
[3] Interview with Jean Flory, 3 December 2003.
[4] Letter from Edmund P. Wellenstein to the author, 25 August 2005, p. 3.
[5] *Bulletin of the EC*, No 9, 1972, p. 11, and further details provided by Edmund P. Wellenstein in a letter to the author of 7 September 2005, p. 4.

[6] The OECD was founded at the Paris Conference of 13 and 14 January 1960. Its members were: Belgium, Canada, the United States, France, Italy, Japan, Portugal, the Federal Republic of Germany, the United Kingdom, the Netherlands and the EEC Commission. The OECD set up the Development Assistance Committee (DAC). HAEC, DGER, report 453, De Baerdemaeker, 'Joint action in international organisations, end of the transitional period', 15 December 1969. PV spéc. 94, EEC Commission, 23 February 1960, XXII3, pp. 8–10.
[7] Council decision of 22 June 1971.
[8] PV spéc. 206, EC Commission, 1972, I, pp. 3–4.

were not subject to the GATT rules since most of these countries were not members. Poland and Hungary, however, with the Commission's encouragement, joined the GATT in 1967 by means of a special protocol (¹). Negotiations were confined to quotas for the goods traded and the duration of the agreement. Relations were bilateral. The Commission would seek to bring the bilateral agreements within the Community sphere by including in them, following a Council decision of July 1960, an 'EEC clause' allowing them to be renegotiated to include provisions of the common commercial policy (²). The entry into force of the Community's agricultural regulations (14 January 1962) basically meant that quantitative restrictions on imports of the products covered by market organisations were abolished, but this seemed impossible to apply to trade with the Eastern Bloc, where agricultural export prices did not reflect market forces; and it was impossible to persuade them to grant the Community compensatory measures. The Commission therefore wanted, at the very least, some coordination of the Member States' trading policies with the Eastern Bloc, something the Council rejected (³). In the end, the Commission proposed abandoning the system of agricultural quotas with the Eastern Bloc and replacing it with a more flexible system of estimates which, if exceeded, would trigger a halt to imports (⁴).

Strangely, although it refused to recognise the Communities, the USSR nevertheless asked them for tariff concessions. But it did so through certain Member States which would have been only too happy to liaise with it on the Community's behalf. Jean Rey refused to let the Council deny him the right to negotiate tariffs in his own good time (⁵). The Council nevertheless agreed, at the Commission's proposal, to facilitate imports of certain Russian products (vodka, caviar, tinned crab). The Commission then proposed, as the definitive period of the Community neared, that Member States limit the duration of bilateral trade agreements, which was often very long, standardise quota lists and adopt identical import and control arrangements (⁶). Furthermore, owing to the start of the definitive period of the Communities, the Commission notified all the state-trading countries that it alone had the power to negotiate trade agreements, thereby laying down a major political marker in relations with the East. Not until 5 November 1968 did a Soviet diplomat, Buzykin, first secretary at the USSR's Brussels embassy, make an official visit to the Commission, and that could not be construed as recognition (⁷).

Following the invasion of Czechoslovakia by Warsaw Pact forces in August 1968, the Commission scaled down its contacts with the Eastern Bloc countries that took part, although it maintained unofficial relations with some of them (⁸). Notwithstanding this, the Commission, so quick to deplore French bilateralism, accepted, for political reasons, a trade agreement between Germany and Poland that did not contain an EEC clause. In contrast, it demanded an explanation after France signed a long-term agreement with the Soviet Union on 26 May 1969, there having been no prior consultations between the Six (⁹), and a 10-year economic cooperation agreement with Poland in 1972. The Commission did all in its power to establish sound economic cooperation with the East on an equal, non-discriminatory basis. It strove to persuade the USSR to recognise it as the Mem-

(¹) Letter from Edmund P. Wellenstein to the author, 7 September 2005, p. 5.
(²) S/03412 final, clause for insertion in the future bilateral agreements of Member States of the EEC (proposal of the Commission to the Council), 7 July 1960. The clause stipulated that, where necessitated by obligations arising from the EEC Treaty and relating to the gradual introduction of a common commercial policy, negotiations would be opened as soon as possible to make the requisite amendments to the agreement concerned.
(³) 'Imports of agricultural products from the Eastern Bloc', COM(62) 101 final addendum, 26 June 1962.
(⁴) 'Commission proposal to the Council on the arrangements for imports from State-trading countries of agricultural products subject to regulation', COM(63) 7, 9 January 1963.
(⁵) PV spéc. 212, EEC Commission, 1963, II.2, p. 5; PV spéc. 214, EEC Commission, 1963, XV.3, p. 15.
(⁶) Colonna di Paliano, G., 'East–West trade relations', Bulletin of the EEC, No 11, 1965.
(⁷) 'First official visit by a Soviet diplomat to the Commission, information memo distributed on Mr Deniau's instructions', SEC(68) 3799, 5 November 1968.
(⁸) PV spéc. 47, EC Commission, 11 September 1968, VI.D, pp. 7–9.
(⁹) PV spéc. 80, EC Commission, 1969, XVI, XIX, pp. 11–14.

ber States' sole representative ([1]). The arrangements introduced in 1968 to subject these relations nonetheless to the rules of the common commercial policy was a success for the Commission on what was a highly sensitive political issue, feels Edmund Wellenstein ([2]), referring to the ultimately successful efforts to harmonise at least the Member States' quota lists. By 1973 the common commercial policy would be fully applicable to the state-trading countries and the Commission would have taken control of the old bilateral trade agreements between the Member States and the Eastern Bloc countries.

The Commission was particularly supportive of a Communist country that had broken with the USSR, Yugoslavia, with which it opened trade negotiations ([3]). The draft agreement had a political impact in that it would, as the Commission put it in 1967 ([4]), give Yugoslavia a degree of political and psychological relief. On 19 March 1970 the Council agreed to sign a three-year agreement covering adjustments to the system of levies on baby beef (40 % of Yugoslavia's exports to the Community) and price guarantees for wine imports. A series of visits were made to Belgrade: Deniau visited in 1970 and was followed in June 1971 by Commission President Malfatti. Marshal Tito asked them to classify Yugoslavia as a non-candidate EFTA country rather than an Eastern Bloc country ([5]).

Relations with Romania were not purely commercial either and, when the Federal Republic of Germany negotiated a bilateral trade agreement with Romania in 1963, the Commission wrote in the following terms: 'Since there are no diplomatic relations per se, the Federal Government must view the conclusion of such agreements with the Eastern Bloc countries as an opportu-

nity to discuss issues other than economic relations per se.' ([6]) Romania was highly active towards the Commission, and its ambassador was the only Eastern Bloc ambassador to frequent the Commission's offices. In the 1970s the Commission, Wellenstein adds ([7]), proposed that certain Romanian products be eligible for generalised preferences owing to the country's low level of development.

Mutual consultation agreements with South America and Asia

Relations with Latin America had been difficult since 1958 because the common market had, from the very outset, inspired unease and anxiety on the South American subcontinent, which, in 1959, wanted technical assistance to create a Latin American common market based on the experience acquired in Europe ([8]). Latin America feared capital flight to the common market and vehemently objected to the preferences granted to the countries and overseas territories linked to the Six by the Yaoundé Convention and to a Community external tariff that it judged too high. Latin American insecurity threatened to complicate matters for the Community at the GATT.

The Commission therefore wanted to talk, but the consultation agreements project met with a frosty reception. Hallstein sent Berthoin on a tour of the Latin American capitals in 1961 ([9]). The Commission proposed ties with the Organisation of American States (OAS) and the US 'Alliance for Progress' and offered placements for Latin American trainees. The Community campaigned

([1]) PV spéc. 202, EC Commission, 1972, XIX.A.

([2]) Letter from Edmund P. Wellenstein to the author, 10 August 2005.

([3]) PV spéc. 201, EEC Commission, 10 October 1962, VII1, p. 6.

([4]) Commission communication to the Council concerning the Community's relations with Yugoslavia, G (67) 43, 31 January 1967.

([5]) HAEU, EN 1518, Émile Noël to Renato Ruggiero, memo on Franco Maria Malfatti's visit to Yugoslavia, 21 June 1971. See also HAEU, EN 204, Émile Noël to Renato Ruggiero, 10 November 1970.

([6]) HAEC, Commission, Executive Secretariat, I/G/796/63, 10 December 1963, telegram from the Government of the FRG concerning the conclusion of a trade agreement between Germany and Romania, Harkort, President and DG I of the EEC Commission, 'Commission proposal concerning the conclusion of a four-year trade agreement between the FRG and Romania'.

([7]) Letter from Edmund P. Wellenstein to the author, 7 September 2005, p. 6.

([8]) PV 69, EEC Commission, 22–25 July 1959, VI, p. 8; PV 271, EEC Commission, 24 and 25 April 1964, VIII, p. 17, Colombia/Venezuela regional integration project.

([9]) In his interview (31 January 2003), Georges Berthoin recalls visiting Argentina, Brazil, Chile, Costa Rica, Cuba, Ecuador, El Salvador, Honduras, Panama, Paraguay, Peru, Uruguay and Venezuela.

in defence of the international agreements on tropical products. The Commission recommended that the Council grant more generous access to the European market for finished and semi-finished products from the Latin American countries. This proposal was crowned with resounding political success when the Community supported the concept of non-reciprocal generalised preferences (GSP) for developing countries and decided to apply them on a large scale. Jean Rey also asked the Member States to refrain from piecemeal contacts with the Latin American countries, to keep the Commission closely informed and to forgo national rivalries (¹). He argued with conviction for the introduction of a single charter for economic cooperation between Europe and Latin America.

Now that trust had been established, the Commission received a flurry of requests to negotiate trade agreements in 1969. In December 1971 a mechanism for dialogue with the Community was established at the request of the United Nations Economic Commission for Latin America (Unecla) (²). On 8 November 1971 the Community and Argentina signed a three-year non-preferential trade agreement on regular meat exports. Brazil called for an association agreement but, like other Latin American countries, was looking for a mechanism for consultation with the Community to limit the impact of the European common tariff and the preferences granted to the African countries.

At the time, Asia was uncharted territory. Because Japan was a low-wage economy, the Community had a special safeguard clause inserted in the Member States' trade agreements with Japan; this clause was a source of continual friction. The grounds for an agreement with Japan were, the Commission wrote to the Council in 1963, that there was now a more obvious political interest in closer ties with Japan, which was not just a leading power in Asia but a country on a relatively exposed frontier of the free world (³). The Commission, having at last obtained the Council's authorisation, opened negotiations for a Community trade agreement in 1969 (⁴). But there were to be no more than bilateral agreements between Japan and the European countries and an EEC–Japan agreement on the voluntary limitation of exports of cotton textiles concluded on 3 November 1970 (⁵). Japan was not willing to accept the special safeguard clause for its trade with the Community in exchange for the end of the exception system it enjoyed in the GATT (⁶).

Georges Berthoin reports contacting the Chinese chargé d'affaires in London in 1971: 'I asked the Commission for authorisation. It is the only time I did so. It was, after all, a little sensitive. Dahrendorf was External Relations Commissioner, and he sent me a note saying: "You are establishing contact at your own risk." I have kept the note, it is great. So, I had a five-and-a-half-hour conversation with the Chinese chargé d'affaires in London. He sent out the interpreter who was supposed to advise or, rather, spy on him' (⁷). Berthoin believes the Communities' recognition by the People's Republic of China in 1975 can be traced back to these contacts.

The Member States were not happy about the Commission's repeated interventions to standardise their bilateral trade agreements with the Eastern Bloc or Japan. Avoiding tackling them head-on, the Commission promised them that it would, if necessary, process their requests for derogations under Article 115 in two days. The Council decision of 16 December 1969 conferring on the Commission exclusive powers — rather than powers shared with the Member States — for negotiations concerning commercial

---

(¹) Memo from Mr Rey on the contents of a Community action programme for Latin America, COM(62) 35, 24 February 1962.

(²) In 1984 this UN regional organisation became the Economic Commission for Latin America and the Caribbean (ECLAC).

(³) Commission proposal to the Council concerning Member States' trade relations with Japan, COM(63) 245, 26 June 1963.

(⁴) 'Japan — economic power and partner for the common market', *Bulletin of the EC*, 1969, No 12, 1969, pp. 17–20.

(⁵) *Bulletin of the EC*, No 1, 1972, p. 43.

(⁶) Letter from Edmund P. Wellenstein to the author, 25 August 2005, p. 5.

(⁷) Interview with Georges Berthoin, 31 January 2003.

relations made standardising bilateral trade agreements easier ([1]).

A Mediterranean policy of good-neighbourly relations

The Commission wanted to develop a coherent Mediterranean policy since peace and cooperation in the area were historically, politically and economically vital to Europe, regardless of whether the Mediterranean countries were eligible to join the Community.

The Commission raised the possibility of an association agreement with Israel in May 1960 and backed the country's accession to the GATT ([2]). It opposed any attempt to boycott Israel when that country asked to open preferential trade negotiations ([3]). A first trade agreement was signed on 4 June 1964 and a second on 29 June 1970. These agreements facilitated Israeli citrus exports to the Community, but US President Lyndon B. Johnson entered the fray. Deniau was visited by the US ambassador, who told him that the United States was the world's biggest citrus producer and had to be given the same treatment ([4]). When dealing with Egypt, the Commission took account of Egypt's behaviour towards Israel and of the attitude of the Federal Republic of Germany, which had broken off relations with Egypt under the Hallstein doctrine ([5]). A preferential agreement was signed with Egypt on 18 December 1972. In the Maghreb, the end of the war in Algeria got things moving again. Tunisia and Morocco wanted association agreements. Association agreements, effectively free-trade agreements, were signed with Tunisia and Morocco on 28 and 31 March 1969 respectively. Despite independence, Algeria remained eligible for EDF aid under commitments given by France prior to July 1962 ([6]). But, before negotiating an agreement, the Commission wanted France and Algeria first to sign a definitive framework agreement. It therefore called for caution ([7]). There would be no cooperation agreement with Algeria until 26 April 1976. A global Mediterranean policy would first be worked out in 1978.

The Common Market Commission (which became the Commission of the European Communities in 1967) had therefore conducted association negotiations with European countries, regardless of whether they were candidates for accession; it had also negotiated trade agreements with the Mediterranean countries. It had worked to win the trust of the Latin American countries and Japan. The association and trade agreements gave the European Community, writes Jean-François Deniau, 'a European dimension that supplemented the national dimension, which was necessary for us and useful for the rest of the world' ([8]). Looking back, Edmund Wellenstein very rightly points out that non-member countries differed in the objectives they pursued through association. There were those that wished to develop trade relations in the GATT (the US, Canada, Japan and, later, certain Eastern Bloc countries) and those that wanted a non-preferential trade agreement (including Yugoslavia and Iran). Others were associated by virtue of Part IV of the Treaty of Rome, which later became the Yaoundé Convention. Some wanted association because they had once had a

([1]) Deniau, J.-Fr., 'A new stage in the implementation of the common commercial policy', *Bulletin of the EEC*, No 2, 1970, pp. 5–7.

([2]) PV spéc. 184, EEC Commission, 4 April 1962, XXXIV, p. 13; C/138/62, 3 and 4 April 1962.

([3]) PV spéc. 262, EEC Commission, 19 February 1964, VII, p. 8; G/59/64; SE, I/S/04037/61, Memo to the Commission on the aide-mémoire from the Government of Israel concerning that country's request to enter into negotiations with the Community on questions arising in relations with Israel, 18 July 1961.

([4]) Interview with Jean-François Deniau, 3 November 2004.

([5]) Hallstein doctrine: The Federal Republic of Germany broke off diplomatic relations with any country that recognised the German Democratic Republic. PV spéc. 76, EC Commission, 30 April 1969, XXXV, p. 23; PV spéc. 146, EC Commission, 10 December 1970, XVIII, p. 7; PV spéc. 146, EC Commission, 9–10 December 1970, XXII, pp. 9 and 10; SEC(70) 4413.

([6]) PV spéc. 236, EEC Commission, 17 July 1963, XIII, p. 13.

([7]) HAEC, Secretariat, VIII/G/85/63, memo to the Commission concerning the working paper on the Community's relations with Algeria, 29 January 1963; VIII/A/1, ML working paper on relations between the European Economic Community and Algeria, 22 January 1963; HAEC, I/G/355/64 final, interim report by the Commission on exploratory talks with Algeria, 9 September 1964.

([8]) 'Agreements with the EFTA states not applying for membership', *Bulletin of the EC*, No 9, 1972, p. 22.

Development of the EEC's external trade between 1958 and 1970

1. Development of EEC imports

	1958		1970	
	%	million USD	%	million USD
Industrialised countries	*53*	*8 526*	*58*	*26 411*
EFTA	22	3 608	23	10 715
Other European countries	5	834	6	2 887
North America	20	3238	23	10 298
Other industrialised countries	5	845	6	2 511
Developing countries	*42*	*6 824*	*35*	*16 105*
Associated overseas countries and territories	10	1 546	8	3 517
Central Africa	6	1 048	8	3 510
Latin America	10	1 647	8	3 591
Western Asia	11	1 803	9	3 899
Other countries of Asia	5	779	3	1 588
State-trading countries	*5*	*789*	*7*	*3 050*
Total	**100**	**16 156**	**100**	**45 621**

2. Development of EEC exports

	1958		1970	
	%	million USD	%	million USD
Industrialised countries	*54*	*8 638*	*66*	*29 836*
EFTA	31	4 970	33	14 884
Other European countries	7	1 143	11	4 954
North America	12	1 901	16	7 362
Other industrialised countries	4	623	6	2 636
Developing countries	*39*	*6 125*	*26*	*11 546*
Associated overseas countries and territories	12	1 860	7	3 253
Central Africa	6	941	3.5	1 597
Latin America	10	1 604	6.5	2 945
Western Asia	4	693	4	1 831
Other countries of Asia	6	1 027	4	1 921
State-trading countries	*6*	*980*	*8*	*3 405*
Total	**100**	**15 911**	**100**	**45 198**

Source: Bulletin of the EC, No 6, 1972.

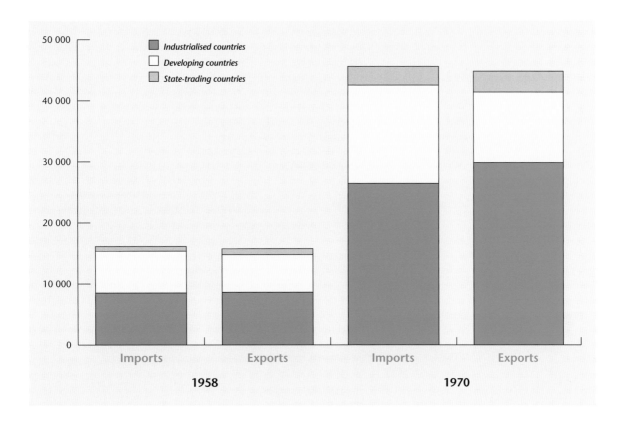

special relationship with a member country (North Africa) while others wanted a preferential agreement (Spain, Israel). And there were European countries that hoped to accede, some of them seeing association as a stepping stone (¹). The Commission considered each request on its merits but noted that the Treaty was an organic whole and that the objectives of the common market were political as well as economic (²).

Fourth challenge: the Commission in international organisations

At the time of the Merger Treaty, which, on 6 July 1967, brought the EEC and Euratom Commissions and the ECSC High Authority together

within the Single Commission, the Communities were involved in the following international organisations (³):

The EEC Treaty gave no details on the Community's relations with certain international organisations or negotiation forums. Article 229 provided for the Commission to liaise with the GATT and the UN. Articles 230 and 231 of the Treaty also spoke of suitable cooperation to be established by the Commission with the Council of Europe and the OEEC. But the Commission would seek to represent the Community in international organisations and all international negotiations of an economic nature, as its Executive Secretary Émile Noël explained in 1958 (⁴).

How was the Commission to silence those who denied its right to be the Member States' sole rep-

(¹) Letter from Edmund P. Wellenstein to the author, 10 April 2005, p. 2; see also the same author's '25 années de relations extérieures de la Communauté européenne', European Documentation, No 4, 1979, p. 16.
(²) Dahrendorf, R., Speech, 25 January 1971, Deutsche Gesellschaft für Auswärtige Politik (Bonn), published in Europe Document, 12 March 1971.

(³) HAEC, BAC 3/1978 503, memo to Jean Rey, 26 June 1967.
(⁴) FJME, ARM 19/2/1, memo by Émile Noël on current European issues, 26 July 1958, p. 6.

369

The Commission in international organisations

UN	UN specialised agencies	Regional organisations in Europe	Non-European regional organisations	Trade agreements
Economic and Social Council	ILO	OEEC/OECD	Afro-Malagasy Union for Economic Cooperation	International Coffee Council
Regional Commission:	FAO	Council of Europe		International Wheat Council
— Economic Commission for Europe	Unesco	WEU	Organisation of American States	
— Economic Commission for Asia and the Far East	WHO	Customs Cooperation Council	General Treaty on Central American Economic Integration	International Olive Oil Council
— Economic Commission for Latin America	IBRD	EFTA		International Sugar Council
— Economic Commission for Africa	IMF	European Conference of Ministers of Transport		International Cotton Council
	UNIDO	Central Office for International Carriage by Rail		General Agreement on Tariffs and Trade
		Central Commission for Navigation on the Rhine		
		Intergovernmental Committee for European Migration		
		International Institute for the Unification of Private Law		

resentative in international institutions? The Commission would, in all international negotiations, seek the formula that best represented the Community interest and would, where powers were shared, accept the Community's representation by one member from the Commission and a representative from the Member State holding the Council Presidency (¹). Where the Community

had exclusive powers, a memo explained (²), it was no longer possible for Member States, whether individually or collectively, however much prior coordination there may have been, to draft or express the Community's point of view. But the Commission constantly found itself having to

---

(¹) PV spéc. 382, EEC Commission, 29–30 November 1966, XI, p. 8.

(²) HAEC, SEC(70) 1229 on the Community's participation in the work of international organisations, I/5169/70-F, memo to the Commission on the Community's participation in the work of international organisations, 1 April 1970.

point out that the Treaties gave it responsibility for preparing and conducting trade negotiations, assisted by a special committee appointed by the Council (¹). Deniau recalls this problem when he was mandated to negotiate the United Kingdom's accession to the Communities: 'When there was talk of my being appointed to head the team of negotiators as the Commission's representative, Boegner (²), on behalf of the French Foreign Ministry, made special representations to tell the Commission: "Don't do it! France is against it."' (³)

The Commission did not always — at least, not in its early days — succeed in ensuring a presence in those international forums where it thought its participation was essential. For instance, in December 1958 it was not invited to a meeting of the UN Economic Commission for Africa, a fact Jean Rey attributed to 'the attitude of the European Member States of the Economic Commission for Africa', a not-so-veiled reference to France and Belgium (⁴). It was, however, present at Unecla, but it had to settle for joint representation with a senior official from the country holding the Council Presidency (⁵). The Commission refrained from requesting observer status at the UN Economic Commission for Europe (UNECE) in Geneva because the Council for Mutual Economic Assistance (Comecon), an organisation of Eastern Bloc countries controlled by the USSR, might claim identical status and so undermine the common front presented by the free world (⁶). In 1959, the Commission, with the backing of the United States, wanted to represent the European Economic Community at the UN Food and Agriculture Organisation (FAO); some of the Six's delegations opposed this, preferring the Commission to be confined to a liaison role (⁷). The Commission and the FAO would conclude a working agreement in 1962. In July 1958 the Commission signed a liaison agreement with the International Labour Office and,

like the ECSC High Authority before it, a mutual consultation and cooperation agreement with the International Labour Organisation (⁸). In 1964 the Commission exchanged observers with the United Nations Education, Scientific and Cultural Organisation (Unesco). In late 1958 the Commission attended meetings of the United Nations Economic and Social Council (Ecosoc) as the 'guest of the Secretary-General'. It was an observer at the 1964 Unctad, where the USSR and the underdeveloped countries accused the European common market of being a 'closed economic grouping' (⁹). There was very little agreement between the Six and the Commission at Unctad (¹⁰). The Commission proposed organising commodity markets, whereas the Member States rejected the tax on coffee and cocoa and the harmonisation of their taxes (¹¹). The Member States did, however, back the Commission on the introduction of generalised preferences for developing countries.

More surprisingly, the Commission was invited in 1958 to attend the meeting of the Board of Governors of the International Monetary Fund (IMF) in Delhi. Marjolin had to go. The Commission asked the Member States not to take a position before it had drawn up proposals (¹²). In 1965 the Commission began negotiating procedures for reforming the international monetary system (IMS) with the US Treasury (¹³).

(¹) Article 111 and Article 113.

(²) Jean-Marc Boegner was the French representative to the European Community.

(³) Interview with Jean-François Deniau, 3 November 2004.

(⁴) PV 44, EEC Commission, 7 January 1959, V, pp. 6–7.

(⁵) PV 57, EEC Commission, 23 April 1959, IV1, pp. 6–7.

(⁶) PV 22, EEC Commission, 19 March 1963, VIII, p. 8.

(⁷) PV 79, EEC Commission, 28 October 1959, IV.5, pp. 7–8.

(⁸) Liaison agreement of 7 July 1958 between the International Labour Organisation and the EEC, PV 21, EEC Commission, 7 July 1958; PV 90, EEC Commission, 3 February 1960, XII, p. 20; PV 123, EEC Commission, 9 November 1960, XI, p. 12, text of the agreement approved by the Commission on 18 June 1958.

(⁹) HAEC, DGER, I-A-3, I/8318/62, information memo on meeting of a global conference on trade under the aegis of the UN; HAEC, S/07767/62, 26 November 1962, memo to the Commission concerning the communication on the global conference on trade and development; DGER, I/S/07767/62, information memo from Jean Rey on the global conference on trade and development, Brussels, 16 November 1962.

(¹⁰) HAEC, memo to Ralf Dahrendorf concerning Commission's discussions on President's attendance at the third Unctad conference, 1 April 1972.

(¹¹) HAEC, DGER, I/S/0332/64 of 12 February 1964, United Nations Conference on Trade and Development, memo from Jean Rey.

(¹²) PV 68, EEC Commission, 15 July 1959, XI, pp. 8–9.

(¹³) PV spéc. 328, EEC Commission, 9 September 1965, XIV6, pp. 11–12. See also paragraph on the Commission's external trade policy.

In contrast, relations with the OEEC were an obligation under Article 231 of the Treaty. Suspicious of the European Economic Community, the OEEC revised its policy after the failure of the free-trade area. Strict reciprocity of representation was not possible because the Commission refused to countenance external observers in its directorates-general, but it did accept regular meetings (¹). The Paris Convention of 14 December 1960, which reconstituted the OEEC as the Organisation for Economic Cooperation and Development, laid down the form of the European Communities' representation. The Commission was even invited by the French government to make proposals on economic cooperation in the West. With some difficulty, the Commission obtained Coreper's consent for the Commission to be the Community's sole representative to the OEEC. As Henri-Marie Varenne recalls (²), Jean Rey, who chaired the special committee from the Commission and the Member States, used the fact that the Commission managed the European Development Fund (EDF) to obtain for it a seat on the OECD's Development Assistance Committee (DAC) (³). The Commission was also active in the Group of 20+1, the OECD's 20 member countries plus the Commission handling trade policy in the OECD, by virtue of the common commercial policy (⁴). For the Commission, the OECD was a forum for consultation and coordination upstream of global negotiations in the GATT (⁵). By virtue of Euratom, the Single Commission was automatically involved in the European Nuclear Energy Agency (ENEA) and the Dragon and Eurochemic joint ventures. In 1970 the progress made by the Community caused the relationship with the OECD to develop (⁶). For the first time, an official meeting was organised between Commission President Jean Rey and OECD Secretary-General Emile van Lennep (⁷).

Links were established with other organisations, among them NATO (though ties were confined to the exchange of economic, i.e. non-military, information) and, above all, the Council of Europe. Hallstein took care of this personally in 1958 (⁸). The two organisations exchanged annual reports, the Secretary-General of the Commission and the Committees of Ministers met at least once a year, and Commission officials were involved in the activities of the Council of Europe, although that organisation was given no formal role in the Commission's decision-making system. Cooperation was planned on social affairs, education and a range of legal issues (⁹). Coreper criticised Hallstein for this close relationship (¹⁰). Observers began to be exchanged with the Western European Union (WEU) in 1958. The two organisations did not always cover the same issues; in 1969 the Commission was not invited to a ministerial session because the topic was not economic and the French government did not want the Commission at the meeting (¹¹).

When the Non-Proliferation Treaty (NPT) opened for signing by States on 1 July 1968, the Commission demanded that Euratom monitor compliance by the signatory Community Member States; this was opposed by the Soviet Union and the United States, which backed the IAEA. The Commission feared that application of the NPT would be incompatible with the Euratom Treaty. It therefore asked the Community Member States not to ratify the NPT until the Commission and the IAEA had

---

(¹) HAEC, Secretariat, 03912, 25 May 1959, memo to the Commission, DGER, Directorate for association with third countries, I-2466/59-F, 'Information memo on relations to be established with the OEEC'.

(²) Interview with Henri-Marie Varenne, 17 December 2003.

(³) PV and PV spéc. 110, EEC Commission, 6 July 1960, VII–VIII, p. 7 and p. 4 respectively.

(⁴) PV spéc. 89, EEC Commission, 27 January 1960, IV, pp. 4–7; 20 Member States + the Commission.

(⁵) Commission's response to the questionnaire from the Group of Four, COM(60) 36, 10 March 1960.

(⁶) BAC 3/1978 572, Permanent delegate to the OECD, DGER, Report No 461, 7 April 1970, 'Relations between the Commission of the European Communities and the OECD.'

(⁷) Report from the Commission Delegation to the OECD on relations between the Commission of the European Communities and the OECD, 15 April 1970.

(⁸) PV 7, EEC Commission, 5–6 March 1958, XIII.b, p. 9; PV 22, EEC Commission, 23 June 1958, Xd, p. 9.

(⁹) HAEC, DGER, memo to the directors-general on the information meeting between the European Commission and the Secretary-General of the Council of Europe (Strasbourg, 16 March 1972), 12 April 1972.

(¹⁰) PV 56, EEC Commission, 16 April 1959, IV.1, p. 6.

(¹¹) PV spéc. 79, EC Commission, 21–22 May 1969, XVIII2–XXX, pp. 6–9; (doc. G/69/98); PV spéc. 80, EC Commission, 4 June 1969, XXIV, p. 22; SG, doc. G (69) 98, 23 May 1969, European Commission President Jean Rey to Gaston Thorn, President of the Council of Foreign Ministers; telegram 'viens d'apprendre [...]'; telex from Gaston Thorn to Jean Rey, 23 May 1969, No 210/69, Comeur, 18, 59.

concluded a monitoring agreement that ensured compliance with the EAEC Treaty. The NPT was signed by Luxembourg on 14 August, the Netherlands on 19 August and Belgium on 20 August 1968; Italy and Germany signed in 1969. The European Community and the IAEA signed an agreement in September 1972 that took account of Euratom and avoided needless duplication of the Community's inspections [1].

The growth in the Community's foreign trade was remarkable — the period 1957–67 saw imports from EFTA increase by 96 %, from the developing countries by 68 %, from the state-trading countries by 183 % and from the United States by 108 % — and the Communities' external relations developed rapidly [2]. Served well by the Commission, the Community became a recognised and envied partner for non-member countries. The Member States, however, were not yet ready to allow the Commission to develop an external economic policy encompassing areas other than tariffs and trade. In 1972 the commercial policy, let alone the external economic policy, had still to be fully standardised.

But successes in the GATT brought a trend towards standardisation. Although the 'empty chair' crisis was something of a discouragement, it did not cause the Commission to give up its plans to develop a common commercial, economic and industrial policy [3]. According to Jean-François Deniau, it also met with violent reactions on the part of the United States: 'With Johnson, we were at daggers drawn: "You've cheated us! We helped you. You couldn't have built Europe without us. And now you're com-

peting with us!" [4]' The monetary crisis that began in 1969 brought home to the Community the pressing need for a common monetary policy. In response to external monetary problems, the Commission confined itself to asking the Member States to adopt cohesion measures after US President Nixon decided to tax imports and float the dollar on 15 August 1971. Commission President Malfatti issued the following warning: 'The problem of our currencies' value against the dollar is important, but I have to be honest and tell you that the Community currencies' value against each other is still more important.' [5] The Commission developed a doctrine in response to the monetary crisis; the doctrine was based on the general realignment of exchange rates, the creation of new international cash reserves in the form of special drawing rights (SDR) and, above all, the creation of a Community mechanism for monetary solidarity.

In the 14 years since the foundation of the institutions of the Treaties of Rome, the European Commission had successfully asserted its authority, despite resistance from some Member States, because it had been able to organise dialogue with governments and had proved itself a competent partner in world trade negotiations. In short, the common external trade policy handed the controls to new decision-makers in the persons of the directors-general for external relations and external trade and the Commissioners, determined to achieve the objectives of the Treaty, persuaded of the benefits of European unity for the free world, capable of innovating in relations with the developing countries and cautious with regard to the American superpower. Ever since the Communities had been established, the European 'federalists', inside and outside the Commission — Monnet being at the heart of the action — had strengthened the role of the Commission, an institution invested with powers that could be used to facilitate political integration. As far back

[1] ECSC, EEC, EAEC, Commission *General Report on the Activities of the Communities in 1972*.

[2] *Bulletin of the EEC*, No 3, 1969; see also HAEC, SEC 474 507 1965, Com. Pol., DGERR, I/14388/64-F Rev 1, 'The EEC's external trade: 1958–1963 (general overview)', December 1964.

[3] BAC 25/1980 1098, DG VIII, Secretariat 862, Brussels, Hans-Broder Krohn, Memo to Klaus Meyer, Deputy Secretary-General, on Community action for Berlin, 18 February 1972.

[4] Interviews with Jean-François Deniau, 3 and 10 November 2004.

[5] 'International monetary events', *Bulletin of the EC*, No 9/10, 1971; Idem, 1971, No 11; Idem, 1972, No 1; Idem, 1972, No 3.

as 1960, Émile Noël explained that Community action demanded agreement on a common defence policy [1]. In the absence of political union, the Commission pursued external political activities rather than an external policy. The insistence with which the Commission demanded a right to interpret the guidelines is, however, quite striking [2]. In 1971 Dahrendorf declared, with considerable foresight, that external relations would one day be the Communities' third pillar of activity. Little by little, the Commission put together Community external policies that went beyond trade policy: it brought Berlin into the Community's external relations, it designed a new Mediterranean policy and formed a new relationship with Latin America and the developing countries in the GATT and Unctad [3]. A common foreign policy was not yet on the agenda and, on the eve of the first enlargement, the Commission confirmed the importance of the political objectives that gave the Community its scope and purpose, as if the 'empty chair' crisis had never happened [4]. Before the 1972 Paris summit the Commission decided to make its contribution to the debate on economic and monetary union, the Community's role in the world and the institutional development of the enlarged Community. The Commission, explained a memo from the Secretariat-General, intended to give greater thought to issues that were not, strictly speaking, within the Community's powers for the moment but which called for Europe to assert its solidarity on the international stage [5]. It was not therefore indifferent to the European political cooperation begun in the early 1970s. It was time to move on from external trade relations to economic relations that reflected political relations, explained

Noël in 1972, noting that, in the sphere of external relations, the Council and the delegations harboured great reservations about any increase in the Commission's remit and were already reluctant to allow it to exercise the powers conferred on it by the Treaty [6].

In its eagerness to voice the common project, to explain what unity should mean, the Commission had found itself embroiled in a rivalry with governments since 1958. Compromise was nevertheless sought by the Commission and accepted by the governments. The Commission's offices or permanent representations abroad soon became delegations, and the head of delegation was accredited to the minister for foreign affairs or the Head of State, thereby acquiring a new prestige. Thus, thanks to the crises and thanks to the Commission's remarkable determination to represent the spirit of unity, Community diplomats held their own, alongside the Member States' foreign offices, proposing common solutions to major international problems and taking account of the diverse interests of the Member States and non-member countries, albeit with a tendency to consider the Atlantic world the centre of gravity of international relations. On 1 July 1968, upon completion of the customs union 18 months ahead of schedule, the European Commission stated that: 'At a time when the organisation of the world on the scale of the old sovereign nations is yielding place to organisation at the level of continents, it is important that the errors of the past should not be repeated at this higher level, that the clash of nations should not give way to the clash of entire continents. Consequently, it is Europe's duty to organise its cooperation and association with the other main groups in the world' [7]. In 1972 Ralf Dahrendorf, the Commissioner responsible for external relations, expressed the view that the experiment in European

[1] HAEU, EN 878, Émile Noël to Jean Monnet, 27 October 1960.

[2] FMJE, AMK C 33/1/249, translation of interview given by Ralf Dahrendorf to *Europäische Gemeinschaft*.

[3] BAC 25/1980 1098, DG VIII, Secretariat 862, Brussels, Hans-Broder Krohn, memo to Klaus Meyer, Deputy Secretary-General, on Community action for Berlin, 18 February 1972.

[4] HAEU, EN 85, preparations for Conference of Heads of State and Government, draft report of ad hoc group to ministers, 6 September 1972.

[5] HAEU, EN 148, draft memo to President Malfatti and Jean-François Deniau containing first thoughts on a Commission contribution for the Conference of Heads of State and Government in 1972, 17 January 1972.

[6] HAEU, EN 159, memo to the Commission on external relations and the Community's responsibilities in the world, 8 March 1972. HAEU, EN 1046, memo to President Malfatti containing observations on the Commission's role and tasks, 22 June 1970.

[7] 'Declaration by the Commission on the occasion of the achievement of the Customs Union on 1 July 1968', *Bulletin of the EEC*, No 7, 1968, p. 5.

Frank Borman, a NASA astronaut who was part of Apollo 8, the first mission to fly round the Moon, visits the Commission on 7 February 1969. Before he left for Europe, Richard Nixon stated: 'So I think it is very appropriate for Colonel Borman to go to western Europe and to bring to them not only the greetings of the people of the United States, but to point out what is the fact: that we in America do not consider that this is a monopoly, these great new discoveries.' (Remarks by Richard Nixon announcing a goodwill tour to western Europe by Colonel Frank Borman, USAF, 30 January 1969, in Woolley, J., and Peters, G., *The American Presidency Project* (online). Santa Barbara, CA: University of California (host), Gerhard Peters (database). Accessible at: http://www.presidency.ucsb.edu/ws/?pid=1997. From left to right: Frank Borman, Jean Rey and Fritz Hellwig.

unity, conducted in the middle of the Cold War, showed that the free countries were capable of holding their own against the duopoly formed by the United States and the Soviet Union. The last word should be left to Jean Rey: 'The Community, and still more the Commission, has always considered itself a beginning rather than an end.' [1]

GÉRARD BOSSUAT and ANAÏS LEGENDRE

[1] HAEC, 144/92 867, Jean Rey, *New trends in the economic organisation of the world*, speech delivered on 12 September 1966 to the XXXVIth International Congress on Industrial Chemistry, Brussels, 10–21 September 1966.

Chapter 18

From 'overseas countries and territories' to development aid

The Community's relationship with the overseas countries and territories was a particularly important issue during the negotiation of the Treaties of Rome and in the first years of the EEC Commission's operation.

Part Four of the EEC Treaty deals with the association of the overseas countries and territories. Although the intentions of the six Member States were generous, the objectives were more prosaic. As a result, the implementation of the Treaty in this field was to prove difficult, despite the conventions that were drafted and signed with the overseas countries and territories.

Cold War and decolonisation

In this area, more than any other, the geopolitical context at the time Community policy was being developed and implemented was of crucial importance. In the grip of the Cold War, the United States and the USSR were locked in a titanic struggle to establish their influence in the southern hemisphere. Meanwhile, the colonial empires continued to disintegrate. Africa followed Asia in the struggle for independence. France, which had suffered the painful loss of Indochina and then recognised the independence of Morocco and Tunisia, saw the problem of Algeria descend into a tragedy which would continue to reverberate until 1962. The French colonies in sub-Saharan Africa gained their independence in the years after 1958, but with the establishment of a Franco-African Community.

The Belgian Congo was an exception. A plan conceived as recently as 1955 did not envisage Belgium's 'tenth province' obtaining independence for another 30 years! The reality check was all the more brutal when it came in 1960. The failed independence of Congo-Léopoldville would continue to affect Belgium's image and credibility in matters relating to the African overseas countries and territories for many years to come.

This was an area subject to particularly rapid change, where the six Member States had very different concerns. Two aspects of relations with the overseas countries and territories were dealt with in the EEC Treaty. The first was trade, the second the Member States' contribution to 'the investments required for the progressive development of these countries and territories' (Article 132(3)).

Aims and objectives of association

'Article 131

[…] The purpose of association shall be to promote the economic and social development of the countries and territories and to establish close economic relations between them and the Community as a whole.

In accordance with the principles set out in the Preamble to this Treaty, association shall serve primarily to further the interests and prosperity of the inhabitants of these countries and territories in order to lead them to the economic, social and cultural development to which they aspire.

Article 132

Association shall have the following objectives:

1. Member States shall apply to their trade with the countries and territories the same treatment as they accord each other pursuant to this Treaty.

2. Each country or territory shall apply to its trade with Member States and with the other countries and territories the same treatment as that which it applies to the European State with which it has special relations.

3. The Member States shall contribute to the investments required for the progressive development of these countries and territories.

4. For investments financed by the Community, participation in tenders and supplies shall be open on equal terms to all natural and legal persons who are nationals of a Member State or of one of the countries and territories […]'.

The conventions between the EEC and the overseas countries and territories

1957

Article 136 of the EEC Treaty states that 'For an initial period of five years after the entry into force of this Treaty, the details of and procedure for the association of the countries and territories with the Community shall be determined by an implementing convention annexed to this Treaty'.

1963

On 20 July the Community and 18 African states and Madagascar signed the Yaoundé Convention.

1969

The second Yaoundé Convention was signed on 29 July. It entered into force on 1 January 1971.

Trade and investment

As far as trade was concerned, the principle adopted at EEC level could in some ways be traced back to the open door principle at the heart of the final act of the Berlin Conference of 1885, as it applied to the traditional basins of the Congo and Niger Rivers. But although the legal conditions were identical for the six Member States, the intensity of the colonial tie had created special channels and networks which the dawn of the post-colonial era did not immediately destroy.

The same was true of the contribution to investments which would take the form of a European Development Fund (EDF) to be managed by the EEC Commission. The Belgians, having continued to regard central Africa as their private preserve, hoped to play a crucial role in running a policy where they claimed to have the benefit of experience. They were to be disappointed. The Luxembourgers, who admitted to having no great interest in the dossier, felt that their contribution satisfied the requirements of political realism. Until the fruits of their economic miracle prompted them to expand their presence in Africa, the Italians tended to view it merely as a potential outlet for their surplus labour. The Dutch distrust-

Yaoundé II was signed in the presence of the representatives of the Member States. A Commission official remembers the negotiations: 'It was a long-drawn-out, meticulous and tiring process, but it was a positive, enriching experience. Anyway, every time we came out, we had without a doubt consolidated the partnership.' 'It was a long experience, but it was enriching since, as we got to know each other, we understood each other far better. After a few weeks of negotiating, lots of prejudices had been overcome.' (Interview with Jean Durieux, 3 March 2004)
Below (left to right): Heinrich Hendus and Henri Varenne.

ed France's African ambitions and did not want it to be forgotten that they still had responsibilities outside Europe. Together with the Germans, they were the main opponents of the French, whom they suspected of trying to grab the richest pickings; in other words, advocating the spreading of risks while planning to reap the lion's share of the economic and political rewards of what would come to be known as development aid.

Development aid?

The concept of development aid, like that of the Third World, was still a nebulous one at the beginning of the 1960s. It contained elements from western Marxist intellectuals, North African anti-colonialists and Christian thinkers. The Cuban revolution and its aftermath, the war in Vietnam and the Chinese Cultural Revolution only reinforced the idea of a world divided between rich and poor. In its pronouncements the Catholic church denounced this dichotomy, calling for peace and justice.

The evolution of association policy paralleled the global trends which formed the backdrop to it. Having originally been inspired by the desire to maintain a privileged link between the former metropolitan countries and their ex-colonies, and underpinned by an ideology that was heavily influenced by the motto 'rule to serve' of Pierre Ryckmans, former governor of the Belgian Congo, this policy evolved with the changing sensitivities and accession of the United Kingdom to the Community, into a more global vision of what genuine development aid was supposed to be. Within the Commission, Sicco Mansholt ([1]) and Jean-François Deniau spearheaded the move to rational generosity as opposed to ruthless calculations of realpolitik. In this sense, the Commission was for a time (albeit a very short time) the setting for an intense public debate, not least about development.

A significant evolution

In terms of the history of the EEC Commission, the response of the administrative system to the paradigm shift can be seen in the successive name changes undergone by DG VIII. As a result, 'overseas countries and territories' eventually became 'development aid', after a spell as 'overseas development'.

Headed by French Commissioners (Lemaignen, Rochereau and Deniau), although other Commissioners, not least the President, took an interest in Africa, the directorate-general represented an average of just over 8 % of the Commission's total staff. They were divided between four directorates, the two main ones, from the strategic point of view, being responsible for the EDF: the Development Studies and Programmes Directorate and the EDF Financial and Technical Directorate.

The directorate-general was based in rue du Marais, physically removed from the other directorates-general, perhaps subconsciously marking the distance between Europe and the overseas countries and territories. It was a microcosm of the ambitions and objectives expressed more or less clearly by the Member States ever since the negotiation of the EEC Treaty. So, while the opportunities for working with other directorates-general such as external relations and agriculture, were relatively limited, the bulk of DG VIII's activities were focused on managing the EDF, which of course entailed contacts with the European

([1]) See p. 180.

The Third World, pawn in the Cold War (1)

'I had a Senegalese friend who, at the time of independence, sent me the material he received in his letter box from the Soviet Union, in French […]. Then there was the World Trade Union Federation, which was based in Prague […]. An incredible amount of propaganda! Based on that, and working via the African press, I would buy newspaper space to publicise who was financing what […]. We had an exhibition in Tananarive. The President of the Republic at the time was pro-association […]. There was minimal opposition […]. In Senegal, there was a Communist party headed by a chemist. It was the only Communist party funded by the Americans, because it called itself the "African Independence Party" […]. That was how I came to fall out with the American Vice-Consul.'

Interview with Pierre Cros, 8 December 2003.

The Third World, pawn in the Cold War (2)

'My Director sent me on a trip to Somalia […]. [It was connected with] the scholarships the Commission was offering Somalis. But, for every one we offered, the USSR and Czechoslovakia provided 20. […] In the case of the scholarships it was all about self-interest. We would meet the Prime Minister and the Foreign Minister, and the others from Education. The USSR's influence and approach were intelligent and very pervasive. The Prime Minister told me they had signed the convention with the European Community but were undecided about the next one. Why? The Somalis were really uncertain. Somalia was afraid of being stifled by the USSR politically. So they were very cautious. Another restraining factor for Somalia was the spirituality (if not exactly religious belief) of the population. They feared the economic and military power of the United States, which is why they were hesitating. As far as Europe was concerned, they feared a covert form of colonialisation. They still bore the scars of the old regime […]. So, as they saw it, the choice was between freedom with uncertainty and security in servitude. On my return in November 1959 I drafted quite a long memo in which I said that Africa was a continent in its own right, not an extension of Europe, as we liked to think of it. Our relationship had to change.'

Interview with Umberto Stefani, 26 January 2004.

Gemeinsamer Markt

„Los, Michel —
schließe die Augen
und denk' an Europa!"

'Gemeinsamer Markt. "Los, Michel — schließe die Augen und denk' an Europa!" ('Common market. "Come on Michel — close your eyes and think of Europe!"') The Federal Republic was at pains to avoid upsetting French political interests in black Africa, but in 1955 it was extremely reluctant to go along with large-scale French investment projects in North Africa. It remained reluctant as it saw no reason why it should join in highly expensive but substantially unrealistic plans. On the other hand, Germany would be quite happy to join a political association with the former French colonies, provided the process was properly 'Europeanised'.

Commissioners' trips to Africa

1. Jean Rey in Africa

'Jean Rey was interested in the same way as Hallstein was, because they understood, and saw on the spot, that this was an area of application of the Treaty where the Commission had considerable means and wide-ranging powers of decision. That naturally corresponded to their aspirations for a Europe where the Commission was the real executive among the other institutions. Because of his background and nationality, Rey was familiar with many of the problems, especially of African countries through his experience of the Congo, and I have to say that — I accompanied him on several trips to Africa that I organised for him at his request — he always struck just the right note. I witnessed many of his talks with men such as Senghor, Houphouët Boigny, and Modibo Keita in Mali. He operated on an equal level with them, took time to familiarise himself with matters of interest to these Heads of State or Government. He expressed his satisfaction at what had been achieved both to his colleague Henri Rochereau and to his collaborators, of whom I was one.'

Extract from the interview with Jean Chapperon,
23 January 2004.

2. Visit by Henri Rochereau, Commissioner for Co-operation and Development, to Côte d'Ivoire in 1965

'One example of a huge agricultural development project is the palm grove project in Côte d'Ivoire. It is thanks to the EDF that the Côte d'Ivoire has become the leading producer of oil palms in the world. This was a project wholly funded by the EDF.'

'The palm oil project involved rooting out 4 million trees and replacing them by 4 million oil palms. This was no mean feat. It transformed Côte d'Ivoire into a leading producer. Was that a good thing or not? For many years it was one of Côte d'Ivoire's main resources. Then, as always, other countries, in particular countries such as Indonesia and other countries in the Far East, began to make palm oil. [...] Côte d'Ivoire suffered the effects of recession on palm oil markets [...] but it was a project which, at the time, seemed glaringly obvious when the world needed palm oil.'

Extracts from the interview with Jacques Ferrandi,
29 May 2004.

3. Von Staden accompanied Hallstein to Léopoldville for the celebrations to mark the independence of Congo-Léopoldville on 30 June 1960

'Belgium had undertaken a huge civilising mission and created a remarkable infrastructure [...], but the colonial regime had remained exceptionally patriarchal. All the important posts were held by Belgians. There were almost no Congolese with a university education. The future for a young, multi-ethnic state did not augur well [...].

The new Prime Minister, Patrice Lumumba [...], was a powerful orator and a born revolutionary. A man without higher education and a former postal worker, he was remarkable for his sharp mind but could also be a victim of his own impetuousness at times. Far from thanking the Belgians for their civilising efforts, he criticised their colonial rule and the patriarchal nature of the regime in terms that must have seemed offensive to them [...]. That evening I found myself at the banquet seated next to the former head of the German delegation. Opposite us sat the King of Rwanda, a Watutsi (or Tutsi). He was a very tall, very handsome man dressed in national costume, and he bore a striking resemblance to the king in the famous film of King Solomon's Mines. The Minister of Housing, who was clearly enchanted, observed in clearly audible tones that someone should invite this fantastical figure to Germany to exhibit him on the stage. Clearly, the idea that a monarch from a former German colony might understand the language of Goethe never even occurred to him.

On the last day of our visit to Léopoldville we had an audience with Lumumba [...]. [He] spoke about future relations of his country with the West and the Community in moderate and realistic terms, without committing himself too much. Yet the impression he gave was completely different: this was a dangerous, ambitious man driven by strong feelings who, I thought, still had a few nasty surprises in store for us. In the plane on the way home I concluded in my report to the Commission that it would not be possible

to work with him. Unfortunately, Hallstein asked me to replace this pessimistic prediction with a much more moderate assessment […].'

Staden, B. (von), *Ende und Anfang. Erinnerungen 1939– 1963*, IPa, Vaihingen/Enz, 2001, pp. 223–226.

Investment Bank. The importance of the EDF increased as a result of the Yaoundé Convention in July 1963, and several possible scenarios for the future were considered in the run-up to the merger of the executives.

The challenges and difficulties, hopes and achievements of DG VIII were evoked, often in lively terms, by those who embodied the spirit of the organisation in the years of transition from the colonial era to one of development aspirations.

MICHEL DUMOULIN, ON BEHALF OF THE CONSORTIUM

More about Stabex

'The attempts at price regulation and market organisation — which ran counter to what our colleagues in external relations were up to with UNCTAD and GATT — [...], were doomed to failure. The Stabex formula [...] was a sort of [...] last resort, which the beneficiary countries themselves did not really use in the spirit of the institution. They simply thought of it as a way of obtaining some extra funding by showing losses in export revenue by adroitly and, we hope honestly, presenting their statistics. Then [...] it was a matter of doing the calculations: losses of so many millions and, with that, you undertook projects which were supposed to directly benefit the producers or producing regions concerned. But I'm not sure that anyone ever checked up on that very carefully.'

Interview with Jean Chapperon, 23 January 2004.

'Deniau the African': 'A true demonstration of our solidarity'

'As far as internationalism is concerned, Europe must always be one step ahead [...]. The same question will arise as regards the association of African countries. I firmly believe that the preferential customs treatment that was the main instrument of this association is doomed in the long term. That leaves aid and the European Development Fund. I suggest another instrument which would be a true demonstration of our solidarity. Studies show that the survival of these developing countries depends almost entirely on the quantities and export price of a small number of agricultural and mineral commodities: groundnuts, cocoa, copper, etc. Europe must set up a fund to stabilise this revenue, which is too dependent on the vagaries of climate and international speculation. Before talking about development, let us combat anti-development. I did the rounds of the European governments and succeeded in winning them all over, despite the "liberal" objections of the United States. This is the system which, after my departure, my successor, Claude Cheysson, would apply with such success under the name Stabex.'

Deniau, J.-Fr., *Mémoires de sept vies. 2. Croire et oser*, Plon, Paris, 1997, pp. 293 and 294.

A Dutch view of DG VIII

'I was actually inspired by what we had done in the Netherlands in the area of aid to developing countries. It was an area that interested me a lot, in the Treaty of Rome too. But it was not at all popular in the Netherlands. In fact the Dutch wanted nothing to do with it. It was something imposed on us by the French. But I was in favour of it and so was Mansholt. So that is how I ended up in DG VIII [...]. I got to meet the African presidents and ministers, it was a very worthwhile experience. These were ties that have lasted for many years. [...]. I also played a very active role in the association of Surinam with the Community. I was in charge of negotiations between Nigeria and the Community. I received a lot of support from Lemaignen, and later Rochereau, to open up what was a very close-knit association built around the French and Belgian colonies. We wanted to involve English-speaking Africa too. I had a lot of contact with London. So I played quite an active role in bringing the English-speaking countries of Africa closer to the Commission — although I would not go so far as to say I succeeded. Lemaignen approved and so did Rochereau. But Paris didn't [...]. Boegner tried to oust me as Director by a diplomatic manœuvre [...] because he felt (and Paris agreed) that I wasn't the man for the job.'

Interview with Jacob Jan van der Lee, 15 December 2003.

Exchange of best practice

Jean Chapperon explained his work as *chef de cabinet* at the Commission:

'We're in a state of permanent negotiation. "If you don't make life difficult for me about the development of vanilla growing in Madagascar, I won't cause you any trouble about the agricultural rules you're drawing up on the manufacture of ice cream, to which you want to add artificial vanilla flavouring made from coal." I exaggerate somewhat but I use this example because it is compelling. One day, as I could not be sure that I would have the agricultural Cabinet's support on a matter concerning projects in Madagascar, I cornered my friend and said that "I don't believe that Rochereau will agree with his colleague Mansholt on this matter".'

Extract from the interview with Jean Chapperon, 23 January 2004.

Bending the rules?

'The Commission immediately decided to limit the checks on Development Fund expenditure. It was a matter of allowing more freedom to cajole the heads of government in Africa into admitting the Commission with its charitable projects. That was the line taken at the time. There was a Commission decision [...] to the effect that financial control would not monitor the "sound management" of the Development Fund's expenditure.'

Interview with Hubert Ehring, 4 June 2004.

The Ortoli Report's comments on the Development Studies and Programmes Directorate and the EDF Financial and Technical Directorate (1961)

'The Directorate consists of a Programme Division and a General Studies Division, both of them very large.

In fact, the Programme Division is more of a "projects" division, in that its job is to examine the economic quality of the requests submitted to the Fund. It is therefore legitimate to wonder whether it ought really to be in the Fund Directorate. However, its future seems to lie in evolving towards a genuine programme division with studies of infrastructure and global long-term forecasts.

The General Studies Division seems to have a highly complex and hierarchical structure [...].

The EDF Financial and Technical Directorate is essentially a technical body. Because of the role of the Programme Division of the Studies Directorate in the economic evaluation of projects, its functions are limited to financial, accounting and auditing aspects [...].

It might be better to bring together the issues affecting the Fund into a single directorate, thus giving one authority the responsibility for operations from start to finish where the unity of such operations is beyond dispute.'

AHUE, FMM 3, *Rapport sur l'organisation des services de la Commission de la Communauté Économique Européenne*, [1961] VIII-3 and 4.

March 1965, the European Development Fund finances the construction
of a dam at Yaramoko in Upper Volta (now Burkina Faso).

An EDF (^{1})-funded project from design to implementation (1963)

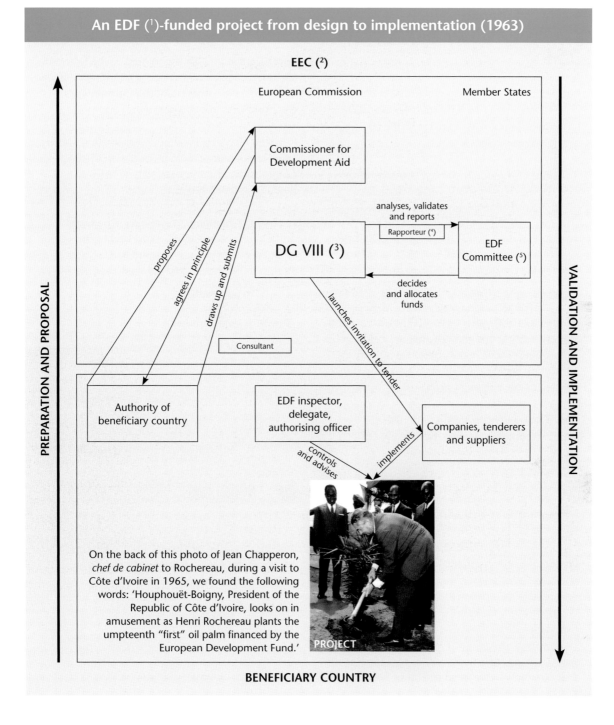

EEC (^{2})

European Commission — Member States

PREPARATION AND PROPOSAL

VALIDATION AND IMPLEMENTATION

Commissioner for Development Aid

DG VIII (^{3})

analyses, validates and reports

Rapporteur (^{4})

EDF Committee (^{5})

decides and allocates funds

proposes

agrees in principle

draws up and submits

launches invitation to tender

Consultant

Authority of beneficiary country

EDF inspector, delegate, authorising officer

Companies, tenderers and suppliers

controls and advises

implements

On the back of this photo of Jean Chapperon, *chef de cabinet* to Rochereau, during a visit to Côte d'Ivoire in 1965, we found the following words: 'Houphouët-Boigny, President of the Republic of Côte d'Ivoire, looks on in amusement as Henri Rochereau plants the umpteenth "first" oil palm financed by the European Development Fund.'

PROJECT

BENEFICIARY COUNTRY

(^{1}) European Development Fund.
(^{2}) European Economic Community.
(^{3}) Directorate-General for Cooperation and Development.
(^{4}) The Rapporteur is the EDF Director.
(^{5}) The EDF Committee comprises representatives of the Member States and votes by qualified majority.

Possible scenarios for DG VIII in 1967

'[...]

(a) Retain the present structure, based on management of a fund (or granting loans) and development of links with the countries of sub-Saharan Africa.

(b) Transfer the purely political activities to the external relations DG, while management of the Fund — or loans (to a possibly larger number of beneficiaries) — would be entrusted to a separate technical department.

(c) Extend activities if the Community agrees and implements a general development aid policy.

In the current climate, option (c) has to be ruled out on political grounds. The majority of Member States (and France in particular) are against the idea of extending the Community's competence to general development problems.

There is no very convincing argument for adopting option (b) while the effective action undertaken by the Community in the development aid field is confined to the EDF and the reservations outlined above continue to apply as regards any extension of the Community's responsibilities in this area [...].

It should be noted that some research has already been carried out, in conjunction with the Euratom Commission, into the possibility of the EDF funding certain projects that have been examined by Euratom in the area of the phytosanitary applications of atomic techniques. The High Authority has consistently expressed to the associated African countries and Madagascar an interest in prospecting for mineral deposits and extending the use of steel.'

AHCE, BDT 144-92 643, *Rapport du secrétaire général de la Haute Autorité et des secrétaires exécutifs des Commissions de la CEE et d'Euratom sur l'organisation des services de la Commission des Communautés Européennes*, SEC(67)3001, 1 July 1967, pp. 28 and 29.

'Pragmatic, rough-and-ready work'

'I found [in 1964] that the EDF worked in a very pragmatic, highly intuitive way. It was to some extent an extension of the colonial practice. The competent people were essentially French — Ferrandi, Auclert, Cellerier [...]. There were other nationalities apart from the French, but the ones with experience of Africa were obviously French in most cases. There were some Belgians too, but they weren't best placed as authorities on development given the dramatic turn of events in the Congo. So, essentially, it was the former officials from the French overseas administration who were at the helm and who exerted an influence. It was a pragmatic, rough-and-ready approach.'

Interview with Jean Durieux, 3 March 2004.

Jacques Ferrandi before he joined the Commission

'So I graduated from the École coloniale in 1938. During the war I served as an officer in a Senegalese infantry regiment. I returned to France in 1945 and was appointed to the Ministry for French Overseas Territories. I then spent a year working for the minister, Pierre Pfimlin, and in 1953 was appointed Director-General of Economic Services for French West Africa (AOF), so I returned to Africa in March that year. I stayed there for five years and the final year marked something of a turning point in my career. In November 1957 we had a visit from Maurice Faure, who was accompanied by his *chef de cabinet* Jean François-Poncet [...]. They stopped in Dakar. They explained the ins and outs of the Treaty of Rome and in particular Part 4 of the Treaty, which dealt with the association of the overseas countries and territories [...]. I had a problem. The Deferre Act of 1956 would put an end to the West African Federation in 1958 and give the eight territories, if not full independence, at least a large measure of autonomy. All of this was due to start in January 1958 and from that date onwards the Government-General of French West Africa would cease to exist [...]. I had no plans, no future, no career prospects [...]. I was available [...] It came as a surprise to me to learn, at the end of December 1957, that one of the two

French Commissioners in Brussels was to be [...] Robert Lemaignen, whom I knew very well for one very simple reason. He was an important figure in the French employers' association, the CNPF, at the time. He was the chairman of a very big French company, SCAC (Société commerciale d'affrètements et de combustibles). It was particularly important because it had the monopoly on supplying coal and various other fuels to all French ports. But Robert Lemaignen also had a second role, which he indulged in on the side, as it were, because it was something he did for fun: he was chairman of a subsidiary of SCAC called Socopao, Société commerciale des ports de l'Afrique occidentale. In this capacity he made frequent trips to Africa and, of course, he often stopped over in Dakar. So we had got to know each other there and had become quite close friends. I was delighted to hear of his appointment, but that was it. So I was quite surprised when a mutual friend asked me if I would agree to head Robert Lemaignen's cabinet in Brussels. This mutual friend was Governor Rey [...], the Governor of Senegal [...] and later Robert Lemaignen's adviser on Africa.'

Interview with Jacques Ferrandi, 28 May 2004.

Lack of communication between a French official and his non-French colleagues in DG VIII

'Ferrandi [...] was a typical ex-colonial official who knew the colonies inside out and in this sense was undeniably competent, but he felt absolutely no need for contact with anyone who wasn't French.'

Interview with Jacob Jan van der Lee,
15 December 2003.

Jean Chapperon, born in 1921, describing his career before joining the Commission

'When I finished secondary school, I took the exams for what was at the time still known as the *École coloniale* (Colonial College), which became the *École de la France d'outre-mer* (College for the French Overseas Territories) shortly after I went there. I passed the exams in 1940 and did a year there before the war took me away from my studies. Thanks to an arrangement organised by the director of the college to protect the students from conscription or problems with the occupying forces, I was able to go to Africa on an initial placement even though I had not completed my studies. I had not graduated, but an exception was made because of the war.

My first spell was in Guinea. There I was called up because of my age. I served until 1945 [...] in a Senegalese infantry regiment, first in Senegal and Morocco, then in the 1st Free French Division, where my unit was brought up as reinforcements after the heavy losses suffered by the Free French Division in the North Africa campaign, in Tunisia, and then Italy.

After demobilisation I was appointed to the Ministry for French Overseas Territories, where, on the advice of some of my ex-fellow students who had become friends, I gravitated towards development aid procedures [...] and their organisation in both Paris and the various French colonies [...].

The work was very interesting. It did rather take me away from the romantic role of colonial administrator, out in the bush, on tour. I did spend some time in the bush, but mine was a different job. It was also the time when the first representative political institutions were being set up in Africa, particularly the territorial assemblies and then the two federal assemblies for French West Africa (AOF) and French Equatorial Africa (AEF). I did a lot of work in this area. In very practical terms it was a matter of explaining the texts, teaching the elected representatives about parliamentary committees, budgets, dossiers, regulations, laws and so on. Well anyway, this was how I approached the job of administrator, and one way or another I continued like that more or less to the end. And it was by virtue of this training and the experience I had acquired that at some point an old school friend who was working for the European Commission ([1]), asked me if I would be interested in a job there. This was at the end of 1961. And, on the basis of the job description and the terms of employment, I accepted. So that is how I found myself in Brussels in the spring of 1962 taking up an appointment as *chef de cabinet* to Henri Rochereau, who was starting his term as European Commissioner with prime responsibility for the association policy provided for in the Treaty of Rome and the conventions annexed to it.'

Interview with Jean Chapperon, 23 January 2004.

([1]) Jacques Ferrandi.

Chapter 19

Moves towards an economic and monetary policy

Establishing a Community economic and monetary policy has been a major concern of the Commission since its inception. As the customs union and the common market in agriculture were being put in place, what mattered was safeguarding the Community's internal cohesion, coupled with the determination to ensure that the common policies being mapped out remained intrinsically coherent. But the external pressures associated with the destabilisation of the international monetary system and its growing fragility during the 1960s meant that the six Member States had to strive to consolidate regional monetary stability while asserting a monetary identity on the world scene.

Economic policy coordination and monetary unification were, therefore, two of the main preoccupations of the Commission for many years.

Towards the 'convergence' of economic and monetary policies

The Treaty framework and the players involved

In the economic and monetary spheres, the EEC Treaty imposed few constraints on Member States and afforded the Commission little room for manoeuvre. Most of the projects launched during the interwar period with a view to achieving the economic unification of Europe had underscored the need for a monetary union but, since the establishment of the European Payments Union in 1950, stabilisation and the return to currency convertibility in Europe were just two of the major concerns facing what was at the time an economically weakened Europe. Since the 1930s many governments had become accustomed to regarding the currency not only as an attribute of their sovereignty but also as a key element in the economy. They reserved the right to intervene in this area under comprehensive policies for which, in their view, they were solely responsible. Nevertheless, it was clear that on several occasions the weakness of certain currencies, including the French franc, frustrated the attempts at restoring free trade in Europe during the 1950s. If such a situation had been repeated, this would have jeopardised the establishment of the customs union. And so it was around the concepts of joint responsibility and solidarity that Articles 103 to 109 of the Treaty of Rome were framed.

Article 103 stated that Member States were to regard their short-term economic policies as a 'matter of common concern' and to consult each other and the Commission on measures taken in this connection. Article 104 stipulated that each Member State was to aim for a high level of employment, price stability, 'the equilibrium of its [overall] balance of payments' and the maintenance of 'confidence in its currency'. Accordingly, stability and currency convertibility were identified as prime objectives without which the customs union could not be established and could not operate effectively. The content of subsequent articles follows on logically from these objectives by laying down the principle of economic policy coordination (Article 105) and the principle whereby each Member State was to treat its exchange rate policy as 'a matter of common concern' (Article 107).

The persistent instability in those areas when the Treaty was being negotiated led those at the negotiating table to envisage a number of crisis situations: a country facing balance-of-payments difficulties liable to impede the functioning of the common market would have its position investigated by the Commission and could be recommended to take economic policy measures while, where appropriate, being granted 'mutual assistance' by its partners (Article 108). However, France saw to it that the possibility of 'necessary protective measures' being taken in the event of a sudden balance-of-payments crisis was written into the Treaty (Article 109). Clearly, such a crisis would be evidence of a sort that the objectives referred to earlier had not been met, and the Commission was determined that it should not come to that.

The institutional means assigned to the Community by the Treaty at the outset in the area of economic and monetary policy were slender. A Monetary Committee, provided for in Article 107 of the Treaty, was soon set up. Alongside the two Commission representatives, who also provided the secretariat, the Committee comprised one representative of the economics and finance ministry in each Member State and one representative of the central bank in each Member State,

ensuring that both economic policymakers and monetary policymakers were represented.

Since it rapidly became clear that this economic framework was insufficient, the Commission persuaded the governments to set up new bodies with the task of strengthening concerted action.

First, Robert Marjolin and then Raymond Barre took charge of economic and financial matters within the Commission. Both were economists and had sound practical experience at both international and European level. Robert Marjolin was influenced by Keynesian ideas and was a proponent of economic planning, two factors that shaped to quite a large extent the options he proposed to the Commission. Raymond Barre, an economics professor who was more liberal in outlook than his predecessor, subsequently adhered to the Gaullist view that the opening up of the French economy to Europe was a powerful means of modernising it. And, lastly, the two men were different physically: Michel Albert referred to Marjolin's 'youthful rangy physique' and liked to recall Raymond Barre's witty reference to himself as 'a square man in a round body' [1].

Although largely the fiefdom of economists, the Commission's Directorate-General for Economic and Financial Affairs (DG II) was successively entrusted to two senior Italian civil servants, both former diplomats and both experts in European matters: Franco Bobba and Ugo Mosca. Under the authority of the director-general, three and then four directorates whose individual remits closely reflected the main concerns of the day were set up: National Economies and Short-Term Economic Policy, Monetary Matters, Economic Structure and Development (all 1965) and, lastly, Budgetary and Financial Matters (1968). Both because of the nature of the interests at stake and given the personality of the men in charge of these matters at the Commission, there was a marked French influence at the time within the directorate-general. This influence cannot though

[1] Interview with Michel Albert, 18 December 2003.

be likened to the influence that the government offices on the rue de Rivoli in Paris exerted over the institutions in Brussels. If we are to understand fully the different influences exerted at the time, we need to look at the role played by Robert Triffin in his capacity as adviser to the Commission from 1958 onwards. Robert Triffin's influence was particularly marked in the case of Robert Marjolin. The two men had known each other in Washington during the war and had met up again in Paris at the beginning of the 1950s, when Marjolin was Secretary-General of the OEEC (Organisation for European Economic Co-operation) and Triffin headed up the IMF's Paris office. Triffin also had a marked influence on Boyer de la Giroday, a former IMF official who, under Raymond Barre, was in charge of the Monetary Matters directorate. Another person influenced by Triffin was Roland de Kergolay, who had worked at the OEEC following his studies in the United States and who became Secretary of the Monetary Committee between 1962 and 1969 following in the footsteps of Alain Prate, who later became economic adviser to General de Gaulle. A former student of Triffin at Yale, Claudio Segré also spent a short time within the Monetary Matters directorate. Last but not least, there were the links that existed between Monnet and Triffin as members of the Action Committee for the United States of Europe, which counted the Belgo-American economist as its adviser, as well as those that existed between a certain Boyer de la Giroday and the Action Committee [1].

Improved economic policy coordination

It was not very long at all before Robert Marjolin cautioned that the provisions of the Treaty were insufficient as practices in the field of economic policy coordination. He took the view that a Community economic policy did not exist but that there were national policies which, fortunately, moved in parallel and did not clash, although there was no assurance that this fortunate state of affairs would continue indefinitely. He went on to recall the importance of a 'coordinated' Community economic policy and to call ultimately for a 'unified' [2] economic policy. Marjolin's arguments suggesting such a new departure were prompted by factors within the Community. He maintained that such unification would become necessary as the common market took shape and that the consequences of different or indeed contradictory economic policies, of inflationary or deflationary crises or of far-reaching adjustments in exchange rates between Community countries would be such as to jeopardise the rapid progress that was being made [3]. As the EEC began to assert its presence on the international scene and given the risks to which the project for the economic unification of Europe was exposed as a result of the deterioration in the workings of the international monetary system, the Commission decided to make its move. In Marjolin's view, as the free world's second most important power, Europe had to assume its responsibilities [4].

Aware of the need to take action, albeit within a restricted institutional framework, the Commission fairly quickly set about strengthening the role of the existing institutions and setting up new bodies. The role of the Monetary Committee initially consisted of a six-monthly examination of the situation in each country, based on reports submitted to the Council and the Commission. Those reports provided details of credit policy and the size and financing of deficits. However, it quite soon

[1] Maes, I. and Buyst, E., 'Triffin, the European Commission and the project of a European Reserve Fund' in Dumoulin, M., (ed.) *Réseaux économiques et construction européenne/Economic networks and European integration*, Euroclio, Études et documents/Studies and documents, No 29, PIE-Peter Lang, Brussels [...], Vienna, 2004, pp. 431–444. *Robert Triffin, conseiller des Princes,* documents compiled by Catherine Ferrant and Jean Sloover, with the collaboration of Michel Dumoulin and Olivier Lefebvre, Ciaco, Louvain-la-Neuve, 1990.

[2] Marjolin, R., 'Pour une politique économique commune', statement to the Economic and Social Council, *Revue du Marché Commun*, October 1959, p. 393 et seq.
[3] Ibid.
[4] Secret report, Harmonisation des politiques monétaires nationales des pays de la Communauté, Brussels, 30 August 1960, referred to by Bottex, A. 'La mise en place des institutions monétaires européennes (1957–1964)', *Histoire, économie et société*, No 4, 1999, pp. 753–774.

Robert Triffin, the European Commission and monetary union

Born in Flobecq (Belgium) on 5 October 1911, Robert Triffin graduated from Leuven University and in 1938 presented his doctorate on monopolistic competition and general equilibrium theory at Harvard. After taking US nationality in 1942, he was recruited by the Federal Reserve and then joined the IMF in 1946. A fervent advocate of European integration, he was seconded in December 1949 to the Economic Cooperation Administration, where the political approach pursued was more in line with his ideals than at the IMF. He managed to convince the US Delegation and then the OEEC (through Robert Marjolin, its Secretary-General) that the arrangements for the European Payments Union (EPU) should include a unit of account with technical characteristics such that its value would remain as stable as possible and which would unofficially serve as the cornerstone of monetary union. In 1951 Triffin was appointed to the Chair of Economics at Yale University but he was still attentive to European concerns. In 1957 he returned to join the team set up by Jean Monnet.

In 1958 Triffin embarked on a dual role at the Commission. He was personal adviser to Robert Marjolin but he also exerted considerable influence within DG II, thanks especially to Frédéric Boyer de la Giroday and Franco Bobba. He took advantage of this to encourage the Commission to use the unit of account that had been adopted by the ECSC for managing its current transactions and to defend the planned European Reserve Fund, which was designed to pave the way for the monetary unification of Europe.

However, this initiative met with mixed success. The Monetary Committee, which consisted primarily of central bank representatives, was opposed to Triffin's ideas. Instead, it welcomed the July 1961 Accession Agreement between the EEC and Greece, which provided for use of the dollar. Triffin and Marjolin failed to get their views across. Raymond Barre subsequently came up with his own ideas for moving towards economic and monetary union and his successor, Wilhelm

Robert Triffin (1911–93) addressing the Japan Economic Research Center in Tokyo in 1967. The Belgian economist, who acquired American nationality but reverted to his original nationality at the end of his life, played a major role at the Commission, on the ACUSE and in major commercial banks in fostering the project for a single European currency.

Haferkamp, called into question Triffin's contract at the Commission. Even so, Triffin was always behind the scenes: initially, at the Hague Summit in December 1969, where, at Jean Monnet's request, he acted as adviser to Willy Brandt, and then, in 1977, in the entourage of the Commission President, Roy Jenkins. In 1979, a currency basket (the ECU) was adopted, and the supporters of a single currency used it on private markets as one way of promoting their ideal. The success achieved on this front facilitated progress towards the future economic and monetary union.

On his return to Belgium, this 'Atlantic citizen', as Kennedy called him, pressed ahead with his research work and continued to exert an influence that very often went beyond the strict framework of economics. He died in Ostend on 23 February 1993.

J. W.

See Wilson, J., 'Triffin (Robert)', *Nouvelle Biographie Nationale*, Académie royale des sciences, des lettres et des beaux-arts de Belgique, Brussels, 2003, pp. 344–347.

became clear that, with the Monetary Committee being content to examine *ex post* the main economic and monetary developments in each Member State and to issue opinions, a new body was needed.

A short-term economic policy committee (the 'Conjunctural Policy Committee') was set up following the initiative taken in the spring of 1959 by the German Secretary of State for Economic Affairs, Alfred Müller-Armack. The Commission, in the shape of DG II, had been monitoring short-term economic developments in the different countries in consultation with national experts from the economic institutes and research centres in each country. The Committee was set up in March 1960 with a view to stabilising and strengthening contacts with national policymakers in the interests of, where possible, more precise and more upstream coordination: as Brussels saw it, regular meetings with those who were more directly responsible in their countries for short-term economic policy would make it possible not only for the administrations tasked with managing external relations but also for all the departments with short-term economic policy-making powers to become involved ([1]). The Committee was made up of prominent individuals with responsibility for 'the conduct of economic and monetary policy at the highest level' ([2]) and one of its prime objectives was to draw up a code of conduct for defining the measures that the Member States would commit themselves to taking or, on the contrary, to not taking, in order to render their short-term economic policies compatible with those of the other Member States and of the Community ([3]). Lastly, the Committee was given the task of drawing up, on the Commission's behalf, the programmes of jointly agreed short-term economic policy measures that might need to be taken to deal with changes in the economic situation.

These objectives were dictated by what had happened in the very recent past. In France the external account difficulties in 1957–58, the weakness of the national currency and the resulting uncertainty, both economic and political, regarding the country's effective participation in the common market are etched in everyone's memory. However, the remedial measures taken by France in December 1958 defused those concerns. As early as the following year, the Commission was, therefore, in a position to envisage what was, for it, one of the important milestones in achieving genuine economic integration, namely the first stage in the liberalisation of capital movements within the Community, as provided for in Articles 67 to 73 of the Treaty. But the lack of a detailed timetable meant that a measure of caution was called for in view of the vulnerability of some countries' external balances and the determination of others to retain control of potentially disruptive capital flows. At the same time, the Commission quite rightly regarded the eventual establishment of a Community capital market as one of the building blocks of an economically integrated Europe. The first step, therefore, was to interpret Article 67(1) of the Treaty, which stipulated that all restrictions on capital movements were to be abolished during the transitional period 'to the extent necessary to ensure the proper functioning of the common market'. The deliberations on this matter between the Member States and the Commission within the Monetary Committee paved the way for the publication of a first liberalisation directive in May 1960, followed by a second, supplementary directive in December 1962. These directives removed restrictions on, in particular, direct investment flows and personal transfers because the very broad measure of autonomy enjoyed by the Member States in the economic policy field prevented any wider-reaching liberalisation. At the same time, the restrictions in existence pointed to the need for increasingly close coordination of national economic policies.

([1]) Coordination of Member States' short-term economic policies, proposal for a regulation presented by the Commission to the Council, annexed to PV 87, EEC Commission, 19 January 1960.

([2]) Marjolin, R., 'The economic situation and policy relating to economic trends', *Bulletin of the EEC*, No 2, 1960.

([3]) Draft regulation on the coordination of the short-term economic policies of the Member States; Commission statement to be inserted into the minutes of the Council discussions of the draft regulation.

As one of Marjolin's priority objectives, such coordination was particularly justified as turmoil on foreign exchange markets resulted in the revaluation of the German mark and the Dutch guilder on 6 and 7 March 1961 respectively.

Economic programming and new institutional developments

The Community action programme for the second stage of the EEC, which was presented in October 1962, was the Commission's comprehensive response to all the concerns and constraints evident at the time. In the economic field, the action programme was, to a large degree, inspired by the views of Marjolin and distinguished between economic development policy, structural policy and monetary policy. As for economic development, the Commission envisaged strengthening its role as an expert in order to usher in gradually a Community short-term economic policy that would bring together all the national policies. Faithful to the method developed by it since its inception, the Commission reckoned on achieving this by way of more refined preliminary studies, comparisons of national macroeconomic data and budgets, and an increasingly close dialogue with the Member States.

The major innovation in all this was medium-term programming, which was justified by the need to shed light on national and Community decisions the effects of which would be discernible only after a certain time-lag, to explain how government resources were allocated and how the governments themselves set about planning and implementing common policies, to clarify regional and industrial redevelopment policies, and to pave the way for an incomes policy. This extensive programme was based on comparisons of national programmes, which were incorporated into a Community programming exercise that was drawn up in 1963 and initially covered the period 1964–68.

The second strand of the programme concerned monetary affairs. The objective was to complete the transitional period, bringing about, according to the Commission memorandum, both economic union and fixed exchange rates, not to mention monetary union. This prospect was hemmed in by both internal and external constraints as the cohesion of the common market could not fail to be seriously affected by deep-seated monetary upheavals, even if those upheavals occurred in the first instance in countries other than the Member States. In this respect, the action programme called for a stronger institutional base involving the setting up of a committee of governors of the Central Banks of the EEC, thereby giving substantial shape to the unofficial meetings that had been held in Basle at the headquarters of the Bank for International Settlements (BIS) since 1959. The extension of monetary cooperation between the Six had to take place not only within the Community but also vis-à-vis the rest of the world. Internally, decisions were needed on creating a currency. From an international viewpoint, action was needed to promote the emergence of an external monetary policy involving relations between the Community and the IMF and the reform of the international monetary system. With such a policy, consultations would have to take place before any important decisions were taken, and there would have to be a procedure for issuing recommendations. Likewise, the Member States would have to introduce mutual assistance arrangements under Article 108 of the Treaty. These arrangements would at last impart fresh impetus to the programme for liberalising capital movements, which had been set in motion by the first two directives. The overall ambition was to move gradually from coordination to centralisation of monetary decisions, with monetary union becoming the objective of the third stage of the common market [1]. It should here be pointed out that the conflicting short-term economic developments in a number of European countries and the resulting monetary strains from 1963 onwards justified the Commission's approach [2].

[1] Action programme for the EEC during the second stage.
[2] Extract from the speech given on 29 October 1963 before the Economic and Social Committee by Robert Marjolin. *Revue du Marché Commun*, No 64, December 1963.

Some of its proposals were proactive and called into question the traditions of national self-reliance. The determination to incorporate Community decisions in a more rigorous programming framework than in the past was challenged by those of liberal persuasion, both within the Commission and outside. In monetary matters, governments were not prepared to undertake the transfers of power needed to strengthen first coordination and then the Community's monetary remit.

The medium-term economic programming arrangements were quite clearly inspired by Marjolin's experience as a colleague of Monnet at the National Planning Agency (Commissariat au Plan) in France, and the spirit of the proposals recalled some of the ideas put forward by France in the very early days of the OEEC (¹). At the beginning of the 1960s, French planning received a further strong boost from the return to power of General de Gaulle, and it was this model that clearly provided the basis for the arrangements proposed by Marjolin. 'European programming' was the theme of the symposium held in Rome in December 1962 but it left ample room for discussion of national models, of which it was designed to be a sort of extension. At the symposium, Pierre Massé, who headed the National Planning Agency and was the most prominent proponent of French planning under the Fifth Republic, presented the French model (²). The setting up of the Medium-Term Economic Policy Committee thus seemed to be geared to adapting the French model to the circumstances of the Community by coordinating the national plans through regular consultation of policymakers at national level, with back-up from the experts in DG II. The general thrust of the common policies and, to some extent, of the future industrial or regional policy was decided within that committee. It was quite clear that such an initiative called for general agreement on the main principles of planning at the level of the Member States, followed by acceptance of the step change sought by Marjolin and his colleagues. Marjolin was well aware that, by itself, the idea of planning gave rise to much opposition, hence the care taken in presenting it, preference for the term 'programming' as opposed to planning, and enumeration of the virtues of competition. That said, Marjolin's aims were the subject of much criticism. As Jean Flory explained after the event, things did not go particularly well at the outset because some of France's partners, Germany in particular, took the handy expression 'medium-term policy' to mean planning (³). At a more fundamental level, the French liberal economist, Jacques Rueff, was certainly doubtful as to whether programming as practised was, in reality, the effective instrument that outsiders envied (⁴). For their part, the employers' organisations, through UNICE, voiced their opposition to state intervention in any form, demanding that programming safeguard entrepreneurial freedom, while economic policymakers in Germany showed scant interest in programming, which they readily likened to state intervention. Ludwig Erhard himself was critical, and the virtues of a planned economy were challenged at a conference organised by the List Society and bringing together Alfred Müller-Armack, State Secretary for Economic Affairs, and a number of renowned German economists, but also Walter Hallstein and Hans von der Groeben (⁵).

Within the Commission itself, and especially the Competition Directorate-General (DG IV), criticisms were levelled at a form of European planning that called into question the central role played by competition in the integration process. The clash between these two schools of thought resulted in a number of compromises. It was

(¹) Bossuat, G., *La France, l'aide américaine et la construction européenne*, 1944–1954, CHEFF, Paris, pp. 192–195.

(²) Massé, P., 'Rapport sur la programmation économique en France', *Revue du Marché Commun*, No 53, December 1962.

(³) Interview with Jean Flory, 3 December 2003.

(⁴) Maes, I., 'Projects d'intégration monétaire à la Commission européenne au tournant années 1970', in Bussière, E., Dumoulin, M. and Schirmann, S. (eds), *Milieux économiques et intégration européenne au XXᵉ siècle — La crise des années 1970*, Euroclio. Études et documents, No 35, PIE-Peter Lang, Brussels [...] Vienna, 2006, pp. 35–50.

(⁵) Maes, I., *Macroeconomic and monetary policy-making at the European Commission, from the Rome Treaties to the Hague Summit*, Working papers. Research series, No 58, National Bank of Belgium, Brussels, August 2004.

Robert Marjolin

Born into a modest family in Paris on 27 July 1911, Robert Marjolin left school at 14. His capacity for work, his determination and his enormous intellectual curiosity allowed him, however, to return to his studies some years later. After passing the equivalent of the baccalaureate, he first read philosophy and then economics and law.

At the age of 21, he won a one year scholarship at Yale University. His discovery of the United States marked him deeply. He was at the time a young socialist militant — he joined the Socialist Youth in 1929 — and was, if anything, critical of things American. It was his time at Yale that gave him his first insight into the benefits that economic liberalism could bring society. He wrote: 'The truth is that I was then, as I was often to be subsequently, intellectually and emotionally torn between a desire for social justice and equality and a deep aspiration towards an efficient and productive society.
It could be that this kind of tension is the key to my personality.' ([1]) Throughout his life, he remained good friends with senior officials in the US administration.

In 1934 Léon Blum appointed him economics editor of the socialist newspaper *Populaire*. Two years later he became a special adviser to the Popular Front government. Following a disagreement, he resigned and published a series of articles in the review *L'Europe nouvelle* in which he called for an economic and social policy in France that was geared primarily to preparing for war.

During the Second World War, he met Jean Monnet, who in January 1944 appointed him head of the French purchasing agency in the United States. In 1945 Monnet arranged for the Provisional Government of the French Republic (GPRF) to appoint him Director for External Economic Relations and subsequently brought him onto his team to assist in implementing the French modernisation and infrastructure plan. His

activities and his visits to London and Washington gave him food for thought and led him to believe that abandoning protectionism was the only way in which France could be modernised. His preference for opening up the French economy was associated with a strong belief in the benefits of Keynesianism and planning. When the Marshall Plan was launched, he became head of the French delegation to the Committee for European Economic Cooperation (CEEC).

As Secretary-General of the Organisation for European Economic Cooperation (OEEC) in 1948, he attempted, without much success, to convince the European countries of the need for a customs union. He resigned in 1955 and soon after joined the team headed by Christian Pineau at the Foreign Affairs Ministry, where he took part as an expert in the negotiations on the Treaty of Rome. He was not in favour of just any kind of European unity. He believed above all in the common market. This was why he defended the EEC against the British proposal for a free trade area (1956–58). His commitment to Europe was, though, free of any idealism or lyricism. And so it did not come as a surprise that, for him, the central role of the European Commission was confined to applying the Treaty of Rome: 'Marjolin did not believe that the concept of "nation" could be replaced by the concept of "Europe" in a single generation or even over several generations, simply by creating new institutions.' ([2])

He left the European Commission in 1967 and shortly afterwards joined the world of business, being appointed, among other things, as a board member of Royal Dutch Shell and economic adviser to IBM.

He died in Paris on 15 April 1986 after putting the finishing touches to his memoirs *Architect of European unity*.

A. L.

([1]) Marjolin, R., *Architect of European unity — Memoirs, 1911–1986*, Weidenfeld and Nicolson, London, 1989, p. 41.

([2]) Ball, G. W., *The past has another pattern*, Norton and Company, New York, 1982, p. 102.

decided, for instance, that the studies on medium-term programming were not to be regarded as setting targets but simply as mapping out prospects. For its part, the Council was at pains to prune back the independence of the future Medium-Term Economic Policy Committee by asserting Member States' responsibility for economic policy coordination.

After being amended by the Commission itself and then by the Member States meeting within the Council, the Commission programme led to the setting up of a number of new committees: the Committee of Central Bank Governors, the Budgetary Policy Committee and the Medium-Term Economic Policy Committee. Alongside this, the tasks of the Monetary Committee were reinforced. Generally speaking, prior consultation and in-depth coordination were needed for budgetary policy, exchange-rate adjustments and positions to be adopted on the functioning and possible reform of the international monetary system.

Coordination with modest results

The wide-ranging objectives spelt out in the 1962 action programme and the institutional innovations introduced in May 1964 gave way to more modest prospects in the ensuing years. At international level, discussions focused on the key questions posed by the difficulties with the US balance of payments and the dollar and by the reform of the international monetary system. The Europeans agreed on one thing: the domestic imbalances in the United States and unduly large capital outflows were largely responsible for the difficulties encountered by the dollar and hence by the international monetary system. Consequently, the United States had to show the discipline that was essential to safeguard the international monetary system, while the Six had to play a role commensurate with their economic stature both in the discussions on the reform of the system and within the international monetary institutions. However, views diverged widely on the attitude to be adopted to the reform of the inter-

national monetary system. At the same time, the pronouncements by General de Gaulle on the matter from March 1965 onwards meant that the discussions became tougher and cast a shadow over the attempts by the Commission to help bring about a solution acceptable to all ([1]).

But any common approach at international level necessitated effective coordination of economic policies. This, though, remained elusive. At the beginning of 1967, the Chairman of the Monetary Committee, Émile van Lennep, raised the matter of a new phase in the strengthening of economic policy coordination involving the introduction of rules on budgetary policy, monetary policy and payments balances. While approving this approach, Marjolin pointed out that it was the misgivings voiced within the Council that restricted the scope of the Commission's initiatives in this respect. The Competition Commissioner, Hans von der Groeben, was even more pessimistic, drawing attention to a gap between the efforts made and the coordination procedures laid down, on the one hand, and the actual situation, on the other. For him, as for President Hallstein, who was, though, less pessimistic overall, the Community and each individual Member State had to find ways of taking on board what was needed for Europe at the political level.

Generally speaking, it was the attitude taken by the different governments that accounted for the less-than-satisfactory headway made towards coordination and frustrated any new advances in liberalising capital movements. Marjolin, who was convinced of the need for a Community capital market and aware of the risks involved, claimed that jumping in at the deep end was the way to learn how to swim provided that all the necessary safeguards were in place.

In January 1967 van Lennep described the actual situation with regard to economic policy integration in the following terms: 'We need to act with

([1]) 'La CEE et les questions monétaires internationales', statement by Mr Robert Marjolin to the European Parliament, 23 March 1965.

perseverance, even if no spectacular progress is made, and we need to tighten the constraints on independent action by national governments in order to offset the weaknesses that political necessity often introduces into measures taken by national governments and, in so doing, to achieve an increasingly close degree of effective coordination' ([1]).

The first attempt at economic and monetary union

The 'first Barre plan'

The years 1968–72 remain in the collective memory as those that witnessed the first attempt at economic and monetary union. Paradoxically, the circumstances at the time seemed, in the words of Jean-Claude Paye, both to offer optimism and to portend danger: optimism was in the air because growth was buoyant and the impression was that it would continue. In addition, the construction of Europe had recently registered some major advances ([2]). There was, however, a feeling of anxiety following a series of monetary developments that confirmed the extreme vulnerability of the international monetary system and threatened to undermine a still fragile European edifice. The sterling crisis that led the United Kingdom government to devalue its currency under difficult conditions in the autumn of 1967 was the last scare before a dollar crisis that heralded the demise of the international monetary system. A few months later, the crisis of May 1968 exploded in France, one of the key members of the Community. According to Paye, viewed from Brussels and in the day-to-day practice at the Commission, these events alerted him and his colleagues to the

fact that progress towards the construction of Europe was fragile and could be undone. Moreover, there was no reason why the same should not happen elsewhere at a later stage and perhaps with more serious repercussions ([3]). Hence the feeling that urgent action was needed to preserve 10 years of achievement in the economic construction of Europe, the argument being that, thanks to political determination underpinned by increasingly close cooperation, the dangers threatening the construction of Europe could probably be averted provided that the situation was not just left at that and progress was made in strengthening coordination and solidarity. For Raymond Barre, it was crucial to shelter the Community ([4]). Benefiting from the experience of his predecessor and given his perfect mastery of international monetary matters and of what rapidly became close contacts with the Committee of Central Bank Governors, he wasted no time in launching the first initiatives to that end.

The memorandum on Community action in the monetary field, presented to the Council in February 1968 and then kept secret because of an extremely strained international monetary environment, emphasised that the Six had no choice but to become more cohesive in the face of the new storms that were brewing: this involved mutual agreement prior to any exchange-rate adjustment, abolition of the margins of fluctuation authorised until then between Member States' currencies, establishment of a mutual assistance mechanism and a European unit of account, along with jointly agreed action within the international monetary institutions.

May 1968 seemed initially to cast doubt on whether a truly coordinated economic and monetary policy was actually possible. In France, the introduction of safeguard measures of a protectionist nature at a time when the customs union between the Six had just come into being on 1 July 1968, and the inflationary environment expected in the

---

([1]) FJME, AMK 13, Émile Noël to Klaus Meyer, discussion with Mr van Lennep during the Commission meeting on 6 September 1967.

([2]) Paye, J.-Cl., 'Vers le plan Werner: le rôle de la Commission des Communautés, 1967–1973', *Le rôle des ministères des finances et de l'économie dans la construction européenne (1957–1978), Histoire économique et financière de la France*, t. II. Animation de la recherche CHEFF, Paris, 2002, p. 114. Jean-Claude Paye here discusses his experience as the *chef de cabinet* of Raymond Barre, the new Commissioner responsible for economic and financial affairs.

([3]) Ibid., p. 116.
([4]) Interview with Raymond Barre, 20 February 2004.

wake of the wage agreements between the unions and employers appeared to run counter to what was needed at the time. Raymond Barre sought to safeguard what was essential. During the summer months he was at pains to persuade the French government to comply with the requirement to consult on safeguard measures while at the same time he endeavoured to make things easier for it in its dealings with the Commission. He later recalled that the discussions with the Commission on the French safeguard measures were often very tense, going on late into the night until a vote was taken ([1]). A few months later, in November 1968, when the French franc suffered a new bout of weakness on the foreign exchange market and both the cooperation and the solidarity between the Six appeared to be quite inadequate, Raymond Barre approached General de Gaulle and persuaded him not to devalue the French franc as this would have had serious repercussions at both national and Community level. Satisfied with the outcome, the Commission concluded from this that monetary solidarity and economic cooperation between the Six needed to be strengthened as a matter of urgency since this was the only way of creating, at the heart of the EEC, the cohesion it needed to prepare for the gathering storm clouds.

On 5 December 1968, the Commission presented to the Council a memorandum 'on the possible Community policy to deal with present economic and monetary problems'. The memorandum of 12 February 1969, which is now commonly referred to as the 'first Barre plan', fleshed out the Commission's proposals for both economic policy convergence and monetary cooperation ([2]). Reflecting the Commission's concerns since the beginning of the 1960s, it advocated medium-term economic policy consultations — particularly the prospects for economic growth and employment, the inflation rate and the external payments equilibrium — by more closely synchronising national economic programmes and dealing in a coordinated manner with the structural problems facing each economy. The coordination of short-term economic policies, themselves built around each country's medium-term programmes, had to be stepped up via consultations prior to economic policymaking and through the introduction of early-warning indicators. The corollary of closer coordination involved, among other things, establishing a short-term monetary support mechanism between central banks to be activated in response to a simple request from the country concerned but subject to a ceiling and to a posteriori consultations, and granting medium-term financial assistance following a Council decision for countries for which the short-term monetary support was not sufficient. In point of fact, the first Barre plan differed from the February 1968 memorandum in that it placed greater emphasis on the need for economic policy coordination, since the events of 1968 had shown that, more than ever, internal cohesion and the ability to withstand external shocks were linked. There was also no doubting the fact that, within the Monetary Committee, the Dutch and German representatives regularly stressed the need for discipline on the inflation front and that the February 1969 memorandum took this into account.

Towards economic and monetary union?

The initiatives leading to the decisions taken by the Six at the Hague Summit, one of the most symbolic of which was the attainment of economic and monetary union in Europe by 1980, stemmed from numerous factors.

In May 1969, the markets were buffeted by a fresh bout of turmoil that caused the German mark to appreciate but the German government, isolated from its partners, failed to decide on a date for a revaluation. The devaluation of the French franc

---

([1]) Paye, J.-Cl., 'Vers le plan Werner [...]', op cit., p. 116. Interview with Raymond Barre, 20 February 2004.

([2]) The Commission memorandum to the Council on economic policy coordination and monetary cooperation within the Community has been the subject of numerous publications. The text of the memorandum can be found in *Le rôle des ministères des finances et de l'économie dans la construction européenne (1957–1978)*, t. II, CHEFF, Paris, 2002.

Raymond Barre

Caricature of the Commissioner responsible for economic and financial affairs from 1967 to 1972, Raymond Barre, in the December 1972 issue of *30 jours d'Europe*, a periodical put out by the Information Office in Paris.

on 8 August 1969 followed by the revaluation of the German mark on 27 October eased the strains and paved the way for discussions between the Member States while two new governments, led by Georges Pompidou in France and Willy Brandt in Germany, showed themselves willing to relaunch the construction of Europe. For its part, the Action Committee for the United States of Europe, advised by Robert Triffin, urged, as a prelude to the creation of a European currency and a European central bank, the launching of the ambitious project to set up a European Reserve Fund. At the Commission, Raymond Barre, who was very much aware of the difficulties of intergovernmental cooperation as a result of deliberations within the Monetary Committee, argued though for a more cautious policy. In Mons, in April 1969, he explained to the finance ministers that completion of the customs union necessitated monetary cooperation, pointing out that the Commission's monetary proposals were rea-

sonable and that, if they were to be jettisoned, this should not have been done on 1 July 1968. In his opinion, something was needed in the place of the levers that external foreign trade provided ([1]). While he persuaded the ministers to set up a short-term support mechanism in January 1970, he knew just how difficult it would be to obtain more in the way of mutual assistance. On 21 February 1970 he explained to Monnet that the approach taken by the German finance minister, Schiller, was to defer any discussion of monetary organisation until the programme for economic and monetary union had been completed. According to Monnet, Barre was of the opinion that monetary measures were needed beforehand and the idea of a European Reserve Fund scared him. Monnet went on to say that, in Barre's view, this difficulty could be sidestepped by not using this term and by securing successive agreements that gradually committed national currency reserves, just like the agreement on automatic assistance had begun to do. Monnet maintained that Barre now had experience of central banks and finance ministries and that they had to become accustomed to this and to move forward one step at a time ([2]).

On the basis of the conclusions reached at the Hague Conference, the Commission set about drafting a proposal for a stage-by-stage plan leading to the attainment of economic and monetary union; this plan soon became known as the 'second Barre plan'. It was presented to the Council on 4 March 1970, two days before the Werner Group was set up by the Finance Ministers of the Six with the task of examining the economic and monetary union project. The Commission communication to the Council on the plan took further the ideas spelt out earlier in this connection. Economic and monetary union was to be seen against the background of moves to create a 'frontier-free economic area' and a distinctive entity on the international scene. National instruments

[1] AMAEF, F 30, B 50 479, Mons Conference, Handwritten notes: 20–21 April 1969.
[2] FJME, AMK C 33/1/126, Conversation with Raymond Barre, 19 February 1970.

Raymond Barre

Raymond Barre was born at Saint-Denis on the French island of Réunion on 12 April 1924. After fighting with the Free French forces in 1943, he had a brilliant academic career, which was not typical for French politicians of his generation: he graduated from the Institute of Political Studies in Paris (IEP) but did not apply to study at the École nationale d'administration (ENA), choosing instead to pursue his university career. In 1950 he passed the examination to become a lecturer in economics.

He became professor of economics (Caen, Tunis, Paris, IEP) and was a man of convictions: as a liberal, he was opposed to French protectionism.

Alongside Jean-Marcel Jeanneney, the Industry Minister from 1959 to 1962, whose private office he headed, Barre devoted his energies to bringing about France's economic regeneration. He then joined the board of the Centre for Income and Cost Studies (CERC) at the National Planning Agency (Commissariat général du plan) in 1966 before taking up his appointment in Brussels in 1967.

Regarded at first as 'de Gaulle's man' by the other Commissioners, who were somewhat wary of him when he arrived, Barre soon made an impression with his pro-European views extending across a whole range of issues.

In Brussels, Barre was in regular contact with Valéry Giscard d'Estaing, at the time the Economic and Financial Affairs Minister in Georges Pompidou's government. His relationship with the future President of the French Republic had a determining influence on his subsequent career. On 12 January 1976, following a ministerial reshuffle, Raymond Barre was appointed Minister for External Trade in the government of Jacques Chirac. Seven months later, when Chirac resigned, he became Prime Minister, the first non-Gaullist head of government in the Fifth Republic.

With France in the throes of a full-blown economic and financial crisis, Barre became not only Prime Minister but also Economic and Financial Affairs Minister. He brought in a series of remedial measures and asserted his determination to give priority to restoring the main economic aggregates and to redressing the economic situation. It was during his term of office that France took an active part in setting up the European Monetary System (EMS).

He stood as a candidate in the presidential elections of 1988 and obtained 16 % of the votes in the first round.

Raymond Barre played a determining role in shaping economic policy in France, regardless of who was in power, the Left or the Right. The discipline he introduced into the conduct of the economy influenced the Left, and in particular Pierre Bérégovoy, as well as the Right, including Édouard Balladur. Between 1995 and 2001, Raymond Barre was Mayor of Lyon.

G.L.

Extract from the interview given by Barre on 20 February 2004 concerning his experience at the Commission:

'I would say that my experience at the Commission helped to round off my training. I had no problem with the idea underlying the construction of Europe. I believe it is important for my country. But talking about Europe is not enough. One needs to have experienced it. The relationships between governments. The tension. The political influences. The trade-union influences. It is all a game in which you had to have taken part. Secondly, there are the relationships between Europe and the rest of the world. Here too, I must say, nothing was straightforward. In other words, both at European level and at international level, you gain what is extremely useful experience. An experience that served me well when I became Prime Minister, by the way. If Giscard d'Estaing appointed me, it was in large part because I had had that experience. So there you are. I have very good memories of my five and a half years at the Commission.'

(Translated from the French)

would thus have to be replaced by Community instruments as a means of directing and exerting overall control of the economy and developing a structural policy that would reduce the disparities between economies. The objective was to create a stable and distinctive monetary area in the context of a weakened international monetary system. There was a sense of urgency at the time regarding the contribution that such an area could make to providing monetary stability. Action had to be taken before the final crisis within the international monetary system brought about the demise of the Community experience. The arrangements proposed by the Commission were in response to the Member States' wish for a progressive approach, the need to balance out the constraints imposed by coordination and the requirement for solidarity between Member States. The first two stages, the preliminary stage (1970–71) and the preparatory stage (1972–75), covered four areas in which cooperation would be stepped up: coordination of economic policies, establishment of a single capital market, tax harmonisation and monetary solidarity. It was only during the third stage (1976–78) that the institutional adjustments needed to complete the process would be made: establishment of a Committee of Governors, creation of a European Reserve Fund, the irrevocable fixing of exchange rates, totally free movement of capital and abolition of tax frontiers. Ambition and caution were thus the watchwords of the Commission's proposals: parallelism between the efforts at economic convergence and the efforts to achieve solidarity, institutional adjustments involving the transfers of sovereignty that would be needed at the end of the day, and implementation of the medium-term economic policy programme for the years 1970–75 as the test of progress towards economic convergence.

The deliberations of the Werner Group took place between March and October 1970. The Commission had plenty of contact with its members, if only because of the respect and friendship that existed between Bernard Clappier (Chairman of the Monetary Committee) and Hubert Ansiaux (Chairman of the Committee of Central Bank Governors), on the one hand, and Raymond Barre, on the other. This was also the reason why, once the Werner Report had been published, Barre had no difficulty in demonstrating that a good number of the report's recommendations were 'the very ones which the Commission has not merely been recommending but has set out in detail for months, not to say years' (¹). Even so, the proposals sent by the Commission to the Council on 29 October 1970 and based on the recommendations of the Werner Plan testified to the same concern for pragmatism and caution as was evident in the plan presented to the Council on 4 March. It was in connection with the institutional arrangements — a matter of great sensitivity to the French government, as Barre was only too aware — that this pragmatism was most marked. Where the Werner Group referred to the setting up of an economic policy decision-making centre that would be politically answerable to a European Parliament and a set of institutional reforms that would be drawn up during the first stage of EMU, the Commission's proposals referred to the transfer of certain powers that would have to be limited to what was necessary for the cohesion of the Union and the effectiveness of Community action and did not touch on the nature of the bodies to be set up or on the allocation of powers between them. Following several meetings of the Council and then a meeting between Brandt and Pompidou, an overall compromise was reached between the Member States on 9 February 1971 and the foundations of the first stage of EMU were adopted on 22 March. Under the proposals, economic policy coordination and monetary cooperation would operate in parallel. In practice, the decision to narrow the Community currencies' permissible margin of fluctuation against the dollar with effect from 15 June was the first step towards setting fixed parities between the Community currencies. For this to succeed, however, the Member States would have to be capable and to have the requisite political resolve to coordinate their actions

---

(¹) 'The economic and monetary union: its objective and its problems', statement by Mr Raymond Barre to the European Parliament, 18 November 1970', *Bulletin of the EC*, No 1, 1971.

UNE DÉCISION QUI FERA DATE DANS L'HISTOIRE DES SIX

En 1981, une monnaie unique pour l'Europe du Marché commun

(Photo-montage J.-L. Debaize)

The *Courrier du personnel* on 18 February 1971 highlights the decisions taken by the Council to establish economic and monetary union and presents a photomontage which points the way towards the euro.

sufficiently to cope with the final convulsions of a moribund international monetary system and with the strains that its demise would create within the EEC.

Disillusion sets in

The speculative crisis that took hold in the spring and summer of 1971 scuttled the options decided on in March. In the face of a massive inflow of footloose capital attracted by the safe haven being offered to an increasing extent by the German mark, the Bundesbank decided on 5 May to abandon support for the dollar and to close the foreign exchange market. The central banks of Belgium and the Netherlands followed suit. For the general public, this crisis, which provided confirmation that the warnings issued by the Commission over a number of years had been justified, raised the question of the ability of the Six to agree on a common approach. At a meeting on 8 May, the finance ministers of the Six failed to reach agreement. Since it wished to preserve the monetary cohesion between the Six within a stable international system, the Commission had proposed fixed parities between the Community currencies, alongside measures to monitor movements of footloose capital so as to protect the Community from further disruptive inflows. The German government, for its part, proposed a coordinated floating of the Community currencies against the dollar as a means of ensuring Community cohesion. The failure to reach agreement led to the break-up of the European currency area. The German mark, and then the Dutch guilder, floated upwards against the dollar. The French and Italian authorities sought to hold their parities steady by introducing exchange controls. The Belgian authorities set up a two-tier foreign exchange market. In the wake of the crisis, Raymond Barre insisted on giving his substantive analysis of the situation to the European Parliament: 'So long as the Member States do not arrive at some measure of political consensus on certain major problems, we shall always have to live — despite declarations of principle expressing good intentions — with qualified commitments and, in difficult situations, with decisions designed mainly to safeguard what each country considers to be its own vital interests'. [1]

The decision by the US government on 15 August 1971 to suspend the gold convertibility of the dollar and to introduce a 10 % import surcharge threw down a new challenge to the Community that was not taken up immediately. At their meeting on 19 August, the finance ministers were unable to agree on a common approach, and so the European currency area remained divided

---

[1] Statement by Mr Barre to the European Parliament, 18 May 1971, *Bulletin of the EC*, No 6, 1971.

The EEC and international monetary instability: sequence of events

1958	**27 December:** return to currency convertibility in 10 European countries
	29 December: devaluation of the French franc
1961	**6–7 March:** revaluation of the German mark and the Dutch guilder
1964	**8 May:** establishment of the Committee of EEC Central Bank Governors
1967	**18 November:** devaluation of sterling
1969	**12 February:** 'Barre plan' on economic policy coordination and monetary support
	8 August: devaluation of the French franc
	24 October: revaluation of the German mark
	1–2 December: Hague Conference: first EMU project
1970	**9 February:** EEC sets up short-term monetary support mechanism
	16 October: presentation of the Werner Report
1971	**22 March:** adoption of the three-stage EMU programme — EEC sets up medium-term financial assistance mechanism
	10 May: floating of the German mark and the Dutch guilder
	15 August: suspension of the gold convertibility of the dollar, floating of the dollar
	17–18 December: Washington Agreements, currency parity readjustments
1972	**24 April:** establishment of the European currency snake (Basle Agreements)
	1 May: sterling enters the snake
	23 June: sterling leaves the snake
1973	**12 February:** devaluation of the dollar
	13 February: Italian lira leaves the snake
	19 March: floating of the dollar
1974	**19 January:** French franc leaves the snake

between a German mark that was appreciating, a Benelux currency area centred on a jointly agreed float of the Dutch guilder and the Belgian franc, and exchange controls in Italy and France. The Europeans immediately realised that this complicated matters for agricultural prices since, as uniform prices were no longer guaranteed because of the divergent fluctuations in the Community currencies, the common agricultural policy, which had been so painstakingly put in place, came under threat. As a result, a complicated system of monetary compensatory amounts (MCAs) was introduced and was, for many years, a source of controversy between Member States.

Faced with the threat posed by the dollar's depreciation and the import surcharge, which might impede exports to the United States and, more generally, to the dollar area, the Six managed to reconcile their differences in September and to agree to make one last-ditch effort to preserve their cohesion. A series of bilateral meetings between European Heads of State or Government enabled them to present a united front to the Americans at the conference held at the Smithsonian Institute in Washington on 17 and 18 December 1971. The US import surcharge was dropped while the parities of the dollar, the yen and the Community currencies were readjusted within the context of an international monetary system with more flexible rules.

The full significance of these decisions at international level can be understood only in the light of the efforts made by the Europeans to resolve their differences. The establishment of the 'snake in the tunnel' ('currency snake') was, in effect, the second strand of a comprehensive programme that had, as its first strand, the agreements reached in Washington. The decision taken by the Six on 21 March 1972 to narrow the permissible margins of fluctuation between their currencies to 2.25 % against the dollar was prompted by the need to secure cohesion and by the view that the Community currencies should, in the place of the dollar, play a more important role than in the past in transactions between European economic operators. The sound performance of the snake was, however, due to a complex range of factors: effective coordination of economic policies, and in particular measures to combat inflation; solidarity between Europeans in matters of monetary cooperation, which seemed to be foreshadowed by the agreement signed between central banks in Basle on 10 April 1972; serious resolve on the part of the US government to help defend the system and on the part of the Six to organise themselves in such a way as to control speculative capital flows. As Raymond Barre put it in a statement made before the European Parliament on 18 January 1972, reflecting the general philosophy that had been his since 1968: 'In an inter-

national context which provides the Community with an exceptional opportunity to organise and strengthen monetary cooperation between its members [...] the Commission proposes that the Member States strive for concrete progress that is economically reasonable, technically possible and politically acceptable' ([1]).

In point of fact, the external shocks attributable to the US authorities' weakness of resolve in stabilising their economy very soon put paid to the European efforts, which were themselves insufficient. At of the end of June 1972, the UK authorities refused to join the 'snake', while the Bank of Italy secured certain changes in the way it financed market intervention. While the Paris Summit of Heads of State or Government reaffirmed, in October 1972, the European resolve to implement the project of economic and monetary union, it became increasingly likely that this would take place against the background of a generalised floating of currencies, something which Raymond Barre had not ruled out back in July 1972 ([2]). Under the circumstances, alongside the strengthened solidarity arrangements, the sound coordination of national economic policies became even more necessary than in the past, particularly as regards the fight against inflation. This was one of the conditions of European monetary stability mentioned by Raymond Barre in his statement before the European Parliament on 18 May 1971: 'Today it must once more be reiterated that the trend of wages and prices remains a cause for concern, that a tight policy on credit and public finance is absolutely necessary and that this policy must be accompanied by restraint on the part of the two sides of industry in the matters of incomes and prices.' In October 1972 the Commission presented to the Council a communication on the measures to be taken to combat inflation. The differences of opinion as to the magnitude of the inflationary danger and the differences in attitude on the part of politicians in

---

[1] Statement by Mr Barre to the European Parliament, 18 January 1972, *Bulletin of the EC*, No 3, 1972.
[2] Statement by Mr Barre to the European Parliament, 4 July 1972, *Bulletin of the EC*, No 8, 1972.

the face of this phenomenon were clearly not conducive to policy coordination in this field. The 1973 oil shock simply accentuated the divergences and made it more difficult to preserve the Community's economic and monetary cohesion.

ÉRIC BUSSIÈRE

'What type of growth, and with what objectives for the population of Europe and mankind?': debate between Sicco Mansholt and Raymond Barre at the Commission in 1972

This debate took place between Mansholt and Barre ([1]), who had, according to his adviser Jean Degimbe, 'gone onto the offensive' ([2]), in the form of an exchange of correspondence during 1972. It quickly became public knowledge and had a marked impact on many Commission officials, including Degimbe and Rencki ([3]), who took the view that, when the Commission was capable of triggering a debate within society, it gave proof of its existence and showed that it was irreplaceable.

On 9 February 1972, echoing the concerns expressed by the Club of Rome and by his friend Professor Tinbergen, the Nobel Prize Winner for Economics, and in response to a report from the Massachusetts Institute of Technology on the limits to growth, Mansholt wrote to the members of the Malfatti Commission, expressing the hope that certain economic policy problems with serious implications for the future of Europe but also for the future of mankind would be discussed by the Commission with a view to presenting well thought out proposals to the Council.

These problems stemmed from the following:

— world population trends (twofold increase by the year 2000), at a time when lowering the birth rate was conditional on improvements in living standards (India, Latin America, China, etc.);

— food production, which was increasing but at the same time was upsetting the ecological balance (pesticides and insecticides discharged into the river system, deforestation, water shortages, etc.);

— industrialisation, at a time when the consumption of raw materials and energy in the industrialised countries was some 25 times higher than the average in the developing countries;

— pollution;

— use of natural resources;

— equality of opportunity for all, a principle that must underlie any reform;

— the industrialised countries' relations with the developing countries at a time when the pursuit of growth in the West was widening the gap in living standards between both groups of countries.

Replying on 9 June 1972, Raymond Barre disagreed with Mansholt's findings. For him, technology could resolve the problems it created provided that it was used to that end.

For Mansholt, a radical policy rethink was needed. He wondered what 'Europe' as such could do and what needed to be done to prevent the machinery from seizing up. He even questioned whether anything could actually be done, whether Europe was capable of intervening and whether this was not a matter for the world as a whole.

([1]) Sicco Mansholt came over as a convinced supporter of the Club of Rome report and a fervent advocate of 'zero growth' in the book *La Crise*, published in 1974.

([2]) Interview with Jean Degimbe, 15 December 2003.

([3]) Interview with Georges Rencki, 13 January 2004.

Mansholt did not believe that there would be a change at global level. In his opinion, only Europe, therefore, could exert real influence in the world and, by strengthening its institutions, could pursue an effective policy in the years to come since the United States was on the decline and did not have the political presence necessary to guide the world towards a solution for this major problem.

For Mansholt, the key issue was population trends throughout the world. Assuming a stable world population, he wanted to see the number of births restricted to a replacement family size, i.e. two children. Barre emphasised that this was one of the recurring themes in the history of economic thought and maintained that technological progress gave reason to believe that agricultural production would grow faster than the world's population.

Mansholt retorted that, even if world population growth was brought under control, action would still be needed to ensure the survival of mankind and that this would entail:

1. priority being given to food production, with investment also going into agricultural products deemed to be 'uneconomic';

2. a marked reduction in the per capita consumption of tangible goods, to be offset by an increased supply of intangible goods (social welfare, intellectual pursuits, organisation of leisure and recreational activities, etc.);

3. a significant increase in the useful life of equipment by preventing waste and avoiding the production of non-essential goods;

4. measures to tackle pollution and raw material depletion by redirecting investment towards recycling and anti-pollution measures, and this would naturally lead to a shift in demand and hence in production.

As regards non-reproducible mineral resources, Raymond Barre stressed the need to know fairly rapidly that a particular resource was running out so that prices and hence consumption could adjust. But he also had recourse to more optimistic statistics, maintaining that proven fossil energy resources (coal, oil) would satisfy the needs of 10 billion people with a level of consumption double that in the United States for 40 years. Above all, he felt that rapid reactors could be developed that, given proven raw material resources, could satisfy those same needs for a million years. For him, the most serious problems were those involving the distribution of resources and people between the regions of the world, and the relationship between man and his environment could be brought under control provided that social relationships between individuals could also be brought under control.

Mansholt took the view that the society of tomorrow could not be growth oriented, at least not in the material sense. He thus suggested replacing GNP with gross national utility or 'gross national happiness' (even so, it remained to be seen whether such a concept could be quantified). Barre underscored the extent to which the well-being of a community could not be quantified because this was an eminently subjective concept. That said, he was not in favour of forcing the pace of growth since, in his opinion, this might benefit productivity more than employment, might raise expectations more quickly than they could be met and might aggravate rather than help mitigate industrial unrest.

For Barre, though, the consumer society was a success and his objectives were quite different:

— broad sections of society did not yet have access to a decent material standard of living;

— job insecurity still weighed heavily on many people;

— the problem of a fairer distribution of incomes was all the more pressing in that global income had increased more strongly over the previous 20 years;

— lastly, as regards the quality of life, living conditions in modern urban areas were affected by many more factors than just pollution, e.g. housing, transport or working conditions.

Whereas Mansholt proposed focusing on the problems of planning and tax policy so as to safeguard the ecological balance, Barre replied that there should not be too many illusions about what national or supranational plans could achieve since the market economy had already been substantially modified by the intervention of the public authorities. Whereas Mansholt sought to put in place a non-polluting system of production ('Clean and Recycling'), to promote the durability of consumer goods via taxation or even to prohibit non-essential goods or to tax them very heavily, Barre drew a distinction between industrial plant and consumer durables: he was opposed to extending the useful life of the former since he was concerned that this would hamper the dissemination of technical progress, but he actually proposed abolishing VAT on second-hand goods.

G.L.

Sources: Letter from Mansholt to Malfatti, Brussels, 9 February 1972; Reflections on the letter from Mr Mansholt to the President of the Commission (Memo from Mr Barre), SEC(72)2068, Brussels, 9 June 1972.

See also the interviews with Mansholt, and in particular those published in the *Nouvel Observateur*, 12–18 June 1972 and 19–25 June 1972, and in his book, *La Crise*, Stock, Paris.

Chapter 20

European regional policy: the foundations of solidarity

The duty of the European Economic Community to assist the regions is laid down in the preamble to the Treaty of Rome, where the Six state that they are 'anxious to strengthen the unity of their economies and to ensure their harmonious development by reducing the differences existing between the various regions and the backwardness of the less-favoured regions'.

An almost silent Treaty

Article 2 of the Treaty itself, which sets as the task of the Community the establishment of a common market, simply refers to the harmonious development of economic activities throughout the Community, without, however, providing for a financial instrument to achieve that end.

However, some of the ways in which the competition rules were applied could be seen as a sort of 'negative image' of a regional policy. Articles 92 and 93, which banned State aid for investments in firms, included an exception for 'areas where the standard of living is abnormally low or where there is serious under-employment'.

These provisions allowed the Commission to check whether a region was genuinely eligible

for this exceptional treatment but, in the end, amounted to no more than a framework for national regional policies [1].

By reading the preamble in conjunction with Article 2 of the founding text, certain 'maximalists' who sought, here as elsewhere, to exploit to the full the opportunities offered by the Treaty set themselves two goals. The first was the harmonious development of the Community's territory, and hence of each of its regions. The second was the convergence of economic policies, which also implied regional policies [2].

Some governments went beyond highlighting the existence of striking imbalances between the various regions which would form the future Community of Six and were aware of the importance of this topic in terms of securing assistance for their own national policies. Italy was a case in point. Since its unification, it had been faced with the serious problem of the Mezzogiorno. After

---

[1] Dossier of Georges Rencki to Michel Dumoulin, 9 April 2006.
[2] Romus, P., *Économie régionale européenne*, fifth ed., Presses universitaires de Bruxelles, Brussels, 1989, pp. 53–54. By the same author: *Expansion économique régionale et Communauté européenne*, Sythoff, Leiden, 1958, and *L'Europe et les régions*, Labor/Nathan, Brussels/Paris, 1979.

Members of Commission responsible for regional policy	
10 January 1958 to 5 July 1967	Robert Marjolin
6 July 1967 to 1 July 1970	Hans von der Groeben
2 July 1970 to 5 January 1973	Albert Borschette

the Messina Conference, one of the aims of the Italian government was to use the common market to promote the economic development of the south [1].

The protocol on Italy explicitly addressed the question of the Mezzogiorno, and the situation of the regions was also mentioned as an essential element in achieving various objectives of the Treaty from agricultural to transport policy and including the free movement of labour [2].

When it began to implement the Treaties of Rome, the Commission decided to set up within DG II (Economic and Financial Affairs) a Directorate for Economic Structure and Development, including a regional development division. In the beginning this was little more than a name. Paul Romus, a Belgian Commission official who was to play an important role in this field remembers that, when he joined it, there was no one there. He met Duquesne de La Vinelle (Director of the Directorate for Economic Structure and Development), who said to him: 'Well, Romus, you're the

first, here's your office and we'll get a few more people.' [3] In any event, until the early 1960s the division, headed by the Italian Emanuele Tosco, comprised only a few A grade officials: Romus, two Frenchmen, an Italian and a German.

Virtually virgin territory

However, various Community countries were becoming increasingly interested in regional questions, as was reflected in the establishment of bodies to develop these policies: DATAR in France and the Cassa del Mezzogiorno in Italy, and research institutes such as Svimez, again in Italy. Furthermore, the ECSC had already planned a series of actions based on the idea of tackling certain economic problems on a regional basis, as had been done with the Belgian coalfields since 1958 [4]. For the time being, the Commission did no more than collect statistics and studies on regional matters, while seeking to define the concept of 'region' and ranking the regions by their level of development. Immediately after the Commission had been set up, at the initiative — it appears — of Robert Marjolin, the member responsible for DG II [5], an initial group of specialists in regional policies within the national administrations of the Six was established to create links between the Community body and those involved in the various Member States. From 6 to 8 December 1961, again under the aegis of the Commission, a conference on the regional economies was held in the Palais des Congrès in Brussels.

The aims of this meeting were: to establish the closest possible contacts between those responsible for the design and implementation of regional policy in each of the six countries; to identify clearly and precisely the lessons to be drawn

[1] See, for example, the references to this topic in the memorandum presented by Italy to the Messina Conference; see ASMAE — Servizio Storico e Documentazione, *Gaetano Martino e l'Europa dalla conferenza di Messina al Parlamento Europeo*, Istituto Poligrafico e Zecca dello Stato, Rome, 1995, pp. 173–176.

[2] See the points made in Beutler, B., Bieber, R., Pipkorn, J., Streil, J. and Weiler, J. H. H., *L'Unione Europea — Istituzioni, ordinamento e politiche*, Il Mulino, Bologna, 1998, pp. 609–610.

[3] Interview with Paul Romus, 20 January 2004.

[4] Spierenburg, D. and Poidevin, R., *The history of the High Authority of the European Coal and Steel Community: Supranationality in operation*, London, Weidenfeld and Nicolson, 1994, pp. 395–417.

[5] On Marjolin's commitment as a member of the European Commission, see Marjolin, R., *Architect of European unity — Memoirs 1911–1986*, London, Weidenfeld and Nicolson, 1989, pp. 245–368. However, this work makes no mention of regional policy.

Regional policy as such was a late add-on. But the awareness of the need to develop it dates back to the early days of the EEC. From 6 to 8 December 1961 the Commission organised a conference on regional economies. On the platform, from left to right: Hans von der Groeben, Robert Marjolin and Sicco Mansholt.

from the efforts made in those countries to achieve a more harmonious development of the major regions within each national economy; to draw attention to the aspects of regional problems which were of shared interest (including the impact of the common market on these problems and possible solutions to them); to enlighten governments and the Commission on certain basic principles underlying regional policy; and to look at how the Commission could help the Member States in this area (¹).

Some 300 delegates attended, of whom about 20 spoke. Work was divided between two commit-

tees, the first headed by Sicco Mansholt (²) (responsible for the common agricultural policy) and the second by Hans von der Groeben (responsible for competition policy). Marjolin's two speeches, opening and closing the conference, were particularly striking. He opened the conference by noting the existence of regional imbalances within the EEC and the extent to which they could hinder the economic development of the Six, without, however, ignoring the social

(¹) See 'La conférence sur les économies régionales', *Revue du Marché Commun*, No 41, November 1961, p. 391.

(²) Sicco Mansholt's presence at this conference was all the more appropriate because, as far back as the conference of the Member States at Stresa, he had stressed his view that the Community needed a regional policy, partly to resolve the problems of European agriculture itself (Stresa agricultural conference, points 5 and 9 of the final resolution; Mansholt's speeches at Bad Godesberg on 10 June 1961 and at Milan on 6 April 1962). See the chapter on the common agricultural policy, pp. 333–339.

aspects of these problems. He then reviewed the work done by various countries in this field and emphasised the influence which the common market was already exerting, in particular the concentration of wealth in certain central regions and the concomitant growth in disparities between these regions and the EEC's less-developed regions. He pointed at the same time to the work already being done by the Community indirectly through the agricultural, social, energy and transport policies. Turning to direct assistance, Marjolin mentioned the work of the EIB, the ESF, and a series of studies launched by the Commission [1]. Winding up, he commented that the meeting should provide the Commission with suggestions on how to tackle certain problems, among which Marjolin included those associated with the frontier regions, with the dispersal or concentration of new investments, with the nature and extent of the aid given by the various governments to private enterprises, looked at from both the positive and the negative point of view, with social and cultural infrastructure, which was an essential aspect of regional development, and with the regional aspect of the transport problem [2]. Marjolin was reserved about the work of the Commission, considering that, at that juncture, the institution should concentrate on cooperating with governments and incorporate regional requirements in other policies. His only reference to a more proactive role for the Commission was the possibility of stepping up studies on the subject in order to establish a number of industrial centres in the Community [3].

Despite this restrained attitude, the Brussels conference encouraged the Commission to set up three working groups: the first to look at ways of promoting the development of outlying regions which were lagging behind the rest of the Community, the second to identify remedies for the decline of certain economic sectors in areas which had been heavily industrialised, and the third to examine the link between aid to firms for regional development purposes and the implementation of the Community's competition policy. Progress was certainly slow, mainly because the Commission officials involved in the project were operating in largely uncharted territory, where information and statistics were often lacking and it was even difficult to define the word 'region' [4]. However, some suggestions were made, such as the establishment of a development centre for southern Italy in the Bari-Taranto area, the launching of forms of cooperation between southern Belgian Luxembourg and northern Lorraine, and development of the Eifel–Hunsrück region.

First communication on regional policy

The three working groups completed their tasks at the end of 1964 but it was not until the following May that the Commission issued its *First Commission communication on regional policy in the European Economic Community*. The Commission's reticence in a sector where the Treaty offered only vague regulatory guidance is confirmed by the choice of the word 'communication' rather than 'report'. Paul Romus stated that it was also necessary to align the work of the division responsible for regional matters in DG II with DG IV's objectives as regards the competition rules designed to prevent measures which could result in market distortion. Despite these restrictions, the communication was an event of major importance. It began by setting out the aims of the regional policies pursued in the various countries of the Europe of Six and then reviewed the instruments used by the Member States in this

[1] Marjolin, R., 'Les économies régionales', *Revue du Marché Commun*, No 41, November 1961, pp. 393–401.
[2] Marjolin, R., 'Summing-up of the Conference on Regional Economies', *Bulletin of the EEC*, February 1962, p. 27.
[3] Ibid., p. 28.

[4] See interview with Paul Romus, 20 January 2004. Romus provided the secretariat for the study group on the old industrial regions, chaired by the Belgian E. Persoons, Deputy Director of the Banque de Bruxelles. The first group was headed by the Secretary of State at the German Ministry of Economic Affairs and the third by the Frenchman Mr Bloch-Lainé, Director-General of the Caisse Dépôts et Prêts. The chairmen of all three groups were therefore drawn from outside the Commission.

Original features of the project to promote an industrial centre in southern Italy, Taranto-Bari

On 19 November 1964 the Commission sent the Italian government a study on the promotion of an industrial centre in southern Italy.

The study proposed using a novel method to launch industrial development in large outlying regions, based on the role of exchanges of intermediate goods and services in the economy of industries with a complex cycle: specifically, it proposed the simultaneous establishment of all the activities required for the operation of the industrial sector to be promoted, and of an adequate number of industries in this sector to justify the existence of these activities, which were linked in economic terms.

In Italy the authorities rapidly developed policies for the south, where serious regional problems and economic difficulties had long been only too evident. The first development aid was effective in attracting capital-intensive heavy industries and stimulating processing industries aimed at the local market. But the impact on the other processing industries, such as engineering or second-stage chemicals, was limited.

The development possibilities for primary industries are obviously limited; and, if they are aimed at the local market, they are subject to the expansion of export activities to stimulate the regional economy.

This requires the development of processing industries with much broader markets. Hence, in 1960, the Commission considered promoting growth centres in southern Italy designed to draw on the primary industries so as to establish centres for the processing industry using a method similar to that which had given birth to the main industrial centres in the United States and western Europe.

When it prepared its study, the Commission found that this method could not be used here because the technical and economic conditions which had allowed this type of development in the past had changed substantially.

Because each industrial plant was increasingly specialised — in order to be competitive and to increase its productivity — so that each industry was concentrating on a single activity, the Commission decided to change its approach to the problem.

Because a businessman would consider manufacturing a finished product only in industrial centres where he could find all the activities linked to his sector and because a subcontractor would set up in business only if he had an adequate number of client businesses locally and the related activities which he himself needed, the Commission considered it necessary to establish all the activities needed for the industrial area in the Bari-Taranto project at the same time.

G. L.

area: from financial aid to the construction of infrastructure, and taking in administrative and financial structures. It also noted that each of a series of Community policies for which there was express provision in the Treaty (agriculture, transport, energy and vocational training) exerted its own influence on the various situations of the regions and confirmed the role played by a variety of Community financial instruments: the EIB, loans from the ECSC High Authority, the EAGGF, the ESF and 'study appropriations'.

In its conclusions based on these prime considerations, the Commission put forward a number of suggestions on the regional policies being pursued by the various governments. It stressed in particular the need for well-considered and coordinated measures. It proposed the establishment in outlying regions of development centres to host industrial plants, services and infrastructure. As for the areas of long-standing industrialisation, the Member States should not simply encourage the establishment of new industries but should also promote the regeneration of urban areas and the reskilling of the labour force through vocational training. It proposed better cross-border coordination to help frontier areas and underlined the importance of a policy for the construction of infrastructure in the broadest sense (communications routes, educational measures, town planning). The Commission renewed its commitment to pursuing a study programme and its desire to take regional requirements into account in devising other policies, particularly the CAP and policy on vocational training, and to promoting cooperation between those responsible in the various Member States, noting the work which had already been carried out for several years by the group of senior national officials, who would be joined by representatives of the EIB and the ECSC High Authority [1]. It should be noted that over that period the High Authority, which had broader powers, had developed vigorous mea-

sures, in a way 'regional' in nature, to cope with the persistent crisis in the coal industry, particularly in Belgium [2].

In the months following this communication, concrete measures were therefore limited.

But in 1966 the Medium-Term Economic Policy Committee looked at the possibility of a European regional policy. This body, which drew heavily on the Commission's suggestions [3], included, besides the representatives of the administrations of the Six, Marjolin, Levi Sandri, von der Groeben, plus Bobba, Director-General for Economic Affairs, and Prate, Director-General for the Internal Market.

Creation of a specific directorate-general

It was, however, the merger of the executives of the three Communities which played a decisive role in the creation in 1967 of the Directorate-General for Regional Affairs, marking a turning-point in the work of the Commission. We know that the ECSC had already proposed some initiatives in this field. As Paul Romus notes, several senior officials from the High Authority joined the Commission. It is not surprising that the Frenchman Jacques Cros, who came from the High Authority, was appointed Director-General of the new DG XVI [4], while the German von der Groeben became the member of the Commission with responsibility for this sector.

The von der Groeben programme

These changes in the structure of the Commission, no doubt influenced by the boost given to the regional policies of some of the Member States, raised awareness of these topics. The new

---

[1] *Première communication de la Commission sur la politique régional dans la Communauté économique européenne*, SEC(65) 1170, 11 May 1965.

[2] Spierenburg, D. and Poidevin, R., op. cit., pp. 600–614.

[3] BAC 20/1979 28, 'Avant-projet de premier programme politique et économique à moyen terme 1966–1970', Brussels, 25 March 1966.

[4] Interview with Paul Romus, 20 January 2004.

The European Investment Bank

The European Investment Bank grants loans for investment projects, including those intended to assist the less developed regions of the Member States. It finances projects for the modernisation and conversion of businesses as well as projects, mainly of a cross-border nature, involving several Member States.

A financial contribution to assisting less developed regions was the Bank's first field of assistance. Originally, funding was provided for primary industries and energy production; it was then extended to processing industries and the development of agriculture.

Then, when the Commission had defined a number of priorities in the transport field, the Bank provided assistance there too.

Between 1958 and 1973 Italy received over half the total amount of loans, followed by France and Germany, with about 20 % each; Belgium, the Netherlands and Luxembourg shared the remaining 10 % or so.

It is important to remember that the European Investment Bank was not set up to finance each and every investment. It dealt only with those which offered a reasonable return, even if this took time to come to fruition. No operating assistance is provided.

The Bank has its own rules about carrying out operations which comply with banking standards but which are limited to the objectives laid down by the Treaty. Its aims are to ensure both that the region participates in general economic progress and that it contributes to it.

It is not acceptable for either the Commission or the Bank for there to be regions whose development is entirely dependent on Community assistance.

G. L.

Commission President, Jean Rey, in a speech to the European Parliament in May 1968, identified regional policy as one of the sectors where the merger of the executives could provide a fresh stimulus [1]. In any case, the customs union had been completed and discussion begun on introducing a monetary policy. More generally, after 1968 there was a tendency for the political balance in Europe to slide towards the left, with greater attention being paid to social problems, a field which it was felt should include regional disparities in some form. It was in this propitious climate that von der Groeben placed the question before the Strasbourg Assembly in May 1969.

After detailing the results secured by the EEC in achieving a common market, the member responsible for DG XVI drew attention to the continuation of contradictions and economic disparities, particularly at regional level. The Commission was to seek solutions to three problems: 'the creation of conditions similar to those obtaining on a domestic market, the effective coordination of economic control through common economic and monetary policies, a common structural and regional policy' [2]. He went on to refer to the serious problems being caused in certain regions by the decline in the number of agricultural workers and the often chaotic growth of urban areas;

[1] See *Bulletin of the EC*, No 6, 1968, pp. 10–11.

[2] Von der Groeben, H., 'Regional policy: an essential and urgent Community task', *Bulletin of the EC*, No 6, 1969, p. 13.

Organisation chart of the departments responsible for regional policy

Organisation chart of Directorate-General II: Economic and Financial Affairs (1958–63)

	1958	1959	1960	1961	1962	1963
Director–General	Bobba	Bobba	Bobba	Bobba	Bobba	Bobba
Assistant	Malavasi	Malavasi	Malavasi	Malavasi	Malavasi	
Directorate C: Economic Structure and Development	Duquesne de La Vinelle	Duquesne de La Vinelle	Duquesne de La Vinelle	Millet	Prate	Prate
Division 2: Regional Development	Tosco	Tosco	Tosco	Tosco	Tosco	

Organisation chart of Directorate-General II: Economic and Financial Affairs (1964–67)

	1964	1965	1966	1967
Director–General	Bobba	Bobba	Bobba	Mosca
Assistant	Stefani	Stefani	Stefani	Stefani
Directorate C: Economic Structure and Development	Prate		Albert	Albert
Division 2: Regional Development	Paelinck		Solima	Solima

Organisation chart of Directorate-General XVI: Regional Policy (1968–72)

	1968	1969	1970	1971	1972
Director–General	Cros	Cros	Cros	Cros	Cros
Assistant	Baré	Baré	Baré	Baré	Baré
Directorate A: Studies and Documentation	Dutilleul	Dutilleul	Dutilleul	Dutilleul	Dutilleul
Division 1: Analysis and Documentation	Wäldchen	Wäldchen	Wäldchen	Wäldchen	Wäldchen
Division 2: Objectives and Methods of Regional Programming	Sünnen	Sünnen	Sünnen		
Specialist department: Policy Instruments for Regional Development	Romus	Romus	Romus	Romus	Romus
Directorate B: Development and Conversion	Solima	Solima	Solima	Solima	Solima
Division 1: Harmonisation and Coordination	Stabenow	Stabenow	Stabenow	Stabenow	Stabenow
Division 2: Regional Policy Measures	Bonnemaison	Bonnemaison	Bonnemaison	Bonnemaison	Bonnemaison

hence the need for a regional policy which should not only promote economic development but also provide solutions to certain social problems. Von der Groeben touched on the need for the Community to place the individual at the centre of its concerns so that the public authorities would be more involved. He ended by including among the Commission's objectives: '(a) coordination of aims and means by joint work on development prospects and confrontation of aims and priorities [...], (b) directing efforts towards the solution of problems arising in the various categories of regions as a result of changes in the various sectors of the economy [...], (c) escalation of aid is another problem requiring solution' (¹). New studies were required in specific cases, and in this connection he mentioned the Aachen/Liège/Belgian Limbourg/Maastricht triangle and the Twente-Westmünsterland frontier region. These references are particularly interesting because in recent years there had been experiments with cross-border forms of cooperation, particularly between France and Belgium, which had caught the eye of Commission officials (²).

A proposal for a decision

In the spring of 1969 the Institut d'études européennes of the Université Libre de Bruxelles (ULB) scheduled for November of that year a symposium on the 'frontier regions in the age of the common market'. It contacted Commission staff, including the Director-General of DG XVI, Cros, and von der Groeben (³). The Commission responded positively and, at the gathering on 27 and 28 November, von der Groeben gave the introductory and final speeches, while a number of Commission officials also spoke: Jacques Cros himself, Georges Michel, director in the Social Affairs DG, Jean-Paul Rey, principal administrator in the Transport DG, Robert Sünnen, head of division in Directorate-General XVI, and Chris-

tophe Dupont of the EIB (⁴); Paul Romus was also present as a lecturer at the ULB and Secretary-General of the symposium.

This symposium was particularly timely. A month earlier, the Commission had sent the Council a proposal for a decision on the organisation of Community instruments for regional development, accompanied by a note on the Community's regional policy detailing the regional problems which existed in the Community, setting out the themes and objectives of regional policy and considering ways of achieving them. The proposal for a decision was of the utmost interest. The Commission, while noting that regional policy initiatives were a matter for the Member States, drew attention to studies showing that, 12 years after it was founded, the EEC's regional disparities had grown, so undermining the effectiveness of a series of Community policies. It concluded by arguing for more powers for the Community, for which it would need adequate financial resources. The proposal gave the Commission the task of examining, along with the Member States, the various problems of a regional nature and gave it the power to make recommendations to the Member States if it so wished. A Regional Development Committee was to be set up and an interest rebate fund for regional development, managed by the Commission and funded from budget appropriations (⁵), was planned. This document constituted a further turning-point because the Commission, mainly thanks to the direct involvement of certain senior officials, sought an extension of its powers in this area and enhanced budget resources. But, as Rosario Solima, then Director for Development and Conversion in Directorate-General XVI says, the proposal had not been drawn up without internal discussions with the Commission member responsible, who originally favoured more modest financing arrangements (⁶). Furthermore, this

(¹) Von der Groeben, H., 'Regional policy: an essential and urgent Community task', *Bulletin of the EC*, No 6, 1969, pp. 15–16.
(²) Interview with Paul Romus, 20 January 2004.
(³) See correspondence in BAC 20/1979.
(⁴) BAC 20/1979, Programme of the symposium 'Les régions frontalières à l'heure du marché commun', 27 and 28 November 1969, Institut d'études européennes — Université Libre de Bruxelles.
(⁵) ACEU, Dossier 9099, R/1887/69 (ECO 200) (FIN 339), 22 October 1969. See also the speech by von der Groeben, H., 'Regional policy in the Community', *Bulletin of the EC*, 12/1969, pp. 5–7.
(⁶) Evidence from Rosario Solima, 28 December 2005.

The common agricultural policy and the less-favoured regions

Agricultural productivity in Europe grew substantially between 1958 and 1973, although this success was not equally spread. One of the features of this period is the decline of certain less-favoured agricultural regions in the Community.

Growth in this period did not enable the agricultural regions with the lowest incomes to catch up with the richer ones — indeed the gap between them widened. The index of agricultural incomes in the poorest and richest regions was 89 and 112 in Germany, 73 and 112 in the United Kingdom, 54 and 165 in Italy, and 53 and 338 in France. At Community level, the gap was still more striking.

Why was this so? The common agricultural policy was not the only culprit. Until the creation of the ERDF in 1975, regional policy had had no real resources. In the absence of any genuine regional policy in the period, the rapid reduction in the agricultural population had only rarely been offset in the less-favoured regions by the creation of jobs in other sectors within those regions. This had led to large-scale migrations to distant regions, or even abroad (in the case of the Mezzogiorno, for example), and to substantial human and economic problems.

To what extent was the common agricultural policy responsible? In accordance with contemporary economic thinking, it helped deprive the regions of instruments for structural action by giving priority to a system for organising agricultural markets which was inevitably centralised and comparatively rigid. This economic thinking was also perfectly happy with regional inequalities and a major flight from the land, which benefited industrial activity elsewhere (90 % of farm workers left for the cities with no vocational training).

How did the officials in charge of the CAP see this development? Georges Rencki argued that the defect of the old-style economic thinking was not the refusal to maintain unviable agricultural holdings but the inadequate consideration given to a limit on the migration to the cities. No thought was given to the longer-term consequences of a haphazard exodus for either the regions of origin or those which became overpopulated — what we now call the megalopolis of the north of the Community.

During that period it was the dynamic young farmers who left the less-favoured regions, so the population aged. In the regions where production conditions were difficult (mainly mountainous regions), there was a danger of depopulation and the low population density made any sort of community life impossible in such regions. Businesses and craftsmen disappeared because they had no customers, and public services such as roads lacked maintenance because not enough taxes were being paid. State services such as schools were kept going only at an enormous cost per person.

This depopulation had a price, as did the swelling of the large urban areas.

Accordingly, the Commission decided to alter the role of the CAP: from 1972 it ceased to be merely a common market in agriculture and became in addition an instrument for the modernisation of holdings, supported by substantial Community finance for the less-favoured agricultural regions. Two resources were provided: the offer of early retirement to heads of holdings, aged at least 55, and help for young farmers to purchase, enlarge and modernise holdings in these regions. But these measures were not applied in the same way in all countries, with France and Italy remaining on the sidelines. Rencki notes that this regional approach was supported by the public announcement in 1972 that the Commission intended to put forward a directive on agriculture in mountainous and less-favoured areas that would be adopted later. The directive provided for direct income support to compensate for natural handicaps to production and avoid depopulation. This represented a move away from simple reliance on market forces to the adoption of a regional planning approach ([4]).

G. L.

position reflected a 'social', and not merely economic vision of a European regional policy that would give the Community greater room for manoeuvre. This stance, it should be remembered, was consonant with the link the Commission had established between its proposals for structural reform in agriculture, the 'Mansholt Plan', its opinion on the reform of the European Social Fund and this draft decision ([1]).

The Council considered the Commission's proposal on 10 November 1969 and sent it to the European Parliament and the Economic and Social Committee, which gave their opinions in April and May 1970 ([2]). Meanwhile, the Hague Summit in 1969 had set the ambitious aims of enlargement, completion and deepening, which seemed to call for new policies, including more vigorous action on regional matters ([3]). The entry of countries such as the United Kingdom, with its severe regional imbalances, must also have made this question appear more urgent.

Slow progress

Results, however, were not up to expectations. This was partly because of differences of opinion on regional matters between countries such as Italy which were attached to the needs of the outlying regions and others such as Belgium which were concerned with the needs of the frontier areas or declining industries. Nor was there a single vision of what the Commission should be doing. Under the new Malfatti Commission, responsibility for Directorate-General XVI went to the Luxembourger Albert Borschette. At the end of October 1970 the Council confirmed that different positions existed. The Italian representatives, supporting the Commission's positions, naturally concentrated on the needs of the outlying regions and matters related to agriculture. They also supported the introduction of instruments to provide financial assistance and the establishment of a Standing Committee for Regional Policy. The French position was much more reserved while the Belgian delegates stressed the needs of the frontier regions. Several delegations simply asked for further studies and Luxembourg was unenthusiastic about setting up an ad hoc committee ([5]). The Council then concentrated on three key points: financing a regional policy, setting up a standing committee and the priorities for a policy of this sort. But the discussion ended with scarcely any concrete results because of the continuing differences between the representatives of the various countries. The Italian delegation vigorously defended the dynamising role of a standing committee in defining the objectives and resources for regional policy. Here supported by the German representatives, it considered that these tasks could be carried out by a committee assisting the Commission. By contrast,

([1]) Introduction to the proposals concerning implementation of the memorandum on the reform of agriculture in the EEC, 11 April 1970, pp. 1–2, and communication from the Commission to the Council and proposal for a resolution on the new guidelines for the common agricultural policy, 15 February 1971, COM(71) 100, p. 10.

([2]) ACEU, Dossier 9097, Note R/1979/69 (ECO 210) (FIN 368), 30 October 1969 and memorandum from the Council Secretariat, 15 May 1970.

([3]) See Guasconi, M. E., *L'Europa tra continuità e cambiamento — Il vertice dell'Aja del 1969 e il rilancio della costruzione europea*, Storia delle relazioni internazionali, No 8, Polistampa, Florence, 2004.

([4]) Dossier of Georges Rencki to Michel Dumoulin, 9 April 2006.

([5]) ACEU, Dossier 9101, R/2276/70 (ECO 229) (FIN 468), 10 November 1970.

the French delegation proposed that the committee should be part of the Council so that it could have a constructive role because its constituent delegations would commit their governments ([1]). Once again, there was clear opposition between those countries favouring a supranational approach and those preferring an intergovernmental system.

The plan for a European Regional Development Fund

Meanwhile, the Commission had not been idle. At the end of December 1970 it decided to develop a work programme to identify instruments to finance a regional policy ([2]). This led in 1971 to the plan for a European Regional Development Fund, the future ERDF, despite the continuing division within the Council as to the methods of finance and the duties of the standing committee. This deadlock was, however, in the process of being overcome as a result of certain external events. First of all, in June 1971 the Italian government presented a long memorandum on employment policy in the Community, stressing the need for Community action to resolve the problems of unemployment in certain regions of the EEC, particularly the Mezzogiorno. This text, which stressed the need to tackle existing regional imbalances ([3]), was carefully considered by the Commission, especially the DGs concerned with social affairs and regional policy. The latter in particular found in the arguments put forward by Italy a confirmation of its own views on the need for Community assistance entailing the mobilisation of appropriate financial resources. It was therefore not surprising that Commissioners Coppé (social affairs) and Borschette (regional policy) concluded their communication to the Commission in April 1972 by stating that, although the

resources currently available to the Community were inadequate to cope with the scale of the problems posed by the particularly significant imbalances in regional economic structure in certain Member States, their implementation as part of Community programmes could pave the way in the Community's priority regions for the activation of an autonomous development mechanism which could intervene when the availability of adequate resources meant that the required mass and rhythm of investment could be achieved ([4]).

It is also significant that in the same month the Commission organised a conference in Venice on Industry and Society, attended by over 120 representatives of trade union and employers organisations. One of the subjects on the agenda was how to reduce social and regional disparities.

Another major event was the enlargement of the EEC. Even in the negotiating phase, the British authorities had made the introduction of an effective regional policy one of the priority aims of their strategy vis-à-vis the Community, nor did their interest wane subsequently ([5]). Defining Community regional measures, especially for the development of other policies being considered by the Nine (monetary, industrial and social policies), was henceforth considered important. In addition, increasingly vigorous interest groups put clear pressure on Brussels to take concrete initiatives ([6]).

([1]) ACEU, Dossier 9101, T/39 f/71 (AG), Brussels, 27 January 1971.

([2]) ACEU, Dossier 9101, T /64/72 (AG), Brussels, 9 February 1971. See statements by the Commission representative.

([3]) See the text of this memorandum in Ballini, P. L. and Varsori, A (eds), L'Italia e l'Europa (1947–1979), Vol. II, Rubbettino, Soveria Mannelli, 2004, pp. 768–800.

([4]) BAC 20/1979 22, Interim report on the Italian memorandum on employment policy in the Community (communication from Mr Coppé and Mr Borschette to the Commission), annexed to memorandum SEC(72) 1283, 5 April 1972.

([5]) Poggiolini, I., 'La Grande-Bretagne et la politique régionale au moment de l'élargissement (1969–1972)', in Bitsch, M.-Th. (ed.), Le fait régional et la construction européenne, Organisation internationale et relations internationales, Bruylant, Brussels, 2003, pp. 133–152.

([6]) See, for example, ACEU, Dossier 9332, letter from Domenico Morpurgo, President of the Trieste Rotary Club to the President of the Council of Ministers of the European Community, 12 April 1972; letter from Bucholz, Secretary-General of the Standing Conference of EEC Chambers of Commerce to Christian Calmes, General Secretary of the Council of the European Communities, 17 April 1972; letter from Théo Rasschaert, Secretary-General of the European Confederation of Free Trade Unions to Christian Calmes, 26 July 1972. The question of regional autonomies and the role of regional bodies was becoming important, see on this point Bitsch, M.-Th. (ed.), op. cit., particularly the contributions by J.-M. Palayret, L. De Rose, etc.

N° 125   Décembre 1968 - 1,50 F

communauté
européenne

explosion régionale
en Europe

The regional question steadily gained in importance during the 1960s. This was highlighted in an article entitled 'Explosion régionale en Europe' in *Communauté européenne*, issue No 125 (December 1968).

The European Regional Development Fund: convincing the Commissioner

'After moving in 1966 from the High Authority of the ECSC (where I was concerned with Community assistance to industrial regions undergoing conversion) to the Commission, where I was Head of Division and then Director for Regional Development, one of my priorities was to convince Mr von der Groeben, the member of the Commission responsible for regional policy, of the need to set up a fund for the development of the regions which were lagging behind and the conversion of industrial regions in difficulties.

His first reaction was negative because he thought that Community help to these regions should come from the EIB, via its loans. However, after lengthy discussions during which I drew his attention to the fact that EIB loans were granted at market rates and after an extremely rigorous selection process (which meant that the EIB was an excellent instrument for "finance" but not for "development"), Mr von der Groeben favoured the establishment of a fund of 50 million units of account financed from budgetary resources (one billion units of account, I think) for the agriculture sector, the famous "Mansholt Reserve".

Initially, Mr von der Groeben wanted a "revolving fund", i.e. an instrument making interest-free loans, like the finance provided to Germany from the financial resources originating in the Marshall Plan. After further discussions he accepted that the impact of such a fund would be minimal and agreed to a fund that would make grants. However, the option selected was grants in the form of interest-rate subsidies, in order to provide leverage for the resources available, which were necessarily limited.

It was only later that the formula selected was that of the European Regional Development Fund making grants to investment projects.'

Reminiscences written by Rosario Solima,
28 December 2005.
(Translated from the French)

In June 1972 a communication from the Commission to the Council recalled the importance of establishing a regional development fund and suggested setting up a regional development company. At the Paris European Summit from 19 to 21 October 1972, the leaders of the Nine at last decided to tackle the question of regional policy. In the final statement, they made resolving problems relating to regional imbalances a top priority, principally to avoid these contradictions compromising the introduction of economic and monetary union. The European Summit asked the Commission to carry out a specific study on the subject, while the Member States undertook to coordinate their regional policies and invited the Community institutions to set up a Regional Development Fund the following year ([1]). This was, in fact, only a first step in a process which was to encounter many obstacles and difficulties because of the enduring divergences among the Member States ([2]). For its part, the Commission continued to put pressure on the national governments. In May it issued a report on regional disparities within the Community and, more importantly, in July it made a proposal for a Council decision to set up a Regional Policy Committee, a proposal for a Council regulation setting up a Regional Development Fund and a proposal for a financial regulation on the special provisions applicable to the European Regional Development Fund ([3]). Meanwhile, particularly because of the accession of new countries to the Community, Directorate-General XVI was somewhat altered. Jacques Cros, the Frenchman who had led it during a particularly delicate phase, felt forced to leave, marking the end of an era in this sector. As Paul Romus remembers, the end of his term was difficult. 'He just said to me in his office one day: "Mr Romus, I'm going." What could a humble

---

[1] ACEU, Dossier 9157, Conference of Heads of State or Government of the Member States and of acceding countries to the European Communities, extract from the final declaration.

[2] See, for example, ACEU, Dossier 9157, R/2941/72 (PV/CONS/R 7) Extr. 1, Extract from the draft minutes of the 216th meeting of the Council, held in Brussels on Monday, 4 and Tuesday, 5 December 1972.

[3] ACEU, Dossier 9264, doc. R/2055/73 (ECO 200) (FIN 517), 3 August 1973.

official like myself say? He told me his reasons: regional policy was under way and, since he had nothing more to expect, he was going home' ([¹]).

But the ERDF was not adopted until 1975. It was to provide capital assistance for productive investment and infrastructure. In other words, it took a further two years of effort to achieve this result. Once again, the Commission and its officials had helped develop a Community policy for solidarity for which there was originally no provision in the Treaty and which one day would play a crucial role in promoting the building of Europe.

ANTONIO VARSORI

([¹]) Interview with Paul Romus, 20 January 2004.

Chapter 21

The emergence of a social Europe

In the tense climate of the Cold War, Jean Monnet and the Six could not fail to make the workers in the two sectors covered by the ECSC aware of the fact that the first attempt at European integration along functionalist lines would not merely take account of the interests of employers and of Member States' economic policies but would also represent an opportunity for all those working in the coal and steel industries. There was a clear will to launch a constructive dialogue with the representatives of the trade unions unaffiliated to the Communist Party. The Treaty of Paris of 1951 and the ECSC in its initial form seemed to meet these requirements.

Two trade union representatives were members of the first College of the High Authority, presided over by Monnet. A consultative committee was set up, comprising representatives of the trade unions, employers, and 'users and stockholders' [1]. The High Authority, taking as its basis the provisions of the Treaty, also encouraged a number of initiatives which heralded the advent of a true European social policy: studies on the improvement of working conditions, financial compensation and funding for vocational training courses for workers affected by the restructuring of the mining and steel industries, and plans for the construction of housing for workers and their families [2]. It was therefore no coincidence that several trade unions formed a good relationship with Monnet [3], having been impressed by the action taken by the High Authority in this area.

---

[1] Regarding the ECSC, see Spierenburg, D. and Poidevin, R., *The History of the High Authority of the European Coal and Steel Community. Supranationality in operation*, London, Weidenfeld and Nicolson, 1994.

[2] Regarding the action taken by the ECSC in the social field, see in particular Mechi, L., 'Una vocazione sociale? Le azioni dell'Alta Autorità della CECA a favore dei lavoratori sotto le presidenze di Jean Monnet e di René Mayer', *Storia delle relazioni internazionali*, X-XI, 1994/1995, No 2, pp. 147–183; Idem., 'L'action de la Haute Autorité de la CECA dans la construction de maisons ouvrières', *Journal of European Integration History*, Vol. 6, No 1, 2000, No 1, pp. 63–88.

[3] Jean Degimbe: 'The fathers of Europe (Robert Schuman, Alcide De Gasperi, Konrad Adenauer and Paul-Henri Spaak) wanted a democratic and liberal Europe in which competition and the market economy would be accompanied by solidarity mechanisms. This was the characteristic feature of the ECSC Treaty. While it is true that Jean Monnet wanted to launch a constructive dialogue with the non-communist trade unions, it should be remembered that in 1950, when Robert Schuman launched the "Schuman Plan", very little time had passed since the end of the war, during which the major trade unionists had played an active role in the resistance and, in doing so, had often established bonds of mutual trust with employers. Jean Monnet, at the end of his Presidency of the High Authority, set up the Committee for the United States of Europe, in which the main leaders of the employers' organisations and trade unions of the Six were actively involved. This Committee played a very influential role in European issues at the time.' (Translation) (Note from Jean Degimbe, 10 March 2006).

The individual as an economic operator — living and working conditions

The economic and political context in which the European Economic Community was 'revived' and created was different from that in which the ECSC had come into being. The EEC was built on the principles of economic liberalism — at least within the market formed by the Six — and was set up and developed at a time of sustained economic growth. The negotiators of the Treaties focused their attention on the economic objectives of the project, to which they appeared to give precedence over the other aspects of the Treaties.

This was evident in the social field. Under the EEC Treaty, individuals were regarded primarily as economic operators. The problem concerned freedom of movement (Articles 48 to 51) and freedom of establishment (Articles 52 et seq.), which formed the foundations of the internal market. The provisions governing them had direct effect.

However, the Treaty referred very tentatively to a policy on the living and working conditions of workers in a separate title (Articles 117 to 128).

Yet, as some would not fail to point out, there were plenty of reasons for tackling both issues together [1], particularly as it was an area in which Community law would change significantly in order to take into account the way in which the Court of Justice interpreted the law over the years [2]. Social issues thus constituted a minor aspect of the EEC Treaty, and the Community's powers in this area were in fact nothing more than simple instruments for implementing an efficient market which could be used to promote economic growth [3].

With Articles 48, 49 and 51 being included at the request of Italy and Article 119 at the request of France, the Treaty affirmed the need to improve living and working conditions, advocated increased cooperation between the social partners, and made provision for freedom of movement for workers and the equal treatment of men and women. The Treaty also set up a European Social Fund, which would 'have the task of rendering the employment of workers easier and of increasing their geographical and occupational mobility within the Community' (Article 123). In practical terms, this meant implementing a policy of assisting workers who found themselves with less work or no work at all after their company had been converted to other types of production. Assistance of this kind was designed to ensure 'productive re-employment' of workers by means of vocational retraining and/or resettlement allowances (Article 125).

A particularly important aspect of this strategy was the development of a common policy in the field of vocational training. An Economic and Social Committee was also set up on a tripartite basis (representatives of trade unions, employers and other activities) as an advisory body responsible for giving opinions to the Commission and, to a lesser extent, to the Council on a number of economic and social issues relating to implementation of the Treaty [4].

Right from the start of the negotiations, Italy, as the country which had the weakest economy and was furthest behind in social terms largely because of the serious problem posed by the Mezzogiorno (southern Italy), showed considerable interest in framing a specific social policy for the EEC. The Italian authorities hoped that this would enable them to tackle any adverse effects associated with the establishment of the EEC while also helping to resolve the 'southern question' [5]. It was undoubtedly no coincidence that

[1] Fallon, M., *Droit matériel général des Communautés européennes*, Academia Bruylant, Louvain-la-Neuve, and L.G.D.J., Paris, 1997, p. 387.

[2] Ibid., p. 409.

[3] See the arguments put forward in Degimbe, J., *La politique sociale européenne du Traité de Rome au Traité d'Amsterdam*, Institut syndical européen, Brussels, 1999, pp. 60–62. For an interpretation of the features of European social policy, see Ciampani, A., 'La politica sociale nel processo d'integrazione europea', *Europa Europe*, X, No 1, 2001, pp. 120–134.

[4] Calandri, E., 'La genesi del CES: forze professionali e strategie nazionali', in Varsori, A. (ed.), *Il Comitato Economico e Sociale nella costruzione europea*, Marsilio, Venice, 2000, pp. 47–65.

[5] See Varsori, A., 'La scelta europea dal centrismo al centro sinistra', in Ballini, P., Guerrieri, S., Varsori, A. (eds), *Le istituzioni repubblicane dal centrismo al centro-sinistra 1953–1968*, Carocci, Rome, 2006.

Articles 48, 49 and 51 of the EEC Treaty

'Article 48

1. Freedom of movement for workers shall be secured within the Community by the end of the transitional period at the latest.

2. Such freedom of movement shall entail the abolition of any discrimination based on nationality between workers of the Member States as regards employment, remuneration and other conditions of work and employment.

3. It shall entail the right, subject to limitations justified on grounds of public policy, public security or public health:

(a) to accept offers of employment actually made;

(b) to move freely within the territory of Member States for this purpose;

(c) to stay in a Member State for the purpose of employment in accordance with the provisions governing the employment of nationals of that State laid down by law, regulation or administrative action;

(d) to remain in the territory of a Member State after having been employed in that State, subject to conditions which shall be embodied in implementing regulations to be drawn up by the Commission.

4. The provisions of this Article shall not apply to employment in the public service.'

'Article 49

As soon as this Treaty enters into force, the Council shall, acting on a proposal from the Commission and after consulting the Economic and Social Committee, issue directives or make regulations setting out the measures required to bring about, by progressive stages, freedom of movement for workers, as defined in Article 48, in particular:

(a) by ensuring close cooperation between national employment services;

(b) by systematically and progressively abolishing those administrative procedures and practices and those qualifying periods in respect of eligibility for available employment, whether resulting from national legislation or from agreements previously concluded between Member States, the maintenance of which would form an obstacle to liberalisation of the movement of workers;

(c) by systematically and progressively abolishing all such qualifying periods and other restrictions provided for either under national legislation or under agreements previously concluded between Member States as imposed on workers of other Member States conditions regarding the free choice of employment other than those imposed on workers of the State concerned;

(d) by setting up appropriate machinery to bring offers of employment into touch with applications for employment and to facilitate the achievement of a balance between supply and demand in the employment market in such a way as to avoid serious threats to the standard of living and level of employment in the various regions and industries.'

'Article 51

The Council shall, acting unanimously on a proposal from the Commission, adopt such measures in the field of social security as are necessary to provide freedom of movement for workers; to this end, it shall make arrangements to secure for migrant workers and their dependants:

(a) aggregation, for the purpose of acquiring and retaining the right to benefit and of calculating the amount of benefit, of all periods taken into account under the laws of the several countries;

(b) payment of benefits to persons resident in the territories of Member States.'

responsibility for the Directorate-General for Social Affairs (DG V) was for a long time entrusted to an Italian member of the Commission: Giuseppe Petrilli, a Christian Democrat who initially held the post, was succeeded by Lionello Levi Sandri, an expert in labour law with close ties to the Social Democratic Party. Although Petrilli did not hold the post for long as he left the Commission in 1960, Levi Sandri remained in office until 1970.

Article 119 of the EEC Treaty

'Each Member State shall during the first stage ensure and subsequently maintain the application of the principle that men and women should receive equal pay for equal work.

For the purpose of this Article, "pay" means the ordinary basic or minimum wage or salary and any other consideration, whether in cash or in kind, which the worker receives, directly or indirectly, in respect of his employment from his employer.

Equal pay without discrimination based on sex means:

(a) that pay for the same work at piece rates shall be calculated on the basis of the same unit of measurement,

(b) that pay for work at time rates shall be the same for the same job.'

The Commission proceeds with great caution

In its early stages, the Commission proceeded with considerable caution in the social field. Petrilli himself, in a long document written in 1959, pointed out that the Treaty ruled out almost any possibility of the Commission taking direct action in this area [1]. In the same communication, the Italian Commissioner said, however, that the implementation of an effective social policy was one of the key objectives of the EEC Treaty and he listed the areas in which the Community should take action: freedom of movement for workers, the European Investment Bank, the European Social Fund, vocational training in the agricultural sector and the coordination of economic and social policies. As regards the Commission's role, Petrilli stressed that use should be made of studies, consultations and opinions [2]. In fact, from the moment of its inception until the

early 1960s, the Commission did use these instruments in most cases. In 1959, for example, it supported the plan for an initial conference on the social impact of automation in the common market [3], focusing in particular on subjects such as changes in employment and wage levels [4].

Although the Commission chose to adopt a cautious approach, it did so also because the Commission's staff had to familiarise themselves with complex subjects and therefore needed to have specialist knowledge and to be able to access data which were not always easy to find. During this 'settling-in' period, the Commission also had to develop a clear relationship with the other Community bodies, in particular with the Economic and Social Committee (ESC), and with those responsible for the various interest groups involved in social issues.

The ESC embarked on its work with considerable enthusiasm. It counted among its members leading trade unionists and employers and sought above all to enhance its responsibilities. The Commission imposed strict limits on the powers of the ESC, based on the provisions of the Treaty. Although the ESC saw itself as an auxiliary body, was essentially technical in nature and could provide relevant information, it would not have been appropriate to have launched a dialogue with it in the belief that its views reflected those of the social partners [5]. The Commission also realised that, because of the structure and procedures of the ESC, its opinions ultimately reached the Commission too late in the decision-making process. Faced with this problem, which came to light very quickly,

---

[1] 'La politique sociale — traits généraux et programme', by Giuseppe Petrilli, COM(59) 143, 20 November 1959.

[2] Ibid.

[3] PV 57, EEC Commission, 23 April 1959, Item XIV, pp. 11–12, 'Note on the automation conference', by Giuseppe Petrilli, COM(59) 42, 18 April 1959.

[4] PV 104, EEC Commission, 18 May 1960, Item V, pp. 6–7, PV 69, EEC Commission, 22 July 1959, Item XII, pp. 11–12, 'Enquête sur les salaires', by Giuseppe Petrilli, COM(59) 101, 16 July 1959; PV 153, EEC Commission, 6 July 1961, Item V, pp. 8–10, 'Étude des problèmes conjoncturels de main-d'oeuvre dans la Communauté', COM(61) 100 final, 28 June 1961.

[5] On these aspects, see Dundovich, E., 'I presidenti del CES: personalità e orientamenti 1958–1968', and Guasconi, M. E., 'Il CES e le origini della politica sociale europea 1958–1965', in Varsori, A. (ed.), op. cit., pp. 89–100 and 155–167.

A European Social Fund meeting in 1963.
From left to right: Lamberto Lambert (second), Lionello Levi Sandri (fourth) and Antonino Arena (fifth).

Petrilli raised the issue of relations between DG V and the representatives of the various interest groups. Nevertheless, caution was the watchword here too, and the Commissioner himself seemed to rule out the possibility of establishing direct and structured ties with the ESC, which could give the impression of being an attempt to launch a 'European social dialogue' ([1]). Although hopes were high initially, the negative experience of relations between the ESC and the Commission meant that the trade unions scarcely believed that it was still possible to establish a working relationship with the Commission on the social issues valued by workers' organisations ([2]).

However, the Commission was urged to take action: first by Italy and then by the European Parliamentary Assembly. The EPA, for which social issues were very important, hoped that a European policy in this area would strengthen the supranational powers of the Community and thus also of the Commission. In response to these appeals, the Commission set about creating the ESF, paying particular attention to the way in which it would be formed. Examining the question of the Social Fund regulation in May 1959, Petrilli wrote

---

([1]) PV 59, EEC Commission, 6 May 1959, Item XXI, pp. 16–17, 'Consultation d'experts et de représentants des diverses branches d'intérêt', by Guiseppe Petrilli, COM(59) 50, 5 May 1959.

([2]) For the position of the trade unions, see Gobin, C., *L'Europe syndicale entre désir et réalité*, Labor, Brussels, 1997, *passim*.

The Petrilli memorandum on the social policy of the Community (November 1959) [1]

This was the first report by the Commission which gave an outline of social policy and set out the Community's programme in this area. In this document, the member of the Commission responsible for social affairs, Giuseppe Petrilli, took as his inspiration the preamble to the Treaty of Rome, which states that the essential objective of the Community is the constant improvement of living and working conditions in the Member States. Economic integration was therefore not an end in itself but subordinate to a social objective. Although it was true that the common market itself constituted a means to economic and social progress, it was not enough in itself to guarantee progress of this kind; this was why positive political action had to be taken, one aspect of which was social policy.

Petrilli thus defined the general objectives of the Community in the light of their social implications. The harmonious development of economic activity called for the elimination of unemployment and structural underemployment within the Community and thus the progressive harmonisation of living and working conditions in the different regions and economic sectors. A prerequisite for steady and balanced expansion was the need to ensure the balanced expansion of employment through constant monitoring of the Community's economic and social development, in particular demographic growth and the technical conditions of production. With regard to the latter point, the increasing availability of female labour and the need to retrain workers in order to respond to changes in the supply of jobs and to the creation of the common market called for a coherent policy on vocational training. Moreover, GDP growth in each of the Member States had to be combined with the distribution of wealth between workers in such a way as to meet the social objectives of the Community. It was therefore necessary to coordinate the economic and social policies of the Member States in order to make full use of productive resources and to even out the social and cultural differences between the various populations concerned.

The social impact of these general objectives of the Treaty was encapsulated in the concept of making harmonisation possible while ensuring that improvement was maintained [2], in other words, enabling individuals, social classes, geographical regions and economic sectors to contribute equally to fostering social progress and hence also to raising the standard of living. In this context, however, the aim of social policy seemed to be defined increasingly by what it should **not** do: it should aim to ensure that economic integration did not interrupt or undermine social development instead of actively promoting the conditions necessary to making harmonisation possible while ensuring that improvement was maintained. This was nevertheless a realistic aspect of social policy, which was only in its infancy at that time.

V. S.

---

[1] COM(59) 143, 20 November 1959.

[2] See Article 117 of the Treaty of Rome.

that there was a clear link between the action taken through the Social Fund and the Commission's implementation of a general employment policy which sought to promote and maintain a dynamic balance in the labour market by providing workers with vocational training in order to continuously adapt demand for employment to the types of jobs on offer ([1]).

The Commission began to put the finishing touches to the ESF and thus showed how determined it was to take action in areas such as vocational training, employment levels, the labour market and hence also worker mobility. In May 1960 the Council adopted Regulation No 9, giving the go-ahead for action to be taken through the Fund, which would be managed by the Commission with the help of a committee composed of representatives of the governments and the social partners and chaired by Petrilli ([2]). That same year, however, Petrilli left his post at the Commission to become President of the Institute for Industrial Reconversion in his home country.

A social policy with a human face

The appointment of Levi Sandri came at a time when the Commission was taking a greater interest in European action in the social field. As early as 1958 the Social Affairs DG had turned its attention to the rights of migrant workers. This was of particular interest to Italy. Emigration to countries in the EEC was still taking place on a large scale. Tens of thousands of Italians were working in the Federal Republic of Germany, Belgium, France and the Grand Duchy of Luxembourg ([3]). Regulations to improve allowances for migrant workers,

mainly in the field of social security (pensions, sickness benefit, unemployment benefit, etc.), were adopted from the start ([4]). In 1961, largely at the Commission's instigation, other regulations were approved which laid the foundations for the free movement of workers from Community countries, with regulations benefiting seasonal and cross-border workers being adopted the following year ([5]). From then on, the Commission appeared to be willing to maintain some form of regular contact with the social partners and argued, for example, that representatives of UNICE, the ICCTU and the ICFTU should be included in the Administrative Committee on Social Security for Migrant Workers ([6]). Levi Sandri also set about improving the effectiveness of the decisions taken in favour of workers in this category. The Italian Commissioner was the prime mover behind a particularly valuable initiative to create a joint programme of exchanges between young workers. On the basis of Article 50 of the EEC Treaty and the existing bilateral agreements, which had achieved only meagre results, Levi Sandri drew up a plan through which the Community would undertake to promote exchanges between trainees. Without overlooking the part played by the Member States, he stressed that the Commission would play a key role, in particular by providing information to the social partners and youth organisations and by allocating grants to meet the needs of young trainees ([7]).

During the first half of the 1960s the Commission came up against serious obstacles which stood in the way of any major initiative in the social field. Apart from Italy, the other countries in the EEC did not really seem ready to strengthen Commu-

---

([1]) 'Note introductive concernant le projet du Règlement du Fonds Social' by Giuseppe Petrilli, COM(59) 62, 27 May 1959.

([2]) On the emergence and activities of the ESF in the 1960s, see Mechi, L., *Les États membres, les institutions et les débuts du Fonds Social Européen*, Varsori, A. (ed.), *Inside the European Community — Actors and policies in the European integration — 1957–1972*, 'Groupe de liaison des professeurs d'histoire contemporaine auprès de la Commission européenne, 9, Nomos-Verlag/Bruylant, Baden Baden/Brussels, 2006, pp. 95–116.

([3]) On the question of emigration, see Romero, F., *Emigrazione e integrazione europea 1945–1973*, Edizioni Lavoro, Rome, 1991.

([4]) PV 39, EEC Commission, 26 November 1958, Item V, pp. 4–5, Communication from Giuseppe Petrilli, COM(58) 257, 24 November 1958.

([5]) PV 167, EEC Commission, 30 November 1961, Item XIV, pp. 16–17, Proposals from the Commission to the Council, COM(61) 175 final, 1 December 1961.

([6]) See, for example, PV 208, EEC Commission, 27 November 1962, Item XV, p. 16, Proposal from the Commission to the Council, COM(62) 127 final, 22 June 1962.

([7]) PV 217, EEC Commission, 13 February 1963, Item X, pp. 12–14, 'Projet d'un premier programme commun pour favoriser l'échange de jeunes travailleurs', Annex 1, COM(63) 14 final, 3 April 1963.

Article 50 of the EEC Treaty

'Member States shall, within the framework of a joint programme, encourage the exchange of young workers.'

nity powers in a field in which the welfare state took different forms on a strictly national basis. The period of prolonged economic growth and the temporary weakness of the trade unions at European level certainly did nothing to encourage a debate on the ways in which European integration might help to resolve the main problems in the social sphere [1]. One important example was that of vocational training: having been one of the areas of action which the High Authority of the ECSC considered most important, its harmonisation was explicitly referred to in the EEC Treaty. This objective was taken up again by Levi Sandri, with the support of the ESC and of one of its members in particular, the German trade union representative Maria Weber [2]. The Commission thus set out a number of guiding principles for policies on vocational training. However, its efforts met with stiff opposition from the French and German governments and the compromise solution, devised primarily by the Italian authorities, had only limited success.

The Commission addressed the question again in 1965, drawing up a draft 'action programme' to develop a number of initiatives in the vocational training sector. This again met with opposition from a number of governments, in particular that of France. A discussion on the Commission's plans was launched by the government represen-

tatives in 1966. With the exception of the Italian delegation, they acknowledged that the Commission's objectives were sound but criticised the financial aspects of the programme and its political implications, in other words the powers of the Commission itself. Not surprisingly, this initiative ultimately failed too [3], but Levi Sandri's unstinting efforts in the interests of migrant workers bore fruit. The fact that the Council approved Regulation (EEC) No 1612/68 of October 1968 meant that Articles 48 and 49 of the EEC Treaty could finally be applied in full [4]. In view of the merger of the Executives of the ECSC, the EEC and Euratom, Levi Sandri pointed out, albeit cautiously, the large number of social areas in which the European Community could take effective action in a 'Report on the social policy of the Community', which he produced in December 1967. He stressed the importance of a 'positive' attitude which could reconcile economic and social requirements, and underlined the role which the Commission might play, calling on it to help by working more closely with the Council and with each of the governments of the Member States in the firm belief that only by forging cooperation and mutual trust would it be possible to lend a human dimension to the large number of economic and technological problems faced by the Community and thus achieve the social objectives formulated by the promoters of the European Treaties [5].

Towards the end of the 1960s European social policy seemed to undergo its first change of direction. In a document dating from late 1966, the Council acknowledged that problems existed with regard to the implementation of social policy but seemed to attribute them to disagreements between the Commission and the Member States [6]. In 1967 a number of organisations,

[1] On the welfare state, see Ritter, G., *Storia dello stato sociale*, Laterza, Rome-Bari, 1996, pp. 142–208; Silei, G., *Welfare State e Socialdemocrazia. Cultura, programmi e realizzazioni in Europa occidentale dal 1945 ad oggi*, Lacaita, Manduria, 2000. On the position of the trade unions in western Europe at this time, see, for example, Maiello, A., *Sindacati in Europa — Storie, modelli, culture a confronto*, Rubbettino, Soveria Mannelli, 2002, *passim*.

[2] On this subject as a whole, see Petrini, F., 'The common vocational training policy in the EEC from 1961 to 1972', *Vocational Training European Journal*, No 32, May–August 2004/II, pp. 45–54 (http://www2.trainingvillage.gr/download/journal/bull-32/32_en_petrini.pdf).

[3] Ibid.

[4] Degimbe, J., op. cit., pp. 62–70.

[5] ACEU, Dossier No 29692, 'Relazione sulla politica sociale della Comunità' by Lionello Levi Sandri, Memorandum SEC(67) 5014 final, 18 December 1967.

[6] ACEU, Dossier No 29648, 'Memorandum sulla politica sociale nella Comunità Economica Europa', Annex to Note No 1321/2/66 (SOC 190 Rev. 2), 9 December 1966.

Meetings of the miners' trade unions on a social Europe held in Dortmund-Westfalenhalle in September 1965.
Coal consumption in the Six fell spectacularly between 1950 and 1968 (from 74 % to 29.3 % of total consumption),
while the share of oil rose (from 10 % to 52.6 %) and gas consumption began to take off (6.4 % in 1968).
The situation was dramatic for the mining world. The principle of conversion that the ECSC was keen to put into practice
helped to mitigate the social catastrophe that flowed from the pit closures in the old industrial areas.
The need for convergence in policies to secure what came to be known as economic and social cohesion was being felt.
But progress towards that objective was slow and difficult.

including the ICCTU, the ICFTU, COPA and UNICE, criticised the action taken by the Community in the social field. The trade unions, in particular, wanted the Commission — implicitly regarded as the driving force behind integration in this sector — to take on a more influential role [1]. The Commission therefore took new measures, while pointing out in several documents the need for firm action on the part of the Community [2].

These encouraging developments very probably influenced the stance of the German government, which was led at the time by a coalition including the SPD. In November 1967, the German Representation to the Communities put forward a proposal for a resolution calling on the Commission to gather information and present a report on the links between social policy and the other Community policies with a view to possible coordination of the measures taken by the various Member States in the field of social policy [3]. This was discussed by the Social Affairs Council at the end of December. It is telling that the Commission, as represented by Levi Sandri, openly supported the

[1] ACEU, Dossier No 29683, Copy of a letter from Jan Kulakowski (IFCTU) and Harm G. Buiter (ECTUS ICFTU) to the President of the Council of the EEC, 16 January 1967; letter from H. M. Claessens (UNICE) to the President of the Council of the EEC, 16 December 1966; letter from André Herlitska (COPA) to the President of the Council of the ECSC, 5 June 1967.

[2] The Council documents provide extensive information on this subject.

[3] ACEU, Dossier No 29692, 1593/67(SOC 185), 28 November 1967.

German proposal ([1]), which was finally approved at the end of February 1968 ([2]).

A May 1968 in social policy?

The stance on social policy was nevertheless still open to discussion.

The transitional phase experienced by the Community at political level did not come to an end until 1969, with the change of governments in France and Germany. However, attitudes to social problems were shaped by other developments too. The events of May 1968 triggered the emergence of new needs and demands for new rights and, in several European Community countries, served to strengthen the trade union movement (in Italy, for example) and the forces of the left (such as in the Federal Republic of Germany) ([3]). The period of European economic expansion finally drew to a close, revealing serious problems which were to have repercussions in the social field. At the Hague Summit in December 1969, the leaders of the Six argued that the Community should take more incisive action in social terms. One of the initial effects of this was to launch the process which would very quickly lead to a reform of the ESF ([4]). While taking important steps to lay down the rules for using the funds made available through the ESF ([5]), the Commission continued to maintain that the ESF should not be limited to *ex post* action but should also be used to launch initiatives on its own account ([6]).

Pressure from Italy

Following the Hague Summit, the Italian authorities, who had expressed their support for the objectives set during the summit, voiced their concerns about the economic effects of a number of European initiatives, ranging from the introduction of value added tax (VAT) to plans for monetary integration. Rome felt that it had to defend its own interests, particularly in view of the 'southern question', which remained as yet unresolved, and the high unemployment rate in Italy compared with the other Community countries. The Italian government therefore again made the point that a European social policy should be implemented which was truly effective. Following Italy's 'hot autumn' of 1969, the trade unions were now united in their efforts and exerted a strong influence on the government, whose Minister of Labour, the Christian Democrat Carlo Donat Cattin, had close ties with the Italian trade union, the CISL ([7]).

At the instigation of the Italian government, a tripartite conference of government representatives, the social partners and the Commission was held in Luxembourg in April 1970. The topic of discussion was the problem of employment in the EEC countries. The Italian delegation, led by Donat Cattin, vigorously advocated the need for Community action to promote employment — an argument forcefully endorsed by Levi Sandri ([8]). In May the Council of Ministers finally approved the plan to create a Standing Committee on Employment, which the Commission was asked to set up. In the meantime, the European Commission underwent a change of membership, with the Belgian Commissioner, Albert Coppé, taking responsibility for the Directorate-General for Social Affairs. During the second half of 1970, the Commission started work on setting up the Employ-

([1]) ACEU, Dossier No 29692, 1792/67 (PVB/CONS 16), Extraordinary Council 3, 19 January 1968.

([2]) ACEU, Dossier No 29700, 351/68 (AG55), 'Communication à la presse', 29 February 1968.

([3]) Silei, G., op. cit., pp. 251–270.

([4]) See Mechi, L., *Les États* […], op. cit.

([5]) See, for example, PV 150, EC Commission, 27–28 January 1971, Item XXIII, pp. 41–44, 'Réforme du Fonds social européen', Memorandum COM(71) 17 final, 24 March 1971.

([6]) PV 114, EC Commission, Item VII, pp. 9–11, SEC(70) 902 final, 11 March 1970.

([7]) On Italy's position, see Varsori, A., 'La questione europea nella politica italiana', in Giovagnoli, A. and Pons, S. (ed.), *L'Italia repubblicana nella crisi degli anni Settanta — 1. Tra guerra fredda e distensione*, Rubbettino, Soveria Mannelli, 2003, pp. 331–350.

([8]) Guasconi, M. E., 'Paving the way for a European social dialogue', *Journal of European Integration History*, Vol. 9, No 1, 2003, pp. 87–110.

The Coppé memorandum on Community social policy [1]

This document, which was adopted by the Commission in March 1971, was intended to trigger extensive discussions within the Council, the Parliament and the Economic and Social Committee with a view to establishing a coherent action programme on social policy, in accordance with the wishes expressed at the Hague Conference in December 1969. The general objectives of the programme, which all the Member States regarded as priorities, were the following:

— greater satisfaction of collective needs, particularly as regards education, public health and housing;

— increased efforts to combat the harmful effects of productive activities on the environment, considered for the first time in the light of its social impact;

— greater equality of initial opportunities for everyone through the improvement of education and training policy;

— greater justice in the distribution of income and wealth;

— adaptation of social welfare schemes to modern needs and, in particular, increased provision for those worst affected by structural changes and technical progress and for those unable to take part in the productive process.

In order to achieve these objectives, the Commission indicated that the economic policies of the Member States should not only take these objectives into account but also form part of a Community strategy. With regard to employment, the Standing Committee on Employment was to be responsible for ensuring dialogue, negotiations and consultation between the Council, the Member States, the Commission and the social partners, while the reformed Social Fund was to be used to make the changes which were recognised as being in the public interest in the various sectors of production by guaranteeing financial solidarity and establishing a link with Community policies in general, thus making it an essential tool in furthering progress towards economic and monetary union.

The key position occupied by employment was indicative of the profound changes experienced by the Community since the late 1960s: unemployment started to become a serious problem for economic development and the Community's third programme on medium-term economic policy also attached considerable importance to an active employment policy. The complex nature of the factors which had a negative impact on employment (different pace of development in different regions; movements of workers between sectors; technological development; problems concerning certain categories of workers, i.e. young people, women, elderly people, disabled people and migrant workers) meant that this issue had to be dealt with from the point of view not only of general economic policy but also of structural and regional policies.

V. S.

ment Committee. As Coppé mentioned in a memorandum, the Commission contested the position adopted by the Council, which would have wanted to control the future Committee. On this point, Coppé wrote that to accept the Council's point of view would ruin the balance between the institutions. The Commission would suffer by losing many of its powers of initiative and consultation. He said that to set up the Committee in this way would create an exceptional situation, as all the other committees — apart from two, which were less important — had been set up within the

[1] SEC(71) 600, 17 March 1971.

The regulations on freedom of movement and social security for migrant workers

Among the key measures taken by the European Economic Community in the field of social policy, the regulations on social security for migrant workers (Nos 3 and 4 of 1958) and freedom of movement (1968), whose provisions on social security were extended by the regulation adopted in 1971, were particularly significant. They were the culmination of many years of effort by the Commission, which had been working on them since its inception. Negotiations were hampered by the different positions adopted by the Member States on social policy. In particular, Italy's interests were completely at variance with those of the other Members of the EEC, which were the destination countries for emigration from Italy.

Under the regulation on freedom of movement for workers (Regulation (EEC) No 1612/68), the principle of giving priority to national workers was replaced by the concept of giving priority to Community workers. The regulation stipulated that workers from countries within the Community should be treated equally. Workers from within the Community could receive assistance from national employment offices when seeking work and benefit from the provisions of collective agreements; they could have access to vocational schools and retraining centres and they enjoyed the same social and tax advantages as national workers. More generally, Community workers were entitled to the same living and working conditions as national workers in the Member States in which they were pursuing their activities.

The Member States were required to grant their nationals the right to leave national territory by showing a simple identity card or valid passport while having to accept on their territory, under the same conditions, nationals from the other Member States. The same rules applied to family members who accompanied migrant workers. Similarly, the Member States had to grant Community workers the right to reside on their territory. However, they were at liberty to refuse right of entry and right of residence to

Community workers on the grounds of public order, public security or public health.

Finally, Regulation (EEC) No 1612/68 made provision for the creation of a European Coordination Office to maintain a balance between supply and demand in the labour market and of an Advisory Committee to ensure cooperation between the Member States. This subsequently led to the creation in December 1972 of the European system for the international clearing of vacancies and applications for employment (Sedoc, now known as EURES).

The regulation on social security for migrant workers (Regulation (EEC) No 1408/71) applied to employed persons, self-employed persons and their families; it was to be supplemented by implementing Regulation (EEC) No 574/72. These provisions also applied to Community nationals who moved to another country for personal reasons or on business.

The regulations in question made provision for the coordination of the social security systems of the Member States, in accordance with the principle that only one legislation was applicable, namely that of the country in which the worker was pursuing an activity. With regard to the conflict of laws, Regulation (EEC) No 1408/71 stipulated that the legislation of the country in which the worker was pursuing an activity was applicable even if the worker in question was covered by insurance as a resident of another Community country. The second coordination principle was that of equality of treatment: the regulation stipulated that persons resident in the territory of a Member State were subject to the legislation of that Member State under the same conditions as nationals of that State. The third principle was that of maintaining acquired rights: pensions and benefits in respect of accidents at work or occupational diseases to which an individual was entitled under the legislation of a Member State had to be paid to the person concerned even if he was resident in the territory of another Member State. The fourth principle related to the maintenance of rights which were in the process of being acquired, with provision being made for the overlapping of periods of insurance or residence in order to establish entitlement to pensions or benefits.

The provisions of Regulation (EEC) No 1408/71 applied to all social security benefits, with only social assistance, benefit schemes for war victims and special schemes for civil servants being excluded from its scope.

With a view to ensuring the coordination of national legislation on social security, two bodies were set up through the Community regulations: the Administrative Commission and the Advisory Committee on Social Security for Migrant Workers. The former was an administrative and management body and the latter a tripartite advisory body. The Administrative Commission, comprising one government representative from each of the Member States, was responsible for dealing with all administrative matters and issues concerning the interpretation of the regulations or the regularisation of the accounts relating to expenditure incurred by the Member States. It examined proposals from the Commission on the drafting or revision of the regulations and was also responsible for promoting cooperation between the Member States and for the payment of benefits.

The Committee was composed of two government representatives from each Member State (one of whom was a member of the Administrative Commission), two trade union representatives and two employers' representatives. It was given the task of examining general issues and questions of principle and the problems associated with implementing the regulations. It also gave opinions, which were submitted to the Administrative Commission with a view to possible revision of the regulations.

V. S.

Commission ([1]). To resolve the matter, a compromise was reached whereby some of the Commission's powers were retained ([2]). Employment remained one of the Community's main concerns, particularly in the light of a new initiative by the Italian government, which presented an important memorandum on this subject in the spring of 1971 and urged the Community to take firm action. The document sparked wide and sometimes heated debate between the Member States. Among the various subjects discussed, Italy drew particular attention to the opportunities available to migrants in terms of where they could work, saying that Germany, for instance, preferred to employ workers from outside the Community (Yugoslavs and Turks, etc.) rather than from within it (such as Italians). The German authorities rejected these accusations. Although the Italian memorandum actually had little immediate impact, it helped to draw attention to the problems of southern Italy and, more generally, to the problem of regional balances, thus helping to bring about the launch of a European regional policy ([3]).

This period was marked, moreover, by a number of initiatives to promote a radical change in European social policy. These came from various quarters, including the European Parliament, the social partners and the Economic and Social Committee. The main concern of the ESC was vocational training, which the Commission had

([1]) 'Création d'un Comité européen de l'emploi et convocation périodique d'un Conseil ad hoc de l'emploi', by Albert Coppé, Memorandum, COM(70) 1072, 25 September 1970.

([2]) Guasconi, M. E., *L'Europa tra continuità e cambiamento — Il vertice dell'Aja del 1969 e il rilancio della costruzione europea*, Storia delle relazioni internazionali, No 8, Polistampa, Florence, 2004, pp. 149–172.

([3]) Varsori, A., op. cit., pp. 339–340.

tried to deal with in previous years but without achieving convincing results. The ESC wanted to see a turnaround in Community action in the social field that would be based on the principle that effective action could help to resolve the problems identified previously, such as employment levels or the situation faced by migrant workers. These proposals were put forward by Maria Weber, a member of the Standing Committee on Employment. Among other things, they included setting up a European Centre for Study on Vocational Training ([1]). It was important at this stage for the Commission to adopt a firm position on an issue which appeared to have become a source of wide and growing interest among various stakeholders. This was illustrated very eloquently in a document drawn up by the Commission in March 1971.

Developing a Community social policy programme

Entitled 'Preliminary guidelines for a Community social policy programme', the document drawn up by the Commission took as its starting point the idea that the process of integration should enjoy a wide consensus. This would involve 'the establishment and strengthening of economic and social democracy, involving both the democratisation of economic and social structures and enhancement of the role and independent responsibilities of employers' and workers' organisations at Community level' ([2]).

One of the points stressed in the document was the fact that governments tended to turn their national social policy objectives into Community objectives. The document examined the situation in the EEC countries regarding employment, income levels, and living and working conditions and set a number of priority objectives: better employment, greater social justice and a better quality of life.

The Commission argued that the plans for economic and monetary union, set out in the Werner Plan, would make it possible to launch a real Community social policy programme. A number of priorities were identified: (a) speedier achievement of the common labour market, (b) absorption of under-employment and structural unemployment, (c) improvement of safety and health conditions at work and outside, (d) improvement of women's working conditions, (e) integration of handicapped persons into active life, (f) the establishment of a social budget, and (g) collaboration between employers and employees ([3]). Between 1971 and 1972 the Commission did all it could to ensure that studies were carried out and action taken in these areas, frequently pointing out that it had acted as a driving force in this regard ([4]). As Jean Degimbe made clear, progress did not start to be made until after 1972 ([5]). The action taken in this area made the governments more determined to use Community instruments in order to achieve a number of specific objectives in the field of social policy.

At the conference of the Heads of State or Government in October 1972 and at the meeting of the Council of Social Affairs Ministers in November of the same year, it was officially recognised that, during the previous two years, the Commission had worked to reform the ESF, set up the Standing Committee on Employment and put forward an important memorandum for a coherent European social policy ([6]). At the European Summit in Paris in December 1972, the European

([1]) See Varsori, A., 'Vocational education and training in European social policy from its origins to the creation of Cedefop', *Towards a history of vocational education and training (VET) in Europe in a comparative perspective — Proceedings of the first international conference, October 2002, Florence*, Vol. II, Cedefop *Panorama* series, 101, Office for Official Publications of the European Communities, Luxembourg, 2004 (http://www2.trainingvillage.gr/etv/publication/download/panorama/5153_2_en.pdf).

([2]) ACEU, Dossier 29705, 'Preliminary guidelines for a European social policy programme', SEC(71) 600 final, 17 March 1971.

([3]) Ibid.

([4]) See ACEU, Dossier No 24950, which contains a number of communiqués from the Commission's Directorate-General for Press and Information on the Commission's initiatives in this area. See also Degimbe, J., op. cit., pp. 93–116.

([5]) Interview with Jean Degimbe, 15 December 2003.

([6]) ACEU, Dossier No 24950, IP(72)194, 20 November 1972, which summarises a declaration by Albert Coppé.

The difficulty of building Europe

With regard to the problem of harmonising social policies, Ezio Toffanin ([1]) said that harmonisation was a myth and the approximation of laws was pointless. There were as many employment policies as there were job situations throughout the Community. He said that it was possible to draw up an employment policy, perhaps on the basis of a few general principles which could be devised in Brussels, but that these could not then be called a common policy. According to Toffanin, there was a simple reason for this: the labour market was not like water and the workers were not liquid.

Summing up the activities of the Social Affairs DG, Jean Degimbe ([2]) observed that it was a large directorate-general which held a huge number of seminars, meetings and conferences, although social dialogue was not taking place at the time. According to Degimbe, many discussions took place, although not much action was taken, and it was not until after 1972 that things took off.

With regard to the problems faced by the Commission in the field of social policy, a former official of the Social Affairs DG who was subsequently attached to the Marjolin cabinet noted that the subjects they dealt with, such as equal pay between men and women, met with fierce opposition ([4]). Moreover, equal pay had still not been achieved after so many years. All matters relating to social affairs were very delicate and the DG had to proceed very carefully, because it was not an appropriate time for the people involved to be having discussions which were too heated.

Regarding freedom of movement for workers, Heinz Henze ([5]) gave an idea of the different ways in which the Member States and the Commission interpreted the concept. He commented that the only problem was the degree to which workers should have freedom of movement. What could Italian workers do and not do? Did they have the right to bring their families with them? None of the other five Member States wanted that. Foreign workers were considered to be seasonal workers. To some extent, the representatives of the Member States still believed that workers would return to their countries of origin. It was what Hallstein had always said in his speeches: that he wanted to turn migrant workers into militant disciples for the European cause. Henze felt that foreign workers and workers from within the Community had come to be regarded as being a massive unifying force for Europe.

leaders again pointed out that they attached as much importance to strong measures in the social sector as to the completion of economic and monetary union ([3]) and gave the Commission the task of drawing up a European social action programme. This was the starting point for a coherent and complex European social policy which was to become one of the distinctive features of the integration process.

Antonio Varsori

([1]) Interview with Ezio Toffanin, 17 February 2004.
([2]) Interview with Jean Degimbe, 15 December 2003.
([3]) ACEU, Dossier No 24950, Information note: 'The social situation in the Community in 1972', May 1973. For subsequent developments in social policy, see Degimbe, J., op. cit., p. 117 *et seq.*

([4]) Interviewed in January 2004.
([5]) Interview with Heinz Henze, 18 December 2003.

Chapter 22

Transport: 'bastion of nationalisms'

Transport loomed large as a sectoral integration challenge before, during and after the Messina relaunch. However, while transport may be one of the few areas where the Treaty provides for the formulation of a common policy, the provisions of Articles 74 to 84, which make up Title IV, consist of anything and everything. A formidable system of locks and bolts had been put in place, thereby transforming the transport sector into a 'bastion of nationalisms' [1].

A poisoned chalice

The vital importance of the transport sector is self-evident, particularly at the economic level, where transport plays a complex role. By virtue of its pervasive role in the economy, transport is a factor of production for other goods and hence represents a cost that may involve pricing policy elements. Furthermore, it is, by definition, an indispensable instrument for the development of trade flows, while at the same time being exposed to national interventionism. Yet the challenge, however complex, is not limited merely to the economic dimension. A territory criss-crossed by a set of land communication routes displays facets of a social, military and, ultimately, political nature.

The development of the railways since the 19th century, and of the motor car during the 20th, has led governments to adopt a policy varying in time and space. In the rail sector, for instance, the pendulum has swung. The granting of concessions to private companies has been followed by an era of state control. The consequences of this are multiple and, at times, paradoxical. Example: whereas the digging of tunnels through the Alps, based on bilateral technical cooperation, enables Italy to be linked to France and to Switzerland, it is impossible to imagine a link between Brussels and Milan that would not involve a change of locomotive at each frontier crossing-point. The technical argument alone fails to take account of this situation. Each State keeps a jealous watch over its rail network.

However, the transport of persons, important though it is, not least in terms of compliance with the principle of public service, is not the only kind involved. Obviously, the transport of goods

[1] Interview with Henri Étienne, 12 January 2004.

is fundamental. Yet harmony was far from being the order of the day among the Six, whether from the tariff or from the tax point of view. Moreover, in the case of rail transport, the national operator faced no competition. And, whereas on the Rhine and the Moselle, competition was rife among the boat and barge operators, road transport, likewise, encountered numerous difficulties.

The position in 1970 was such that 50 % of all trade in goods between the Member States was by road. Depending on relations, international traffic was free or, alternatively, subject to various types of authorisation, either arranged in advance or on a quota-linked basis. A host of other measures relating to customs provisions and formalities, to the question of transit or 'cabotage' or to the 'return laden' notion for lorries illustrate the particularly arduous nature of the challenge facing the Transport DG.

Nonetheless, the problems specific to transport had long been the focus of attention. Ever since the 19th century, international railway congresses had been held on a regular basis. While they served as a forum for presenting and discussing technical matters, more often than not the real business of international cooperation was relegated to the category of wishful thinking. The same impression is given by the work of the recently created European Conference of Ministers of Transport (ECMT). In other words, the desire to cooperate clashes at grassroots level with interests of a strictly national nature, with the exception of the railways since the national rail companies 'have more or less concomitant interests and are used to cooperating.' [1] At the same time, they exercise a veritable monopoly closely linked to the interests of the State. Because of this total dependence, 'their tongues are tied' [2].

Complex at the technical level and sensitive at the political level, the transport sector has caused major difficulties right from the inception of the

ECSC. These difficulties also characterised the work of the Spaak Committee and, subsequently, the negotiation of the Treaties. The ambitions set out in 1956 were gradually revised downwards. The various projects, confides Nicola Bellieni 50 years later, were so severely emasculated as to render them devoid of any real substance and, in the case of certain provisions, incomprehensible [3]. Ultimately, it was left to the Council, acting unanimously, to take decisions in the future on the content of a policy still to be formulated for want of a positive definition.

The director-general as 'stationmaster'

Because of the technical complexity of the material to be dealt with and the vague nature of the policy to be formulated, responsibility for the sector did not exactly whet the appetite of the Commissioners. In June 1958, after succeeding his recently deceased compatriot, Rasquin, the Luxembourger, Lambert Schaus, inherited the transport portfolio in the absence of any other candidate. His *chef de cabinet* was Lucien Kraus. This former Luxembourg judge took direct charge of this 'very difficult' dossier, which 'no one wanted'. He was assisted by his compatriot, John Peters. The latter attended the transport meetings, particularly those involving the representatives of the three executives and those provided for under Article 83, which established a committee of national experts. But this committee 'performed no useful purpose. These people met quietly and had their travelling expenses paid.' [4]

The directorate-general was headed by an Italian, Renzetti. A product of Ferrovie dello Stato (Italian State Railways), he was the first of the Italian 'set', some of whom had a railway background, to head DG VII. Minoletti, who succeeded him in 1962, was a specialist in maritime matters. Likewise, Rho, who took over in 1965, was also an ex-railwayman.

---

[1] Interview with John Peters, 29 January 2004.
[2] Interview with Nicola Bellieni, 19 December 2003.

[3] Note from Nicola Bellieni, May 2006.
[4] Ibid.

Paris–Brussels, Brussels–Paris. The mythical TEE used by French officials going back to Paris at the weekend. The famous 'Decalogue' is said to have been written on the train (see box pp. 106–107): (Interview with Henri Étienne, 12 January 2004.)
The publicity material refers to the diesel motor cars for the first Trans Europ Express trains (entry into service in June 1957), which were replaced in 1964 by hauled trains with TEE coach components in stainless steel (see photograph).

The DG and his Commissioner

'The director-general was Renzetti, an Italian. If necessary, he was contactable. But I never really needed to contact him. Still, it was reassuring to know that I could. His assistant was Mr Vittorelli. So it was like a small family. The atmosphere was very convivial. We all worked quite well together. I have no negative memories. That applies also to Mr Schaus, who was the Commissioner. I was always made to feel welcome, we went on trips together. I recall that there was a good collaborative atmosphere. Although there were lots of minor disagreements between Mr Schaus and Mr von der Groeben, the real problem arose from the difficulties affecting relations with the Member States.'

Interview with Nicola Bellieni, 19 December 2003.

Despite the highly convivial ambiance — all the more so as Schaus, a great Italophile (he was chairman of the 'Italian–Luxembourg friendship society'), spoke impeccable Italian — one might be forgiven for observing that the directorate-general did not come across as particularly dynamic. Under Bodson and Coppé, it remained rail-oriented 'to the core' (¹), just like Paolo Rho, head of division in 1958, and director-general in 1965.

In operational terms, therefore, the establishment of the directorate-general was very gradual. This was largely due to the imprecise, even downright cryptic, terms used in the Treaty about transport. Furthermore, the weight of ECSC experience, which was known to be conflictual, was the decisive factor, and this contributed significantly to the meandering nature of the directorate-general. While this factor set the tone of the early days, it was not, of course, the only one that helps to explain why the common transport policy dossier was 'a sorry dossier' (²).

'A sorry dossier'

From its inception, the DG comprised three directorates. Two were horizontal, while the third, vertical one, was concerned with 'development and modernisation'. It was responsible for the three modes of transport covered by the Treaty (³): rail, road and inland waterways. Each of them came under the responsibility of a division.

If a common policy was ever to become a reality, then it was going to be at the heart of this directorate. There was a link here with the directorate which, within the DG, focused on tariffs and prices and with collaboration with the Competition DG, despite 'the "petty" disagreements between Schaus and von der Groeben' (⁴).

The details of the problem were well explained, under Schaus's name, in an article published in *Revue du Marché Commun* in April 1959.

First, the following point was made:

'Tariff dismantling could cease to have any practical impact if the Member States were able to offset or water down the effects of reductions in customs duties by maintaining or introducing discriminatory measures affecting rates and conditions of carriage.'

This was followed by an implied question and a declaration of intent:

'There is a question mark as to whether the EEC's transport policy will be liberal or prescriptive. The general tendency of the Treaty is to promote trade liberalisation. Yet this does not preclude — rather it even implies — a need to take regulatory measures to guarantee such free trade. We want economic freedom, but we also want a freedom that is orderly.'

Here, as elsewhere, in the past as in the present, this remains the knotty heart of the problem.

(¹) Note from Nicola Bellieni, May 2006.
(²) Interview with Nicola Bellieni, 19 December 2003.

(³) Article 84.
(⁴) Interview with Nicola Bellieni, 19 December 2003 (see box above).

Although a competent lawyer and diplomat, Schaus was no politician. Deliberately mischievous, with a tendency to say out loud what others were thinking but keeping to themselves ([1]), he and his administration were faced with making a choice or, at the very least, laying the foundations. Hence the plethora of studies and reports which marked, and would continue to mark, the life and the image of the DG.

In itself, however, this was not enough since the real prerequisite was a reply to the question of whether the competition rules laid down in the Treaty applied to transport or not.

In October 1960, in a speech to the Grosser Verkehrsausschuss beim deutschen Industrie- und Handelstag (Main Transport Committee within the German Association of Chambers of Commerce), meeting in Bremen, the Commissioner laid his cards on the table before the representatives of Germany's trade and industry. In the Commission's view, the general rules on competition applied to the land transport sector. In addition, however, there also had to be progress in air and sea transport.

This interpretation of the Treaty was maximalist or, rather, universalist. On 12 November 1960 the memorandum issued by the Commission confirmed this. Subsequently, the DG went on to draw up a memorandum on the future direction of the common transport policy. Endorsed by the Commission in April 1961, it was followed a year later by the common transport policy action programme.

The line adopted in 1960 was confirmed. In practice, however, there was no movement. Rather the national administrations, trade organisations and specialised press were at pains to lay into the Commission's universalist pretensions tooth and nail. And this, despite the fact that Article 75 provided for derogations.

Recollections concerning Lambert Schaus

'An extremely interesting person. He was a lawyer and the son of a goldsmith ([2]). From his goldsmith-watchmaker father he appears to have inherited, in addition to the extreme sense of precision associated with gold and fine objects, a certain *joie de vivre*. He had been closely involved with the Nouvelles Équipes Internationales (a Christian Democrat movement including Schuman, De Gasperi and Adenauer), of which he was a founder member. This was the ideological base to which he remained faithful all his life. He did not spend the war years in London like his brother. Instead, he was in the Resistance. The Germans sent him to the work camps. He had a very good war. Afterwards, he became a lawyer and then Minister for Supply. In my newspaper, I had launched savage attacks on him at the time. When he arrived at the Commission, I said to myself: 'This is the end!' Then, after some time his *chef de cabinet* quits. He sends for me. He was so amused by the articles I had written about him that he had insisted on meeting me. The upshot was that he offered me a job on his staff. This gives you some idea of the character of the man: a good sport.'

Interview with Henri Étienne, 12 January 2004.

'Lambert Schaus was a diplomat, he was not a politician. He was a lawyer before becoming a minister. He resigned from the Luxembourg government and became an ambassador in Brussels. A co-signatory, with Joseph Bech, of the Treaty of Rome, he understood the Treaty, and all its vagaries, admirably well. Thus, his appointment was testimony to his thorough grasp of the facts and there was no way he could be regarded as an amateur. He was also a good negotiator. But the obstacles he faced proved too much for him. Whether it was the national groupings or the industry circles that eventually got the better of him, they were able, through their country's permanent representations, to prevent things from getting done. A very upright and highly cultured man […], Schaus was unfortunate enough not to be in the right place at the right time. All the things he worked on, developed or thought out at the time have endured and eventually been realised. There can be no talk of failure. It was simply that his ideas did not catch on in the era that spawned them […]'

Interview with John Peters, 29 January 2004.

([1]) Interview with John Peters, 29 January 2004.

([2]) The father of Lambert Schaus was a jeweller-watchmaker.

Article 75 of the EEC Treaty

'1. For the purpose of implementing Article 74, and taking into account the distinctive features of transport, the Council shall, acting unanimously, until the end of the second stage and by a qualified majority thereafter, lay down, on a proposal from the Commission and after consulting the Economic and Social Committee and the Assembly:

(a) common rules applicable to international transport to or from the territory of a Member State or passing across the territory of one or more Member States;

(b) the conditions under which non-resident carriers may operate transport services within a Member State;

(c) any other appropriate provisions.

2. The provisions referred to in (a) and (b) of paragraph 1 shall be laid down during the transitional period.

3. By way of derogation from the procedure provided for in paragraph 1, where the application of provisions concerning the principles of the regulatory system for transport would be liable to have a serious effect on the standard of living and on employment in certain areas and on the operation of transport facilities, they shall be laid down by the Council acting unanimously. In so doing, the Council shall take into account the need for adaptation to the economic development which will result from establishing the common market.'

The foregoing requires a level of explanation, given that the situation is paradoxical, to say the least.

By way of reminder, the date of publication in the Official Journal of the famous Regulation 17/62 laying down the procedure for implementing Articles 85 and 96 was 21 February 1962. In paving the way for the eradication of cartels and monopolies, it represented an important victory for the Commission (¹). The latter, riding on the crest of a wave, now felt the time was right for further advances. On 27 February, the Council turned its attention to the question of transport. It concluded its meeting by calling on the Commission to submit, together with a timetable, general proposals on the implementation of the common policy in the context of a global and balanced action programme. Two months later the programme was ready.

This caused what can only be described as a general outcry, or rather a shouting match, between the interested parties and the Commission, between the latter and the Council, and even within

the Commission, caused by differences among the protagonists regarding their ability to act.

Regulation 17/62 was certainly an important victory for the Commission. It was a victory for DG IV and, more particularly, for von der Groeben. But did this mean, for all that, that DG VII could rush into the breach? Nothing was less certain. This DG was weak. On the basis of a recent diagnosis, the need to reorganise its work was absolutely vital.

'Services not directly involved in the action'

The situation looked pretty clear. The 1961 guidelines and the 1962 programme appeared to trigger a dynamic transition between a period of gestation and a period of action. Hence it was important, on the one hand, to have a clearly defined system for allocating tasks within the DG itself and, on the other, to parcel out some jobs, such as tax, social and legal aspects, to other directorates-general (²). In other words, although

---

(¹) See pp. 317–318.

(²) HAEU, FMM 3, *Rapport sur l'organisation des services de la Communauté Économique Européenne*, 1961, VII-1.

transport was centre stage, the DG itself lacked coherence. Accordingly, lines of authority were in need of 'remodelling'; 'vagueness in the allocation of tasks' had to be avoided. In short, as the Ortoli report explained with consummate euphemism, the main thrust must be thought through with sufficient energy to avoid having to bother as well about managing services not directly involved.

The weak link in the design was therefore the directorate-general directly concerned. Certainly, without forgetting the 'applicability of the general rules' credo, the action programme was an excellent document. Taking into account the special features associated with the issues, the action programme developed the notion of a form of organised competition designed to lead, ultimately, to the elimination or, at the very least, the neutralisation of those features.

To put it another way, the common policy should lead to the establishment of a genuine competitive market aimed at keeping the overall cost of transport as low as possible, so as to meet the needs of the economic players in all regions of the Community. Such a programme called for decisions to be taken in compliance with a graduated timetable covering the following four areas: access to the market, tariffs and prices, conditions of competition and the question of infrastructures.

At the methodological level, the gradualness of the process was realistic. Rather than define a final scheme, the Commission preferred to lay down transitional arrangements that might differ according to the countries and modes of transport. Moreover, if the ideal approach was to conduct the action as much as possible in the various sectors concerned, then parallelism between those sectors need not be constraining. To act otherwise would create blockages.

On 14 June 1962 the Council took a close look at the action programme. The main question, as far as the Council was concerned, was whether

John Peters on lobbyists

'I had contacts with the railways, I had personal contacts [...] with the hauliers. I was even on friendly terms with some of them. The trade bodies made it their business to choose good lobbyists. The lobbies are not a nuisance in themselves; they are only a nuisance in the eyes of the politicians. This is understandable as they are short-circuited, so to speak. But when it comes to laying the foundations of a policy, they are extremely useful. They provide you with information which you yourself would never have been able to find. Or which you would have discovered only much too late. In this way, you are able to take account of the technical possibilities, the political possibilities and the human possibilities. All this is something you can only get to know by talking to the trade insiders. You are not necessarily at their mercy [...] I know of only two cases where officials were bribed. All in all, my colleagues were always interested in having conversations with the lobbyists because they were intelligent people. They didn't beat you with a stick. Nor were they the sort of people who would try to bribe you, because they knew the whole thing could backfire on them. All of these considerations formed an integral part of our exploration of a subject. As with the literature, or as with the economic theories. We needed to have these contacts in order to work effectively.'

Interview with John Peters, 29 January 2004.

Regulation 17 applied to the transport sector. It was a matter of legal verification, but not purely and simply. Indeed, one official, idiosyncratically describing the Council's attitude, declared that the Council was 'enchanted' and found the programme 'magnificent yet again'. But the enthusiasm was superficial. In reality it was a game — one could even go so far as to say an infantile game — between, on the one hand, a directorate-general and a Commissioner, both of them eager to find a solution, and, on the other, the Council [...] [1].

_____

[1] Interview with Nicola Bellieni, 19 December 2003.

Article 80 of the EEC Treaty

'1. The imposition by a Member State, in respect of transport operations carried out within the Union, of rates and conditions involving any element of support or protection in the interest of one or more particular undertakings or industries shall be prohibited as from the beginning of the second stage, unless authorised by the Commission.

2. The Commission shall, acting on its own initiative or on application by a Member State, examine the rates and conditions referred to in paragraph 1, taking account in particular of the requirements of an appropriate regional economic policy, the needs of underdeveloped areas and the problems of areas seriously affected by political circumstances on the one hand, and of the effects of such rates and conditions on competition between the different modes of transport on the other.

After consulting each Member State concerned, the Commission shall take the necessary decisions.

3. The prohibition provided for in paragraph 1 shall not apply to tariffs fixed to meet competition.'

In point of fact, DG VII, having been invited to carry out more of its beloved studies, could not afford to drag its feet over Regulation 17.

What the transport undertakings were calling for was an end to the uncertainty caused by the conflict between the 'universalist' thesis and the thesis propounded by the believers in the special nature of the sector.

Complete U-turn by the Commission

Pressed to come up with an answer, the Commission prepared a draft regulation seeking to exclude transport from the scope of Regulation 17! The turnaround was total. Certainly, the measure was conservative inasmuch as there was no question now of having to decide between the two theses. Yet observers of these events were not taken in. Indeed, the rapporteur of the European Parliament Internal Market Committee declared that the Commission, contrary to the view it had been defending not so long previously, had now fallen into line, apparently at the insistence of the national governments [1].

In the event, on 26 November in Paris, the Council adopted Regulation No 141 exempting transport from the application of Council Regulation No 17 until 31 December 1965. Shortly before the expiry of this deadline, a new Regulation (165/65/EEC) extended this measure until the end of 1967.

It goes without saying that the introduction of a common policy turned out to be a veritable fiasco. Worse, the measure adopted in November 1962 had the effect of exempting the undertakings from serving notification of any agreements they might enter into. And then voices were raised denouncing the fact that not only the governments themselves but also some people within the Commission had been urging the transport operators to keep mum and not to budge [2].

Between late 1962 and December 1967, the transport 'policy', although not entirely fruitless, chalked up only meagre results. And these results were only in certain sectors. Thus it was that, as far as freedom to provide services is concerned, it was in the road transport sector that a few advances were recorded.

In 1964, in the infrastructure investment sector — an area so very sensitive on account of the risks of distortion caused by the existence of State

---

[1] European Parliament, Session document No 107, 16 November 1962, p. 3. On the progress of the draft regulation: Bernard, N., 'Regulation No 17 and the common transport policy', in Gerbet, P. and Pépy, D. (eds), *La décision dans les Communautés européennes — Colloque de l'Association pour le développement de la science politique européenne, organisé par l'Institut d'études politiques de Lyon,* Presses universitaires de Bruxelles, Brussels, 1969, pp. 343–365.

[2] European Parliament, *Débats, session 1962–1963,* 19 November 1962, p. 15. Gerhard Kreyssig for the Socialist Group.

aid and the possibility of having recourse to the EIB — DG VII launched an investigation into the cost. Two years later it urged that all investments having Community-wide implications should be subject to a consultation procedure.

When all is said and done, however, the essential issue was the system of prices and terms of carriage. Discriminatory practice in this area was rife. For the same goods and within the same transport link, prices and conditions of carriage could vary depending on the country of origin and the country of destination. As early as 1960, measures had been adopted with the aim of gradually ending this state of affairs. The next stage, much more sensitive in nature, involved the prohibition of 'any element of support or protection in the interest of one or more particular undertakings or industries' (Article 80). However, the prohibition of aid does not, in itself, constitute a policy since, in order for such a measure to be enacted, tariffs would need to comply with common rules. The question was on the table in 1965 and 1966. The main thrust of the argument was that 'bracket tariffs' should be introduced which would be compulsory for all modes of transport, whether international or domestic. Such a system would mean devising a reference tariff scheme to serve as an average. Once again, the general outcry was spectacular. Yet it had the advantage of forcing further clarification as the deadline of 31 December 1967 approached.

In October 1966, the Council asked the Commission to implement the harmonisation of the conditions of competition as well as the harmonisation of capacities since, once again, the two positions were in conflict. On the one hand, the position of the proponents of maximum and minimum tariffs; on the other, the position of those opposed to this option, who advocated that restrictions on access to the market should be regulated on the basis of capacity, i.e. the volume of potentially transportable goods.

This was the basis on which the DG, in its efforts to reconcile two highly opposed approaches,

**Opposition to the role
of the transport sector**

'As regards the role of the transport sector, opposition was forthcoming from all sides. The high-level lobbyists operated not just at Commission level but also at the level of the Permanent Representations, which were closest to them and with which they were most familiar. As with a tree, this opposition rose from the roots to the trunk, re-emerging even during the discussions at the Commission.'

Interview with John Peters, 29 January 2004.

conducted its work. In February 1967, it presented its communication, and in December, the Council took its decision on a three-stage programme designed to implement the common policy. Numerous measures were adopted between 1968 and 1973. Being the work of a remodelled directorate-general, these measures did not necessarily express a policy reflecting an ambitious vision of the role that transport should play in the Europe of the Six on the basis of a clear conception of the role of the related infrastructures ([1]). These infrastructures were supposed to form the hitherto missing links that would ensure the structuring or integration of the European area. But there was still a very long way to go.

A 'new' directorate-general

In July 1967, the Luxembourger, Victor Bodson, who, according to John Peters, was a somewhat Spaakian personage, albeit not on such a grand scale, a liberal in socialist clothing ([2]), replaced Schaus, and the Secretaries-General of the three executives signed their report on the organisation of the departments. As far as transport was concerned, Bodson took account of the 'undeniable

---

([1]) Interview with Nicola Bellieni, 19 December 2003.
([2]) Interview with John Peters, 29 January 2004.

imbalance between the imminent completion of the customs union and the retention of profoundly divergent systems [...] in the Six'. He felt that the three original directorates should 'work alongside' the ECSC's Transport Directorate, whose staff of 11 was very much reduced. Accordingly, 'since the quest for greater integration depends on the progress made with the implementation of the common policy, attempts to increase the number of staff are not necessary'. DG VII looked forward, therefore, to seeing its staff of 107 expanded only by their colleagues from the High Authority (¹).

The 1967 programme

As announced, the 1967 programme was phased over three stages. Its elaboration and adoption were accompanied — encouraged even — by the agitation caused in some cases by the attitude of certain governments and in others by the activism of the head of DG VII himself, exasperated by the constant blockages occurring within the Council.

In this last-mentioned case, the fact that the head of the DG was Italian, coupled with the fact that Rome had no policy, meant that this activism was doomed to failure.

'My director-general intervened', recalls Nicola Bellieni, 'in an attempt to persuade the Italian government to call for the relaunching of the common transport policy. But the whole thing was too obvious. Given that the Italians did not have a position on the matter, there was no way there could be a result.' Furthermore, the fact that 'efforts were under way to relaunch a transport policy from Rome on the basis of papers drafted in Brussels, coupled with the fact that the head of the Italian Minister of Transport's private office was a personal friend of the direct-

---

(¹) HAEC, BDT 144-82 643, *Rapport du secrétaire général de la Haute Autorité et des secrétaires exécutifs des Commissions de la CEE et d'Euratom sur l'organisation des services de la Commission des Communautés européennes*, SEC(67) 3001, 1 July 1967, pp. 68–69.

Italy's instructions

'The Permanent Representative of Italy used to come to the "transport" meetings. It was obvious that all the countries had their instructions. Except for Italy. But I remember very well how an attempt was made to telephone Rome. From a technical point of view, that was more difficult in those days than it is today. At a certain moment the Permanent Representative left the room. Ten minutes later he returned and announced: "On behalf of the Italian government, I would like to make the following statement, etc." We were astonished. We all wondered where he had been to get this information. He confided to us afterwards that he had been to the toilet [...]'

Interview with Nicola Bellieni, 19 December 2003.

ERTA

'The desire to regulate driving hours and resting time and to install tachographs in lorries was German-inspired. Germany feared that the Dutch might operate illegally by getting their lorry drivers to drive for more hours than were permitted. And they were the great champions of this idea [...] Furthermore, everyone agreed that neither other road users nor, above all, passengers on coaches as you see them nowadays should be exposed to traffic hazards simply because the driver was suffering from excessive overtiredness. The idea was noble to begin with, very Christian and very open, but, when it came down to it, nobody wanted to grasp the nettle. Because that would have restricted the freedom of individual firms to use the various tools at their disposal, including their drivers, in such a way as to meet the requirements of the market.'

Interview with John Peters, 29 January 2004.

---

or-general' was not necessarily a guarantee of success. The document from the DG adopted 'a virulent position in favour of the common policy'. When taken up by the Italian government,

Motorway construction in the 1960s and a degree of 'Europeanisation' of the transport business are two of the factors behind the perception of European integration as a fact of life.

it looked odd, raised questions and, ultimately, 'had no effect' (¹).

Having potentially graver implications, the German position in 1967 shook the governments and played a decisive role in shaping the Council decision in December. Fed up with waiting, Bonn, through its Transport Minister, Georg Leber, drew up a programme specific to the Federal Republic for the years 1968 to 1972. This project to reorganise the transport sector conflicted with the ECSC Treaty. Adopted on 8 November 1967, it illustrated the German government's wish to uphold the interests of its inland waterways sector on the

Rhine by opposing all forms of regulation, while at the same time demonstrating a more open attitude as far as the rail sector was concerned. Once again, a shouting match ensued. Indeed, in matters extending beyond the three-stage programme of 17 December 1967, the Bonn government never lowered its guard, forcing the Commission to react by issuing recommendations aimed at getting Bonn to change tack. At the same time, in the Netherlands, and not just in the HGV sector, where there was opposition to measures aimed at regulating the working hours of lorry drivers, but in the inland waterways sector as well, attempts were being made to increase the number of obstacles.

In other words, while the Commission's desire to implement the programme thus adopted might

(¹) Interview with Nicola Bellieni, 19 December 2003. On this question, see BAC 3/1974 76.

The three stages of the 1967 programme

'First stage:

harmonisation of working conditions in road transport;

application of the competition rules to transport;

rules governing aid to transport;

elimination of double taxation on motor vehicles;

standardisation of the provisions governing the duty-free admission of the fuel contained in the fuel tanks of commercial motor vehicles;

introduction of a Community quota for the carriage of goods by road between Member States;

establishment of a graduated charging scheme for the carriage of goods by road between Member States.

Second stage:

'regulation on action by Member States concerning the obligations inherent in the concept of public service;

'regulation on the normalisation of the accounts of railway undertakings.

Third stage:

harmonisation of vehicle tax structures;

introduction of a standard and permanent accounting system for expenditure on infrastructure in respect of each mode of transport.'

Communication from the Commission to the Council of 10 February 1967 on the development of the common transport policy following the Council resolution of 20 October 1966.

amount to 'an altogether thankless task' [1], this desire also prompted it to place some degree of hope in the Court of Justice. The point at issue was to settle, at institutional level, the question as to how far the Commission could impose its decisions on a Member State. In 1969, the Court, in a case relating to the rates charged by — of all bodies — the Italian railways, gave a ruling on the scope of the Commission's discretion, with a view to limiting it [2]. Two years later, another case demonstrated the extent to which the Commission could become paralysed in the absence of a common policy. The case in question concerned the European Agreement on Road Transport (ERTA), in respect of which, according to the ruling by the Court after the matter had been brought before it by the Commission, the power to conclude agreements was firmly vested in the Member States. Indeed, powers could not be conferred on the Community 'because the common transport policy was not yet sufficiently developed' [3].

Yes, the task is thankless, and it is also frustrating. Indeed, the transport sector continues to be exempt from common rules. According to a decision taken by the Council in 1969, States must remove the 'obligations inherent in the concept of a public service'. But it goes on to add: 'save where it is essential to maintain such obligations in order to ensure the provision of adequate transport services' [4].

Thus, despite producing 'an infinity of texts' forming 'quite a coherent whole, when taken together' [5] — amounting, however, to a Community policy and not a common policy — more often than not the Transport DG came across as impotent. This does not mean that its staff were not doing any work. On the contrary, like this head of division for infrastructures, an Italian,

[1] Interview with John Peters, 29 January 2004.
[2] ECJ, Case 1/69 *Italy* v *Commission* (9 July 1969).
[3] ECJ, Case 22/70 *Commission* v *Council (European Agreement on Road Transport)* (31 March 1971).
[4] Council Regulation (EEC) No 1191/69 of 26 June 1969, OJ English special edition, Series I, Chapter 1969 (I), p. 283.
[5] Interview with Nicola Bellieni, 19 December 2003.

The weight per lorry axle is not a purely technical problem

'The question of harmonising the weights and dimensions of lorries in the Member States is not an empty question. It is covered by Article 75 of the Treaty. On the ground, there are two opposing factions: the proponents of 10 tonnes per axle and the proponents of 13 tonnes. France defends the latter position. The implications are not purely technical. In fact, they are economic since the adoption of common rules would have consequences for the manufacturers, who are not slow in bringing this to the attention of their national political authorities. So it is that the Berliet company defends tooth and nail the 13-tonne option, inasmuch as having to replace the fleet would not only be very costly but would also be tantamount to offering the German manufacturers of 10-tonne per axle lorries a golden opportunity on a plate.

In 1971, the Berliet company is particularly active. Jean Chamant, the French Transport Minister, 'when setting out the French position, seems to draw his inspiration from the notes prepared by our company for the Administration', writes a Berliet employee. Satisfied with the Minister's attitude in Brussels, Paul Berliet tells him: 'I would like to thank you for having defended [...] the French HGV manufacturers' position [...]. Consequently, despite the attacks you will inevitably face, I would urge you to uphold the position you have adhered to so firmly hitherto.' In February 1972, Georges Pompidou and Willy Brandt address this question at their summit meeting [...]'

Moguen-Toursel, M., 'Lobbying, compromis, rapprochements transversaux: les manœuvres autour de la définition d'un nouveau code européen pour le transport routier (1950–1980)', in Moguen-Toursel, M. (ed.), *Stratégies d'entreprise et action publique dans l'Europe intégrée (1950–1980): Affrontement et apprentissage des acteurs/Firm strategies and public policy in integrated Europe (1950–1980): Confrontation and learning of economic actors*, Euroclio, Études et documents, No 37 © PIE–Peter Lang, 2007. (Translated from the French)

who 'is working his fingers to the bone' on the planned link between Brussels, Luxembourg and Strasbourg, 'a project for which an abundance of plans existed', other people are producing remarkable papers in other areas. 'But there is no evidence to show that anything of even the slightest significance has ever come from that quarter.' [1].

The transport policy thus started off on the wrong foot. This Community 'fata morgana' left both players and observers somewhat disillusioned [2]. According to them, the ideas were there, and an overall concept existed in the minds of many [3]. 'All the things worked on, developed or thought out at the time have endured — and eventually been realised.' [4] Indeed, it is only now, several decades later, that what was in a state of intellectual gestation has finally begun to see the light of day.

Michel Dumoulin

[1] Ibid. (Translation)

[2] De l'Écotais, Y., *L'Europe sabotée*, Rossel, Brussels, 1976, pp. 162–163.
[3] Interview with Henri Étienne, 12 January 2004.
[4] Interview with John Peters, 29 January 2004 (see box p. 453).

Chapter 23

An improbable industrial policy

While industry and those involved in it were at the heart of the process of economic integration which got under way in 1958, there was scarcely any provision in the Treaty for the direct involvement of the EEC. The introduction of the free movement of manufactured goods throughout the Community, coupled with competition legislation which left to market forces the job of fashioning economic structures, formed the basis of the Commission's work in this field. One of the originators of Community industrial policy commented at the start of the 1970s that, when the EEC Treaty was being drafted, nobody realised that there was a need for an industrial policy and there was hardly any general thought given to its content and definition [1]. Only some countries had some experience in this area, giving rise to differences of opinion which more or less matched those that were causing division in relation to economic planning.

It should therefore come as no surprise just how few people the Commission had at its disposal for a policy which was not mentioned in the Treaty of Rome. In the organisation chart which

appeared at the beginning of 1958, industry came under the Internal Market DG and, inside the DG, it was represented by a division attached to the Directorate for Industry, Craft Trades and Commerce, which Fernand Braun headed from 1962.

This situation remained unaltered until the merger of the executive bodies. This resulted in the creation of a Directorate-General for Industrial Affairs headed by Robert Toulemon, with Fernand Braun as his deputy and Jean Flory at the head of a Directorate for Studies and Industrial Policy. These changes were made between 1964 and 1970 by the Member of the Commission responsible for the internal market and then industrial affairs, Guido Colonna di Paliano. Although the overall effect was fairly limited in terms of what was actually achieved during the period, this change of direction reveals a series of slight shifts in thinking, the nature and elements of which deserve explanation.

One of the first officials in the division responsible for industry has explained just how vague the Commission's task was in this area: 'What was the point of an industry division when the European Economic Community began? What was it supposed to

---

[1] Toulemon, R. and Flory, J., *Une politique industrielle pour l'Europe*, Presses Universitaires de France, Paris, 1970, p. 79.

do? Were there any articles in the Treaty which specifically referred to industrial policy? Practically, there was none.' (¹) The questions which were put to the Member States were met with a response which could be summed up as 'It's none of your business', either because the representatives of the country in question thought that the relevant initiatives were inappropriate or because they thought that industrial matters were basically national concerns. The upshot was: 'What direction should we go in? It took us some time to find out.' (²)

From sectoral action to an overall policy

The first ideas on industrial policy were very sectoral in nature and scarcely regarded as having anything to do with a policy as such. The introduction of the customs union, coupled at times with falling international rates, caused serious difficulties for some sectors. These difficulties were anticipated when the Treaty was drafted, with provision under Article 226 for protective measures during the transitional period in the event of serious sectoral or regional difficulties. The Italian government in fact decided to make use of this option at the end of 1960 for sulphur, lead, zinc, iodine and silk. The Commission consequently decided temporarily to isolate the Italian market, provided that measures allowing only profitable firms to survive were brought in. It was clear to the Commission that restrictive import measures of this kind could result in serious drawbacks for consumer firms and should not take the place of resolving the structural problems which these difficulties revealed.

Battle in the shipyards

A new series of difficulties affecting larger sectors in the Community provided the Commission shortly afterwards with a chance to consider matters more thoroughly. At the beginning of the 1960s

Europe's shipyards were facing growing competition from the Japanese, who were rapidly winning a larger share of the market. The Member States reacted in a haphazard manner with aid schemes to rectify the differences in prices with their competitors: France from 1959, Germany in 1962, followed by Italy and then the Netherlands and Belgium as well. These schemes, sometimes in conjunction with restructuring programmes which turned out to be inadequate, needed to be extended beyond the periods originally planned. The shipbuilding sector thus provided an ideal test bed for an overall approach to the matter by the Internal Market DG. The first move, which took the form of a proposal for a directive in April 1965, was to align national practices on subsidies. This directive, adopted by the Council after a lengthy delay (July 1969), was devised at the time only as an interim solution, pending a more comprehensive policy which was still to be defined. The Internal Market DG worked hard on it in the summer of 1965. Shipbuilding in Europe was beset by structural difficulties caused simultaneously by supply conditions which were technologically ill-matched to demand, by the fragmentation of its structures of production and also by a series of disparities in relation to the facilities provided for Japanese shipyards in terms of raw material prices, research aid, credit arrangements, customs protection, etc. The fundamental approach for which the Internal Market DG opted was based on the idea that a 'passive attitude' would eventually lead to European constructors being ousted from the world market, contrary to the decisions of the governments which had opted to maintain a shipbuilding industry even though the consolidation policies followed by some Member States tended to be protective and conservative in nature. The recommended policy thus called for shipyards to be rationalised and geared to the construction of new types of vessel and for national programmes to be compared with a view to determining certain options at Community level (³).

(¹) Interview with Jean Durieux, 3 March 2004.
(²) Ibid.

(³) *Problèmes posés par une politique des structures dans le domaine de la construction navale*, communication by Mr Colonna di Paliano, SEC(65) 2880, 13 October 1965.

The note on shipbuilding which the same directorate-general prepared two years later showed further thinking about the kind of policies to be followed. On the one hand, structural action was advocated for which aid from the national authorities could be justified on a temporary and selective basis. On the other, specific action was called for on credit arrangements and credit insurance so that European shipyards could enjoy the same conditions of access to financing as their Japanese rivals. At Community level, the plan was for no import taxes on supplies for shipbuilding from non-member countries and, in particular, the coordination of national research efforts and even the pooling of human and financial resources for certain programmes ([1]).

Textiles and high-tech industries

Similar findings and conclusions emerged for the textiles industry: competition from countries with low labour costs, direct intervention by the authorities in some Member States, need for structural change and greater research efforts. The idea which emerged at Community level was for a common commercial policy on imports from low-cost countries, tax incentives to encourage the modernisation of equipment, coordination of national research efforts and approximation of company law to encourage groupings of companies at European level ([2]).

The sector-by-sector approach was also applied to some high-tech industries which were studied and examined by working parties set up by the Medium-Term Economic Policy Committee. The data-processing sector symbolised these concerns. The Europeans were lagging behind the Americans in the case of computers and components, and there was a risk that the consequences could be dramatic in the medium term, at the economic level as well as in political and human terms. The causes of this situation were companies' limited capital resources, inadequate means devoted to research and little support from the public sector in terms of orders compared with the United States. The Commission therefore came up with a proposal to improve the structures of the sector and to create companies on a European scale, to introduce 'jointly decided' public financing, to consider (i) the possibility of pooling public orders for research and development and for the purchase of equipment while avoiding any discrimination among enterprises in the Member States on the grounds of nationality, and (ii) major joint projects on research and development ([3]).

An overall approach

The outcome of this sector-by-sector approach was a more overall view prompting some debate which was then taken up by the press and various analysts. In an article in *Le Figaro* of 9 March 1965, Raymond Aron criticised what he called the 'failure of the common market' and wrote that, when a French or Italian firm was in difficulties, it usually turned to an American company, rather than to a firm in the same sector in another country in the common market. The sources which fuelled the public debate sometimes even came from within the Commission itself. It is a known fact that *The American Challenge*, which was written by the French politician, Jean-Jacques Servan-Schreiber, and which sold in millions around the world, was based on a series of internal Commission studies.

There is no doubt that, in line with a tradition which had emerged at the beginning of the century, comparing Europe as it developed as a

([1]) BAC 116/83 815, Directorate-General for the Internal Market, Directorate-General for Competition: sectoral structures policy, shipbuilding, 9 June 1967.

([2]) 'Textile industry in the Community', *Bulletin of the EEC*, No 5, 1966, pp. 5–8.

([3]) BAC 118/83 815, Industrial structures policy, electronics industry, document for the Medium-Term Economic Policy Committee, 25 July 1967; Medium-Term Economic Policy Committee, 'Sectoral aspects of the structures policy' working party, opinion of the working party concerning the directions of economic policy to be followed in the electronics industry, especially the computer industry, 25 July 1967.

Community with the model represented by the United States was one of the main lines of thought of many analysts and of many officials at the Commission.

The thinking on the medium-term economic policy programme proposed by the Commission and adopted by the Council at the end of April 1966 contributed to the first general consolidation of ideas on industrial policy. The introduction to the programme referred to the need for 'industrial policy measures' for the sectors experiencing difficulty in adapting, the introduction of a structural policy, the encouragement of intra-Community industrial mergers, a better understanding of foreign investment within the EEC and more extensive research efforts.

Memorandum on Community industrial policy (July 1967)

All the concerns which were gradually coalescing towards the definition of a Community industrial policy were analysed by Alain Prate, Director-General for the Internal Market, in September 1966.

The introduction of the tariff union, which was in the process of completion, was not enough to create an economic community, which in the industrial sphere posed certain problems that 'could not be resolved just by eliminating barriers to trade' [1] and threatened to result in muddled and even contradictory direct intervention by countries. In the industries which had come out of the first industrial revolution, where growth was slow and where the first signs of decline were apparent, the problems which arose concerned structural change. In these branches of activity the primary objective of a Community industrial policy was to avoid muddled and contradictory intervention by the authorities which 'distorted the conditions of competition among Community enterprises' [2].

The other matter which Alain Prate raised concerned US investment. He was referring particularly to the rapidly expanding sectors representing the future where it was somewhat embarrassing to have technically healthy European firms being bought up, often at a knockdown price, with the consequence that 'dominant positions dependent on decision-making centres in non-member countries were being created in some important industrial sectors of the Community' [3]. The problems which arose in these sectors concerned structures and financial resources. Lastly, attention was drawn to the likely consequences of the ongoing Kennedy Round talks and their effects on industry in Europe with regard both to Europe's own inadequacies and to the US tariff structure. There were several reasons why all these matters demanded a common European response. In the case of the sectors beset by structural difficulties, the idea was to stop the Member States 'outbidding' each other, and this prompted a desire for 'coordinated industrial policy measures taken by the Community so that the necessary changes could be made in a gradual and concerted manner while ensuring freedom of competition and the free movement of goods within the common market' [4]. As for the industries of the future, such as nuclear power, aerospace, electronics and pharmaceuticals, Alain Prate's cautious aim of rediscovering a 'degree of autonomy' needed to involve 'coordination of national efforts, possibly reaching outside the Community' [5], i.e. by using the resources of the Six in conjunction with those of the United Kingdom.

The proposed action was thus divided into several parts, with the idea of creating a genuine common market within which technical regulations in particular would no longer constitute artificial barriers to trade. The idea was also to coordinate and develop efforts in connection with scientific and technical research and for conversion of the industries which had emerged

---

[1] HAEC, BDT 118/83 807, *Politique industrielle et marché commun*, note signed Alain Prate, 12 September 1966.
[2] Ibid.

[3] Ibid.
[4] Ibid.
[5] Ibid.

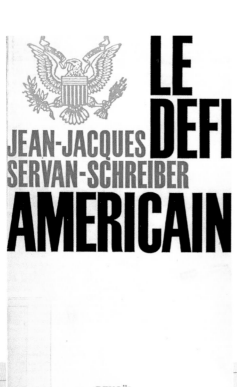

'My God! said God, I forgot to create Europe':
Piem, or Pierre de Barrigue de Montvallon, the cartoonist who
worked for *Le Figaro* among others, illustrates the growing
awareness of the gap between the United States and Europe,
which Jean-Jacques Servan-Schreiber, editorialist, director
and founder of *L'Express*, took as his subject in an essay that
has not yet been forgotten: *Le défi américain*,
(*The American Challenge*). As Michel Albert puts it:
'*The American Challenge* is a profession of faith in Europe.
That is how it was seen in America, all over Europe and in
Japan too. The Japanese found it most inspiring.'
(Interview with Michel Albert, 18 December 2003.)

from the first industrial revolution. Lastly, the idea was to encourage the creation of enterprises which were big enough and had adequate financial resources to 'stand up to the competition from enterprises in non-member countries' (^{1}) while ensuring that the European countries did not outbid each other in their efforts to attract foreign investment. The idea was thus to create a 'business Europe' by means of a series of measures affecting company law, taxation and the capital market.

The proposals put forward by Alain Prate in 1966 thus tended towards a middle way, combining a series of institutional measures to complete and extend the tariff union and open up competition among operators with a series of Community moves which were justified because of the risk of distortion as a result of measures by the Member States. Prudence was therefore the watchword in order to ensure, in the light of what had gone before, that there was no repeat of discussions which were as pointless as the disputes over the comparative merits of 'competition and planning' (^{2}).

The proposals contained in the note by Alain Prate in September 1966 provided the basis for a communication by Colonna di Paliano to the Commission on 2 March 1967 and then a 'Memorandum on Community industrial policy', published at the beginning of July 1967. Colonna di Paliano's note to the Commission in March was thus broadly inspired by the ideas put forward by Alain Prate, albeit with slightly less emphasis on competition with the United States. The Commission memorandum, which differed little in terms of structure and ideas from the document presented by Colonna di Paliano in March, managed to present a rather more favourable balance between the market and competition. On the one hand, the Commission responded on the basis of the facts: the Member States were prompted to act in response to the difficulties

connected with the decline of certain activities and it was important to harmonise such action. On the other hand, the proposed policy was presented as an environment policy based on freedom of competition for enterprises but providing them with an institutional framework and resources to allow them to adapt to the demands of a 'large open market' and 'international competition' (^{3}). The July 1967 memorandum consequently insisted on the responsibility incumbent on enterprises: 'The main effort needs to be made by the enterprises themselves, especially with regard to management, while the Community must endeavour to remove the barriers which enterprises encounter when attempting to become more efficient, especially by removing discrimination, distortion and other inequalities in the conditions of competition which are contrary to the Treaty and prevent the functioning of the common market.' The balance between necessary structural concentration and competition thus constituted one of the tricky points of a policy which was also the subject of difficult talks with those representing employers in Europe (^{4}). The liberal slant of the memorandum also appeared in the guidelines on trade policy which it recommended, with the need to 'eliminate distortions of competition which could arise from differences in the trade policies followed by the Member States', a trade policy devised 'as liberally as possible' and 'harmonisation of export subsidy policies' (^{5}). The Member States' own responsibility was also emphasised in the memorandum: sectoral actions at European level were all the more effective if they were properly linked to macroeconomic policy initiatives.

The industrial policy gradually mapped out by the Commission thus emerged as a synthesis of the discussion and experience which occurred during the first years of its work: response to

---

(^{1}) HAEC, BDT 118/83 807, *Politique industrielle et marché commun*, note signed Alain Prate, 12 September 1966.
(^{2}) Ibid.

(^{3}) 'Memorandum on Community industrial policy', SEC(67) 1201, 4 July 1967.
(^{4}) UNICE, *L'industrie européenne face à l'intégration économique et sociale*, November 1966, p. 12.
(^{5}) 'Memorandum on Community industrial policy', SEC(67) 1201, 4 July 1967.

Exchange of views between the Commission and a Union of Industries in the European Community (UNICE) delegation, 7 April 1967, on industrial problems in the common market. UNICE saw the light of day in March 1958 in the wake of the Council of Industrial Federations in Europe (CIFE) and the Union of Industries of the Countries of the European Community. It brought together the national industrial federations of the six ECSC Member States. At the outset, it aimed at 'uniting the central industrial federations to foster solidarity between them; encouraging a Europe-wide competitive industrial policy; and acting as a spokesperson body to the European institutions' (http://www.unice.org/content/default.asp?PageId=212). UNICE ensures permanent liaison with the Community institutions, studies problems arising in that context and coordinates as far as possible responses and public statements of opinion by central industrial federations. Lastly, it promotes the emergence of a common policy through studies and exchanges and extends its activity to problems arising in relations between the Community and non-member countries, as explained by Jean Meynaud and Dusan Sidjanski at the time (*Les groupes de pression dans la Communauté européenne, 1958–68 — Structure et action des organisations professionnelles*, Éditions de l'institut de sociologie de l'université libre de Bruxelles, IEE de l'ULB, Brussels, 1971).

sectoral difficulties, desire to promote growth industries, need to take account of the actions of individual countries while stressing the ideas of the single market and freedom of competition. This all gradually took shape through continual dialogue with the Member States, but also with employer organisations such as UNICE which were keen to maintain firms' freedom of action and to stand up for their interests at interna-tional level, especially during the Kennedy Round talks. Industrial policy thus gradually charted a course between internal market pol-icy, competition policy and trade policy. As Fernand Braun put it, 'It made sense, and it was in everyone's interest.' [1]

[1] Interview with Fernand Braun, 8 December 2003.

The memorandum of 1970 and its consequences

The merger of the executive bodies and the ensuing reorganisation resulted in the creation of a Directorate-General for Industry. This was the logical consequence of the observation made by Commissioner Colonna di Paliano in March 1967, when he remarked, 'There is no specific responsibility for industrial policy' [1]. The set-up which he headed in 1968 was, to some extent, the culmination of the thinking that had gone on over the previous years.

The memorandum on Community industrial policy, which the Commission adopted on 18 March 1970, stemmed from earlier concerns but outlined some areas for priority action. On the one hand, the Commission move was in line with the logic of completing the single market. As Robert Toulemon wrote in the *Revue du Marché Commun* in September 1970, the stated aim was to 'place industry in the six countries in a coherent framework as close as possible to that of a national market' [2]. This completion of the single market thus involved the removal of barriers and divisions slowing down the integration of economic activities. The programme to harmonise regulations creating barriers to trade, especially in the case of standards, which the Council adopted in March 1969, was an initial part of the response, in spite of the foreseeable delays in its implementation. Another objective was the removal of barriers to the development of enterprises' strategies within the Community. The idea was to allow establishments to be set up and alliances and mergers to go ahead which hitherto had not been possible and which had justified the criticism some years earlier by Raymond Aron, and to introduce a European company statute, together with measures on taxation and the European financial market. But the aims went beyond establishing this simple framework, which was a prior but preliminary condition for the introduction of an industrial policy that was at last being viewed in a more positive light. Robert Toulemon noted that all these measures 'affected industry but did not come under what was generally understood as industrial policy' [3]. The thrust of the plan put forward by the Commission was presented to Jean Monnet by Robert Toulemon on 12 February 1970. The objective was to bring about the creation of multinational European enterprises, standardise public procurement and create technological development contracts, in order to thwart a trend which threatened Europe's technological independence and its future growth because these were industries where the 'market was currently developing most' [4].

The proposed policy took its inspiration from the policies followed until then by some countries at national level (as in France), the idea being to transfer them to the Community level by exploiting orders and public funding for research for the benefit of European enterprises. They would thus be encouraged to form groups with a view to reaching critical mass. And so the Commission was focusing its action where competition policy intersected with a more active policy. Competition policy was involved in the sense that there was a need to move away from particularly adverse practices in sectors where public procurement or orders from enterprises closely linked to the State represented the bulk of the market: major electrical installations, equipment for nuclear power stations, computers, telecommunications and aircraft. The aim of the Commission was not, as some people had thought, to 'limit competition but to establish it where it did not exist' [5]. Another aim was to move beyond the stage of intergovernmental cooperation, on which the Member States had until then focused their attention, with all the difficulties that this approach entailed in terms of financing, 'diplomatic'

---

[1] 'Problèmes de la politique industrielle', Communication by Mr Colonna di Paliano, SEC(67) 672, 27 February 1967 (Commission meeting of 2 March 1967).

[2] Toulemon, R., 'Des idées nouvelles en politique industrielle', *Revue du Marché Commun*, September 1970, pp. 385–393.

[3] Ibid.

[4] FJME, AMK C 33/6/112, Conversation with Robert Toulemon, Hotel Astoria, 12 February 1970.

[5] Toulemon, R., 'Des idées nouvelles [...]', op. cit.

Declaration of the Heads of State or Government at the end of the conference in Paris from 19 to 21 October 1972 (extract)

Industrial, scientific and technological policy

'7. The Heads of State or Government felt there was a need to try and provide a uniform foundation for industry throughout the Community.

This entails the removal of technical barriers to trade and elimination, especially in the field of taxation and law, of obstacles hindering alignment and concentration among undertakings, swift adoption of a statute for the European company, the progressive and effective opening up of public contracts, the promotion on the European scale of competitive undertakings in advanced technology, the adaptation and redevelopment, under socially acceptable conditions, of industrial branches in difficulty, the preparation of provisions to guarantee that concentrations affecting undertakings established in the Community are compatible with the Community socioeconomic goals and fair competition under the Treaty provisions both within the common market and on the outside markets.

Objectives should be defined and the development of a common scientific and technological policy ensured. This policy implies coordination of national policies within the Community institutions and the joint carrying out of action in the Community interest.

To this end, an action programme with a precise schedule backed by appropriate means should be drawn up by the Community institutions before 1 January 1974.

The environment

8. The Heads of State or Government stress the value of a Community environment policy. They are therefore requesting the Community institutions to draw up an action programme with a precise schedule before 31 July 1973.

Energy

9. The Heads of State or Government feel there is a need for the Community institutions to work out as soon as possible an energy policy which ensures a reliable and lasting supply on economically satisfactory terms.'

Bulletin of the EC, No 10, 1972, p. 19.

management of programmes and an emphasis on a 'fair return'. The suggestion in the memorandum was thus to combine the change of scale with the effect of integration by implementing industrial development contracts funded by Community resources in order to encourage the desired 'multinational groupings' of enterprises. A policy of this kind needed to be all-embracing in order to cover a wide range of sectors so that each Member State could be offered a satisfactory package of benefits and sacrifices. As the Commission memorandum put it, 'The balance of interests must be sought on the broadest possible basis' [1]. This policy also needed to take into consideration the responsibility of the Community bodies and of manufacturers. It also assumed that the objectives of such a programme would be considered when implementing competition policy. In this regard, the positions taken by the Member of the Commission with responsibility for competition, Emmanuel Sassen, offered a series of opportunities by recognising the need for Europe to catch up with the United States in a

---

[1] *La politique industrielle de la Communauté*, Memorandum from the Commission to the Council, COM(70) 100, 18 March 1970.

variety of areas and the need for greater concentration in some sectors in order to attain critical mass while avoiding any 'national flagship' or 'European monopoly' approach. What the Commission had to do was to give a clear indication of the types of cooperation which either were not outlawed by the Treaty provisions or could be exempted from any such prohibitions. It was also a matter of authorising support in conjunction with Community action programmes if the growth industries were not to be 'irretrievably left behind' [1].

The Commission memorandum was discussed by a group of senior officials who had been asked by the Council to consider the various points which it raised. In this way, the issue of a Community industrial policy was taken up again in the autumn of 1972. It was the subject of one of the chapters in the declaration published at the end of the Conference of Heads of State or Government in Paris from 19 to 21 October (see box p. 471).

The results of the conference fell short of the Commission's objectives. In the spring of 1971, in fact, the Commission had put to the Council a proposal for the creation of an Industrial Policy Committee, organised along the same lines as the Medium-Term Economic Policy Committee, with the task of promoting consultation among the Member States and between them and the Commission. The idea was to encourage consultation on the general outlines of industrial policy, national sectoral policies, structural problems, the opening of public contracts to technological development and technological cooperation with non-member countries [2]. The Commission's major objectives also included consultation among major purchasers of capital goods, often in the public sector, and consultation on standards, research and joint purchasing in sectors such as electricity, transport, telecommunications,

television, etc. The hope was also to see the conclusion of a series of decisions concerning taxation of mergers and to witness the introduction of legal instruments for joint projects or undertakings (joint undertaking status, European economic interest grouping) [3]. While the main objectives defined by the Commission could be found in the conclusions of the Paris Summit with regard to the opening up of markets, the introduction of a legal and tax framework conducive to the emergence of enterprises on a Community scale, the promotion of high-tech sectors and the conversion of industries in difficulty, the actual introduction of an industrial, scientific and technological policy was deferred pending an action programme to be decided by 1 January 1974, with no provision for any specific institutional mechanism for its implementation.

In actual fact, the discussions prompted by the publication of the 1970 memorandum confirmed the differences in basic approach among the Member States. When considered in conjunction with the priority accorded to the negotiations on accession, this explains how little response they met with [4]. While the Dutch were reluctant about any new development until the question of UK membership was settled, the French government was aware of the overall objectives pursued by the Commission and distanced itself from the Commission's stance on the implementation process to be adopted. Rather than an integrated policy at Community level, it preferred an approach involving sectoral actions by countries working together without any Commission involvement [5]. The French were therefore against the idea of the proposed Industrial Policy Committee, for which the Commission would have provided the secretariat. In the same way, the French government was reluctant to accept the idea of the Commission arranging consultations among purchasers in the public sector or the thought of losing any scope for manoeuvre in relations with

[1] HAEC, BDT 118/83 808, Speech by Emmanuel Sassen on industrial policy in the European Community, 12 December 1968.
[2] 'Industrial development, technical and scientific policy', *Bulletin of the EC*, No 6, 1971.
[3] FJME, AMK C 33/6/115, Note by Robert Toulemon, 14 March 1972.
[4] Toulemon, R., *L'Europe*, Desclée de Brouwer, Paris, 1992, p. 109.
[5] Toulemon, R., *Une politique industrielle pour l'Europe*, Presses universitaires de France, Paris, 1974, p. 103.

'Industry and Society in the European Community' conference in Venice from 20 to 22 April 1972.
From left to right: Luigi Ferro (Direzione Studi e Relazioni Culturali Fiat);
at the back, Marcello Pacini (Agnelli Foundation), and Cesare Sacchi; in the centre, Giovanni Agnelli (President of Fiat).
Identified by Elisabetta Rumerio and Alberta Simonis, Fiat Archives, Turin.

non-member countries on scientific or techno-logical matters (¹). At the other extreme, the German government tended to favour completing the internal market and removing barriers to business activities but showed little interest in the more positive measures which the Commission was pursuing in line — as Robert Toulemon put it — with the 'most traditional liberal ideas' (²). In a more general sense, in addition to the differing ideas about the process of integration and the role that common policies were supposed to play, there were other differences of analysis with regard to the attitude to be adopted on the issue of US investment in Europe. In actual fact,

each Member State was eager to strike a balance between the benefits and drawbacks which could affect it as the result of any Community action in these new fields. The Commission's approach relied on the Member States accepting a 'growing degree of mutual dependence in very sensitive policy fields' (³). Consequently, as Robert Toulemon was able to state in September 1970, the introduction of such a policy at Community level 'depended on a sense of realisation which had barely taken shape' (⁴). Overall, the lack of any legal basis constituted one of the major obstacles to introducing an industrial policy, the general lines of which had been progressively mapped out.

(¹) HAEU, EN 2452, *Indices d'une évolution négative des positions du gouvernement français dans le domaine de la politique industrielle, technologique et scientifique*, 2 November 1971.
(²) Toulemon, R., 'Des idées nouvelles […]', op. cit.

(³) Toulemon, R., *Une politique industrielle* […], op. cit., p. 112.
(⁴) Toulemon, R., 'Des idées nouvelles […]', op. cit.

467

The beginnings of environment policy according to Michel Carpentier

Commissioner Spinelli handed responsibility for the environment to Robert Toulemon, Director-General of Industrial Affairs in 1969. 'The idea was, from the outset, to incorporate in the ambitious objectives but also in the strictly economic aims of the EEC a new political dimension which was still fairly vague but which was encouraging because of its appeal to the general public and because of its integration effect. The aim was at the same time to reduce the adverse repercussions of economic development on the environment and natural resources and to provide a qualitative dimension to such development by improving the quality of life' ([1]). Robert Toulemon asked Michel Carpentier to take on the task and to become the head of the new Environmental Affairs Division. He agreed and threw himself into the task: 'Without being unduly modest, I can say that we had to start practically from scratch. The little we did have in legal and political terms — but with the help of a lot of enthusiasm, thinking, hard work and a bit of luck — helped us to establish the basis on which the environment policy gradually took shape.'

The first task for Michel Carpentier and his Division — 'a small group of people at the Commission, with lots of ideas for the Community, who made the most of the Treaty and who, in addition, rode the wind of change from outside to help them in their task' — was to define a method and an approach. 'The method consisted of devising an ambitious policy plan, of seeing to what extent the plan and its underlying philosophy could be squared with the philosophy of the objectives of the Treaty, of looking also to see how the plan could be started by using the legal resources of the Treaty, and then of drawing

up and submitting to the Member States and Parliament communications and initial proposals for an environment policy, to be used as a basis for getting a discussion going.'

As for the approach, the new division needed to cooperate and talk with various bodies. In this way, with the support of his Commissioner and his Director-General, Michel Carpentier established a dialogue with the authorities responsible for the environment in the Member States and in the four candidate countries. He was met with a 'deeply courteous welcome in every country, albeit with strong differences in the response to the idea of a new Community policy'. The Commission was supported by Parliament, which quickly became interested in environmental issues and 'stepped up its involvement through written and oral questions, opinions, comments and criticisms'. As for the Commission, opinions were divided: 'On the one hand, I recruited some extra staff from the Joint Research Centre at Ispra, people who were keen to find a new direction. On the other hand, we went through a period of "grey areas": the Commission, which was a regular victim of soul-searching over whether the work of some of its officials fitted in with the priority objectives of the Community, decided to persuade the Secretariat-General to conduct a survey on whether the work carried out in the fields of the environment and education was justified in relation to the objectives of the Treaty. Thanks to the good sense and understanding of my colleagues conducting the survey, I was found "not guilty" of straying off course!'

J.C.

Industry and growth objectives

Altiero Spinelli was appointed Member of the Commission with responsibility for industrial af-

fairs and research in June 1970 and immediately began to think in terms of extending the scope of the Commission's analysis and action in these areas. The Conference on Industry and Society in the European Community, which was held in Venice from 20 to 22 April 1972 at the instigation of the new member of the Commission, set out to

([1]) For all quotations: Carpentier, M., 'La naissance de la politique de l'environnement', *Revue des affaires européennes*, 1989, No 384, pp. 284–297.

Spinelli writes in his diary (*Diario europeo, II, 1970–1976*, Il Mulino, Bologna, 1991–92, p. 291):
'In Venice to inaugurate the Conference on Industry and Society with an address of which I had drafted the first and last sections, which were ideally formulated and offered a political perspective, and left it to Layton to write the middle section on the conference topics. The address went down really well. There were large numbers of industrialists and trade unionists. I think it was a great success. The Community's industrial policy will no longer bear the imprint of the "Colonna memorandum" but of the "Spinelli conference". Just as I intended. In particular, I had the support of all the European trade unions, even the CGIL, and only the CGT is still fighting "mock battles against a non-existing society".'

involve everyone in defining a Community industry policy with a broader perspective. On the one hand, Spinelli believed that a definition of industrial policy could not come only from the Commission, even if it was involved as part of its institutional dialogue with the Council. As he saw it, this needed discussion, agreement and a much broader political advocacy and should provide a link between what could be achieved with the instruments of the Treaty and the subsequent phase which would call for stronger political commitment. On the other hand, making it an integral part of society's concerns required the 'qualitative objectives of industrial development' to be taken into account.

In this latter regard, the sudden upsurge of concern about the environment and about the objectives of growth, which was fostered by the publications of the Club of Rome, prompted Spinelli and his colleagues, in the same way as Mansholt [1], to turn their attention to such data. This meant that the policy to be followed by the Commission needed not only to be geared to the industrial development of the Community but also to involve measures ensuring that this kind of development was part of the general development of society. The topics of the wide-ranging

[1] See Chapter 8, pp. 175–178 and box pp. 414–416.

discussion in Venice were thus inspired by the main ideas proposed by the Commission in the 1970 memorandum and at the same time by the social and regional aspects of industrial issues. Particular attention was given to questions such as the linkage of individual and collective needs and problems relating to the environment. The placing of European policy in its international context, the role of multinationals, cooperation with the United States or Japan and Europe's responsibilities with regard to the industrial development of the Third World were also among the topics listed for discussion [1]. Even the title of the publication which came out of the Venice Conference — *Pour un modèle européen de développement* (A European development model) — showed how the Commission had brought all these ideas into focus [2].

This approach led to a reaffirmation of the need for planning which placed industrial policy in the context of future economic and monetary union.

It was part of a broad view of development which brought together industry, research and technological development and also took heed of the environment. While the outline it proposed did not question the need for industrialisation and rapid growth, it wanted them to be better managed and better balanced and to be born of a greater democratic say in decisions through an expanded dialogue with the social and economic partners [3]. The conclusions of the Paris Summit of October 1972 to some extent reflected these new ideas when they referred to environment policy or the fact of involving the social partners in the 'economic and social decisions' of the Community. If the implementation of such a programme then seemed far in the future, the first hints of a Community environment policy which appeared at that time showed that there was justification for these new concerns.

ÉRIC BUSSIÈRE

[1] *Organisation de la conférence sur 'l'industrie et la société dans la Communauté européenne'*, Communication by Altiero Spinelli, SEC(71) 185, 15 January 1971.

[2] *Pour un modèle européen de développement, conférence 'Industrie et société dans la Communauté européenne'*, La librairie européenne SA, Brussels, 1972/Armand Colin, Paris, 1973.

[3] BAC 53/1987 275, Note de synthèse sur les travaux de la conférence 'Industrie et société dans la Communauté européenne'.

Chapter 24

Energy:
from synergies to merger

'Energy is the daily bread of our nations' [1] in the words of Fernand Spaak, Director-General of the Directorate-General for Energy from 1967 to 1975. A society without access to energy cannot function, survive or prosper because energy forms the basis of all industrial activity. Moreover, the development of the European economy is possible only thanks to a plentiful supply of low-cost energy.

Between 1957 and 1967 the Commission of the European Economic Community was responsible for producing proposals in the field of energy, although not for all forms of energy. From a legal and institutional point of view, there was no single common energy market: instead, there were several. The Euratom Commission produced proposals for the nuclear sector, the ECSC High Authority for the coal sector, and the EEC Commission for other energy sources such as oil and natural gas. In November 1960 Robert Marjolin summarised the situation in the following terms: 'The Treaties do not have the same content, the procedures are different and are over-seen by different authorities (the ECSC High Authority, the EEC Commission and the EAEC Commission). Nowhere in these Treaties is energy policy treated as a whole; no one is dealing with the relationship between the different forms of energy.' [2]

During this period, the energy economy of the six Member States of the Community was undergoing major change. Energy consumption was rising, but the increase in demand could not be met by Community coal production, particularly owing to its high price. A shift from coal to oil was taking place, facilitated by the fact that no one was overly concerned at the sharp increase in dependence on oil-producing countries. However, caution had not been abandoned altogether. Although no one was expecting a genuine shortage of oil, Europe sought to secure its energy supply. Armed with their past experiences, the European countries maintained strategic energy reserves. At the same time, nuclear energy research was continuing apace and the first nuclear power stations were coming on stream.

---

[1] FJME, AMK 128/3/12, 'Une stratégie européenne de l'énergie' conference given by Fernand Spaak on 6 June 1974 to the Société royale d'économie politique de Belgique, June 1974.

[2] FJME, ARM 26/6/55, 'Exposé sur la politique énergétique', presentation by Robert Marjolin to the ESC, 29 November 1960, pp. 1–2.

The Commission was also at this time encouraging research into new energy sources and innovative ways of using existing energy sources.

Following the merger of the executives, the Single Commission was entrusted with producing proposals for all energy sources. Likewise, the administrative structure of the European Executive was adapted accordingly. As a result, the Directorate-General for Energy was born, taking over the responsibilities of the Energy Economy Division and broadening its remit.

The Energy Economy Division

In 1958 the Directorate-General for Economic and Financial Affairs took over responsibility for energy matters, which were placed under the remit of the Energy Economy Division of the Structures and Economic Development Directorate.

At the time, the Director-General for Economic Affairs was Franco Bobba (1958–66), with Louis Duquesne de La Vinelle, the first Director of the Structures and Economic Development Directorate, reporting to him on energy matters. Duquesne de La Vinelle has been described as 'impeccable in every respect, showing true distinction of thought and conduct, for whom actions spoke louder than words. He [Duquesne de La Vinelle] was unselfish and did not particularly seek to obtain power, but would often clash with Bobba.' ([1]) His successors were three Frenchmen: Pierre Millet (1961), Alain Prate (1962–64) and Michel Albert (1965–66). The latter two, both high-ranking Treasury officials, evidently were interested above all in economic and financial affairs ([2]), as borne out by their subsequent careers.

Duquesne de La Vinelle himself stated that his approach to establishing a coordinated energy policy was to concentrate on problems that related to the structure of the industry, which he regarded

as the key to all other aspects of energy policy. It was necessary to make the various governments aware of the exact nature of the differences separating them, to point out to them the importance of reducing these differences and to make suggestions to them in this respect. For each country, this meant seeking a balance between the benefits they could obtain and the concessions required of them. Ideally, negotiations would be carried out among the real decision-makers on energy policy: if this could not be achieved, it would be very difficult to prevent the various sides from focusing on certain points of principle ([3]), which they had no power to influence. Clearly, it was not the intention of the EEC Commission to work in isolation on this matter.

Louis Duquesne de La Vinelle chose Georges Brondel as head of the Energy Economy Division. The two men had met when Duquesne de La Vinelle represented Belgium at the OEEC, where Brondel was the Secretary. Brondel recalled that one day he received a telephone call from Professor Duquesne de La Vinelle, who told him that he was working at the Commission as director in charge of finances in the Directorate-General for Economic and Financial Affairs, which also had responsibility for energy matters. Duquesne asked Brondel if he would be prepared to take charge of the energy division. Brondel accepted the job on the spot and immediately headed for Brussels to take up the post ([4]). Brondel was head of division from 1958. He continued at the Directorate-General for Energy in 1967, devoting the rest of his career to working in this field.

In addition to the splintering of responsibilities relating to energy across the different Communities, there were also areas of overlap in energy matters between the different directorates-general of the Commission, particularly between the Competition DG and the Internal Market DG. In a report on the organisation of the Commission

---

([1]) Interview with Paul Romus, 20 January 2004.
([2]) Interview with Georges Brondel, 25 February 2004.

([3]) BAC 156/90 2053, Louis Duquesne de La Vinelle, 'Les éléments d'une politique coordonnée de l'énergie dans la CEE', 16 June 1959, p. 7.
([4]) Interview with Georges Brondel, 25 February 2004.

	Officials responsible for energy matters in DG II (Economic and Financial Affairs)		
	Director-General	Director of the Structures and Economic Development Directorate	Head of the Energy Economy Division
1958			
1959		Louis Duquesne de La Vinelle	
1960			
1961		Pierre Millet	
1962	Franco Bobba		Georges Brondel
1963		Alain Prate	
1964			
1965		Michel Albert	
1966			

departments, François-Xavier Ortoli noted that: 'The Energy Economy Division is taking shape after a difficult beginning, but it appears to run the risk of becoming more a division that coordinates the positions in the energy sector of several directorates-general than a division working at the forefront of policy development.' The rapporteur wanted to see the Energy Economy Division take the lead in its field. Consequently, any issues relating to oil, coal, gas, etc. that emerged were to be examined with the participation of the division in order to be incorporated into the overall energy policy that the Commission wanted to promote. He finished by stating that his earlier comments should not disguise the fact that the existence of an Energy Economy Division was currently justified only by the distribution of tasks among the different executives and that, once a merger of the executives became possible, it would make sense to set up a Directorate-General for Energy [1]. The implications of

these findings would only gradually be taken into account.

The Commissioner

The Commissioner responsible for energy matters was Robert Marjolin. 'No one quarrelled with this assignment since things seemed so quiet in that domain' [2], he remarked. Energy matters interested him. 'Already at the time of the Marshall Plan and European reconstruction, Europe's energy supplies and the cost of imported oil were among my major concerns.' [3] As the future showed, energy would continue to interest Robert Marjolin: after leaving the Commission, he joined the board of directors at Royal Dutch Shell.

The role of the Commission in the energy sector, as defined by the French Commissioner, was to contribute to the development of an energy policy that would be regarded by all the Member

---

[1] HAEU, FMM 3, 'Rapport sur l'organisation des services de la Commission de la Communauté Économique Européenne', 1961. This report is also known as the Ortoli Report. The report was drawn up by the Rationalisation Committee, made up of Franco Bobba, Pieter VerLoren van Themaat and François-Xavier Ortoli.

[2] Marjolin, R., Architect of European unity — Memoirs 1911–1986, Weidenfeld and Nicolson, London, 1986, p. 395.

[3] Ibid., p. 394.

States as the most favourable for the Community in the long term. In so doing, the Commission would need to keep in mind constantly that the proposals it was producing did not concern one isolated sector of the economy but were part of an overall economic policy in which it could one day come to play a key role ([1]). Consequently, in order to ensure the unity of the common market for energy, it was vital to adopt an approach that was as comprehensive as possible, to establish a common trade policy and to harmonise the tax burden and competition rules ([2]). The main objective of the policy was to supply energy to industry, and to economic activity in general, at the lowest possible price compatible with security of supply ([3]). These were happy times when the Commission was able to regard the fall in energy prices as a favourable factor contributing to more rapid development of the EEC.

In its early years, the Commission took part in the Inter-Executive Group for Energy with the ECSC and Euratom and developed measures intended to establish a common market for hydrocarbons.

Coordination with the other executives: the Inter-Executive Group for Energy

The Inter-Executive Group for Energy (1959–66) was a permanent working group responsible for presenting to the Special Council of Ministers of the ECSC 'general guidelines on energy policy, proposals for implementing the policy, and the wording of the specific measures relating to the implementation of the common energy policy ([4]).

The working group comprised representatives of the executives, accompanied by officials. Robert Marjolin and Hans von der Groeben represented the EEC. From 21 February 1959 they were accompanied by a third member, Giuseppe Caron. Their ECSC counterparts were Pierre-Olivier Lapie, Albert Coppé and Fritz Hellwig, while Paul De Groote and Emmanuel Sassen represented Euratom.

The activities of the Inter-Executive Group were marked by frequent disagreement between the representatives of the ECSC High Authority and the representatives of the EEC Commission, with the representatives of Euratom regularly siding with the EEC. Daniel Cardon de Lichtbuer took part in the meetings of the group, first as an official of the EEC Commission and then after 1960 as an official of the High Authority, having been appointed as Albert Coppé's *chef de cabinet*. He recalled how 'everyone tended to argue on behalf of the product they represented. But, overall, the ECSC was on the defensive and the European Commission on the offensive. The Commission was arguing for the opening up of the energy market, for cheap oil and for cheap energy in general'. Relations between Lapie and Marjolin have been described by some as excellent ([5]) and by others as difficult. Gérard Olivier, at the time legal adviser to the ECSC High Authority, recalled that relations between Lapie and Marjolin were not particularly friendly and that they did not particularly have confidence in one another but that they managed to work together ([6]).

The group started by bringing together the documents that would make it possible to establish basic statistics and forecasts. It was certainly necessary to undertake analyses making sure, above all, that the same methods were used despite the different countries and different energy sources ([7]). The work yielded two types of document for publication: the annual forward estimates and the long-term energy outlooks for 1970–75.

([1]) HAEC, Speech given by Robert Marjolin at the Institute of Energy of the University of Cologne, 14 June 1962.

([2]) CEAB 13 303, Summary report of the meeting of 22 November of the Working Group of the Inter-Executive Group for Energy, Strasbourg, 24 November 1960, p. 4.

([3]) Presentation by Robert Marjolin to the Economic and Social Committee (plenary session of 29 and 30 November 1960), quoted in *Europe Documents*, 20 December 1960, pp. 1–2.

([4]) BAC 118/1986 2455, Groupe interexécutif 'Énergie', création et but.

([5]) Wilson, J., *La politique pétrolière et énergétique dans l'Europe des Six (1957–1966) — Entre économie et politique: les tergiversations d'une autruche à six têtes — Étude à travers les archives de la Communauté européenne*, dissertation, UCL, Louvain-la-Neuve, 1997, p. 159.

([6]) Interview with Gérard Olivier, 4 December 2003.

([7]) CEAB 2 3759, Pierre-Olivier Lapie, 'Les institutions européennes et les problèmes énergétiques de l'Europe', communication delivered at the 13th study days of the Economic Institute of Energy of the University of Cologne, 25 and 26 March 1965, p. 5.

Working together

'The mere fact that we said "The three have to work together in the area of energy policy" helped pave the way for the merger.'

Interview with Fritz Hellwig, 3 June 2004.

A difficult coordination

Hallstein, President of the first Commission, also refers to the difficulties in coordinating policies between the three executives in his memoirs:

'In fairness, however, it must be pointed out that efforts to form three separate energy policies into one were bound to lead to futility until the three administrations of the three Communities were merged. [...] On the whole, it was inevitable that the institutions of the three Communities should, despite all efforts to coordinate their approach to matters of energy, think in terms not of a common overall policy for power but in terms of the coal industry, of oil or of nuclear energy.'

Hallstein, W., *Europe in the making*, Allen & Unwin, London, 1972, p. 221.

During group meetings, problems linked to the competition between coal and oil were regularly raised. Marjolin wanted the subject to be examined because 'the fundamental problem is the competition between coal and the new forms of energy (oil and natural gas)'. For Marjolin it was better to concentrate on what he saw as 'the essentials' rather than studying a whole series of issues that he regarded as being of secondary importance, such as the conditions for competition or cyclical instability [1]. Faced with the threat to European coal production, some wanted oil to be subject to the same competition rules as coal. However, the Treaties provided for different rules for coal and oil. As von der Groeben noted, in order to introduce identical sets of rules, one would need an identical market, which was not the case [2]. The two products were in different situations, and so Marjolin reflected that, if one could theoretically remove coal from the equation, it was very likely that the EEC would move towards a free market without any protection, with the exception of imports from eastern Europe, for which some precautions would have to be taken. Even if a degree of control were to be imposed on the market to avoid excessively sharp price fluctuations and duplication of investments, the overriding aim would clearly be to achieve the lowest possible prices in the long term [3]. The difficulty lay in the fact that the coal market and the decline of the European coal industry could not be ignored.

A number of documents were drawn up and presented to the Council of Ministers. Having received its terms of reference from the Council of Ministers, the Inter-Executive Group adopted on 25 June 1962 its memorandum on energy policy, presenting the prospects for the energy market and proposals to achieve the gradual opening up of the energy market by 1970. However, in the interim, the memorandum remained in limbo as the Member States felt it was necessary to await the merger of the Communities before deciding on the key choices that would lay the foundations for a common energy policy. Marjolin did not share this point of view as it gave governments the opportunity to do nothing until the merger took place. Worse still, it was likely to encourage them to delay the merger [4].

---

[1] CEAB 13 303, Draft minutes for the meeting of 27 July 1959 of the Inter-Executive Working Group for Energy, 26 July 1959 [*sic*].

[2] CEAB 9 624, Minutes for the meeting of 27 April 1959 of the Working Group for Energy Policy, 4 May 1959.

[3] BAC 25/1975 334, Minutes for the meeting of 9 May 1961 of the Inter-Executive Group for Energy, 27 June 1961.

[4] CEAB 2 2793, Minutes of the 37th meeting of the Inter-Executive Working Group for Energy, held on 5 February 1964, pp. 2–3. For Hellwig, however, 'It is logical to link the date of the merger of the Communities with the intended date for implementation of a common energy policy. Regarding the linking of the two as an obstacle to achieving the merger indicates a certain degree of pessimism.' Ibid., p. 6.

Finally accepted by the Council in April 1964 in the form of a memorandum of understanding (^{1}), the memorandum established the objectives of the energy policy: cheap and secure energy supplies, gradual substitution, stability in energy supply in terms of both cost and available quantities, free choice for the consumer, fair competition on the common market between the different sources of energy, and a general economic policy.

The merger of the executives heralded the end of the Inter-Executive Group, depriving it of its *raison d'être*. From then on, the Single Commission would oversee coordination of the former competences in the energy sector.

Oil's growing dominance

The European Commission did not wait for the energy crisis of 1973 to start tackling issues relating to oil. From the beginning, it was understood that oil was extremely important. The closure of coal mines was to begin, and competition from imported coal was fierce. However, competition from oil imports was even greater: prices were relatively low, and everything was falling into place. Natural gas was being discovered on the territory of the European Community, at Lacq in France and in the Po valley in Italy. In fact, all manner of things were being discovered and, a few years later, it would also be discovered that the era of coal was over (^{2}).

Faced with these developments in the energy market, the reactions of the governments differed, as far as both external trade policy and domestic taxes or measures with equivalent effect were concerned (^{3}). The Commission thus attempted to organise the market for crude oil and its derivatives on a European scale and to apply certain rules,

Pierre-Olivier Lapie on the Inter-Executive Group for Energy

Pierre-Olivier Lapie, Chairman of the Inter-Executive Group for Energy from October 1959, explained how the group worked:

'In 1960 we knew little about the real energy problems facing the Community as a whole. The institutions in Brussels had only just come into existence, although the ECSC, which was older, had sufficient instruments to monitor the coal market. The first and crucial stage consisted in assembling the precise documentation and agreeing on a consistent working method. There were also a good deal of general and philosophical reflections on oil replacing coal as an energy source. However, in this new and dynamic field, there was little concrete analysis. Global estimates of energy consumption were not enough: we also needed to identify the mechanisms for sharing out energy requirements among the different competing energy sources. Moreover, we could no longer restrict ourselves simply to an inventory of what existed; in order to develop a policy, we also needed to work with future projections. For example, it's one thing to vaguely observe that ships no longer run on steam and locomotives increasingly less so, another to calculate precisely the energy costs for maritime and rail transport, and yet another to transpose the figures to cover the period 1970–75. The three Communities had numerous problems to resolve: producing equivalent statistics and calculation methods, resolving terminology issues; to complete these tasks, they needed to collaborate with national civil services who were prepared for such tasks to varying degrees and to overcome the fears of some in industrial circles.'

Lapie, P.-O., 'La politique énergétique européenne — Ses étapes, ses difficultés', *Revue du Marché Commun,* No 100, 3/1967, pp. 135–136. (Translated from the French)

(^{1}) Memorandum of understanding on energy matters entered into by the governments of the Member States of the European Communities on the occasion of the 94th session of the Special Council of Ministers of the European Coal and Steel Community, held on 21 April 1964 in Luxembourg.

(^{2}) Interview with Daniel Cardon de Lichtbuer, 12 November 2003.

(^{3}) EEC, Commission, *Third General Report on the Activities of the Community (21 March 1959 to 15 May 1960),* May 1960, p. 159.

Sondage BERGA N° 1 (SAHARA)

After 10 years of geological surveys in the Sahara, France discovered oil deposits in 1956. The French Minister for Industry, Jean-Marcel Jeanneney, proposed that the six Member States take special measures to promote the sale of crude oil of Community origin by giving it the benefit of Community preference. Crude oil refined in the Community from crude oil originating in the Member States would be tax free. The proposal was rejected.

with the aim of producing a genuine common market for petroleum products. In 1961 it noted that this aim was far from being achieved. Trade between the Member States still involved only small quantities and there were disparities in prices between the different markets, which had even been widening during the previous few years [1]. Six months later, a more optimistic Marjolin declared that 'a whole series of events suggest that 1962 will be a decisive year for European energy policy. Public opinion has been made aware of the success achieved by the EEC in agriculture and we should take advantage of this psychological factor. The common market is increasingly taking shape and the establishment of a common market for petroleum products is imminent'. [2]

[1] EEC, Commission, *Fourth General Report on the Activities of the Community (16 May 1960 to 30 April 1961)*, July 1961, p. 121.

[2] CEAB 2 2323, Minutes of the meeting of 22 and 23 January 1962 of the Inter-Executive Group for Energy, 12 February 1962.

Key dates in the implementation of an energy policy

25 May 1959:	Establishment of the Inter-Executive Group for Energy.
21 September 1960:	Robert Marjolin and Hans von der Groeben present a draft memorandum to the Commission on coordinating the different energy policies.
22 December 1960:	The Inter-Executive Group adopts an emergency programme.
6 January 1961:	Robert Marjolin and Hans von der Groeben present to the Commission a draft set of measures for coordination of the energy policies, adopted by the Inter-Executive Group on 22 December 1960.
5 April 1962:	Informal meeting of the Council of Ministers in Rome, granting a mandate to the Inter-Executive Group to develop proposals for a common energy policy within three months.
25 June 1962:	Adoption by the Inter-Executive Group of the memorandum on the common energy policy.
21 April 1964:	Memorandum of understanding on energy matters adopted by the Member States at the Council.
16 February 1966:	The Commission sends the Council a note on the Community's policy on oil and natural gas.
3 December 1968:	Wilhelm Haferkamp presents to the Commission a communication on the initial guidelines for a common energy policy, submitted to the Council on 18 December.
17 December 1969:	The Commission adopts a proposal for a Council regulation on the communication to the Commission on programmes for the import of hydrocarbons, and another on the communication on investment projects of Community interest in the oil, natural gas and electricity sectors, presented to the Council on 22 December 1969.
22 July 1971:	The Commission adopts a communication to the Council on the implementation of an initial guideline for a common energy policy.
4 October 1972:	The Commission examines a number of documents to be presented to the Council. They relate to the progress necessary for the common energy policy; the problems of and approach to energy policy for the period 1975–85; a new system of Community aid for coking coal and coke for the iron and steel industry in the Community; establishing a uniform system for imports of hydrocarbons from third countries (cross-border oil and gas pipelines); measures intended to attenuate the effects of problems in the supply of hydrocarbons.

Starting in March 1959, meetings were organised between the Commission and national petroleum experts on fixing common external tariffs applicable to petroleum products from List G (petroleum oil, petroleum gas, etc.). From April 1960, meetings were held, under the chairmanship of Marjolin, in the form of a permanent working group made up of high-ranking national officials responsible for oil and natural gas matters and representatives of the three executives (EEC Commission, Euratom Commission and ECSC High Authority). The aim of the working group was to study oil-related problems in the Community and to propose common solutions. The Commission produced studies in collaboration with these experts on matters such as imports of oil and petroleum products from third countries, particularly from the East, and on investment in the petroleum industry.

Marjolin reportedly considered oil to be a political or geopolitical matter rather than economic because it affected international politics and was in this respect an absolutely fundamental issue [1]. Worried by Europe's growing dependence on Middle Eastern oil, the Commissioner wanted to meet with the oil companies and embarked on a tour of them. The response was on the whole favourable: 'In the space of two months, we went first to London, where we met with the chairmen of Shell and BP, spending an entire day with them. Next we travelled to the United States, where we visited Esso, Mobiloil, Gulf, Chevron and Texaco. In other words, we covered all of the seven sisters.' [2] In addition to these visits to the heads of the leading American and European oil companies, Marjolin also organised a meeting in Brussels with the representatives of the companies. 'This initiative caused some fuss in an industry which was shrouded in mystery and whose American members lived in constant fear of stringent antitrust legislation. But such was the prestige of the European Economic Community at the time that the people I had invited agreed without demur to come to Brussels. I seem to remember that nothing specific came out of that meeting, since there was no serious problem then and no one seemed to have any presentiment of all the trouble to come a few years later.' [3]

The Commission and its officials also had to deal with other oil-related issues, including oil in the Sahara, the Netherlands' request to establish the Association of the Netherlands Antilles, France's

A great opportunity for the common energy policy

'The common energy policy will be the major issue in the merger of the Communities, while the merger of the Communities will be the great opportunity for the common energy policy.'

CEAB 2 3759, Pierre-Olivier Lapie, 'Les institutions européennes et les problèmes énergétiques de l'Europe', Declaration made during the 13th study days of the Economic Institute of the University of Cologne, 25 and 26 March 1965, p. 22. (Translated from the French)

special arrangements relating to the oil sector, and the external oil tariff.

Against this backdrop, in February 1966 the Commission issued a memorandum on oil and natural gas policy. The document covered oil-related issues independently of the common energy policy [4] and, as a result, did not deal with the question of the price of petroleum products. In July 1967 the Council approved the guidelines that were to form the basis of Community policy in this field once the new Directorate-General for Energy had come into existence.

The Directorate-General for Energy

The Directorate-General for Energy, DG XVII, was to be 'the Commission's instrument in a sector in which it was expected to take priority action to develop and implement a common energy policy' [5]. It was active in all matters that related directly or indirectly to this aim. In the first instance it could be asked to prepare a proposal for the Commission whereas, in the second, it would

---

[1] Interview with Georges Brondel, 25 February 2004.
[2] Ibid.
[3] Marjolin, R., op. cit., p. 396.

[4] CEAB 9 2237, Declaration made by Robert Marjolin during the meeting of 20 January 1965 of the Inter-Executive Group for Energy in Strasbourg, p. 1.
[5] HAEC, BDT 144-92 643, 'Rapport du secrétaire général de la Haute Autorité et des secrétaires exécutifs des Commissions de la CEE et de l'Euratom sur l'organisation des services de la Commission des Communautés européennes', SEC(67) 3001, 1 July 1967, p. 108.

issue an opinion or provide comments on a proposal dealing with energy matters, even if it was not the main subject of the proposal. Consequently, the Directorate-General for Energy was frequently and regularly called upon.

The Directorate-General for Energy was organised along classic Commission lines. It was divided into horizontal generalist directorates and into vertical directorates dealing with a specific energy source. Among the horizontal directorates, there was a division reporting to the Director-General and an Energy Economy Directorate. The three vertical directorates were responsible for coal, oil and nuclear power respectively as well as other primary sources and electricity. The Euratom Safeguards Directorate was set up in 1971.

Fernand Spaak, the son of Paul-Henri Spaak, was Director-General of the Energy DG from 1967 to 1975. A Belgian, he worked first for the Belgian National Bank (1950–52) and then for the ECSC High Authority together with Jean Monnet and René Mayer, before becoming Director-General of the Euratom Supply Agency in 1960. This meant that he had experience of working at two of the three European executives. Fernand Spaak was described as a man of considerable elegance and charm who was a very able politician because of his diplomatic manner. He was very popular with his colleagues [1]. At the Energy DG, he was assisted initially by Marcello Buzzonetti and then from 1970 by Philippe Loir, both of whom came from the Euratom Commission.

The new directorate-general brought together coal experts from the ECSC High Authority, nuclear sector specialists from the Euratom Commission and EEC Commission officials who were specialists in other energy sources. Some of these officials had already worked together in the Inter-Executive Group for Energy. Officials from the Other Energy Sources Directorate of the ECSC were not limited to working on issues relating to coal. Lucio Corradini, the former head of this

directorate, became the head of the Energy Economy Directorate. Herbert Mirschinka, who had been the head of the Electricity and Manufactured Gas Division of the High Authority, became Director of the Electricity Division.

The Commissioner placed in charge of energy in 1967 was Wilhelm Haferkamp (1967–72). He was also in charge of Euratom's Supply and Safeguards Agency. He did not have any experience of the energy sector and is reported to have found his brief difficult but of great importance and, by some accounts, he even found the job enjoyable [2]. He hoped that ending the compartmentalisation of responsibilities for the energy sector would give fresh impetus to the development of an energy policy. He knew that the task would not be easy: 'The existence of three European Commissions, each with certain responsibilities in the energy field was certainly an obstacle to the establishment of a common energy policy, despite serious efforts to ensure effective and close cooperation. We must however realise that, even after the removal of this obstacle, establishing a European energy policy remains a very difficult task.' [3]

Haferkamp defined the task given to the Energy DG thus: it 'consists in defining in definite terms the Community interest in relation to energy policy and applying the appropriate means of promoting this interest. We are well aware that identifying the Community interest in the medium and long term will not be an easy task. We face major differences of opinion and conflicting interests in this field, although this is not peculiar to energy. Still, in the past, national governments have formulated energy economy policies to very different degrees. We must not, however, allow ourselves to be discouraged by this state of affairs or by the fact that at present we still have to apply three Treaties that are not based on a uniform approach to energy'. [4]

[1] Interview with Serge Orlowski, 29 November 2004.

[2] Interview with Franz Froschmaier, 19 January 2004.
[3] Introductory note on energy policy, presented by Wilhelm Haferkamp, SEC(68) 1570, 3 May 1968, p. 1.
[4] Ibid.

Organisation chart of the Directorate-General for Energy

	1968	1969	1970	1971	1972
Director-General for Energy	Fernand Spaak (E-ECSC)				
Assistant	Marcello Buzzonetti (E)		Philippe Loir (E)		
Division attached to the Director-General: Energy Policy	Georges Brondel (EEC)			Jean Leclercq (E)	Jean Leclercq (E) + Giorgio Longo (E)
Energy Economy Directorate	Lucio Corradini (ECSC)				
			Michel Teitgen (ECSC)		Michel Teitgen (ECSC)
			Gerrit van Duijn (EEC)		Robert De Bauw (EEC)
Coal Directorate	Oskar Schumm (ECSC)			Karlheinz Reichert (ECSC)	
	Casper Berding (ECSC) Gustav Wonnerth (ECSC) Louis Calibre (ECSC) Siegfried von Ludwig (ECSC) François Long			Casper Berding (ECSC) Louis Calibre (ECSC) Siegfried von Ludwig (ECSC) François Long	
Hydrocarbons Directorate	Jacques Hartmann (ECSC)			Georges Brondel (EEC)	
	Berthold Daniels (ECSC)			Piero Davanzo Berthold Daniels (ECSC) Gerhard Wedekind	
Directorate for Nuclear Energy, Other Primary Sources, Electricity	Abraham De Boer (E)				
	Jean Leclercq (E) Gabriele Genuardi (E) Herbert Mirschinka (E)		Jean Leclercq (E) Gabriele Genuardi (E)	Jean-Claude Charrault (E) Gabriele Genuardi (E) Hans Eliasmöller (EEC)	
Euratom Safeguards Directorate				Enrico Jacchia (E)	
				Ugo Miranda (E) Pierre Bommelle (E)	Ugo Miranda (E) Pierre Bommelle (E) Manfred Schmitt

NB: The institutions mentioned are the original institutions.

E = Euratom

Haferkamp worked closely with Fernand Spaak ([1]). The Commissioner underlined the importance of close collaboration with the leading officials of the Member States' governments, both in developing Commission proposals and in applying the principles of a common energy policy ([2]). He also supported positive forms of business cooperation, as well as cooperation between the Commission, national governments, producers and energy consumers. Increased internal cooperation should not however lead the Commission to turn in on itself. Internal cooperation also needed to be complemented by cooperation with partners in third countries ([3]). With this aim in mind, he established contacts with the United States, which he visited in the spring of 1969. The meetings he held in Washington and New York focused on issues of cooperation in energy policy between the European Community and the United States, on coal, oil and natural gas policies, and on issues relating to the development of nuclear energy, the Community's fissile materials supply problems, safety controls in the Community and the Verification Agreement with the International Atomic Energy Agency ([4]).

An initial guideline

In December 1968 the Commission presented the Council with a document entitled 'Initial guideline for a common energy policy'. Commissioner Haferkamp aimed from the beginning, when drawing up the document, to define the basic principles of a common energy policy. Since the end of the war, he had been the head of a trade union in Germany and was well prepared for negotiations with industry. Over the course of several months, he met with his staff at

DG XVII ([5]) to present a homogenous set of measures ([6]).

In the initial guideline, the Commission stated that, unlike for the products of other industrial sectors and agricultural products, there continued to be serious obstacles to the trade in energy products within the Community. If the situation remained unchanged and a common energy market were not achieved in the near future, the level of integration achieved up to that point would be endangered. Only a Community policy that fully integrated the energy sector into the common market could prevent such a dangerous development ([7]). The Commission made use of its power of initiative to bring about a change in the situation.

The text was presented as 'an outline of policy action fixing the general aims and the instruments by which a Community policy can be established' ([8]). The initial guideline also made provision for measures establishing a common market and a supply policy. It was also important that interests of the consumer be placed at the heart of the policy, which sought to achieve security of supply and prices that were relatively stable and as low as possible. For the Commission, competition 'must play the leading role'; it also needed to be 'vigorous, effective and fair. Instruments must be created that provide improved supervision of supply flows and prevent interruptions in supply. The most important instrument is supervision, while intervention should be regarded as a last resort'. ([9])

Commission officials presented the initial guideline to different interest groups and the other European institutions. In the words of one official: 'the most constructive conclusion that can be drawn from ex-

---

([1]) Interview with Franz Froschmaier, 19 January 2004.

([2]) *Constitution d'un groupe énergie composé de fonctionnaires dirigeants des États membres (Communication de M. Haferkamp)*, SEC(68) 1573, 3 May 1968.

([3]) Introductory note on energy policy, presented by Wilhelm Haferkamp, SEC(68) 1570, 3 May 1968, p. 6.

([4]) PV 82, EC Commission, 1969, XV.3, p. 22; *Bulletin of the EC*, No 8, 1969, p. 58.

([5]) The Directorate-General for Energy.

([6]) Brondel, G., *L'Europe a 50 ans — Chronique d'une histoire vécue — Politique énergétique — Perspectives pour demain*, M&G Éditions, Bourg-en-Bresse, 2003, pp. 53–54.

([7]) *Première orientation pour une politique énergétique communautaire (Communication de la Commission au Conseil)*, COM(68) 1040, 18 December 1968, p. 2.

([8]) *Bulletin of the EC*, No 2, 1969, pp. 60–61.

([9]) BAC 156/1990 2134 Sigrist, Note for the attention of the members of the Commission, Subject: 59th session of the Council of 17 and 18 January 1969, 28 [29] January 1969, p. 2.

Working method in the 'little' Europe of Six, Georges Brondel

'As an official, I would contact [the Member States] any time there was a problem to be resolved. I would visit each of the capitals in turn, by which I mean I went to see those in charge of energy matters in each of the Member States. I reached the point where I could do the trip in three days. I would go first to Luxembourg, and from there I would go to Bonn. From Bonn I would fly to Rome. I would return from Rome via Rotterdam and Paris. For each proposal I produced, I would go to all the capitals to gauge their reactions before drafting the document for the Council. That meant that when the paper was finally submitted to the Council, it had every chance of being accepted. Afterwards, when there were nine, 12 and then 15 Member States, this approach was no longer possible. One could no longer contemplate visiting all the capitals and the atmosphere had changed.'

Interview with Georges Brondel, 25 February 2004.

amining the response to the initial guideline is that it is now time to move beyond declarations of intent and commit ourselves to proposals which, given the differing interests and conceptions, could constitute a viable and effective solution.' [1]

Starting from 1969, after the Council gave its approval to the principles, the Commission studied the document and attempted to implement it. The Council called on the Commission to submit concrete proposals. Haferkamp declared that he could not have hoped for a better outcome [2] and would work together with his team towards achieving this goal [3].

----

[1] BAC 38/1986 1011, Note for the attention of the Director-General, Analysis of the different positions on the 'Initial guideline for a common energy policy', 10 November 1969.

[2] HAEU, EN 1387, Emile Noël's notebook, Handwritten notes taken during the meeting of the Commission of 19 November 1969.

[3] Also *La mise en œuvre de la 'Première orientation pour une politique énergétique communautaire'* (Communication de la Commission au Conseil), COM(71) 810, 30 July 1971; *Les problèmes et les moyens de la politique de l'énergie pour la période 1975–1985* (Communication de la Commission au Conseil), COM(72) 1201, 4 October 1972; *Progrès nécessaires de la politique énergétique communautaire* (Communication de la Commission au Conseil), COM(72) 1200, 4 October 1972 (see box overleaf).

A report judged harshly

Fernand Spaak presented the initial guideline to the Economic and Social Committee. A handwritten note was discovered in the archives, written by one of the audience who is quite critical of the report:

'Spaak report on energy policy

An amateur's overview

A vague description of the situation in the various energy sectors (the promising future of nuclear energy, our good fortune in having underground natural gas, coal in decline, the advantages of oil […]

And the Commission's "political guidelines"? A series of banalities an economics student wouldn't dare come out with:

— competition, "an essential component of energy policy"!!!

— intervention when necessary,

— coordination,

— establishing general targets or indicative programmes […],

— not forgetting social aspects,

— integrating everything into "trade policy mechanisms",

— oh, and also "we need an action framework that will incorporate all the behaviour [sic] of businesses, of governments and of the Community itself",

— and 'regional policy' of course.

The question is: what are we going to do?'

BAC 177/1995 296, annex to summary report of the fourth meeting of the section specialised in energy matters, held in Brussels, 6 February 1969, Presentation by Mr Spaak, 5 March 1969. (Translated from the French)

Environmental protection and energy conservation

In a document entitled 'Progress necessary on the common energy policy' (¹), the Commission reported on various developments that were causing major concern and which required energy policy measures (²). These included environmental protection and energy conservation.

As regards environmental protection, the problems were of an immediate nature and remain an issue today. The main problems were: pollution of the atmosphere by sulphur compounds and vehicle exhausts, rising temperatures in some rivers and lakes due to the discharge of water used for cooling in power stations, the safety of nuclear installations and the storage of radioactive waste (³).

The foreseeable rise in energy costs, supply problems and concerns about protecting the environment all led to the promotion of energy conservation. The Commission highlighted certain areas for which it judged it necessary to take action by all appropriate means and as soon as possible. The areas in question were as follows:

— 'recovery of residual heat resulting from heat conversion in district heating installations;

— the early replacement of old, low-performance heating systems;

— better insulation of industrial furnaces;

— heat insulation for buildings and private houses;

— achieving a reduction in vehicle fuel consumption by means of the appropriate technology.' (⁴)

This initial guideline did not have as great an impact as had been hoped for. In this context, legal adviser Bastiaan van der Esch wrote in 1972 to the Director-General for Energy, stating that 'four years ago, the approach laid out in the initial guideline seemed justified, given that the aim at the time was to improve awareness and to look for a common basis for future action. However, during the talks on the initial guideline, a number of Member States would support only a report by the permanent representatives to the Council commenting on the initial guideline, with the proviso that they would keep their options open with regard to possible formal Commission proposals. As a result, the discussions on the initial guideline did not pave the way for a political consensus that could be used in support of specific formal initiatives from the Commission. Subsequent experience has shown that the decision-making process launched by the initial guideline has, in fact, para-lysed the Commission's power of initiative, without making it any easier to achieve a successful outcome for the few specific formal proposals submitted to the Council. This is borne out by the slowness in obtaining the Council's approval for the two regulations on providing information concerning investments and imports'. (⁵)

Problems with oil and uncertainty over energy

As has been seen, the initial guideline was slow to translate into concrete proposals. Even so, the effects of the Six Day War and the closure of the Suez Canal in 1967, which led to a sharp increase in crude oil prices, did not pass unnoticed. The Commission was preoccupied by Europe's energy dependence. In 1971 President Malfatti stated that 'this year, given the situation regarding supply in

---

(¹) *Progrès nécessaires de la politique énergétique communautaire* (Commission communication to the Council), COM(72) 1200, 4 October 1972.
(²) Ibid., p. 9.
(³) Ibid., p. 10.

(⁴) Ibid., p. 11.
(⁵) BAC 156/1990 2139, Esch B. (van der), Note for Mr Spaak, Subject: your notes: (a) Problems and methods relating to energy policy and (b) New proposals for a common energy policy, 14 September 1972, pp. 3–4.

Press conference by Altiero Spinelli to explain the general principles of the reorganisation of Euratom, Brussels, 12 November 1970.

the medium term, the Commission will aim to develop and intensify, to a greater extent than has so far been the case, its efforts in terms of security of supply. When one considers the problem of safeguarding the Community's supply of hydrocarbons, the importance and urgency of establishing a common policy become manifest. In addition, the Commission will make every endeavour to ensure that the proposals it has already submitted to the Council in a number of energy policy areas are adopted in the course of this year'. (¹)

The Commission proposed various measures to avert an interruption in supply. In October 1972 it produced a proposal for a directive on measures intended to attenuate the effects of problems in the supply of petroleum. As an alternative to dependence on oil and in order to diversify sources of supply, it encouraged the generation of electricity from nuclear energy and proposed a draft Council decision on a Community contribution to financing nuclear power stations by raising loans on the market. This was because the investment required for a nuclear power station remained greater than that for a classical power station (²). In addition to its concerns about security of supply and diversification of energy sources, the Commission was also concerned about environ-

(¹) HAEC, Franco Maria Malfatti, Speech of the President of the Commission before the European Parliament, Strasbourg, 10 February 1971.

(²) 'Annexe 3 de La mise en œuvre de la «Première orientation pour une politique énergétique communautaire» (Communication de la Commission au Conseil)', COM(71) 810, Brussels, 30 July 1971.

Great uncertainty and alarmist forecasts

The uncertainty is great and the forecasts alarmist. This is how the head of the Energy Policy Unit wrote to his director-general:

'On the one hand, the situation regarding our energy needs remains crucial to economic development and social progress [...] On the other hand, the future of the energy sector, which must be prepared over a long period of time, is clouded in uncertainty. Changes in the rate of growth in energy requirements, the effect of concerns relating to the environment, the development of new technologies, and the structure of the international market for the most important energy products are all examples of areas in which developments can occur that cannot be predicted by simply reading the past.

Concerns about the future have led to a proliferation of hypotheses regarding these issues. The combination of some of these factors creates scenarios that are serious or even catastrophic enough that policies have to be developed to deal with them at the expense of immediate problems, giving up on economic and social progress as we understand it today in order to prevent or delay catastrophes presented by some as being certain in the long term.

It is clear that, by simply extending development trends observed in the recent past, for which in the short term there appears to be no alternative, within about 50 years we will find ourselves in a situation for which humanity is largely unprepared.'

BAC 31/1980 151, Outline of thinking
on a second guideline, April 1972.
(Translated from the French)

mental protection, energy conservation, and scientific and technological research. Clearly, there was no denying the 'intellectual ebullience' [1] of the Commission at this time. It was facing a worrying situation in terms of resources, while at the same time offering some people the opportunity to reflect on the prospects for the sector, given the issues and challenges created by the changes in the economic and international climate.

The activities of the Commission in the energy sector between 1958 and 1973 produced mixed results. In November 1972 François Long, head of the Supply Division, sent an executive summary to Fernand Spaak that was particularly eloquent in this respect. In it, Long wrote that 'In view of the difficulties in building a coherent and comprehensive system covering all the key issues of energy policy, such as cheap supply, security of supply and stability in supply, limited but nonetheless effective instruments have been put in place, such as the recently obtained agreement on declaring investments in oil. At the same time, the growing understanding of the Community's energy structures and of likely developments in the coming years constitutes a solid base on which to build'.

'We are increasingly discussing these issues with the relevant circles. In the absence of a coordinated policy in the proper sense of the word, experience shows that working together in this way with representatives of governments and industry leads, if only partially, to the adjustment of individual and national policies to take account of a Community perspective. Doubling our

[1] Comments by Philippe Loir, 1 August 2005.

The Chinon nuclear power station on the banks of the Loire, inaugurated in 1963,
is the first commercial-scale power station built on the French model — natural uranium, graphite and gas.

efforts in order to achieve more intensive collaboration and translating the ideas in our documents into concrete results can only facilitate the implementation of an energy policy. In any case, these efforts can only promote and expand the necessary contacts with the "outside".' (¹)

JULIE CAILLEAU

(¹) BAC 31/1980 151, François Long, Note for the attention of Mr Fernand Spaak, 24 February 1972.

The contribution made by the Commission of the European Atomic Energy Community (Euratom)

In 1967 the Euratom acquis *in the area of nuclear energy and research was brought within the purview of the single Commission. But it was back in January 1958, before the Directorate-General for Energy and the Directorate-General for Research and Technology were created, that the Euratom Commission had set about implementing the Euratom Treaty.*

Existing side by side with the EEC, Euratom covered a specific energy source.

Implementing the Treaty involved first and foremost putting in place a regulatory framework. This consisted of establishing a Supply Agency, with Fernand Spaak as the first Director-General, adopting a regulation on controlling the security of fissile materials, setting up a Security Control Directorate under Jacques Van Helmont and laying down rules on the ownership of such materials, which, in the words of Article 86 of the Euratom Treaty, 'shall be the property of the Community'. These measures, which were closely linked, were absolutely essential in that they ensured the unity of the European internal market in nuclear energy under conditions of the highest security.

To these must be added measures to protect health against ionising radiation, knowledge-dissemination activities, and the adoption of rules on investment and the creation of joint ventures.

Then, in order to 'contribute to […] the speedy […] growth of nuclear industries', to quote Article 1 of the Euratom Treaty, the Commission set about organising research, inter alia by setting up the Joint Research Centre, or JRC, where it envisaged installing 'large apparatus and special equipment', carrying out 'studies' and building 'experimental, test and prototype (including propulsion) reactors'. The hope was that the research would lead to the development of one or more types of power reactor to generate energy or even, following the American example, to propel ships. The choice of reactor type was a key issue that was to colour the relationship between the world of research and the electricity-generating industry.

Lastly, the Commission proceeded to develop its international relations. In this area, the initial plans for creating a nuclear energy community took account of the need to collaborate with the United States. The visit by the 'Three Wise Men' Committee in 1957 bears witness to this. As early as 1958, the Commission concluded a cooperation agreement with the US authorities and cemented a close relationship with them by sending to Washington, in November of that year, a personal representative, Curt Heidenreich.

The United States provided the Community with a steady supply of fissile materials and was prepared to share with it its knowledge and research findings, including in the power reactor area, with a first prototype being built in Belgium as part of a Franco-Belgian joint venture. Euratom thus paved the way for the future French and Belgian nuclear programmes.

With the merger of the executives, the Commission of the European Communities became, in 1967, the guardian of this acquis *created by the Euratom Commission. It defended and preserved Euratom's contribution to the future European Commission, which to this day applies the provisions of the* acquis. *There were, however, difficulties along the way.*

Foremost among these was the struggle to retain a separate European security control system.

The 1968 Nuclear Non-Proliferation Treaty (NPT) entrusted control of fissile materials to the International Atomic Energy Agency, a United Nations body. The Euratom system could not be replaced, however, by bilateral arrangements as these would have made impossible the functioning of the Community's internal market, rendering inoperative the Supply Agency as keeper of the fissile material accountancy data.

After long and difficult negotiations, a tripartite agreement was reached between the Member States (apart from France, which was not an NPT signatory at the time and which, when the Treaty was concluded, was not subject to its safeguards), the Atomic Energy Community and the IAEA.

This outcome enabled the five Member States which did not possess nuclear weapons to sign the NPT, the conflict of laws with the Euratom Treaty having been avoided and Euratom's functioning safeguarded. This was the first time that the Community as such concluded with a United Nations agency a close cooperation agreement setting out precise obligations.

Of course, the security control obligations were not to everyone's taste. Once General de Gaulle came to power, the application in France of this treaty requirement proved difficult on occasion and pragmatic arrangements had to be introduced. As Heinrich von Moltke recounts, one method of camouflaging reality was to lessen Euratom's visibility when the executives were merged. Euratom no longer appeared as such in the new Single Commission's establishment plan. Instead of being under the umbrella of one directorate-general, it was broken up piecemeal and distributed among various departments. Could it be, in von Moltke's words, that this facet of European integration was not something to be very proud of (¹)?

A second difficulty was the difference of opinion with France over supply. This turned on whether the supply provisions of Title Two, Chapter VI of the Euratom Treaty were null and void because the Council had not confirmed or amended them, as provided for in Article 76. The Commission brought France before the Court of Justice, which ruled that the Treaty's original provisions remained in force. The Commission's counsel, a member of its Legal Service, Jean-Pierre Delahousse, had succeeded in persuading the Court that the supply regime should be maintained.

A third difficulty lay in the Commission's choice of reactor type, namely the natural uranium reactor, as a springboard for nuclear research in Europe. This choice was to have serious consequences for the JRC when this technology, which had originally been advocated by France, was not taken up by any manufacturer, the European electricity industry preferring the enriched uranium reactor type already tried and tested in the United

States. Even France subsequently opted for the enriched uranium reactor in the wake of the Franco-Belgian prototype. The Commission gradually faced up to this difficult situation for the JRC and successfully managed the switchover.

Speaking of the Euratom Treaty in 1957, Robert Marjolin said that it was not set in stone, the central factor in its success or failure being the attitude of the governments involved.

He was right: the Euratom Treaty contained the basics for the industry's development, but political will was the key to its implementation. This political will was lacking, as witnessed by the absence of an overarching energy policy. Herein lay the source of the difficulties encountered by the EEC Commission, the ECSC High Authority and the Euratom Commission. The position did not change with the merger of the executives in 1967, nor has it changed to this day despite the new-felt urgency.

This problem notwithstanding, the Euratom Commission, and the EEC Commission after it, made maximum use of the possibilities offered by the Treaty to take such regulatory measures as were essential to include and maintain nuclear energy in a single Community market.

By establishing the Joint Research Centre, the Commission confirmed that the development of a leading-edge industry, with the economic progress that ought to ensue, was not possible without a combined effort. The difficulties in this area stemmed in part from the fact that the nascent industry and the research communities in the various countries did not follow up sufficiently on the JRC's work.

Ivo Dubois

(¹) Interview with Heinrich von Moltke, 22 January 2004.

Chapter 25

Research and technology, or the 'six national guardians' for 'the Commission, the eternal minor' [1]

In the aftermath of the Second World War, the whole nature of science policy was profoundly altered. The vast military research programmes, deploying heavyweight equipment and large research teams, achieved spectacular results, notably the nuclear bomb, and the governments wanted to continue with the organisation of this type of programme for civilian purposes.

However, the scope of this new 'Big Science' was clearly beyond the capacities of even the largest European states. From the beginning of the 1950s, this led to the establishment of various forms of European cooperation in the field of research and technology: the European Atomic Energy Community (1956–57), the European Organisation for Nuclear Research (CERN, 1952) in the field of particle physics, the OECD European Nuclear Energy Agency (ENEA, 1957), the European Molecular Biology Organisation (EMBO, 1964) in the field of molecular biology, the European Space Research Organisation (ESRO, 1962), the

European Launcher Development Organisation (ELDO, 1962) and the European Conference on Space Telecommunications (ECST, 1964) in the field of space, as well as several examples of cooperation in the aviation sector, the most famous being Concorde (1962) and Airbus (1967).

The examples of European cooperation are many and varied. From an organisational point of view, some were just bilateral (e.g. in the aviation sector), while others resulted in intergovernmental organisations (such as CERN and EMBO and the space agencies) and only Euratom became a Community institution. Some of the forms of cooperation had purely scientific objectives, while others were more or less directed at commercial applications. The number of members also varied considerably, ranging from 21 countries for ENEA to 13 for CERN, six for Euratom and two for Concorde.

The link between scientific research and economic growth

Since the beginning of the 1960s, the work of the OECD had highlighted the crucial link between scientific research and economic growth. The

---

[1] HAEU, JG77, Jules Guéron, Memorandum on the Euratom programme, 18 June 1968.
For a short résumé of Community research policy up to the mid-1990s, see the reference work by Guzzetti, L., *A brief history of European Union research policy*, Office for Official Publications of the European Communities, Luxembourg, 1995.

Euratom and the JRC

In order to develop its research activities, Euratom set up the Joint Research Centre, the main task of which was to carry out programmes in this field. This essential component was provided for in the Euratom Treaty of 1957. It was restructured in 1971.

The JRC was based in four places. Ispra in Italy and Petten in the Netherlands had a general remit. The other two centres, the Central Bureau for Nuclear Measurements in Geel, Belgium, and the European Institute for Transuranium Elements in Karlsruhe, Germany, had more specific tasks. These were either existing research centres or Community laboratories located in existing national facilities. The Member States ceded ownership of the land and the existing infrastructure to the Community for 99 years, and undertook to contribute financially to new investments. The Community, for its part, would build new centres or develop existing ones. This arrangement would save both money and time.

The largest centre, Ispra, was also the first for which an agreement was signed, in July 1959. This centre was very active: 'We had plenty of resources, both in terms of personnel and in terms of money for equipment. The only limit was our imagination and ability to work.' [1] Nevertheless, at the end of the second five-year research plan, the Council failed to agree on a third plan. From 1968 to 1972 the JRC operated on the basis of annual programmes, resulting in a deterioration in research activities.

In 1969 'the crisis erupted. We no longer had five-year programmes but programmes of survival, and of transition from one year to the next. We were in a situation in which funds were cut. We were threatened with staff dismissals on account of the lack of a long-term programme. There was even talk of doing away with the Joint Research Centre altogether.' [2] The ORGEL project to develop a heavy-water reactor was stopped. This was followed at the Ispra Centre by a period of strikes and occupations.

Following the Hague Conference in 1969, the JRC was reorganised and reformed in 1971 both at management level and as regards its activities. It was now able to pursue non-nuclear scientific and technological research activities. In February 1973, the Council finally adopted a new multiannual programme.

J.C.

reports concerning the 'technology gap' pointed to the weaknesses of European research as the cause of the economic divide between Europe and the United States. To enable Europe to catch up, they advocated not only the establishment of national research policies but also greater cooperation between European countries. Not only was it necessary to put an end to the duplication of research programmes and to pool official aid but also to establish a truly European market for high-technology products so as to encourage the emergence, on a European scale, of sufficiently large leading-edge industries to rival their American competitors. These arguments were widely propagated in the press and in various publications, including *The American Challenge*, the best-seller by Jean-Jacques Servan-Schreiber [3].

A degree of consensus developed on the need to combine European efforts on research and technology, but there were serious differences of opinion about the practical arrangements. Given the chaotic nature of the existing forms of cooperation, there were those who were in favour of an overall strategy in the context of the European Communities. René Foch, a senior Commission official responsible for relations with the OECD,

[1] Interview with Philippe Bourdeau, 5 March 2004.
[2] Interview with Gianluigi Valsesia, 4 December 2003.
[3] See Chapter on Industrial Policy, pp. 465 and 467.

observed that, given the global nature of the issue involved, a sectoral body such as ELDO or Euratom could hardly provide a framework for an overall policy. The Commission of the European Communities, with its general responsibilities for economic matters, was in a better position to do so ([1]). However, this option would entail a loss of sovereignty for the Member States, a question that was all the more delicate since very advanced technologies not only had economic but also military implications. Others proposed setting up a European Armaments Agency ([2]). Questions were also raised about whether or not the United Kingdom should be included in this cooperation: there was not as yet any agreement about its possible membership of the EEC, but at the time its scientific and technological potential was generally regarded as being at least equivalent to that of the six EEC countries combined ([3]). What about the United States, an economic competitor but above all an ally which had defended Europe? Not to mention the European subsidiaries of American companies, regarded by some as Trojan horses but by others as a springboard for Europe to catch up in terms of technology. And what about the respective roles of the public authorities and companies?

The Commission's first thoughts

The EEC and Euratom Treaties and rivalry

The Treaties establishing the European Communities were largely silent on the question of research, with the notable exception of the Euratom Treaty, which provided for the creation of a Joint Research Centre responsible for direct research

activities, the financing of cooperative research programmes, the promotion of information, the dissemination of technical knowledge, the harmonisation of safety standards, the control of fissile material, the creation of joint undertakings and other actions relating to industrial property and patents. The ECSC Treaty provided for the encouragement of research in the coal and steel sectors (Article 55). The EEC Treaty, for its part, provided an explicit basis only for an agricultural research policy (Article 41). However, the EEC Commission took the view that the Community should concern itself with research and development in all sectors since Article 2 of the Treaty gave it the task of promoting the harmonious development of economic activities and continuous and balanced growth. However, the Commission's powers to act pursuant to that article were extremely limited: it could only establish procedures for the coordination of the policies of the Member States, which retained complete powers as to the substance.

Under Article 2, in July 1963 the Commission proposed the creation of a Medium-Term Economic Policy Committee, as provided for in the Industrial Policy Chapter. This committee of representatives of the Member States would have the task of establishing a five-year economic policy programme aimed at coordinating the economic decisions of the governments and the Community, including in the field of scientific and technical research. In November 1963, the Euratom Commission suggested to the ECSC High Authority and the EEC Commission the setting-up of an Inter-Executive Research Working Party, but the idea was rejected by the latter ([4]). The Euratom and EEC Commissions disagreed about which of them should play the leading role in the development of a common research policy. The Euratom Commission advocated a broader interpretation of the Treaty — extending beyond the nuclear sector — since this approach would allow there to be a relatively

([1]) Foch, R., *L'Europe et la technologie: un point de vue politique*, (Les cahiers atlantiques, 2), Institut atlantique, Paris, 1970, p. 46.

([2]) For example, Foch, R. (op. cit.) and Calmann, J., *Defence, Technology and the Western Alliance*, The Institute for Strategic Studies, London, 1967.

([3]) See, for example, the assessment by Firmin Oulès: 'In the nuclear field Great Britain can contribute a potential as great as that of all six of the EEC countries together. In the other fields of scientific research, Great Britain has 59 % of the research personnel in the common market.' Oulès, F., *Planification et technologie dans l'Europe unie*, Centre de recherches européennes, Lausanne, 1968, p. 213.

([4]) BAC 118/86 1388, Enrico Medi at the EAEC Commission, 30 October 1963; ibid. Enrico Medi at the EAEC Commission, 6 April 1964.

ORGEL

The choice of ORGEL dates back to 1958–59 or thereabouts. At that time, there was no 'battle of the systems'. The nuclear world was divided into two: the countries which produced enriched uranium (USA, USSR) and the countries which did not and had to use natural uranium, entailing the use of graphite or heavy water as moderators. Graphite resulted in enormous reactors that were not very economic in producing energy. In fact, they were intended to produce plutonium. The heavy-water reactors were better and the Canadians, with CANDU (CANada Deuterium Uranium), were fairly successful. However, in both cases, on-power fuelling was necessary, which was very favourable for the production of plutonium for military purposes but was technically complicated and sometimes resulted in serious operating difficulties.

However, the countries which did not have enriched uranium had no choice. The Americans at the time exploited their monopoly position and, opting for enriched uranium, entailed unacceptable dependence. That was why the British and the French started with 'Magnox' reactors in Britain and 'graphite-gas' reactors in France. To improve matters, the British decided to enrich their fuel slightly, leading to the AGR (¹). The French chose the heavy-water route, with carbon-dioxide cooling. This was the EL 4 project. It was against this background that ORGEL came into being. The idea was to give a 'backbone' to the JRC, whose main establishment was in Ispra and which already had a heavy-water reactor that had been built by the CNEN (Centre national d'équipement nucléaire). At the time (1960) there was no battle of the systems. The CEA (Commissariat à l'énergie atomique) proposed to Euratom, in good faith, the study of a variant of the heavy-water reactor cooled by an organic liquid.

During the 1960s the enriched-uranium reactors developed by the Americans (PWR (²) and BWR (³)) gradually gained the upper hand.

Following their success with military marine reactors, the Americans decided to derive civil reactors from them for the production of electricity: the Shippingport PWR designed by Westinghouse, and the Dresden BWR supplied by General Electric. They acted with determination and speed and were able fairly rapidly (within five years) to propose power reactors in the 200 Mwe range: Chooz 1, SELNI, Garigliano, etc.

Euratom was involved in these developments through the US–Euratom programme and the joint undertakings. Jules Guéron attached great importance to this.

Meanwhile, despite a great deal of effort, the heavy-water reactors did not really take off. This was the case both with the French project (EL 4) and with ORGEL. And the Germans were clearly opting for the enriched-uranium reactors of the American type.

From 1965 to 1966 EDF began to have doubts about the possibility of designing competitive natural-uranium reactors. However, its position was opposed by the CEA and especially by General de Gaulle. It took EDF four to five years to get its point of view accepted, and that was what was known as the 'battle of the systems'. It was very heated and, in 1969, resulted in the abandonment of the 'French' system, i.e. natural-uranium reactors, with the assent of the general, who was much less obstinate than legend would have us believe! The rest is history.

Unfortunately, however, Euratom was swept along by the current, unable to react on account of the cumbersome and slow Community procedures. By 1967–68 it appeared that ORGEL would never be built by an electricity company, with the result that interest in the project dwindled. It therefore slowed down and stopped completely in 1969, when Euratom was in all sorts of difficulties. However, the overall balance sheet as far as ORGEL was concerned was not as negative as some people claim, since a lot of interesting work of high quality was carried out at Ispra and elsewhere while it was being developed.

(¹) AGR: advanced gas-cooled reactor.
(²) PWR: pressurised-water reactor.
(³) BWR: boiling-water reactor.

'Community-based' policy. The EEC Commission, for its part, stressed the need for research and development policy to be part and parcel of economic policy, even though the EEC Treaty only gave the Community institutions the right to coordinate intergovernmental activities.

In a note to the Council in March 1965, the French government advocated the establishment of a common research policy for the EEC (¹). Later that month, the Medium-Term Economic Policy Committee, established by a Council decision of April 1964 (²), set up a Working Party on Scientific and Technical Research Policy (PREST). The Euratom Commission would have preferred to have the task of running the Secretariat for the new Working Party, but this responsibility was shared between the EEC, Euratom and the ECSC, under the direction of an official in Directorate-General II (Economic and Financial Affairs) of the EEC Commission. In May 1965 the ECSC High Authority successfully relaunched the idea of an Inter-Executive Research Working Party; this was finally set up in October 1965 with the primary task of defining a common position for the executives within PREST, drawing on the experience of the three Communities. It also prepared their joint representation within international organisations such as the OECD.

Setting up PREST failed to bring an end to the rivalry between the EEC and Euratom Commissions, as can be seen from the debates on research in the European Parliament in October 1966. De Groote, a Member of the Euratom Commission, repeated once again that Euratom did not think it appropriate to establish an organic link between economic affairs and scientific research, while his colleague Marjolin, on the other hand, stressed the link between research and economic development (³). This power struggle complicated and slowed down Community initiatives in the research field until the merger of the executives in May 1967.

Composition and mandate of PREST

PREST was composed of two representatives from each Member State (with the exception of Luxembourg, which had only one representative), either civil servants or experts, plus two members for each of the executives of the Communities. Its first Chairman was André Maréchal, who was very pro-European (⁴) and was Director in the French Directorate-General for Scientific and Technical Research. Its mandate was to examine the problems involved in the preparation of a coordinated or common policy for scientific and technical research and to propose measures for the inauguration of such a policy, with due regard for the possibilities of cooperation with other countries; this examination was to be linked as closely as possible with the general economic policy of the Member States and of the EEC (⁵).

(¹) BAC 118/86 1388, French Permanent Representation to the EC, R/251/65, 9 March 1965.

(²) Council Decision 64/247/EEC of 15 April 1964 setting up a Medium-Term Economic Policy Committee, OJ English special edition, Series I, Chapter 1963–64, p. 133.

(³) Debates in the European Parliament of 18 October 1966. See Caty, G., *L'Europe technologique*, U2, dossiers, 89, Colin, Paris, 1969 pp. 22–28.

(⁴) Interview with Philippe Bourdeau, 5 March 2004.

(⁵) BAC 118/86 1390, Council Note, R/180/67, 21 February 1967.

The proposals made by Amintore Fanfani and Harold Wilson

In 1966, the question of a European research policy was still on the agenda following proposals from Amintore Fanfani, the Italian Minister for Foreign Affairs, and Harold Wilson, the British Prime Minister. In June 1966, Fanfani addressed the NATO Council, requesting the United States to help the countries of western Europe catch up in the field of research and development through a Marshall Plan for technology bringing together and strengthening the western bloc in the context of the cold war. When he put forward his ideas to the Council of the European Communities in December, Fanfani also stressed the need for cooperation between European States. The Fanfani project was not taken up by NATO owing to a lack of interest on the part of the United States.

Wilson launched his idea of a European Technological Community in his Guildhall speech on 14 November 1966. The British Prime Minister put forward his country's scientific and technological strength as an argument in support of its application for membership, hoping that de Gaulle would appreciate this contribution. While not purely rhetorical, Wilson's phraseology was extremely vague. The British were afraid that projects of a more specific nature would be open to criticism from de Gaulle, especially as they would have liked a new type of research policy focusing much more on cooperation between, or the merger of, private companies on projects with a directly commercial scope. At the same time as he was advocating a European Technological Community, Wilson was in fact distancing himself from major European projects such as ELDO and Airbus, which were regarded as being too expensive and inefficient. The British government was also divided on the fundamental review of the special relationship with the United States that a strengthening of European cooperation would entail. The French government also had serious reservations about Wilson's ideas. De Gaulle was afraid that the British would in fact prefer to cooperate with the United States and that the UK's technological lead would enable it to dominate a European Technological Community, replacing American domination by British domination ([1]).

The EEC Commission was opposed to the transatlantic cooperation route proposed by Fanfani. The memorandum of the Inter-Executive Research Working Party of March 1967 supported this position, indicating that, for cooperation between the United States and Europe to be established on a firm basis, it was necessary for the United States to have a valid partner able to establish relations based on genuine reciprocity and capable of contributing a share comparable to that of the United States in the context of any joint undertakings. What the EEC Commission wanted above all was a strengthening of technological cooperation between European countries. In the Commission's view, the Community of Six was the ideal framework for this cooperation because of its economic cohesion and its institutions. Furthermore, the compensation mechanisms necessary to resolve the 'fair return' problem would be easier to establish in the context of the numerous activities of the EEC. However, the Commission did advocate the closest possible association with European non-member countries, in particular the United Kingdom ([2]).

The Euratom or research policy crisis

The first Council meeting on research and the work of PREST

In the wake of the wide-ranging discussions following the Fanfani and Wilson proposals, the Council decided, at the end of 1966, to organise a special session on research questions. The prepara-

([1]) Young, J. W., 'Technological cooperation in Wilson's strategy for EEC entry', in O. J. Daddow, (ed.), *Harold Wilson and European integration. Britain's second application to join the EEC*, British Foreign and Colonial Policy, Frank Cass, London, 2003, pp. 95–114. The quote is from F. Oulès, op. cit., p. 219.
([2]) BAC 11886 1391, Memorandum on the problems of scientific and technical progress in the European Community, Communication from the ECSC High Authority and the EEC and EAEC Commissions to the Council, EUR/C1711/2/67, 20 March 1967.

De Gaulle and nuclear safeguards

'The controversy about "control" reminds me of another event which had taken place shortly before, namely the crisis between France and Euratom concerning safeguards which formed part of the political core of the Treaty. At the time, the French military programme was already in full swing. There were reactors at Marcoule producing electricity but also plutonium and, under the Euratom Treaty, all special fissile material was owned by the Community and subject to Commission safeguards unless it was used for military purposes. However, de Gaulle did not want any controls carried out by the Commission at Marcoule or in other installations regarded by the French authorities as military, and a crisis erupted. In this situation, the question arose as to whether the Euratom Commission would bring a complaint against France before the Court of Justice.

At the time, I was instructed to sound out the opinion of the German "*cabinets*" at the EEC Commission. I therefore saw Mr Narjes, who was Mr Hallstein's *chef de cabinet*, and subsequently a Member of the Commission, and Ernst Albrecht, who was Mr von der Groeben's *chef de cabinet*, a brilliant economist who later became Prime Minister of Lower Saxony. The outcome of these meetings was not unequivocal and rather paradoxical. The economist told me: "You really must refer the matter to the Court. It's a question of principle. We cannot tolerate a Member State being in breach of the Treaty." However, Mr Narjes, the lawyer and diplomat, had a different point of view: "On no account do that. It is clear that de Gaulle will not abide by the verdict of the Court. That will damage the prestige of the Court, which is an institution common to the three Treaties. The entire construction of Europe is founded on law and, if the Court is no longer respected, the entire mechanism is called into question." This was what I had to report to my superiors.

To resolve the conflict, the President of the Euratom Commission, Étienne Hirsch, an extraordinary man, decided to go and see General de Gaulle. After returning from Paris, he reported to me the following dialogue between them: "General, the Treaty bears the signature of France; it seems clear to me that France is obliged to respect it to the letter." To which General de Gaulle replied: "Mr President, treaties are like young girls, they fade." There was an impasse. We knew that it was impossible to convince the general, and the Euratom Commission decided not to bring the matter before the Court of Justice. Subsequently, compromises were found so as to camouflage the conflict without risking any diversion of fissile materials from their declared uses. One of the ways of camouflaging things was to reduce the visibility of Euratom when the executives were merged. As a result, Euratom no longer appeared in the organisation chart of the new Single Commission. Bits of it were to be found scattered around in the various departments, but not in any one particular directorate-general. Was this because there was no great pride in this facet of European integration?'

Interview with Heinrich von Moltke, 22 January 2004.

---

tions for this first Council meeting on research were complicated by the Euratom crisis, which came to a head at the beginning of 1967, and also delayed by the merger of the executives in May. The situation was paradoxical. Focusing its attention and energy on the formulation and implementation of a policy to shape the common market, the EEC Commission did not pay particular attention to basic research. In inheriting the JRC, it now had a major research instrument at its disposal. However, this wobbly institution seemed very cumbersome to some, which was why they wanted to reduce it in size if they could not do away with it altogether.

The JRC officials joining the new Single Commission brought with them a specific culture and felt out of place. According to Serge Orlowski, speaking of Euratom as a whole 'when the executives were merged, Euratom was like a naughty little brat that nobody in the family knew what to do with. The EEC Commission made a takeover bid for Euratom, absorbed it and then from one day to the next it ceased to exist. The furniture and the family jewels were shared out.' [1]

[1] Interview with Serge Orlowski, 29 November 2004.

Within Coreper, only the Italian and Belgian governments were really in favour of the immediate establishment of a Community policy. Germany, the Netherlands and Luxembourg wanted to settle the problem of Euratom before embarking on other areas of research. They first of all sought to create a large market and a tax and legal climate conducive to the merger of businesses and to leave it up to private enterprise to catch up on the technological front. The French delegation was also opposed to a general discussion of the problems of research, stressing that all research matters remained the responsibility of the Member States unless otherwise stipulated in the Treaties [1].

In July 1967, PREST submitted its first report — the 'Maréchal Report' [2] — to the Medium-Term Economic Policy Committee. Stressing above all the economic importance of research, it was based to a large extent on the memorandum of the Inter-Executive Working Party on Research of March 1967. Basing themselves on the American model, the European governments should encourage the establishment of international businesses and increase their financial contribution to research. This aid should be coordinated at European level to avoid a dispersion of efforts and, in particular, should take the form of research contracts and joint public procurement. In addition, industrial research should enjoy the benefits of a European patent. The Commission and the Member States published a preliminary draft convention on European patent law in October 1962. However, the negotiations had broken down, a major stumbling block being the possible participation of countries that were not members of the EEC [3]. The

Maréchal Report also recommended a regular comparison of the national research programmes so as to determine the areas in which joint action would be the most effective. It indicated six areas in which there was a need to examine the scope for cooperation rapidly: information technology and telecommunications, transport, oceanography, metallurgy, air, water and noise pollution, the monitoring of foodstuffs, and meteorology.

The first meeting of the Council of Research Ministers was finally held in Luxembourg on 31 October 1967. Community competence in this area nevertheless remained explicitly limited: the final resolution was adopted jointly by the Council, the Commission and the representatives of the Member States. The resolution instructs the Medium-Term Economic Policy Committee to continue with the comparison of national policies and examine the scope for cooperation in the areas indicated in the Maréchal Report.

In October 1967, the new Directorate-General for Research and Technology (DG XII) of the Single Commission was not yet in place. That is why the Commission's participation in PREST was entrusted to a steering group consisting of Commissioners Hellwig, Barre and Colonna di Paliano, assisted by the relevant directors-general. A small task force of officials prepared the group's work [4].

In late November 1967, PREST set up specialised working parties to examine the priority sectors indicated in the Council resolution, but their work rapidly came to a halt. After the Council meeting of 18 and 19 December, when de Gaulle vetoed Britain's membership for the second time, the Dutch and Italian governments, followed by the Belgian government, suspended their participation in PREST. These three countries wished to collaborate with the United Kingdom in areas, such as technology, which were not covered by the Community Treaties. After several attempts by the Commission and the Belgian and German governments, the Council finally decided, in

---

[1] BAC118/86 1390, Note on the discussion within Coreper on scientific and technical research of 23 February 1967, R/272/1/67, 1 March 1967, and errata of 10 and 22 March 1967; BAC 118/86 1391, Note on the discussions within Coreper of 9 June 1967 on scientific and technical research, R/918/67, 27 June 1967.
[2] CEAB 2 3743, Report by PREST, July 1967.
[3] BAC 118/86 1392, SEC(68) 7, 4 January 1968. The first significant step towards European cooperation on patents was to be the Munich Convention of October 1973, an international treaty outside the framework of the European Communities. On the history of the European patent, see Kranakis, E., *Industrialisation and the dynamics of European integration: the quest for a European patent, 1949–2003*, presented at the first plenary conference of the ESF network 'Tensions of Europe — Technology and the making of 20th century Europe' (Budapest, 18–21 March 2004).

[4] PV 15, EC Commission, 19–23 November 1967.

December 1968, to resume the work of PREST. France agreed that the applicant countries could be mentioned as potential participants in the future cooperation, but they would not be allowed to take part in PREST meetings.

PREST's report to the Council in March 1969 — called the 'Aigrain Report' after the new Chairman of the Working Party — was a fairly slim programme, 'but it was a beginning' ([1]), to quote Heinrich von Moltke. It contained 47 proposals for research in the sectors indicated in the 1967 resolution. After they were examined in Coreper, a process that lasted until October, the Council finally approved 30 or so proposals in areas such as information technology, the environment, meteorology and metallurgy. The Community invited non-member countries to take part in finalising the projects and establishing the legal framework for carrying them out. The interministerial conference held in Brussels on 22 and 23 November was finally attended by the six EEC countries plus the United Kingdom, Ireland, Denmark, Norway, Sweden, Switzerland, Austria, Spain, Portugal, Finland, Greece, Yugoslavia and Turkey. The 19 countries adopted a resolution on European cooperation in the field of science and technology (COST) and signed cooperation agreements on seven projects (with a total budget of around 21 million units of account). COST was not set up as an international organisation but rather as a pragmatic procedural framework for the conclusion and implementation of intergovernmental agreements. Moreover, it did not have joint funds at its disposal. The secretariat for the Committee of COST Senior Officials was provided by the General Secretariat of the EEC Council and the technical secretariats for COST projects were the responsibility of the Commission, which made relations between COST and the Community institutions rather ambiguous. France initially refused to allow any Commission participation in COST but, after lengthy discussions, the general resolution finally refers to the 'European Communities represented by the Council and the

---

([1]) Interview with Heinrich von Moltke, 22 January 2004.

IL CENTRO RICERCHE DI ISPRA RISCHIA DI ESSERE SMANTELLATO

« L'Euratom di Ispra? Lei gira qui a destra, poi va diritto fino all'aeroporto e prende il primo volo per gli Stati Uniti; non può sbagliare ».

A witty reaction to the threatened dismantling of the Joint Research Centre in Ispra: 'The Euratom Centre in Ispra? Take the first on the right, then go straight on to the airport and take the first flight to America. You can't miss it.' December 1968.

The Euratom setback

'I have memories of an immense mess. Ispra, Petten, Mol and Karlsruhe had been developed, setting up a Joint Research Centre which the Europeans had never really appropriated for themselves. The large research machinery and the big laboratories remained "national" and, with a few rare exceptions, the Euratom laboratories and machinery merely complemented them. The quality of the Community teams of scientists and researchers was not in question. There was also the fact that the focal project was the test reactor ORGEL, which did not have the success it was expected to have and never got further than the experimental stage. The attempted relaunch when the executives were merged failed. Attempts were made to divert to Ispra experiments that could have been conducted anywhere in Europe, even in the small research reactors and especially in the "loops" of the big reactors. Activities were carried out in areas such as the resistance of materials, and so on. This was useful and done well, but in no way did it justify the existence of Ispra as the main JRC establishment. For us at Euratom, it was a source of bitterness and sadness, but in the Member States and in Brussels nobody really had any illusions about the future of the centre. It should also be remembered that the bulk of Community research in this field was in fact connected with the production of electricity from nuclear energy and that, as is still the case, the likelihood of European patents giving rise to European industrial property shared equitably between the six partners, with all the attendant economic, commercial and social consequences, was remote since one of the partners also had political and military ambitions which were not shared by four of the others and could not, in any case be shared by the fifth.'

Interview with Manuel Santarelli, 4 March 2004.

Commission'. The Commission also signed three project agreements, allowing the Community to collaborate on the establishment of a European information technology network (COST11) and research in the field of materials and the environment (COST50 and COST61a) [1].

More than five years after the setting-up of PREST, the Community initiative resulted in seven 'à la carte' intergovernmental agreements involving non-member countries. The overall approach of the national research programmes was abandoned completely. The Commission officials running the secretariat for PREST were not very impressed by its activities. While those activities may have shown the governments, scientists and industry that a common research policy could gradually be established, the direct results did not seem to be in proportion to the time and outlay devoted to them: 12 000 days of work by the experts and 2 million units of account of expendi-

ture. Because of the slowness of the Community institutions' decision-making process (over the four years since the resolution was adopted in 1967, only 18 months were devoted to scientific work), many projects were already obsolete. Furthermore, all the interruptions, hesitations, changes and the enlargement of the institutional framework had made the experts consulted sceptical. Lastly, the Commission could no longer launch new initiatives in the sectors handled by PREST. According to the new Commissioner, Spinelli, 'a mountain had given birth to a mouse' [2].

There were many factors which impeded the establishment of a common research policy: the question of Britain's membership, the major difficulties with Euratom, the 1968–69 crisis in the space agencies (particularly concerning the merits of developing a satellite-launching capability independent of the United States and the coordi-

[1] On COST: Roland, J.-L., *A review of COST cooperation since its beginning*, EC Commission, Luxembourg, 1988 (EUR 11640).

[2] BAC 5479 49, Draft report by PREST to the Medium-Term Economic Policy Committee, II/382/71, 1 September 1971; Spinelli, A., *Diario europeo, II, 1970–1976*, ed. E. Paolini, Il Mulino, Bologna, 1991–92, p. 229.

COST projects

'In 1971 the first big COST agreement was signed. Spinelli officialised this cooperation in a number of projects. There were six or seven COST environmental projects. We succeeded in placing the scientific secretariat for at least two of these projects in Ispra. These were COST61 on the physico-chemical behaviour of atmospheric pollutants and COST64 on the behaviour of organic micropollutants in water. These projects had a very long lifespan since, even after Britain joined, the COST system was used for scientific cooperation outside the multiannual research programme.'

Interview with Philippe Bourdeau, 5 March 2004.

Community or intergovernmental?

'At first we wondered, as is almost always the case when a measure is launched by one or more governments, whether an attempt was being made to replace Community teams and the Community method by intergovernmental teams with, of course different working methods, and in particular anything to do with the method of voting.

Where PREST was concerned, we had the good fortune that it was Mr Aigrain who dealt with it. Pierre Aigrain was by nature "European" in spirit. Similarly, as was later the case for the environment, responsibilities were shared between the Community and the Member States in accordance with what was subsequently called by Jacques Delors the principle of "subsidiarity".'

Interview with Michel Carpentier, 5 January 2004.

nation of the different bodies), and the slowing-down of work following the merger of the executives. More basically, the Commission lacked a solid legal basis for establishing a Community research policy. It therefore organised several symposiums on the legal aspects of European technological cooperation, one of which (Nice, 1971) even considered a draft of an additional protocol to the Treaty of Rome on technological policy ([1]). However, until the Single European Act of 1986, the Commission's subsequent proposals would be based on Article 235 of the EEC Treaty, 'that catch-all' to quote Gianluigi Valsesia ([2]), which authorised the Council to decide, acting unanimously, on any measure which, while not provided for in the Treaty, was necessary to attain one of the objectives of the Community. Progress towards a common research policy would therefore depend on the common will of the Member States.

From a modest restart to greater ambitions

The final communiqué of the Hague Summit Conference held in December 1969 emphasised both the importance of research and development and the Community's essential role in this field. More particularly, the Heads of State or Government expressed their 'readiness to continue more intensively the activities of the Community with a view to coordinating and promoting industrial research and development in the principal advanced sectors, in particular by means of common programmes, and supply the financial means for the purpose' ([3]). This seemed to indicate the abandonment of the national and transatlantic solutions of the past in favour of European collaboration ([4]). It was rather ironical, however, that it should come at a time when the

---

([1]) EC Commission, *Les cadres juridiques de la coopération internationale en matière scientifique et le problème européen* — Proceedings of the symposiums held in Aix-en-Provence (1 and 2 December 1967) and Nice (6 and 7 December 1968), Brussels, 1970; idem., *La politique technologique de la Communauté européenne — Aspects juridiques et institutionnels*. Symposium organised in the framework of the Institut du Droit de la Paix et du Développement and the Faculty of Law and Economic Sciences of Nice (Nice, 10 and 11 December 1971), special edition of *Revue du Marché Commun*, No 153, April 1972.

([2]) Interview with Gianluigi Valsesia, 4 December 2003.

([3]) ECSC, EEC, EAEC, Commission, *Third General Report on the Activities of the Communities in 1969*, 1970, point 208.

([4]) Cf. Zimmerman, H., 'Western Europe and the American challenge: conflict and cooperation in technology and monetary policy, 1965–1973', *Journal of European Integration History*, Vol. 6, 2000, pp. 109–110.

Space and nuclear energy: reserved questions

'At the time, space and nuclear power were considered by the leaders in the Member States in much the same way. These were matters for intergovernmental agreements. There was no question of turning them into "Community" matters in the strict sense of the term. Accordingly, we could consider to what extent we could at least exchange information, know in advance what was going to be done, and what the relations would be with other countries, the United States in particular and even the Soviet Union, but that was about as far as it went.'

Interview with Michel Carpentier, 5 January 2004.

Ispra Centre was experiencing a wave of strikes before being occupied by officials threatened with unemployment because of the lack of a research programme that was not one of 'survival, and of transition from one year to the next' [1].

While Ispra continued to resemble a 'floating island' [2], the reactions to the communication on Community industrial policy, which was submitted to the Council in March 1970 [3], showed that the Member States were very reluctant to honour the commitment given at The Hague. This communication, known as the 'Colonna Memorandum' after the Commissioner Guido Colonna di Paliano, had been prepared by the Directorate-General for Industrial Affairs (DG III) under the direction of Robert Toulemon [4]. The memorandum gives pride of place to advanced industries. To promote these sectors, it proposed in particular the dovetailing of policies relating to public or semi-public procurement, the creation of Community contracts for technological development and the adoption of common positions in relations with non-member countries. Following a year of discussions, Coreper could only conclude that it was impossible to reach agreement on any of these questions [5].

Following the Colonna Memorandum, the Commission submitted more specific proposals to the Council. A note submitted in June 1970 suggested a procedure for regular consultation between the Six on their national research and development projects, whether nuclear or non-nuclear [6]. In September 1971, the Commission proposed extending the joint undertaking status provided for under the Euratom Treaty beyond the nuclear sector, so that it could be granted to any new enterprise that resulted from the merger of firms established in at least two Member States and was intended to exercise a major activity of common interest from a European standpoint in the field of technological development. 'Joint undertaking' status would facilitate the establishment of transnational firms and make it possible for tax and customs advantages to be conferred and for loans or guarantees to be granted by the Community [7]. In July 1972, the Commission also put forward its final proposal concerning the implementation of Community contracts, as announced in the Colonna Memorandum. These subsidies, managed by the Commission in collaboration with the European Investment Bank, would support medium-sized technological projects carried out on the basis of cooperation by firms from different Member States or meeting a public need not yet satisfied at Community level [8]. None of these three Commission proposals resulted in a decision being taken by the Council.

Meanwhile, in July 1970, Altiero Spinelli had been appointed as Commissioner for industrial, technological and scientific affairs. Remaining true to his

---

[1] Interview with Gianluigi Valsesia, 4 December 2003. Cf. www.anniruggenti.net
[2] Interview with Serge Orlowski, 29 November 2004.
[3] Community industrial policy. Memorandum from the Commission to the Council, COM(70) 100 final, 18 March 1970.
[4] See Chapter on Industrial Policy, p. 470.

[5] Cf. EC Commission, *Sixth General Report on the Activities of the Communities in 1972*, 1973, point 291.
[6] BAC 79/82 222, Note from the Commission to the Council, 17 June 1970.
[7] Proposal for a Council regulation on the setting-up of joint undertakings under the EEC Treaty (presented by the Commission to the Council), COM(71) 812 final, 14 September 1971.
[8] Proposal for a Council regulation on the implementation of Community contracts (presented by the Commission to the Council), COM(72) 710 final, 18 July 1972.

The Joint Research Centre, a floating island

'I was still at the Joint Research Centre in 1969. We were a floating island. I still reported to Brussels but had become, so to speak, the captain of a raft that had no direction and no engine. We were waiting to return to Brussels. I went by train once a week to Brussels to go and see the Director-General, to see how he was going to allocate the staff, repatriate people. We were on the outside. Ispra was collapsing. The entire Centre was very happy to be free, but didn't really know what to do, which also explains the strikes, as it was a good opportunity for the Italians to go on strike. We didn't really know who was doing what. It was chaotic until everything was reorganised much later. The researchers took advantage of the situation to do their own research, etc. People were very happy there, they certainly did not want to move. However, in the departments, there were a number of people working in the scientific services for Orgel but not part of the Orgel team who, having seen the Orgel project stopped and not wanting to become researchers looking through microscopes for ever, returned to Brussels. About 100 people came back. The Centre was in limbo for some time, followed by the restructuring about which I know little.'

Interview with Serge Orlowski, 29 November 2004.

federalist convictions, 'something of a visionary but a great man' (¹), Spinelli had ambitions for the establishment of a strong and independent technological policy as a result of Community institutions with wide-ranging decision-making and executive powers. However, he was more interested in major Community policy and institutional questions than in industry or research, to such an extent that some people spoke of a 'casting error' (²).

His technological projects were very largely inspired by Christopher Layton, who in 1969 published a work entitled *European advanced technology: a programme for integration* (³).

According to von Moltke: 'It was a very good book. It had real public support.' (⁴) An adviser to Spinelli from 1971 (i.e. before Britain joined the Community), Layton became his *chef de cabinet* following the signing of the Enlargement Treaty.

Spinelli first of all regrouped the old Directorates-General III (Industrial Affairs), XII (Research and Technology) and XV (Joint Research Centre) into a single DG III (Industrial, Technological and Scientific Affairs), under the direction of Toulemon. 'A DG with imagination which needs to acquire power', as Spinelli wrote in his diary (⁵).

In November 1970, the Commission formulated its first proposals for comprehensive structures for implementing the ambitious Community decisions taken at the Conference at The Hague. Given the dispersed nature of the Member States' technological projects and, in some cases, the competition between them, it seemed urgent to pool all these efforts in projects and contracts on a Community scale, in order to achieve a minimum critical mass. In the Commission's view, the Community had few reasons for and no interest in remaining inactive pending the conclusion of the enlargement negotiations.

Accordingly, the Commission first of all recommended setting up a European Research and Development Committee (CERD), which would prepare joint projects. It would replace the many existing working parties of experts (⁶) or at least coordinate their work. On the basis of the work of CERD, the Commission would make proposals to the Council concerning a wide range of joint measures: organisation of information centres, measures for the harmonisation of public initiatives, training schemes, financial aid for research and development projects, granting of joint undertaking status,

(¹) Interview with Serge Orlowski, 29 November 2004.
(²) Interview with Robert Toulemon, 17 December 2003, for example.
(³) Layton, C., *European advanced technology: a programme for integration*, Political and Economic Planning, London, 1969.

(⁴) Interview with Heinrich von Moltke, 22 January 2004.
(⁵) Spinelli, A., op. cit., pp. 53–54 ('una DG di immaginazione che deve conquistare un potere').
(⁶) PREST, Euratom's Scientific and Technical Committee, the Council's Working Parties on Research, Industrial Policy and Atomic Questions, and COST. Cf. BAC 27/85 63, Note from the Secretariat of the Medium-Term Economic Policy Committee, 18797/II/70, 16 December 1970.

participation in the activities of other scientific organisations, and the direct implementation of research programmes. Along the lines of the American NASA, a European Research and Development Agency (ERDA) under the Commission's control would manage the financing of Community projects. To this end, it would have funds from the Community's own resources. Lastly, the Commission proposed the establishment of the European Science Foundation (ESF) to encourage European cooperation on basic research. The Board of this foundation would include members responsible for the major scientific institutions in the Member States ([1]). In other words, it was a question of 'creating what is now known as the European Research Area. Spinelli fully supported the initiatives of his services', according to Philippe Bourdeau ([2]).

However, the question of research remained in abeyance until the conclusion of the accession negotiations. In June 1972, the Commission submitted a new communication to the Council calling on it to recognise that the Community's remit covered all areas of research and development. While not absorbing the independent European scientific organisations, the Community should formulate the overall strategy and act as a catalyst. The proposals concerning CERD, ERDA and ESF were re-tabled, with some amendments. CERD would comprise experts chosen on a personal basis and not as representatives of the Member States. ERDA was now considered to be a medium-term solution to be implemented when the joint or Community programmes envisaged or developed were sufficiently diverse and of a suitable scale. For the time being, preference was given to partial and provisional solutions. To finance the work of the European Science Foundation, COST projects, Euratom's multiannual programme and the industrial development contracts, the Commission requested, for a three-year period, an annual budget averaging 120 million units of account, corresponding to 2 % of the national public-sector budgets for research and development. It also announced that it was preparing proposals for a European venture capital fund, a European network for scientific and technical information and documentation, and programmes in the key sectors of aeronautics, information technology and telecommunications. Economic research was at the heart of the Commission's concerns, but its communication also paid considerable attention to the environmental and social dimensions of technology ([3]). Accordingly, the first two 'indirect action' research programmes (shared-cost contracts) adopted by the Council under Article 235 of the EEC Treaty concerned the environment, and the BCR (Community Bureau of Reference) (1972).

At the Paris Summit on 19 and 21 October 1972 the Heads of State or Government of the enlarged Community called upon the Commission to draw up an action plan in the field of science and technology, entailing the coordination of national policies within the Community institutions and the joint implementation of projects of importance to the Community as a whole. This programme, together with a detailed implementation timetable, was to be adopted by the Council before 1 January 1974 ([4]). At the beginning of 1973, the Council finally adopted a new four-year programme for the Joint Research Centre, which had been surviving since 1968 on temporary annual budgets. However, the institutional reforms proposed by Spinelli went much too far for the Council, which rejected entirely the idea of the ERDA. CERD was set up in April 1973 but was never to be more than yet another advisory body. The European Science Foundation was set up in November 1974, but outside the Community framework.

In other words, as the Commission itself put it in 1972, where European technological cooperation was concerned, the previous 15 years had been a

([1]) 'Commission memorandum to the Council concerning overall Community action on scientific and technological research and development', SEC(70) 4250, 11 November 1970 (published as Supplement 1/71 to the Bulletin of the EC).
([2]) Interview with Philippe Bourdeau, 5 March 2004.
([3]) 'Objectives and instruments of a common policy for scientific research and technological development', COM(72) 700, 14 June 1972 (published as Supplement 6/72 to the Bulletin of the EC).
([4]) ECSC, EEC, EAEC, Commission, Sixth General Report on the Activities of the Communities in 1972, 1973, point 5.

Spinelli (second from the right) visits British Aerospace during the development of Concorde, which made its first commercial flight on 21 January 1976.

period in which experience had been gained rather than one in which achievements had been made ([1]). This highlights, in this sector as in many others, the essential importance of political will in terms of the Community dimension.

Without this will, there can be no technological cooperation since, according to Jean Flory writing in the early 1970s, where science and technology are concerned, 'it is impossible to make completely rational choices. It is not uncommon, therefore, in our countries, for such problems to be settled by the head of government. In the Community, when a consensus cannot be reached, it is no longer pos-

sible to take a decision.' ([2]) This point of view is shared by Heinrich von Moltke. Commenting on the ideas of Toulemon and Flory, who called for European programmes which, like the major American projects, would stimulate research by large firms by ordering prototypes from the most competitive among them, he explained that: 'To be able to do this, as in the United States we need a President capable of motivating a nation to agree to this sort of expenditure. We haven't got one.' ([3])

Éric Bussière and Arthe Van Laer

([1]) *Objectives and instruments* [...], Supplement to the *Bulletin of the EC*, op. cit., p. 14.

([2]) Flory, J., 'Historique et problématique de la politique technologique de la Communauté', in EEC Commission, *La politique technologique de la Communauté européenne. Aspects juridiques et institutionnels* [...], op. cit., p. 307.

([3]) Interview with Heinrich von Moltke, 22 January 2004.

Chapter 26

What information policy?

In the brief address that he gave at Val-Duchesse on 16 January 1958 at the first constitutive meeting of the EEC Commission, Hallstein, after stating that the Commission's work 'will be able to bear fruit only if there is good cooperation with the other institutions', stressed that it 'is one of those whose supranational nature is the most pronounced'. The President set out his stall. The new Commission fully intended to play a central part in the implementation of this new phase in the construction of Europe, a task which required support and encouragement. That was why Hallstein added: 'We earnestly request the organs of public opinion to follow our work with a critical interest and to help us instil strong and rich life into the new ideas.' [1]

The invitation to the media could not have been any clearer. It was not enough to keep abreast of current events in Europe and give a constructive account of them. The media also had somehow to convey or even (dare we say it), legitimise the Commission's ambition to embody the nascent Europe.

But the fulfilment of this ambition was not and would not be an easy matter. The debate on the usefulness and, where appropriate, the nature and scale of the information effort was a long-running one. Moreover, when Hallstein sought the cooperation of the media, he could not have been unaware of the effort that 'big sister' [2] in Luxembourg had launched in this sector over the last five years.

The impact of the ECSC

Since 1953 the ECSC High Authority had made every effort to ensure that not only the spirit which inspired it, and the tasks which fell to it, but also the results that it garnered were better known. This was done *à la Monnet*. Moreover, the institutional distinctions were rather blurred, and this created extremely strong personal relations between people, as Georges Berthoin stressed [3].

---

[1] PV 1, EEC Commission, 16 January 1958, Annex II, p. 2.

[2] Rabier, J.-R., 'La naissance d'une politique d'information sur la Communauté européenne (1952–1967)', in Dassetto, F. and Dumoulin, M. (eds), *Naissance et développement de l'information européenne — Actes des journées d'étude de Louvain-la-Neuve des 22 mai et 14 novembre 1990*, Euroclio, Études et documents, Vol. 2, Peter Lang, Bern [...] Vienna, 1993, p. 28.

[3] UCL, GEHEC, Interview with Georges Berthoin by Béatrice Roeh, 28 March 2000.

The President of the High Authority, 'anxious for the utmost discretion in drawing up plans and preparing decisions [...], was equally anxious to inform citizens and their elected representatives, as well as the press, what we call "public opinion"', recalled Jacques-René Rabier (¹). He spoke wisely. He was one of the key players in the field of information throughout the period under consideration.

Having come to Luxembourg in January 1953 at the request of Monnet, with whom he had spent 'a few years of study' (²) at the Commissariat du Plan, Rabier was given the task of drawing up a report for the ECSC Assembly and gradually put in place 'a sort of spokesman's group' responsible for informing the press. This group included others who were close to Monnet: François Fontaine, who came from the Commissariat du Plan, and François Duchêne, former correspondent of the *Manchester Guardian* in Paris. A Belgian Christian trade unionist, Jef Moons, joined the team in 1954. They did not have very many people to talk to: 23 journalists accredited to the ECSC in 1956. Some of them, such as Fernand Braun (³), began in their ranks a career that would end up at the EEC Commission. Others, such as Rainer Hellmann of the agency VWD (⁴) and, above all, Emanuele Gazzo, would become veritable pillars of the world of press correspondents in Brussels. On 12 March 1953 Gazzo published the first issue of the *Bulletin de l'Agence Europe*. Covering the ECSC, it was joined, from 9 December 1957, by a new daily bulletin entitled *Marché commun/Euratom*. The two publications merged on 2 January 1968.

In Luxembourg the service's activities expanded. The people were competent. They had that pioneering spirit which would earn them the nickname, along with others, of *fonctionnaires-militants* from the renowned journalist Jean Boissonnat. The task was a difficult one. The hopes that had sprung from the EDC Treaty and then from the framing of the statute of a European Community collapsed in 1954. As in other more recent circumstances, it would seem that European integration was suffering from a lack of education.

But while the task was enormous, the resources were derisory. As at 1 January 1956 the service directed by Rabier, whom the High Authority had appointed on a proposal from Monnet before his departure, employed 25 persons, only 18 of whom were in Luxembourg because the information service was partly decentralised to Bonn, Paris, Rome, London and Washington.

Its activity was channelled in two directions: wide-ranging general action through the media and through fairs and exhibitions, on the one hand, and specific action aimed at target groups such as trade unions, professional organisations and teachers, on the other.

While it is true that, originally, the question of information was far from being the focus of attention, its importance increased as the ECSC and its policies asserted themselves, putting others either temporarily or permanently in the shade. Decisions, which needed to be explained on account of their technicality, were taken. They were liable to displease some sector of industry or other or even some government or other. This was because the very idea of a Community, i.e. the Six as a whole, was revolutionary compared with the national approach. Through having to inform, attack or counter-attack, the ECSC gained credibility and legitimacy, thus forging the basis of an identity of which the High Authority constituted the spearhead. Needless to say, those who already did not appreciate the supranational nature of the ECSC very much were exasperated by information which they would have liked to be voiceless. Likewise, is there any need to stress that the brief but substantial experience of the

(¹) Rabier, J.-R., 'Les origines de la politique d'information européenne (1953–1973)', in Melchionni, M. G. (ed.), *Fonti e luoghi della documentazione europea — Istruzioni per l'uso*, Università degli Studi di Roma 'La Sapienza', Facoltà di Economia, Rome, 2000, p. 85.
(²) AMK C 33/5/104, Letter of Jean Monnet to Jacques-René Rabier, Paris, 20 February 1970.
(³) Interview with Fernand Braun, 8 December 2003.
(⁴) UCL, GEHEC, Interview with Marcel Mart by Béatrice Roeh, 7 April 1998.

Jacques-René Rabier at work. Jacqueline Lastenouse recalls: 'His desk was always covered with a mass of books, theses, dissertations and articles about Europe, and there were piles of all sorts of documents and publications on the floor, on his desk, on his cupboards. There was stuff everywhere.' (Interview with Jacqueline Lastenouse, 21 January 2004.)

ECSC had to be taken into account when the new institutions were born?

The Joint Press and Information Service (^{1})

On 14 January 1958 the Presidents of the three executives held a joint meeting in Luxembourg. The agenda included in particular the development of certain services common to the three

Communities, such as press and information. As early as the second meeting of the college, von der Groeben said that it would be a good idea to have a joint service in this area, specifying that two tasks would have to be carried out: 'Firstly, to make public opinion aware, in an even-handed manner, of the solutions set out in the Treaties and, secondly, to inform the Commission every day about what is in the newspapers'. With regard to the High Authority's information offices, he added that they would be able to continue their activities for the benefit of the three Communities. Lastly, he stressed the need to have a Spokesman for the EEC Commission as soon as possible (^{2}).

___
(^{1}) This chapter does not deal with four types of publication which are also information tools, namely: the products of the Publications Office, the *Official Journal of the European Communities* (OJ), the first issue of which appeared on 20 April 1958, the *General Report* to the Parliamentary Assembly and, lastly, the *Bulletin of the EEC*, publication of which was decided on 19 November 1958.

___
(^{2}) PV 2, EEC Commission, 24, 25 and 27 January 1958, Item XV, p. 8.

On 31 January 1958 in Luxembourg, at a meeting with all the members of the High Authority and with Sassen for Euratom, the EEC Commission heard a statement by Rabier about the operation of his service. Following this presentation, it seemed possible 'to establish, on the basis of the High Authority's Press and Information Service, a Joint Press and Information Service', while it was 'necessary to nominate for Brussels a Spokesman responsible for the Commission' ([1]).

What at first sight seemed straightforward soon became complicated. Luxembourg was one jump ahead. It showed this by temporarily placing four officials at the disposal of the EEC Commission, with one of them acting as liaison between Brussels and the High Authority ([2]). Was the latter on the inside lane? In May the Commission decided that Rabier would go to Brussels regularly for contacts with the members of the college 'with a view to the smooth operation of the Press Service' ([3]). And this at a time when the Belgian capital was the scene of the International and Universal Exhibition, where the presence of the Six was marked solely by the ECSC pavilion.

Imperceptibly, the question of information was subjected to stealthy attacks. Indeed, it was not without reluctance over a long period that the EEC Commission endorsed the solution of a joint service based on the ECSC template because 'the sovereignties of institutions are no less tenacious than national sovereignties' ([4]).

The Joint Service, administered by the Inter-Executive Group, was given a number of tasks: to organise the Communities' representation at events such as fairs and exhibitions, to increase the coverage of Community actions by radio, television and cinema, to produce information programmes aimed at trade unions, farmers, educational circles and non-member countries, as well as to bring out a range of publications and to organise visits and study trips.

However, one fundamental question was not resolved: the Spokesman's place in the set-up. On 16 December 1958 the Commission adopted a memorandum which it submitted to the Inter-Executive Group ([5]).

The Commission proposed that a director-general be given responsibility for ensuring the Joint Service's technical, administrative and budgetary cohesion. He would receive his instructions from the Inter-Executive Group but would be bound by each executive's instructions in its own sphere of responsibility. In consultation with the Spokesmen of the executives, who received their instructions directly from the latter, he would be responsible for coordinating press policy ([6]).

The options announced reflected the existing tensions between the executives and the future tensions between the Joint Service and the Spokesman. These tensions, which were illustrated by several refusals on the part of the EEC Commission to discuss compromise proposals presented by the Euratom Commission ([7]), explain why an agreement on the general rules for the management and organisation of the Joint Services was not reached until 1 March 1960, whereas the establishment plan of the Spokesman's Group had been decided back in October of the previous year ([8]).

Under the March 1960 agreement, the Press and Information Service would be run by a management board comprising at least one member from

---

[1] PV 3, EEC Commission, 31 January 1958, Item IV.a, pp. 3–4.
[2] PV 11, EEC Commission, 24–27 March 1958, Item XVI, p. 15.
[3] PV 18, EEC Commission, 20–23 May 1958, Item VI, pp. 7–8.
[4] Rabier, J.-R., 'La naissance d'une politique [...]', op. cit., p. 28.

[5] PV 41, EEC Commission, 10 December 1958, and PV 42, 16 December 1958.
[6] PV 30, EEC Commission, 24 September 1958, Item XIV, p. 12; PV 31, 1 October 1958, Item XI, p. 8; PV 34, 21 October 1958, Item XIV, p. 8; PV 36, 5 November 1958, Item VII, pp. 2–4; PV 42, 16 December 1958, Item XII, pp. 2–6.
[7] PV 54, EEC Commission, 16 March 1959, Item XIV, p. 4; PV 77, 12 October 1959, Item II.2.b, p. 5.
[8] PV 54, EEC Commission, 16 March 1959, Item XIII, pp. 3–4; PV 57, 23 April 1959, Item XII, p. 10; PV 79, 28 October 1959, Item XII, pp. 6–7.

The senior officials in the Spokesman's Group

Before 1968

— Spokesman	Giorgio Smoquina (1959–61)
	Beniamino Olivi (1961–68)
— Deputy Spokesmen	Paul Collowald (1959–61)
	Joachim von Stülpnagel (1959–61)
— Head of Section, 'Information for Community countries'	Paul Collowald (1961–67)
— Head of Section, 'Information for non-member countries'	Joachim von Stülpnagel (1961)
	Dietrich Behm (1962–67)

From 1968

— Spokesman	Beniamino Olivi (1968–1972)
— Deputy Spokesman	Paul Collowald (1968–72)

each of the three institutions ([1]) and chaired by the EEC Commission.

With regard to the Spokesman, the EEC Commission reluctantly accepted the proposal from the High Authority and the Euratom Commission to attach each Spokesman's Group to its executive rather than to the Joint Service ([2]). An important nuance was, however, introduced a few weeks later when the EEC Commission arranged for the Spokesman's Group to be able to issue opinions on the Joint Service's drafts ([3]).

On 24 March 1960 the management board held its first meeting and adopted the establishment plan. The Joint Press and Information Service, headed by Rabier, comprised, on the one hand, sections spe-cialised by information target (trade unions, agriculture, overseas, universities) and resources (fairs/exhibitions, radio/TV/cinema, publications, visits and training courses) and, on the other hand, press and information offices in the Member States and certain non-member countries (London and Washington). But the skirmishing continued, whether about the appointment of officials and their attachment to other DGs ([4]) or about the balance between nationalities, which was deemed insufficient.

However, there was also internal skirmishing, particularly about the struggle for influence relating to the Spokesman and his Group, and between the latter and the Joint Service.

The Spokesman and his Group

The position of Spokesman was inspired by the German practice of the *Sprecher der Regierung* ([5]).

([1]) Ludlow, P., 'Frustrated ambitions: the European Commission and the formation of a European identity, 1958–1967', in Bitsch, M.-Th., Loth, W. and Poidevin, R. (eds), *Institutions européennes et identités européennes*, Bruylant, Brussels, 1998, p. 311.

([2]) In January Sicco Mansholt and Giuseppe Petrilli issued a communication on this subject. On 17 February the majority of the college voted in favour of attaching the Spokesman's Group to the Joint Service, but only to the extent that the Commission was responsible for administrative management of the latter. Giuseppe Caron, Jean Rey and Lambert Schaus voted against. PV 88, EEC Commission, 22 January 1960, Item X.a, p. 9; PV 95, 2 March 1960, Item V.1, pp. 8 and 9; PV 93, 17 February 1960, Item XXXI.B, pp. 14–16.

([3]) PV 98, EEC Commission, 23 March 1960, Item XIII.B, p. 14.

([4]) The agricultural information and overseas information sections remained an integral part of the Joint Service, while seconding officials to the Spokesman's Group. See PV 106, EEC Commission, 31 May 1960, Item XXXVI, pp. 10–15.

([5]) Interview with Bino Olivi, 26 January 2004.

Hallstein wanted a German. His colleagues were reluctant because the Commission's Spokesman did not necessarily have to be the President's Spokesman. Moreover, his candidate was Joachim von Stülpnagel, who was 'a young diplomat, very go-ahead' [1]. He was 'a must' [2]. But there was one snag. He was related to General Otto von Stülpnagel, the German military commander in France until the summer of 1941. In the College of Commissioners, Lemaignen protested, as did Marjolin [3]. In order to resolve the situation, an Italian diplomat, Giorgio Smoquina, was appointed on 10 December 1958. He stayed in the post until April 1961.

In order to complete the set-up and, probably, to satisfy the Germans and the French, the College appointed two deputy Spokesmen in October 1959. Hallstein, who was nothing if not persistent, chose von Stülpnagel, who would deal mainly with external problems. Marjolin's choice was a former journalist — Paul Collowald — who had worked for *Le Nouvel Alsacien* as well as being correspondent for *Le Monde* in Strasbourg before being recruited by the High Authority at the end of 1957 to develop information in the fields of universities, education and youth [4].

After the departure of Smoquina in 1961, the efforts to identify a successor came to nothing and the Executive Secretary suggested a consensus choice, namely the official responsible for handling the dossier in Caron's office [5]. The official in question was Beniamino — known as Bino — Olivi. An Italian jurist, he had briefly been a magistrate in his native country before joining the Commission, where in DG IV he had dealt with patents before being summoned to join Caron's office.

Olivi, who would become 'an Italian shooting star' [6], considered that his role was to explain the Commission, its positions and its decisions to the press [7]. 'I "am" the press', he said. 'The press "goes" via me' [8]. But the way of doing the job had to be invented. Olivi 'will remain, in the collective memory of the press and European officials, as the pioneer and founder of this original profession in the context, itself original, of the Community institutional system' [9].

Olivi was not on his own. Firstly, the 'new old hands' of the Spokesman's Group initiated him somehow into a job with which he was not familiar and, secondly, the Group, officially attached to the executive from 1 January 1961, expanded rapidly. Immediately after the Stresa Conference in 1958, Mansholt had taken on Clara Meyers, from the Council of Europe [10]. Information for the British and Americans was not forgotten. It was an aspect on which Jean Monnet was already keen in Luxembourg. Richard Mayne and, later, John Lambert performed this task in Brussels.

The people to whom the Spokesman and his Group talked were the journalists. Weekly meetings were held with them at midday on Thursdays 'in a rudimentary little room, almost like a living-room, for around 40 journalists' [11] who were informed about the previous day's deliberations of the Commission. Meetings for the lobbyists were also organised every Thursday until the end of the 1960s [12]. Paul Collowald explained in this regard that 'as Bino Olivi wanted to reserve the press room for accredited or passing journalists, the presence of lobbyists was not allowed' [13]. However, information for UNICE, ETUC and a few other European-level organisations was not to be taken lightly. The Executive Secretary, Émile Noël, in agreement with the Spokesman, proposed the following compromise to the organisations in question: 'Every Thursday, Paul Collowald, Deputy Spokesman, will receive the six or seven

---

[1] Interview with Paul Collowald, 2 December 2003.
[2] Interview with Manuel Santarelli, 4 March 2004.
[3] Ibid. and interview with Bino Olivi, 26 January 2004.
[4] Interview with Paul Collowald, 2 December 2003.
[5] Ibid.
[6] Interview with Daniel Cardon de Lichtbuer, 12 November 2003.

[7] Interview with Bino Olivi, 9 February 2004.
[8] Ibid., 26 January 2004.
[9] Interview with Manuel Santarelli, 4 March 2004.
[10] Ibid.
[11] De l'Écotais, Y., *L'Europe sabotée*, Rossel, Brussels, Paris, 1976, p. 144.
[12] Interview with Manuel Santarelli, 4 March 2004.
[13] Note by Paul Collowald, December 2005.

Commission Press Room in the Joyeuse Entrée building. Relations with the press were built up gradually on a pragmatic basis.
On the counter to the right, information material is available for accredited journalists.
At the main table: Camille Becker, Paul Collowald, Bino Olivi, Clara Meyers, Stephen Freidberg and Robert Cox.
To the right of Camille Becker: Norbert Kohlhase.

approved representatives in his office to present and comment on the Commission's decisions' (¹).

The work within the Group was the subject of trade-offs. Olivi, the Spokesman, who attended Commission meetings except when there was a restricted meeting, gave a verbal report to his colleagues. Depending on the outcome of the meeting, it was decided who would speak about what and how.

While the main task of the Spokesman and his deputies was to 'reply brilliantly or otherwise to the journalists' (²), it was also necessary to provide

the national information offices with the where-withal to answer the questions that were put to them. Smoquina drafted what soon came to be known as 'BIO notes' for *Bureaux d'information only'*. They were sent by telex on Thursdays. In June 1960 the 'Information memos' were launched. They presented the substance of issues in article form and summed up the situation generated for this or that sector by the development of the common market (³).

Olivi pursued and developed his predecessor's initiatives. Having apparently gained Hallstein's confidence, despite the latter's mania for secrecy

(¹) Note by Paul Collowald, December 2005.
(²) Interview with Daniel Cardon de Lichtbuer, 12 November 2003.

(³) BAC 243/1991 13, Note from Giorgio Smoquina to the national offices, 1 June 1960.

noted by many observers, he undoubtedly occupied a key position in the Commission's set-up. His personality and talent matched those of the Director of the Joint Service. Olivi and Rabier were 'two personalities who respected but did not like each other', according to one observer ([1]). 'With Rabier, there has always been a rivalry', declared Olivi ([2]): over and above questions of personality, talent, even commitment — 'Rabier more committed in a radical federalist way; Olivi [...] less dogmatic and more convinced of the need to take account of national realities and the risks for Europe of a rampant supranationality' ([3]).

What information policy?

The Commission not only needed a structure to carry out its information policy. Above all, it had to define its goals. Did it want to design and implement a policy whose objective was to contribute to the formation of a 'European public spirit', a 'European awareness', in accordance with the undertakings of the 'founding fathers' and the proclamations in the preambles to the Treaties of Paris and Rome, or merely to disseminate news about the day-to-day activities of the institutions? This choice was the crux of the information policy, especially when it had to be shared with the Member States.

As regards the intentions, it would appear that, despite the results of opinion polls showing that the general public was very poorly informed about the construction of Europe ([4]), it was preferable to target the opinion formers, those 'sociological chequer-boards' as they were termed by Raymond Rifflet, quoted liberally by Rabier. 'As a chequer-board you have to take all the different European, national and regional circles, professional and otherwise, political, journalistic, the [various associations]. And ensure that these groups and persons get to know each other, see

what they have in common. This is also the method of Monnet, who did not talk about sociology but simply spoke about making citizens aware of what was being done on their behalf and, if possible, with their participation.' ([5])

While the saga of the status of the Joint Service was unfolding, men and women were working. However, the Commission was not happy. Indeed, the public information campaign on dismantling of quotas, which was due to start on 1 January 1959, did not get off the ground ([6]). Lemaignen took this opportunity to criticise sharply a way of informing that he would have liked to be more ambitious at the same time as being served by leading writers such as Raymond Aron. Next it was the turn of the Assembly to have its say. In this regard, the complicity between certain officials and MEPs was flagrant, on both this and other matters. Rabier collaborated with the Dutch Christian-Socialist MEP Wilhelmus Johannes Schuijt, former correspondent of the *Tijd* in Paris and former deputy Secretary-General of the *Nouvelles Équipes Internationales*, on drafting 'just the two of them' the report on information that would be submitted to the Strasbourg Assembly on the occasion of the debate on the budget for 1960.

On 20 November 1959, after the German MEP Gerhard Kreyssig, on behalf of the Socialist Group, had asked for (and obtained) a special appropriation to be voted 'for expenditure intended exclusively to intensify at national level in the six countries information for the general public about the European Communities, particularly by developing the training of young people in a European spirit', Schuijt, in a fiery speech, criticised the shillyshallying of the executives in organising the Joint Service and defining a common conception of information ([7]). At the end of the

([1]) Interview with Manuel Santarelli, 4 March 2004.
([2]) Interview with Bino Olivi, 26 January 2004.
([3]) Interview with Manuel Santarelli, 4 March 2004.
([4]) Ludlow, P., op. cit., p. 316.

([5]) Interview with Jacques-René Rabier, 8 January 2004. What might be called the 'doctrine' of the Joint Press and Information Service was outlined in a communication from its head to the Institut d'études européenne — Université Libre de Bruxelles (17–18 February 1965) entitled 'L'information des Européens sur l'intégration de l'Europe'.
([6]) PV 37, EEC Commission, 10 November 1958, Item IV, pp. 4–6; PV 52, 3 March 1959, Item VIII, p. 7.
([7]) JO, APE, meeting of 20 November 1959, pp. 35–39.

debate, on 24 November, the Assembly reaffirmed 'the capital importance' of an efficient information policy of the European Community with a view to fostering the shaping of a European public opinion aware of the main cultural and material values of the unification of Europe.

This way that some in the Commission had of practising activism, with or without the help of members of the Assembly, was not to everyone's taste, as shown by the fact that, on 13 June 1960, the Ministers for Foreign Affairs decided to organise a meeting of the heads of their ministries' press services to examine a number of information issues, most of which concerned the Communities, without the participation of the Joint Service [1]. This significant incident contributed ultimately to placing the issue on a political footing because the scale of the budget resources made available for information depended on the choices that would be made.

In October 1962 the Council, while acknowledging the need for a debate with the executives, put off holding one. The Assembly saw things differently [2]. In November it adopted a resolution which, while setting the general objective that had been pointed out, firmly underlined the vital importance of an information policy and the urgency of discussing it within the Council [3].

It was probably not just this resolution, no more than the Commission's point of view as expressed by Caron, which led to the situation being resolved. The virtual end of the negotiations on the accession of the United Kingdom in January 1963 provided an opportunity for France to settle a number of scores.

In March 1963 Coreper asked the Commission to present a document that would form a basis for discussion [4]. The memorandum adopted by the Commission on 26 June 1963, in agreement with the other two executives, was augmented by the suggestions from the Spokesman's Group. It did not mention, as a result of the reservations expressed by Mansholt, the administrative problems but only the policy to be followed with a view to 'contributing to the formation of a European civic awareness' [5].

After the memorandum had been examined by Coreper and an ad hoc working party, the Council gave its opinion in October 1963 on four important points:

— development and rationalisation of the Communities' information policy;

— creation of a group of national experts on information;

— increased use of the services of the Member States' embassies in associated and non-member countries, whose activity would have to be coordinated [6], while a positive response would be given to the Commission's suggestion to open two new information offices in New York and Geneva;

— creation of a Council working party to supervise the Commission's action [7].

This working party, the creation of which reflected the concern to place the Commission under supervision that year, which can be termed the year of 'press leaks' [8], saw at its very first meeting the French representative launch a vitriolic attack on the information policy pursued up to then by the Commission and suggest a redirection of expenditure within the budget allocated to the sector. A budget which, in 1963 precisely, was reduced significantly before being revised

---

[1] PV 107, EEC Commission, 15 June 1960, Item V, pp. 3–4.
[2] Ludlow, P., op. cit., p. 321.
[3] Ibid.
[4] Ibid.

[5] Presented to the Commission on 19 June by Henri Rochereau, the memorandum was adopted by the Commission on 26 June. PV 232, EEC Commission, Item XXXV, pp. 31–32; PV 233, Item IV, pp. 6–8.
[6] Clavel, J.-Cl. and Collet, P., op. cit., p. 50.
[7] Ludlow, P., op. cit., p. 324.
[8] Between 1958 and 1972 the College discussed the matter of press leaks on 26 occasions. The year 1963 alone accounted for 19.2 % of this total.

upwards, as if this warning shot was expected to change the direction of the Joint Service, which the Council, following in France's footsteps, would like to see pay more attention, in close consultation with Coreper, to non-member countries rather than to the Member States (¹). This was because France was not too pleased, for example, that the Paris office had developed since 1959, at the initiative of Marjolin, 'parallel circuits' (²) in the form, particularly, of *Notes d'information* intended for a 'small number of initiates' (³). The kingpin of the enterprise, the head of the office in the rue des Belles Feuilles, the urbane François Fontaine, another of those *fonctionnaires-militants* who had the gift of exasperating Paris, was aware that the 'goal of providing arguments and guidelines would quickly come up against political difficulties' (⁴). There was and would be no shortage of the latter. In February 1968, to give one example, Fontaine published in the magazine *France Forum* an article entitled 'Une dégradation de l'ordre international'. Jean Rey, noting that it contained 'specific criticisms with regard to the French government's foreign policy that were expressed, in certain places, in very vivid terms', remonstrated with the author: 'I consider that, in acting in this way, you have gone beyond the bounds that must be observed. While the officials of our press offices must enjoy a degree of freedom in expressing their thoughts, they must also show restraint and refrain from publicly criticising the Member States' policy [...] I would be grateful if you would abide by this line of conduct in the future.' (⁵)

It was not therefore surprising that the Joint Service and, later, the Information DG did not enjoy a good press, both outside and inside the Commission. In addition to the 'overlaps' between the Joint Service and the Spokesman's

Group (⁶) and to the lack of 'rotation of officials' assigned to the information offices (⁷), what some people complained about was the activism from which the sector was suffering. In 1964 Émile Noël (about whom some said that 'as regards relations with press and information, he was not necessarily an ally' (⁸) because he wanted them to be more targeted) wrote to Fontaine: 'I have always deplored the dispersion among many sectors of our information activity, which can have only a sprinkler effect.' (⁹) The Secretary-General was probably right. Not only did the Joint Service have to 'sail as closely as possible to its management board' (¹⁰) but, with the means at its disposal, it could not do everything.

What resources?

In 1961 the Joint Service had a staff of 82, including the information offices in Bonn, Paris, The Hague, Rome, London and Washington, and had a budget of BEF 87.2 million. Some, even within the College of Commissioners, thought that this was too much. Thus, the decision taken by the College to commit in 1964 the appropriations needed for fitting and equipping a recording studio managed by the 'Radio, Television, Cinema' section of the Joint Press and Information Service on the Commission's premises was not unanimous. In fact, Schaus abstained, as did Colonna di Paliano, the latter because he had not been consulted, despite the fact that he was head of the sector concerned! (¹¹)

The Joint Service's tendency to go ahead regardless did not founder so much on the refusal to increase the appropriations as on the failure to increase staff numbers. As far as the budget was

(¹) Ludlow, P., op. cit.
(²) AMK C 34/1/93, note by François Fontaine with a view to a meeting in Brussels with Robert Marjolin, Paris, 20 January 1959. The note was forwarded to François Duchêne on 21 January (AMK C 34/1/94).
(³) Ibid.
(⁴) Ibid.
(⁵) AMK C 34/1/170, Jean Rey to François Fontaine, Brussels, 10 April 1968.
(⁶) AMK C 33/4/302, Clara Meyers, Note to Beniamino Olivi, Brussels, 2 December 1963.
(⁷) AMK C 33/4/297, Richard Mayne, Note to Beniamino Olivi, 18 July 1963.
(⁸) Interview with Paul Collowald, 2 December 2003.
(⁹) AMK C 33/4/106, Émile Noël to François Fontaine, Brussels, 10 September 1964.
(¹⁰) Interview with Manuel Santarelli, 4 March 2004.
(¹¹) PV 296, EEC Commission, 1964, Item XVI, p. 22.

Renato Ruggiero, Franco Maria Malfatti and Rudolf Dumont du Voitel in the Commission TV studio.
Rudolf Dumont du Voitel, Head of the Radio, Television, Cinema Division in DG X, recalls: 'What we said was this:
"After technology, we also have to be able to supply information to broadcasters, make suggestions and give assistance."
But we couldn't recruit. There were no posts for the purpose. In order to recruit, I had to get up to all sorts of tricks.
Take on temporary staff. Then I had this idea: why not arrange for the broadcasters to second an editor to Brussels for a year
at a time. It was in their interests to have a representative in Brussels who could witness developments at first hand and,
as the representative of his language and his country, make his qualities available to our information bulletin, and the upshot
was that we were able to put out a "bulletin" in four languages every day. It was entitled 'Nous pouvons vous aider'
(We can help you). So we had a multilingual editorial team that met at the beginning of each week. Later we changed
the system and set up a production team. We had cameras we could use and we had film transmission equipment.
And so, when important things were going on in the Council, we prepared animated films using the film techniques available
at the time (before modern electronic aids) on decisions concerning agriculture, external relations, the customs union
or what have you. The editorial team not only supervised production but also wrote the texts for the animated films
in the various languages and prepared daily bulletins for the then six Member States of the Community.
They also did the rewriting and fine-tuning work.' (Interview with Rudolf Dumont du Voitel, 1 December 2003.)

concerned, the warning shot in 1963 was followed by an increase in the sums allocated. In 1965 they were more than double what they had been in 1961. That being so, this budget was particularly complex because it was a Joint Service. Hence, 'specific common information expenditure' was implemented according to a distribution key between the three executives ([1]) that bore the hallmark of real 'Chinese book-keeping' ([2]).

The number of statutory staff, 85 in all, remained unchanged. But this figure was deceptive because the Joint Service seemed to have been a fertile ground of inventiveness to offset the gaps in the organisation chart. That is why 'support staff' have to be added to statutory staff. They officially numbered 29 in 1965, divided between Brussels and the information offices. But this was not all. Account must also be taken of the contracts offered to personnel working in Brussels under the label of experts and the 'personnel taken on by associations whose activity is entirely or partially subsidised' by the Joint Service and then by the DG ([3]). As Rabier explained: 'Ways were found' not only of increasing staff numbers but also, and probably above all, of conveying information where officially the services could not act openly ([4]). Fausta Deshormes-La Valle knew these 'ways'. Between 1961 and 1973, the date of her establishment as an official, she had '21 contracts as an expert, auxiliary, temporary and then auxiliary again [...]' ([5]).

Placing under supervision?

The year 1965 therefore began in a climate that can be termed relatively satisfactory, provided that the ingenious ways found to increase staff numbers are viewed likewise. The situation deteriorated rapidly, however. In June 1965, foreshadowing in a way the 'empty chair' crisis, the repre-

sentatives of the French government stopped attending the meetings of the working parties where the Joint Information Service and national administrations were represented, while a visit to the French Conseil d'État, organised by Gaudet in agreement with the Keeper of the Seals, was cancelled by Paris at the last minute. At issue was a letter from Rabier 'presenting to the Members of the Assembly an American questionnaire regarding General de Gaulle's policy' ([6]). This was only one of a number of incidents. Yann de l'Écotais, special envoy of AFP in Brussels from 1965 onwards, recounts that the Commission's television studio was inaugurated during the actual crisis. France's Permanent Representation was neither informed nor invited. Scandal mingled with paranoia because 'we imagined that from "his" studio [...] President Hallstein was going to address "live" the peoples of Europe' ([7]). Yet another incident. During the French presidential election campaign, a booklet in a silver cover about the Church and Europe 'was widely distributed in the "religiously" sensitive regions that were a naturally favourable ground for Jean Lecanuet', the General's adversary. 'Prepared with editorial help from the Office catholique d'information sur les problèmes européens (OCIPE) and financed at the request of the Paris office' ([8]), the booklet was published by the Joint Service. What happened next is easy to imagine ([9]).

Information policy, which no longer claimed, at least officially, the Commission's attention during the crisis, was subjected in Luxembourg in January 1966 to particularly close scrutiny by France through the famous heptalogue intended to 'put the Commission in its place' ([10]).

([1]) Interview with Robert Pendville, 16 December 2003.
([2]) Interview with Jacques-René Rabier, 8 January 2004.
([3]) COM(70) PV 146 final, meeting of 9 December 1970, p. 18.
([4]) Interview with Jacques-René Rabier, 8 January 2004.
([5]) Interview with Fausta Deshormes-La Valle, 2 February 2004.

([6]) AMK C/34/1/150, memorandum of a conversation between Van Helmont and Fontaine, 6 July 1965. The letter introduced the author of the survey, Professor Daniel Lerner, and not the questionnaire, stated Jacques-René Rabier in a note of 12 December 2005. The results of the survey were published by Lerner, D. and Gordon, M., *Euratlantica — Changing perspectives of European elites*, The MIT Press, Cambridge and London, 1969, who thanked, among others, Émile Noël and Jacques-René Rabier (p. VIII).
([7]) De l'Écotais, Y., op. cit., p. 34.
([8]) Note by J. Rabier of 12 December 2005. The OCIPE, created in Strasbourg in 1956, opened an office in Brussels in 1963.
([9]) De l'Écotais, Y., op. cit., p. 34.
([10]) Interview with Paul Collowald, 2 December 2003.

The material origin of the 'empty chair' crisis, according to the Spokesman

'The agenda for the meeting of the Commission held during a part-session of the European Parliament on 24 March 1965 included the discussion and, if need be (but President Hallstein intended to obtain it "at all costs"), approval of the draft regulation on financing of the common agricultural policy. The Spokesman had had a lengthy discussion with Hallstein before the meeting and had been strongly encouraged to talk to the press about it, which was altogether exceptional for him. Several journalists had therefore waited for the end of the meeting (late afternoon) to have some news. Hallstein authorised (and encouraged) the Spokesman to convene the press before the extraordinary meeting of Parliament, which took place that very evening. A summary of the document approved by the Commission (by a majority after a very tense debate) was quickly prepared by the Spokesman's Group and handed out to the press (before the Members of Parliament received the document, sparking off a brief incident between the officials of Parliament and those of the Commission). It was therefore the Spokesman who was — materially — at the origin of the "empty chair" crisis [...]

The episode is worth mentioning because the "abnormal" behaviour of Hallstein revealed his determination to provoke the crisis or, at the very least, a confrontation between France and its partners.'

Correspondence from Bino Olivi
to Michel Dumoulin, May 2006.
(Translated from the French)

Paris clearly called for changes to be made in the conduct of information policy, which had to observe a degree of neutrality vis-à-vis the Member States' overall policy and had to be managed by both the Council and the Commission. Whereas the other five partners sought to cushion the impact of France's demands somewhat ([1]), the Commission expressed its willingness to cooperate. Colonna di Paliano suggested consulting Coreper

about the broad lines of the information programme before it was adopted by the three executives. The Commissioner felt that the executives should reaffirm their full authority over the Joint Service, while taking account of developments concerning the future merger ([2]). Finally, on the strength of the relative support of the Five, the Commission preserved its autonomy in the field of information as the time approached to organise the Single Commission, which, in the Joint Service, had been the focus of attention since March 1964 ([3]).

The Single Commission

On 28 July 1967 Karl-Heinz Narjes, hitherto head of Hallstein's *cabinet*, was given the task of producing under the authority of Coppé, who was responsible for press and information, a draft organisation chart of the new Directorate-General for Press and Information ([4]), DG X, of which he would be the first Director-General.

DG X was created in November 1967. 'It was a relief', recalled Rabier and Pendville. 'For us, this simplified the budgets. We no longer had some people attached to Euratom and others to the other two executives, with bits and pieces of the budget.' ([5]) At the same time, it was 'a big split' because Rabier, 'who is not known for his "Gaullist" sentiments' ([6]), was discarded in favour of Hallstein's *chef de cabinet*, for whom a place had to be found ([7]).

The Spokesman's Group, which had merged with those of the other two executives, came under President Rey. The Spokesman of the EEC Commission, Olivi, was appointed to head the new service. He had a lot on his plate. In 1967 the

---

([1]) Ludlow, P., op. cit., p. 323.

([2]) PV 347, EEC Commission, 1966, Item VI, pp. 8–9; PV 349, Item V.9, pp. 4–5; PV 350, Item III.3, pp. 5–7.
([3]) AMK 113/1/6, Richard Mayne, Note to Mr Beniamino Olivi, Brussels, 6 March 1964.
([4]) PV, EC Commission, 28 July 1967, 4, Item XXI.B, p. 34.
([5]) Interview with Jacques-René Rabier, 8 January 2004.
([6]) AMK C 33/5/100, Jean-Jacques Servan-Schreiber to Jean Monnet, Paris, 3 November 1969.
([7]) Interview with Robert Pendville, 16 December 2003.

Senior officials in the Joint Press and Information Service and then in DG X (1960–72)	
— Director of the Joint Service	Jacques-René Rabier (1961–67)
— Director-General for Press and Information	Karl-Heinz Narjes (1968–70)
	Jacques-René Rabier (1970–72)
— Director of information and information media (Press and Information DG)	Louis Janz (1968–72)
— Director of information for particular sectors (Press and Information DG)	Jacques-René Rabier (1968–70)

number of journalists accredited to the Commission was getting on for 500, making it one of the leading services of its kind in the world.

In practical terms, the College of Commissioners was preoccupied by the questions relating to the staff cuts proposed by Levi Sandri, which were accepted without too much ado by Coppé (¹). In return, while there was still a lot of discussion about the staff of the DG and the Spokesman's Group, von der Groeben proposed resorting to temporary recruitments in order to make savings while allowing the work to continue (²).

As the problems relating to staff seemed to be on the way to being resolved, not without giving some the impression that the merger was an opportunity to bring to the Information DG 'people from the ECSC, Euratom […] who were not always the best' (³), the Commission turned its attention to the aims and organisation of information policy.

Drawn up in connection with the restructuring of the services, the proposed programme was discussed in March 1968. The main areas of focus were improving citizens' knowledge of the working of the Communities, increasing the appropriations allocated to information for the applicant countries, and the importance of information for universities and adult education. Nothing unexpected there! However, the discussion dragged on. At issue was the way in which the Council and the Commission could agree on the use of the appropriations for information.

This thorny question remained on the table throughout 1968 (⁴). In the spring of the following year, Coppé formulated proposals which purported not to resolve the question of relations with the Council but to decide the Commission's position with regard to determining the policy to be pursued. The scope of the one or two general principles outlined by the Commissioner on 26 March 1969 was far from negligible. On the one hand, the Commission would have to hold a debate each year on the press and information policy in order to determine the general line of information activities, before translating it into budgetary terms. On the other hand, the Commission had to allocate more appropriations to its public relations. Lastly, stressing the

---

(¹) PV 15, EC Commission, Items VIII.8 and XII.1–2, pp. 22–23, 29–30; PV 23, EC Commission, 1968, Item IV.2, p. 4.

(²) PV 54, EC Commission, Item VII, pp. 42–43; PV 63, Item XX.1–2, p. 36; PV 68, Item XVI.c, p. 20; PV 69, Item XIV.b, pp. 22–23; PV 72, Item XLIII.1, p. 35; PV 73, Item XXVII.2, pp. 17–18; PV 103, Item XXII.b, p. 11.

(³) Interview with Robert Pendville, 16 December 2003.

(⁴) PV 30, EC Commission, Item XXVIII, pp. 8–12; PV 31, Item XVII.7, p. 28; PV 32, Item XIV, p. 15; PV 34, Item IX, pp. 15–16. The discussion about the budget did not resume until November 1968. See PV 58, Item VII, p. 11.

importance of genuine cooperation between the Press and Information DG and the other directorates-general, Coppé proposed the appointment in each of them of an official responsible for maintaining ongoing contacts with DG X. This could be the official already responsible for liaison with the Spokesman (¹).

The proposal was not without interest. But it was likely to cause difficulties if some did not play the game, or played it too well. So, in the weeks following Coppé's proposal, the College was obliged to consider on two occasions the allegation that DG X had given the text of the Aigrain Report, which is dealt with in the chapter on research, to a number of journalists, whereas the Commission had decided not to publish it. Even worse, as Raymond Barre stressed, *Communautés européennes*, a Commission publication, made public certain information that was not intended to be in the public domain (²). Similar incidents were observed inter alia in The Hague and Bonn.

Decidedly, the question of control of information was becoming more important at the very time when the increase in the number of accredited journalists was strengthening the role of the Spokesman. But, whereas with Coppé things happened in a relatively good-natured way — 'they let Albert amuse himself' with information, reported Daniel Cardon (³) — they changed after 1 July 1970.

The responsibility — or should that be guardianship? — for information was handed to the Luxembourger Albert Borschette. The former Spokesman and former members of DG X agreed on one thing: the former Permanent Representative of Luxembourg intended to wipe the slate clean. While Narjes declared that he demolished everything (⁴), Olivi complained that he 'wanted to be the Commission's Spokesman and bring in his

> **Monnet encourages the appointment of Rabier to succeed Narjes**
>
> 'From the beginning of the ECSC, I had put Rabier in charge of information. He handled it remarkably well. I think [...] that you have under you an exceptional man from every point of view, experienced in these difficult tasks relating to information.'
>
> AMK C 33/5/198, Jean Monnet to Jean Rey, Paris, 8 November 1969. (Translated from the French)

Luxembourgers in place of Rabier and myself' (⁵). He 'really did a lot of harm' to DG X (⁶), he 'paved the way for the break-up' of the university and youth information teams that followed enlargement (⁷).

Rabier was appointed on 4 March 1970 to succeed Narjes, who had become Minister for Economic Affairs and Transport of Schleswig-Holstein in November 1969, and there was no doubt that relations between the Commissioner and the Director-General were fraught. A particularly significant anecdote bears witness to this.

Borschette, whose literary talent was acknowledged, had been conscripted into the ranks of the Wehrmacht and had fought on the eastern front. This 'against our will' past was far from being always well perceived. In 1959 the Commissioner had published a volume of war memoirs. Rabier, whose humour could be lethal, was embittered by the Commissioner's behaviour with regard to information and offered his staff a copy of the work whose title said it all: *Continuez à mourir* [...] (continue dying [...]) (⁸).

Borschette therefore intended to take information in hand. The study of reforms was started in July 1970. One of the main ideas was that 'the improve-

---

(¹) PV 73, Commission, 1969, Item XXXIII, pp. 38–44.
(²) PV 76, EC Commission, 1969, Item XXXIII, p. 19; PV 78, Item IX, p. 4.
(³) Interview with Daniel Cardon de Lichtbuer, 22 November 2003.
(⁴) Interview with Karl-Heinz Narjes, 24 May 2004.

(⁵) Interview with Bino Olivi, 26 January 2004.
(⁶) Interview with Fausta Deshormes-La Valle, 2 February 2004.
(⁷) Interview with Jacqueline Lastenouse-Bury, 21 January 2004.
(⁸) Interview with Jacques-René Rabier, 8 January 2004.

ment of information for the public on the problems of the construction of Europe depends on the convergence of the efforts of all the information services: those of the European institutions and those of the national governments', according to the programme of information activities for 1971 [1] — a programme that went hand in hand with the reorganisation of the DG adopted on 5 May 1971 [2].

The new organisation chart seemed clear. In contrast, the distribution of responsibilities was somewhat ambiguous and a source of conflict and confusion between units. While four services were directly attached to the Director-General, the two directorates — Information Target Groups and Information Resources — now seemed to be seen as being able to carry out activities likely to come into conflict with those carried out under the direct authority of Rabier. For example, a group on economic and social information, under the direct authority of the Director of Information, was 'responsible for the design of information on subjects relating to social policy', in particular [3]. However, directly attached to Rabier was a Directorate for trade union information, of which it could be said at the very least that it was primarily interested in social policy. Similarly, within the Directorate for Information Resources, the Division for Audiovisual Media seemed authorised or even encouraged (which was nothing new — see below) to go it alone, as shown by the secondment to it of three journalists from radio and television organisations in Member States [4]. Borschette kept a very close watch of this operation with the head of division concerned, Dumont du Voitel.

This being so, the Commission devoted more time to examining the annual activity programme, and

this gave rise to certain choices in terms of priorities for action. Thus, in 1971, it highlighted consumer information, intensification of agricultural information in connection with the new CAP guidelines and the need to develop information measures in Belgium [5]. The following year, the emphasis was on social information [6], although the change in public opinion prompted some concern. 'The political and even economic integration of Europe is no longer something that is self-evident for large sections of the population within the Community', read the introduction to the information policy programme for 1972 [7]. Even more disturbing, 'the strongest criticisms of Community policy come nowadays from a section of the young population, especially those who are politically committed' [8]. In the light of this situation and the challenges posed by economic and monetary union, enlargement and the position of the Community in the world, the principles of information policy were listed in 21 points, including 'information policy must follow uniform guidelines laid down specifically for this purpose by the Commission or its competent member in or as a supplement to the annual programme [...]. The Directorate-General [...] and the Spokesman's Group shall cooperate closely and complement each other.' [9] Moreover, DG X 'will henceforth make sure even more that the results of its work are checked. The information resources deployed must give results commensurate with the expenditure committed.' And, the sting in the tail, DG X 'must be aware that its scope in terms of personnel and administration is limited. Its actions must be circumscribed in a way that does not compromise effectiveness and transparency.' [10]

While approving the programme, the Commission stressed strongly, at the end of 1971 and the beginning of 1972, that the decision to award grants,

[1] 'Programme d'activité d'information pour 1971', SEC(71) 590 final, p. 2.

[2] PV 162, EC Commission, 1971, 1, Item VI.b, pp. 8–14. On the discussions prior to the adoption of the new provisions, see PV 156, EC Commission, 1971, Item XVIII.b, p. 5; PV 159, Item XXII, p. 20; PV 161, Items X.1 and XVIII.d, pp. 18 and 16.

[3] 'Réorganisation de la direction générale presse et information', 30 April 1971, SEC(71) 1626, p. 3.

[4] 'Note à l'attention de MM. les membres de la Commission', 7 December 1971, Annex II, 'Projet de réponse à la question écrite No 401/71 de M. Vredeling', SEC(71) 4395.

[5] PV 154, EC Commission, 1971, Item XXIII, p. 16; PV 159, Item XXII, p. 20; PV 161, Items X.1 and XVII, pp. 18 and 24.

[6] PV 188, EC Commission, 1971, Item XXV.a, p. 21; PV 189, Item XXIII, pp. 19–22; PV 199, 1972, Item XX, pp. 19–22.

[7] 'Programme de politique d'information 1972', Brussels, 9 December 1971, SEC(71) 4483, p. 1.

[8] Ibid.

[9] Ibid., p. 6.

[10] Ibid., p. 8.

Se non è vero [...] (¹)

'Mr Rabier was a man who was at war with the administration.'

Interview with Robert Pendville, 16 December 2003.

particularly to 'information multipliers', had to be taken at a meeting of the Commission (²). Admittedly, the Commission had been granting subsidies for a long time already — the first had been to the Centre universitaire de Nancy in May 1959 (³) — but what was significant was the reminder. As though the screws had to be tightened on a DG whose business culture, since the time of the Joint Service, had been shaped too ingeniously. It was probably this spirit that had made it possible to work wonders in many sectors, such as youth, adult education and universities.

Youth and universities

While stressing the fact that this sector was not the only one where imagination ruled the day, it was definitely one of those where the policy introduced over the years best illustrated the spirit of the pioneers and its enduring nature (⁴).

In Luxembourg the High Authority was not unaware of the role of universities. In particular, it 'created a European prize for theses on European integration, awarded grants to the newly created institutes of European studies, organised university meetings and initiated a dialogue with the student world by bringing together the national associations of students of the six Member States at a meeting held in Rome in 1958' (⁵).

But there was a difference between the university world in particular and that of youth in general. In a context which was marked by the reconciliation and, shortly, by the rapprochement between France and Germany, action for youth seemed essential once the adventure of the European Youth Campaign had come to an end in 1959, after failing in its attempt to be replaced, under the auspices of the new institutions, by an 'Office for European information and education' (⁶). In the same year the Socialist MEP Gerhard Kreyssig obtained, as we have seen, the Parliamentary Assembly's approval for the creation of a specific budget heading to 'develop a European civic education programme, particularly for young people'. An appropriation of BEF 10 million was allocated to it, 'giving greater legitimacy to the Joint Service to act in these circles, which were rapidly becoming particularly sensitive' (⁷).

However, once it had been obtained, the manna had to be managed. Émile Noël had an idea on this subject. At the time of the exhibition train organised by the Camarades de la Liberté, he was helped by Jean Moreau, who was responsible in Baden-Baden for youth and education policy between 1946 and 1951. This disabled war veteran, a specialist in matters relating to youth, had subsequently launched the European Youth Campaign, at least two members of whose political bureau, Georges Rencki and Jean Degimbe, had later become senior officials at the EEC Commission. But it was another former member of the campaign, Charles Maignal, to whom Noël entrusted the task of finding Moreau in order to put him in charge of this action and its budget heading (⁸). Appointed to a Euratom post in July 1960, Moreau therefore dealt with youth, adult education and above all university circles. In 1964 Noël gave his approval for 'top priority being given to

---

(¹) *Se non è vero, è ben trovato* ('If it's not true, it's a good story'). Italian proverb.

(²) PV 173, EC Commission, 1971, Item XI.d, p. 3; PV 189, Item XXIII, p. 19; PV 195, 1972, Item III, p. 3.

(³) PV 59, EEC Commission, 4 May 1959, Item V, p. 8.

(⁴) Lastenouse, J., 'La Commission européenne et les études universitaires sur l'intégration européenne, 1960–2000', *Temas de Integraçao*, No 15–16, 2003, pp. 12–36.

(⁵) Note by Fausta Deshormes-La Valle and Jacqueline Lastenouse, December 2005.

(⁶) Palayret, J.-M., 'La Campagna europea della gioventù, I movimenti per l'unità europea 1954–1969', in Pistone, S. (ed.), *I movimenti per l'unità europea, 1954–1969 — Atti del convegno internazionale, Genoa 5-6-7 November 1992*, Pime, Pavie, 1996, p. 346.

(⁷) Note by Fausta Deshormes-La Valle and Jacqueline Lastenouse, December 2005.

(⁸) Interview with Jacqueline Lastenouse-Bury, 21 January 2004.

action for universities' (¹). This interest and this belief were confirmed by Rabier and Jacqueline Lastenouse (²).

After starting from a tiny nucleus, the action carried out among universities ultimately involved numerous people. In a way, this illustrated the process of contamination through cohesion. Hence the importance of the welcome given to visitors, of whom there were many. These visits also involved, on account of their responsibilities, officials from other DGs, who were usually happy to establish contacts with an outside world from which they were generally far removed. Again aimed at the outside world, the introduction of research grants, the sending of the Communities' documentation to European Documentation Centres (EDC) in universities, the subsidies for the organisation of symposia and seminars, the effort made to disseminate research work, and the setting-up, including in the United Kingdom, of university associations to bring together specialists in European studies slowly but surely brought the European university area into being — and had a multiplier effect. At secondary education level, the Paris office produced in 1966 dossiers that were sent to 5 000 history and geography teachers. Drawn up by university staff and disseminated by the association Europe Université, they were intended to offset the shortage of school manuals by constituting 'an in-depth operation in schools' (³).

This initiative, which was just one of many, was characteristic of the will to make up for the lack of interest in cooperation 'on the part of the ministries of education. The initiatives for "European updates" of subjects such as history, geography or civic education did not receive any official support in the Member States, with the notable exception of the European Schools Day. Cooperation with the national ministries in the field of statistical comparisons was not continued after the "empty chair" crisis. However, from 1967, co-

operation was instituted with school television programmes, resulting in the production of a number of joint broadcasts.' (⁴)

This specific impetus in the field of education was redoubled by the Parliamentary Assembly 'adopting unanimously on 9 May 1966 the proposal by the MEP Scarascia-Mugnozza to create, at European level, youth institutions that were representative of the national ministries and youth organisations. This proposal led the Joint Information Service to consolidate a policy of rapprochement with these bodies culminating, at the major symposium on Youth organised in May 1970, in the creation of the European Youth Forum, which would thereafter be the vehicle for dialogue between young people and the European institutions. The Summit of Heads of State or Government held in The Hague on 3 and 4 December 1969, confirming the importance of a youth policy, gave the seal of approval to the role of the Commission. The Parliament–Commission joint strategy really brought about a political breakthrough in this area.' (⁵)

Lastly, 'in the field of adult education, initiatives were taken, particularly with regard to women's magazines and women's associations, which expected Europe to improve their status and represented important vectors of information at the heart of society. With time, the baton was passed to social policy, which would give priority to equality of treatment as laid down in the Treaties. This too was the beginning of a political breakthrough.' (⁶)

What is impressive, it must be repeated, is that so many initiatives had been taken by, what was, when all is said and done, a small number of people. In this regard, the 'contacts' factor as applied to what looked very much like a cause was decisive. Whether it had existed before these people had joined the Commission or over the years thereafter, this factor made a substantial contribution to the development of networks serving ini-

(¹) AMK C 33/4/106, Émile Noël to François Fontaine, Brussels, 10 September 1964.
(²) Interview with Jacqueline Lastenouse-Bury, 21 January 2004.
(³) AMK C 34/1/154, François Fontaine to Jean Monnet, Paris, 24 March 1966.

(⁴) Note by Fausta Deshormes-La Valle and Jacqueline Lastenouse, December 2005.
(⁵) Ibid.
(⁶) Ibid.

The policy of the Joint Press and Information Service and subsequently of the Directorate-General for Information (DG X) is to develop activities targeting specialised sectors and circles that could act as information relays. Here representatives of women's magazines visit the Commission.

tiatives that were designed to bring an idea to fruition. In this connection, the breeding ground that was the European Youth Campaign played a role that has already been touched on. However, it is important to come back to it in order to stress how many 'new old hands' — particularly women in this case — from the campaign formed the initial nucleus of a highly motivated team attached to Jean Moreau and Jacques-René Rabier: Fausta Deshormes-La Valle, the linchpin of *Giovane Europa*, Irène Scizier, etc.

From overseas to audiovisual

In other cases, the experience that was placed at the service of information had been acquired

elsewhere. For example, Pierre Cros was head of the press office of the French High Commissioner in Dakar when Lemaignen's *chef de cabinet* proposed that he come to Brussels. He came. 'It started in rue du Marais'; he recounts. 'With an empty desk, an armchair, a cupboard and nothing else. Everything would have to be done. There was no archive. There was nothing because it was brand new. That's what was extraordinary.' [1] Head of the Information and Development Division both at the time of the Joint Service and within DG X, Cros used his knowledge of Africa for the benefit of information where there was a great deal to be done, in that decolonisation entailed an enormous amount of

[1] Interview with Pierre Cros, 8 December 2003.

work to counter Soviet propaganda. What better response could there be than to highlight the achievements on the ground of the DG responsible for overseas matters, as can be seen in an earlier chapter [1].

Dumont du Voitel, who up to 1973 was responsible for the audiovisual sector, also had previous experience. Having worked in Bremen for television, he found himself in Brussels 'in the role of a sort of adviser on televised communication for President Hallstein'. The task was a difficult one. The President lacked humour [2]. He did not smile easily. He had to be taught how to behave in front of the cameras so that people could say: 'Good heavens, the President can laugh too!' [3].

This account by Dumont du Voitel is revealing. In fact, information continued to be conveyed primarily via the press and radio. However, television experienced exceptional development. In the United States first, and then in Europe, General de Gaulle used it with consummate skill. A challenge in terms of information, it also became one in terms of communication. The Member States understood this and maintained a monopoly over it. As a result, the oft proclaimed but rarely achieved ambition of developing an audiovisual service worthy of the name came up against difficulties that were far from being solely technical. It was one thing to encourage television productions such as Robert Jung's series for the German channel ARD and the film *Continent sans frontières*, on which the colossus of journalism, Raymond Cartier, collaborated. It was another matter entirely to create a studio and to broadcast. On a number of occasions, staff from Member States' TV stations were invited to Brussels. They came from RAI and ARD in 1962–63 [4]. A similar operation was conducted in 1971. Nothing came out of it. Yann de l'Écotais writes, not without malice, about the television studio inau-

gurated in 1965 and 10 years later 'still not able to broadcast to RTB, Belgian television, which would act as a link to the various other stations in Europe' [5]. Technical incompetence or obstructionism by the Member States? Could we imagine the ORTF of General de Gaulle, or even of Georges Pompidou, providing the link with Brussels?

Even though 'information was never a major portfolio for the Commissioners' [6], it did in fact prove to be an important issue. In this connection too, the activities of the information offices, which have been referred to a number of times, should be discussed.

The press and information offices

The aim of the press and information offices in the capital cities was to inform the public and, at the same time, to gauge its reactions and pass this information on to the executives. In addition, they collaborated closely on the production and implementation of the programmes and initiatives devised by the DG in Brussels.

The ECSC information offices were the first to be used, namely those in Paris, Rome, Bonn and London [7]. The new needs led to the creation of an office in The Hague. Others were refurbished, such as the one in Paris, which moved to a building in the rue des Belles Feuilles acquired by the High Authority and the EEC Commission [8]. Opening an office in Berlin was also mooted, but the project could not be realised despite the agreement of the executives.

The main question was to know from whom the offices received the information and to whom they passed it on. In 1958 the memorandum from the EEC Commission to the other two executives proposed inter alia that the heads of the offices be

---

[1] See Chapter 18, pp. 377–395.
[2] 'Humorlos', Interview with Rudolf Dumont du Voitel, 1 December 2003.
[3] Ibid. 'Donnerwetter, der Präsident kann ja auch lachen'.
[4] Ibid.

[5] De l'Écotais, Y., op. cit., p. 34.
[6] Interview with Jacqueline Lastenouse-Bury, 21 January 2004.
[7] PV 2, EEC Commission, 24 January 1958, Item XV.c, p. 8.
[8] PV 14, EEC Commission, 21 April 1958, Item VIII, p. 6; PV 24, 9 July 1958, Item IX.d., p. 12; PV 26, 22 July 1958, Item XXIV.f, p. 32.

subordinate to the Joint Service and that the offices themselves be common to the three executives. They would receive from the Spokesmen the day-to-day information and the authorisation to pass it on. Their role would also be to coordinate information in the country where they were [1].

Generally very active, the offices suffered from a structural shortage of staff [2], even though their number was increasing slowly but surely. For example, in 1967 the German government's request for an office to be created in Berlin was met almost 10 years after the first attempt. Jean Rey inaugurated what was designed as an annex to the Bonn office on 11 June 1968 [3]. Brussels and Luxembourg were also the subject of requests for the creation of offices at the time of the general administrative reorganisation in 1967 [4].

This development raised not only the question of staff numbers — Borschette managed to get a ceiling imposed on the number of DG X officials in Brussels in order to reinforce the staff of the offices — but also that of the decentralisation of work and the exploitation of each office's initiatives [5]. This was a tricky question. We have seen that François Fontaine, in Paris, while extending the scope of his task somewhat, certainly managed to stir things up. Now, what was tricky in a Member State was even more so in non-member countries.

Information for non-member countries

Generally speaking, the Council showed itself to be suspicious about information initiatives in non-member countries. The risks of interference

	List of press and information offices	
Member States	Bonn (ECSC office)	
	Berlin (1968)	
	Brussels (1968)	
	The Hague (1958)	
	Luxembourg (1968)	
	Paris (ECSC office)	
	Rome (ECSC office)	
Non-member countries	London (ECSC office, press and information office, 1960; creation of a mission 1971)	
	Washington (ECSC office, press and information office, 1960)	
	New York (press and information office, 1964)	
	United States (creation of a mission comprising the Washington and New York offices, 1971)	
	Geneva (press and information office, 1964)	
	Canada (Community representation)	
	Tokyo (press and information office)	
	Latin America: Montevideo (Community information office, 1964) [6]; Santiago, Chile (ECSC liaison office, 1965 [7]; EC office from 1968)	
	Turkey (documentation centre)	

[1] PV 42, EEC Commission, 16 December 1958, Item XII, pp. 2–6.
[2] Thus, on 23 March 1960, the College asked S. Mansholt to examine with the management board of the Joint Service whether it was possible to increase the staff of the Bonn, Paris and Rome offices. See PV 98, EEC Commission, 23 March 1960, Item XIII.c, p. 15.
[3] PV 6, EC Commission, 1967, Item III, p. 8; PV 7, Item XI, pp. 13 and 14; PV 8, Item XIII, pp. 14 and 15; PV 40, 1968, Item XXX, p. 26.
[4] PV 15, EC Commission, 1967, Item VIII.8, pp. 22 and 23; PV 17, Item X.4.a, p. 28.
[5] PV 156, EC Commission, 1971, Item XIX.c, p. 9; PV 173, Item XXVIII.f, p. 34.

[6] 1964 was the year when the Council of the EEC decided to open the office (Spierenburg, D. and Poidevin, R., *The history of the High Authority of the European Coal and Steel Community — Supranationality in operation*, Weidenfeld and Nicolson, London, 1994, p. 583.
[7] 1965 was the year when it was decided to open the office (ibid., p. 583).

were obvious. From time to time, the Commission, without any overall vision, took initiatives in two directions. First, the opening of information offices in non-member countries and, second, participation in the universal exhibitions of the period: Montreal and Osaka.

Without overlooking the fact that this question has to do more generally with the problems of the affirmation of the Communities and then of the Community on the international stage, it must be stressed that the EEC Commission had to fight hard, from the outset, to persuade Coreper, for example, to recognise its competence and prerogatives in the preparation of documentation for non-member countries [1]. This having being attained, the irony of history meant that Jean Rey's idea of having the periodic information notes prepared by the Spokesman's Group, in collaboration with the External Relations DG, led to the decision that they would be intended not for the Community information offices but for the Member States' embassies in non-member countries [2].

Over the years, the EEC Commission gave in to occasional impulses, where the subject was a sensitive one. The only way that seemed open to it therefore was to go along with the offices while making sure not to run the risk of being accused of transforming them into 'parallel embassies' or 'hotbeds of propaganda' [3].

Everyone at Expo

Among the events likely to serve as a showcase for European integration, the universal exhibitions played a definite part. In Brussels in 1958, the ECSC pavilion pointed the way. But the subsequent exhibitions showed once again that the Council and the Community executives were rarely on the same wavelength when it came to information and representation. Thus, from November

1964 to February 1965, the Communities' participation in the Montreal exhibition seemed to be compromised because the Council refused to approve the sum proposed by the EEC Commission as being necessary for participation, which Schaus and, especially, Rey deemed important [4]. In the end, it was not without difficulties that the Communities' pavilion was eventually erected and inaugurated on 10 September 1967.

The favourable impression left by the experience in Canada [5] and the obvious matters at stake in good relations with Japan meant that a positive response was given to the invitation to take part in the Osaka exhibition.

Unlike in the case of the Montreal exhibition, the Council quickly marked its approval of the principle. With regard to the budget, Coppé proposed that, before negotiations with Coreper began, a limited sum below which participation would not be possible should be set. Thanks to this arrangement, which was (in all senses of the word) reasonable, a compromise was found with the Permanent Representatives. With the financial aspect settled, Coppé then worked together with von der Groeben, Sassen, Rochereau and Colonna di Paliano, and with the DGs concerned, on the choice of the plan of the pavilion and on its contents. What was finally produced seemed to meet expectations. The Belgian Minister for Foreign Affairs and President-in-Office of the Council, Pierre Harmel, had nothing but praise for the pavilion, which he visited in April 1970 [6]. Once again, the combination of circumstances and the people involved obviously played a crucial part in the information strategy, its implementation and reception.

---

[1] PV 56, EEC Commission, 13 April 1959, 1, Item IV.2, 6.
[2] PV 87, EEC Commission, 18 January 1960, Item XXV, p. 18.
[3] See also Chapter 17, pp. 339–376.

[4] PV 292, EC Commission, Item XX, p. 11; PV 302, Item III.3, pp. 5–6; PV 303, Items VII.1 and XXVII, pp. 16 and 36; PV 305, Item III.3, p. 7.
[5] PV 392, EC Commission, Item XVII, p. 18; PV 399, Item III.5, pp. 10–11; PV 4, Item XXVI.2, p. 40; PV 5, Item XI.1, p. 18; PV 6, Item VIII, pp. 11–12.
[6] On participation in the Osaka exhibition, see PV 23, EC Commission, Item XXXVIII, p. 39; PV 34, Item X, pp. 16–17; PV 48, Item XV, p. 17; PV 51, Item XXXII, p. 36; PV 52, Item XI.3, p. 22; PV 56, Item XX.2, p. 16; PV 57, Item XVIII, pp. 15–16; PV 61, Item VI.m, p. 14; PV 117, Item XXXVI, p. 31.

ECSC Pavilion at Expo 58, designed by the architects Eugène Delatte and Robert Maquestiau.

The end of an era?

Paul Collowald's account of the decisions taken at the time of the first enlargement is worth quoting: 'In 1973 the British arrived. There was a big stir at director-general level, where at three or four in the morning Ortoli had finally to distribute the portfolios between the Commissioners — the infamous night of the long knives — and then immediately, as a corollary, had to appoint the directors-general. There absolutely had to be a director-general with the nationality of one of the three countries that were joining. At four o'clock in the morning, Ortoli kicked out Jacques Rabier. And it was Sean Ronan, an Irishman, who became director-general [...]. He was most likeable, did not speak a word of French, had never concerned himself with information [...]. A new director had also been appointed from academia, Roy Price. He was the Englishman.' (¹)

The ensuing upheaval can be interpreted in two ways. The first of these consists, not without some nostalgia, in emphasising a break between the period of Europe of the Six and that of Europe of the Nine. The second highlights the fact that men and women who had been trained in the 'operational doctrine' of the Joint Service and were therefore aware that the objective of

---

(¹) Interview with Paul Collowald, 2 December 2003.

Members of the Commission with responsibility for information

January 1958	Michel Rasquin represented the Commission in the Inter-Communities Working Party on Information.
18 April 1958	Pending the return of Michel Rasquin, Hans von der Groeben replaced him. Michel Rasquin died at the end of April 1958.
16 December 1958	Hans von der Groeben wished to be relieved of his responsibilities in the field of press and information. Sicco Mansholt replaced him in the Inter-Executive Group, which supervised the management of the Joint Service and that of the Spokesman's Group. Each Commissioner gave him instructions in the areas for which he was responsible.
5 April 1960	Sicco Mansholt asked to be relieved of his responsibilities in the field of press and information on account of the tasks that he had to take on in relation to the CAP. The Commission appointed Giuseppe Caron, who would have to chair the management board of the Joint Press and Information Service. It also created a working party on 'Press and Information', composed of Giuseppe Caron (Chairman), Sicco Mansholt, Robert Marjolin and Hans von der Groeben.
29 May 1963	Following the resignation of Giuseppe Caron from his post as Commissioner, the Commission had to appoint his replacement as chairman of the working party on 'Press and Information' and to represent the Commission on the management board of the Joint Service. Hans von der Groeben declared that he could not accept this responsibility. On a proposal from Robert Marjolin, Henri Rochereau was appointed. He also replaced Robert Marjolin as a member of the working party, with Lionello Levi Sandri replacing Giuseppe Caron.
1964–67	In 1964 Guido Colonna di Paliano became Commissioner responsible for press and information.
6 July 1967 to 1 July 1970	Within the new Commission, Albert Coppé was responsible for press and information, while Jean Rey, President of the Commission, was responsible for the Spokesman's Group.
2 July 1970 to 23 February 1972	Albert Borschette was responsible for press and information, while Franco Maria Malfatti, President of the Commission, was responsible for the Spokesman's Group.
24 February 1972 to 5 January 1973	Albert Borschette's term of office was renewed, while Sicco Mansholt replaced Franco Maria Malfatti and was therefore in charge of the Spokesman's Group.

information policy was not simply to disseminate news but to contribute to the formation of a 'European public spirit' intended in 1973 to provide the link between 'Little Europe' and the enlarged Europe.

MICHEL DUMOULIN

'Something had to give'

The day after the 'night of the long knives', Ortoli summoned Rabier. 'Last night something had to give', he told him. 'I understand, Mr President. That something is me', replied Rabier, who was offered the post, unpaid, of 'special adviser', a job in which he would create the Eurobarometer.

Interview with Jacques-René Rabier, 8 January 2004.

Chapter 27

Enlargement: the Commission seeks a role for itself

The first rumours of a possible UK application for EEC membership were immediately treated with suspicion on the Continent, where doubts were expressed about the sincerity of the UK's intentions. The Commission representative in London, Georges Berthoin [1], relayed with some concern Prime Minister Macmillan's alleged comment: 'We must embrace them, destructively.' [2] Would the Community, which was still in its infancy, be able to easily integrate such a colossus among its members? It also very soon became clear that membership applications would not be confined to the United Kingdom. In the wake of the latter's application, Denmark, Ireland and Norway showed signs of interest. What would be the impact on the Community and, in particular, on the European Commission, the policy initiator and guardian of the Treaties?

This chapter explores the Commission's position before and during the enlargement negotiations (1961–63 and 1970–73), focusing on their procedural aspects. What powers did the Commission have under the Treaty, what margin of man-

oeuvre did the Member States allow it as negotiator and to what extent was it able to exploit this margin? Who were involved in enlargement at the Commission and how have their contributions been assessed? And, lastly, what are the principal points of convergence or divergence between the two rounds of negotiations? These are the points which will be addressed here. Scant, if any, attention will be paid to the technical aspects or content of the negotiations themselves. Although of undoubted importance, the talks on imports of New Zealand dairy products and sugar from the Commonwealth countries, the integration of the future members' agricultural and fisheries sectors, and the question of financial contributions will not be discussed here. The political significance of some of these aspects should, however, not be forgotten: financial contributions to the Community (now European Union) budget continue to be a thorny issue for governments as the arrangements agreed in 1972 leave an imprint to this day. Equally, the organisation of the sugar market, including Commonwealth sugar, still taxes agricultural ministers. Finally, this chapter will focus on United Kingdom accession rather than that of Ireland, Denmark and Norway, as negotiations with the

[1] FJME, AMK C 30/1/174, Letter from Georges Berthoin to Jean Monnet, 17 June 1960.
[2] See box, p. 363.

British took centre stage, for the Commission too, and were by far the most time-consuming ([1]).

1961–63

In late 1960 Commission leaders expressed their reservations about UK accession. Commission President Walter Hallstein was concerned about London's sudden volte-face after the failure of the free-trade area. Fearing it would cause disruption of the Community, he indicated that there would be no question of renegotiating the Treaty of Rome or slowing down the European project. Vice-President Robert Marjolin even concluded that UK membership would be a bad thing as, psychologically, the British lived in a different world from that of the Community. Not aware of any Englishman who might be appointed a member of the Commission and take an independent position, Marjolin considered that, in the circumstances at the time, no more than some form of association could be envisaged ([2]). A month later he softened his line, although he still had reservations. He accepted that the Commission should approve the accession of the United Kingdom but only if it were ready to embrace the common market. For him, this was doubtful. UK membership was not, in his eyes, so much a trade issue as a sentimental and political one. Following a recent trip to the United Kingdom, where he had met Frank Figgures, Secretary-General of EFTA, Marjolin questioned whether accession was in the Community's interest or even in that of the British themselves. Figgures warned him that UK accession could even blow the common market apart. This was a warning the Commission Vice-President took extremely seriously, wondering whether the UK government would not do better to cultivate its links with the Commonwealth as these links would inevitably suffer in the wake of any accession ([3]).

The *cabinets* and DGs also had their say. Hallstein's *chef de cabinet*, Berndt von Staden, underlined the threat that enlargement could pose to European unity as it could compromise the future strategy of Germany, which was caught in a defensive position between the Russians and the United States. Alfred Mozer, Mansholt's *chef de cabinet*, believed the British were not yet ready to take their place in a Europe which was still at a formative stage and in which they had played no part in the previous decade. Jean-François Deniau, Director for European Affairs, pointed to the time factor. The common agricultural policy had to be worked out first and, according to him, this would take 18 months. Then work would have to begin on the Community's foreign policy and this would take at least three years. UK membership of the common market would be possible only if the British made a clear political choice. Martin Meyer-Burckhardt, Director of General Affairs in Agriculture, considered that, before any agreement was entered into with the United Kingdom, the implications of introducing some form of competition in the EEC's agricultural sector would have to be examined in detail. The impact on European agriculture of Greece's and Turkey's association, which was also under discussion at that time, also needed to be considered. Harmonisation of agricultural prices between the EEC and the United Kingdom would take 20 to 30 years ([4]).

However, these reservations were clearly not shared by all. From the outset, Vice-President and Agriculture Commissioner, Sicco Mansholt, was optimistic about the UK's membership application provided that it was prepared to accept the Treaty and the principles and main components

---

[1] Two excellent accounts of the Commission's work during the first round of accession negotiations can be found in Ludlow, N. P., 'Influence and vulnerability: the role of the EEC Commission in the enlargement negotiations', in Griffiths, R. T. and Ward, S. (eds), *Courting the common market: the first attempt to enlarge the European Community*, Lothian Foundation Press, London, 1996, pp. 139–155; and in 'A welcome change: the European Commission and the challenge of enlargement, 1958–1973', *Journal of European Integration History*, Vol. 11, No 2, 2005, pp. 31–46.

[2] FJME, AMK 55/2/3, Conversation between Max Kohnstamm and Robert Marjolin, 18 October 1960. Interview with Robert Toulemon, 17 December 2003.

[3] HAEU, MK 18, François Duchêne report, 15 November 1960.
[4] Ibid.

of the CAP. In March 1961 he gave a speech to Europe House in London, where he had the opportunity to engage in a wide-ranging exchange of views with the representatives of UK agricultural organisations. Although obviously highlighting the huge problems involved in bringing UK agricultural policy into line with the CAP, he indicated that this was not an impossible task [1].

Association or accession?

In the wake of these initial reactions, doubts were expressed about whether an association or an accession should be considered for the United Kingdom. In mid-April 1961 a Commission communiqué was issued stating that the provisions of the Treaty of Rome would have to be accepted in their entirety from the outset and that, otherwise, the possibility of association could always be considered [2]. This created confusion in national capitals and speculation that this could have something to do with the UK's application. Was this an implicit reference to the possible replacement of UK membership by mere association? It quickly emerged that the communiqué had not been discussed or approved beforehand by the Commission as a whole and that the final text had not been seen by President Hallstein or the Commissioner for External Relations, Jean Rey. Although some members of the Commission did not agree with its content, it was not considered expedient to put out an amended version of the communiqué as this would only complicate matters. It was indicated that no particular importance should be attached to it, nor should it be interpreted as the Commission's policy line on the UK's accession application [3].

This was not an isolated incident. A similar situation arose in September 1961. Hallstein stated in his defence that he was sometimes misrepresent-

ed by the press. It should be added that, at the time, he was known for his hostility to the press [4].

Despite these minor incidents, which reveal the indecision reigning at the time on this very sensitive issue, the Commission had come to the conclusion that too reserved an approach would be counterproductive, especially as most Member States, and first and foremost the Netherlands, were in principle in favour of the UK's membership application. It obviously did not wish to run the risk of antagonising Member States and potential members.

Events took a decisive turn on 31 July 1961, when Prime Minister Harold Macmillan announced to the House of Commons that the UK government intended to apply for UK membership of the EEC. A closer look at his statement reveals the real aim of the application: to ensure that satisfactory conditions for the United Kingdom could (or could not) be obtained in the negotiations. Once this point of no return had been reached, the Commission knew that it should play a leading role in the future negotiations by virtue of its expertise and experience. Since this was the first enlargement and there was no precedent, it was obviously essential that 'Brussels' take a procedural position.

What was the Commission's role in the negotiations to be?

This was crucial. Indecision reigned at the highest level. Should the Member States, the Council or the Commission conduct the negotiations? Things did not look good for the Commission. Even before the official membership application, talks had been held between the British and the Member States, but mainly at bilateral level between the United Kingdom and France. Furthermore, both the British and the French made it known that the Commission would not play a

---

[1] FJME, AMK C 33/3/182, *Agriculture in the common market conference*, 28 March 1961.
[2] ABZN, 996.0 EEG 1955–64, Dossier 421, van Schaik report, 19 April 1961.
[3] ABZN, 996.0 EEG 1955–64, 421, Report 134 Linthorst Homan, 24 April 1961.

[4] Interviews with Beniamino Olivi, 26 January and 9 February 2004.

Communiqué issued by the EEC Commission on 1 August 1961 concerning Macmillan's statement in the House of Commons (31 July 1961) (on the United Kingdom's accession to the EEC)

'The Commission considers this a turning point in post-war European politics. [...] regards it as fresh recognition of the economic and political value of the work of European integration undertaken since 1950.'

EEC Bulletin, 9/10, 1961, p. 10.

major role in the future official negotiations. The UK representative in Brussels, Michael Tandy, set out from the principle that the Commission would take part in the talks but not as a negotiator [1]. France did not want the Commission to have direct contacts with the British, even if, unofficially, Hallstein could be kept up to date by the accredited UK Ambassador [2].

The Anglo-French position which emerged from the *pas de deux* between London and Paris was not, naturally, to the Commission's liking. Jean Rey indicated that, in principle, the procedure to be used for accession should be the same as that for association, along the lines of that adopted for Greece, with which negotiations were being conducted under Article 228 of the Treaty. However, Article 237, which governed accession, gave the Commission much less influence as membership applications had to be addressed to the Council, which took a unanimous decision on them after consulting the Commission. Furthermore — and this was even more crucial — the conditions of admission and the necessary adjustments to the Treaty could be the subject of an agreement be-

tween the Member States and the applicant State. This meant that the accession arrangements would be determined not by the Commission but by the Member States for their negotiations with the applicant State and that the Council itself would play no official role. This approach was also underpinned by Article 236, which was linked to Article 237, governing the amendment of the Treaty. According to this Article, it was for the Council to take a decision in principle on amendments to the Treaty after consulting the Commission and Parliament. However, the Member States had sole responsibility for the drafting of any amendment [3]. The accession procedure was clearly an intergovernmental affair in which the capitals played a dominant role. Legally speaking, the Commission had very few arguments to rely on.

But this was no more than skirmishing. Things took a more serious turn when the UK, Danish and Irish applications [4] arrived in Brussels between July and September 1961 followed by Norway's application in April 1962. In a press release the Commission talked about a decisive turning point in post-war European politics, declaring that it was firmly committed to offering its full cooperation and contributing to the completion of this new phase in Europe's economic and political unification and to a rapprochement between the free world on both sides of the Atlantic [5].

Nor did the Commission intend to play a subordinate role. It had the support of a number of Member States, as the record of Coreper's discussions on 23 August 1961 shows. The Permanent Representatives Committee played an important role in preparing the decisions taken by the Council. These discussions are a graphic illustra-

[1] ABZN 996.0, EEG Part III, 'EEG en het VK', June 1961, Report 180 Linthorst Homan, 5 June 1961.
[2] ABZN 996.0, EEG Part III, 'EEG en het VK', June 1961, Report 343 Beyen, 27 June 1961.
[3] ABZN 996.0 EEG 1955–64, 439, Note from Jaap Kymmell (Directie Integratie Europa (DIE)) on the accession negotiation procedure, 21 August 1961.
[4] Officially, in the case of the United Kingdom, this was not an accession application but an application to open negotiations to find an agreement on accession to the common market. Interviews with Beniamino Olivi, 26 January and 9 February 2004.
[5] ABZN, 996.0, EEG 1955–64 423, European Commission press communiqué, 23 August 1961.

The Treaty and enlargement
Article 237 of the EEC Treaty

'Any European State may apply to become a member of the Community. It shall address its application to the Council, which shall act unanimously after obtaining the opinion of the Commission.

The conditions of admission and the adjustments to this Treaty necessitated thereby shall be the subject of an agreement between the Member States and the applicant State. This agreement shall be submitted for ratification by all the Contracting States in accordance with their respective constitutional requirements.'

Article 228 of the EEC Treaty

'1. Where this Treaty provides for the conclusion of agreements between the Community and one or more States or an international organisation, such agreements shall be negotiated by the Commission. Subject to the powers vested in the Commission in this field, such agreements shall be concluded by the Council, after consulting the Assembly where required by this Treaty.

The Council, the Commission or a Member State may obtain beforehand the opinion of the Court of Justice as to whether an agreement envisaged is compatible with the provisions of this Treaty. Where the opinion of the Court of Justice is adverse, the agreement may enter into force only in accordance with Article 236.

2. Agreements concluded under these conditions shall be binding on the institutions of the Community and on the Member States.'

tion of the prevailing views at the time and warrant some examination.

Rolf Lahr, the German Permanent Representative, who was chairing Coreper at the time, took the view, in contrast to the objections described above, that it was not inconceivable for the Commission to play a specific role in the negotiations on the basis of Articles 236 and 237. Neverthe-

less, he would prefer such a decision to be taken on the basis of 'practical and political' arguments. He underlined that the Commission had been a driving force in the association negotiations, and that it had expertise and experience which should be drawn on, pointing to its position as the most neutral spokesperson and, finally, to its expertise in particular fields such as the Common Customs Tariff. The Belgian Permanent Representative, Joseph Van der Meulen, also considered the Commission's participation in the negotiations to be essential at all levels. Like his German colleague, his view was based on practical and political considerations. He also believed that in many areas the Member States no longer had a prerogative to take decisions. The Community's activities had always progressed as a result of proposals by, and on the initiative of, the Commission and, the Belgian diplomat added, it was essential that there be interaction between the proposals formulated by the Commission and the results achieved in the negotiations. The Luxembourger Albert Borschette took the same view, adding that it would be a good idea, from the very start, for the British to be made aware of the existence and working methods of the Brussels institution.

Linthorst Homan of the Netherlands was more critical. Although he agreed that for 'practical and utilitarian' reasons, the Commission should be given a role, this should be on condition that it was not considered legally necessary or a *droit acquis*. This position was due to the reluctance of the Dutch government, which was furious at the recent failure of the free-trade area and discussions on political cooperation in Europe, to give the Commission an autonomous role. The Hague considered that, in both instances, the Commission had attached too much importance to France's views. Although he accepted all the arguments put forward in the Commission's favour, the Italian Giulio Pascucci had doubts, like Linthorst Homan, about the weight of the legal arguments.

The French representative, Jean-Marc Boegner, was in no doubt whatsoever: the Treaty provided no legal basis for the Commission to claim any leading role for itself. He was surprised that his colleagues Rolf Lahr and Joseph Van der Meulen had referred to Article 236, especially as there was no question of amending the Treaty. A practical approach was required. If the Commission attended the negotiations, would it have the right to speak? In other words, France's representative in Coreper doubted whether the Commission's participation in the process was of any use at all.

Coreper Chairman Rolf Lahr thought that it was humanly and practically impossible to oblige the Commission to keep silent. He also considered it inconceivable that the Six should not make use of the firm grasp of the subject and excellent negotiating skills of figures such as Hallstein, Marjolin and Mansholt. He concluded that none of the Committee's members were prepared to let the Commission take the reins in the negotiations but that all the Permanent Representatives, with the exception of France, considered its involvement desirable for political and practical reasons.

Coreper was also divided on who should be appointed as the chairman or spokesman for the Six. Lahr, Van der Meulen, Borschette and Pascucci proposed Spaak and Hallstein — the latter in a personal capacity and not as President of the Commission — as they combined breadth and experience in negotiating with a commitment to the Community.

Linthorst Homan preferred Spaak as it was unreasonable to expect Hallstein to cope with the Commission's day-to-day work and the extremely full negotiating schedule for the months ahead. In the Dutchmen's view, Spaak should not negotiate with the British on the basis of Community viewpoints worked out in advance but as a neutral conference chairman within an autonomous multilateral structure. Linthorst Homan disagreed on this point with his colleagues, who advocated a strictly bilateral form of negotiation between the EEC Member States, speaking with one voice, and the UK delegation.

Opposition, once again, came from the French side. Boegner admired Spaak and Hallstein but was not in favour of appointing a Community representative or a Community spokesperson on behalf of the Member States.

Having discussed the Commission's role and the need for a coordinated stance, Coreper turned to the venue for the negotiations. Five of the six Permanent Representatives preferred Brussels. The fact that the Commission's administration was located here was considered to be an advantage. Once again, Boegner took a different view. The atmosphere and spirit of Brussels should not be dominated by the accession negotiations, he said, as normal work had to continue. And he added that France had thought of Venice because of the splendour of its setting or the capital of the country holding the Council Presidency (¹).

France was clearly at odds with its partners on most points, and the Netherlands had reservations. The United Kingdom's initial position was that the Commission should have no negotiating role, but it gradually took a more conciliatory line. At the beginning of 1961 the British indicated that London would be surprised if the Commission were excluded from the negotiations (²). As Jean-François Deniau reported, the British had laid their cards on the table: their plan was to systematically play off the so-called Friendly Five against France without having to take a stand themselves (³).

Encouraged by the support of Germany, Italy, Belgium, Luxembourg and [...] the United Kingdom, the Commission continued to demand a prominent role for itself in the negotiations. Boegner's and Linthorst Homan's interpretation of Article 237 was questioned. On 7 September

---

(¹) ABZN, 996.0 EEG 1955–64, 439, Report by the Permanent Representative in Brussels (Gecombineerd Nederlandse (Permanente) Vertegenwoordging (GNV)) on the Coreper meeting on enlargement, 23 August 1961.
(²) ABZN, 996.0 EEG 1955–64, 439, Report 7369 by Brussels Permanent Representative, 6 September 1961.
(³) Deniau, J.-Fr., *Mémoires de 7 vies — 2. Croire et Oser*, Plon, Paris, 1997, p. 187.

Commission players in the accession negotiations

1961–63 Commission	**Walter Hallstein:** President, head of the Commission delegation to the enlargement negotiations at ministerial level
	Jean Rey: Commissioner for External Affairs, member of the Commission delegation to the enlargement negotiations
	Robert Marjolin: Commissioner for Economic and Financial Affairs, Vice-President and member of the Commission delegation to the enlargement negotiations
	Giuseppe Caron: Commissioner for the Internal Market, Vice-President and member of the Commission delegation to the enlargement negotiations
	Sicco Mansholt: Commissioner for Agriculture, Vice-President and member of the Commission delegation to the enlargement negotiations
	Jean-François Deniau: head of the delegation of Commission officials in negotiations at Permanent Representative level
	Émile Noël: Secretary-General
1970–73 Commission	**Franco Maria Malfatti:** President
	Jean-François Deniau: Commissioner for External Trade and head of enlargement negotiations at ministerial level
	Edmund Wellenstein: head of task force for enlargement negotiations at Permanent Representative level, with Roland de Kergolay, Manfred Caspari, Klaus Otto Nass and Fernand Braun and others
	Sicco Mansholt: Commissioner for Agriculture and Vice-President (President from 2 March 1972)
	Raymond Barre: Commissioner for Economic and Monetary Affairs and Vice-President
	Émile Noël: Secretary-General

1960–63: Bange, O., *The EEC crisis of 1963 — Kennedy, Macmillan, de Gaulle and Adenauer in conflict*, Macmillan Press and St Martin's Press, Houndmills, etc., 2000; Edwards, G. and Spence, D., *The European Commission*, Frank Cass, London, 1994; 1970–73: Hannay, Sir D., *Britain's entry into the European Community — Report by Sir Con O'Neill on the negotiations of 1970–1972*, Frank Cass, London and Portland, 2000.

1961 the Commissioners discussed a report by Michel Gaudet, head of the Legal Service. The Commission let it be known that not only did it want to be directly involved in the negotiations but that it should also act as spokesman for the Six ([1]). It would be unfair to rely solely on the relevant Treaty articles and the matter should be approached from a wider perspective. Apart from purely institutional matters, such as the composition of bodies and the weighting of votes within the Council, very few negotiating points concerned the Member States alone. Most of the talks to be held concerned the Community as a whole. Some of the main points relating to UK accession, such as trade with the Commonwealth, adaptation of British agriculture or relations with EFTA

([1]) HAEC, BDT 38/84, No 99, S/04880/61, 7 September 1961.

countries, were crucial political issues in which the Commission could, on the basis of the Treaty, at least demand to be involved.

The Commission was not, however, optimistic about the outcome. Axel Herbst, Deputy Secretary-General, grew suspicious about the Member States' real intentions as Coreper's meetings progressed. He feared the worst for the Council meeting on 26 and 27 September, at which the procedure to be followed was to be decided (¹).

In the run-up to the meeting, Brussels prepared itself for the negotiations, focusing on the composition of its own delegation and its administrative back-up. There were some internal frictions owing to Hallstein's solo initiatives. The Commission President made a number of appointments to enlarge the administration team without consulting many of his colleagues. Deniau was promoted to A1 so that he could play a leading role in the negotiations. Although there was much admiration in the Commission for Deniau, who had done sterling work in the association negotiations with Greece, his promotion brought the number of A1 officials to 11, of whom five were French. This unequal distribution was naturally not appreciated by the other nationalities. Since they could not reverse the decision (²), the Commissioners made sure that Hallstein did not grab the entire enlargement dossier for himself. They decided to appoint the Commission President, the three Vice-Presidents (Mansholt, Marjolin and Caron) and Jean Rey to chair the working party led by Deniau, who was responsible for negotiations at Coreper level. This working party was to be responsible for contacts at ministerial level.

Hallstein's attempt to claim sole responsibility for himself failed when Jean Rey was appointed against opposition from the French, who, in the light of the negotiations with Greece, did not expect him to make any significant contribution (³).

After the divergences of opinion at the Coreper meeting on 23 August on the role to be played by the Commission, Member States began to change their minds. The Benelux countries came to a compromise that lay between the bilateral position of Belgium and Luxembourg and the multilateral position of the Netherlands. They took the view that the Six should, as far as possible, coordinate their positions in advance but that divergences of opinion between Member States should not be excluded a priori. These three small countries' joint position was that the conference should be led by a general permanent chairman who would also act as a mediator in the case of conflict between one or more Member States and the British. The Benelux countries proposed Spaak, since Hallstein, who had been put forward in Coreper, was no longer a potential candidate. They also called for the Commission to play a consultative role. Italy and Germany adopted a bilateral negotiating formula: the Six — on a strictly coordinated basis — and the United Kingdom. The Six's delegation would also include a Commission representative with extensive consultative powers. This left France, which fought to the bitter end against any substantial participation by the Commission (⁴).

At the Council meeting on 26 and 27 September 1961, a final decision was taken on the procedure to be followed in the negotiations.

(a) The negotiations under Article 237 would be negotiations between the six Member States and the United Kingdom. The Member States would, as far as possible, put forward common viewpoints to the United Kingdom.

(b) The Commission would participate in the conference in an advisory capacity with the right to speak.

(¹) HAEC, BDT 38/84, No 99, S/04880/61, Herbst report following the Coreper meeting of 18 September 1961. See also Ludlow, etc., 'Influence and vulnerability […]', op. cit., pp. 141–142.

(²) ABZN, 996 EG 1955-64, 382, Report 353 Linthorst Homan, 26 October 1961.

(³) ABZN, 996.0 EEG, 439, EEC accession procedure, report, Paris embassy, 23 August 1961.

(⁴) ABZN, 996.0 EEG, 439, EEC accession procedure, May 1964 […], The future negotiations between the EEC and the UK, 12 September 1961.

(c) The Commission would also play a full part in the Six's coordination work.

The conference was chaired by the Member States on a three-monthly rotating basis. This excluded the Benelux candidate Spaak, who was opposed by the French and others. It was also decided — Germany and Italy dissenting — that the negotiations would be conducted largely at multilateral level. However, any concession by the 'Friendly Five' was subject to France's acceptance that the Commission's role should not be subordinate. In the talks with the British the Commission would advise the Six and would be authorised to speak freely in meetings between them. It was also decided that negotiations would be held in Brussels. After the frustrating course of the preparations, during which it had nearly been marginalised, the Commission now had reason to be relieved.

The Commission's role in the negotiations

Once the negotiations began, the Commission's role proved much broader than the consultative role it had been given might have indicated.

For one thing, the choice of a multilateral negotiation formula gave it an opportunity to encourage the Member States to come up with harmonised attitudes and a joint approach. The Commission devoted much of its energies to this task and attempted to act as honest broker for the Six.

The Commission's second task, for which it was eminently qualified, was to oversee compliance with the provisions of the Treaty of Rome and Community secondary legislation. It did sterling work in producing reports and opinions which were gratefully accepted by Member States' delegations. It provided all but one of the reports used in the negotiations [1]. Finally, Hallstein and Deniau were able, despite initial opposition, to take the floor at interministerial and Coreper meetings.

The Commission was represented in the negotiations by a small team comprising Hallstein and his right-hand men, von Staden and Deniau. As is always the case, much was achieved behind the scenes or in circumstances of which there is no record. Every month Hallstein invited the head of the British delegation, Edward Heath, and his strategist, Sir Eric Roll [2], to a private dinner with von Staden and Deniau. On the menu: the state of negotiations and proposals for progress in the negotiations [3]. At the end of April 1962 the Commission was putting together a package of proposals. Hallstein and von Staden, who had been in the United States, returned on the *Queen Elizabeth*. These six days aboard ship were used to work with Deniau, who had flown to New York at the President's behest to accompany them on the return voyage [4]. Although a working trip, it also provided an opportunity for relaxation, thanks to Deniau, who combined 'Brianz und Phantasie' (intellect and imagination), wrote von Staden.

Deniau's participation in the negotiations was considered to be particularly useful. As one of the few to attempt to stimulate the negotiations by putting forward constructive ideas [5], Deniau, who was still young, was generally considered to be a man of vision, instinct and courage [6], with solid European convictions [7]. Although very different in character, he had a good relationship with his superior, Commissioner Rey. The one an austere Belgian Protestant and former parliamentarian, and the other a French Catholic, inclined to be autocratic and sometimes insolent [8].

The Commission was accused, in particular by the Dutch, of often taking the French side in controversial issues such as the length of the transitional period for UK agriculture [9]. This might

---

[1] ABZN 996.0 EEG 1955–64, 394, Statement by Hallstein concerning negotiations with the United Kingdom to the European Parliament on 5 February 1963.

[2] Deniau, J.-Fr., op. cit., p. 187.
[3] von Staden, B., *Ende und Anfang: Erinnerungen 1939–1963*, IPa, Waihingen/Enz, 2001, p. 222.
[4] Ibid., pp. 217–218.
[5] ABZN, 996.0 EEG 1955–64, 384, 8 February 1962.
[6] Interview with Fernand Braun, 8 December 2003.
[7] Interview with Pierre Duchâteau, 22 December 2003.
[8] Interview with Pierre Duchâteau, 22 December 2003.
[9] Ibid.

Negotiations fail (1963)

'This event has had a psychological impact and a negative influence on the functioning of the Community institutions in recent months. My Commission has attempted from the outset to be a solid rock in the face of this situation. We have been guided by two concerns: that everything we have accomplished in the European project might be destroyed and that our venture may perhaps not be taken further.'

Hallstein, W., 1963 — A testing year, speech by the EEC Commission President at the annual conference of the Bundesverband Deutscher Zeitungsverleger, Frankfurt am Main, 4 July 1963, p. 6. (Translated from the Dutch)

Charles de Gaulle — press conference in the Élysée Palace — 14 January 1963

'The United Kingdom has lodged its application to join the common market after refusing to participate in the Community we are building and after creating a sort of free-trade area with six other States [...] after exerting some form of pressure on the Six to prevent the common market from coming into force. England has applied to join but on its own terms.'

De Gaulle, Ch., *Discours et Messages — Pour l'effort Août 1962–Décembre 1965*, Plon, Paris, 1970, p. 68.

appear somewhat surprising after the initial scepticism shown by the French about any form of participation by the Commission, but they welcomed the fact that the Commission, like them, stuck firmly to the Treaties and the Community *acquis*. Hallstein and Mansholt played a leading role here. However, the rapprochement between Paris and the Commission was also due to the Commission's realisation that time was running out. As von Staden reported, Hallstein pressed Heath and Roll in the autumn of 1962, at one of those private dinners, to make headway on agriculture as it was strongly rumoured in Paris that General de Gaulle was beginning to lose patience [1].

Despite the many hurdles encountered on the way, there was for some time a belief that negotiations would reach a successful conclusion, but this was not to be. On 14 January 1963 they faltered at the hurdle of the French veto. To the surprise of many, including the Commission [2], de Gaulle announced at one of his memorable press conferences that he would not agree to UK membership. The British were not sufficiently 'European' in his eyes and, consequently, were not yet ready to accept the Community's political

goals. It was not simply a question of accepting the Community *acquis* since accession was also a political act demonstrating a certain 'European commitment'.

The General's political bombshell, which he justified on the grounds that the United Kingdom would have to accept the Treaty of Rome unreservedly and unconditionally, was also a rejection of the Anglo-American agreements concluded in the Bahamas on 21 December 1962 on the creation of a multilateral nuclear force and the supply of Polaris missiles to the United Kingdom by the United States.

'There was much wailing and gnashing of teeth. Righteous indignation and rending and tearing of hair in the capitals', wrote Deniau graphically [3].

The last negotiating session was dramatic. Couve de Murville was the butt of criticism and unpleasant remarks from all quarters, with the exception of the Commission [4]. It made no difference. France stuck stubbornly to its position.

[1] von Staden, B., op. cit., p. 222.
[2] Interview with Willem-Jan van Slobbe, 6 January 2004.

[3] Deniau, J.-Fr., op. cit., p. 190.
[4] von Staden, B., op. cit., p. 222.

A second attempt

In 1967 history repeated itself. The four previous applicants made new applications which de Gaulle unilaterally torpedoed despite a relatively positive prior opinion from the European Commission ([1]).

Two years later in October 1969 the Commission presented an opinion on the accession applications. Robert Toulemon, one of the main drafters, recalled a meeting with the French Permanent Representative Jean-Marc Boegner. The Commission had proposed extending, in accordance with the Treaty, the possibility of majority voting in the Council of Ministers to facilitate enlargement. Toulemon's response was: 'But my dear friend, you are suggesting something we don't like, the United Kingdom's accession, and to get us to accept it you have added something we like even less, supranationality! You have no chance of persuading us.' ([2]) Enlargement was obviously not going to happen just yet.

1970–73

General de Gaulle's departure as French President in 1969 and the summit in The Hague in the same year provided an opportunity for the accession applications to be reconsidered. Insofar as the applicant States accepted the Treaties and their political aims, the decision taken since the entry into force of the treaties and the options adopted in the sphere of development, the Heads of State or Government had indicated their agreement to the opening of negotiations between the Community on the one hand and the applicant States on the other. ([3]).

The summit in The Hague endorsed two basic principles for the Community's future: firstly, Community accession (the three Treaties were

Cartoon which appeared in the British press in January 1963 after the French veto on UK membership:
'Learning French is not easy,
But Mac seems remarkably slow.
We can only repeat,
That a kick in the seat,
In plain, basic English means NO.'

considered as a whole, irrespective of the different accession procedures) in order to silence, once and for all, both within and outside the Community, the tendency in some quarters to consider accession as being the sole prerogative of the Member States. Secondly, the 'Community *acquis*' was to be treated as forming part of an entity with the Treaties of Rome and Paris.

On 1 July 1970 negotiations with the United Kingdom were once again envisaged. However, despite the constructive role it had played in the first round of negotiations and the two crucial 'opinions' it had subsequently issued (in 1967 and 1969), the Commission was not assured a leading role in this new phase. The Member States, and in particular France, continued to defend vigorously their previous position.

([1]) 29 September.
([2]) Interview with Robert Toulemon, 17 December 2003.
([3]) Extract from the communiqué issued by the summit of Heads of State or Government in The Hague, 1 and 2 December 1969.

Once again the Commission did not simply sit back. In January 1970, well before the negotiations began, President Rey told Jean Monnet that the Commission could not be excluded and that Mansholt, Barre and other members of the Commission expected the Commission to be involved in the conduct of the negotiations. He suggested that the Commission's term of office be extended until the conclusion of the negotiations with the British. He proposed that a small coordinating committee be set up within the institution, to be chaired by the President, for the duration of the negotiations (¹). There is a clear parallel with the 1960s. Jean Rey also made reference to the recent Kennedy Round, in which the Commission had successfully acted as principal negotiator on behalf of the Member States. In his view, the Council should ask the Commission to formulate proposals on the points to be addressed before the start of the negotiations. Once they had been approved by the Council, these proposals would form the basis for negotiations between the Commission and the Member States (²). Rey was optimistic about the negotiating space that national governments would give him. He pointed to the good personal contacts he had with the French President, Georges Pompidou, his Foreign Minister, Maurice Schumann, and the German Chancellor Willy Brandt. But Monnet was not entirely convinced. In his view, Rey expected too much from informal individual conversations with heads of government and attached too much importance to the need for the Commission to have an energetic and clearly defined position. He noted that it was the Commission which was negotiating, not an individual (³).

Monnet's doubts proved correct. In March 1970 the national governments decided to appoint a new Commission whose President had to be an Italian under the agreed rotation system. It also

became clear that foreign ministers intended to play the leading role in the negotiating procedure itself (⁴). Once again the Commission had to abandon its hope of acting as spokesman.

On 1 July 1970 Franco Maria Malfatti replaced Jean Rey as President of the Commission. His *chef de cabinet* was the astute Renato Ruggiero, future Director-General of the WTO. Shortly before, in a conversation between the Secretary-General Émile Noël and members of the Action Committee for the United States of Europe, there was huge speculation about who would lead the Commission delegation in the negotiations at ministerial level. Malfatti, Deniau, Borschette and Dahrendorf were mentioned. The pros and cons of each case were discussed. Malfatti had the advantage of being able to negotiate in his capacity as President, as Hallstein had done in the first negotiations. On the other hand, he did not have the experience — or perhaps the capabilities — of his predecessor. Deniau had acquired experience as head of the task force during the first negotiations. However, in the new Commission he was responsible for development aid for associated countries, and his directorate-general was not directly involved in enlargement. As external relations and external trade had been given to Commissioner Ralf Dahrendorf, the enlargement negotiations were basically part of his portfolio. What counted against him was his lack of experience in the Commission since he had come straight from Bonn, where he had been State Secretary for Foreign Affairs. The argument against Albert Borschette, Luxembourg's Permanent Representative during the first negotiations, was that he had recently proposed that the Council be the Community's main spokesman instead of the Commission! This obviously counted against him. The Action Committee's discussions failed to reach any practical conclusion (⁵).

On 8 and 9 June 1970 the Council finally decided what the Commission would be required to do. Its tasks would be: (a) to give its opinion on mat-

---

(¹) FJME, AMK C, 33/5/207, Conversation between Jean Monnet and Jean Rey, 13 January 1970.
(²) HAEU, EN 113, SEC(69) 4733, Memo to members of the Commission, 11 December 1969.
(³) FJME, AMK C 33/5/207, Conversation between Jean Monnet and Jean Rey, 13 January 1970.

(⁴) FJME, AMK C 33/4/222, Conversation with Émile Noël, 19 March 1970.
(⁵) FJME, AMK C 33/4/227, Conversation with Émile Noël, 1 June 1970.

The British accession steeplechase. Leapfrog with the Belgian (BE), Dutch (NE) and Luxembourg (LUX) partners is easy enough, but General de Gaulle represents an insurmountable obstacle.

ters arising during the negotiations; (b) to define and defend Community policy already agreed; (c) to propose, at the Council's request and in collaboration with the applicant countries, solutions to problems; (d) to conduct exploratory talks with non-applicant EFTA countries.

The ministerial negotiations were to be led by the President of the Council according to the six-monthly rotation system. Rey's plea for the Commission to be given a central role was ignored. However, in contrast to the first round of negotiations, the Commission had more scope to influence things. It was made clear that, at the Council's request, it could propose solutions to problems in consultation with the delegations of the applicant countries. Even though this was solely in already established Community policy areas, it pro-

vided a huge opportunity for the Commission, whose role as guardian of the Treaties and the Community *acquis* had steadily grown since the early 1960s. The huge increase in primary and secondary legislation and in the policy areas in which the Community was active meant that there were few topics on which the Commission could not claim to have some authority. What was also interesting was that the Council had put itself at the centre of the negotiating process instead of the Member States, reinforcing the Community nature of these negotiations. Talks were also conducted at a more bilateral level — between the Member States and the United Kingdom — than they had been in the early 1960s [1].

---

[1] HAEU, FMM 41, General Report., *Negociations avec les pays candidats*, pp. 282–284.

Jean-François Deniau recollects on his discussions with Georges Pompidou

'The President of the French Republic, Georges Pompidou, trusted me. I met him regularly throughout the whole of this complex affair. [...]

To keep Pompidou up to date on the progress of the negotiations I drafted a note [...] with, in the left column, arguments in favour of the UK's entry and, in the right column, arguments against. He asked me point blank what my feelings were on the matter. Reply: "France cannot impose a veto for a second time even if the first was justified [...]"

"What do you think Deniau?"

"We can't say no if the UK really wants to join. What we have to decide is whether it is because of us they want to join."

"What would be the best thing for us?"

"There are huge problems in both cases. But it would be easier for the UK to block the Community by remaining outside as this would give any member who didn't want to act a cast-iron alibi. Don't let us forget that Westminster is the mother of democracies and we owe our freedom to the Battle of Britain pilots."

Pompidou is a passionate hunter, a countryman. He said:

"Stay under cover." (He snuggled down in his chair like a hunter-in-waiting). "Never be the first to break cover."

A month later another tête-à-tête.

"And if we decide to block the UK's entry?"

"The same rules apply, Mr President. We won't say no — it will be the British who say no."

"?"

"They will if they feel that the European Community is unacceptable for them because the political and, in particular, institutional disadvantages outweigh the commercial advantages."

"And how would we persuade them of this?"

"In theory it's very simple, Mr President. All we have to do is ensure that, under the Community *acquis*, the Six agree to strengthen the European Commission's powers, there is a return to qualified-majority voting in the Council of Ministers, there is at least a limited interpretation of a country's vital interests and the Strasbourg Assembly, which the French delegation still stubbornly refuses to call Parliament, is elected by universal suffrage. These are magic words like abracadabra or *vade retro satana*. The English will retreat saying 'not for us'. Our partners will not be able to enter any opposition in view of everything they have said."

I remember my discussions with the Dutch Minister for Foreign Affairs, Joseph Luns:

"How can you be in favour of the UK's entry and also be in favour of European political integration when the two are totally contradictory?"

"If we are going to build a British-style Europe that you, the French, want to impose on us, we may as well do it with the British."

Silence. Pompidou drew on his Marlboro.

"But, Deniau, institutional progress à la Six would mean a marriage with the Germans?"

"Yes, Mr President. And not only a civil marriage. Europe is a religion."

One month later, I saw Pompidou again after sending him a personal warning: "We can't wait any longer; the negotiating machinery is in motion. Up to now, we have been able to linger over the preparations and discussion of dossiers. Now we have to decide what we want or what we don't want. There are no good negotiations without objectives."

Pompidou was stretched out in his chair. He watched his smoke rings rise to the gilded ceiling of the presidential palace. He got up and put his cigarette in the ashtray.

"Let them join Deniau. It will be easier."

Just as I was leaving, he called me back.

"And don't say anything to the Quai. If they knew the half of it, they would go on and on. Not a word! I have enemies as well as friends."'

Deniau, J.-Fr., *Mémoire de 7 vies — 2. Croire et Oser*,
Plon, Paris, 1997, pp. 273–274 and 276–279.
(Translated from the French)

The Commission 'machine'

Instead of dwelling on formal procedures, the new Commission focused on the practical ways in which it could use its influence, expertise and experience.

Firstly, it was essential to put in place solid internal 'machinery'. Hardly had he entered office than Malfatti set up a working party for the negotiations. This was headed by the Commissioner for Development, Jean-François Deniau, who was preferred over previously nominated candidates. He was given responsibility for Directorate B in DG I, which was concerned with enlargement, association and preferential agreements. This put him at the centre of two areas of the negotiations. In the early 1960s he had represented the Commission in Coreper, but now he was involved in the ministerial discussions. He had the support of a task force responsible not only for the accession negotiations with the United Kingdom, Ireland, Denmark and Norway but also for talks with non-applicant EFTA countries such as Sweden and Austria. This task force was headed by Director-General Edmund Wellenstein, who had come from the ECSC High Authority and had headed the Directorate-General for External Trade at the Commission since 1967. He was preferred ahead of the more natural candidate, the Director-General for External Relations, Helmut Sigrist. Wellenstein had known Deniau since his time as Commissioner for External Trade (1967–70) and enjoyed the confidence of Deniau, who called him the 'miracle worker' ([1]). During his long European career he had acquired a reputation as a skilled negotiator with considerable energy and an extremely good grasp of the matter at hand. Such qualities were obviously extremely useful in meeting the challenges of enlargement. Wellenstein was not, however, on his own. He was ably assisted in the task force by his deputies Roland de Kergolay and Manfred Caspari. The direct participation of other senior officials was crucial. These included Louis Rabot and Helmut von Verschuer (Director-General and Director in the Directorate-General for Agriculture) as the agricultural issues were some of the most sensitive. Fernand Braun (Deputy Director-General in the Directorate-General for Industry) dealt with everything relating to the internal market: customs union, industry, etc. and Gérard Olivier (Deputy Director-General in the Legal Service) handled institutional and general legal matters. Francesco Fresi, head of division responsible for accession and secretary to the delegation, reported directly to Wellenstein and coordinated all the delegation's work on the preparations for the negotiation dossiers and represented the delegation in the committee drafting the future Accession Treaty. Jos Loeff and Paolo Cecchini (head of division responsible for the EFTA countries) underscored, by their presence, the importance of the links that existed between the negotiations with the accession countries and those with the EFTA countries. Lastly, a number of other officials were also involved in the preparatory work or in the work of the many working parties. These included Dieter Maltzahn, Jacques Leconte, Klaus Otto Nass, Luigi Boselli, Adriaan Kouwenhoven and Hans Beck ([2]).

([1]) Deniau, J.-Fr., op. cit., p. 273.

([2]) Interview with Klaus Otto Nass, 2 April 2004.

Drafting the Treaties — this was obviously a key area as it involved several aspects. At the risk of revealing the subsequent course of the negotiations, a few comments would be apposite here.

The first issue which had to be addressed by the Commission's and Council's Legal Services was whether there should be a single treaty with all the accession candidates or a separate treaty with each of them. Should there be a single treaty for all the three Communities or a separate treaty for each of them?

For the Legal Service, the answer to the first question was simple. There should be a single accession instrument but this technique should not prevent any matter concerning only particular applicant countries from being addressed or resolved either in the Treaty itself or in the annexed protocols (¹).

The second question, however, was much more complex. Accession to the ECSC required a Council decision followed by the deposition by the applicant countries of a unilateral accession instrument, whereas an inter-State treaty was required for the other two Communities (²). This meant that a simpler and legally feasible solution had to be found so that only one act was necessary. The Commission's Legal Service deployed all its resourcefulness in interpreting Community law but had to conclude that a political decision was required (³) that reflected the guidelines adopted at the Summit of Heads of State or Government in The Hague, which enshrined the principle that the three treaties had to be regarded as a whole irrespective of the different accession procedures, thereby putting an end to the tendency to regard accession as a matter for the Member States. The Community *acquis* henceforth formed a whole with the Treaties of Paris and Rome.

The solution finally adopted with a view to ending any uncertainty was ingenious. The new members would accede to each of the three Communities on the basis of a treaty in respect of the EEC and Euratom and a decision in respect of ECSC, with an act of accession crowning all of them as it were (⁴).

There was no doubt that in this, as in other cases, the lawyers played a decisive role. But they were not the only ones. This was a strategy involving both the Commission delegation for the Community enlargement negotiations and officials from the Commission's directorates-general.

In the first round of negotiations all the Commissioners had claimed a say in the matter, but responsibility now lay in Deniau's hands alone. Unlike Hallstein, Malfatti kept a discreet distance. Even Mansholt, who had always been in charge of agriculture, was less involved than in the first round. He had become a sort of tactician, leaving the technical details of the complex agricultural dossier to Director-General Louis Rabot, a man with vast experience, and the Director for International Affairs, Helmut von Verschuer.

One of the few Commissioners, apart from Deniau, to be directly involved in the negotiations was Vice-President Raymond Barre. Being responsible for economic and monetary matters, he was closely involved in the sterling dossier and the United Kingdom's integration into the European market. He was no enthusiastic partisan of UK accession, and the UK delegation had long suspected him of wanting the negotiations to fail (⁵). Wellenstein rejected this allegation. Barre might be critical, severe and opposed to the concession of optouts for the British, but he was never destructive, Wellenstein was reported to have said (⁶).

There were nevertheless some serious arguments between the French Commissioners Deniau and Barre. According to Pierre Duchâteau, a member

---

(¹) Francesco Fresi personal archives, Note from the Legal Service, p. 4.
(²) Ibid., p. 8.
(³) Francesco Fresi personal archives, p. 12.

(⁴) Ibid. Note from Edmund P. Wellenstein to Jean-François Deniau, 18 January 1972 (FRF/ma).
(⁵) Hannay, D. (ed.) *Britain's entry into the European Community. Report by Sir Con O'Neill on the negotiations of 1970-1972*, Frank Cass, London, 2000, pp. 306–307.
(⁶) Interview with Edmund P. Wellenstein, 17 December 2003.

The final agreement on UK entry into the European Community came in the night of 22 to 23 June 1971.
The journalists and technical crews from the world's press waited hours for the decision after yet another marathon sitting.
With the discussions going on into the early hours, some of them tried to sleep as best they could.

of Deniau's *cabinet*, his boss tended to view Barre as an obstructive and boring professor, whereas Barre saw Deniau as a superficial diplomat ([1]). Deniau was certainly a consummate diplomat. During the negotiations he maintained close links with French politicians and officials and with Jean Monnet's Action Committee, and used them to overcome the differences of opinion which emerged in the course of the negotiations. He regularly talked directly to President Pompidou ([2]). Within the Commission he kept up-to-date, thanks to his relationship with Wellenstein, who played an important part in the preparatory work through his task force ([3]).

Wellenstein too exerted a growing influence in the course of the negotiations as he was perhaps the only director-general who could talk directly in the Council with ministers ([4]).

The work involved was enormous. Overtime became standard procedure. Talks continued through the night. The poor quality of the coffee and sandwiches had a visible impact on spirits.

Not only on the spirits of the top-level negotiators such as Deniau and Wellenstein, but also on the officials responsible for drafting the Commission's proposals to be included in the Accession Treaty ([5]). At times, the pressure was intense. Such was the case in the second half of 1971, when the

([1]) Interview with Pierre Duchâteau, 22 December 2003.
([2]) Interview with Francesco Fresi, 5 February 2004.
([3]) HAEU, FMM, 18 December 1970 (Adhésion No 91/70), 19 April 1971 (No 52/71), 2 May 1971, 7 May 1971 (No 65/71), 14 May 1971 (No 72/71), 2 July 1971 (No 103/71), etc.

([4]) Interview with Francesco Fresi, 5 February 2004.
([5]) Interview with Francesco Fresi, 5 February 2004.

Memories of the negotiations: disgusting coffee and poor sandwiches

Patrick Hillery, 1971

'All-night sessions means sometimes leaving for the hotel and without going to bed, eating and flying to London. The memories of the night sessions are of poor sandwiches and disgusting coffee [...] and pressures like a visit from President Malfatti of the Commission to try to convince me that I was holding everything up. Perhaps my early training as a house doctor in the Mater Hospital in Dublin was good preparation for this.'

Hillery, P., *How I negotiated Irish entry to the EEC*, IPA, Dublin, 1999, p. 24.

Jean-François Deniau, summer 1962

'A dramatic all-night session [...] bad coffee and cold cigars. We were in a small room, two for each delegation [...] impasse [...] The President sent round another cup of disgusting coffee. This sometimes provides a breathing space to work out a compromise.'

Deniau, J.-Fr., *Mémoires de 7 vies — 2. Croire et Oser*, Plon, Paris, 1997, pp. 187–188. (Translated from the French)

Italian Presidency pushed for the Accession Treaty to be signed before the end of its term. To no avail, as it was not signed until the beginning of 1972 under the Luxembourg Presidency [1].

Nevertheless, negotiations were less formal than they were to become subsequently. Many points were settled at informal dinners and talks squeezed in between official meetings. Personal contacts were essential and the main progress was achieved outside the meeting room [2].

From a formal viewpoint, in the 1961–63 negotiations power was largely in the hands of the Member States and national capitals, whereas the negotiations in the early 1970s were conducted at Council and Permanent Representative level. This gave the Commission a fair degree of freedom to deliver its opinions and make proposals. They may not have been adopted but this was not the fault of the Commission but of ministers. Wellenstein talked about a 'dream' position [3].

This did not mean that emotions did not sometimes run high. Duchâteau reported that one day Deniau irritated the British negotiator Geoffrey Rippon so much that, in pure frustration, he overturned the glasses of whisky on his interlocutor's table [4]. From time to time the Commission also committed some manifest errors. Introducing the common fisheries policy (CFP) just before the negotiations began, admittedly on the basis of a unanimous Council decision, was a tactical error which led to serious conflicts with the delegations of the applicant countries. The CFP gave fishermen free access to Member States' territorial waters. This would mean that the four applicant countries would no longer have control over their fishing waters once they joined. Their impression was that the Six had taken this decision so that they could address the issue of overcapacity in the future new members' fishing fleets. Violent clashes and long and painful negotiations ensued. Finally, a transitional period of 10 years was fixed during which the applicant countries would continue to be able to freely dispose of the greater part of their fishery resources.

This account would not be complete without mentioning the inevitable corollary of the accession of the United Kingdom, Ireland and Denmark: future relations with the non-applicant partners of the European Free Trade Association (EFTA), established in 1959 on the United Kingdom's initiative. In parallel to the accession negotiations, Wellenstein's task force had to prepare talks with the six countries in question: Austria, Switzerland, Portugal, Finland, Sweden and Iceland. Negotiations with these

[1] Interview with Francesco Fresi, 5 February 2004.
[2] Interviews with Jean-Claude Eeckhout, 3 December 2003, and Edmund P. Wellenstein, 17 December 2003.

[3] Interview with Edmund P. Wellenstein, 17 December 2003.
[4] Interview with Pierre Duchâteau, 22 December 2003.

Herzog Krag von Dänemark gibt Europa sein Ja-Wort Zeichnung: Hartung

The cartoonist Hartung depicts the 'yes' vote in the referendum on Denmark's accession to the European Community in *Die Welt*: 'Duke Krag of Denmark says 'yes' to Europe'.

countries also had to be concluded in sufficient time to enable their outcome to come into force at the same time as the Accession Treaty. Otherwise, this would have created a hiatus in trade relations. The political choice to be made concerned the nature of the agreements in question. However, there was a precedent. Independently of the United Kingdom, Austria had been seeking association with the Communities for some years. For Austria, the Commission had opted for harmonisation of policies, including agricultural policy, but this had proved complicated and unsuccessful. Deniau and the task force persuaded the Commission, and then the Council, to change tack. After consulting the applicants, the new approach was endorsed: simplify negotiations by aiming for the simplest arrangement possible, namely free trade for industrial products (along the EFTA model). This would involve dismantling tariffs and quotas between partners, but

each partner would be free to pursue its own policy with the rest of the world. No harmonisation, but partners would have to comply with competition rules equivalent to those of the Community or free trade in the products concerned would be suspended. This rather technical explanation is crucial as it shows why the Commission alone acted as negotiator on this issue, which came under EEC common commercial policy. The agreements negotiated by the task force were adopted by the Council on 22 July 1972 (with Finland in the autumn of 1972). This marked the conclusion of the first wave of enlargement negotiations, which had taken a little over two years [1].

---

[1] Paragraph written by Edmund P. Wellenstein (memo from Edmund P. Wellenstein to Julie Cailleau and Natacha Wittorski, late February 2006, p. 10).

Enlargement milestones

1961

31 July: Prime Minister Harold Macmillan announces to the House of Commons that the United Kingdom is going to apply for EEC membership.

Official application submitted by Ireland.

9 September: Official application submitted by the United Kingdom.

10 August: Official application submitted by Denmark.

13 September: The Commission sets up a working party comprising Commissioners Rey, Caron, Mansholt and Marjolin and chaired by President Hallstein to coordinate the accession negotiations and take part in the Council negotiations.

12 October: Task force made up of officials from various DGs and headed by Jean-François Deniau is established.

8 November: Negotiations open with the United Kingdom.

1962

10 April: The British negotiator Edward Heath announces that the United Kingdom will take part in negotiations on political union.

30 April: Official application submitted by Norway.

11 and 12 May: Agreement in principle on a customs union between the United Kingdom and the Six.

22 and 23 October: The Council decides to approve Ireland's application for membership of the EEC.

1963

14 January: General de Gaulle announces that he will use his veto in the Council to block UK membership.

29 January: Accession negotiations with the United Kingdom are deferred.

1967

10 and 11 May: The United Kingdom, Ireland and Denmark apply for a second time to join the Community.

31 May: General de Gaulle declares that the United Kingdom must make far-ranging economic and political reforms before it can join the Community.

6 July: The Rey Commission takes office.

21 July: Official application submitted by Norway.

29 September: The Commission gives its opinion on UK, Irish and Danish membership.

18 December: Second French veto on UK accession.

1969

1 October: The Commission delivers another opinion to the Council on enlargement.

1 and 2 December: European summit in The Hague. Renewed confidence in the EEC. The new French President Georges Pompidou agrees to stop blocking the opening of enlargement negotiations.

1970	**14 January:** Press release issued by Commissioner Martino on the organisation of preparations for negotiations with the United Kingdom. The Commission sets up a working party under Martino to prepare accession negotiations.
	30 June: Diplomatic conference in Luxembourg on enlargement. At the Council's request, the candidates declare that they will accept in their entirety the Treaty and Community secondary legislation.
	21 July (United Kingdom) **and 21 September:** (Ireland, Denmark, Norway) Negotiations open. Jean-François Deniau, the Commissioner for Development Aid, heads the negotiations on behalf of the Commission. A task force is set up and chaired by Wellenstein (Directorate-General for External Trade).
	2 July: The Malfatti Commission takes office.
1971	**7 June:** Agreement between the Community and the United Kingdom on the future role of sterling.
	23 June: Luxembourg agreement between the Community and the United Kingdom on its accession to the common market.
1972	**22 January:** Signing of the Accession Treaties with the United Kingdom, Ireland, Denmark and Norway.
	2 March: The Mansholt Commission takes office.
1973	**1 January:** The United Kingdom, Ireland and Denmark join the EEC.

Clavel, J.-Cl. and Collet, P., *L'Europe — Au fil des jours — Les jeunes années de la construction européenne 1948–1978*, 'Notes et Études documentaires, No 4509–4519, La documentation française, Paris, 1979; PV, EEC Commission, 1958–73; Derek, U., *The community of Europe — A history of European integration since 1945*, Longman, London and New York, 1991; Boudant, J. and Gounelle, M., *Les grandes dates de l'Europe communautaire*, Larousse, Paris, 1989.

Seize the opportunities available

The Commission underwent far-reaching changes between 1960 and 1973. Enlargement, spread over several rounds of negotiations, created not only opportunities but also dangers for the Commission. The main dangers were apparent from the very beginning, i.e. in the first half of 1961. Article 237 of the EEC Treaty gave the Commission very little opportunity to play a role in the process. Responsibility lay clearly in the hands of the Member States. The Commission, which nevertheless attempted to carve out a role for itself, initially encountered strong resistance from certain Member States, in particular France and the Netherlands, in the pursuit of its goals. This initial experience was frustrating for the Brussels institution. It clearly felt itself sidelined as a result of the Member States' reluctant attitude. However, its luck changed once the negotiations began.

The Commission was involved on several fronts, meeting and advising Member States, assuming its role as guardian of the Treaties and producing important documents and reports. Governments' initial distrust gradually dissipated and Commission delegates were able to play a freer and more autonomous role in talks between ministers and between their representatives.

The negotiations failed in January 1963 but the blame could not be laid at the Commission's door. This was due to the unilateral manoeuvrings of France and General de Gaulle.

In the second round of negotiations the Commission was able to exploit the credibility it had gained. Instead of becoming involved in endless procedural discussions, it exploited the margin of manoeuvre it had been given by the Member States. The capitals no longer had the same

The signing of the Accession Acts, an expression of political will

'What is taking place today is not due solely to the **momentum of history**, it is the fruit of a tenacious desire which has manifested itself in the **action of individuals** and institutions (¹).

The signing which took place on Saturday was not simply a notarial act certifying the existence of a particular situation. It is the expression of a **European political will** which has succeeded in overcoming enormous difficulties and is a real gamble on the future.

[...]

Let us remind the new members of the responsibility they bear. They have joined the Community because it is a dynamic grouping. They have joined the Community because it is the only way of being able to play an international role. It is also a huge gamble. They must do everything to make it succeed.'

Emanuele Gazzo in *Europe*, 21 January 1972.
(Translated from the French)

Think 10

'The Community has embarked on a new adventure. This applies both to its founding and to its new members. We must stop looking backwards. In some ways this is a new beginning but it is also true that everything continues. The leap in the dark, of which Robert Schuman spoke in 1950, has now been followed by a new leap into the dark but this is much less dangerous given the valuable experience and successful results we have gained. The Community of 10 will be different from that of Six but the spirit, principle and bases will be the same. Let's look ahead to a future full of problems but also of promises.

In the weeks and months ahead, the euphoria of the signing of the Acts will fade away and a number of practical problems will have to be tackled and resolved [....] The Community institutions now have to **think 10** and not succumb to the temptation to **reject the graft because it is biologically incompatible.**

Emanuele Gazzo in *Europe*, 24–25 January 1972.
(Translated from the French)

influence. The centre of gravity had shifted to the Council and Coreper. The Commission's tactical and practical contribution was of crucial importance in drafting the agreement which led to the accession of the United Kingdom, Denmark and Ireland on 1 January 1973.

This accession, which was marked by the signing of the Treaty in the Egmont Palace in Brussels on 22 January 1972, was undoubtedly a victory. At the same time, this signing immediately preceded the tragic *Bloody Sunday* events in Northern Ireland that gave such a bad image of Britain to continental public opinion. It would not, however, have been complete if the Community had not been allowed to participate in the Treaty of Accession alongside the Member States. In a memo to

Franco Maria Malfatti two weeks before the signing of the Treaty, Émile Noël set out the arguments for such participation, reflecting the spirit rather than the letter of Article 237 of the EEC Treaty and Article 205 of the Euratom Treaty. This was in effect Noël's doctrine: 'It is not with one or more Member States that the applicant State wishes to establish new relations, but with the Community. It is the Community legal order that the new member wishes to join and it is this legal order which will be concerned by enlargement: it is therefore up to the institutions responsible for the Community order and which are the only ones in a position to assess the implications of the negotiations

---

(¹) Original emphasis.

Signing of the Treaty of Accession of the United Kingdom, Ireland and Denmark to the European Community
in the Egmont Palace in Brussels on 22 January 1972.
At the table, the British delegation, from left to right: Alec Douglas-Home, Foreign Secretary, Edward Heath, Prime Minister,
and Geoffrey Rippon, Chancellor of the Duchy of Lancaster and Minister in charge of the accession negotiations.
In the front row of the guests present, from left to right: Joseph Bech, Paul-Henri Spaak and Jean Monnet. Jean-Charles Snoy
et d'Oppuers, signatory of the Treaties of Rome for Belgium together with Paul-Henri Spaak, is sitting behind the latter.

that should decide.' (¹) He continued that it would be legally appropriate for the final act to be signed not only by the plenipotentiaries of the 10 Member States but also by the plenipotentiary of the Council of the European Communities (the President or members of the Commission) (²).

However, despite the fact that the Commission was required by the Treaties to submit an opinion on accession to the Council (³), or perhaps

because this was only an opinion, 'the French delegation in Brussels', wrote Deniau, 'focused its diplomatic efforts on one objective: to prevent me from signing in order not to acknowledge that the Commission had a role to play.' (⁴) And yet was this opposition not itself recognition of something nobody could deny?

Over the period as a whole, the Commission clearly increased its influence thanks to its work during the first accession negotiations. It could therefore be expected to play a greater role in subsequent enlargement negotiations.

(¹) Francesco Fresi personal archives, Émile Noël, Note for President Malfatti, 7 January 1972 (P/21/72), p. 1.

(²) Ibid., p. 2.

(³) Francesco Fresi personal archives, Note from Edmund P. Wellenstein to Jean François Deniau of 18 January 1972 referred to in footnote p. 555 and annexes including opinion for the Council.

(⁴) Deniau, J.-Fr., op. cit., p. 288.

Can the first enlargement be said to have been a total success? No, is the reply of many officials who were working at the time and who regret the fact that the institution changed as a result of the first enlargement. The early years when the Commission had a relatively solid administrative apparatus were never to return. According to some, the growing use of English has also helped to change the spirit and thinking of the Commission. Ivo Schwartz commented that British accession had a much greater and more dangerous impact on European integration than the Gaullist convictions of the 1960s [1].

Jan van der Harst

---

[1] Interview with Ivo Schwartz, 16 January 2004.

ANNEXES

Sequence of events

25 March 1957	Treaties establishing the European Economic Community and the European Atomic Energy Community signed in Rome
16–17 April 1957	First meeting of the Interim Committee
1 January 1958	Treaties of Rome enter into force

Commission from 10 January 1958 to 9 January 1962

Composition: Walter Hallstein (President), Robert Lemaignen, Piero Malvestiti (replaced by Giuseppe Caron on 9 December 1959), Sicco Mansholt, Robert Marjolin, Giuseppe Petrilli (replaced by Lionello Levi Sandri on 22 February 1961), Michel Rasquin (in office until 27 April 1958, replaced by Lambert Schaus on 19 June 1958), Jean Rey and Hans von der Groeben.

1958

14 January	Presidents of the three executives (High Authority of the ECSC, EEC Commission and EAEC Commission) meet in Luxembourg
16 January	First meeting of the Commission at Val-Duchesse
March	Émile Noël is appointed Executive Secretary of the EEC Commission
10 April	Commission agrees to publish a single Official Journal as proposed by the President of the Parliamentary Assembly. The first issue of the *Official Journal of the European Communities* is published on 20 April.
15 April	Under the first EEC Council regulation, the official languages and the working languages of the Community institutions are Dutch, French, German and Italian
July	Members of the Commission and their private offices move into the Joyeuse Entrée building
3–11 July	Conference in Stresa of the agriculture ministers of the Community

1959

1 January	First stage of customs union completed
31 July	Turkey requests an association agreement with the EEC

1960

4 January	Convention establishing the European Free Trade Association (EFTA), which brings together Austria, Denmark, Norway, Portugal, Sweden, Switzerland and the United Kingdom, signed in Stockholm
March	Agreement between the presidents of the three executives on the general administrative and organisational rules for the three joint services (legal, statistical, information)
20 September	European Social Fund regulation enters into force
14 December	Convention on the OECD signed in Paris

1961

1 January	Spokesman's Service in the Joint Information Department is split up, with each part being attached directly to the executive for which it is responsible
31 July	Official accession application by Ireland
9 August	Official accession application by the United Kingdom
10 August	Official accession application by Denmark
2 November	France presents the Fouchet Plan
8–9 November	Accession negotiations open with the United Kingdom
30 November	Accession negotiations open with Denmark
18 December	Staff Regulations of Officials of the EEC and Euratom adopted by the Council and take effect on 1 January 1962
	First agriculture marathon

Commission from 10 January 1962 to 5 July 1967

Composition: Walter Hallstein (President), Giuseppe Caron (replaced on 9 September 1964 by Guido Colonna di Paliano), Lionello Levi Sandri, Sicco Mansholt, Robert Marjolin, Jean Rey, Henri Rochereau, Lambert Schaus and Hans von der Groeben

1962

14 January	Council adopts the first regulations concerning the common agricultural policy (CAP), which is designed to create a single market in agricultural products and to ensure financial solidarity through a European Agricultural Guidance and Guarantee Fund (EAGGF). It also decides on the changeover to the second stage of the transitional period on 1 January 1962.
18 January	Accession negotiations open with Ireland
March	Dillon Round ends
17 April	Fouchet Plan abandoned
30 April	Official accession application by Norway

1 July	Customs duties on industrial products moving between Member States are reduced to 50 % of their 1957 level
1 November	Association agreement between Greece and the Community enters into force
12 November	Accession negotiations open with Norway

1963

9 January	Commission adopts its rules of procedure
14 January	De Gaulle vetoes UK membership
5 February	Judgment in *Van Gend en Loos,* in which the Court of Justice rules that the Community constitutes a new legal order for the benefit of which the Member States have agreed to limit their sovereign rights
7–8 May	Giuseppe Caron resigns and portfolios are reallocated between Commission members
20 July	Yaoundé Convention signed between the Community and 18 African States and Madagascar
25 July	Commission presents to the Council a recommendation on the Community's medium-term economic policy. It envisages forward-looking economic studies as a first step and the definition of a medium-term economic policy programme (1966–70) as a second step. Lastly, it proposes setting up a Medium-Term Economic Policy Committee.
16–23 December	Second agriculture marathon

1964

4 May	Kennedy Round opens officially
1 June	Yaoundé Convention enters into force
1 July	European Agricultural Guarantee and Guidance Fund (EAGGF) established
15 July	Judgment in *Costa/ENEL,* in which the Court of Justice lays down the principle that Community law takes precedence over national law
30 September	Commission presents 'Initiative 1964' action programme
1 December	Association Treaty between the EEC and Turkey enters into force
12–15 December	Third agriculture marathon

1965

8 April	Treaty on the merger of the European executives (Merger Treaty) signed
30 June	Onset of the 'empty chair' crisis
22 July	Commission presents to the Council a memorandum on the financing of the CAP and on the Community's own resources
26–27 July	EEC Council meets without France

1966

1 January	Start of the third and final stage in the transitional period preceding the establishment of the common market

1967

28–29 January	Meeting in extraordinary session in Luxembourg, the Council reaches an agreement, the 'Luxembourg compromise'; end of the 'empty chair' crisis

10 February	Council adopts the first medium-term economic policy programme (Commission draft dated 29 April 1966)
	Commission presents a communication on the common transport policy
10–11 May	Second accession applications by the United Kingdom, Ireland and Denmark
21 June	Commission adopts a working paper concerning industrial policy within the Community
30 June	Commission signs the Final Act of the Kennedy Round negotiations

Commission from 6 July 1967 to 1 July 1970

Composition: Jean Rey (President), Raymond Barre, Victor Bodson, Guido Colonna di Paliano, Albert Coppé, Jean-François Deniau, Hans von der Groeben, Wilhelm Haferkamp, Fritz Hellwig, Lionello Levi Sandri, Sicco Mansholt, Edoardo Martino, Henri Rochereau and Emmanuel Sassen

1967

1 July	Merger Treaty enters into force; Single Commission established
	Common market for cereals, pigmeat, eggs and poultrymeat established
21 July	Second accession application by Norway
27 November	Second veto of UK membership by General de Gaulle

1968

1 July	Customs union completed
26 July	Association agreement signed between the EEC and three East African States in Arusha
18 December	Commission presents to the Council the 'Agriculture 1980' memorandum on the reform of agriculture (Mansholt Plan)

1969

12 February	Commission presents to the Council a memorandum on the coordination of economic policies and on monetary cooperation within the Community, generally referred to as the 'Barre plan'. According to this, Member States must enter into joint consultations to coordinate their short-term economic policies; in the monetary field a system of financial assistance is provided for to allow Member States to cope with a temporary balance-of-payments deficit.
16 July	Commission presents to the Council a memorandum proposing that Member States' financial contributions be replaced by the Communities' own resources and that the budgetary powers of the European Parliament be increased
29 July	Second Yaoundé Convention signed
15 October	Commission presents to the Council a draft decision assigning to the Community the means necessary to promote a regional development policy
1–2 December	Summit in The Hague
19–22 December	Agriculture marathon
31 December	End of the 12-year transitional period laid down by the EEC Treaty for implementation of the common market

1970

January	Changeover from the transitional period to the definitive period for the EEC
4 March	Commission presents to the Council a communication on drawing up a plan for economic and monetary union
18 March	Commission adopts a memorandum on industrial policy

Commission from 2 July 1970 to 5 January 1973

Composition: Franco Maria Malfatti (President until 21 March 1972), Sicco Mansholt (President from 12 April 1972), Raymond Barre, Albert Borschette, Albert Coppé, Ralf Dahrendorf, Jean-François Deniau, Wilhelm Haferkamp, Carlo Scarascia-Mugnozza (from 12 April 1972) and Altiero Spinelli

1970

21 July	Accession negotiations open with the United Kingdom
21 September	Accession negotiations open with Denmark, Ireland and Norway
27 October	Adoption of the report of the Member States' foreign affairs ministers on the problems of political unification, called the 'Davignon report'
26 November	Council decides to reform the European Social Fund (ESF) in order to provide the Commission with an appropriate instrument for linking together social policy and the other common policies

1971

1 January	Second Yaoundé Convention and the Second Arusha Agreement enters into force
31 March	European agreement concerning the work of crews of vehicles engaged in international road transport (AETR) adopted
1 July	Tariff preferences for developing countries enter into force

1972

22 January	Accession Treaty signed with the United Kingdom, Ireland, Denmark and Norway
13–15 March	Agriculture marathon
21 March	Franco Maria Malfatti, Commission President, resigns and is replaced by Sicco Mansholt
	Council adopts a resolution based on the proposals presented by the Commission relating to the conditions that would permit achievement of the first stage of economic and monetary union
25 March	Report of the ad hoc group for examining the problem of increasing the powers of the European Parliament, known as the 'Vedel report'
24 April	Establishment of the 'currency snake', whereby the Six undertake to restrict to 2.25 % the fluctuation margin for the parities between their currencies
1 May	The European Social Fund (ESF), as renewed by the Council decision of 1 February 1971, becomes operational
25 September	Referendum in Norway sees a majority reject accession to the European Communities
19–21 October	Paris Summit

1973

1 January	Communities enlarged to take in Denmark, Ireland and the United Kingdom
6 January	A new college of 13 Commissioners takes office

Commission organisation charts (1964, 1968, 1972)

Organisation chart of the Commission of the European Economic Community on 1 August 1964 ([1])

College

Executive Secretariat

DG I: External Relations

Director-General

Directorate A: General affairs — Multilateral trade policy

Directorate B: Western Europe — Accession and association

Directorate C: Trade policy towards developing countries

Directorate D: General trade policy

Director with special responsibilities, including negotiations

DG II: Economic and Financial Affairs

Director-General

Secretary to the Monetary Committee

Adviser

Directorate A: National economies and short-term economic policy

Directorate B: Monetary matters

Directorate C: Structure and Economic Development

DG III: Internal Market

Director-General

Adviser

Directorate A: Movement of goods

Directorate B: Customs matters

Directorate C: Right of establishment and services

Directorate D: Industry, craft sector and distributive trades

---

([1]) Organisation chart as presented in the *Annuaire de la Commission de la Communauté économique européenne*, Brussels, 1 August 1964.

DG IV: Competition

Director-General

Adviser

Directorate A: Restrictive practices and monopolies, dumping, private forms of discrimination

Directorate B: Approximation of legislation

Directorate C: Tax matters

Directorate D: State aid, discriminations by States

DG V: Social Affairs

Director-General

Directorate A: Labour

Directorate B: Manpower

Directorate C: Social Fund and vocational training

Directorate D: Social security and social services

DG VI: Agriculture

Director-General

Deputy Director-General

Directorate A: General affairs

Directorate B: Organisation of markets in crop products

Directorate C: Organisation of markets in livestock products

Directorate D: Organisation of markets in specialised crops, fishery products and forestry products

Directorate E: Agricultural structures

Directorate F: Agricultural economy and legislation

DG VII: Transport

Director-General

Directorate A: Organisation of the transport market

Directorate B: Transport prices and conditions

Directorate C: Coordination of investment and economic studies

DG VIII: Overseas Development

Director-General

Directorate A: General affairs

Directorate B: Development studies

Directorate C: European Development Fund

Directorate D: Trade

DG IX: Administration

Director-General

Directorate A: Staff

Directorate B: Budget and finances

Directorate C: Internal matters

Spokesman's Group

Spokesman

'Information for the Community' section

'Information for non-member countries' section

Joint services of the executives of the European Communities in 1964

Press and Information Service of the European Communities

Director

Adviser responsible for links with the ECSC

Offices in capital cities:

— Paris

— Bonn

— Rome

— The Hague

— London

— Washington

— New York

— Geneva

Legal Service of the European Executives

Director-General with special responsibility for EEC affairs

Director-General with special responsibility for ECSC affairs

Director-General with special responsibility for EAAC affairs

Assistant to the Directors-General with special responsibility for EEC and ECSC affairs

Statistical Office of the European Communities

Director-General

Directorate A: General statistics

Directorate B: Statistics on energy and overseas associated countries; data processing

Directorate C: Statistics on external trade and transport

Directorate D: Industrial and craft-sector statistics

Directorate E: Social statistics

Main Sector F: Agricultural statistics

Organisation chart of the Commission of the European Communities on 22 August 1968 ([1])

College

Secretariat-General

Legal Service

Spokesman's Group

Statistical Office of the European Communities

Director-General

Adviser on mathematical models

Directorate A: General statistics and associated countries

Directorate B: Energy statistics

Directorate C: Statistics on the distributive trades and transport

Directorate D: Industrial and craft-sector statistics

Directorate E: Local statistics

Directorate F: Agricultural statistics

DG I: External Relations

Director-General

Directorate A: General affairs, external relations in the scientific, technical and nuclear fields

Directorate B: External relations with European countries, accession, association, preferential agreements

Directorate C: General policy on the developing countries, bilateral relations and economic organisations of the United Nations

External offices:

— Delegation to the United Kingdom

— Delegation to the international organisations in Geneva

— Delegation to the OECD

— Liaison Office in Washington

— Liaison Office in Santiago (Chile)

DG II: Economic and Financial Affairs

Director-General

Secretariat to the Monetary Committee

Directorate A: National economies and short-term economic policy

Directorate B: Economic structure and development

Directorate C: Monetary matters

Directorate D: Budgetary and financial matters

DG III: Industrial Affairs

Director-General

Principal Adviser

Directorate A: Studies and industrial policy

Directorate B: Steel

Directorate C: Sectors and industrial applications

Directorate D: Customs

Directorate E: Movement of goods

DG IV: Competition

Director-General

Directorate A: General competition policy

Directorate B: Restrictive practices, dominant positions, private forms of discrimination (except in the energy and steel sectors)

Directorate C: Restricted practices, concentrations, private forms of discrimination (energy and steel)

Directorate D: State aid, discrimination and public enterprises, State monopolies

Directorate E: Oversight

([1]) Organisation chart as presented in the *Courrier du personnel*, No 30, 22 August 1968.

DG V: Social Affairs

Director-General

Administrative unit attached to the
Director-General:

— Reports, analyses and social aspects of
Community policies

Directorate A: Labour

Directorate B: Re-employment and rehabilitation

Directorate C: Social security and social action

Directorate D: Living and working conditions and
industrial relations

Directorate E: Health protection

Directorate F: Occupational safety and health

DG VI: Agriculture

Director-General

Deputy Directors-General

Directorate A: International matters concerning
agriculture

Directorate B: Organisation of markets in root
crops

Directorate C: Organisation of markets in
livestock products

Directorate D: Organisation of markets in
specialised crops, fishery products and
forestry products

Directorate E: Agricultural economy and structure

Directorate F: European Agricultural Guidance
and Guarantee Fund

DG VII: Transport

Director-General

Directorate A: General development of the
common transport policy and market access

Directorate B: Transport prices and conditions

Directorate C: Harmonisation — coordination
and infrastructure charging

DG VIII: Development Aid

Director-General

Directorate A: General matters and training

Directorate B: Development policy and studies

Directorate C: European Development Fund

Directorate D: Production and trade

DG IX: Personnel and Administration

Director-General

Deputy Director-General in Luxembourg

Directorate A: Staff, recruitment and careers

Directorate B: Management and individual rights

Directorate C: Administration

Directorate for Publications

DG X: Press and Information

Director-General

Directorate A: Information and media

Directorate B: Information for particular sectors

Offices outside the Community:

— Washington

— New York

— London

— Geneva

— Montevideo

Offices in the Community:

— Bonn

— Berlin

— Brussels

— The Hague

— Luxembourg

— Paris

— Rome

DG XI: External Trade

Director-General

Deputy Director-General

Directorate A: Trade policy — multilateral matters and agricultural matters

Directorate B: Trade policy — objectives, instruments and industrial matters

DG XII: General Research and Technology

Director-General

Administrative units attached to the Director-General:

— Education, training, fundamental research

— General guidelines for nuclear programmes

Directorate A: Scientific and technological policy

Directorate B: Programmes and means of action

Directorate C: Technological operations

DG XIII: Dissemination of Know-How

Director-General

Directorate A: Transfer of technical know-how and industrial property

Directorate B: Information and documentation centre

DG XIV: Internal Market and Approximation of Legislation

Director-General

Administrative unit attached to the Director-General:

— Harmonisation policy, analyses and coordination

Directorate A: Right of establishment, services

Directorate B: Approximation of commercial and economic legislation

Directorate C: Banking and insurance, company law

Directorate D: Taxes

DG XV: Joint Research Centre

Director-General

Directorate A: Programmes

Directorate B: Administration

Directorate C: Structures and organisation

DG XVI: Regional Policy

Director-General

Directorate A: Studies and documentation

Directorate B: Development and conversion

DG XVII: Energy

Director-General

Administrative unit attached to the
Director-General:

— Energy policy

Directorate A: Energy economy

Directorate B: Coal

Directorate C: Hydrocarbons

Directorate D: Nuclear energy, other primary
sources, electricity

DG XVIII: Credit and Investment

Director-General

Directorate A: Credit

Directorate B: Investment

DG XIX: Budgets

Director-General

Directorate A: Operating budget and finances

Directorate B: Research budget, investment,
redeployment

DG XX: Financial Control

Director-General — Financial Controller

Deputy Director-General — Financial Controller
(for all areas controlled and with special
responsibility for control in connection with
atomic research)

Euratom Supply Agency

Director-General

Technical Adviser

Security Control

Director-General

Director for Security Control

Security Office

Director

Principal Adviser

Adviser

Organisation chart of the Commission of the European Communities in June 1972 ([1])

College

Secretariat-General

Legal Service

Spokesman's Group

Statistical Office of the European Communities

Director-General

Adviser on Mathematical Models

Directorate A: General statistics and associated countries

Directorate B: Energy statistics

Directorate C: Trade and transport statistics

Directorate D: Industrial and small business statistics

Directorate E: Local statistics

Directorate F: Agricultural statistics

Commission Delegation for negotiations on enlargement of the European Communities

Administration of the customs union

DG I: External relations

Director-General

Adviser

Directorate A: General affairs, external relations in the scientific, technical and nuclear fields

Directorate B: External relations with countries of the Mediterranean basin

Directorate C: General policy towards developing countries, bilateral relations and economic organisations of the United Nations

External offices:

— Washington

— London

— Paris (Delegation to the OECD)

— Santiago (Chile)

— Geneva (Delegation to the International Organisations)

DG II: Economic and Financial Affairs

Director-General

Adviser

Secretary to the Monetary Committee

Directorate A: National economies and economic trends

Directorate B: Economic structure and development

Directorate C: Monetary affairs

Directorate D: Budgetary and financial matters

Office for liaison between the Commission and the European Investment Bank

[1] Organisation chart as presented in the *Annuaire de la Commission des Communautés européennes*, June 1972.

DG III: Industrial, Technological and Scientific Affairs

Director-General

Deputy Director-General responsible for industry and technology

Deputy Director-General responsible for scientific and research policy

Adviser

Administrative units attached to the Director-General:

— Environmental matters

Administrative units attached to the Director-General:

— Environmental matters

Administrative units attached to the Deputy Director-General responsible for industry and technology:

— Industrial and technological problems with third countries

— Harmonisation of industrial policy with the policy on development cooperation

Directorate A: Movement of goods

Directorate B: Industry — Technology — Steel

Directorate C: Industry — Technology — Nuclear and energy sectors

Directorate D: Industry — Technology — Electronics, data processing, aviation, space, new means of transport

Directorate E: Industry — Technology — Various sectors

Directorate F: Industrial and technological policy

Directorate G: Scientific policy and coordination of research

Scientific programmes

Attached administratively to DG III and answerable directly to the competent Commission member: Group on Teaching and Education

DG IV: Competition

Director-General

Directorate A: General competition policy

Directorate B: Restrictive practices, dominant positions, private forms of discrimination (except in the energy and steel sectors)

Directorate C: Restrictive practices, concentrations, private forms of discrimination (energy and steel)

Directorate D: Aid, discrimination and public enterprises, State monopolies

Directorate E: Inspection

DG V: Social Affairs

Director-General

Principal Adviser

Administrative unit attached to the Director-General:

— Reports, analyses and social aspects of Community policies

Directorate A: Manpower

Directorate B: Social Fund and readaptation

Directorate C: Social security and housing

Directorate D: Living and working conditions and industrial and trade relations

Directorate E: Health protection

Directorate F: Industrial safety and medicine

DG VI: Agriculture

Director-General

Deputy Directors-General

Directorate A: International affairs relating to agriculture

Directorate B: Organisation of markets in crop products

Directorate C: Organisation of markets in livestock products

Directorate D: Organisation of markets in specialised crops, fisheries and forestry

Directorate E: Economy and agricultural structure

Directorate F: European Agricultural Guidance and Guarantee Fund

DG VII: Transport

Director-General

Principal Adviser

Directorate A: General development of the common transport policy and market access

Directorate B: Transport rates and conditions

Directorate C: Harmonisation — Coordination and infrastructure charging

DG VIII: Development Aid

Director-General

Adviser

Deputy Director-General

Administrative unit attached directly to the Director-General:

— Regular reports

Administrative units attached directly to the Deputy Director-General:

— Financial questions relating to the EDF

— Secretariat of the EDF Committee

Directorate A: General affairs and training

Directorate B: Trade and development

Directorate C: EDF programmes and projects

Directorate D: EDF technical operations

DG IX Personnel and Administration

Director-General

Adviser

Deputy Director-General in Luxembourg

Principal Adviser

Unit attached to the Director-General:

— Medical service

Directorate A: Staff

Directorate B: General services and equipment

Directorate C: Translation, interpreting and library

DG X: Press and Information

Director-General

Administrative units attached to the Director-General:

— Youth, adult education and university affairs

— Trade union information

Directorate A: Information

Directorate B: Means of information

Offices in the Community ([1]):

— Brussels

— Bonn

— The Hague

— Luxembourg

— Paris

— Rome

Press and information offices attached directly to the Head of Delegation (see DG I):

— United States

— United Kingdom

— Latin America

— Geneva

DG XI: External Trade

Director-General

Director-General a.i.

Special unit: Matters relating to the formulation of external economic policy

Directorate A: Trade policy: multilateral and agricultural matters

Directorate B: Trade policy: objectives, instruments and industrial matters

DG XIII ([2]): Dissemination of Knowledge

Director-General

Technical Adviser (Coal research)

Committee for Information and Documentation in Science and Technology (CIDST)

Directorate A: Transfer of know-how and industrial property

Directorate B: Information and Documentation Centre

DG XIV: Internal Market and Approximation of Legislation

Director-General

Administrative unit attached to the Director-General:

— Harmonisation policy, analysis and coordination

Directorate A: Right of establishment, services

Directorate B: Approximation of commercial and economic legislation

Directorate C: Banking and insurance, company law

Directorate D: Taxes

DG XVI ([3]): Regional Policy

Director-General

Directorate A: Studies and documentation

Directorate B: Development and conversion

([1]) Attached directly to the Director-General.
([2]) Within the meaning of Article 53 of the Euratom Treaty.
([3]) There was no DG XV.

DG XVII: Energy and Control of Safety at Euratom

Director-General

Administrative units attached directly to the Director-General:

— Energy policy

— General affairs

Directorate A: Energy economy

Directorate B: Coal

Directorate C: Hydrocarbons

Directorate D: Nuclear energy, other primary sources, electricity

Directorate E: Euratom safeguards

DG XVIII: Credit and Investments

Director-General

Directorate A: Borrowing and cash management

Directorate B: Investments and loans

DG XIX: Budgets

Director-General

Principal Adviser

Programme Evaluation Unit (PEU)

Directorate A: General budget and finances

Directorate B: Methods and operating budgets

DG XX: Financial Control

Director-General — Financial Control

Principal Adviser

Joint Research Centre

Director-General of the JRC

Principal Adviser

Special Adviser acting as Deputy Director-General

Institute in Geel (Central Office for Nuclear Measurements)

Institute in Karlsruhe (European Institute for Transuranium Elements)

Institute in Ispra

Euratom Supply Agency

Director-General ([1])

Technical Adviser

Security Office

Director

Adviser

Office for Official Publications of the European Communities

Director

Principal Adviser

Publications

Sales

([1]) Within the meaning of Article 53 of the Euratom Treaty.

SOURCES
AND BIBLIOGRAPHY

Sources

Archives of the European Community institutions

Historical archives of the European Commission, Brussels (HAEC)
   ECSC collection: CEAB
   EEC and ECSC collections: BAC
   Minutes of the meetings of the Commission of the European Economic Community, 1958–67
   Minutes of the meetings of the Commission of the European Communities, 1967–72.
Archives of the Council of the European Union, Brussels (ACEU)
Historical archives of the European Union, Florence (HAEU)
   EEC Council collection
   European Parliament collection: EP

Archives of European personalities and bodies

Personal archives of Francesco Fresi, Paris
Personal archives of Marianne Noël-Bauer, Paris
Personal archives of Georges Rencki, Tervuren
Archives of the université libre de Bruxelles, Brussels (AULB)
   Papers of Jean Rey: 126 PP
Bundesarchiv, Koblenz (BA)
   Papers of Walter Hallstein: WH
Fondation Jean Monnet pour l'Europe, Lausanne (FJME)
   Collection of the Action Committee for the United States of Europe: AMK
   Collection of the correspondence of the Action Committee for the United States of Europe: AMK C
   Robert Marjolin collection: ARM

Collections deposited with the Historical Archives of the European Union, Florence
(HAEU)
Émile Noël collection: EN
Franco Maria Malfatti collection: FMM
Altiero Spinelli collection: AS
Étienne Hirsch collection: EH
Jules Guéron collection: JG
Emanuele Gazzo collection: EG
Klaus Meyer collection: KM
Albert-Marie Gordiani collection: AMG
Fondation Paul-Henri Spaak, Brussels (FPHS)
Papers of Paul-Henri Spaak: PHS
Internationaal Instituut voor Sociale Geschiedenis, Amsterdam (IISG)
Mansholt archives: AM
Université catholique de Louvain (UCL), Archives of the Groupe d'étude 'Histoire de
l'Europe contemporaine', Louvain-la-Neuve (GEHEC)
Pierre Bourguignon papers: PB

National archives

Belgium
Archives du service public fédéral des affaires étrangères (formerly Ministère
des affaires étrangères) de Belgique, Brussels (AMAEB)

France
Archives du ministère des affaires étrangères de France, Paris (AMAEF)
Centre des archives économiques et financières, Savigny-le-Temple (CAEF)
Archives nationales françaises, Centre historique des archives nationales, Paris
(ANF-CHAN)
555 AP: Georges Pompidou collection (GP)
Archives nationales françaises, Centre des archives contemporaines, Fontainebleau
(ANF-CAC)

Italy
Servizio Storico, Archivi e Documentazione, Rome (ASMAE)

Germany
Politisches Archiv des Auswärtigen Amts, Bonn (PAAA)

Netherlands
Archief ministerie van Buitenlandse Zaken, The Hague (ABZN)

Oral archives

Historical archives of the European Union, Florence (HAEU)

The transcription of these interviews will be available as from June 2007 at http://www.eui.eu/EUArchives, section 'Oral History', heading 'European Commission Oral History 1958–1972':

— Group interview with Fernand Braun, Giuseppe Ciavarini Azzi, Jean-Claude Eeckhout, Jacqueline Lastenouse-Bury and Robert Pendville, conducted by Marie-Thérèse Bitsch and Yves Conrad, Louvain-la-Neuve, 19 October 2004.

— Michel Albert, Paris, 18 December 2003, by Éric Bussière, Ghjiseppu Lavezzi and Émilie Willaert.

— Ernst Albrecht, Burgdorf/Beinhorn, 4 March 2004, by Jan van der Harst and Veronika Heyde.

— Clément André, Louvain-la-Neuve, 9 February 2004, by Yves Conrad and Julie Cailleau.

— Raymond Barre, Paris, 20 February 2004, by Marie-Thérèse Bitsch, Éric Bussière and Ghjiseppu Lavezzi.

— Camille Becker, Louvain-la-Neuve, 4 March 2004, by Yves Conrad and Anaïs Legendre.

— Nicola Bellieni, Brussels, 19 December 2003, by Ghjiseppu Lavezzi.

— Odile Benoist-Lucy, Paris, 27 January 2004, by Marie-Thérèse Bitsch and Anaïs Legendre.

— Georges Berthoin, Paris, 31 January 2004, by Gérard Bossuat and Anaïs Legendre.

— Jean-Jacques Beuve-Méry, Brussels, 3 March 2004, by Yves Conrad and Myriam Rancon.

— Philippe Bourdeau, Brussels, 5 March 2004, by Yves Conrad and Julie Cailleau.

— Fernand Braun, Brussels, 8 December 2003, by Michel Dumoulin and Julie Cailleau.

— Georges Brondel, Paris, 25 February 2004, by Éric Bussière, Julie Cailleau and Armelle Demagny.

— Claude Brus, Paris, 5 December 2003, by Gérard Bossuat and Ghjiseppu Lavezzi.

— Paul-Henri Buchet and Élisabeth Buchet née Gangloff, Brussels, 20 January 2004, by Yves Conrad and Julie Cailleau.

— Marcello Burattini, Brussels, 18 February 2004, by Yves Conrad and Julie Cailleau.

— Daniel Cardon de Lichtbuer, Brussels, 12 November 2003, by Michel Dumoulin and Myriam Rancon.

— Michel Carpentier, Paris, 5 January 2004, by Éric Bussière and Arthe Van Laer.

— Manfred Caspari, Munich, 18 February 2004, by Veronika Heyde.

— Jean Chapperon, La Garde-Freinet, 23 January 2004, by Jean-Marie Palayret and Anaïs Legendre.

— Giuseppe Ciavarini Azzi, Brussels, 6 February 2004, by Yves Conrad and Myriam Rancon.

— Paolo Clarotti, Brussels, 28 November 2003, by Éric Bussière and Ghjiseppu Lavezzi.

— Paul Collowald, Brussels, 2 December 2003, by Yves Conrad and Myriam Rancon.

— Leo Crijns, Maastricht, 3 December 2003, by Jan van der Harst and Nienke Betlem.

— Pierre Cros, Brussels, 8 December 2003, by Yves Conrad and Anaïs Legendre.

— Pierre Defraigne, Brussels, 16 December 2004, by Michel Dumoulin and Julie Cailleau.

— Jean Degimbe, Brussels, 15 December 2003, by Michel Dumoulin and Ghjiseppu Lavezzi.

— Frans De Koster, Brussels, 14 November 2004, by Gérard Bossuat and Myriam Rancon.

— Margot Delfosse née Frey, Brussels, 25 October 2004, by Yves Conrad and Ghjiseppu Lavezzi.

— Jean-François Deniau, Paris, 3 and 10 November 2004, by Gérard Bossuat and Anaïs Legendre.

— Yves Desbois, Tervuren, 3 December 2003, by Yves Conrad and Myriam Rancon.

— Fausta Deshormes née La Valle, Brussels, 2 February 2004, by Michel Dumoulin and Julie Cailleau.

— Gaetano Donà, Padua, 21 January 2004, by Antonio Varsori and Veronica Scognamiglio.

— Wilma Donà née Viscardini, Padua, 25 February 2004, by Antonio Varsori and Veronica Scognamiglio.

— Ivo Dubois, Brussels, 22 December 2003, by Yves Conrad and Anaïs Legendre.

— Pierre Duchâteau, Brussels, 22 December 2003, by Yves Conrad and Anaïs Legendre.

— Rudolf Dumont du Voitel, Tervuren, 1 December 2003, by Veronika Heyde and Myriam Rancon.

— Jean Durieux, Brussels, 3 March 2004, by Anaïs Legendre.

— Jean-Claude Eeckhout, Brussels, 3 December 2003, by Julie Cailleau.

— Claus-Dieter Ehlermann, Brussels, 29 January 2004, by Yves Conrad and Myriam Rancon.

— Hubert Ehring, Brussels, 4 June 2004, by Yves Conrad and Myriam Rancon.

— Henri Étienne, Strasbourg, 12 January 2004, by Marie-Thérèse Bitsch and Myriam Rancon.

— Carlo Facini, Brussels, 18 February 2004, by Michel Dumoulin and Veronica Scognamiglio.

— Jacques Ferrandi, Ajaccio, 28 and 29 May 2004, by Jean-Marie Palayret and Anaïs Legendre.

— Jean Flory, Paris, 3 December 2003, by Marie-Thérèse Bitsch, Éric Bussière and Anaïs Legendre.

— Francesco Fresi, Paris, 5 February 2004, by Gérard Bossuat and Anaïs Legendre.

— Franz Froschmaier, Brussels, 19 January 2004, by Michel Dumoulin and Julie Cailleau.

— Renée Haferkamp-Van Hoof, Brussels, 12 February 2004, by Yves Conrad and Myriam Rancon.

— Victor Hauwaert, Tervuren, 30 March 2005, by Yves Conrad and Corinne Schroeder.

— Fritz Hellwig, Bonn, 3 June 2004, by Wilfried Loth and Veronika Heyde.

— Heinz Henze, Brussels, 18 December 2003, by Veronika Heyde and Myriam Rancon.

— Axel Herbst, Bonn, 25 May 2004, by Wilfried Loth and Veronika Heyde.

— Michel Jacquot, Brussels, 19 December, by Ghjiseppu Lavezzi.

— Andreas Kees, Berlin, 17 November 2004, by Veronika Heyde.
— Norbert Kohlhase, Strasbourg, 26 May 2004, by Marie-Thérèse Bitsch and
  Myriam Rancon.
— Max Kohnstamm, Fenffe, 30 May 2005, by Jan van der Harst and Anjo Harryvan.
— Jacqueline Lastenouse née Bury, Brussels, 21 January 2004, by Michel Dumoulin
  and Julie Cailleau.
— Régine Leveugle-Joly, Sint-Stevens-Woluwe, 1 October 2004, by Yves Conrad and
  Anaïs Legendre.
— Guy Levie, Brussels, 3 March 2004, by Yves Conrad.
— Paul Luyten, Brussels, 21 October 2004, by Yves Conrad and Anaïs Legendre.
— Manfredo Macioti, Brussels, 6 July 2005, by Michel Dumoulin and
  Corinne Schroeder.
— Alfonso Mattera Ricigliano, Brussels, 25 November 2004, by Ghjiseppu Lavezzi.
— Klaus Meyer, Bonn, 16 December 2003, by Wilfried Loth and Veronika Heyde.
— Bernhard Molitor, Remagen, 19 February 2004, by Veronika Heyde.
— Karl-Heinz Narjes, Bonn, 24 May 2004, by Wilfried Loth and Veronika Heyde.
— Klaus Otto Nass, Paris, 2 April 2004, by Wilfried Loth and Veronika Heyde.
— Beniamino (Bino) Olivi, Brussels, 26 January and 9 February 2004,
  by Michel Dumoulin and Myriam Rancon.
— Gérard Olivier, Paris, 4 December 2003, by Gérard Bossuat and Myriam Rancon.
— Serge Orlowski, Brussels, 29 November 2004, by Julie Cailleau.
— Aurelio Pappalardo, Brussels, 26 January 2004, by Michel Dumoulin and
  Veronica Scognamiglio.
— Robert Pendville, Brussels, 16 December 2003, by Yves Conrad and Julie Cailleau.
— Riccardo Perissich, Rome, 2 February 2004, by Antonio Varsori and
  Veronica Scognamiglio.
— John Peters, Woluwé-Saint-Pierre, 29 January 2004, by Ghjiseppu Lavezzi.
— Detalmo Pirzio-Biroli, Udine, 16 June 2004, by Antonio Varsori and
  Veronica Scognamiglio.
— Ernesto Previdi, Wezembeek-Oppem, 26 January 2004, by Yves Conrad and
  Julie Cailleau.
— Jacques-René Rabier, Brussels, 8 January 2004, by Yves Conrad and Julie Cailleau.
— Giovanni Ravasio, Genval, 7 July 2004, by Éric Bussière and Ghjiseppu Lavezzi.
— Georges Rencki, Tervuren, 13 January 2004, by Ghjiseppu Lavezzi.
— Gianfranco Rocca, Brussels, 7 July 2004, by Michel Dumoulin and
  Veronica Scognamiglio.
— Dieter Rogalla, Sprockhövel, 18 December 2003, by Wilfried Loth and
  Veronika Heyde.
— Paul Romus, Brussels, 20 January 2004, by Michel Dumoulin and
  Ghjiseppu Lavezzi.
— Renato Ruggiero, Milan, 15 July 2004, by Veronica Scognamiglio.
— Armand Saclé, Paris, 28 January 2004, by Éric Bussière, Veronika Heyde and
  Laurent Warlouzet.
— Manuel Santarelli, Kraainem, 4 March 2004, by Yves Conrad and Myriam Rancon.
— Carlo Scarascia-Mugnozza, Rome, 24 March 2004, by Antonio Varsori and
  Veronica Scognamiglio.
— Ivo Schwartz, Tervuren, 16 January 2004, by Veronika Heyde and Myriam Rancon.

— Jean-Claude Séché, Brussels, 8 June 2004, by Yves Conrad and Myriam Rancon.
— Claudio Segré, Geneva, 3 March 2004, by Éric Bussière and Ghjiseppu Lavezzi.
— Marc Sohier, Brussels, 3 June 2004, by Yves Conrad and Myriam Rancon.
— Umberto Stefani, Brussels, 20 January 2004, by Michel Dumoulin and Julie Cailleau.
— Ernest Steinmetz, Louvain-la-Neuve, 5 March 2004, by Yves Conrad and Julie Cailleau.
— Jean Stenico, Brussels, 24 February 2004, by Michel Dumoulin and Ghjiseppu Lavezzi.
— Robert Sünnen, Overijse, 25 February 2004, by Ghjiseppu Lavezzi.
— Anne Maria ten Geuzendam, Brussels, 17 December 2004, by Yves Conrad and Corinne Schroeder.
— Ursula Thiele, Brussels, 20 October 2004, by Michel Dumoulin and Anaïs Legendre.
— Ezio Toffanin, Louvain-la-Neuve, 17 February 2004, by Michel Dumoulin and Veronica Scognamiglio.
— Robert Toulemon, Paris, 17 December 2003, by Éric Bussière, Gérard Bossuat and Anaïs Legendre.
— Gianluigi Valsesia, Brussels, 4 December 2003, by Yves Conrad and Julie Cailleau.
— Jacques Vandamme, Brussels, 21 January 2004, by Michel Dumoulin and Julie Cailleau.
— Jacob Jan van der Lee, The Hague, 15 December 2003, by Jan van der Harst and Nienke Betlem.
— Guy and Lydia Vanhaeverbeke, Brussels, 25 February 2004, by Michel Dumoulin and Anaïs Legendre.
— Karel Van Miert, Beersel, 19 August 2005, by Michel Dumoulin and Julie Cailleau.
— Willem-Jan van Slobbe, Nijmegen, 6 January 2004, by Nienke Betlem.
— Henri-Marie Varenne, Paris, 17 December 2003, by Gérard Bossuat and Anaïs Legendre.
— Pieter VerLoren van Themaat, Bilthoven, 13 February 2004, by Jan van der Harst and Nienke Betlem.
— Marcell von Donat, Munich, 18 February 2004, by Veronika Heyde.
— Hans von der Groeben, Rheinbach, 16 December 2003, by Wilfried Loth and Veronika Heyde.
— Astrid von Hardenberg, Berlin, 16 November 2004, by Veronika Heyde.
— Heinrich von Moltke, Tervuren, 22 January 2004, by Julie Cailleau and Arthe Van Laer.
— Helmut von Verschuer, Nentershausen, 3 March 2004, by Jan van der Harst and Veronika Heyde.
— Pierre Wathelet, Brussels, 8 June 2004, by Yves Conrad and Ghjiseppu Lavezzi.
— Edmund P. Wellenstein, The Hague, 17 December 2003, by Jan van der Harst and Nienke Betlem.
— Johannes Westhoff, Laren/Eemnes, 7 January 2004, by Anjo Harryvan and Nienke Betlem.
— Erich Wirsing, Tervuren, 2 March 2004, by Veronika Heyde and Myriam Rancon.

NB: The interviews have been translated as required for the different editions of this work.

Bibliographical breakdown

Bibliography

Retrospective bibliography

No retrospective bibliography exists. If necessary, consult:

— Dumoulin, M. and Trausch, G. (eds), *Les historiographies de la construction européenne — Actes du colloque de Louvain-la-Neuve des 11 et 12 septembre 1991*, number of the *Lettre d'Information des Historiens de l'Europe contemporaine/Historians of Contemporary Europe Newsletter*, Vol. 7, Nos 1 and 2, 1992).

— Kaiser, W., 'From State to society? The historiography of European integration', in Cini, M. and Bourne, A. K., *Palgrave advances in European Union studies*, Palgrave Macmillan, Basingstoke, 2006, pp. 190–208.

— König, M. and Schulz, M., 'Die Bundesrepublik Deutschland und die europäische Einigung: Trends und Kontroversen der Integrationshistoriographie', in König, M. and Schulz, M. (Hrsg.), *Die Bundesrepublik Deutschland und die europäische Einigung, 1949–2000, Politische Akteure, gesellschaftliche Kräfte und internationale Erfahrungen — Festschrift für Wolf D. Gruner zum 60. Geburtstag*, Franz Steiner Verlag, Stuttgart, 2002, pp. 15–36.

— Varsori, A., 'La storiografia sull'integrazione europea', *Europa/Europe*, nuova serie, Vol. X, No 1, 2001, pp. 69–93.

Since the works mentioned above do not claim to be exhaustive, consultation of the *European Yearbook — Annuaire Européen*, Vol. XXX, Nijhoff, The Hague/Paris, 1984, which contains a cumulative list of the articles published in Volumes I to XXIX, is recommended. It should be noted that many of these articles are in the nature of source works. In addition, the *Nouvelles Universitaires Européennes/European University News*, published by the University Information Unit in DG X (last part published: No 202–203, January 1999), is a high-quality source of bibliographical information.

For national historiographies, see:

— Bossuat, G., *Histoire des constructions européennes au XXe siècle — Bibliographie thématique commentée des travaux français*, 'Euroclio' collection, *Références* series, Peter Lang, Berne [...] Vienna, 1994.

— Dumoulin, M., 'La Belgique et la construction européenne: un essai de bilan historiographique', in Dumoulin, M., Duchenne, G. and Van Laer, A. (eds), *La Belgique, les petits États et la construction européenne — Actes du colloque de clôture de la VIIe chaire Glaverbel d'études européennes 2001–2002 (Louvain-la-Neuve, les 24, 25 et 26 avril 2002)*, Peter Lang, Brussels [...] Vienna, 2003, pp. 15–37.

— Gerbet, P., *La France et la construction européenne — Essai d'historiographie*, 'Euroclio' collection, *Références* series, Peter Lang, Berne [...] Vienna, 1995.

— Nies-Berchem, M., 'L'historiographie luxembourgeoise et la construction européenne', in Trausch, G. et al., *Le Luxembourg face à la construction européenne/Luxemburg und die europäische Einigung*, Robert Schuman European Study and Research Centre, Luxembourg, 1996, pp. 253–262.

Current bibliography

A current bibliography of the books, articles, memoirs and theses on the history of European integration has been published at Louvain-la-Neuve (1987–95), in *Historiens de l'Europe contemporaine/Historians of Contemporary Europe*. The *Journal of European Integration History* (Luxembourg) has, since 1995, provided an up-to-date record of research in this field. Other scientific reviews regularly publish contributions to the history of European integration during the period covered by this publication. See in particular *Contemporary European History*, the *Journal of Common Market Studies* and the *European Review of History*.

For the sources, see:

— Melchionni, M. G. (ed.), *Fonti e luoghi della documentazione europea — Istruzioni per l'uso*, Università degli Studi di Roma 'La Sapienza', Facoltà di Economia, Rome, 2000.

Method

— Descamps, Fl., *L'historien, l'archiviste et le magnétophone — de la constitution de la source orale à son exploitation*, 'Histoire économique et financière de la France' collection, *Sources* series, 2nd edition, ministère de l'économie, des finances et de l'industrie, CHEFF, Paris, 2005.

— Wallenborn, H., *L'historien, la parole des gens et l'écriture de l'histoire — le témoignage à l'aube du XXIe siècle*, Labor, Brussels, 2006.

Chronologies

In general:

— Boudant, J. and Gounelle, M., *Les grandes dates de l'Europe communautaire*, 'Essentiels' collection, Larousse, Paris, 1989.

— Clavel, J.-Cl. and Collet, P., *L'Europe au fil des jours — Les jeunes années de la construction européenne 1948–1978*, 'Notes et Études documentaires' collection, No 4509–4510, La Documentation française, 10 April 1979.
— Olivi, B., *L'Europe difficile — Histoire politique de l'intégration européenne*, nouvelle édition, Gallimard, Paris, 2001, pp. 775–870.
— Vanthoor, W. F. V., *A chronological history of the European Union, 1946–2001*, Elgar, Cheltenham, 2002.

From 1958 to 1969:
— Dörsch, H. J. and Legros, H., *Les faits et les décisions de la Communauté économique européenne — Chronologie des Communautés européennes 1958–1964*, Vol. 1, Éditions de l'université de Bruxelles, Brussels, 1969.
— Dörsch, H. J. and Legros, H., *Les faits et les décisions de la Communauté économique européenne — Chronologie des Communautés européennes 1965–1968*, Vol. 2, Éditions de l'université de Bruxelles, Brussels, 1973.
— Dörsch, H. J., *Les faits et les décisions de la Communauté économique européenne — Chronologie des Communautés européennes 1969*, Vol. 3, Éditions de l'université de Bruxelles, Brussels, 1978.

Edited sources

— *Akten zur Auswärtigen Politik der Bundesrepublik Deutschland 1966 (AAPD)*, Vol. 2, Oldenbourg, Munich, 1997.
— Ballini, P. L. and Varsori, A. (eds), *L'Italia e l'Europa (1947–1979)*, 2 vols, Rubbettino, Soveria Mannelli, 2004.
— Harryvan, A. G. and Harst, J. van der, *Documents on European Union*, Palgrave Macmillan, Basingstoke, 1997.
— *Le rôle des ministères des Finances et de l'Économie dans la construction européenne (1957–1978)*, Vol. II, 'Journées préparatoires tenues à Bercy le 14 novembre 1997 et le 29 janvier 1998', 'Histoire économique et financière de la France' collection, *Animation de la recherche* series, CHEFF, Paris, 2002.
— Ministère des affaires étrangères (Paris), direction des archives, *Documents diplomatiques français*, 7ᵉ série, Vol. 1–29, 1954–1966, PIE-Peter Lang, Brussels […] Vienna, 1987–2006.

Printed sources

— *Bulletin de la Communauté économique européenne*, 1958.
— *Bulletin of the European Economic Community*, Brussels, 1959–67.
— *Bulletin of the European Communities*, Luxembourg, 1967–72.
— *Courrier du personnel*, Commission of the European Communities, Internal information bulletin, 1967–72.
— *General Report on the Activities of the European Economic Community*, Brussels, 1958–67.
— *General Report on the Activities of the European Communities*, Brussels, 1967–72.

Memoirs, recollections, reminiscences

— *Benelux, 'laboratoire' de l'Europe? Témoignage et réflexions du comte Jean-Charles Snoy et d'Oppuers*, éd. Thierry Grosbois, 'Histoire de la construction européene — Études, instruments et documents de travail' collection, Ciaco, Louvain-la-Neuve, 1991.

— Beyen, J. W., *Aperçu sur le développement de l'intégration européenne*, Rome, 1957.

— Beyen, J. W., 'Europese verbondenheid', *Europa, eenheid en verscheidenheid, Acht colleges in het kader van het Studium Generale 1963 aan de Rijksuniversiteit te Leiden*, Leiden, 1964.

— Brondel, G., *L'Europe a 50 ans — Chronique d'une histoire vécue — Politique énergétique — Perspectives pour demain*, M&G Éditions, Bourg-en-Bresse, 2003.

— Deniau, J.-Fr., *Mémoires de 7 vies — 1. Les temps aventureux*, Plon, Paris, 1994.

— Deniau, J.-Fr., *Mémoires de 7 vies — 2. Croire et oser*, Plon, Paris, 1997.

— Groeben, H. von der, *Aufbaujahre der Europäischen Gemeinschaft — Das Ringen um den Gemeinsamen Markt und die Politische Union (1958–1966)*, Nomos Verlag, Baden-Baden, 1982.

— Groeben, H. von der, *Deutschland und Europa in einem unruhigen Jahrhundert — Erlebnisse und Betrachtungen*, Nomos Verlag, Baden-Baden, 1995.

— Groeben, Hans von der, *The European Community, the formative years. The struggle to establish the Common Market and the Political Union (1958–66)*, EC, Commission, Luxembourg, European perspectives, 1987.

— Hallstein, W., *Der unvollendete Bundesstaat — Europäische Erfahrungen und Erkenntnisse*, Econ, Düsseldorf/Vienna, 1969; *Europe in the making*, George Allen & Unwin Ltd, London, 1972.

— Lastenouse, J., 'La Commission européenne et les études universitaires sur l'intégration européenne, 1960–2000', *Temas de Interaçao*, No 15–16, 2003, pp. 12–36.

— L'Écotais, Y. de, *L'Europe sabotée*, Rossel, Brussels/Paris, 1976.

— Lemaignen, R., *L'Europe au berceau — Souvenirs d'un technocrate*, Plon, Paris, 1964.

— Mansholt, S. L., *La Crise — Conversations avec Janine Delaunay*, Stock, Paris, 1974.

— Mansholt, S. L., *The common agricultural policy — Some new thinking*, Suffolk Soil Association, London, 1979.

— Marjolin, R., *Architect of European unity — Memoirs 1911–1986*, Weidenfeld and Nicolson, London, 1989.

— Monnet, J., *Memoirs*, Collins, London, 1978.

— Narjes, K.-H., 'Walter Hallstein in der Frühphase der EWG', in Loth, W., Wallace, W. and Wessels, W. (Hrsg.), *Walter Hallstein — Der vergessene Europäer?*, Europa-Union Verlag, Bonn, 1995, pp. 139–163.

— Pisani, E., *Le Général indivis*, Albin Michel, Paris, 1974.

— Rabier, J.-R., 'Les origines de la politique d'information européenne (1953–1973)', in Melchionni, M. G. (ed.), *Fonti e luoghi della documentazione europea — Istruzioni per l'uso*, Università degli Studi di Roma 'La Sapienza', Facoltà di Economia, Rome, 2000, pp. 84–98.

— Snoy et d'Oppuers, J.-Ch., 'Les étapes de la coopération européenne et les négociations relatives à une zone de libre-échange', *Chronique de la politique étrangère*, Vol. XII, No 5–6 (September–November 1959).

— Snoy et d'Oppuers, J.-Ch., *Rebâtir l'Europe — Mémoires — Entretiens avec Jean-Claude Ricquier*, FJME/Duculot, Paris – Louvain-la-Neuve, 1989.

— Spaak, P.-H., *Continuing battle*, Weidenfeld and Nicolson, London, 1971.
— Staden, B. von, *Ende und Anfang — Erinnerungen, 1939–1963*, IPa, Vaihingen/
Enz, 2001.
— Uri, P., *Penser pour l'action — Un fondateur de l'Europe*, Odile Jacob, Paris, 1991.
— Van Helmont, J., *Options européennes, 1945–1958*, Office for Official Publications
of the European Communities, Luxembourg, 1986.
— Wellenstein, E. P., *25 années de relations extérieures de la Communauté
européenne*, Office for Official Publications of the European Communities,
Luxembourg, 1979.

General works

— Bitsch, M.-Th. (ed.), *Histoire de la construction européenne*, 3rd edition,
Complexe, Brussels, 2004.
— Bitsch, M.-Th. (ed.), *Le couple France-Allemagne et les institutions européennes:
Une postérité pour le plan Schuman?*, 'Organisation internationale et relations
internationales' collection, No 53, Bruylant, Brussels, 2001.
— Bitsch, M.-Th. (ed.), *Le fait régional et la construction européenne*, Bruylant,
Brussels, 2003.
— Bitsch, M.-Th., Loth, W. and Poidevin, R. (eds), *Institutions européennes et
identités européennes*, Bruylant, Brussels, 1998.
— Bossuat, G., *'Faire l'Europe sans défaire la France', 60 ans de politique d'unité
européenne des gouvernements et des présidents de la République française,
1943–2003*, 'Euroclio' collection, *Études et documents* series, No 30, PIE-Peter
Lang, Brussels, 2005.
— Bossuat, G., *Les fondateurs de l'Europe unie*, 'Histoire Belin Sup' collection, Belin,
Paris, 2001.
— Commission européenne, *40 ans des Traités de Rome ou la capacité des Traités
d'assurer les avancées de la construction européene*, Bruylant, Brussels, 1999.
— Degryse, Ch., *Dictionnaire de l'Union européenne*, 2nd edition, De Boeck
Université, Paris/Brussels, 1998.
— Deighton, A. and Milward, A. (ed.), *Widening, deepening and acceleration: the
European Economic Community, 1957–1963*, Nomos Verlag, Baden-Baden, 1999.
— Deniau, J.-Fr., *L'Europe interdite*, Seuil, Paris, 1977.
— Gerbet, P., *La construction de l'Europe*, 3rd edition, Imprimerie nationale, Paris, 1999.
— Gerbet, P. and Pepy, D. (eds), *La décision dans les Communautés européennes —
Colloque de l'Association pour le développement de la science politique
européenne, organisé par l'Institut d'études politiques de Lyon*, Presses
universitaires de Bruxelles, Brussels, 1969.
— Lecerf, J., *Histoire de l'unité européenne*, preface by Jean Monnet, 'Idées'
collection, No 80, Gallimard, Paris, 1965.
— Lecerf, J., *La Communauté en péril — Histoire de l'unité européenne 2*, 'Idées'
collection, No 333, Gallimard, Paris, 1975.
— Lecerf, J., *La Communauté face à la crise — Histoire de l'unité européene 3*,
'Idées' collection, No 501, Gallimard, Paris, 1984.
— Lindberg, L. N., *The political dynamics of European economic integration*,
Stanford University Press, Stanford (California), 1963.

— Loth, W. (ed.), *Crisis and compromises — The European project 1963–1969*, 'Groupe de liaison des professeurs d'histoire contemporaine auprès de la Commission européenne' collection, 8, Nomos Verlag/Bruylant, Baden-Baden/Brussels, 2001.
— Loth, W., *Der Weg nach Europa — Geschichte der europäischen Einigung 1939–1957*, 3rd edition, Vandenhoeck & Ruprecht, Göttingen, 1996.
— Loth, W. (ed.), *La gouvernance supranationale dans la construction européenne*, Bruylant, Brussels, 2005.
— Milward, A., *Politics and economics in the history of the European Union*, Routledge, London/New York, 2005.
— Moravcsik, A., *The choice for Europe, social purpose and State power from Messina to Maastricht*, Cornell University Press–Routledge/UCL Press, Ithaca NY/London, 1999.
— Spierenburg, D. and Poidevin, R., *The history of the High Authority of the European Coal and Steel Community — Supranationality in operation*, Weidenfeld and Nicolson, London, 1994.
— Toulemon, R., *La construction européenne: histoire, acquis, perspectives*, new edition, 'Livre de poche — References' collection, Librairie générale française, Paris, 1999.
— Varsori, A. (ed.), *Inside the European Community — Actors and policies in the European integration, 1957–1972*, 'Groupe de liaison des professeurs d'histoire contemporaine auprès de la Commission européene' collection, 9, Nomos Verlag/Bruylant, Baden-Baden/Brussels, 2006.

Works and articles on the personalities involved
— Amouroux, H., *Monsieur Barre*, Robert Laffont, Paris, 1986.
— Association Georges Pompidou, *Georges Pompidou et l'Europe*, Complexe, Brussels, 1995.
— Balace, F., Declerq, W. and Planchar, R., *Jean Rey — Liégeois, européen, homme politique*, Les éditions de l'université de Liège, Liège, 2002.
— Bossuat, G., 'Émile Noël dans la tourmente de la crise communautaire de 1965', in Loth, W. (ed.), *La gouvernance supranationale dans la construction européenne*, Bruylant, Brussels, 2005, pp. 89–113.
— Brouwer, J. W. and Merriënboer, J. van, *Van Buitengaats naar Binnenhof — P. J. S. de Jong, een biografie*, Sdu Uitgevers, The Hague, 2001.
— Collowald, P. and Fontaine, Fr., *La naissance de l'Europe contemporaine — Interview du comte Snoy et d'Oppuers*, 'Histoire de la Communauté européenne' collection, DG X, Brussels, 1984.
— Condorelli Braun, N., *Commissaires et juges dans les Communautés européennes*, Librairie générale de droit et de jurisprudence, Paris, 1972.
— Elvert, J., 'Hans von der Groeben: Anmerkungen zur Karriere eines Deutschen Europäers der Ersten Stunde', in König, M. and Schulz, M. (Hrsg.), *Die Bundesrepublik Deutschland und die europäische Einigung, 1949–2000 — Politische Akteure, gesellschaftliche Kräfte und internationale Erfahrungen — Festschrift für Wolf D. Gruner zum 60. Geburtstag*, Franz Steiner Verlag, Stuttgart, 2002, pp. 85–103.
— Fenaux, R., *Jean Rey, enfant et artisan de l'Europe*, Labor, Brussels, 1972.

— Harryvan, A. G., Harst, J. van der and Voorst, S. van (eds), *Voor Nederland en Europa — Politici en ambtenaren over het Nederlandse Europabeleid en de Europese integratie, 1945–1975*, 'Horizonreeks' collection, 2, Instituut voor Nederlandse Geschiedenis/Boom, The Hague/Amsterdam, 2001, p. 347.

— *Hommage à Émile Noël, Secrétaire général de la Commission européenne de 1958 à 1987 — La fonction publique européenne*, Office for Official Publications of the European Communities, Luxembourg, 1988.

— Loth, W., Wallace, W. and Wessels, W. (Hrsg.), *Walter Hallstein — Der vergessene Europäer?*, Europa-Union Verlag, Bonn, 1995; Loth, W., Wallace, W. and Wessels, W. (eds), *Walter Hallstein — The Forgotten European?*, Palgrave Macmillan, Basingstoke, 1998.

— Lukaszewski, J., *Jean Rey*, Fondation Jean Monnet pour l'Europe, Lausanne, 1984.

— Merriënboer, J. van, *Mansholt — Een biografie*, Boom, Amsterdam, 2006.

— Mozer-Ebbinge, A. and Cohen, R. (eds), *Alfred Mozer — Porträt eines Europäers*, Europa Union Verlag, Bonn, 1982.

— Poorterman, J., *Jean Rey nous parle*, Chez l'auteur, Brussels, 1984.

— Preda, D., 'Hallstein e l'amministrazione pubblica europea (1958–1967)', *Storia, Amministrazione, Costituzione — Annale dell'Istituto per la Scienza dell'Amministrazione Pubblica,* Vol. 8, Il Mulino, Bologna, 2000, pp. 79–104.

— Previti Allaire, C., 'À propos des archives Émile Noël: aux origines d'une carrière européenne (1922–1958)', *Journal of European Integration History*, Vol. 10, No 2, 2004, pp. 77–92.

— Rochard, B., *L'Europe des Commissaires — Réflexions sur l'identité européenne des traités de Rome au traité d'Amsterdam*, Bruylant, Brussels, 2003.

— Roussel, É., *Jean Monnet*, Fayard, Paris, 1996.

— Smets, P.-F. (ed.), *Les Pères de l'Europe: cinquante ans après — Perspectives sur l'engagement européen — Actes du colloque international des 19 et 20 May 2000, Bruxelles, Palais d'Egmont*, 'Bibliothèque de la Fondation Paul-Henri Spaak' collection, No 9, Bruylant, Brussels, 2001.

— Tindemans, L. and Cardon de Lichtbuer, D. (eds), *Albert Coppé*, Garant, Antwerp-Apeldoorn, 2006 (with a CD-ROM).

— Zuleeg, M. (Hrsg.), *Der Beitrag Walter Hallsteins zur Zukunft Europas*, Nomos Verlag, Baden-Baden, 2003.

Works and articles on specific topics

— Badel, L., Jeannesson, S. and Ludlow, P. (eds), *Les administrations nationales et la construction européenne, une approche historique (1919–1975)*, 'Euroclio' collection, *Études et documents* series, No 31, PIE-Peter Lang, Brussels, 2005.

— Bitsch, M.-Th. and Bossuat, G., (eds), *L'Europe unie et l'Afrique — De l'idée d'Eurafrique à la convention de Lomé I — Actes du colloque international de Paris, 1er et 2 avril 2004*, 'Groupe de liaison des historiens auprès des Communautés' collection, 10, Bruylant/L.G.D.J./Nomos Verlag, Brussels/Paris/Baden-Baden, 2005.

— Bloes, R., *Le 'plan Fouchet' et le problème de l'Europe politique*, College of Europe, Bruges, 1969.

— Bourrinet, J., *La politique commerciale de la CEE: forces et faiblesses*, Europa-Institut, Universität des Saarlandes, Saarbrücken, 1991.

— *Bruxelles, l'Européenne*, UCL, Institut d'études européennes/Tempora, Louvain-la-Neuve/Brussels, 2001.

— Bussière, É. and Feiertag, O. (eds), *Banques centrales et convergences monétaires en Europe (1920–1971)*, special edition of *Histoire, économie et société*, No 4, 1999.

— Bussière, É., Dumoulin, M. and Schirman, S. (eds), *Europe organisée, Europe du libre-échange? — Fin XIXe siècle–Année 1960*, 'Euroclio' collection, *Études et documents* series, No 34, PIE-Peter Lang, Brussels, 2006.

— Carpentier, M., 'La naissance de la politique de l'environnement', *Revue des affaires européennes*, No 384, 1989, pp. 284–297.

— Conrad, Y., 'L'organizzazione amministrativa della Commissione europea "mercato comune" (1958–1961)', *Storia, Amministrazione, Costituzione — Annale dell'Istituto per la Scienza dell'Amministrazione Pubblica*, Vol. 8, Il Mulino, Bologna, 2000, pp. 157–187.

— Conrad, Y., 'Prolégomènes d'une histoire de l'administration européenne — La mise en place de la Commission de la CEEA', in Dumoulin, M., Guillen, P. and Vaïsse, M. (eds), *L'énergie nucléaire en Europe — Des origines aux débuts d'Euratom*, 'Euroclio' collection, *Études et documents* series, No 4, Peter Lang, Berne, 1992, pp. 131–149.

— Dassetto, F. and Dumoulin, M. (eds), *Naissance et développement de l'information européenne — Actes des journées d'étude de Louvain-la-Neuve des 22 mai et 14 novembre 1990*, 'Euroclio' collection, *Études et documents* series, No 2, Peter Lang, Berne [...] Vienna, 1993.

— Degimbe, J., *La politique sociale européenne du Traité de Rome au Traité d'Amsterdam*, Institut syndical européen, Brussels, 1999.

— Demey, Th., *Bruxelles, chronique d'une capitale en chantier*, Vol. II, *De l'Expo 58 au siège de la CEE*, Paul Legrain, Brussels, 1992.

— De Michelis, A. and Chantraine, A., *Mémoires d'Eurostat — Cinquante ans au service de l'Europe*, Office for Official Publications of the European Communities, Luxembourg, 2003.

— Dimier, V., 'De la dictature des drapeaux au sein de la Commission européenne? Loyautés multiples et constitution d'une identité commune au sein d'un administration multinationale', VIIe congrès de l'Association française de science politique, Lille, 18, 19, 20 et 21 septembre 2002, http://congres-afsp.univ-lille2.fr/docs/tr5_dimier.doc

— Dimier, V., 'L'institutionnalisation de la Commission européenne (DG Développement) — Du rôle des leaders dans la construction d'une administration multinationale 1958–1975', *Revue Études internationales*, Vol. XXXIV, No 3, September 2003, pp. 401–427.

— Dinan, D., *Europe recast — A history of European union*, Palgrave Macmillan, Basingstoke, 2004.

— Dumoulin, M., 'Les travaux du Comité Spaak (juillet 1955–avril 1956)', in Serra, E. (ed.), *Il rilancio dell'Europa e i trattati di Roma/La Relance européene et les traités de Rome/The relaunching of Europe and the Treaties of Rome*, Actes du colloque de Rome, 25–28 mars 1987, 'Groupe de liaison des historiens auprès des Communautés' collection, 3, Bruylant [...] Nomos Verlag, Brussels [...] Baden-Baden, 1989, pp. 195–210.

— Dumoulin, M. (ed.), *Réseaux économiques et construction européenne/Economic networks and European integration*, 'Euroclio' collection, *Études et documents* series, No 29, PIE-Peter Lang, Brussels [...] Vienna, 2004.

— Dumoulin, M. and Bussière, É. (eds), *Les cercles économiques et l'Europe au XXe siècle*, recueil de textes, Louvain-la-Neuve – Paris, 1992.

— *Du plan Fouchet au traité franco-allemand de janvier 1963*, special edition of the *Revue d'Allemagne et des pays de langue allemande*, Vol. 29, No 2, 1997.

— Eck, J.-Fr., *Les entreprises françaises face à l'Allemagne de 1945 à la fin des années 1960*, 'Histoire économique et financière de la France' collection, *Études générales* series, CHEFF, Paris, 2003.

— Europeus (Uri, P.), *La crise de la zone de libre-échange — Un document E.P.I.*, 'Tribune libre' collection, Plon, Paris, 1959.

— Gerbet, P., *1957, La naissance du Marché commun*, 'La mémoire du siècle' collection, No 50, Complexe, Brussels, 1957.

— Gillingham, J., *European integration 1950–2003 — Superstate or new market economy?*, Cambridge University Press, Cambridge, 2003.

— *Grenzen aan veeltaligheid? Taalgebruik en bestuurlijke doeltreffendheid in de instellingen van de Europese Unie*, SdU Uitgevers, The Hague, 1991.

— Griffiths, R. T., 'The Beyen Plan', *The Netherlands and the integration of Europe 1945–1957*, NEHA, Amsterdam, 1990, pp. 165–182.

— Griffiths, R. T., 'The Mansholt Plan', *The Netherlands and the integration of Europe 1945–1957*, NEHA, Amsterdam, 1990, pp. 93–111.

— Griffiths, R. T. and Ward, S. (eds), *Courting the common market — The first attempt to enlarge the European Economic Community and the French veto, 1961–1963*, Lothian Foundation Press, London, 1996.

— Guasconi, M. E., *L'Europa tra continuità e cambiamento — Il vertice dell'Aja del 1969 e il rilancio della costruzione europea*, 'Storia delle relazioni internazionali' collection, No 8, Polistampa, Florence, 2004.

— Guzzetti, L., *A brief history of European Union research policy*, Office for Official Publications of the European Communities, Luxembourg, 1995.

— Hannay, D. (ed.), *Britain's entry into the European Community — Report by Sir Con O'Neill on the negotiations of 1970–1972*, Frank Cass, London and Portland, 2000.

— Harst, J. van der (ed.), *The 1969 Hague Summit — a new start for Europe?*, special edition of the *Journal of European Integration History*, Vol. 9, No 2, 2003.

— Hein, C., *L'implantation des Communautés européennes à Brussels — son historique, ses intervenants*, travail de fin d'études, Institut supérieur d'architecture de La Cambre, Brussels, 1987.

— Hemblenne, B., 'Les problèmes du siège et du régime linguistique des Communautés européennes (1950–1967)', *Die Anfänge der Verwaltung der Europäischen Gemeinschaft/Les débuts de l'administration de la Communauté européenne*, Nomos Verlag, special edition of the *Jahrbuch für Europäische Verwaltungsgeschichte*, Baden-Baden, 1992, pp. 107–129/144.

— Heyen, E. V. (Hrsg.), *Die Anfänge der Verwaltung der Europäischen Gemeinschaft/Les débuts de l'administration de la Communauté européene*, special edition of the *Jahrbuch für Europäische Verwaltungsgeschichte*, 4, Nomos Verlag, Baden-Baden, 1992.

— Hulet, C., 'L'instauration d'une politique de coopération administrative entre les trois exécutifs des nouvelles institutions communautaires — Naissance du Service commun de presse et d'information (1958–1961)', *Douze études sur l'Europe — Contributions de jeunes diplômés de l'Université catholique de Louvain présentées dans le cadre d'"Euromémoforum"*, Institut d'études européennes, Pôle européen Jean Monnet, Louvain-la-Neuve, 1999, pp. 219–236.

— Kaiser, A., *Dänemark und die Europäische Union (1972–1993)*, Mosbach, 1994.

— Kaiser, W., *Using Europe — Abusing the Europeans — Britain and European integration, 1945–63*, Macmillan, London, 1996 (reprinted 1999 with new preface).

— Kaiser, W. and Elvert, J. (eds), *European Union enlargement — A comparative history*, Routledge, London/New York, 2004.

— Keogh, D., *Ireland and Europe, 1919–1989*, Hibernian University Press, Cork/Dublin, 1989.

— Krige, J. and Guzzetti, L. (eds), *History of European scientific and technological cooperation, Firenze, 9–11 November 1995*, Office for Official Publications of the European Communities, Luxembourg, 1996.

— Küsters, H. J., *Fondements de la Communauté économique européenne*, 'Europe' collection, Office for Official Publications of the European Communities/Labor, Luxembourg/Brussels, 1990.

— *L'administration de l'Union européenne*, special edition of the *Revue française d'administration publique*, No 95, Paris, 2000.

— Landuyt, A. and Pasquinucci, D. (ed.), *Gli allargamenti della CEE/UE 1961–2004*, 'Storia del federalismo e dell'integrazione europea' collection, 2 vols, Il Mulino, Bologna, 2005.

— *La politique technologique de la Communauté européenne — Aspects juridiques et institutionnels — Colloque organisé dans le cadre de l'Institut du Droit de la Paix et du Développement, et de la Faculté de Droit et des Sciences économiques de Nice (Nice, 10 et 11 décembre 1971)*, special edition of the *Revue du Marché Commun*, No 153, April 1972.

— Lauring Knudsen, A.-Chr., *Defining the policies of the common agricultural policy — A historical study*, doctoral thesis, EUI, Florence, 2001.

— Layton, Chr., *European advanced technology — A programme for integration*, Political and Economic Planning, London, 1969.

— Legendre, A., 'Jalons pour une histoire de la diplomatie européenne — la représentation des Communautés européennes à Londres (1954–1972)', not yet published.

— *Le rôle des ministres des Finances et de l'Économie dans la construction européenne (1957–1978)*, Vol. I, 'Histoire économique et financière de la France' collection, *Animation de la recherche* series, CHEFF, Paris, 2002.

— Lethé, M., *L'Europe à Bruxelles dans les années 1960: le pourquoi? et le comment?*, History degree in dissertation, UCL, Louvain-la-Neuve, 2003, p. 133.

— Lord, Chr., *British entry of the European Community under the Heath government of 1970–1974*, Dartmouth, Aldershot, 1993.

— Loth, W., 'Français et Allemands dans la crise institutionnelle de 1965', in Bitsch, M.-Th. (ed.), *Le couple France-Allemagne et les institutions européennes — Une postérité pour le plan Schuman?*, 'Organisation internationale et relations internationales' collection, No 53, Bruylant, Brussels, 2001, pp. 229–243.

— Loth, W. (ed.), *Crisis and compromises — the European project, 1963–1969*, 'Groupe de liaison des professeurs d'histoire contemporaine auprès de la Commission européenne' collection, No 8, Nomos Verlag/Bruylant, Baden-Baden/Brussels, 2001.

— Ludlow, N. P., 'A welcome change — The European Commission and the challenge of enlargement, 1958–1973', *Journal of European Integration History*, Vol. 11, No 2, 2005, pp. 31–46.

— Ludlow, N. P., *Dealing with Britain — The Six and the first UK application to the EEC*, Cambridge University Press, Cambridge, 1999.

— Ludlow, N. P., *The European Community and the Crisis of the 1960s: Negotiating the Gaullist Challenge*, Routledge, London, 2005.

— Ludlow, N. P., 'The making of the CAP: towards a historical analysis of the EU's first major policy', *Contemporary European History*, Vol. 14, No 3, 2005, pp. 347–371.

— Maes, I., *Macroeconomic and monetary policy-making at the European Commission, from the Rome Treaties to the Hague Summit*, Working papers — Research series, No 58, National Bank of Belgium, Brussels, August 2004.

— Maes, I., 'The ascent of the European Commission as an actor in the monetary integration process in the 1960s', *Scottish Journal of Political Economy*, Vol. 53, No 2, 2006, pp. 222–241.

— Malandrino, C., *'Tut etwas tapferes' — compi un atto di coraggio — L'Europa federale di Walter Hallstein (1948–1982)*, 'Storia del federalismo e dell'integrazione europea' collection, Il Mulino, Bologna, 2005.

— Mestmäcker, E.-J., Möller, E. and Schwarz, H.-P. (Hrsg.), *Eine Ordnungspolitik für Europa — Festschrift für Hans von der Groeben zu seinem 80. Geburtstag*, Nomos Verlag, Baden-Baden, 1987.

— Molegraaf, J. H., *Boeren in Brussel — Nederland en het Gemeenschappelijk Europees Landbouwbeleid, 1958–1971*, doctoral thesis, Universiteit Utrecht, 1999.

— Nême, J. and Nême, C., *Économie européenne*, PUF, Paris, 1970.

— Neville-Rolfe, Edition, *The politics of agriculture in the European Community*, Croom Helm, London, 1984.

— Newhouse, J., *Collision in Brussels — The common market crisis of 30 June 1965*, Norton, New York, 1967 (Faber and Faber, London, 1968).

— Noël, É., *Les rouages de l'Europe — comment fonctionnent les institutions de la Communauté européenne*, preface by François-Xavier Ortoli, 2nd edition, Nathan/Labor, Paris/Brussels, 1979; Noël, É., *The European Community: how it works*, European perspective series, Office for Official Publications of the European Communities, Luxembourg, 1979.

— Noël, G., *Du pool vert à la politique agricole commune — Les tentatives de Communauté agricole européenne entre 1945 et 1955*, Economica, Paris, 1988.

— Nugent, N. (ed.), *European Union enlargement*, Palgrave Macmillan, Basingstoke, 2004.

— Olivi, B., *L'Europe difficile — Histoire politique de l'intégration européenne*, new edition, Gallimard, Paris, 2001.

— Paye, J.-Cl., 'Vers le plan Werner: le rôle de la Commission des Communautés, 1967–1973', *Le rôle des ministères des Finances et de l'Économie dans la construction européenne (1957–1978)*, Vol. II, 'Histoire économique et financière de la France' collection, *Animation de la recherche* series, CHEFF, Paris, 2002.

— Perron, R., 'Les débats transatlantiques et le GATT', *Milieux économiques et intégration européenne au XXe siècle*, CHEFF, Paris, 2001–2002, http://www.comite-histoire.minefi.gouv.fr/seminaires/les_seminaires/premiere_annee ___200/downloadFile/attachedFile/MEIE_4.pdf?nocache=1112259302.73, pp. 9–16.

— Peterson, J. and Shackleton, M. (eds), *The institutions of the European Union*, 'The New European Union Series' collection, Oxford University Press, Oxford, 2002.

— Pineau, Chr. and Rimbaud, Ch., *Le grand pari, l'aventure du traité de Rome*, Fayard, Paris, 1991.

— Pistone, S. (ed.), *I movimenti per l'unità europea, 1954–1969 — Atti del convegno internazionale, Genova 5–6–7 November 1992*, Pime, Pavia, 1996.

— Preston, Ch., *Enlargement and integration in the European Union*, Routledge, London, 1997.

— Puissochet, J.-P., *L'élargissement des Communautés européennes — Présentation et commentaire du traité et des actes relatifs à l'adhésion du Royaume-Uni, du Danemark et de l'Irlande*, PUF, Paris, 1973.

— Rochard, B., *La Commission et l'identité européenne (janvier 1958–decembre 1969)*, Institut des hautes études internationales, Geneva, 1997.

— Roland, J.-L., *Bilan de la coopération COST depuis ses origines*, EC Commission, Luxembourg, 1988 (EUR 11640).

— Romus, P., *Économie régionale européenne*, 5th edition, Presses universitaires de Bruxelles, Brussels, 1989.

— Romus, P., *L'Europe et les Régions*, Labor/Nathan, Brussels/Paris, 1979.

— Serra, E. (ed.), *Il rilancio dell'Europa e i trattati di Roma — La Relance européenne et les traités de Rome — Actes du colloque de Rome, 25–28 mars 1987*, 'Groupe de liaison des historiens auprès des Communautés' collection, 3, Bruylant/Nomos Verlag, Brussels/Baden-Baden, 1989.

— *Storia, Amministrazione, Costituzione — Annale dell'Istituto per la Scienza dell'Amministrazione Pubblica*, Vol. 8, Il Mulino, Bologna, 2000.

— Thiemeyer, G., *Vom 'Pool vert' zur Europäischen Wirtschaftsgemeinschaft: europäische Integration, Kalter Krieg und die Anfänge der gemeinsamen europäischen Agrarpolitik 1950–1957*, Oldenbourg-Verlag, Munich, 1999.

— Toulemon, R. and Flory, J., *Une politique industrielle pour l'Europe*, Presses universitaires de France, Paris, 1970.

— Tracey, M., *Government and agriculture in western Europe 1880–1988*, Harvester Wheatsheaf, London, 1989.

— Tristram, F., *Une fiscalité pour la croissance — La Direction générale des Impôts et la politique fiscale en France de 1948 à la fin des années 1960*, 'Histoire économique et financière de la France' collection, *Études générales* series, CHEFF, Paris, 2005.

— Van Lierde, Cl., *La querelle des sièges des institutions européennes*, mémoire de licence en sciences politiques, UCL, Louvain-la-Neuve, 1993.

— Varsori, A., 'Alle origini di un modello sociale europeo: la Comunità europea e la nascita di una politica sociale (1969–1974)', *Ventunesimo Secolo*, No 9, March 2006, pp. 17–47.

— Varsori, A. (ed.), *Il Comitato Economico e Sociale nella costruzione europea*, Marsilio, Venice, 2000.

— Warlouzet, L., 'Du Plan français à la politique économique de la CEE — La mise en place du Comité de politique économique à moyen terme, 1962–1964', in Dumoulin, M. (ed.), *Socio-economic governance and European identity/ Gobernanza Socioeconomica e Identidad Europea, Cuadernos de Yuste, 1*, Fundación Academia Europea de Yuste, Yuste, 2005, pp. 41–58.

— Westerman, F., *De graanrepuubliek*, Olympus, Amsterdam, 2005.

— Willaert, É., 'La Banque Européenne d'Investissement: des réseaux au service de l'intégration économique à travers le cas de la France', in Dumoulin, M. (ed.), *Socio-economic governance and European identity/Gobernanza Socioeconomica e Identidad Europea, Cuadernos de Yuste, 1*, Fundación Academia Europea de Yuste, Yuste, 2005, pp. 77–92.

— Willemarck, L., 'Het taalgebruik in de instellingen van de Europese Unie — Een kluwen van politieke, culturele en management problemen', *Studia Diplomatica*, Vol. LVI, No 3, 2003, pp. 49–92.

— Wilson, J., 'Europe et politique pétrolière: aperçu du (non-)fonctionnement des institutions entre 1957 et 1966', *Douze études sur l'Europe — Contributions de jeunes diplômés de l'Université catholique de Louvain présentées dans le cadre d''Euromémoforum'*, Institut d'études européennes, Pôle européen Jean Monnet, Louvain-la-Neuve, 1999, pp. 197–217.

— Wilson, J., *La politique pétrolière et énergétique dans l'Europe des Six (1957– 1966) — Entre économie et politique: les tergiversations d'une autruche à six têtes — Étude à travers les archives de la Communauté européenne*, dissertation, UCL, Louvain-la-Neuve, 1997, p. 159.

— Young, J. W., *Britain and European Unity, 1945–1999*, 2nd edition, Palgrave Macmillan, Basingstoke, 2000.

— Young, J. W., 'Technological cooperation in Wilson's strategy for EEC entry', in Daddow, O. J. (ed.), *Harold Wilson and European integration — Britain's second application to join the EEC*, 'British foreign and colonial policy' collection, Frank Cass, London-Portland, 2003, pp. 95–114.

— Zwaan, J. W. de, *The Permanent Representatives Committee — Its role in European decision-making*, Nijhoff, Amsterdam, 1995.

— Zwaenepoel, R., *Ekonomische beoordeling pro en contra het Europees landbouwbeleid en het Mansholtplan*, licentiaatsverhandeling, KUL, Louvain, 1971.

TABLES AND INDEX

List of authors

Authors of articles

Marie-Thérèse Bitsch
Professor Emeritus, Université de Strasbourg III-Robert Schuman

Éric Bussière
Professor, Université de Paris IV-Sorbonne
Jean Monnet Chair of History of the Construction of Europe

Gérard Bossuat
Professor, Université de Cergy-Pontoise
Jean Monnet Chair of History of European Integration

Julie Cailleau
Doctoral student in history, Université catholique de Louvain, Louvain-la-Neuve

Yves Conrad
Guest lecturer, Université catholique de Louvain, Louvain-la-Neuve

Michel Dumoulin
Professor, Université catholique de Louvain, Louvain-la-Neuve
Jean Monnet Chair of Contemporary European History

Anaïs Legendre
Diploma of advanced studies (DEA) in foreign civilisations and international relations, Université de Paris I Panthéon-Sorbonne

Matthieu Lethé
History graduate, Université catholique de Louvain, Louvain-la-Neuve

Wilfried Loth
Professor, Chair of Modern and Contemporary History, Universität Duisburg-Essen
Jean Monnet Chair in the History of European Integration

Jan van der Harst
Senior lecturer in international relations and international organisations,
Rijksuniversiteit Groningen, Groningen
Jean Monnet Chair in the History and Theory of European Integration

Arthe Van Laer
Doctoral student in history, Université catholique de Louvain, Louvain-la-Neuve

Antonio Varsori
Professor, Università degli studi di Padova, Padua
Jean Monnet Chair in the History of European Integration

Table of boxes

J. C.: Julie Cailleau
Doctoral student in history, Université catholique de Louvain, Louvain-la-Neuve

A. D.: Armelle Demagny
Doctoral student in history, Université de Paris IV-Sorbonne

G. L.: Ghjiseppu Lavezzi
Diploma of advanced studies (DEA) in modern and contemporary history,
Université de Paris IV-Sorbonne

A. L.: Anaïs Legendre
Diploma of advanced studies (DEA) in foreign civilisations and international
relations, Université de Paris I Panthéon-Sorbonne

M. R.: Myriam Rancon
Diploma of advanced studies (DEA) in 'History of Europe in the 20th century',
Université de Strasbourg III-Robert Schuman

C. S.: Corinne Schroeder
Doctoral student in history, European University Institute, Florence

V. S.: Veronica Scognamiglio
Graduate in political science, Università degli Studi di Firenze

J. W.: Jérôme Wilson
Doctoral student in history, Université catholique de Louvain, Louvain-la-Neuve

N. W.: Natacha Wittorski
Research assistant, Université catholique de Louvain, Louvain-la-Neuve

The authors have written their contributions in their mother tongue.

Index of names

Table of abbreviations and acronyms

AACM	Associated African Countries and Madagascar
ACUSE	Action Committee for the United States of Europe
AETR	accord européen relatif au travail des équipages des véhicules effectuant des transports internationaux par route (European Road Transport Agreement)
AFP	Agence France-Presse
ARD	Arbeitsgemeinschaft der öffentlich-rechtlichen Rundfunkanstalten der Bundesrepublik Deutschland (Consortium of German public broadcasting services)
Benelux	Economic Union of Belgium, Luxembourg and the Netherlands
BIS	Bank for International Settlements
BRGM	Bureau de recherches géologiques et minières, Orléans, France
CAP	common agricultural policy
CCFOM	Caisse centrale de la France d'outre-mer
CDU	Christlich Demokratische Union
CEA	Commissariat à l'énergie atomique
Celpom	Comité d'étude et de liaison du patronat de l'outre-mer
CERC	Centre d'études des revenus et des coûts (Centre for Income and Cost Studies)
CERD	European Research and Development Committee
CERN	European Organisation for Nuclear Research
CET	Common External (Customs) Tariff
CFP	common fisheries policy
CGIL	Confederazione generale del Lavoro
CGT	Confédération générale du travail

CIFE	Conseil des fédérations industrielles d'Europe
CISC	International Federation of Christian Trade Unions
CISL	Confederazione Italiana Sindacati Lavoratori
CJEC	Court of Justice of the European Communities
CNEN	Centre national d'équipement nucléaire
CNJA	Centre national des jeunes agriculteurs (young farmers' trade union organisation)
CNPF	Conseil national du patronat français (French employers association)
COCOR	Coordination Committee of the Council of Ministers
Comecon	Council for Mutual Economic Assistance
COPA	Comité des organisations professionnelles agricoles
Coreper	Committee of Permanent Representatives
COST	European cooperation in the field of scientific and technical research
CPC	Commercial Policy Committee
CSCE	Conference on Security and Cooperation in Europe
CSU	Christlich-Soziale Union (Christian Social Union)
DAC	Development Assistance Committee
DATAR	Délégation à l'aménagement du territoire et à l'action régionale (regional policy agency)
DC	Democrazia Cristiana (Christian Democracy)
DG	directorate-general
DGER	Directorate-General for External Relations
EAC	European Association for Cooperation
EAEC	European Atomic Energy Community
EAGGF	European Agricultural Guidance and Guarantee Fund
EARD	European Association for Research and Development
EC	European Communities (ECSC, EEC, EAEC)
ECJ	European Court of Justice
ECLA	Economic Commission for Latin America
ECLAC	Economic Commission for Latin America and the Caribbean
ECMT	European Conference of Ministers of Transport
ECNR	European Council for Nuclear Research
Ecosoc	Economic and Social Council (UN)
ECRD	European Committee for Research and Development
ECSC	European Coal and Steel Community
ECSC	European Conference on Satellite Communications
ECST	European Conference on Space Telecommunications
EDC	European Documentation Centre
EDC	European Defence Community
EDF	Électricité de France

EDF	European Development Fund
EEC	European Economic Community
EFTA	European Free Trade Association
EIB	European Investment Bank
ELDO	European Launcher Development Organisation
EMBO	European Molecular Biology Organisation
EMS	European Monetary System
EMU	economic and monetary union
ENA	École nationale d'administration
ENEA	European Nuclear Energy Agency
ENI	Ente Nazionale Idrocarburi
EP	European Parliament
EPA	European Parliamentary Assembly
EPC	European Political Cooperation
EPU	European Payments Union
ERDA	European Research and Development Agency
ERDF	European Regional Development Fund
ESC	Economic and Social Committee
ESF	European Science Foundation
ESF	European Social Fund
ESRO	European Space Research Organisation
EUI	European University Institute
Euratom	*see* EAEC
FAO	Food and Agriculture Organisation
FEDOM	Fonds européen de développement pour les pays et territoires d'outre-mer (Development Fund for Overseas Countries and Territories)
FFPE	Fédération de la fonction publique européenne (European Civil Service Federation)
FGTB	Bureau of the Belgian Labour Federation
FIDES	Fonds d'investissement pour le développement économique et social des territoires d'outre-mer (Investment Fund for the Economic and Social Development of the Overseas Territories)
FLN	Front de libération nationale
FNSEA	Fédération nationale des syndicats d'exploitants agricoles (French farmers' union)
FRG	Federal Republic of Germany
GATT	General Agreement on Tariffs and Trade
GDR	German Democratic Republic
GNH	gross national happiness
GNP	gross national product

GPRF	Gouvernement provisoire de la République française (Provisional Government of the French Republic)
GSP	non-reciprocal generalised preferences
HEC	HEC Paris, Graduate Business School
HGV	heavy goods vehicle
IAEA	International Atomic Energy Agency
IBRD	International Bank for Reconstruction and Development
ICCTU	International Confederation of Christian Trade Unions
ICFTU	International Confederation of Free Trade Unions
IEP	Institut d'études politiques (Institute of Political Studies)
ILO	International Labour Office
ILO	International Labour Organisation
IMF	International Monetary Fund
IMS	International Monetary System
ITO	International Trade Organisation
JRC	Joint Research Centre
KVP	Katholieke Volkspartij (Catholic People's Party)
MCA	monetary compensatory amount
MIT	Massachusetts Institute of Technology
NASA	National Aeronautics and Space Administration
NATO	North Atlantic Treaty Organisation
NGO	non-governmental organisation
NPT	Non-Proliferation Treaty
NSDAP	Nationalsozialistische Deutsche Arbeiterpartei
OAS	Organisation of American States
OCIPE	Office catholique d'information sur les problèmes européens (Catholic European Study and Information)
OECD	Organisation for Economic Cooperation and Development
OEEC	Organisation for European Economic Cooperation
OJ	Official Journal of the European Communities
ORTF	Office de radiodiffusion-télévision française
PCF	French Communist Party

PREST	Policy Research in Engineering, Science and Technology
PV	Minutes
PvdA	Partij van de Arbeid (Labour Party)
RAI	Radio Audizioni Italiane
RTB	Radio-Télévision belge
SALT	strategic arms limitation talks
SDR	special drawing rights
SFIE	Syndicat des fonctionnaires internationaux européens
SFIO	Section française de l'Internationale ouvrière (French Section of Workers' International)
SGCI	secrétariat général du Comité interministériel pour les questions de coopération économique européenne (Secretariat-General of the Interministerial Committee for Questions concerning European Economic Cooperation, France)
Sofina	Société financière de transports et d'entreprises industrielles
SPD	Sozialdemokratische Partei Deutschlands
Stabex	system for the stabilisation of export earnings
Svimez	Associazione per lo sviluppo dell'industria nel Mezzogiorno (Association for Industrial Development in the Mezzogiorno)
UCL	Université catholique de Louvain
UK	United Kingdom
UN	United Nations
Unctad	United Nations Conference on Trade and Development
UNECE	United Nations Economic Commission for Europe
Unecla	United Nations Economic Commission for Latin America
Unesco	United Nations Educational, Scientific and Cultural Organisation
UNICE	Union des industries de la Communauté européenne (Confederation of European Business, now Business Europe)
UNIDO	United Nations Organisation for Industrial Development
USSR	Union of Soviet Socialist Republics
VAT	value added tax
WEU	Western European Union
WTO	World Trade Organisation

Credits

Extracts from publications

The European Commission gratefully acknowledges the permission given by the following publishers to reproduce extracts from their works:
— Agence Europe, Brussels
— Bundesverband Deutscher Zeitungsverleger e.V., Berlin
— Contact, Amsterdam
— Deutsche Verlags-Anstalt, Munich
— Éditions Didier Hatier, Namur
— Éditions Plon, Paris
— Éditions Robert Laffont, Paris
— Éditions du Seuil, Paris
— Éditions Stock, Paris
— Éditions techniques et économiques *(Revue du Marché Commun)*, Paris
— Établissements Émile Bruylant SA, Brussels
— Garant-Uitgevers, Antwerp
— Internationaal Instituut voor Sociale Geschiedenis, Amsterdam
— IPA, Dublin
— Le Monde, Paris
— Librairie Fayard, Paris
— Peter Lang, Brussels

Iconography

Below we indicate the holders of rights in documents reproduced, together with the source or place of conservation.

We have made every effort to contact rights holders, but we were unable to locate a few.

For further information, please contact:

European Commission
Secretariat-General — Unit C.3
BERL 6/173
Rue de la Loi/Wetstraat 200
B-1049 Brussels
E-mail: SG-COMMANDE-PUBLICATIONS@ec.europa.eu

Page	Source used or place of conservation / Copyright holder
Front endpaper	European Commission Media Library, P-002378-01-34h © European Communities
35	European Commission Media Library, P-001321/00-05 © European Communities
39	European Commission, DG X. Representation in Luxembourg (ed.), *Europa Grafica, Unir des peuples — Associer des États-nations: exposition Europa Grafica; Luxembourg, 29 avril au 14 mai 1995,* Luxembourg, Office for Official Publications of the European Communities, 1995, p. 21 All rights reserved
43	European Commission Media Library, P-008722/01-35 © European Communities
48	*La Dernière Heure,* 17 January 1958 © Belga et *La Dernière Heure/Les Sports*
56	Private collection, Jean Flory All rights reserved
61	European Commission Historical Archives, BAC 291/1991 1146 All rights reserved
73	European Commission Media Library, P-008368/00-4 © European Communities
80	European Commission Media Library, P-002380-01-16 © European Communities
85	European Commission Historical Archives, BAC 291/1991 287 All rights reserved
88	European Commission Media Library, P-002864-00-1 © European Communities
99	Moisan, R., 'Les instructions pour Bruxelles', *Carrefour,* 16 June 1965, No 1 (accessible at European Navigator, http://www.ena.lu) All rights reserved

101	Cartoon by Jean Remy, cover page of the weekly *Pourquoi Pas?,* No 2442, 16 September 1965
105	European Commission Media Library, P-001349/00-10 © European Communities
113	European Commission Media Library, P-002760/01-22 © European Communities
118	European Commission Media Library, P-003227/01-31 © European Communities
129	European Commission Media Library, P-003170-04-17 © European Communities
139	European Commission Media Library, P-003230/01-3h © European Communities
150	European Commission Media Library, P-009748-06-5h © European Communities
157	European Commission Historical Archives, BAC 291/1991 408
159	European Commission Media Library, P-003388-01-6h © European Communities
167	*Courrier du personnel,* No 184, 15 October 1971 As Clément André, chief editor of the *Courrier du personnel,* recalls, this caricature of Mansholt was very probably taken from another publication of the time.
177	*30 jours d'Europe,* March 1972
179 (left)	European Commission Media Library, P-009698-00-3h © European Communities
179 (right)	Private collection, Georges Rencki
191	European Commission Media Library, P-008949-00-1h © European Communities
193	European Commission Media Library, P-007759/00-2 © European Communities
197	European Commission Media Library, P-008227/00-2 © European Communities
201	European Commission Media Library, P-003232/00-1 © European Communities
203	European Commission Media Library, P-003496/00-2 © European Communities
211	Private collection, Marianne Noël-Bauer
216	European Commission Media Library, P-004539-01-23 © European Communities
223	Illustration by Roger Faut, *Courrier du personnel,* No 4, 19 October 1967, p. 14

233	European Commission Historical Archives, BAC 291/1991 287 All rights reserved
237	Illustration by Roger Faut, *Courrier du personnel,* No 7, 7 December 1967, p. 3 All rights reserved
239	Illustration by Roger Faut, *Courrier du personnel,* No 5, 9 November 1967 All rights reserved
243	Private collection, Michel Dumoulin All rights reserved
249	*Courrier du personnel,* No 40, 31 October 1968, p. 5 All rights reserved
255	European Commission Media Library, P-003222-01-11 h (centre), P-003222-02-4 h (bottom), P-003222-02-16a (top) © European Communities
263	European Commission Historical Archives, BAC 291/1991 244 All rights reserved
265	*Courrier du personnel,* No 170, 12 July 1971, and No 185, 22 October 1971 All rights reserved
267	European Commission Media Library, P-009190-00-12h © European Communities
275	Centre d'archives et de recherches européennes de l'Institut européen de l'université de Genève, Fonds AP and Richard de Coudenhove-Kalergi, correspondence All rights reserved
277	European Commission Media Library, P-002378-01-34h © European Communities
279	European Commission Media Library, P-002388-01-33h Construction of Berlaymont begins in the European quarter All rights reserved
281	European Commission Historical Archives, BAC 291/1991 527 All rights reserved
283	Private collection, Carla De Clercq All rights reserved
285	European Commission Historical Archives, BAC 291/1991 292 All rights reserved
287	Fonds Henri Storck, Brussels © Fonds Henri Storck
291	European Commission Media Library, P-009588-01-4 © European Communities
301	European Commission Media Library, P-009226-2 © European Communities
315	European Commission Historical Archives, BAC 291/1991 1223 All rights reserved
323	European Commission Media Library, P-002388-01-33h © European Communities
325	European Commission Historical Archives, BAC 291/1991 566 All rights reserved

335	European Commission Media Library, P-003328-02-6h © European Communities
337	European Commission Media Library, P-003352-02-9h © European Communities
348–349	Cartography: Guillaume Balavoine © European Communities
351	European Commission Historical Archives, BAC 291/1991 591 All rights reserved
357	European Commission Historical Archives, BAC 291/1991 977 All rights reserved
361	Fondation Jean Monnet pour l'Europe, Archives Jean Monnet, AMK C 30/1/173 Reproduction authorised, provided the source is acknowledged
375	European Commission Media Library, P-002765-02-12 © European Communities
379	Private collection, Henri-Marie Varenne All rights reserved
381	Köhler, H. E., *Pardon wird nicht gegeben: Karikaturen unserer Zeit,* Facketräger-Verlag, Hannover, 1957 © Wilhelm-Busch-Gesellschaft e.V. Hannover
386	European Commission Media Library, P-010594-00-1h © European Communities
387	Historical Archives of the European Union, Florence © Historical Archives of the European Union, Florence
394	Université catholique de Louvain, Archives Robert Triffin All rights reserved
402	*30 jours d'Europe,* December 1972 All rights reserved
405	*Courrier du personnel,* No 151, 18 February 1971 All rights reserved
413	European Commission Historical Archives, BAC 291/1991 572 All rights reserved
423	*Communauté européenne,* No 125, December 1968 All rights reserved
431	European Commission Historical Archives, BAC 291/1991 582 All rights reserved
435	European Commission Media Library, P-009583-01-11 © European Communities
445 (top)	*Le Soir illustré,* 5 December 1957, p. 35 All rights reserved
445 (bottom)	SNCB Holding, service «Archives et photothèque», Brussels © Photo Groupe SNCB
453	European Commission Historical Archives, BAC 291/1991 1223 All rights reserved
461 (top)	*Le défi américain,* Éditions Denoël, Paris, 1967 All rights reserved

461 (bottom)	*30 jours d'Europe,* No 121–122, August–September 1968 All rights reserved
463	European Commission Historical Archives, BAC 291/1991 812 All rights reserved
467	European Commission Media Library, P-003488-01-32h © European Communities
469	European Commission Media Library, P-003488-03-20 © European Communities
477	Photothèque du groupe Total, Paris © Total/All rights reserved
485	European Commission Historical Archives, BAC 291/1991 158 All rights reserved
487	EDF, *Histoire de l'énergie nucléaire,* 1999, p. 6 © EDF Media Library, K2569-209
499	*La Stampa* Archives © *La Stampa*/Giorgio Cavalli
505	Private collection, Gianfranco Rocca All rights reserved
509	European Commission Media Library, B 3127-19 © European Communities
513	European Commission Media Library, P-010426-00-2 © European Communities
517	European Commission Media Library, P-003226-01-10 © European Communities
525	European Commission Historical Archives, BAC 291/1991 965 All rights reserved
529	European Commission Historical Archives, BAC 291/1991 1414 All rights reserved
543	*Daily Worker,* 28 January 1963 © Morning Star
545	*Der Nächste bitte, Zwanzig Jahre Weltgeschehen in 160 politischen Karikaturen,* Saarbach, Cologne, 1971, p. 33 © Fritz Behrendt
549	European Commission Media Library, P-0011619/00-17 © European Communities
551	*Die Welt,* 4 October 1972, p. 4 (accessible at European Navigator, http://www.ena.lu) All rights reserved
555	European Commission Media Library, P-003364/06-01 © European Communities
Back endpaper	European Commission Historical Archives, BAC 291/1991 292 All rights reserved

European Commission

The European Commission, 1958–72 — History and memories

Luxembourg: Office for Official Publications of the European Communities

2007 — 626 pp. — 21.5 × 27.5 cm

ISBN 978-92-79-05494-5

Price (excluding VAT) in Luxembourg: EUR 30